MW00356358

Soldiers of *Barbarossa*

Combat, Genocide, and Everyday Experiences on the Eastern Front, June–December 1941

EDITED BY CRAIG W. H. LUTHER
AND DAVID STAHEL

STACKPOLE
BOOKS
Guilford, Connecticut

Published by Stackpole Books
An imprint of The Rowman & Littlefield Publishing Group, Inc.
4501 Forbes Blvd., Ste. 200
Lanham, MD 20706
www.rowman.com

Distributed by NATIONAL BOOK NETWORK

British Library Cataloguing in Publication Information Available

Library of Congress Cataloging-in-Publication Data Available

ISBN 978-0-8117-3879-8 (cloth : alk. paper)
ISBN 978-0-8117-6882-5 (electronic)

♾™ The paper used in this publication meets the minimum requirements of American National Standard for Information Sciences—Permanence of Paper for Printed Library Materials, ANSI/NISO Z39.48-1992.

We proudly dedicate this volume to David M. Glantz (Col., US Army, ret.) for his unsurpassed contribution to understanding the Russo-German War 1941–1945. As historians of that most terrible conflict in history, we thank him for all that he has taught us, for his many years of graciously given support, for his intellectual generosity, and, most of all, for his patience.

In a few hours it will begin! We Germans face an enemy with a threefold [numerical] superiority; our regiment is in the very front line. The resistance must be broken, in spite of the bunkers, the human hordes, and all kinds of devilry. It's a war for Germany's greatness and future. (Dr. Heinrich Haape, 6 Infantry Division, Army Group Center, 21 June 1941)

We've just got the Sondermeldungen *about the dissolution and destruction of various cauldrons. The numbers are quite incredible. Almost a million prisoners and huge numbers of tanks, aircraft and guns. If that continues, then the end will come quickly.* (Albert Neuhaus, Army Group North, 6 August 1941)

We're experiencing grim times and heavy losses. We've been stuck in the same place [the El'nia salient] for five weeks now and we're badly and constantly tormented by the Russian artillery. I just don't know how much longer our nerves can stand up to this. . . . I think we've already made enough heavy sacrifices. We're also constantly being promised that we'll be going back home, but it always comes to nothing. (Obergefreiter M. H., 268 Infantry Division, Army Group Center, 2 September 1941)

A magnificent day breaks. At 5:30 a.m. the German artillery opens fire and keeps up a heavy barrage for three hours. Our panzers attack. Our own attack is carried out, supported by Stukas, which, in rolling deployments, fight the retreating enemy with bombs. There are also Heinkel and Do [Dornier] aircraft. The roar of the engines never ceases for a minute. Me 109s keep the air clear. At 4:00 p.m. we advance. Everything is pushing forward. In the distance, Stukas bomb a fortified village into flames. A more wonderful combination of weapons, Luftwaffe, *army has hardly been seen. It continues early into the night.* (Gefreiter G., 11 Panzer Division, Army Group Center, 2 October 1941)

Now, I have something unpleasant to tell you. Last night we changed our position to Tikhvin. What I had always suspected has now come true. They've dropped us in the sh** again. . . . A young comrade of mine, Willi Braun, ran off yesterday evening and he is not back yet. Seems to have gone mad. When they find him, he'll probably be shot. Everyone, without exception, is scared for their life but, with the right trust in God, it's all right. . . . Hopefully, we'll be pulled out of here very soon, otherwise our nerves will be completely wrecked. (Erich Dohl, Sixteenth Army, Army Group North, 3 December 1941)

We are standing on a knife edge every day here. That is why we feel so betrayed. . . . We don't care a fig about any crusade, we are fighting for our bare lives here, every day and every hour, against an opponent who is a great deal more superior to us in all areas on the ground and in the air. We are being sent nothing from the rear, on the contrary, three divisions . . . were pulled away prematurely, the Luftwaffe *is pulling almost everything away, and our "winter equipment" is a joke in the current conditions.* (Oberstleutnant Helmuth Stieff, Fourth Army, Army Group Center, 7 December 1941)

Contents

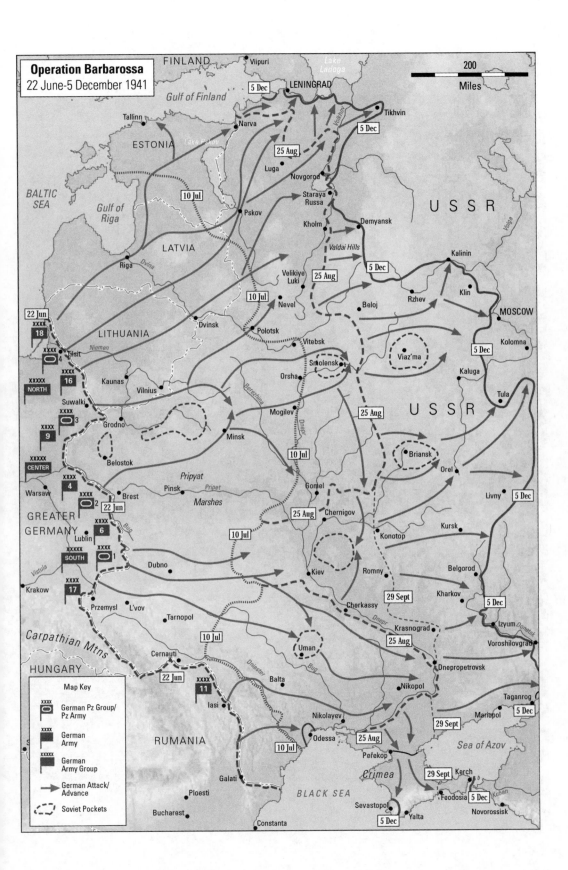

Operation Barbarossa
22 June-5 December 1941

FINLAND

Viipuri

Lake Ladoga

200

Miles

Gulf of Finland

5 Dec
LENINGRAD

Tallinn

Narva

Tikhvin

ESTONIA

Lake Peipus

5 Dec

25 Aug

Luga

Novgorod

USSR

BALTIC SEA

Gulf of Riga

10 Jul

Pskov

Staraya Russa

Volkhov

Kholm

Demyansk

Riga

Dvina

LATVIA

Velikiye Luki

Valdai Hills

Kalinin

25 Aug

5 Dec

Klin

Dvinsk

Nevel

Beloj

Rzhev

MOSCOW

22 Jun

XXXX
18

LITHUANIA

Polotsk

Vitebsk

10 Jul

Viaz'ma

5 Dec

Kolomna

XXXX
4

Tilsit

Niemen

Smolensk

XXXXX
16 NORTH

Kaunas

Orsha

USSR

Kaluga

Suwalki

XXXX
3

Vilnius

Berezina

Mogilev

Dnepr

25 Aug

Tula

XXXX
9

Grodno

Minsk

Briansk

Orel

XXXXX
CENTER

Belostok

10 Jul

Livny

5 Dec

Pripyat

Gomel

Kursk

Warsaw

XXXX
4

Pinsk

Pripet

Marshes

Chernigov

25 Aug

Konotop

XXXX
2

Brest

22 Jun

Belgorod

GREATER GERMANY

XXXX
6

Bug

10 Jul

Kiev

Romny

Kharkov

Lublin

XXXXX
SOUTH

XXXX
1

Dubno

Cherkassy

29 Sept

5 Dec

Krakow

XXXX
17

Przemysl

L'vov

Tarnopol

Dnepr

Krasnograd

Izyum

Donets

25 Aug

Voroshilovgrad

Vistula

Carpathian Mtns

10 Jul

Uman

Dnepropetrovsk

Cernauti

Dniester

Bug

HUNGARY

22 Jun

XXXX
11

Balta

Nikopol

Taganrog

Iasi

Nikolayev

29 Sept

Mariupol

5 Dec

RUMANIA

Odessa

25 Aug

Sea of Azov

10 Jul

Pefekop

Galati

Crimea

29 Sept

Kerch

Ploesti

BLACK SEA

Sevastopol

Feodosia

5 Dec

Kuban

Bucharest

Yalta

Novorossisk

Constanta

5 Dec

Map Key

XXXX
⊡ German Pz Group/ Pz Army

XXXX
■ German Army

XXXXX
▨ German Army Group

→ German Attack/ Advance

⟋⟍ Soviet Pockets

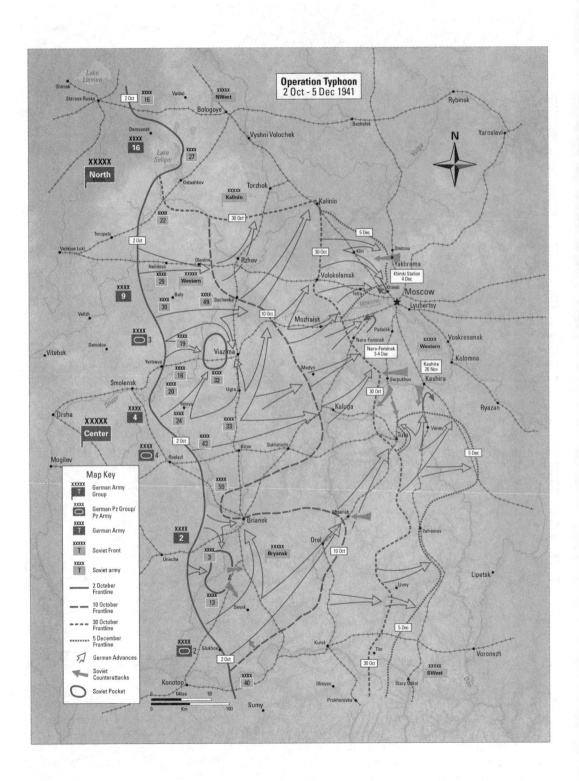

Notes on Style

For consistent spellings of towns, cities, and other geographical features, we have relied on historical maps and map studies (both published and archival). For more obscure towns and villages cited in the field post letters (or, occasionally, in the diary entries) of the German soldiers that make up this collection, we have in many cases simply retained the original German spellings.

We have typically cited the ranks of German rank-and-file soldiers as well as NCOs and officers in the German language—for example, *Gefreiter* Alois Scheuer (in place of Lance Corporal), *Hauptmann* Herbert Pabst (in place of Captain), *Generaloberst* Heinz Guderian (in place of General), and so on. For a comparative listing of equivalent military ranks (German and American) see Appendix 1.

We have sought to employ reasonably consistent protocols for German military units noted in the soldiers' letters or in our own annotations. For example, armies are always spelled out, as in "Fourth Army," while other military units, regardless of their size, are generally referred to with the unit number followed by the type of unit (e.g., 3 Panzer Group, 9 Army Corps, 24 Panzer Corps, 6 Infantry Division, 77 Infantry Regiment). Sometimes shortcuts are taken: for example, 9 AK for 9 Army Corps, 6 ID for 6 Infantry Division, 18 IR for 18 Infantry Regiment. In the soldiers' letters themselves, one will occasionally find abbreviated German unit designations for units below division and regimental level, and we have left these as they are—for example, III./PzRgt 18 (instead of 3rd Battalion, 18 Panzer Regiment); 11./IR 56 (instead of 11th Company, 56 Infantry Regiment); 7./IR 15 (mot.) (instead of 7th Company, 15 Infantry Regiment [mot.]). (Note: Soviet armies are occasionally noted in our chapter introductions, and these are always numbered—e.g., 3 Army.)

Throughout the narrative we have kept the German dating standard in the sequence of day, month, and year. For example, 1.6.41 signifies 1 June 1941, not 6 January 1941, as in American usage. For denoting distances, kilometers are used (with corresponding miles in parentheses). For denoting time, we have made use of several variants (e.g., 0315 hours, 3.15 in the morning, 8:00 a.m., 8 o'clock in the morning).

It should also be noted that each chapter (June through December 1941) begins with a succinct (ca. 2½ pages) introduction to provide the requisite historical context for the letters that follow. Finally, our historical annotations will furnish military historians, as well as military history "buffs" in general, with an array of additional insights into the first six months of the Eastern Campaign.

Foreword

Throughout the twentieth century, Russia exercised a powerful influence on the employment of German military power. With its immense amounts of arable land and material resources, Russia acted like a magnet, first for the *Drang nach Osten* ideas of pan-Germanist thinkers and later for the racially expansionist and murderous ideology of Adolf Hitler and his acolytes. During both world wars, millions of German soldiers served and fought in Russia, thus interacting with both its environment and its people. The remarkable collection of soldiers' writings amassed by the editors here provides the opportunity to compare the experiences of the *Landsers* of the Imperial German Army with those of the Third Reich's *Wehrmacht*.

The continuities revolve around the interconnected issues of culture and environment. German soldiers in both wars were struck by the immensity of Russia. Also noteworthy for soldiers a generation apart was the harshness of the environment. Searing heat, mind-numbing cold, and the almost trackless countryside were things soldiers in both wars invariably mentioned in their letters and diaries. The same went for the effects of snow and mud on both soldiers and horses.

Concomitant with the nature of an area was the people who occupied it and the civilization they had managed to create. While the writings presented here are suffused in a number of cases with Nazi ideology, German soldiers in both world wars held an attitude of cultural superiority. While admiration might be expressed for Russian soldiers as dogged fighters, even soldiers who were not ardent Nazis were taken aback by what they regarded as the primitive state of Russian civilization. Such attitudes were common among soldiers who served in the East from 1914 to 1918 as well. Both culture and environment contributed to a similar general picture of "the East" in both cases—namely, a wild, uncivilized, alien place inhabited by people regarded as certainly culturally, if not racially, inferior.

The peculiarities of the World War II soldier's experience in Russia were related to developments in warfare after 1918. The most notable of these was aircraft. The observations of German soldiers presented here show how quickly general German air superiority disappeared as the power of the *Luftwaffe* was diffused over Russia's enormous air space. If one reads the soldiers' comments carefully, one can see where the *Luftwaffe* is making its major effort at any particular time in the campaign.

The other most notable discontinuity with earlier experience concerned sheer brutality, both inwardly and outwardly directed. The inward brutality was manifested in the enforcement of harsh discipline in the German Army. While death sentences in the imperial army were rare, they were commonplace in the *Wehrmacht*. Also of note was the relative indifference, at least on the part of a number of soldiers, to the murderous brutality directed against Jews and other victims of Nazi occupation policies.

Finally, one last continuity with imperial Germany must be noted, and gratefully at that. Germany's education system created the most literate army in Europe in the nineteenth and twentieth centuries. Without that educational base, this work would not have been possible. It enabled Luther and Stahel to let the soldiers speak for themselves.

Richard L. DiNardo
Professor of National Security Affairs,
Marine Corps Command and Staff College,
Quantico, Virginia

Acknowledgments

The editors of this volume are acutely aware that their efforts would have been for naught without the support and encouragement of colleagues and friends. We would like to take a brief moment to provide the acknowledgment they deserve. Let us begin with Mr. David Reisch, the senior history editor of Stackpole Books, who believed in us and our concept and gave us the intellectual and "artistic" space we required to produce this unique book; David was our advocate every step of the way, and for that we will always be grateful. Among David's colleagues at Stackpole who also deserve recognition are production editor Elaine McGarraugh, assistant editor Stephanie Otto, and copy editor Melissa Churchill. Thanks are also due to proofreader Linda Hoffman and layout artist Karen Weldon for their crucial contributions.

Special thanks are also due Dr. Richard L. DiNardo, professor of national security affairs, Marine Corps Command and Staff College (Quantico, Virginia), for preparing the foreword to *Soldiers of Barbarossa*. Also meriting high praise is Dr. Madeleine Brook (now teaching at the University of Stuttgart, Germany) for her translations of hundreds of field post letters. While we translated a portion of the letters ourselves, Madeleine's expert translations constitute the bulk of this book. Dr. Brook also conducted research and provided us with a large tranche of German letters from the Library of Contemporary History in Stuttgart; in this activity, she was ably supported by Frau Irina Renz, head of special collections at the library.

We would also like to acknowledge (in no particular order) cartographer Joe Youst for drawing the exquisitely detailed maps, Dr. Oleg Beyda for his assistance with research, dear friend and colleague Herr Johannes Haape for permission to use photographs from his Haape Family Archive, Herr Arne Schrader and Christian Reith of the German War Graves Commission for permission to use commission photographs, Mr. Rupert Harding (Pen & Sword Books, UK) for permission to use photographs, and Henley's Photo Shop (Bakersfield, California) for producing the high-quality photographs that grace this book.

CHAPTER 1

Operation *Barbarossa* in the Letters of German Soldiers

David Stahel

"It is completely different from what the unbelievable propaganda shows you."[1]

In the course of the Second World War, estimates suggest that some forty billion German letters were exchanged back and forth between the front and the homeland. More than three-quarters of these (some 76 percent) originated from the homeland with the remaining 24 percent sent in return by soldiers.[2] This disparity may be explained by a number of factors. Most significantly, there were many more civilians in the homeland than soldiers at the front. Yet despite the disparity in numbers, the individual soldier was writing more letters on average than a typical civilian. This is particularly surprising when one considers the time constraints on the men, especially in 1941. As soldiers fought, advanced, or retreated, the demands of the campaign were typically extreme, leaving little time for other duties and even less for personal pursuits like letter writing.

When the front settled down into longer periods of positional warfare, soldiers faced periodic shortages of paper, which was an issue throughout Germany. Nevertheless, German soldiers understood that their letters served as vital "life signs" for families and sweethearts. As a result, the need to write—and write often—was seen as essential. Homesick men wrote copious letters, and while some only seldom put their thoughts to paper, almost no one wrote nothing. Soldiers were also compelled by the powerful allure of receiving post themselves. Field post was the one link back to Germany, to loved ones, and to all that was familiar to the men. In 1941, a daily volume of some fifteen million letters required transport between the front and the homeland,[3] and that would rise to upward of twenty-five million in 1942. Over the course of the war, estimates suggest that letters required between twelve and thirty days to reach their recipients,[4] but owing to numerous transportation problems, longer waits were more typical for field post to and from the Eastern Front in 1941. As an illustration of the sheer volume of paper being transported, the logistics section of a single German panzer division noted that between 2 October 1941 and 31 January 1942, it had moved 530 tons of essential supplies of which some 80 tons was field post.[5] Inadequate and overburdened railways supplying the Eastern Front combined with steadily declining motorization, the increasing depth of German operations, and seasonal rains to delay

1

deliveries of field post by six weeks or more. This had serious implications for the morale of the men. On 9 November, the war diary of Krüger's 1 Panzer Division noted: "The connection with the homeland seems to have been severed." This contributed to a depressed mood among the troops.[6] Three days later, it was reported that some two thousand sacks of post were awaiting delivery to the division in Smolensk.[7]

After going weeks without post, one soldier commented, "You notice that field post is just as important as rations and ammunition, because it has to sustain and nourish our spirits, our emotions. And to sustain the soldier as a human being, to prevent him from becoming a raw brutalized instrument of war, that is the higher task of the letter writer back home."[8] Similarly, William Lubbeck noted that

> when a soldier is fighting a thousand miles away from his native soil, mail from home provides a tremendous boost to morale. Because of military censorship, we could not write about our units, where we were or our battles at the front. At the same time, letters to those back home provided us a momentary release from war's miseries and gave loved ones relief from their constant anxiety over the soldier's fate. . . . Like most soldiers, I read and reread these messages from home and devoted a large portion of my free time to writing letters in reply. In my experience, news from home was one of the most significant factors shaping a soldier's capacity in combat because it determined his state of mind and morale. Throughout the war, these letters were as important to sustaining our souls as food was to sustaining our bodies.[9]

Not surprisingly, the arrival of post was an event of great joy and even celebration among the men. Karl Nünnighoff stated in a letter, "My eyes almost cried with joy when I got my post today."[10] The occasion would typically be followed by hours of shared exchanges of news as well as packages of edible treats, baked by wives and mothers. Many men then set about replying to the letters they had just received. Beyond the joy and camaraderie such deliveries offered, the arrival of post was an irreplaceable emotional support. After a particularly difficult day, Werner Adamczyk noted,

> I turned to the several letters from Rosemarie. Thank God, they were more cheerful. She did not mention the war at all—only her feeling of love and her expectations of me coming home on vacation soon. She wrote about many plans of what we would do together. They were lovely letters and they brought me back to a mental balance. Indeed, with much imagination I projected my thoughts and feelings forward to that much-desired time. But would I make it? That was the question I asked myself, with trembling hands and tears in my eyes.[11]

Another soldier referred to post from his wife as "the nicest and best source of strength," while others dubbed the letters "little brown darlings" and "the only gleam of hope." One soldier wrote of being "as happy as a small child who had just received a present." Likewise, Heinz Heppermann told his wife, "I often have the symptoms of something, sometimes a cold, then many headaches or stomach upsets, here and there also a torn ligament; but soldiers mostly don't pay attention to such things! All of this disappears when a letter from home arrives for us, with caring words, words of faithfulness and of affiliation."[12] In addition to the emotional importance of field post, the army was struggling to provide even the basic essentials for soldiers, meaning that letters sometimes arrived in packages that offered the rare opportunity for "luxury" items. One soldier listed the contents of his latest package, which included a notebook, small envelopes, skin cream, mineral pastilles, vitamin tablets, razor blades, cigarettes, and biscuits.[13]

While receiving news from home was the essential point of interest for the soldiers at the front, it is what they wrote in return that is of such value to military historians. It is only relatively recently that historians of the Nazi-Soviet conflict have begun to chart a view of this conflict from below. The first fifty years of the postwar era saw the war in Eastern Europe represented almost exclusively from a top-down perspective in which the movement of armies, corps, and divisions overshadowed any individual experience. Social histories of the German Army have really only gained traction since the 1990s,[14] and while these have offered us important frameworks for understanding, capturing the many dimensions of a war in the East in which an estimated ten million German men served between 1941 and 1945 will no doubt require more work.

What have we learned so far? Owing to increasing literacy rates, it is really only in the modern era that a view of the everyday soldier may be reconstructed from his own writings. Earlier German conflicts also saw enthusiastic responses from the soldiers, producing voluminous correspondence. In the Franco-Prussian War (1870–1871), some 101 million letters were exchanged, while in the First World War the number reached 28.7 billion.[15] Only a fraction of these survive in archives, museums, and private collections, but as sources they offer a raw and honest authenticity, unencumbered by subsequent developments or the problems of memory. Their linguist form, personal content, and the fact they were typically not intended for a wider audience underline their value in capturing the Zeitgeist of the soldier's experience, social condition, and state of mind. While the study of field post promises so much, in fact, the use of letters in the writing of history has only recently established itself as a serious medium of inquiry. In Nazi Germany's case, critics have argued that postal censorship colored the content of what could be written, while soldiers at the front were in any case distorting their letters through a desire to protect relatives from the harsh truths of war.[16] It is argued that such conscious or unconscious bias undermines the substance of the information and has led to letters from the front being dismissed as "the product of fantasy."[17] Yet such characterizations are misguided.

The organization and distribution of field post within the German Army was controlled by a division of the quartermaster-general. At the top of this department was *Generalmajor* Karl Ziegler, who directed some twelve thousand people across occupied Europe to manage the movement and delivery of the army's letters.[18] Post was not addressed directly to a man's unit or even his area of deployment; in fact, it was not necessary for the sender to know anything about his military service or posting in order for a letter to reach him. A letter was simply addressed with his name and a five-number field post signature. Every unit had a unique number, which for security reasons could be changed at any time during the war. Upon arrival at the front, one man from each company was responsible for the collection of mailbags and the distribution of their contents, typically by reading out names to an impromptu assembly of men.[19]

While Ziegler's department managed the delivery of letters to and from the Eastern Front, the matter of censorship was dictated by the High Command of the Armed Forces (*Oberkommando der Wehrmacht*) and carried out by a "field post examination center" within each army. This was nominally staffed by five officers and fourteen noncommissioned officers, which, not surprisingly, could do little more than sample a fraction of the mailbags passing to and from the front. Figures from examination centers later in the war suggest that an individual censor could reasonably manage to inspect upward of 176 letters a day, but of course such a figure was entirely dependent on the highly variable length of letters. In one of the first substantive attempts to analyze and publish a large sample of German field post, Ortwin Buchbender and Reinhold Sterz concluded, "The letters of the edition clearly show how the censor influenced the mentality of some letter writers. However there remains the impression that after careful examination of some 50,000 field post letters . . . that the mass of soldiers expressed their views and opinions astonishingly openly and unselfconsciously."[20]

Klaus Latzel's study has referred to two forms of attempted censorship, which he has dubbed "external" and "internal." The first referred to the explicit checking of content to identify and reprimand (or potentially charge) culprits,[21] although evidence of serious infractions resulted from less than 1 percent of the total checked mail.[22] The threat, however, of disciplinary action was hoped to have a disproportionate impact on "internal" censorship, in which the letter writer would self-censor his own work.[23] This so-called "scissors in the head" effect was bolstered by a media campaign in which the need for censorship received a high profile. The intent was for soldiers to believe the controls were more rigorous and frequent than was actually the case, although they too must have been aware that the sheer volume of letters mitigated against anything other than a tiny sample being checked.[24] More to the point, one may well question the extent to which soldiers were prepared to self-censor their only medium of communication with home, although concern for relatives may well have led to a considerable percentage playing down the difficulties and dangers they confronted. The urge to freely communicate and share profound experiences had to compete with the desire not to disturb or worry loved ones.

The basis for the censorship of field post was the "Ordinance on Communication," which was published on 12 March 1940 and stipulated that information provided by the troops in their letters was subject to secrecy regulations in six key areas:

1. Distribution of information on army matters that are subject to secrecy
2. Spreading rumors of all kinds
3. Sending photos and pictures of all types, which are subject to secrecy regulations
4. Sending enemy propaganda
5. Critical comments on measures taken by the army and the government of the Reich
6. Statements raising the suspicion of espionage, sabotage, and subversion[25]

As this collection will illustrate, such a directive was by no means always observed, but disregarding the regulations took on both overt and covert manifestations. In practice it was the first of the six regulations that was the most difficult for soldiers to observe and therefore constituted the most contravened of the regulations. It required soldiers to withhold all specific details of their service, such as composition, size, and location of their units; the names of superiors and comrades; information related to equipment and arms; military intentions; and combat losses.[26] Given that many of these subjects formed the basis of their experiences, soldiers could often not resist writing about them, although others adopted codes that allowed them to communicate forbidden details in secret. W. Bremer told after that war how he and his father came up with a system of revealing where he was in any given letter. "The first letter of a sentence and every other first letter of the following sentences spelled out the name of the place in which I was. That was naturally not a small place, but always the bigger cities. One was only supposed to write 'in the East.'"[27] Others adopted even more simple methods for expressing themselves openly, especially in regard to the fifth regulation on expressing criticisms. In one such postal code, a dash at the end of a sentence indicated that the author meant the opposite of what was stated. Such simple adaptations kept postal communication open and honest in spite of official regulations.[28]

While some letter writers proved ingenious at subverting the censor, what is perhaps more remarkable is the relative frankness, especially when it came to military matters, that most letters display. Soldiers, for the most part, seem to have felt at liberty to discuss the war or their personal circumstances as soldiers, including negative aspects, in varying degrees of openness.[29] The exception, which other studies have confirmed, concerned political matters. Criticisms of Hitler or the Nazi party in soldiers' letters from 1941 are far less common than those directed against the shortcomings of the army. The penchant for openness, in spite of the official regulations and the censor, led to some attempts at curbing such behavior. A report dating from the middle of September 1941 by the 263 Infantry Division noted, "Soldiers must be informed that in writing letters it is forbidden to make any mention of supposed or genuine difficulties, especially the unfavorable influence of the war on the morale and health of the soldiers. Letters from home, in which any mention is made of abuses of any kind, or personal anxieties, must be destroyed. We are duty bound to bear with courage any difficulties . . . without providing food for enemy propaganda."[30]

Martin Humburg's study of German field post referred to a "fall crisis" in 1941, which asserted that the increasingly drawn-out war resulted in two psychological episodes affecting the mood of German soldiers. The first was the disappointment of hopes for outright victory in the summer of 1941, and the second was the realization that a winter campaign had become inevitable.[31] Over the summer, the strains of the German advance that demanded constant combat, long marches, and sometimes heavy losses were sustained by the promise of a rapid victory and release from the campaign's many torments. Already in the opening weeks, the mental strains of the Eastern Campaign had been excessive, but as the cumulative toll mounted with no end in sight, homesick, exhausted, and even traumatized men defied regulations to share their fears and frustrations with family and loved ones. The problem was that the *Ostheer* (eastern army) appeared to be winning all the battles but not the war itself. As Helmut Pabst complained in a letter home, "What a country, what a war, where there's no pleasure in success, no pride, no satisfaction; only a feeling of suppressed fury."[32] Similarly, Harald Henry complained that after all the battles he had taken part in, there was still no discernible end in sight. Writing home on 20 October, Henry wrote: "How much longer shall it take! It must finally come to an end or at least we should get some relief. At all the great encirclement battles of Army Group Center, Belostok, Minsk, Mogilev, Roslavl', Desna, Viaz'ma and Briansk we were outstanding and took part with heavy losses. For once one must allow us to have a break. It is not bearable any longer."[33]

Certainly, by the final months of 1941, the men had endured a great deal of personal suffering and loss, which itself led to a form of brutalization. Letters offered a rare outlet for emotions as well as an opportunity to "process" and "rationalize" the events in which they were taking part. It also gave hope that return letters would provide much-needed understanding, encouragement, and love. Under the difficult circumstances, such emotional support acted as a vital coping mechanism and helps explain the extraordinary importance attached to the arrival of post from home. Yet, however important this exchange may have been to the men at the front, the information they were sending to the homeland sometimes radically departed from the triumphalist tone of German propaganda, which created a credibility gap that the Nazi regime did not like.

The best illustration of the divergence in representations of the war from "above" versus "below" was the Reich's press chief, Dr. Otto Dietrich's, declaration of victory following the double encirclements at Viaz'ma and Briansk in early October. Before the international and domestic media, Dietrich declared, "The campaign in the East has been decided by the smashing of Army Group Timoshenko."[34] The following day (10 October) the *Völkische Beobachter*, a Nazi daily newspaper, carried banner headlines extolling the news: "The Great Hour Has Struck!" "Campaign in the East Decided!" "The Military End of the Bolsheviks."[35] This was mimicked in the Romanian daily *Evenimentul*, which led with the full-page headline: "The Russian Campaign Is Over."[36] Yet German soldiers were not the only ones who knew how far from the truth this was; German propaganda minster Joseph Goebbels observed the events with nervous trepidation. The German reporting, he wrote, was "almost too positive and too optimistic. When, for example, the press are given the headline: 'The War Is Decided!' that surely goes too far." Goebbels saw that this risked the prestige of the whole regime. "I hope to God," Goebbels continued, "that the military operations develop so that we don't suffer a psychological reverse."[37] Yet that was already taking place in the East, and such preposterous reporting only compounded the problem as exasperated soldiers increasingly sought to inform their loved ones about the "real war" they were fighting. One soldier complained bitterly of the lack of winter preparations before assuring his family, "The reality is indeed something other than the radio announcements."[38] Likewise, in early December, Werner Beermann contrasted the enduring war with the farcical public depiction of two months earlier: "I can well imagine that you, like many in the homeland, have a very hazy picture of what is happening here. According to the newspapers, radio announcements, and newsreels everything is crystal clear: 'The war in the East is decided!'"[39]

Just as Goebbels had feared, the field post from the East was now directly undermining the propaganda effort, suggesting that the party and high command was out of touch with reality on the ground. Writing on 12 December, the propaganda minister noted, "Actually the impact of letters from the front, which had been regarded as extraordinarily important, has to be considered more than harmful today. The soldiers are pretty blunt when they describe the great problems they are fighting under, the lack of winter gear . . . insufficient food and ammunition."[40] Yet rather than acting to restrain public expectations and recasting the state's message to close the credibility gap, Goebbels's solution was to issue an instruction on the "art of writing letters" for the troops. This called for an emphasis on "manly, hard and clear letters . . . differentiating between impressions best locked deeply in the heart because they only concern soldiers at the front and those which can be, and should be, related at home to keep them informed about the war." In line with National Socialist conceptions of soldiering, the instruction then asserted that anyone who complained was "no true soldier."[41] Not surprisingly, Goebbels's instruction had little discernible impact on the tone in which letters were written, especially since the unexpected Soviet winter offensive was placing extraordinary new demands on the men.[42] Hans Joachim C. wrote home in early December of his plight at having to keep watch both day and night at the front: "I cannot tell you what that means. First, the terrible cold, blizzard, wet feet through and through—the boots never dry anymore and cannot be pulled off—and secondly, the Russians test our nerves. . . . Everyone thinks of the end."[43]

Germany's winter crisis was only just beginning, and for all the censorship and strict directives about letter writing, soldiers typically insisted on a measured or even total independence in the face of official regulations. Personal communication was a rare "private space," off-limits to the draconian world that dominated their lives and inhibited their freedoms. The army, of course, did not simply accept such willful insubordination, and complaints continued to be recorded. *Generalleutnant* Erich Schroeck, commanding the 98 Infantry Division, noted in a report from early December 1941,

> The German soldier at the front is too much given to writing. It is intolerable that the diaries of German soldiers or letters addressed to their relations should fall into the hands of the enemy. The anxiety of relations about a son or husband is interpreted by the enemy as our weakness. . . . It is necessary to remind the troops once again that they must not mention very much in their letters and above all they must not describe heavy losses. By making such statements we merely sadden our relations, whereas we ought to sustain them with cheerful news. Moreover, news of this kind passes from mouth to mouth and may reach the enemy.[44]

Clearly, soldiers' letters offered their own narrative of the war in the East, and it was one that departed starkly from the official representation in the German media and often did not serve as the morale-boosting confirmation of the regime's ideal for "true soldiers." It is this contrasting view of the war in the East "from below" that the current volume seeks to capture and represent. It is a story best told in the soldiers' own words, unfiltered and authentic. It spans excerpts from hundreds of letters (as well as a few diaries), including well over two hundred German soldiers serving in all areas of the Eastern Front during 1941. There is a rough correlation between the size of the German Army groups and the number of excerpts from each. Officers were also included, mostly of junior rank and none above colonel (*Oberst*). This preserves the "view from below," which we have sought to represent by casting as wide a net as possible in terms of subjects and themes. Of course, any "ego documents" produced by historical actors assume certain context, either for the period in which they lived or the specialist knowledge they and their readers possessed. Accordingly, the collected excerpts have been annotated for context and correctives. Apart from orienting the reader on technical terms, army organizational matters, and aspects of the Nazi state, the annotations offer insight into the growing literature on the Eastern Front in 1941.

Broadly speaking, the book canvasses three distinct categories of experience in the East—combat, genocide, and everyday life. Although these form broad areas of discussion, what emerges is anything but uniform. In reality, the men who made up the German *Ostheer* were never as socially, culturally, or politically homogeneous as the collective representation of the *Volksgemeinschaft* (national community) in National Socialist propaganda suggested. At the same time, their experience of the war in the East and how they made sense of it was always an individual one. Their letters reflect diversity and contradiction even sometimes in relation to similar phenomena. As Hester Vaizey noted, "In many senses, there was not a 'typical experience' of the war. Indeed, one major strength of *Feldpostbriefe* as a source is that they offer a multi-perspective view of the impact of war on the private sphere."[45] This tapestry of experience and opinion offers contrasting perspectives on the *Wehrmacht*'s inner workings and tells us much about how the soldiers coped (or did not cope) with the demands of the war. The fact that there can seldom be a single answer or united opinion to any one question does not invalidate field post as a source; it in fact reveals the extent to which top-down histories focused on organizations and structures present at times an artificial uniformity and disguise contradiction. Patterns of dominant behavior can, of course, still be identified among the soldiers, and the question then becomes how these were established and justified.

Combat was the defining experience of the Eastern Campaign and the most celebrated aspirational goal of "manhood" in the National Socialist world. Indeed, "struggle" was at the core of Nazism, and there was no greater enemy than the "Jewish Bolshevik" in Soviet Russia. In many respects this made Operation *Barbarossa* the defining event of Hitler's Third Reich—a campaign that would make or break Germany as a global power because the dictator would brook no compromise. Everything therefore depended on the fighting strength of the *Wehrmacht*, and having cast the war in such binary terms, no sacrifice was too great for victory. This was the war that Germany's soldiers found themselves fighting in 1941. Indeed, as German troops crossed the Soviet border, the utter poverty of Soviet peasantry appeared to substantiate the clash of ideologies that framed the war in German eyes. This also gave German soldiers a sense of righteousness that their values, culture, and even "race" were superior. Although soldiers attributed the abject poverty of the East to the Communist policies of the derided "Soviet paradise," in fact, in many regions, impoverishment long preceded Bolshevik rule. This perception, however, added to the destructiveness of the war and the tendency to view the Soviet people as "backward," "hostile," and "enemy."

Germanic superiority was not only assumed to be culturally evident by the divergent living standards but also given weight by the *Wehrmacht*'s military performance. In the early weeks of the campaign, soldiers evinced a clear pride in their achievements, as Albert Neuhaus wrote in June: "There is simply no stopping the German steamroller."[46] The following month Karl Fuchs excitedly declared that the war would soon be over on account of "our great success" and "because already we are fighting against only fragmented opposition."[47] Yet the *Barbarossa* campaign also highlighted the fallacy of Germany's "natural" superiority. On the first day of the war, Heinrich Haape noted, "Our regiment's losses on this single day are greater than during the entire French campaign."[48] Likewise, Udo von Alvensleben wrote of "the enemy's astounding combat power," which by early July caused him to conclude, "Our losses have been tremendous."[49] The constant exertion, constant danger, and constant proximity of death overwhelmed men as they struggled to articulate what they were experiencing. On only the sixth day of the war, August Sahm tried to find the words to describe what he was enduring:

> Since 22.6. we've been in combat and I really can't describe what I've had to go through. Attack—dig in—artillery fire—attack again. I'm writing to you from a foxhole. Since the start of the fighting I haven't washed or shaved. . . .
> I can't begin to express what I feel. If I only saw some meaning in it all! I simply can't come to terms with it. The only thing that I do is—try to hold on from minute to minute in this maelstrom of strange, unknown forces.
> How it hurts, one's own suffering—and even more that of others.
> Human beings are swept away, fall like withered leaves—human beings.[50]

Sahm's letter makes the trauma of the events almost palpable, and even his incomprehension at what he was observing speaks to the shocking reality of what he was exposed to. As the study by Wolfram Wette observed,

> Those of us who have read collections of battlefield letters cannot avoid the impression at times that many of the *Landser* [German soldiers] were not capable of finding adequate words to describe the events swirling around them. They could not accurately describe what it was like to live on the borderline between life and death, in a chaos that shattered nerves and wore bodies to the bone. Yet it was by no means due to a lack of intelligence, nor merely consideration for the feelings of the recipients of the letters, whom the soldiers did not want to alarm. Many enlisted men were simply struck dumb by the hideous reality of battle; what they were experiencing was an inferno that defied description.[51]

Hannes Heer has described the process of brutalization on the Eastern Front as resulting from a transformative event in which men first experienced "shock" and then a process of "renormalization." Importantly, German soldiers were not simply engaging in warfare but a conflict in which the rules of civil society and the basic codex of armed conflict were being repudiated. The brutalizing effect of their experiences, and sometimes their own actions, initially induced a sense of shock brought on by a loss of orientation, the duration of which varied from soldier to soldier. Men wrote home of becoming "a different person," of being forced to "completely readjust," and of experiencing "inner change." Another wrote that he had been forced to "throw overboard several principles held in the past," while others spoke of a new "split consciousness." The shock, however, soon passed, as the daily exposure to unparalleled violence became, out of necessity, normalized. In identifying this process, Heer was able to point to German soldiers' descriptions of themselves as having become "hard," "indifferent," and "heartless."[52] William Lubbeck observed, "Over time, war hardens your heart and leads you to do brutal things that you could never have imagined yourself doing in civilian life."[53] Likewise, Willy Peter Reese wrote of developing an "armor of apathy" that he used to protect himself "against terror, horror, fear, and madness, which saved me from suffering and screaming." Yet Reese noted that this same apathy "crushed any tender stirring within me, snapped off the green shoots of hope, faith, and love of my fellow men, and turned my heart to stone."[54] Accordingly, the "renormalization" process was a coping mechanism aimed at dealing with the shocking brutality of the war in the East, yet the price was typically a radical desensitization toward violence, allowing for indifference not only toward the horrors of war but also to the acts of violence that governed the German occupation.

The "renormalization" was therefore a transformative process that caused men to "reorder" moral parameters, shifting to what some portrayed as the "laws of war." This was a subtle process of incremental rationalization that often occurred unconsciously, allowing the individual to believe he retained his good moral standing. For the vast majority of German soldiers, there was no question of being on the "right" side, firmly dissociated from any suggestion of inappropriate, much less criminal, behavior. Almost any German action could be justified as ensuring "security," which in turn necessitated "harsh measures." One letter from a German noncommissioned officer captured the cognitive process explicitly:

> Does war actually have its own laws? I read now "Not everyone that saith onto me 'Lord, Lord,' enters into Heaven, but rather those who do the will of my Father in Heaven." Just now, an elder came to me, someone took his pig. Now he wants to get at least something from it. In any case, he also lost his cow. Of course, it is for our kitchen, but this is difficult for those who are affected by it. Should I give my people less to live on to spare the civilian population? Or am I obligated to care for the men so that they live as well as possible? In general, one says that war has its own laws. Thus, the case is settled. . . . You see, the war brings not only a re-evaluation, but a revolution of the moral sphere. [It] has its own law.[55]

Likewise, Hans Albring not only observed that a fundamental "reordering" was taking place but even framed this new age of humanity as a positive evolution: "And, who knows, perhaps this is the metaphysical meaning of the war, that a new and true image of humanity is rising in us, after we have followed a false, and increasingly distorting, image of humanity for so many hundreds of years."[56]

Referring to the renormalization process taking place on the Eastern Front, Hannes Heer described "how amorality became normality,"[57] but importantly this is not how German soldiers saw it. The adaptation of what social psychologists call "basic norms" determined new behavioral boundaries that were intended to safeguard the group. Such a transformation is typically stimulated by the perception of a threat for which a community accepts new rules to cope and ensure survival. Thus, in their self-conception, German soldiers were not becoming amoral but rather the opposite. In a struggle to defend their cherished homeland and *Volk*, the adoption of new basic norms was required to protect the same moral world they had always accepted. Lothar Fritze's study concluded, "It is always the others who are the 'evil' ones. They believed their own actions to be justified. . . . This is also the reason why it was impossible within the framework of their thinking to develop a sense of guilt, which, however, does not rule out that they knew or presumed that others would view their actions as criminal."[58] Of course, some soldiers did develop guilt complexes, but these were typically kept private because the wider community had adapted basic norms to justify and explain harsh actions. It was the weakness of those "too soft" to implement the required response that endangered the community and threatened the righteousness of those expounding the new basic norms. Indeed, National Socialism promoted an ideal type of masculinity that, as Lisa Pine observed, "functioned to exclude whole categories of men that did not fit in to the 'national community,' based on a set of prescriptive norms."[59] The pressure to conform was therefore externally enforced and inwardly desired, allowing for a general conformity around ideas and actions encompassed by "the laws of war," which in practice might better be described as "lawlessness."

A forthcoming study of German field post on the Eastern Front by David Harrisville further demonstrates that soldiers frequently employed a series of moral rationalizations to justify their actions and defend a positive self-image. His study illustrates how traditional values from a broad array of belief systems, including traditional nationalism, military virtues, Christian principles, and middle-class norms, buttressed National Socialist ideology and complemented its aims. As Harrisville concludes,

> There were still differences, however, between the *Wehrmacht*'s conception of the soldier and the "new man" of Nazism. The ideal warrior as the army defined him in the 1930s carried out his job with ruthless efficiency but in principle still operated within established codes of conduct, avoided excessive brutality, and displayed chivalry toward non-combatants. In contrast, the Nazis' ideal man recognized no limits, adopted an attitude of brutal toughness, and showed no mercy in his dealings with lesser races. Overall then, the relationship between traditional values and Nazi innovations in the *Wehrmacht* at the start of the Second World War was rife with ambiguities. In some cases, the two norm systems coexisted in tension, but more and more they appeared to be working together to the Nazis' benefit.[60]

Such research not only adds to our understanding of how the soldiers of *Barbarossa* proved so cohesive but also challenges the postwar myth of the "clean" *Wehrmacht* generated by the memoirs of former generals and veterans' organizations. Instead, Harrisville argues that the coalescence of traditional values with Nazi aims predates the origins of the myth to the war years themselves. The personal justifications varied, and many no doubt obfuscated what was happening in the East through their silence, but the message of a decent, long-suffering *Wehrmacht* dedicated to

Germany and deserving of its admiration was an established message that untold letters typically emphasized.

Thomas Kühne's research into the social world of the German soldier sheds further light on the profound bonds between men that acted to reinforce notions of unit cohesion and group loyalty beyond any reference to duty or patriotism. According to Kühne, German comradeship promoted a profound form of male bonding, allowing groups to forge a surrogate form of family, which provided a powerful source of emotional support to shield against the brutalizing effects of warfare.[61] As Gottlob Bidermann wrote, "We had become old together and had developed a brotherhood between us, a closeness of spirit and trust that those who live in safety throughout their lives cannot know."[62] Likewise, Helmut Günther observed, "Only through such comradeship was it possible to survive all the madness around us."[63] The sense of the unit as "home" and men as "family" was also evident in soldiers' writings. Martin Pöppel wrote in his diary, "Here a man looks at other Germans and sees his brother, his home."[64] Such tight bonds were also linked with Germany's fighting prowess, as Karl Fuchs wrote home in a letter: "A great friendship binds us German soldiers together out here. . . . This loyalty is the essence of the German fighting spirit. We can depend on each other unconditionally. Each one of us sets the example for the other and that makes us strong."[65] It was this intimate form of comradeship, forged through months of fighting in the Soviet Union, that acted as a central prop in maintaining a cohesive group structure and providing substantiation and validation for any group behaviors. Even remarkable acts of violence against passive, nonthreatening groups could be accepted if, according to targeted research by Jeff Rutherford, the result was deemed to have a military benefit.

Rutherford's notion of "military necessity" led the German Army to use any and all means, regardless of their ethical costs, to achieve victory on the battlefield, and it resulted in both impressive combat effectiveness as well as frequent recourse to violent outbursts directed at Soviet civilians.[66] Critically, Rutherford shows a correlation between a perceived "need" and an often ruthless "response." In other words, ruthless actions were typically not random acts undertaken for the sake of sheer malice or cruelty. When, for example, food was short, labor was required, or a suspected partisan threat was identified, German formations were shown to be capable of the most brutal actions against a local population, which they might previously have treated comparatively well. Moreover, Rutherford's work suggests that National Socialist ideology was more an enabling, rather than an instigating, factor for the army's behavior—a conclusion backed by Sönke Neitzel and Harald Welzer, whose own study found that "far more important than ideology for soldiers' perceptions and interpretations, and thus for their concrete decisions and actions, was their military value system."[67] Such studies help us build a picture of the army at the institutional level, which may or may not extend to individual behavior but establishes the prevailing environment that the majority adhered to.

Neitzel and Welzer's study focuses not on field post but on how soldiers spoke to one another in private and what that revealed about their wartime culture and values. Detailed conversations of German POWs were secretly recorded by British and American intelligence, forming a remarkable source base—some hundred thousand pages—of unparalleled evidence. They record the soldiers freely conversing in their own world of normative values, unfiltered by outsiders or postwar ideals. As Neitzel and Welzer demonstrate, the stories they tell include random as well as purposeful acts of violence, which require no explanation within the group and do not appear to cause the interlocutor to question his standing within the group. As Neitzel and Welzer explain, "Stories about shooting, raping, and robbing are commonplace within the war stories. Rarely do they occasion analysis, moral objections, or disagreements. The soldiers understand one another. They share the same world and swap perspectives on the events that occupy their minds and the things that they've seen and done."[68]

The tolerance for violence among the soldiers in the East was exceptional, but while they generally understood and accepted it, this does not mean that they were uniformly violent in a criminal sense. Since the 1990s, an impassioned debate has taken place about the role of the average German soldier in war crimes, especially in the East. Rolf-Dieter Müller concludes that the percentage of German soldiers who participated in war crimes was "if anything smaller still" (*eher noch geringer*) than the estimated 5 percent of German soldiers involved in war crimes in occupied Italy.[69] Christian Hartmann's study of five German divisions on the Eastern Front in 1941 and 1942 concludes that criminal conduct was largely a feature of rear area security formations and not the frontline units, which made up the vast majority of the troops deployed in the East. Hartmann even questions whether the *Wehrmacht* should be regarded as a perpetrator organization of the National Socialist regime.[70] Such conclusions contrast starkly with those reached by Dieter Pohl in his analysis of the *Wehrmacht*'s occupation policies in the Soviet Union. Pohl finds that the number of divisions deployed on the Eastern Front in which no war crimes were committed was "low" and adds that members of the *Wehrmacht* may have constituted the majority of those responsible for mass crimes carried out by the Nazi state.[71] At its most excessive, Hannes Heer suggests some "60 to 80 per cent" of German soldiers who fought in the East participated in war crimes.[72]

Such a range of figures almost poses more questions than it answers and, on the surface, brings us no closer to a conclusion. My own analysis (together with Alex J. Kay) argues for a distinction in how we understand and apply the term "criminality." Most studies discussing the German occupation of the Soviet Union relate to what might be termed "first tier criminality" in which the intention of the perpetrator is to harm, maltreat, or kill a victim. Yet what had been overlooked is the broader category of "secondary criminality" in which the actions of soldiers have serious longer-term implications for their victims but that these were not the intention of the act itself.[73] For example, German soldiers "living off the land" by taking food from impoverished villagers did not intend for their victims to starve to death, but that may well have been the result. Whether death resulted from outright starvation or the complications malnutrition brought on for the old, weak, and very young, the cause was the same, and the role played by German soldiers, even if unwittingly, is hard to ignore. Yet soldiers typically felt no guilt for their actions because the suffering and high mortality rate among Soviet civilians was neither the intended result of their actions nor something that German soldiers remained to witness. In addition, a rationalization of their actions was not difficult to achieve: Soviet peasants had always been poor and were used to dealing with scarcity; it was war and they were acting on orders to secure their own food; retreating

Soviet troops had themselves exploited and deprived the population before the Germans arrived; German troops also had to eat. Accordingly, one must then consider the degree to which German requisitioning was confined to the essentials necessary for their survival. Ivan Ivanovich Steblin-Kamenskii, a Russian interpreter who volunteered to serve with the German 206 Infantry Division, noted in his diary in March 1942, "All in all, it is very hard for me to see this new, unknown face of the German soldier, without any human feeling. Having more than is needed for nutrition, he then takes away the last [food] from women and children. I'm completely overwhelmed, shocked, insulted, and yet I can do nothing and have to serve with them."[74]

Other examples of activities leading to involuntary fatal outcomes and constituting "secondary criminality" would include the common practice of seizing winter clothing or removing peasants from their homes to accommodate Germans in the winter months. Horses and vehicles were also seized, as were scarce medical supplies, tools, and machinery. Movement for civilians was heavily restricted, while formally public facilities, like hospitals, were often confined to German use. The process of dispossessing Soviet civilians of what little they had became so ubiquitous in some regions that civilian death rates soared, and even if German soldiers may not have intended this, their actions contributed to it. How much one therefore associates an average German soldier with the term "criminal" will doubtless remain subjective in view, but any determination must at least take into account the full implications of their activities in the East. Given that more than twelve million Soviet civilians died in only three years of German occupation, such considerations are not peripheral to the debate.

While the worldview constructed for German soldiers encouraged both impunity and superiority toward easterners, the contrasting "otherness" of so many foreign elements acted to emphasize the unique bonds and cultural familiarity of a soldier's comrades. In 1948, Edward Shils and Morris Janowitz explored how German soldiers coped on the Eastern Front and suggested that the ethos of comradeship was underwritten by "primary groups" around which the cohesion of their units was sustained. This points to the strong social networks built on common understandings that underwrote the *Wehrmacht*'s remarkable solidarity.[75] Omer Bartov has argued that the primary groups broke down under the withering casualty rates, but in fact the system of resupply sustained most of these groups long enough to retain a common culture even as men cycled in and out. When groups were wiped out or completely new formations were sent East, the same brutalizing factors that transformed and then "renormalized" the first generation of the *Ostheer* rapidly repeated themselves. This is not to say ideological factors were not a feature in molding German soldiers' views and directing their behavior, but they should not be overstated.[76]

Of course, there were those who refused to accept and adhere to the *Ostheer*'s basic norms or were for whatever reason rejected by the soldiers' community. This, however, meant social isolation and a lack of vital support structures, making for a difficult life. As Hans Frenzel noted in his diary, "I continue to live in isolation. I cannot become intimate with anyone. Solitude. I am surrounded all the time by men who lack any refinement, who are completely egotistical and seeking their own advancement, forever licking boots. Narrow-minded fools. Impossible to converse with them freely; so I keep quiet. . . . A pitiful life."[77] As Kühne's study of comradeship makes clear, the need for companionship on the Eastern Front was an extremely powerful motivation, providing a sense of "power, security and a safe haven" against the parallel fear of isolation in the face of unremitting danger and death.[78]

Not only was there an internal pressure to conform, but the external worldview constructed by German propaganda cast the soldier's options in seemingly existential terms. Propaganda portrayed the Soviet Union as an aggressive colossus threatening European civilization with a corrupted "Jewish Bolshevik" ideology.[79] Such a formidable "foe image" threatened "cultured" Europe with a godless enemy, making any soldier willing to question the maximum use of force to defend against such a daunting menace seem almost heretical. Moreover, racial concepts facilitated a dehumanization of the Soviet population, which enabled excesses by reducing natural inhibitions.[80] Michaela Kipp's study of German field post shows how the war was cast in terms of German "cleanliness" and "purity" against the "filth" of the East both figuratively and literally.[81] It all acted to promote a unity of purpose among German soldiers, which aided combat effectiveness and reduced personal inhibitions about the consequences of their actions.

The radicalization of behavior was further stimulated by early evidence of Soviet atrocities against isolated groups of Germans, which while not a result of state policy were nevertheless alarmingly common and fed every German fear and prejudice. Violence begat violence on both sides, feeding a brutal dialectical logic of atrocity and reprisal, resulting in a surging spiral of violence that dramatically accelerated the incidents of extrajudicial killings. For German soldiers, however, only Soviet excesses and criminality were emphasized, offering both a sense of victimhood and righteousness in whatever retaliatory measures were undertaken.

The purpose here has been to draw a broad outline of how the current historiography evaluates and contextualizes the world of the German soldier in the *Barbarossa* campaign. It underlines many of the broad themes that arise in the letters themselves, but it is the myriad individual perspectives, shaped by different experiences and personalities, that make field post such a compelling source of evidence. The *Barbarossa* campaign has received much scholarly attention in the past two decades, but even in the comprehensive studies that Craig and I have written, which seek to give a voice to the German soldier, the narrative structure limits this medium to short quotations and brief excerpts. This book places the German soldier's perspective in the foreground and aims to represent his impressions of the war through hundreds of letters from rank-and-file soldiers and lower-level officers. The selection of letters is gleaned from a wide variety of sources. Two main collections in Germany have been particularly useful: first, the *Bibliothek für Zeitgeschichte* (BfZ) in Stuttgart and, second, the *Museumsstiftung Post und Telekommunikation* held by the *Museum für Kommunikation* in Berlin. The past twenty-five years have also seen a proliferation of published collections in Germany, many of individual soldiers assembled by their descendants.[82] These sometimes have very small print runs and can be hard to find even in extensive library collections, but this growing body of literature offers some excellent collections of field post. Craig has also made available a considerable personal collection of privately donated letters from his contacts in Germany and many years of association with veterans' organizations. In sum, we hope to have produced the most comprehensive and wide-ranging collection of letters on Operation *Barbarossa* available to an English-speaking audience.

CHAPTER 2

June 1941

Introduction

By mid-June 1941, the massive buildup of German forces in the East was almost complete. The vast migration of men and matériel had begun in earnest in February 1941 and progressed in several stages of rail and road movements. The final stage of the pre-Barbarossa buildup began in early June and embraced two dozen panzer and motorized divisions (twelve of each); however, in an effort to maintain secrecy, only on the final four nights before the start of the attack did these and the other mechanized formations—the sharp tip of Hitler's invasion force—slip into their final assembly areas adjacent or close to the Russo-German demarcation line. In aggregate, the German Ostheer comprised 148 divisions on the main battle front of 1,800 kilometers (1,080 miles) from the Baltic to the Black Sea, with 120 divisions of the three army groups (North, Center, and South) making up the first assault wave (28 were assigned to the OKH reserve).[1] It was the largest invasion force the world had ever seen—more than three million men, 3,500 tanks and assault guns,[2] 7,146 artillery pieces, 600,000 vehicles, and 625,000 horses. This enormous array was supported by a Luftwaffe force structure of about 3,000 aircraft in the East, of which 2,250 were combat-ready.[3] Axis allies participating in Operation Barbarossa included about 500,000 Finnish and some 150,000 Romanian troops.

Facing this imposing juggernaut across the frontier was the Red Army—inexperienced, ill prepared, and ignorant of the fate about to befall it. Of the Red Army's total force structure (more than five million men and 303 divisions), field forces deployed in the western frontier regions (first strategic echelon) boasted a total strength of roughly three million men, organized into 171 divisions, including 40 tank and 20 mechanized divisions (arranged in 20 mechanized corps). In addition to these forces, there was a second strategic echelon composed of five reserve armies under the centralized control of the Soviet High Command; when war came, these reserve armies—virtually invisible to German intelligence—were in the process of assembling along the Western Dvina and Dnepr River lines. Also stationed in the western frontier regions were more than seven thousand aircraft of the Red Air Force, which, with a force structure of almost twenty thousand aircraft, was the world's largest air force. The bulk of its equipment, however, like that of the Red

Army as a whole,[4] *was obsolete and, perforce, posed but a limited threat to the experienced pilots of the* Luftwaffe.

Shortly after 0300 hours, Sunday, 22 June 1941, as the first shafts of sunlight rose tentatively above the horizon in the east, the morning calm was shattered as thousands of German guns, ranging from super-heavy rail-borne artillery to light and medium field howitzers and infantry mortars, opened fire on their targets at the frontier.[5] Overhead, the fighter, divebomber, and bomber squadrons of the Luftwaffe struck Soviet cities, towns, airfields, and other targets, while the initial waves of German infantry and combat engineers swarmed across the frontier. Red Army resistance was at first light to nonexistent—dazed and disoriented, many Soviet troops were caught unprepared in their camps and barracks—and, within a few hours, German assault detachments had secured intact every key bridge along the border rivers. In his personal diary, Generaloberst *Franz Halder, chief of the Army General Staff,* noted that tactical surprise had been achieved across the entire front.[6]

Although Soviet resistance gradually stiffened—indeed, at many points along the front, elite NKVD border guards[7] and Red Army units fought with surprising tenacity from the opening hours of the campaign—the German panzer units, in close cooperation with the Luftwaffe, slashed deep gaps through the Red Army defenses, achieving operational breakthroughs along all three axes of the German advance—toward the coveted objectives of Leningrad, Moscow, and Kiev. Forming the spearhead of Generalfeldmarschall *Fedor von Bock's Army Group Center* were the tanks and motorized infantry of two powerful panzer groups—2 Panzer Group, commanded by Generaloberst *Heinz Guderian, and 3 Panzer Group, led by* Generaloberst *Hermann Hoth (together comprising more than 1,800 tanks). Pushing inexorably through the dense Belorussian forests and tall fields of wheat and rye, they had, by 28 June, captured the flaming city of Minsk 300 kilometers (186 miles) from their start line, shattering Red Army forces in their path and encircling three Soviet armies. A city of about 250,000 inhabitants, Minsk, the capital of Belorussia, had been badly disfigured by a series of savage* Luftwaffe *raids. Those Red Army forces who had retired eastward through the city "saw not a city but a bonfire."*[8]

On the northern wing, the armies and panzer group of Generalfeldmarschall *Wilhelm Ritter von Leeb's Army Group North* attacked on a narrow front of 300 kilometers (186 miles), yet here, too, initial successes were dramatic. As the mist still shimmered in the forests, meadows, and valleys along the East Prussian frontier, German infantry debouched from their assembly areas and plunged over the border, while the panzers of Generaloberst *Erich Hoepner's 4 Panzer Group (six hundred tanks) poured out of the woods. Leeb's first wave of forces shattered partially manned Soviet defenses and began their headlong drive through the Baltic States, through territory once Germanized by the Teutonic knights and Hanseatic traders—regions that for centuries had furnished many of the families that had officered the Prussian and German armies.*[9] *On both 26 and 30 June, German armor seized intact vital crossings over the Western Dvina River, nearly 300 kilometers from the frontier as the crow flies. While Leningrad was still some 500 kilometers (310 miles) away, the Germans were confident they would soon get there.*

On the southern wing of Hitler's Ostheer, the armies and panzer group of Generalfeldmarschall *Gerd von Rundstedt's Army Group South* attacked out of German-occupied Poland into the robust Soviet fixed fortifications covering the Ukraine. On 22 June, the fighting was often bitter, costly, and at close quarters, as the German infantry and combat *engineers cleared lanes through the Soviet bunkers and minefields; by the next day, the tanks of Generaloberst Ewald von Kleist's 1 Panzer Group (715 in all) were lunging into the Ukraine, aiming to forge bridgeheads over the Dnepr River at and near the city of Kiev, the industrial and political center of the Ukraine. It was in the south, however, covering the Ukraine, that the Soviets had stationed their strongest mechanized corps, and, in the days ahead, they unleashed a series of furious counterstrokes that resulted in a "tank battle of unprecedented proportions."10 Yet these Soviet mobile formations—poorly coordinated and inexperienced—attacked in piecemeal fashion and were decimated by German armored and air forces at the very pinnacle of their prowess; on 30 June, surviving Red Army forces in the Ukraine were ordered to pull back to new defenses anchored on the 1939 Soviet-Polish frontier.11*

Although the first nine days of Operation Barbarossa had resulted in spectacular German victories—reinforcing the conviction of Hitler and his General Staff that the campaign would come to a successful conclusion in a matter of weeks—there were, for soldiers at the forward edge of battle at least, disturbing auguries of what the future held in store. Indeed, as underscored in field post letters and diaries too numerous to note, the average German soldier—the Landser, the German equivalent to the American G.I.—quickly became aware that in Soviet Russia he had encountered an adversary who, while far from fully prepared for war, often fought tenaciously, even fanatically, against the supremely confident invaders.12 The German combat soldier soon realized that Russia posed challenges unlike any he had faced in Poland, France, or the Balkans. Severely exacerbating these challenges were the racial and ideological antagonisms that characterized and shaped the Eastern Campaign from its inception and that, inter alia, rendered the shooting of prisoners of war—both German and Russian—a commonplace occurrence across the front. Operation Barbarossa had only just begun, but its extraordinary violence, cruelty, and death were already on full display.

Letters and Diary Entries (15–30 June 1941)

15.6.41: *GEFREITER* HANS B. (269 INFANTRY DIVISION, 4 PANZER GROUP, ARMY GROUP NORTH)13

This morning I located what will probably be our last billeting area in the Reich before all hell breaks loose [*vor dem grossen Krach*]. It's a tent camp under open skies. With the massing of so many troops there's simply no space left in the houses. But if it's not too cold, and the weather stays dry, that should work out fine. There's been quite a run on straw.

Opinions here have changed and are now almost unanimous: in general, no one believes in a peaceful solution any more. I would give almost anything to get a peek behind the scenes of the diplomacy just once, because without question everything is being tried to maintain the peace in eastern Europe. But there's no doubt that we're now on the cusp of a final decision. To be sure, we're living in most interesting times, which historians will still be writing about after thousands of years. I only think with deep sadness in my heart about the years that will be lost to our lives together.

15.6.41: WM. JOSEF L. (129 INFANTRY DIVISION, NINTH ARMY, ARMY GROUP CENTER)[14]

Tomorrow we're leaving this place, so any chance of visiting me is now quite impossible. We'll be going into an area where there are no German-speaking people and where great throngs of soldiers are housed, so we won't have a roof over our heads but will have to camp in the woods in our self-made tents. That's not pleasant, because in spite of the heat during the day, at night it turns uncomfortably cold. So we've now been forsaken by God and every good fortune. What hits me the hardest is to have to be away from you even longer. But despite it all I can't let that disturb me. The day will come when all this is at an end.

16.6.41: REGIMENTAL ADJUTANT (45 INFANTRY DIVISION, FOURTH ARMY, ARMY GROUP CENTER)[15]

Today the order came. So it is getting serious [also es wird Ernst]. The Führer has decided, after the collapse of the peace efforts with England, to first overthrow Russia. Only the How and When still present us with a conundrum. With no declaration of war? But: it will be war against the archenemy [Erzfeind] of our idea, Bolshevism. And we will know how to conduct it, grimly and resolutely [hart und entschlossen].

16.6.41: GEFREITER HANS B. (269 INFANTRY DIVISION, 4 PANZER GROUP, ARMY GROUP NORTH)[16]

The summer in the East is supposed to be quite warm, and the time for swimming will have to be put aside. But the actual advance will at most go on for eight weeks. After that, we'll hopefully have time to swim. Our army has really performed immensely well, and I see the impending operations as having already been won, too. In my view, England will be brought to collapse by the blockade and the air attacks alone. In the East, our food source [Ernährung] will be secured one way or another. Europe, in any case, can't be allowed to starve because those in the most fruitful land can't or don't want to cultivate it. It all turns largely on that. What is also quite right is that order must now be brought at once to all of Europe.

16.6.41: GEFREITER HEINZ B. (291 INFANTRY DIVISION, EIGHTEENTH ARMY, ARMY GROUP NORTH)[17]

There was something up again here last night. We're within view of the Russian border and hardly managed any sleep. Today, however, everything has relaxed a bit again, so that we're able to get some rest. Personally, I don't take what's going on here seriously. I can't imagine that we'd get ourselves into a war with Russia. Of course, the possibility exists, because there are still many Jews in Russia, that Russia would join forces with the English, and that the English might attack us from there, so naturally we have to be on guard against that.

17.6.41: WERNER R. (8 PANZER DIVISION, 4 PANZER GROUP, ARMY GROUP NORTH)[18]

On 17 June we packed up our things again and, leaving behind the motor vehicles we had just received, marched on foot at night until we were right at the Lithuanian frontier, not far from the small border town of Eydtkau, in a humid forested area. Between the thickets of pine and fir trees we built tents for four persons out of triangular shelter halfs and camouflaged them. The region was dominated by an unimaginable plague of mosquitoes. Myriads of these blood-sucking pests [*Plagegeister*] could bring one to the point of desperation. These June days were hot and oppressive and, at least for me, filled with great worry and inner tension.

On one occasion, I was sent to Eydtkau to receive orders and found the town to be oddly unfamiliar and practically deserted by civilians.

21.6.41: DR. HEINRICH HAAPE (6 INFANTRY DIVISION, 3 PANZER GROUP,[19] ARMY GROUP CENTER)[20]

In a few hours it will begin!

We Germans face an enemy with a threefold [numerical] superiority; our regiment is in the very front line. The resistance must be broken, in spite of the bunkers, the human hordes, and all kinds of devilry. It's a war for Germany's greatness and future.

I have been completely calm so far. The world seems silent and untroubled to me, and just now I feel the peace of nature twice as deeply. Despite the fact that a lot, a very great lot of troops have marched up to the border, yet there's not a soldier to be seen! The weather is wonderful, the birds are singing and the trees are wearing a fresh green. A magnificent lake is just close by again and there's the same mood in the air that I described to you at Pentecost. A magical world of a truly living peace. Just before the storm that will make the earth tremble, with all its consequences!

21.6.41: *LEUTNANT* HANS JOCHEN SCHMIDT (ARMY GROUP CENTER)[21]

We then also moved off at dusk and occupied an assembly area in a depression at the Suwalki tip.[22] Each of us received 60 rounds of live ammunition. From that point forward our rifles stayed loaded. There could be no thought of sleep. But we had a radio, which unfortunately quit on us much too early. No one suspected anything yet in the Reich and they were enthusiastically playing dance music, which we let trickle comfortingly over our souls. The route of advance [*Vormarschstrasse*] was alive with traffic. Vehicle after vehicle. At 2400 hours the proclamation of the *Führer* was read out to us, and the tension became almost unbearable.

21.6.41: *GEFREITER* HANS CASPAR VON WIEDEBACH-NOSTITZ (20 PANZER DIVISION, 3 PANZER GROUP, ARMY GROUP CENTER)[23]

Early on Saturday morning there is a lecture conducted by *Oberleutnant* Kischnik and *Leutnant* Behr concerning conduct on operations, especially dealing with the technicalities of driving and then the peculiarities of the Russian armed forces: uniforms, tanks and types of aircraft. At midday the section drives off for about 100 kilometers to the forming-up area of the 20 Panzer Division which is located in the former Lithuania. How enormous is the difference of this area from Germany: dirty ruined houses, ragged population, neglected land and pitiful livestock. Later on, none of this would catch our attention. In the evening the vehicles are serviced, tents are erected and fires [lit]. All that would later become a habit.

Late evening, on the longest day of the year, at a company briefing, we learn of the *Führer*'s proclamation. We are conscious of the historical nature of this moment. Early tomorrow at 0300 hours it was due to become a reality. In the distance one could hear the constant noise of rattling chains of moving tanks and the noise of engines.

21.6.41: *GEFREITER* HUBERT HEGELE (1 MOUNTAIN DIVISION, SEVENTEENTH ARMY, ARMY GROUP SOUTH)[24]

Many rumors have been floating about recently, from the one about Molotov's revolution—which, if need be, we would support—to the right of transit through Russia in order to assist hard-pressed Iraq against its English attackers. An attack on the Soviet Union? Well, we don't believe that at all. First of all, Germany has a friendship pact and a non-aggression pact with the Soviet Union; and secondly—a battle against this vast empire? No, that won't happen. What is truth—what is rumor? What do we little wheels in this vast machinery of war know? Nothing, absolutely nothing. Only the unrest in our hearts about whatever's looming ahead of us. That something is coming, we surely know that.

21./22.6.41: GERD HABEDANCK (WAR CORRESPONDENT WITH 45 INFANTRY DIVISION, 2 PANZER GROUP,[25] ARMY GROUP CENTER)[26]

We came from Warsaw through heat, dust and jam-packed roads to the Bug. We passed tracts of woodland bristling with vehicle parks, artillery batteries in villages and radio relay stations and headquarters staffs under tall fir trees. Silently, absolutely silently we crept up to the edge of the Bug. Sand had been strewn across the roads so that our hob-nailed boots made no sound. Assault sections already grouped moved along the road edges in mute rows. Outlines of rubber dinghies were discernible as they shuttled along, raised up against the light of the northern sky.

21/22.6.41: *OBERLEUTNANT* JUERG VON KALCKREUTH (6 INFANTRY DIVISION, 3 PANZER GROUP, ARMY GROUP CENTER)[27]

The tension is immeasurably high. Everything is being feverishly prepared. And yet there are still a few who believe that the whole affair is just a bluff. . . . It is incredible that the paper war [*Papierkrieg*] could flare up again now, of all times. New orders arrive all the time with deadlines, mostly for "immediately." Many a piece of paper ends up unheeded in a large file marked "outstanding." It can wait until the baggage train moves up again, perhaps only after weeks—already deep in Russia. . . . The 18 IR is to be the "point of main effort" [*Schwerpunkt-Regiment*]. (Now I can write to you about this, because everything will already be well under way long before this letter reaches you). . . .

At 0130 hours, we get ready at the command post in order to go to the observation post, where the commander—in his tent—awaits us. With me is *Leutnant* Sengelhoff. A deathly calm lies over the frontier area. Everybody around us and immediately in front of us moves inconspicuously and quietly forward, to the frontier. The telephone jangles: the units report that they've all completed their preparations. A scouting party receives rifle fire from the direction of Hill 220, no casualties. Around 0215 hours it begins to dawn; the sky reddens in the east and announces a clear day.

22.6.41: HERMANN STRACKE (SOMEWHERE ON THE EASTERN FRONT)[28]

Last night the *Oberleutnant* read out to us the proclamation of the *Führer*, so now this time we will finally be playing our part. . . . If at this moment the designs of fate stand uncertain before me, and one ultimately must be prepared for anything, ready for anything, then believe me that I will go into battle confidently, joyously and undaunted [*unverzagt*]. And that I will proudly take on this trial of life [*Lebensprobe*].[29]

22.6.41: *GEFREITER* HUBERT HEGELE (1 MOUNTAIN DIVISION, SEVENTEENTH ARMY, ARMY GROUP SOUTH)[30]

0255 hours. Still 20 minutes to go until the start of the attack. Good Lord, the minutes pass by so begrudgingly today. Not a sound is to be heard. Only when you really perk up your ears can you detect some gentle whispering. We are just 20 meters from the border fence. The concentration of our assault troops has succeeded perfectly. The enemy has noticed nothing. The Russian sentries standing on their observation post haven't a clue. It's just two men, but they'll be the first to go down.

0306 hours. If I could only smoke a cigarette. The sky is now cloudless and the stars are shining down on us insignificant souls with their cheerful splendor, but the silver gray of the morning intrudes ever more strongly in their twinkling magnificence. You cannot grasp hold of sober thoughts in these final minutes—but you hardly need to. I make a little prayer and ask the Good Lord to stand by my side.

0310 hours. Still five minutes. The faces of my comrades look like gray masks. Their gaze is fixed straight ahead. The pounding in our chests grows stronger and stronger. The *Pioniere* begin—very quietly, so you can hardly hear it—to cut a couple of pathways through the wire with their large shears. We still have two minutes to go. From somewhere, far off in the distance, you can hear the call of a pack animal.

0315 hours. Finally! A hand is raised up and gives the signal. As if drawn by a magnet, all eyes are on the hand of the assault troop leader [*Stosstruppführer*]. And with the raising of his hand, two shots from our sharpshooters resound through the night. The two Russian sentries collapse. The campaign against the Soviet Union has begun.

22.6.41: *FELDWEBEL* HANS M. (79 INFANTRY DIVISION, OKH RESERVE, ARMY GROUP SOUTH)[31]

So, what say you about our new enemy? Perhaps father can still remember how I talked about the Russian army during my last leave. And even then I said that, over the long haul, we cannot maintain friendly relations with the Bolsheviks. Besides, there are still far too many Jews there [*Dazu sind dort noch viel zu viele Juden*]. There's nothing new here. We sit continuously by the loudspeakers and listen to reports from the front.

22.6.41: *UNTEROFFIZIER* WILHELM PRÜLLER (9 PANZER DIVISION, 1 PANZER GROUP, ARMY GROUP SOUTH)[32]

Some of us simply gaped with astonishment, some took it with equanimity, some are horrified . . . [after learning that Germany was now at war with Russia].[33] Personally I think it's a good thing that we face the fight squarely and save our children from having to do it. For this reason: in the long run it would have proved impossible for two such giant nations, living right next to each other and with completely different ways of life, to exist side by side in peace and understanding. The fight between Communism, which is rotting so many peoples, and National Socialism was bound to come. And if we can win now, it's better than doing it later. And the *Führer* will know what he's doing. Above all, I'm sure it'll end well.

22.6.41: *LEUTNANT* HELMUT D. (4 MOUNTAIN DIVISION, OKH RESERVE, ARMY GROUP SOUTH)[34]

Since early this morning at 0300 hours, we have a state of war with Russia. We heard the artillery firing and the planes passing by. We are not in the action yet, but waiting to advance. Russia is very big, but favorable for our mobile troops [*schnelle Truppen*]. We don't know yet where, or when, we'll join the fight. Even for us it came as quite a surprise, but after the explanation of the *Führer* much has become clear. Naturally, the question of food [*Ernährungsfrage*] is also important. With Russia we will be able to feed ourselves.

22.6.41: *LEUTNANT* HEINZ DÖLL (18 PANZER DIVISION, 2 PANZER GROUP, ARMY GROUP CENTER)[35]

At exactly 0310 on 22 June 1941 we were ready to fire. Somewhat restively I followed the minute and second hands of my watch until the firing order came.

At 0315 a lightning bolt of gigantic dimensions tore through the night. Thousands of artillery pieces shattered the silence. I will never forget those seconds. But just what they signified for the world, for Germany—that was beyond comprehension. . . .

The artillerymen told me about an unbelievable experience. At our crossing point, they said, tanks dived into the Bug like U-boats and then reappeared on the east bank. Must be pretty strong tobacco they're smoking, I thought to myself, but it was true.[36]

22.6.41: *GEFREITER* HERBERT R. (45 INFANTRY DIVISION, 2 PANZER GROUP, ARMY GROUP CENTER)[37]

It was early morning and suddenly thousands of guns opened up all at once [on the fortress of Brest Litovsk][38] . . . it was truly an inferno. It was already becoming light, but after a while a wall of black smoke rose into the sky, and it again became black as night—and that only because of the explosions. I was lying on my back in my foxhole, and was so startled by the sudden artillery fire that the burning cigarette, which was up near my service coat, fell on me and burned a hole in my chest. That was my first wound in Russia.

22.6.41: WALTHER LOOS (45 INFANTRY DIVISION, 2 PANZER GROUP, ARMY GROUP CENTER)[39]

[Loos is describing the bombardment of the fortress of Brest-Litovsk.] It seemed that a curtain over the terrors of the underworld rose above our heads. At first we were still hearing the discharges, the thunder and howling of wailing shells passing overhead, streaking in death-dealing trajectories toward the opposite bank from hundreds of barrels ranging from the smallest to the largest caliber. Involuntarily ducking our heads, we were almost forgetting to breathe. However, a second later the artillery fire of a different heavy gun gathered such a deafening and breathtaking strength like I never experienced later. Even those participants in the First World War among us later acknowledged that at that time, they had never experienced fire of such concentrated power. The sky turned red, and even though it was night, it became as light as day. Large trees fringing the Bug swayed wildly and were torn to pieces as if from an invisible force by the atmospheric pressure of the passing shells.

22.6.41: SOLDIER FROM BERLIN (ARMY GROUP CENTER)[40]

The thunder of guns [*Kanonendonner*] awakened us at 0315 in the morning. 34 batteries are firing. We can see the barrage from the edge of the forest, since we are merely 7 kilometers away from the frontier (Bug). Soon towns are burning, white flares [*Leuchtkugeln*] shoot up, the front rages like a storm. When there is flak fire, gray streaks rise into the sky, slowly drifting away. A plane goes down burning. The sky, at first clear and red, gradually turns purple mixed with green. There is a gigantic smoke cloud behind the low silhouette of the horizon and it drifts leadenly to the right. . . . Near Janov Podl three enemy bombers pass right over us. Flak of all types fires like crazy [*wie wahnsinnig*]. A small herd of sheep flees behind the road.

22.6.41: *GEFREITER* GERHARD BOPP (35 INFANTRY DIVISION, 3 PANZER GROUP,[41] ARMY GROUP CENTER)[42]

In the morning, at 0200, we move into our assembly area [*Bereitstellung*]. Around 0300, directly above us, the German bombers drone and the fighters sing as they head east. One can make out the thunder of battle in the distance and sense the earth trembling. We begin our advance at 0330 and cross the border—here only characterized by bundles of straw—at 0403. All along the horizon columns of smoke from burning houses. The populace (Lithuanians) greets us joyfully, some with tears in their eyes. The girls and children throw flowers at us and all the vehicles are decked out with lilac blossoms, like in maneuvers . . . if there were no war.

Around 0700, the first prisoners, shaven bald heads, Mongol faces, etc. Then the first fatalities . . . dead horses, etc.—through artillery fire before reaching the Kirsna River in the Didžioji region. Shells strike to the left and right of the road, but at great distances away. We get through unscathed. We capture the bridge over the Kirsna intact. After a brief stop, we continue to . . . where there has been intense enemy resistance since midday, which is only broken that evening. There, bivouac and provisions are in short supply, because the roads are sandy and in poor condition, and so the field kitchen can barely get through. There is only a little warm food and coffee.

22.6.41: *UNTEROFFIZIER* FRITZ HÜBNER (ARMY GROUP CENTER)[43]

On 21 June, we moved up to the frontier under cover of darkness. The attack was to begin at 0400 hours. A half hour before that the artillery preparation began, and it roared and thundered [*dröhnte und donnerte*] as if the world was going under. At 0400 the firing ceased and the attack got underway.[44] The enemy was certainly knocked on his heels by the force of the attack, but with what doggedness did these Russian soldiers fight! Of course, we had the bad luck on this first day to encounter Stalin cadets. They were aspiring officers and political officers [*Politruks*] who refused to surrender. Rather they fought to the last man and had to be formally beaten or shot to death in their rifle pits.

The nature of the war [*Art der Kriegs*führung] had fundamentally changed; it was alien to us [*sie war uns fremd*]. We soon found the first reconnaissance patrols that had fallen into Russian hands. They had had their genitals cut off while still alive, their eyes gouged out, throats cut, or ears and noses cut off. We went around with grave faces, because we were frightened of this type of fighting. Inevitably, we, too, developed an unnatural ruthlessness [*unnatürliche Härte*] which had not been instilled in us during training.

22.6.41: *OBERLEUTNANT* RICHARD D. (7 PANZER DIVISION, 3 PANZER GROUP, ARMY GROUP CENTER)[45]

And now at [0305] hours it all began, perhaps not as abruptly as it had in the West and not on the scale that it had in the World War, but a quarter of an hour later the first *Luftwaffe* air wings roared back, and now squadron after squadron travels eastward. And all the while the sun shone. . . . You now know more than we do, because there is now no opportunity to listen to the radio, and everything will happen at once, and the spaces will be so vast that you can even find them on our wall map. We have maps that reach a long way to the east, and if you remember Napoleon's army did that on foot, but we're motorized and we'll get it done in 14 days. . . . The supply vehicles clatter along the road, making their way past our quarters. We'll have to force our way between them. Perhaps we'll see the first prisoners this evening.

22.6.41: *PANZER-OBERSCHÜTZE* ERICH HAGER (17 PANZER DIVISION, 2 PANZER GROUP, ARMY GROUP CENTER)[46]

[At 0315] our artillery fire begins. A mighty display of firepower. We are standing ready for attack. However, the Russians skedaddle. At midday we come to the Bug [River], stand for an hour at the bridge, which has been built.

See my first air battle. 8 bombers were shot down by our aircraft. Awful to watch. Crossed the Bug. We come to the first of our dead. Snipers were the culprits? Wounded Russians are still lying here. Password is drive and keep driving. All through the day and night. Firing catches us at the back. 5 tanks kaput. We travel on alone. We had to arrive on time. Our first attack is ahead of us. 200 Russian tanks are against us.

22.6.41: *LEUTNANT* WILLIBALD G. (57 INFANTRY DIVISION, 1 PANZER GROUP,[47] ARMY GROUP SOUTH)[48]

At 0315 hours the spellbinding barrage got underway. We captured the bridge over the Bug at Sokal'. It was a fantastical firework display! Some 400 guns, including *Nebelwerfer*,[49] fired in unison along a five-kilometer front. The infantry made good progress, so we've already been able to make a change of position and cross over [the Bug]. Sokal' is in flames but we had to go through the city. The Russians put up no resistance. They didn't fire a shot across [the river], and there's not a single Russian plane to be seen. The Russians it seems were taken completely by surprise. Of course, the war has only just begun. Hopefully it will continue to go so splendidly! We are waiting in the first rays of sunlight for our horses.

22.6.41: *SOLDAT* WERNER F. (HEAVY FLAK MG BATTALION 52 [MOT.], ARMY GROUP CENTER)[50]

So now the decision has been taken—for all of you surely a blow out of the clear blue sky. Just 14 days ago I wrote that there most likely wouldn't be war with the Soviets. At that time, we thought we'd get passage [through Russia] and go into action in the Near East. In my mind, I already saw myself strolling through the bazaars of Baghdad. . . . Last night the company commander spoke and read out the *Führer's* proclamation. The political revelations were quite simply powerful and surprising. Now that we know what's at stake, I'm all in. . . . We're still posted on territory of the Reich, not far from the frontier in an area that used to be Polish. Everything seems strange here— the little white wood houses, the primitive farmsteads, even in the larger settlements almost everything is of wood; the churches with their bulbous Russian spires; the traces of the battles in Poland.

This morning, at 0305 hours, we witnessed the start of hostilities! Because of all the mosquitoes our tents had become unbearable, so we were already up and about at around 0300. At first just a few aircraft and then, quite suddenly, machine gun and artillery fire announced the start of combat. Later entire Stuka wings came on and in the forests beyond us great clouds of smoke were visible. Then the shelling gradually grew more distant, and now, at 1400, you can only hear something occasionally in the distance. Single Russian planes appeared on a few occasions and were greeted by vigorous fire from our flak. So that's it with my "impressions of war." We're still not in action, just waiting and waiting. We heard Goebbels and Ribbentrop on the radio.

22.6.41: *GEFREITER* HANS ROTH (299 INFANTRY DIVISION, 1 PANZER GROUP,[51] ARMY GROUP SOUTH)[52]

All of a sudden, at exactly 0315 hours, and apparently out of the blue, an opening salvo emerges from the barrels of hundreds of guns of all calibers. . . . It is impossible to comprehend one's world in such an inferno.

Our homeland is still innocently asleep while here death is already collecting a rich harvest. We crouch in our holes with pallid but resolved faces while counting the minutes until we storm the Bug fortifications . . . a reassuring touch of our ID tags, the arming of hand grenades, the securing of our [submachine guns].

It is now 0330 hours. A whistle sounds; we quickly jump out from undercover and at an insane speed cross the 20 meters to the inflatable boats. In a snatch we are on the other side of the river where rattling machine-gun fire awaits us. We have our first casualties.

With the help of a few *Sturmpionieren* [assault engineers] we slowly—much too slowly—eat through the barbed wire barriers. Meanwhile, shells fire into the bunkers at Molnikow. . . .

We finally get out of this mess. In a few short steps we are able to advance to the first bunker, arriving in its blind spot. The Reds fire like mad but are unable to reach us. The decisive moment is near. An explosive specialist approaches the bunker from behind and shoves a short-fused bomb into the bunker's fire hole. The bunker shook, and black smoke emerged from its openings, signaling its final doom. We move on.

Molnikow is completely in our hands by 1000 hours. The Reds, hunted by our infantry, disperse quickly to Bisknjiczo-Ruski. . . . We are ordered to cleanse the village of any remaining enemy combatants. The area is combed house by house. Our shelling has caused terrible damage. The Reds, however, have also done their fair share.

Slowly, our nerves grow accustomed to the all too familiar gruesome images. Close to the Reds' custom house lies a large mound of fallen Russians, most of them torn to shreds from the shelling. Slaughtered civilians lie in the neighboring house. The horridly disfigured bodies of a young woman and her two small children lie among their shattered personal belongings in another small, cleansed house. . . .

We have taken our first prisoners—snipers and deserters receive their deserved reward.

22.6.41: *LEUTNANT* ARNOLD DÖRING (53 BOMBER WING, 2 AIR FLEET, CENTRAL FRONT)[53]

The ground below is covered with haze, but the targets are nevertheless clearly visible. I am surprised that we are not met with any counteraction. This will come as a surprise to those below!

The "eggs" are released. Piles of fire and smoke, fountains of earth and dust, mixed with wreckage parts of all kinds, are shooting vertically upward. Unfortunately, our bomb rows lay to the right side of the ammunition bunkers. But a whole row of bombs goes down across the entire field and plows the runway. The take-off strip receives two hits. As the formation makes a turn I can see fifteen of the parked fighters go up in flames, plus most of the living quarters. Toni cries: "Antiaircraft fire," but we could only see one single shot more than half a mile behind us. We are already out of their shooting range. Then there is a fearsome cry over the radio: "Fighters from behind!" Our machine guns rattle. The formation tightens up. Of course, we offer a large target to the Russians, but our defensive fire is most concentrated. Bullet tracers from twenty-seven planes sprinkle against the Russians, who immediately decide to disappear diving.

22.6.41: *LEUTNANT* RUDOLF MAURER (251 INFANTRY DIVISION, ARMY GROUP NORTH)[54]

At about 11:00 a.m. the company watches 14 Russian bombers being attacked by a single (!) German fighter, which eventually shoots down four of the "Russians." The rest of the bombers turn away. Unfortunately, I slept through this spectacle. In the afternoon, I enjoyed coffee klatsch at the rectory in Kanthausen. The wife of Pastor Schulz tells me that her husband is a staff officer and that she hopes for his speedy return after the end of this "*Blitz-Krieg*." Refugees are coming from Gumbinnen and Königsberg, mostly women and children, stowing their belongings in small suitcases. In the morning we're to get moving, at 0230 hours. So on this Sunday evening we're preparing to move off into the war that's already begun with Russia.

22.6.41: *GEFREITER* W. (137 INFANTRY DIVISION, FOURTH ARMY, ARMY GROUP CENTER)[55]

22.6. In the afternoon an enemy tank attack [*Panzerangriff*]. *Obergefr.* Glaser got a direct hit and was dead immediately. We've now reached our objective for the day and are in a small patch of birch trees. I want to go to sleep, but I can't. So I'll keep writing. Finally our own tanks arrived [most likely he means the assault guns of Battalion 226], and the dreadful fear was finally over. My whole life over I will not forget this tank attack. I've never experienced anything in my life that was so dreadful [*schrecklich*]. As a simple rifleman one is entirely defenseless. But our defensive weapons are first class.

22.6.41: *GEFREITER* LUDWIG B. (296 INFANTRY DIVISION, SEVENTEENTH ARMY, ARMY GROUP SOUTH)[56]

Now I'd like to write you all a few lines on this very first day of the struggle against Russia. It was quite splendid [*ganz schön*] how it all went off this morning at 0315 hours. Of course, our pilots were the very first on the scene, and so far not a single Russian plane has managed to reach our positions. It's now 3.00 in the afternoon. Our guns have all spoken quite nicely, and the collapse of Russia should take about three weeks. So don't worry—it will all go very quickly with the Russians, even if some of us will have to bite the dust. But it won't be in vain, it will be for Germany's better future.

22.6.41: PAUL R. (44 INFANTRY DIVISION, 1 PANZER GROUP,[57] ARMY GROUP SOUTH)[58]

Most of the bunkers on the Bug have been captured. Several are still firing, because the Russians are really tough. At the edge of the wood are a couple of houses, from which snipers are shooting at us. A few hand grenades and the straw roofs are burning like torches in the sun-filled morning. . . . None of the civilians have fled. The war came as too much of a surprise to them.

22.6.41: UNKNOWN SOLDIER (45 INFANTRY DIVISION, 2 PANZER GROUP, ARMY GROUP CENTER)[59]

Storm on the fortress of Brest-Litovsk. . . . Already in the morning the way to the East is free for our panzers, but the most difficult fighting for the fortress goes on.

The battles on the islands extremely difficult.[60] Complex terrain: groups of houses, clusters of trees, bushes, narrow strips of water, plus the ruins, and the enemy is everywhere. His snipers are excellently camouflaged in the trees. Camouflage suits made of gauze with leaves attached to them. Superb snipers! Shooting from hatches in the ground, basement windows, sewage pipes. . . .

First impression: the Bolshevik fights to his very last breath. Perhaps because of the threat of the commissars: those who fall into German captivity are shot. (According to statements by the first prisoners.) At any rate: no slackening of fighting power, even though resistance futile since citadel is surrounded.

Silent night. We dig the first graves.[61]

22.6.41: *GEFREITER* HUBERT HEGELE (1 MOUNTAIN DIVISION, SEVENTEENTH ARMY, ARMY GROUP SOUTH)[62]

The first day of the Russian campaign is over. It was difficult, more than difficult. We now know more than we did last night. Will it always go on here like this? Many of our comrades have already been laid to rest in the burning Polish soil. The 2nd Battalion has suffered the most bloody losses of the regiment.

It takes me ages to fall asleep. The thoughts of the day, particularly of the horror at the castle gardens in Oleszyce, were simply too burdensome. And now a solemn stillness lies over the battlefield at the border. Above, in the cloudless night sky, there is the splendor of a million stars; on the earth, the white recognition flares of the Germans and the red flares of the Russians. They fashion the "magic of the night" [*Zauber der Nacht*].[63] And tomorrow?[64]

22.6.41: DR. HEINRICH HAAPE (6 INFANTRY DIVISION, 3 PANZER GROUP, ARMY GROUP CENTER)[65]

The first day in the campaign against Russia. We have a hard day behind us! The Russians fought like devils and never surrendered, so we engaged in close combat [*Nahkampf*] on several occasions; just now, half an hour ago, another four Russians were struck dead with the butts of our rifles. Our regiment's losses on this single day are greater than during the entire French campaign. . . .[66] We were at the center of the attack [*Schwerpunkt des Angriffes*]. Of the regiment's 6 doctors, one is KIA (shot to the head) and another injured. And 4 medical orderlies are also KIA. We have pushed the Russian back along the whole line, except for a few bunkers that have not yet fallen. There is still hard fighting going on. I had a lot of work to do and frequently had to bandage comrades under heavy machine-gun fire. I have not yet had anything to eat today and only a very little to drink; we are cut off from our supply line!

22.6.41: *GEFREITER* FRANZ B. (198 INFANTRY DIVISION, ELEVENTH ARMY, ARMY GROUP SOUTH)[67]

Since war with Russia has finally broken out, we will soon be receiving extra front pay. We can't really write anything in detail, and there is a very strict control of the mail. Up to the final minute everything was shrouded in secrecy. . . . We were quite surprised [by the outbreak of war], for to the very last minute we had counted on a peaceful settlement with Russia. Last night our *Oberleutnant* visited our quarters and brought the news that tomorrow, at 0300 hours, it was going to start with Russia. So, early this morning, for our baking, we had to bring our steel helmets, gas masks, gas shelters, cartridges, guns and bayonets with us. But today has passed by peacefully. I'm quite eager to see what the night will bring us. We're all prepared for a major struggle [*einen grossen Kampf*]. We brought two light machine guns into position to protect our bakery area. It's the first time that we've had to take such extensive security precautions in our company.

Rumor has it that the *Führer* was supposed to give a radio address today. But we didn't hear anything. It's also rather ridiculous—we don't have a newspaper and don't listen to the radio—so we know nothing in particular about the reasons for the conflict with Russia. For the moment, any thought of going on leave is out of the question.

22.6.41: *GEFREITER* OTTO ST. (SUPERIOR CONSTRUCTION STAFF 5, ARMY GROUP NORTH)[68]

Today is the memorable day of the advance into Russia! My first thoughts were of you—how you're most likely overcome with worry about me. How I wish this letter would reach you in the fastest way possible! But you'll probably have 10 anxious days before this letter arrives. I can well imagine how things look to you now.

I had slept peacefully and awakened about 5.45 in the morning, when a comrade insisted there was an air raid warning. I really had no desire to climb out of my "nest," but then someone burst in our room and said, "The *Führer* is speaking!" and that he'd heard it. So quickly out of bed and turn on the radio—and we heard the news, which astounded us all, of the invasion of Russia. We also heard that a mail embargo [*Postsperre*] was now in effect, so you can't write to me!

Last Sunday I said that on Saturday—that is, yesterday—it would all kick off. I was only off by a few hours! And still, again and again I had my doubts, if it would really begin in the East. But everything that was going on here could not, in the end, lead to any other conclusion. What a remarkable deployment took place here! You simply can't imagine it! You were able to see the preparations back when we crossed the Rhein. But what's happened here is 50 times greater! It's exactly what was announced over the loudspeaker—something the world has never seen before!

And just how fast it's all going. The word is that our troops have already advanced quite far.

Everything is quiet here. In the morning the local population was understandably somewhat agitated, but already by midday it was a typical Sunday. People are taking walks and have complete trust in our *Wehrmacht*. I believe that it will also end very quickly with the Reds. . . . I believe that now the final decision is coming. And as Russia goes, so goes England. So it's at least possible that this accursed killing [*das unselige Morden*] will come to an end this year.

22.6.41: *HAUPTMANN* HERBERT PABST (77 DIVEBOMBER WING, 2 AIR FLEET, CENTRAL FRONT)[69]

Deblin . . . in a barracks camouflaged as a farmhouse on a dreadfully dusty, but beautifully disguised advanced airstrip close to the Bug River.

It's time—the new special reports are coming. Early, at 0200 hours, I got up; at 0330 at first light, I started off into Russia for the first time. At 1900 hours, I've already flown 3 sorties and haven't yet had lunch. But I only noticed that at 1600 hours and it doesn't matter. . . . Over there—at first [we struck] bunker positions and batteries close to the Bug, then our tanks quickly moved forward, and we also flew further ahead.

A tank battle below—sort of rectangular little boxes crawling all over the fields followed by wafting billows of dust—ours? Enemy's? Constant flashes from below—here houses are burning, there smoke in the forest—there, a tank is burning and the ammunition goes up in bright flashes amid the red fire. Lower! It's our own panzers advancing there. Beyond the forest, columns are moving toward them—tanks, trucks, the roads and forests are full.

Attack!—The bomb is already flashing up behind me while I pull up, now another, then another—boom, that must have been an ammunition truck going up. A dazzling flash shoots up, black shards fly, leaving smoldering red fire in its place.

Attack with machine guns! One [plane] after another dives down behind me, putting constant bursts of fire into the motionless motor vehicles. There, one starts to burn. Even the Me 109s flitting round us are coming in low for the attack. Then I gather the *Bumas* [i.e., his *Stukas*] on the return flight. All nine there? Yes, all nine! . . .

We land again soon after that. . . . The mechanics gather round us, eager for news, while the flight commanders report to me that all the machines have landed safely. A hasty meeting. Where were enemy, where friend, sighted? Impact of our attacks? Everything is very grave and hurried. . . . So! And now shirt off, a coffee, a cigarette.

23.6.41: DR. HANS LIEROW (6 INFANTRY DIVISION, NINTH ARMY, ARMY GROUP CENTER)[70]

Decamp at 0700, bright day. Dust and yet more dust. March casualties begin to mount. It is 1100 hours, the sun beats down. At least a fresh breeze. Even so, many exhausted men. The acting medical officer and the ambulance haven't got through to the troops yet. The companies must use their own resources. Officers and enlisted men are able to ride on requisitioned *Panje* wagons.[71] Now that 18 km have already been done, there are still approximately another 50 km to march today.

The great event of the day is not a particularly warlike event, but just a stupid sand track—many kilometers long through a large forest—through which man, horse, and vehicle must plough, having to make the most incredible exertions. Many cases of heatstroke [*viele Hitzeschläge*] with loss of consciousness. No acting medical officer, who should now be 5 km behind us. Insufficient evacuation transport. Eventually, the units drive the heatstroke victims in *Panje* wagons. . . .

The populace is flying Lithuanian colors. They have placed drinking water in buckets along the road. The antitank troops were greeted with cheers. Masses of lilacs were strewn across their vehicles. . . . The village inhabitants and their clerics cheered and prayed for God's blessing on the German colors.

The day stays hot. Teams of horses pull the carriages of the infantry and the artillery; the sweat runs rivulets through the thick dust on the soldiers' faces. On the second day of war, in the evening at 2100 hours, we reach the Neman River at Primar-Preny.

23.6.41: *FELDWEBEL* HERBERT E. (SS "DAS REICH" DIVISION [MOT.], 2 PANZER GROUP, ARMY GROUP CENTER)[72]

The spell is broken, and at home you all know now that our old political foe is to be beaten. We knew about it already the whole of last week, and it gave us a devilish joy that, even on Saturday evening, nothing was given away on the radio. But we already knew that the attack had been ordered for 3:00 in the morning, and that, as a result, somewhat later the declaration of the *Führer* would be broadcast on the radio.

We've yet to be committed to enemy territory. The deployment of so many troops requires a thorough organization, [and] through our wireless [operations] we've now ensured that the enormous columns of troops have been able to move along the roads without a hitch. But we still expect to be relieved this week and to be properly committed to battle.

Yesterday at the front, near Brest-Litowsk, there was air battle after air battle. At times, the Russian planes fell like flies from the clouds. Our fighters have really performed splendidly. Right here, beside us at the cemetery, the Poles buried the dead Russian [airmen].

We're all now rereading everything in the *Führer*'s *Mein Kampf* with great enthusiasm. Our entire mode of conduct at the moment is so precisely described in Chapter 14, that only the *Führer* is able to turn such prophecies into reality. It's my conviction that no more time will be needed to destroy Russia than was needed for France. Then my assumption that I'll get to go on leave in August will still come true.

23.6.41: DR. HEINRICH HAAPE (6 INFANTRY DIVISION, NINTH ARMY, ARMY GROUP CENTER)[73]

These two days were hard, really hard! Today we have had only a few casualties and no dead. But there is still no link to the supply train. In the last two days I have had only 2 slices of bread to eat and only little to drink. The dust mixes with sweat, settles in the skin and eats into it. My lips have swollen and in places they have split from the dryness. It's hot with a blue sky.

The war is even bloodier than I thought it would be, but we are setting a good pace and do not falter. Death is reaping a rich harvest. The battle was tougher yesterday than today. Yesterday we experienced several bombing attacks on our soldiers. We were low about the loss of our dear comrades and asking ourselves what is to become of all this if it goes on like this. There is shooting from every cornfield, from every farmhouse. As I was bandaging up another Russian, the "pigs" ["*Schweine*"] shot at me constantly with machine guns.

The Russians were carrying out another bombing attack, when suddenly German fighters arrived and shot 6 heavy bombers down. A magnificent air battle. . . . Germany's greatness and future is at stake and I can only say that at this moment I don't want to be anywhere else but here. . . .

We will spend the few hours of nighttime rest sleeping in the forest. My gas mask, on which I lay my field cap, has been my pillow for days now. And how wonderfully I do sleep on it—better than in the nicest bed. That's the work of extreme, honest tiredness!

23.6.41: *GEFREITER* RÖDER (ARMY GROUP NORTH)[74]

On 23.6.1941 we crossed the German-Russian frontier at Wirballen. On the same day, we arrived at Kaunas late in the afternoon, and took up quarters in a Russian barracks, the name of which is not known to me. As we were driving through the city of Kaunas, and before we'd reached our barracks, I saw a large gathering of people at a market square. I stopped my vehicle to see what was going on there. Because there were so many people standing around, and also a wall, I had to climb up onto my vehicle to get a better view of the square. What I then saw were Lithuanian civilians, armed with various striking instruments, beating up a number of civilians until they exhibited no more signs of life. I had no idea why these people were being beaten to death in such a dreadful manner, so I asked a medical *Feldwebel*, who was standing by me, but who I didn't know personally, about it all. He told me that those being killed were all Jews, who had been seized by the Lithuanians in the city and brought to the square. Those doing the beating were Lithuanian convicts [*Zuchthäusler*], who had been released from prison. I never learned just why the Jews had been killed. . . . Those watching were almost exclusively German soldiers, who watched the dreadful event out of curiosity. . . . Before they were killed, the Jews prayed or muttered something to themselves. Some of the Jews even went on praying when they were badly injured and already lying on the ground.

23.6.41: ALEXANDER COHRS (ARMY GROUP SOUTH)[75]

I didn't make any notes about this day right away. That was because we struck the forward Russian defensive line and had to overcome it. [The defensive line] consisted of tanks of older construction that were so deeply buried in the ground that only their revolving turrets were above ground. Any normally trained soldier would work his way up to such an island of resistance while taking advantage of every possibility for cover.

Here I experienced for the first time the effects of a National Socialist education, as the Hitler Youth area commander [*Gauleiter*] from Dortmund, Hans Völmcke, a teacher and former German long-jump champion, attacked one of the dug-in tanks without any support by shooting at it with his carbine as he continued to advance toward it. Every other one of us knew quite well that a carbine could, at best, only have an effect on the morale of the tank crew, perhaps in the manner of a very loud knocking sound. Before his death he cried out for a medical orderly. And he came, too, but he had no cover, and so the medical orderly also died after he had leapt from behind shelter—behind which he and I had crouched—without being able to reach Völmcke. It was Emil Klimaschewski from Strasburg in the Uckermark, who had a cheese factory and was the father of five children.

24.6.41: *SOLDAT* H.C. (EASTERN FRONT)[76]

In the past few days the political events have come thick and fast, and, personally, I have never looked into the future with such confidence as right now, as I view this struggle as a member of the German *Wehrmacht*. Despite its necessity the pact with Russia[77] was still something unnatural, and no one had really been comfortable with it.

24.6.41: *LEUTNANT* RUDOLF MAURER (251 INFANTRY DIVISION, ARMY GROUP NORTH)[78]

We crossed the frontier at Waldheide. The last German villages were really quite primitive. It doesn't seem like any fighting took place at the border crossing [and] only the roads were partially destroyed, because we're marching along sections of road that have already been repaired. The first Lithuanian town we reached was Sudargas. And so onward to the East. . . . The population is intimidated [*verschüchtert*]. The houses are all decked out with green-yellow-red flags and flowers, and the people say "Heil." But there is dirt and dust that is indescribable. The poor infantry! Unbelievably, the church in Sudargas is still standing, even the cross! We've seen the first graves and the first prisoners. And the thunder of the guns near Kaunas can be clearly heard.

24.6.41: *LEUTNANT* ERNST-MARTIN RHEIN (6 INFANTRY DIVISION, NINTH ARMY, ARMY GROUP CENTER)[79]

Review of the first two days: A complete success. Breach of the frontier fortifications. The enemy is retreating along the entire front. The regiment [18 Infantry Regiment] has suffered the following losses: 2 officers and 29 NCOs and enlisted men fallen; 1 officer, 57 NCOs and enlisted men wounded; 3 NCOs and enlisted men missing. The high percentage of dead is doubtless the result of the underhanded way of fighting [*hinterlistige Kampfesweise*] of the numerous snipers and partisans. This will be "no humane" war.

24.6.41: DR. HANS LIEROW (6 INFANTRY DIVISION, NINTH ARMY, ARMY GROUP CENTER)[80]

Six hours' sleep in the tent. It is 0630. Heavy gun and machine-gun fire from the Neman [River] wakes us. We're supposed to cross over today. . . . The sun shines down from a cloudless sky. From 1100 to 1200 hours crossing over the Neman with pneumatic boats. Bridge blown up by the Russians 20 minutes before arrival of German spearhead. . . . There are supposedly 130 Russians in the forest. Forests are, for the most part, fleetingly searched or not at all. Loss of time and unnecessary losses. . . .

March continues in the early evening. *Oberstleutnant* Hennicke brings the news that an enemy artillery battery is ahead of us, which is to be captured. The battalion marches toward it with weapons at the ready. 24-pound ammunition boxes on left and right shoulder straps, 15 km in 3 hours straight across very hilly countryside. I took the load from the last ammunition box carrier on one occasion. But I was soon drenched in sweat.

24.6.41: *PANZER-OBERSCHÜTZE* ERICH HAGER (17 PANZER DIVISION, 2 PANZER GROUP, ARMY GROUP CENTER)[81]

We arrive in Slonim and are surrounded. Behind us Russians, in front of us Russians, to the left and to the right. An unpleasant feeling. Meantime, set up next to the road and do technical duty. All of a sudden we are attacked from behind. Tanks. Tanks come and a load of vehicles. We shot all of them. Everything was burning. We were shot at from the cornfields all around. The wounded Russians were even firing at us. We are surrounded. Anything that came into view was shot. 12 Russians and one of our *Uffz.* were shot. Kottendorf and Mertel shot. These were our first wounded. Russians using special bullets.[82] *Uffz.* Feder hit by a special bullet. *Fldw.* Kummistan a shot in the backside.

24.6.41: *UNTEROFFIZIER* WILLY P. (167 INFANTRY DIVISION, ARMY GROUP CENTER)[83]

In our battalion sector there were 23 bunkers and fortifications, of which today alone all but two have been captured. Until now we've been in reserve. We have two dead and six wounded in the battalion. As long as the Russians are in the bunkers, they fight quite well. But once outside of them they're quite cowardly and treacherous. While those in front raise their hands as a sign of surrender, a grenade flies out from behind or one of them starts to shoot. House-to-house combat is thriving in the villages. In short, all those heroic deeds of the Poles [*Polenheldentaten*] are being used by the Russians. The Mongolians are perfectly cowardly figures, but they'll surely see a reckoning! After the final two bunkers here are finished off, then of course we'll continue to advance. . . . Hopefully, it will all come off without a hitch, just as quickly as it did in France.

24.6.41: *LEUTNANT* GEORG KREUTER (18 PANZER DIVISION, 2 PANZER GROUP, ARMY GROUP CENTER)[84]

At 2200 hours, I am summoned to the division. I take another five motorcycle messengers with me. The road is blocked by vehicle columns; it takes a long time for me to get through. At the head of the column, I discover that the division [command post] is surrounded.[85] I continue on alone. It is pretty dark. Now and then, I come across one of our soldiers. Russian tanks may be attacking? I establish a hedgehog position with a few hastily organized people.

When a rifle company continues ahead, I join them. We meet the commander of the combat engineer battalion, Major Rahl. He seems to think that there are absolutely no Russians there at all and that we are simply shooting at each other. When I continue onward, I meet my chief, who is going to get help. I go with him to the division CP. We can't go along the road and must take a long detour.

A crazy shoot-out [*tolle Schiesserei*] is underway and there's nothing to be seen. Close to the location of the command post, we come across some Russians, who are lying ahead of us in the grass. . . . It looks like everything has gone berserk at the command post. A Russian column coming from the west had thrust directly onto our march route. They probably wanted to get out of the cauldron. A few trucks were shot into flames by a tank that just happened to be standing by for repairs. The enemy dismounted from the rest and attacked.

It was a strange group of people. There were even a few German Communists among them. Most of them were in civilian clothes! Even women and children were there. They wore steel helmets, too, and shot at us. Everything around us was in flames. Russian trucks and German gasoline trucks! If only day would come so that we can get some help. The shooting is coming from everywhere! . . . My chief now has command here. The division commander isn't here, but with reconnaissance.

25.6.41: *MAJOR* WERNER HEINEMANN (23 INFANTRY DIVISION, FOURTH ARMY, ARMY GROUP CENTER)[86]

The advance continues with disruptions, we're already deep inside Russia; but *der Russe* fights doggedly, bravely, and with extraordinary cunning [*ausserordentlich verschlagen*].

25.6.41: ERICH KUBY (3 INFANTRY DIVISION [MOT.], 4 PANZER GROUP, ARMY GROUP NORTH)[87]

Forty-nine kilometers beyond Kaunas. Evening about 7:00 p.m. We drove through the entire night despite long stops and in the morning reached Seta, which is totally destroyed. At the exact spot where we stopped there lay a dead woman in uniform. Someone with the advance detachment said that she had been in command, and that she and the remaining Russian soldiers all shot themselves when they realized that resistance was useless. Later, however, a shell must have struck her, because her body was torn apart. If the Soviet leadership succeeds in stirring up their party members to such acts of fanaticism, and to build a national movement out of the rest of Russia, they'll make it awfully difficult for us.

25.6.41: *LEUTNANT* GEORG KREUTER (18 PANZER DIVISION, 2 PANZER GROUP, ARMY GROUP CENTER)[88]

Even the longest night finally comes to an end! Now we can see clearly! Russians are still being pulled out of the trucks, some of them are hidden under the axles; there are even some in our [vehicles]. It is quite a considerable number coming together here. The woman who wailed so madly through the night has now become quieter. She has an infant with her. Her wailing made everyone nervous all night long; she must be mad, because she pounds away and talks as if making a grand speech.

Around 20 of the worst renegades and those who have passed themselves off as German soldiers are executed. And the woman is among them! I am pleased that this chapter is closed. If it is to go on like this, then we'll have to receive fresh supplies of nerves!

25.6.41: KARL-GOTTFRIED VIERKORN (23 ID, FOURTH ARMY, ARMY GROUP CENTER)[89]

In the week we have behind us, we got barely any sleep, only marching, marching. In between times often in firing positions and being shot at with a vengeance. We only advance along sandy tracks. Man and animal are completely exhausted. We seem to have overestimated the Soviet Army—many prisoners, half ape-like and with shaved heads, poorly equipped and, so it would seem, on a low cultural level; many pass us by like that. The country has many charms: endless cornfields, vast forests, some of them primeval in appearance, now and then little farmsteads, and villages with typical wooden houses, draw wells, and cattle herds. The population seems helpful and friendly. Yesterday they showered us with flowers and put water and cool milk along the sides of the road against our infernal thirst and the dust.

25.6.41: *OFFIZIER* HANS HERTEL (STAFF, 39 PANZER CORPS, 3 PANZER GROUP, ARMY GROUP CENTER)[90]

The troops . . . continued their attack . . . at undiminished speed and boxed their way through the enemy resistance everywhere.[91] But the rapid tempo was still not enough for the general of these troops [*General der Panzertruppe* Rudolf Schmidt]. He knew that speed was everything in this offensive. So he gave the order: forward, at any cost! [*Vorwärts um jeden Preis!*] And then began an unprecedented chase. The general, accompanied by only a very few forces from a reconnaissance battalion and a few men from his staff, positioned himself personally at the spearhead, driving ahead in an open jeep in order to reconnoiter the best march routes.[92]

25.6.41: *SOLDAT* S.K. (78 INFANTRY DIVISION, FOURTH ARMY, ARMY GROUP CENTER)[93]

For the time being, our division is advancing in the second wave behind the fighting troops, distance approximately 30 km. Since yesterday, we stopped advancing to the east and are now marching in a more northerly direction. Today, the noise of battle in front of us is very loud; one comrade thinks it is from the fortress of Belostok. According to the map, that could be right. We generally get our tramping done at night; thank God, I have no foot problems, and generally I can't complain about anything. Today, incidentally, we had to really put our backs into our combat vehicles: the horses couldn't manage it alone any more.[94]

25.6.41: ALBERT NEUHAUS (ARMY GROUP NORTH)[95]

My dear Agnes!

Early morning greetings to you! Yesterday we drove along the roads on which our troops had advanced and we saw horrid scenes [*schaurige Bilder*]. Tauroggen [Taurage], a city of about 15,000 inhabitants, was completely in ashes.[96] To the right and left of the road were the recently dug graves of those killed in battle [and] the bloated corpses of horses. Refugees, without even the most basic necessities of life, wandered about. The Russians have already been thrown back quite a way. There are shot-up Russian tanks on the road. The furious German advance is not to be stopped—it's a concentration of forces the world has never seen before. We're not involved in the actual fighting. You can only throw up your hands in admiration for the German organization that stands behind it all. There was quite a commotion at the front again tonight. Even now one can still hear the thunder of the guns. The Russian prisoners make you shudder; they come in all types.

25.6.41: ALBERT NEUHAUS (ARMY GROUP NORTH)[97]

Dear Johanna![98]

Many thanks for your kind note. . . . Agnes has no doubt kept you fully informed about me. I am doing very well and I hope the same for all of you. What times we live in. Yesterday, we drove through burning towns and cities; simply dreadful scenes here. What our country is going through at the moment is, I believe, almost nothing compared to the suffering [in those lands] over which the war has raged. We have quite an aversion to the Russian prisoners; in other words, we're not taking many prisoners. Up here in the former Lithuania there are lots of Jews and so we're giving no quarter [*kein Pardon*].[99]

In the distance we can always hear the thunder of the guns and the explosions of aerial bombs. The advance is continuing, and only the endless Russian distances can make you somewhat uneasy. But you can only marvel at how well organized it all is. There is simply no stopping the German steamroller. When this campaign is over, the fate of the English will also most likely be sealed. I'll be surprised to see just how far we advance. The world has never seen such a concentration of forces. The wagon columns, two or three abreast, never seem to come to an end. As a result, we swallowed lots of dust yesterday.

25.6.41: *OFFIZIER* UDO VON ALVENSLEBEN (16 PANZER DIVISION, 1 PANZER GROUP, ARMY GROUP SOUTH)[100]

It turns slowly to evening and night, the army columns [*Heeressäulen*] move forward even more slowly. Rutted tracks have usually been worn alongside the roads, which are, as a rule, country roads full of deep potholes and sandy pits, which we cautiously leap across. The motorcyclists wriggle and hop their way through it all, like trout. Complete chaos, covered in clouds of dust—a profitable target for the Soviet bombers. There is frequently shoving, tugging; vehicles that get stuck are helped along. We all look like chimney sweeps.

The Ukrainian landscape: Impressions deepen through frequent stops, during which there is contact with the inhabitants of the country. This bit of earth is populated with tough, patient, resigned creatures, who submit to the terrors of this existence with apprehension, circumspection and stoic dignity, and on whose backs, at whose expense, the weight of this world stage falls. The country is a never-ending expanse, but it doesn't seem lonely, as villages and scattered cottages constantly appear, made of mud or wood, with straw-thatched roofs, very poor, but really very highly evocative [*phantasieanregend*]. You imagine such primitive little houses can only be found at the other end of the world. They are frequently burned out. The farming tools and machines are carefully placed outside because of the fire risk. Triple-domed Orthodox churches are a feature of the larger villages. Any number of crucifixes and images of saints stand by the side of the paths. The shadows of the inhabitants squat motionless in front of the houses. Frogs croak in the swamps. The forests exhale freshness and moisture. A ghostly landscape at dusk. A tall, white church stands alone in the landscape; it has a bold baroque façade and sweeping door pillars.[101]

In the direction of the enemy, fires redden the sky. Above us, the starry heavens twinkle through the delicately fragrant branches. There is shooting. Our panzers are engaged in battle.[102] Columns [of military vehicles] roar by. It seems to me that I have fought in every campaign since the creation of the world.

26.6.41: *UNTEROFFIZIER* EGON N. (6 INFANTRY DIVISION, NINTH ARMY, ARMY GROUP CENTER)[103]

The roads today are once again frightful. We sink up to our ankles in the very fine, dusty sand. Our automobiles and horses struggle through it with great difficulty. Of course, riding a bicycle is quite awful. I hope that things improve very quickly.

Up to now we have just two lightly wounded men in the company [12./IR 18]. . . . We don't see much of the Russians, except for a few snipers [*Heckenschützen*] now and then, and to be sure they fight in a beastly and stubborn way.

26.6.41: *GEFREITER* HANS EFFERBERGEN (ARMY GROUP SOUTH)[104]

Two days of fighting behind us. Yesterday my unit was badly messed up in a wheat field.

The Russians are nothing but low-down curs. For one thing, they often let us come up to within twenty yards of them and then start blazing away at us from positions so well concealed that they simply can't be seen. For another thing, they ensconce themselves high up in the trees and before you have any inkling of their presence their guns start popping. For a third thing, they work hand-in-glove with the civilians, put on ordinary clothes and in the twinkling of an eye change into a gang of the most abominable bandits.[105]

The unreaped grain fields greatly facilitate defense operations. Sometimes the bullets from these fields come flying so horizontally that they must be firing standing up.

26.6.41: *OFFIZIER* UDO VON ALVENSLEBEN (16 PANZER DIVISION, 1 PANZER GROUP, ARMY GROUP SOUTH)[106]

Our tanks are advancing rapidly. This has resulted in a very long southern flank that is being protected by two infantry divisions against Russian tank units that are attacking laterally. The woods all around are full of Russians; they're rallying far behind us, but even with artillery support they're suffering heavy losses. We're not coming up against a firm front. The immense areas through which our tanks have long since advanced are still occupied by the enemy and must be laboriously mopped up. So from the very first hours [of the campaign] we've had Russians on all sides of us. That's led to distressing surprises. We recently spent the night on a farm wrapped up in our pale blankets like mummies, protecting our faces from myriads of mosquitoes.

On a rumor that Russian tanks and cavalry have broken through from the south our GHQ artillery [*Heeresartillerie*] flees to the rear [while] rear area services prepare to defend themselves. The local civilians flee into the woods, while at the same time the Russians make a breach from the north and fall upon our surprised [marching] columns. Our march discipline fails.

26.6.41: *GEFREITER* RUDOLF STÜTZEL (5 INFANTRY DIVISION, NINTH ARMY, ARMY GROUP CENTER)[107]

When you visited me back then in Karlsruhe, I had said that there would be war with Russia. And now it's happened. Since the 22nd of this month, at 0305 hours, our troops have been on the offensive. Our assembly area [for the attack] was near Sejni, close to Suwalki. Our division (5 ID) advanced in an easterly direction. The enemy resistance was rapidly broken. The *Luftwaffe* and artillery did great work in advance, so we encountered little opposition from their Russian counterparts. We were attacked by five Russian bombers, whose bombs landed directly beside us in open ground, but only on the first day. We had no losses. Since then we've only seen burning Russian airplanes. In our sector alone 600 were shot down on a single day! The [Russian] air force has been totally eliminated.

Since yesterday we've been in the vicinity of Serijai. We've buried eight of our comrades from the advance detachment there. Countless dead Russians lay all around on the hill here, as well as several burned-out tanks. With five other comrades we took 24 prisoners! Since yesterday we've got orders not to take any more prisoners. . . . This campaign will come to an end just as rapidly as the others, even if the territory is much larger.

26.6.41: *FELDWEBEL* HEINZ R. (ARMY GROUP SOUTH)[108]

We currently find ourselves on a sunken road, to the right the ruins of a number of houses are still smoking somewhat. It is very hot, I have loosened my collar, undone my neckerchief, but it's still not much better. If only it would stop.

I'm now sitting in another vehicle under shady fruit trees. Things are rolling past on the road, everything is being urged on to the front. We are just a few kilometers from the city of [L'vov]. It's a larger city, so it would seem, although I had never heard its name before. It lay to the side of me, with typical Russian domes and churches, although the country has only been [under Russian control] since two years ago.

Now, no doubt you want to hear about how I am getting on. Far in the distance you can hear artillery fire, and in general dust and heat reign supreme here.[109] I last wrote to you from the town of Hr. The day before yesterday, at 2000 hours, I drove away from there with my solo [motorcycle] and a column of fuel trucks [*Tank-Kolonne*], which I was actually supposed to bring to [Officer] Adele. Just beyond the town of

Hr. the road came to an end and a corduroy road [*Knüppeldamm*] began. At the side of the road stood soldiers who guided each vehicle along and immediately banked up the road again. After a few kilometers we went down an embankment and across a narrow river on a makeshift wooden bridge. At the other side a sand path began and there was a small wood. Elevations with barbwire, a dead animal. We were in Russia.

Now we set off on some crazy driving, overtaking entire columns. Fortunately, it was a bright night because we had to drive without any light, only in the distance was there firelight: a burning village. Our overtaking maneuvers were a frequent cause of abusive shouts, until we finally came to a narrow wooden bridge, where everything had come to a standstill. . . . We soon continued, until we finally got stuck. That had the advantage that we could get some shut-eye for 2–3 hours. Only when it started dawning could we continue. The roads were often poor, but since it had rained at least a little, initially, it wasn't so dusty. We often went through fields, as the road was too bad. The houses were primitive, but not especially dirty. . . . The roads gradually got increasingly boggy, the road surface giving way like rubber beneath the heavy vehicle. The road often had to be put to rights with spade and brushwood, but we continued ever onward. Then, after midday, a delay occurred: A small wooden bridge had collapsed and now the bypass route had to be made traversable. So we had a break, which I used to get some sleep. . . . After an hour and a half, it was onward over swamp and field and dusty roads. The dust is as fine as flour. You can't imagine what we look like. . . .

We entered . . . [L'vov] as it got dark. The ruins of a few houses were burning at the approach. The population hadn't fled. A number of soldiers were standing in a small square and speaking vehemently to a Jew, who was so scared for his life that he didn't know what to do. He lay imploringly on the ground. He was accused of complicity in the mutilation of two German pilots who had had to make an emergency landing. Shortly afterward, I heard pistol shots.

That night I slept well in the truck, in the morning I paid out my fuel and went on a tour with Berndt. At noon we saw infantry searching the cornfields and farmsteads and flushing out [Soviet] soldiers. There was some lively shooting, because these snipers [*Heckenschützen*] weren't being taken prisoner. Instead, the farmsteads in which some were found went up in flames. Myself, I soon went on with the motorcycle. At one point there were numerous dead Russians lying on the ground, otherwise just dust and sun.

27.6.41: AUGUST SAHM (ARMY GROUP SOUTH)[110]

Since 22.6. we've been in combat and I really can't describe what I've had to go through. Attack—dig in—artillery fire—attack again. I'm writing to you from a foxhole. Since the start of the fighting I haven't washed or shaved. Please pass this on at once to my parents, since I don't have any more paper with which to write to them.

I can't begin to express what I feel. If I only saw some meaning in it all! I simply can't come to terms with it. The only thing that I do is—try to hold on from minute to minute in this maelstrom of strange, unknown forces.

How it hurts, one's own suffering—and even more that of others.

Human beings are swept away, fall like withered leaves—human beings. But take heart, my friend, for I have learned to pray during these days. . . . We long to be together with HIM, and ask of HIM that HE protect us.

27.6.41: WM. JOSEF L. (129 INFANTRY DIVISION, NINTH ARMY, ARMY GROUP CENTER)[111]

For the last 10 days I have been unable to write to you. Correspondence restrictions are still in place; I don't know when this letter will make its way to you. The last few days were filled with forced marches, defensive battles, and advances through enemy lines and fortifications. . . . Only someone who went through everything in the last Great War can tell you what it's like to march for hour upon hour in swampy terrain, in never-ending flatlands, through dust and beating sun.

27.6.41: *UNTEROFFIZIER* E.J. (CONSTRUCTION BATTALION 44, EASTERN FRONT)[112]

The farther along we get, the more we notice the Communist conditions. The dwellings of the people here are miserable. What we have in comparison is like gold. We've just made a brief stop to rest at the entrance to a town. A column of Jews under German supervision has just marched past us. They're going to clean up the roads. Here there are more Jews than other places.

27.6.41: *OFFIZIER* MARTIN STEGLICH (ARMY GROUP NORTH)[113]

This morning we got ready quickly. Last night we had to fend off a sudden enemy attack [*Überfall*]. It was pitch black. We chased them off. Several of the Reds were killed. I had my men occupy the main battle line. In this war it all depends on making damn sure that when our troops are resting they're protected—anywhere that they are!

The dwellings of the Reds are like they were 20 years ago in Russia. Many of the villages are almost completely empty! There are just piles of corpses lying about, or mutilated and wounded Lithuanians crawling around—horrible, ghastly scenes. Our soldiers are really quite angry, and woe betide the Russian who tries to ambush and shoot at us!

We advanced through the most difficult wooded areas in stifling heat with our weapons at the ready. I arranged for a *panje* vehicle to carry the heavy ammunition. Now we're on the route of advance [*Vormarschstrasse*] . . . in the 30-kilometer-deep woods. Route of advance? What a joke! It's just a forest lane—a path through the woods! Now we've taken up a position for all-round defense in this primeval woodland. The mosquitoes sting like the devil. Utterly repulsive. There's no water for washing up either. But this night shall also pass. We got mail again today.

27.6.41: ALBERT NEUHAUS (ARMY GROUP NORTH)[114]

My dear Agnes!

The burning sun drives the sweat from our pores. You simply don't know how to protect yourself from it. This morning we've already bathed in a little brook, so we feel somewhat better again.

Yesterday we moved up a small distance. What we saw was dreadful. We drove through an area where just days before a furious tank battle had raged. And there they were—these terrible giants that weigh up to 90 tons.[115] These things have such thick armor plating that even 150mm guns are powerless against them. If our magnificent flak[116] hadn't been there, it could easily have turned out badly for us. But the flak took them out and our advance continued. That was really a battle of matériel [*Materialschlacht*], and I believe that much will be said about it later—about the tank battle at Raseinai.[117]

We don't see any Russian aircraft any longer. But once again the Russians have built a monument of shame to our brave soldiers, as they worked over the few prisoners they'd made in a devilish and sadistic fashion. But our revenge for that is hard on their heels. We're taking very few prisoners now, and you can imagine what that means. [Destroyed] Russian tanks were all over the terrain, but unfortunately there were also German antiaircraft guns, antitank guns, radio intercept vehicles, and motorcycles.

27.6.41: *LEUTNANT* ERNST-MARTIN RHEIN (6 INFANTRY DIVISION, NINTH ARMY, ARMY GROUP CENTER)[118]

Dear parents!

Since the six-day-long mail ban will be lifted tomorrow, I wanted to send you a quick word. I am very well, the leaden exhaustion of the last few days and nights has been thoroughly overcome by an extended day of rest, and this evening we have our sights set on new objectives.

The last five days brought some great moments and many valuable experiences. The company proved itself just as I had hoped it would. The most pleasing thing is that I had only 6 casualties in the company, despite tough fighting. . . .

The Russian soldier fights courageously and doggedly, with much more spirit than the Frenchman. On the other hand, their leadership seems to be rigid and lacking any particular initiative. . . . Here in Russian-occupied Lithuania we have seen the most alarming examples of the effects of Communism, which destroys property and wealth. The populace continually pleads with us to protect them against the communist gangs, which ruthlessly shoot dead any nationalistically minded people.

For days now, the heat has been oppressive. Our constant companions are dust, sweat, and thirst. Despite the frequently very primitive conditions in which we are living, the stresses, and the immense heat—not to mention the dusty tracks and roads, often covered in sand 20 cm deep—to a man our mood is marvelous. . . . You should see my boys, how their eyes light up in their dust-encrusted, pinched faces when it is time to go to battle.

27.6.41: *HAUPTMANN* HERBERT PABST (77 DIVEBOMBER WING, 2 AIR FLEET, CENTRAL FRONT)[119]

Cauldron of Belostok outside Slonim.

At first light: Alarm! The encircled Russians have broken through along the road of advance. 40 minutes later I was in the morning air with the squadron. But here, too, I saw a German column at the indicated spot. I go warily deeper to see better—there! Signal lights rise up, signs are hastily unfurled—hey, they are mightily afraid because of the threateningly circling Stukas. But you can rest assured—I'll look closer first. It is difficult to make out from above.[120]

There, a bit farther ahead, two vehicles are burning—the road is otherwise empty—there, too, a shaky white signal light flares up. [A white Very signal light always meant "German troops here!"] But from the forest edge, not far from the road, there is the occasional flash—muzzle flashes! Aha, so something is going on over there after all. I circle and look. Again, a signal light climbs into the air from the road: Be careful! It's us! But in the forest I can see vehicles hidden on a path, gathered densely at the side—nervous quiet, nothing moves. Only at the forest edge is there movement and shooting toward the road. "*Buma*-Attack!" The Germans on the road were probably scared shitless when we laid our eggs. Then there's a flash in the forest, huge columns of smoke shoot into the sky, boom, boom, again—there, a huge jet of flame, then something else exploded. Again and again we attack, bombs rain down into the little wood; as I pull up, I can see more vehicles in a field further away in the distance—I'm out of bombs, now the tracer of my machine gun leaps down in a slanting attack and draws pale threads of smoke into the clear morning air.

Dense columns of our troops are again marching east even on this road today. We will no doubt soon follow.

Otherwise: food, vodka, cigarettes—everything there and everything's fine. I'm sitting bare-chested under shady trees, my radio playing gentle melodies, my trusty "culture hero," even in these distant . . . vistas.

27.6.41: *LEUTNANT* WILLIBALD G. (57 INFANTRY DIVISION, SIXTH ARMY, ARMY GROUP SOUTH)[121]

Since the last letter I wrote to you first thing yesterday we've experienced all sorts of things! A tank attack [*Panzerangriff*]. . . .

I had already written you that we'd been deployed to support the mission of a battalion, which was to extricate a surrounded company. And over the course of the night, that succeeded. The battalion withdrew to a village at the edge of the forest.

We had our observation post on a hill around 3 km away from the village and our gun position just behind that. All hell broke out shortly after 8:00 a.m. We were showered with a hail of shells by the Russian artillery, and this later turned into aimless harassing fire.

During this time, we observed around 30 tanks just beyond the village, moving into position in a forest clearing. The village itself stood in fierce flames as a result of the constant fire from the heavy enemy artillery.

In collaboration with our forward observer [*vorgeschobenen Beobachter*], who was with the infantry at this place, we shelled the concentration of tanks—ourselves constantly under fire at our observation post and gun positions—and we even managed to stop a few of them. We then received the order to advance approximately 2 km with the observation post and to establish it on a hill range just outside the village.

During disassembly, we discovered that enemy tanks had already advanced into the village. We had barely occupied the new observation post than the message came that Russian tanks had skirted round the hill behind which our gun position stood and were now attacking the limber positions and the supply train. They quickly skedaddled and it cost a great deal of trouble to draw everything back together again later.

At the same time, the enemy tanks attacked the village in large numbers, pushing forward beyond it and on the road frontally toward the artillery position. We were lying in the middle of this in the holes we had quickly dug and let the tanks drive past us.

The battery's first platoon was then immediately brought up to the hill and fought the frontally attacking tanks at close range, while the other batteries demolished the rearward tanks or forced them to turn back. This was Ralph Ross's baptism of fire [*Feuertaufe*], which he survived. He was with the forward platoon, which finished off 3 tanks at close range of 120–150 meters, and damaged many more, forcing them to turn back.[122] And all of that under heavy enemy artillery fire! It was a miracle that nobody from my battery was wounded. What's more, Russian aircraft made low-level and bombing attacks, which unfortunately claimed a number of dead and wounded in the battalion. The tanks were 30-tonners![123]

28.6.41: *LEUTNANT* WALTER MELCHINGER (ARMY GROUP SOUTH)[124]

The scenes to the right and left of the roads are just the same as yesterday. It is war. The behavior of the inhabitants [in the Ukraine] is quite touching. They bring us flowers, weep for joy, kneel down before us and kiss our hands, bring us milk, eggs, and water for washing.

Right on the heels of the fleeing enemy. Always toward the front.
It is a delight to be a soldier. Day and Night.
No time for writing.
I've longed so for this. It is the fulfillment of all my wishes.[125]

28.6.41: *PANZER-OBERSCHÜTZE* ERICH HAGER (17 PANZER DIVISION, 2 PANZER GROUP, ARMY GROUP CENTER)[126]

Everything keeps moving. . . . We get 60 liters of fuel from the half tracks and drive on through the line of bunkers. Receive fire and transmit okay. Get stuck in the mud, also *Oblt.* Zinschütz. The Gef pulls us out.[127] We get in, get the shells, and get to the rendezvous point. Drive through the burning town that has been destroyed by Stukas. Outside the bunker there is Pak artillery. We fire at everything and drive on. Firing from the left and right again. The Russians are hiding themselves and firing from an ambush. In any war there has never been such a sniper war, also by civilians. When we found the first objective it was midnight. It was near Slonim. . . .

We drive on at the head and come to a village. Heavy firing here. We come to a corner and it happened there. 3 shots from not more than 20–30 meters away went into our tank. Driver *Uffz.* Wedde dead. . . . We bail out as the tank already on fire. We have only what we have on us. It was so quick. . . . Albert, me, Fuchs, and *Uffz.* Kirsch were the 4 who lay in the ditch. Fuchs and I creep along the ditch. Come to an underpass and huddle into the mud with our only weapon, a pistol. Albert lost his getting out of the tank. We lay in the mud for ¾ of an hour. The Russians were continuing to fire. The enemy all around, we can't get away. We see our last hour coming. But it turns out differently. At the last minute comes a patrol of infantry. They take us with them and we go back. 2 crews come . . . 5 wounded are here. Albert and I are the only healthy ones. The 2 drivers are dead. Fritz is missing. Our tanks come back, can't get any further forward. It was close. I just can't believe that we got away. We went back with 2 MTW [troop-carrying vehicles].

Shots went directly into the driver and next to me [in the tank]. I can only speak of luck that I didn't get hurt. I'm so sorry about Wedde. He didn't give out a sound.

29.6.41: *GEFREITER* EWALD M. (125 INFANTRY DIVISION, SEVENTEENTH ARMY, ARMY GROUP SOUTH)[128]

Today is Sunday, but we notice nothing of it, because the war machine can't rest until the last of the enemy has been felled. After the six-week rest period in Yugoslavia we were on the move again, which did us all good. And now we're living close to nature [*naturverbunden*] in the woods of Russia. Today the *Sondermeldungen* just kept coming and coming.[129] It is staggering what is happening here, and what will happen in the coming days. Yesterday morning 30 of us fought it out with 18 Russians in a village behind the front. Our bullets and grenades took out two of them, one we took prisoner, and the others escaped before we reached the village. One of our comrades was wounded. They were tough chaps, these Russians, mostly very young.

29.6.41: ANONYMOUS (20 PANZER DIVISION, 3 PANZER GROUP, ARMY GROUP CENTER)[130]

The *Luftwaffe* must have visited a major attack on Minsk one or two days previously, leaving only ruins behind. All the Party buildings, schools, tenement blocks, and state grocery stores were destroyed, with the exception of the large Party building by the Lenin monument. Dead Red Army soldiers [*tote Rotarmisten*] lay on the roadsides. Nobody bothered about them. Nothing could better characterize the apathy and indifference of the population [*Apathie und Stumpfheit der Bevölkerung*] than this attitude toward their own dead. Instead, the rabble was very eager to drag away anything of use from the ruins, especially foodstuffs and items of clothing from the warehouses. Women, carrying huge bundles, almost collapsing under the load, stole away into the side streets.[131]

29.6.41: *GEFREITER* HANS CASPAR VON WIEDEBACH-NOSTITZ (20 PANZER DIVISION, 3 PANZER GROUP, ARMY GROUP CENTER)[132]

In spite of the fact that the roads have been rendered soft by the rain our tanks entered Minsk yesterday evening. We also resume our march with the divisional HQ. Bloated Russian corpses, Russian antitank guns, artillery and horses lie shot up on the route. A few kilometers on there is the completely destroyed reconnaissance squad from our company. The crew of the first vehicles are dead and partly burned. Those in the rear vehicle with *Leutnant* Kiesling were able to get away: a gruesome sight.

Toward midday we are coming toward Minsk, which is the first large city that we have seen. Almost 80 percent of it is destroyed.[133] Only the suburbs are still standing. There are giant luxury buildings and factories among wretched wooden huts with poor plaster work, no guttering. Everything is dirty and untidy. The city has still not been completely cleared of the enemy. Everywhere snipers are being flushed out and shot.

29.6.41: *GEFREITER* WILHELM H. (STAFF, CONSTRUCTION BATTALION 46, EASTERN FRONT)[134]

Today was truly a great day! Twelve special reports! I took note of the most important of them. It's simply impossible to grasp the magnitude of these successes, the so-called initial successes, or to comprehend the extent of their significance! You can only be amazed, and thankful for the *Führer* and our brave soldiers! The greatest concentration of forces of all time has been followed, and will continue to be followed, by the greatest successes of all time!

In our sector it's already been, so to speak, quiet since Monday. But not in the air, because the large Ju 52 transports continuously fly back and forth over us, often at a very low altitude; tirelessly, like busy little bees, they carry all sorts of material to the front, and thus contribute in no small measure to the great successes.

Now and then we still see fighters, ground-attack aircraft [*Zerstörer*] and Stukas, but we see less and less of them, because their bases are constantly moving up. . . .

Our comrades from the staff have already advanced far ahead of us, but they're still not moving as rapidly as the combat troops. Red airplanes are no longer to be seen, and there are as many knocked-out Russian tanks lying around on the road as there were automobiles last year in France! Apparently, at one spot someone hanged a sniper.

The Russian inhabitants seem rather indifferent. Already on the second or third day I heard that right after the start of hostilities the Jews were trying to flee in large numbers into the General Government[135] out of fear, but that they weren't being let through. Of course, when there's trouble, they're always the first to beat it!

29.6.41: FRIEDRICH G. (STAFF, 26 DESTROYER WING, 2 AIR FLEET)[136]

And now about this war. I spent the first hours on the airfield. And then I was told to get ready with my people straight away so as to go on ahead to the area we had just occupied and make preparations for the air wing that would follow on behind. On the journey, on dusty roads, through long stretches of pine forests and past lakes, I saw and experienced many consequences of the war at close hand. A lot of Russians are still around in the woods; under cover of darkness they fire from the woods at passing columns. One *Feldwebel* was shot dead on Wednesday morning. We went with two combat patrols to search the area and found four of these bandits and snipers. They were summarily shot. We saw many a soldier's grave, shot-up tanks, fallen and shot Russians, a burned-out village, and other things. In the evening, we came to a rest stop and we spent the night there, too.

The following morning the Russians came with more planes. We had already heard bomb impacts. Three of the machines were on a direct course for us. Came down to perhaps around 4–6000 meters. We had started up all vehicles, all personnel were there. Then it got hairy. Everyone ran in every direction. Everybody thought they could still save themselves. We watched the planes with wary expressions. When will the bombs fall? When will they shoot at us? Those were the thoughts with which we anticipated the next few seconds. But we were lucky, because the effect would have been dreadful. The Russians flew over us and away; either they had no more bombs or some other notion inconceivable to us, because we were left alone.

But we got a real kick out of what started next! Our fighters were in pursuit. We, on the ground, willed on their fighting spirit with our thoughts, and our warmest wishes accompanied our machines. Hardly had the first opened up than [one of the Russian planes was struck by] a sheaf of fire. The airplane was burning and hurtled down into the depths of the forest, trailing a long tail [of smoke] behind. Another fighter sought out the second [Russian plane] and opened fire—it was burning, the pilot parachuted out. The machine fell from the sky. The third was able to carry on for quite some time while on fire, until it, in a beautiful parabola, pitched into the forest with a powerful detonation. At any rate, it still carried a bomb. The same fate quickly befell another three enemy bombers. We on the ground were enthusiastically following our fighter planes and rewarded every air victory with a loud 'Urrah!' But what are six airplanes compared to the 57 that were shot down here on the day just before we arrived at the new location. 57! . . .

I'm excited to see how events progress. It can't go on long.

29.6.41: *UNTEROFFIZIER* ROBERT RUPP (17 PANZER DIVISION, 2 PANZER GROUP, ARMY GROUP CENTER)[137]

Wygora. At dawn a Russian tank drove past (coming from the front). He waved; some are saying he had a white flag. [One of our tanks] pursues him and shoots him up at the corner of the forest behind us. We're bombarded by artillery, pretty close, but just short of us. The vehicles are taken across the road into a clearing in the forest. We're still under artillery fire. We disperse ourselves through the forest. . . . A new route to Minsk has to be found, so it is said. The company is in a forest until around 1330 hours. . . . Panzers are reconnoitering ahead. Traveling over fields, etc. We drive through the village at a fast pace (it is occupied by Russians) and rapidly take the hills. We have occupied the hills, but are met immediately by artillery fire. The impact of the first shell strikes *Unteroffizier* Friedrich Schmidt [and he falls] with outstretched arms. We dig ourselves in on the hill. There is constant artillery and mortar fire. . . .

Behind the village that's being cleared (the Russians are sitting in the foundations of the houses), we smoke out an artillery spotter. He is shot along with around fifteen men! Then the artillery is quiet. . . . A Pak gun has been identified and is subjected to fire. Horses dart out of the bushes (the Pak horses) with the driver, run in circles in the field. Now a bunker has been made out to the right of the Pak gun. And now life emerges over there. Entire hordes [of Russians] flee to the rear. The sandhill is an observation post for our artillery. The escaping Russians are shot at with artillery and machine guns. Terrible effects can be seen. . . .

The Russians flee into the village and an entire battery, horse-drawn, tries to escape to the right. Some of them get through. Next we observe an enemy vehicle column (automobiles), approaching from the left. Are we to be encircled? The vehicles are taken under fire by artillery. Our weapons don't have the range for it. We become a little subdued [*etwas kleinlaut*], we know we could be surrounded. Suddenly, a large number of German tanks emerge from the village. At the same time, we fall in, cross the bridge in the valley and advance on the hills beyond it. We receive heavy fire from all directions. But it's not targeted. . . .

The Russians have positions in which just a single man can stand. The firing of our weapons creates an unheard-of racket. Soon, the villages to the left and right of the road are burning. Some Russians surrender. The second platoon "takes no prisoners." One prisoner, holding something red in his hand, runs anxiously with raised hands through the noise. . . . "Shoot him down!" one of ours yells, races after him and trips his foot so he falls flat on his face. He stands right up again and is taken to a load of other prisoners.

A sheep with a shot-up leg is lying on the ground. Leixner does the merciful thing and shoots it [*Gnadenschuss*]. An old man is sitting in a small cellar. Cows are standing about confused by the noise. A calf is sitting, its rear body shot to pieces. Half a platoon moves to the forwardmost line, pistol shots from every direction. . . . We take our positions and spray the forest with bullets. Behind us, a Pak gun or a tank is shooting. Our opponents in the forest are still, our lead elements can once again move up. And soon after that we all stop for a rest.

We drink a last tea in our trench. I can still see civilians in the burning villages. We are to make sure the forest is secure during the night. Then we're told we have to go farther back. And then we hear that we advanced too far, almost to Minsk, and as a result had almost got ourselves surrounded. So we have to go back to the area we were in last night. So that was all for nothing!

A wounded man is bandaged up next to us in the trench. A tank driver calls for the medic. He has been shot in the head and you can see his brain.

30.6.41: *OFFIZIER* LEO TILGNER (ARMY GROUP NORTH)[138]

We passed the day distributing captured goods. Three small packages are now on their way to you. One of them contains a primitive wood Madonna that I found while underway on the road. It stood on a rotted-out squared timber in a wooden lantern with panes of glass. In the second little package are two packets of Russian tea. In the third is fabric for shirts, fleecy on the reverse side. Each of us received two meters [of fabric], and also soap. We also got Russian military blouses, which I will wear after they've been washed. There were all kinds of other things, but we arrived a little too late. I think that pretty much everything has been pilfered from the captured Russian party members. Apparently, the local inhabitants tortured the Jews today. Some of our people saw it.[139]

30.6.41: HARALD HENRY (ARMY GROUP CENTER)[140]

The line of retreat of the [enemy] army, which has been shattered by our tanks and Stukas, made for a powerful and disturbing impression. Right at the edge of the road were the immense craters left by the Stuka bombs, whose air pressure had tossed even the heaviest tanks into the air and spun them around. Our tanks had finished off what was left of the army, which had been caught by surprise by the bombers, and so we marched for 25 kilometers past scenes of monstrous destruction. Along with perhaps 200 smashed, burned-out, overturned tanks of both the heaviest and lightest armor plating, [there was] artillery, trucks, field kitchens, motorcycles, antitank guns—a sea of weapons, helmets and equipment items of all kind. . . . And between all of that the already black and swollen corpses. Most appalling were the horses—ripped to pieces, swollen up, intestines oozing out, a bloody nose torn off, enveloped in the odor of decay—something ghastly between a slaughterhouse and putrefaction—that had a paralyzing effect on our column. The worse of it all was a pig that, happily smacking its lips, gnawed at one of these horse cadavers; so we were certain that this horse flesh, in a roundabout way, would also taste good to people, including me.

30.6.41: *MAJOR* WERNER HEINEMANN (23 INFANTRY DIVISION, FOURTH ARMY, ARMY GROUP CENTER)[141]

In the field:
    The field kitchen is steaming, and all around the horses are tucking in to plentiful supplies of seized oats, the *Landser* are sitting in the corn and cleaning their gear for the first time in 8 days. It is a profound image of peace, only the continual appearance of Russians from out of the cornfields and the bushes is a reminder of the collapse of the two huge Belostok armies.[142] Whenever possible, they are shot dead, because they have murdered Germans who fell into their hands in the most bestial manner. But we can't always bring ourselves to do that when these utterly shell-shocked, half-starved, and parched half-animals come crawling out of the cornfields.

The never-ending crack of snipers is also dying away, they are too exhausted. But many a motorcyclist or other messenger or ration carrier still meets with danger in the rear areas; one of my motorcycle messengers lay behind his machine in the forest for 3 hours while receiving fire from all directions, after we had already marched along that same route several hours previously without any contact with the enemy. It's a truly barbaric war [*asiatischer Krieg*], but with time we can learn to deal with this, too.

30.6.41: *UNTEROFFIZIER* HEINZ B. (125 INFANTRY DIVISION, SEVENTEENTH ARMY, ARMY GROUP SOUTH)[143]

Now that the letter embargo has been lifted I also hope to hear from you often just as before. Surely you would now like to know something about our participation in this war. We made contact with the front line sooner than expected; we then went into action and managed to shoot up a town. To be sure, only a single battery of our battalion was in action, while we were placed in readiness. As you're aware from the *Wehrmacht* reports, the Russians have committed a large number of tanks in our sector. On a single stretch of some 7 kilometers we encountered no less than 60 shot-up [Russian] tanks. There were four of the super heavies among them. . . . You simply can't imagine what behemoths they are. Their armor plating was 45mm thick—utterly incredible brutes. One of them had driven straight through two houses before it was destroyed. We—by that I mean our infantry division—didn't have any tanks, but were able to take them out with only Pak and flak guns. A really heroic achievement. They let the [tanks] come as close as 5 meters before destroying them. Some of the tanks had driven right over our guns, crushing them to pulp. This morning a panzer corps went into action and has taken Lemberg [L'vov]. Hopefully, we'll go through Lemberg tomorrow, because we're at most just 30 km away.

There's another war being fought here, and that is the battle against the Russian stragglers, who hide out insidiously in the woods and tall fields of corn and take shots at individual soldiers and troops. They're being captured in large numbers. . . . The number of prisoners taken by our battery has already grown considerably; there was even a Russian commissar among them, and he was shot. At the moment the front has advanced quite a distance again, so we most likely won't have any contact with the enemy for a while. Otherwise, I think the war will quickly come to a victorious conclusion, and it will be the greatest victory in world history.

CHAPTER 3

July 1941

Introduction

"On the whole," confided Generaloberst *Franz Halder, chief of the Army General Staff, in his personal diary on 3 July 1941, "it may be said even now that the objective to shatter the bulk of the Russian army this side of the Dvina and Dnepr has been accomplished. . . . It is thus probably no overstatement to say that the Russian campaign has been won in the space of two weeks."[1] During the first half of the month, Halder's euphoric assessment appeared to be confirmed, as the* Ostheer *continued its inexorable push into European Russia along all three axes while registering spectacular new victories. Following in the wake of the German armored spearheads were the* Einsatzgruppen *(murder squads) of the SS, unleashing terror and death against Jews, Communist functionaries, the Soviet intelligentsia, and other "undesirables." Blinded by hubris and racism, the* Führer, *in a notorious policy meeting on 16 July, intimated that the ultimate objective of the Eastern Campaign was to divvy up the "giant cake" that was Soviet Russia so as first to "rule" it, second to "administer" it, and third to "exploit" it.[2]*

Along the combat front, the most impressive gains were made by GFM von Bock's Army Group Center, the largest of the three German Army groups. By the second week of July, organized Soviet resistance in the large pocket between Belostok and Minsk had collapsed, resulting in the destruction of several dozen Red Army formations and yielding several hundred thousand prisoners as well as thousands of captured or destroyed tanks and guns. Meanwhile, mobile units of Guderian's 2 and Hoth's 3 Panzer Group,[3] rumbling relentlessly eastward, forged bridgeheads across the major river barriers of the Western Dvina and Dnepr; indeed, by mid-July, Army Group Center had advanced some 600 kilometers (373 miles) from its start line in occupied Poland,[4] seizing all of Belorussia and inflicting unprecedented losses on opposing Soviet forces. On 16 July, motorized infantry of Guderian's panzer group reached Smolensk, and, in cooperation with Hoth's panzers to the north, began to forge another large pocket around several Russian armies. It was at this point, however, that Bock's advance began to slow abruptly and lose momentum. The Soviet High Command launched a series of desperate counterstrokes, which although poorly executed, blunted and attrited attacking German forces; moreover, with Red Army units trapped around Smolensk furiously resisting their annihilation, it would take the Germans several precious weeks to compress and subdue the pocket. Yet despite stiffening Russian resistance, as well as incipient logistical problems, on 30 July the center of Bock's bulging 700-kilometer (435-mile) front was only 300 kilometers (186 miles) from Moscow.[5]

On the northern axis, Army Group North of GFM von Leeb continued its drive toward Leningrad. Unlike in the center, spectacular encirclements did not characterize the advance of Leeb's group, whose smaller panzer contingent had to negotiate more difficult terrain (including forests, lakes, and swamps) from the very outset. With Soviet forces in precipitous retreat, Hoepner's 4 Panzer Group advanced from the Dvina River, capturing Ostrov on 4 July and Pskov several days later, smashing Soviet defenses along the Stalin Line and entering the Leningrad Oblast (region). By 10 July, after less than three weeks of often bitter combat, Army Group North had advanced 500 kilometers (310 miles), occupying Lithuania, Latvia, and most of Estonia in the process; that same day, the army group began what it hoped would be the final drive on Leningrad, and, in but a few short days, Hoepner's spearheads built bridgeheads across the lower Luga River, barely 100 kilometers (62 miles) from the outskirts of the city. Yet here, too, the pace of operations suddenly slowed to a crawl, as Red Army defenses coalesced and the German armored spearheads had to stop to refit, replenish, and wait for the lagging infantry to catch up. By the end of the month, ammunition stocks in the divisions and corps of Leeb's army group had plunged dangerously and were still dropping. A further advance on Leningrad would have to wait.

On the southern axis, GFM von Rundstedt's Army Group South, after fending off fierce counterattacks by several Soviet mechanized corps, had, by 10 July, penetrated to a depth of 350 kilometers (217 miles) into the Ukraine. Efforts by Red Army forces to establish new defensive positions along the Stalin Line (on the prewar Soviet border) were unsuccessful, as Kleist's 1 Panzer Group, supported by the bombers, Stukas, and fighter-bombers of the Luftwaffe, rapidly smashed through the barrier and, by 12 July, stood with two panzer divisions on the Irpen River on the approaches to Kiev. Despite stubborn Red Army resistance, Rundstedt now sought to roll up Soviet forces west of the Dnepr River and, by late July, his tanks were bearing down on Uman and threatening encirclement of two Soviet armies. Meanwhile, the southern wing of Army Group South had finally attacked out of Romania on 2 July, crossing the Prut River with one weak German Army and supporting Romanian units. Advancing with no armor and little to no air support, they made slow progress in the weeks that followed in the face of aggressive and mobile Soviet armored rear guards and harassing raids by Red Army fighters and bombers.

With victory over Russia seemingly assured, Hitler, in early July, decided that both Leningrad and Moscow were not to be attacked by ground forces; rather, both cities were to be tightly invested, leveled by the Luftwaffe, and starved into submission.[6] A few days later, the Führer ordered that production priorities be switched from the army to the navy and Luftwaffe in preparation for the final struggle for world supremacy against Britain and America. During the second half of the month, however, as the pace of the German Blitzkrieg slackened, the first glimmers of doubt began to plague the German dictator and his General Staff. For it was becoming apparent that neither the Red Army nor the Soviet state was about to collapse as a result of the initial German hammer blows; in fact, Russian resistance was palpably increasing, while German casualties (both men and matériel) were mounting dangerously.[7] In response to such unpleasant realities, Hitler and his generals began to reexamine their strategy for the conduct of the campaign. While the debates that took place at Hitler's remote East Prussian headquarters need not concern us here—simply put, Hitler sought a final decision on the flanks, in the Baltic (Leningrad) and in the Ukraine, while his General Staff kept their eyes squarely on Moscow—suffice it to say that in the weeks that followed (into late August), Hitler, OKW, and OKH were unable to operate with the requisite unity of effort. Beset by indecision, at odds with his General Staff, Hitler would promulgate a flurry of (in part) contradictory directives addressing the future course of operations. Largely due to the fierce Red Army resistance around Smolensk, on 30 July 1941 the Führer *issued Directive No. 34, which,* inter alia, *directed that Army Group Center "go over to the defensive, taking advantage of suitable terrain."*[8] *Much to the disappointment of the Bock's soldiers, the army group would not resume its advance on Moscow for two months.*

Letters and Diary Entries (1–31 July 1941)

7.41 (EXACT DATE UNKNOWN): *OBERLEUTNANT* K. (20 PANZER DIVISION, 3 PANZER GROUP, ARMY GROUP CENTER)[9]

Expanse, never-ending expanse, monotony in form and color, gray cottages, squat and isolated. . . . It is a melancholy country, desolate for people from the West. . . . The huts were most likely built in exactly the same way 1,000 years ago as they are today. The only progress in this time is no doubt the glass windows. Gray on gray, impoverished and depressed, they stand there, far too tiny, incidentally, for the many children who grow up in them, but constructed with very clear proportions. In contrast to the few stone houses, usually party buildings in the towns, which are ugly and loveless constructions, these pitiful cottages are tasteful in the circumstances. . . .

The people live in pitiful conditions, unimaginably poor. They have nothing in their huts; they live with their many children in a single room. . . . The Russians—if you listen to our men—they are something between human and beast [*Mitteldinge zwischen Mensch und Tier*]—"You know, I don't think a peasant like that has even been to the cinema," was something I heard recently. The superior civilization of the West gives the simple man, and not only him, an arrogance without equal toward other life forms, and even more so toward other people who evidently don't want to know anything about all that technological stuff. That is, at a pinch, understandable, and yet we should see it differently. A nation of peasants lives as long as the earth has life. A nation that works between stone and asphalt can only use up its substances, but can't accumulate more.[10]

1.7.41: *LEUTNANT* HEINZ DÖLL (18 PANZER DIVISION, 2 PANZER GROUP, ARMY GROUP CENTER)[11]

The battles increased in severity (*Härte*) from day to day, as Red Army resistance began to coalesce. Even at night we had no peace. We formed hedgehog positions, whereby almost one-third of our battlegroup was always in combat readiness. What we were quite certain of is that we had advanced directly at the border into concentrated Red Army forces.

1.7.41: *LEUTNANT* HELMUT H. (258 INFANTRY DIVISION, FOURTH ARMY, ARMY GROUP CENTER)[12]

We've now gone a bit farther. The scenes on the road leading out of Belostok toward the east are remarkable. It's indescribable what you see there. In France we never encountered anything nearly as bad. Here it's almost exclusively a matter of military equipment and vehicles. Roughly estimated, there are, among other things, well over 100 armored vehicles in this area, among them some of more than 50 tons. Adding to the chaos are trucks, guns, petrol vehicles, etc., too many to count. And all of this is due to the success of our aircraft, for there are no signs of any defensive measures taken by the Russians. How these people could have left all this behind, without giving the slightest thought to defending themselves, is inexplicable. The defeat of Russia seems guaranteed given the look of things here. But if you take a closer look at all this Russian clothing and equipment, you can only conclude that, aside from some artillery totally copied from our own, it might as well be the equipment of "Old Fritz's" army [*Kriegsausrüstung der Armee des Alten Fritz*].[13] Much of this stuff has already found a worthy place in our museums, where it doesn't disturb anyone.

1.7.41: *LEUTNANT* RUDOLF MAURER (251 INFANTRY DIVISION, SIXTEENTH ARMY, ARMY GROUP NORTH)[14]

Everything during the advance is happening too quickly for us. We're experiencing almost nothing at all. The motorized units are racing ahead like maniacs [*fahren mit einem "Affenzahn" los*], and we foot soldiers are merely tasked with moving up behind them and cleaning up the remnants left behind by the enemy. Yesterday afternoon, an *Oberfeldwebel* in our company, while preparing the billets, caught 9 Russians in their hiding place all by himself. The chaps were all armed, but despite that they didn't make any trouble. That was clearly the cleverest thing for them to do, and now they can help with the harvest in Germany. Marching on these wretched roads and with all this dreadful dust, is torture for man and beast. Even our automobiles are having trouble with the dust. My car is already in need of repair and is with the workshop company.

This Sunday I had the opportunity to go to Kaunas, the largest city in [Lithuania]. The city is a curious mixture of American culture and Russian nonculture [*Un-Kultur*]. On the edge of the city are cottages that, like all of them around here, are so wretched that even the most run-down house in Halsdorf,[15] if it happened to be here, would suffice as quarters for the regimental staff. And yet 100 meters from these cottages is a magnificent building that's like an American palace. Half of the inhabitants go barefoot, while the other half is decked out in the latest fashions from Paris. There was nothing to buy there. I had dinner at a local inn. . . . A young girl, who was the interpreter at the inn, told me that, since the Russians occupied Lithuania, they hadn't disturbed the church services. That was why, as I wrote before, you could find crucifixes everywhere. And such are my modest experiences.

1.7.41: *UNTEROFFIZIER* WILHELM PRÜLLER (9 PANZER DIVISION, 1 PANZER GROUP, ARMY GROUP SOUTH)[16]

It's a fabulous sight to watch our tanks move up into position—about 40 of them. At 7.30 we actually move off. At every point of attack we stop, antitank guns go into safety positions, the men demount and the tanks crash through. At the second target we encounter strong tank opposition, but the Russians aren't up to our antitank guns nor to our tanks. When we move up later, the road and the ditches are jammed full of knocked-out enemy tanks.

There are hideous sights in the inside of the tanks—one man without a head, another sliced in two, the brains plastered over the walls—revolting. . . . Our tanks are always quicker on the draw when shooting, even if it's only a split second. I've already counted 15 finished Russian tanks. And that's the way it goes in: we are constantly attacked by enemy tanks, they are constantly repulsed, till we reach the third objective. . . .

Now I learn that we almost suffered a bad defeat. The 8th Company penetrated the woods in front of us—about 100 meters—and received terrible infantry fire, partly from sharpshooters in the trees and partly from marvelously camouflaged MGs. The company lost 80 men. The chief is badly wounded. Those who got back told the most revolting stories you can possibly imagine. The wounded *Kameraden* were worked over by the Russians with gun barrels until they were dead. Many people saw this themselves.

Only the Russians can be that bestial. That's what they are anyway, beasts! No other people on earth, no other soldier in the whole wide world could act like such beasts. . . .

The colonel came by and thanked the battalion for its showing in a day of severe fighting. We have hardly climbed into our car, tired from the day's events, and tired from hunger and thirst, and ready to sleep sitting up, when we get the order to march forward the next morning at 5.30. But not in today's direction. We are to go toward Tarnopol.

1.7.41: ALBERT NEUHAUS (ARMY GROUP NORTH)[17]

My dear girl!

After crossing the Dvina I send you warm greetings from Latvia. First of all, let me say that everything is absolutely tip top with me and all of us.[18] There's butter, eggs, lard in great quantities, and we've also got some terrific soap again, so we've all just done our laundry. There was a wash kitchen available to us and our laundry is now swinging from the clothesline in the radiant sunshine. As for us, we've been running around the entire afternoon in our bathing trunks and that's given us a nice brown tan. We're sitting around on a small hill, and about a 100 meters from us the Dvina is flowing, the hard-fought-for Dvina.

Up until yesterday, the Russian bombers were being rather bold, because our fighters weren't around. But now our planes have an airfield quite close to us, so the Russian swine are hardly to be seen. Today, at midday, three bombers flew over us again; however, as soon as they showed themselves, our fighters attacked and shot them all down. When the fighters returned they proudly "rocked" their wings. We really are as happy as they are when the boys up in the air meet with such success. Yesterday we were forced to take cover on a few occasions, and it's an odd feeling when you see the bombs fall from the sky. But there's no stopping our young fliers.

We no longer hear any artillery fire at all. God only knows how far the front has moved on. Our fighters are now circling over us at all times and that gives us a peaceful and secure feeling. We're shuffling along so far behind that we really haven't got an assignment. In a few weeks this Eastern Campaign will most likely be over. How nice it would be if, in September or October, the watchword was "demobilization," and Albert could once again love his girl.

2.7.41: DR. HEINRICH HAAPE (6 INFANTRY DIVISION, NINTH ARMY, ARMY GROUP CENTER)[19]

I am superbly well! We don't have any contact with the enemy at all right now; we're marching on poor roads, following the motorized units that are hard on the heels of the fleeing enemy. The poor horses! They're emaciated and exhausted to the point of collapse. We go on relentlessly![20]

2.7.41: *MAJOR* HANS MEIER-WELCKER (251 INFANTRY DIVISION, SIXTEENTH ARMY, ARMY GROUP NORTH)[21]

In Kaunas Lithuanian activists have drummed up a large number of Jews, beaten them to death with rods [*Stangen*], and then danced on their corpses to music. As soon as the dead were dragged off, more Jews were herded together and the entire affair repeated!

2.7.41: *GEFREITER* FERDINAND M. (167 INFANTRY DIVISION, ARMY GROUP CENTER)[22]

Now that we're finished with the Russian defensive installations in our sector of the Bug we've begun to advance. That matters less to us than to our vehicles, [because] the roads are in an unbelievable condition. For the infantry there's only one thing to do—to march and march some more; 40, 50, 60 kilometers a day, in a searing heat, isn't easy for even the strongest among them. The terrain here consists of really deep sand,[23] and our vehicles often sink in it right up to their axles, and then it's the pushing details [*Schiebekommandos*] to the front all over again. At the moment, we're in marshy terrain on the southern edge of that giant area in which the main Russian forces have been encircled.

At 4.00 in the morning we were again on the march and, at 10:00 a.m., we'd reached our objective for the day. Our infantry has only now just arrived, at 6.00 in the evening, and they're dog tired [*hundemüde*]. There are more and more prisoners, who are mostly driven out of the woods by hunger. We can only shake our heads when we see their faces. It's a mix of peoples that you simply don't see every day, mostly Asians.

2.7.41: AUGUST SAHM (ARMY GROUP SOUTH)[24]

I think, for the time being, you need not be worried. The worst of it is behind us. Since the day before yesterday we're no longer in contact with the enemy, but just continuing to march. Physically I'm about worn out. Both of my feet are sore and festering; my right thumb was full of pus and was lanced yesterday (so please excuse my handwriting). . . . And I must tell you, again and again, that I strive daily to be with HIM.

When our columns are on the move, the gray clouds of dust over the roads are so thick that sometimes you can't make out anything around you. It's almost suffocating. It's like a grasp into nothingness [*Griff ins Nichts*] and deep within me I tremble before it. Like the blind we move along in this fog of dust.

There's no point in thinking things over during such marches, but still the questions become pressing—so many questions but no answers, none.

2.7.41: *GEFREITER* HANS B. (269 INFANTRY DIVISION, 4 PANZER GROUP, ARMY GROUP NORTH)[25]

Ten days of the war have now already passed, and so I finally have a little time to write. My posting to a booty detail [*Beutekommando*] is certainly interesting, but each day brings tremendous exertions. We're 200 kilometers behind the front today, tomorrow we might be between the tanks and the infantry as usual. Both [possibilities] are bound up with considerable danger due to the woods in between. Of course, any snipers [seized] in the woods are shot at once, and dead Russians are lying around everywhere in large numbers; but sadly, sadly, many comrades have already been killed due to this underhanded way of fighting. Normal combat does not result in as many victims as that against these bandits. We don't get much sleep. Almost every night there's guard duty. Even during the few hours of rest you have to be up and totally alert for sudden attacks, because one sentry's carelessness could mean we are all lost.

2.7.41: *OFFIZIER* UDO VON ALVENSLEBEN (16 PANZER DIVISION, 1 PANZER GROUP, ARMY GROUP SOUTH)[26]

According to General Kempff,[27] the higher-ups [i.e., higher HQs] are operating with unrestrained [*freventlichem*] optimism; but even we, who are in the middle of events, are only beginning—hour by hour—to grasp that we have to relearn everything, that our experiences in earlier campaigns are worthless [*nichts mehr wert sind*]. What had always been the strength of the *Panzertruppe* could now lead to its ruin.

It turns out that the strength of the tactical operations group [*Führungsabteilung*] is insufficient in this very different method of battle. The division is being led from two points that are quite far apart. Hube[28] wishes to keep me in his immediate vicinity. At the moment, the situation is forcing us into action at Dubno and Werba-Kamienna, where a very large tank battle is rapidly developing. Hube is personally commanding the panzer regiment, which has been ordered back from Kremenec, and the reconnaissance battalion. Here for the first time we encountered the Russians' Pak 30—which is superior to our tanks—the enemy's astounding combat power, the excellence of his lower-ranking leadership, and his first acts of inhumanity [*Unmenschlichkeiten*]. Our losses have been tremendous. *Generaloberst* von Kleist, who wants to advance as rapidly as possible, is always driving us to hurry. What's important, he says, is not taking ground, but smashing the enemy.

2.7.41: *SOLDAT* MANFRED V. (32 INFANTRY DIVISION, SIXTEENTH ARMY, ARMY GROUP NORTH)[29]

We're now sitting in a somewhat larger village. It's been raining the entire day. At the moment, I'm sitting with a Russian who is some kind of barber. I haven't had my hair cut for five weeks! You can imagine what I look like.

So, shortly after we came away from the infantry, our platoon was placed under the command of the A.A. (that means reconnaissance battalion [*Aufklärungsabteilung*]). It was great there, because we antitank troops are welcome everywhere. People know very well how valuable we are. Even the infantry likes fighting alongside us; for starters, we can shoot pretty well, and for seconds [having us around] is a huge morale boost for our infantry. . . . On 1 July the division finally formed a really rather nice advance detachment [*Vorausabteilung*] and, again, our platoon was there. With the advance detachment, we made a huge advance . . . ca. 85 km ahead of our own front line. The poor infantry, they had to keep up with all that on foot. Today, we're being pulled out of the advance detachment, going back to the company, to the other two platoons, who haven't done anything yet.

We have been in the town, or rather larger village, the whole day: wonderful. You can always find all kinds of odd things there, but also many useful objects. When fleeing, *der Russe* demolished all the shops to such an extent that you might as well call them garbage heaps in the truest sense of the word. Unfortunately, Russia, or rather Lithuania, is a very poor country, so there's no question of a bit of the good life, like there apparently was in France.

It's almost exclusively Jews living here in this little town. Disgusting people: typical kaftan Jews; they just talk too much, with their hands just as much as with their mouths. *Der Russe* has nothing better to do but flee and he leaves half, but usually most all of his weapons and equipment behind, as well as the wounded and dead. We see awful, dreadful scenes. But you can't ever write that in letters; words can barely describe it. It's just a good thing that you don't get to see such scenes in the *Wochen-schau*.[30] Many a young man would lose his appetite for war.

3.7.41: *GEFREITER* HEINZ B. (23 INFANTRY DIVISION, SECOND ARMY, ARMY GROUP CENTER)[31]

The equipment [*Armierung*] of the Russian troops is good. Every day we ask ourselves where the hundreds of tanks came from, which litter the roads everywhere. Gigantic, completely new types of guns, all of them drawn by tractors, have also been left behind.[32]

3.7.41: *LEUTNANT* RUDOLF MAURER (251 INFANTRY DIVISION, SIXTEENTH ARMY, ARMY GROUP NORTH)[33]

We'll be moving out at 6.00 in the morning. The next towns we'll be advancing through are Raguvele and Troskonai. For the first time in enemy territory we're making camp, in the city of Anyksciai. But the billets have to be shared between our regiment and the division staff. The inhabitants are unusually kind, and they do everything they can to make us feel welcome. I've been billeted with a businessman, who had been living in the woods with his family for 14 days before the outbreak of war with Russia. We find clean beds in a clean room. Unfortunately, the night is just too short.

3.7.41: *LEUTNANT* WALTER MELCHINGER (ARMY GROUP SOUTH)[34]

On these bad roads our rations often don't catch up to us in time; then, for days, we have nothing to eat and, what is worse, nothing to drink. But the Ukrainian inhabitants support us, and in a touching way. At every village they all stand on the road and shower us with flowers, and bring us milk and eggs. They weep with joy to finally be liberated from the Red plague, which wreaked such havoc. I've become so cold-hearted toward this rabble [*Gesindel*] that I have no feeling at all for the dead Russian soldiers lying about. The day before yesterday we nabbed quite a large number of them that had fled wildly into the cornfields. We also made lots of booty, particularly horses.

3.7.41: *LEUTNANT* POHL (18 PANZER DIVISION, 2 PANZER GROUP, ARMY GROUP CENTER)[35]

Early morning 0700 hours, between Borisov and Tolochino, tank alarm. From the right comes a Russian tank battalion at "full speed" [*Drauflosfahrt*] and attacks us. *Hauptmann* Kirn, with the 1st Battalion, fires furiously, but all hits simply slide off: the first T-34s.[36] Horror grips us. Only a wet field separates us from the Russians.

They drive at full throttle into the marshy ground and 11 T-34 tanks get stuck. The remaining tanks turn back, luckily for us. Now we wear the others down with our firing; they slowly climb out and we take 11 tank crews prisoner, with their commander and adjutants. The Russian commander is deeply impressed.

3.7.41: *GEFREITER* FERDINAND B. (125 INFANTRY DIVISION, SEVENTEENTH ARMY, ARMY GROUP SOUTH)[37]

Adolf and I are marching against our great enemy: Russia. And with that, one of my wishes has come true, [because] I've always wanted to go to war against this blasphemous country [*gotteslästerlichen Land*]. This time it's bound to be the end for this pagan power. Unbelievably huge masses of troops are advancing. I would never have believed such a rearmament [*Aufrüstung*] to be possible in such a short time, and yet it is so.

Adolf and I are now marching along as well, or sometimes we ride on bicycles, snaking through the advancing columns. You are witness to Jewish, Bolshevik cruelty the like of which I would never have believed possible. Yesterday, we went through a larger town, Lemberg [L'vov], and passed by a prison. Even from a distance there was an awful stench of corpses. When we came closer, we could hardly bear it. Inside lay 8,000 dead, captured civilians—beaten to death, murdered, certainly not shot, a bloodbath perpetrated by the Bolsheviks just before their retreat.[38] Very similar cases in another town, perhaps even more gruesome.

[The Russian] sniping is a dangerous business,[39] to which yesterday even an SS regimental commander fell victim. The murderer is said to have been a Jew. You can quite imagine that something like that cries out for vengeance, which is carried out, of course. Some soldiers we treated had injuries that were from snipers.[40]

And so the Russians can no longer defend themselves. To the right and left of the advance route lie dead Russians, shot-up and burned-out tanks—the drivers are still inside, completely charred. These are giant tanks, one simply can't imagine, and yet [they are] destroyed.

3.7.41: *UNTEROFFIZIER* WILHELM PRÜLLER (9 PANZER DIVISION, 1 PANZER GROUP, ARMY GROUP SOUTH)[41]

For today's advance we are assigned to the main body of troops. . . . At about 7:00 a.m. we march. It has begun to rain again, worse luck! We halt in front of Kamionka. To our left some flak guns go into position and cover the north. In a hollow we discover Russian cavalry, which the flak begins to fire at. You could see clearly through the binoculars the ruin that the flak is inflicting on the Russians. Horses and men lying about in wild disorder. . . . It's frightful.

In the course of the afternoon we hear a shout near regimental battle headquarters: "Enemy tanks! Pak to the front!" Our battalion is still pulling up, the 1st Battalion is way in front of Kamionka, and there isn't any Pak available. I grab a motorcycle and tear to the rear like a fire engine to bring up some Pak. The road is cluttered up badly enough by stuff coming toward the front, and the disabled enemy tanks lying around make it even worse. It takes a long time for me to get back, grab the Pak platoon and go back with them . . . and by the time I get to regimental headquarters the Pak is no longer needed. A Russian tank came from the north toward Kamionka, drove straight into battle headquarters with the turret open, the tank leader standing straight up, and about 10 Russian soldiers including women sitting on top of the tank. Each one had a pistol. They wanted to break through Kamionka to the east—suicide commando!

One of the Russians got the ordnance officer with a pistol shot. What good do our weapons do against such a huge tank?[42] The thing went through Kamionka almost unscathed, and traveled right across the bridge going east before our flak picked it up. When we passed the demolished tank later, it was completely burned out. Some of the women, completely nude and roasted, were lying on and beside the tank. Awful. All along the whole road of approach you see Russians who have been mashed up by our lorries or tanks. If you look at one of them, you can't believe that it was ever a human being. An arm there, a head there, half a foot somewhere else, squashed brains, mashed ribs. Horrible.

3–8.7.41: DR. HANS LIEROW (6 INFANTRY DIVISION, NINTH ARMY, ARMY GROUP CENTER)[43]

The last few days were filled with putting back around 25–30 km a day. The roads became more bearable. . . . Refreshing baths were taken at a bivouac location. In the afternoons we usually go to our quarters, wash, bathe, eat, drink, and sleep. We don't go into the shabby houses, with their thatched roofs, because of the horrendous number of fleas. We live in tents. . . . If it can be come by, the floor is lined first with straw, then with blankets. At any rate, we all sleep well, because we are dog tired.

I regularly visit the companies after the soldiers have rested for over 3–4 hours. I mostly find abrasion wounds on feet, as well as gastric troubles. The soldiers are permitted to sit up on ammunition and weapons wagons and armored vehicles. . . . The battalion transports 12–15 soldiers with march injuries in this manner. There are also a few who [feign] injuries and they are handled rather roughly and ruthlessly. . . . There has been no contact with the enemy. Individual Russians come out of the forests, are hungry, and come into the prisoners' camp. The populace is poor, very poor.

4.7.41: HARALD HENRY (ARMY GROUP CENTER)[44]

The hours that we're on the advance are endless, 25 or 30 kilometers past smashed and burned-out tanks, vehicle after vehicle, past the skeletal remains of shot-up and burned-down villages. Black and ghostlike, solitary walls rise up and in a little garden a couple of tiger lilies are still blooming, rather eerily. There is that peculiar smell, which will stay with me forever from this campaign—that mixture of fire, sweat, and horse cadavers. The dust masks us all quite literally: those who are blond have an almost white, dull glow to their hair; those with black hair look like the soldiers of Frederick the Great, brightly powdered; while others have gotten curly hair like negroes. And the martial-looking mustaches, which many of us, including myself, continue to grow, are turning gray. We're wet through all over, sweat is running down our faces in rivers, not just sweat but sometimes tears too, tears of helpless rage, desperation and pain [*Tränen der hilflosen Wut, der Verzweiflung und des Schmerzes*], squeezed out of us by this inhuman effort. No one can tell me that someone who isn't an infantryman can possibly imagine what we're going through here. Think of the most terrific exhaustion you've ever known, the searing pain of open, inflamed sores on the feet—and you have my very condition, not at the end but at the beginning of a 45-kilometer march. Only gradually, after a number of hours, do the feet become inured to the pain of the sores with each step taken on these roads, which are rather like broken stone or beach sand.[45]

4.7.41: *STABSFELDWEBEL* HELMUTH A. DITTRI (20 PANZER DIVISION, 3 PANZER GROUP, ARMY GROUP CENTER)[46]

The biggest battle yet was fought out near the village of Bocheikovo. The Russians opened murderous artillery fire against our troops. The boom of heavy antitank guns filled the air. The Russians are crack shots. Their shells fell right on our road. And we had nowhere to turn, as the ground was boggy to the right and left of us. All our guns were in action but the enemy was obstinate; there was no sign of his giving way. One more of our tanks caught fire. . . . We wirelessed for reinforcements and artillery support. . . . Even when they retreat the Russian tank guns blaze away for all they're worth.

We are moving north, toward the village of Ulla [on the Western Dvina River, west of Vitebsk]. Again we met desperate resistance. Again that devilishly accurate Russian artillery fire. Our riflemen suffered severe losses. Many in our company were wounded by shell fragments. The fire from the Russian side became more and more intense. We had to retrace several hundred meters. It is getting dark, but the Russians continue their raking fire.[47]

4.7.41: *LEUTNANT* WILLIBALD G. (57 INFANTRY DIVISION, SIXTH ARMY, ARMY GROUP SOUTH)[48]

I'm doing well, as much as anyone can say such a thing during a strenuous campaign. . . . We haven't fired any weapons for three days now. *Der Russe* has withdrawn to the fortified former Russian border [the Stalin Line]. If you look on the map, you'll see that we're about 30 kilometers north of Tarnopol and 10 kilometers from the Russian border.

Since the day before yesterday it has been pouring rain, and you can imagine just how strenuous it is to make a 15–20-kilometer march at night—across hills and valleys and over roads turned to quagmires, in which the horses either get stuck or slip and fall. But we must continue to advance, and we're doing just that! . . .

The inhabitants are quite touching! We're getting butter, eggs, milk, and bread in large quantities. They're all Ukrainians, and they're glad that the Bolsheviks are gone. It's nice when, as an advance party [*Vorkommando*], you're the first German soldier to enter a village. You're honored and marveled at like a wonder of the world. Everyone scrambles about to be able to offer hospitality to the German officer.

5.7.41: *UNTEROFFIZIER* HEINZ H. (6 INFANTRY DIVISION, NINTH ARMY, ARMY GROUP CENTER)[49]

We were right up front through the first four days. But we can no longer keep pace with the tanks or the motorized divisions. They are already far "to the front," even as our infantry, despite the heat and dust, are performing extraordinary forced marches. At the moment, we're in the vicinity of a larger city at the edge of a woods. It's hot, and we've already turned brown. Every day is hot and humid. Every other day, according to plan, we make a big leap forward, moving at night along sandy, rutted tracks. There's little to do. We're hardly using our radios. The only thing you really have to look out for is the accursed snipers. Especially at the start of it all, because we were facing elite regiments. But believe you me, these "gentlemen" are not being handled with kid gloves. When we come across them, they're shot. . . . It's fortunate that the Russian air activity has completely come to an end here.[50] Now and then small groups [*Schwärme*] of German bombers fly toward the front and drop their loads (most likely near Minsk: you've surely heard and read about the encirclement battle going on there). Yes, indeed, our *Luftwaffe*.

5.7.41: KARL FUCHS (7 PANZER DIVISION, 3 PANZER GROUP, ARMY GROUP CENTER)[51]

My darling wife! My dear boy!

We have fought in battle many days now and we have defeated the enemy wherever we have encountered him. Let me tell you that Russia is nothing but misery, poverty, and depravity! That is Bolshevism![52]

It is late in the evening now and quite dark already. We only wait for our expected orders: Mount your tanks! Start your engines! Move out! Mädi, if you were only here and could see me—tanned by the sun, dusty and dirty, with eyes as clear as a falcon!

Our losses have been minimal and our success great. This war will be over soon, because already we are fighting against only fragmented opposition.

How are the two of you? I cannot wait until the moment of my return. It will be wonderful. My return is certain.[53]

5.7.41: *OBERLEUTNANT* FABICH (INFANTRY REGIMENT "*GROSSDEUTSCHLAND*" [MOT.], ARMY GROUP CENTER)[54]

Rollbahn:[55] enemy in the woods to the left. The assault guns [*Sturmgeschütze*][56] are under *Oblt.* Frantz, with whom we cooperate splendidly; they move across the open fields and seek to destroy the enemy. They come to a stop 400 meters in front of the grain field, at which time [our 3rd Company] advances across a broad front. When we get to the edge of the woods a platoon goes in. Then: "Urrah!"—the Russians attack quite suddenly [*urplötzlich*]. Wild explosions, ricochets—panic. A few men run back to the rail embankment. We build a new holding line here—that was too great a shock. A half hour later, accompanied by a 50mm Pak, the company advances into the woods again to save our wounded comrades. There were 5–6 men. . . . Finally we reach them. There they lay: wickedly mutilated, bestially disfigured—all dead! That was quite a shock that all the men carried with them: everyone knew what it meant to fall into Russian hands.

5.7.41: *GEFREITER* WERNER R. (ARTILLERY UNIT, EASTERN FRONT)[57]

You will be astounded to hear that I was there for the launch of the offensive against Russia on 22 June. It's a reminder of why you're a soldier and trained in Esslingen. It was just a pity that, as a result of the pleasingly rapid progress, I was only in action for two days. Basically, this was due to the same circumstances as in June last year, during the attack on the Maginot Line at the front by the Upper Rhine. In my opinion, the latter was more powerful than what I experienced in Poland [at the start of the Russian campaign]. But on the other hand, back then France was already close to collapse anyway, whereas this time the reaction of the Red Army has had something uncanny and incalculable [*Unheimlich* = *Ungewisses*] about it. For example, during the days beforehand there were no sounds of engines in the sky to be heard. In particular, the fear that the Soviet Union might respond with gas wasn't without cause. . . . But nothing of the kind transpired.[58]

What was odd was that the Poles in the area where I was were saying on the day before that the war would start on Sunday already. By the way, they still had a good memory of German troops from the Polish campaign, whereas they were more frightened of the Bolsheviks, who would set everything ablaze. And, furthermore, the appearance of airplanes had a startling effect on the Poles. They immediately left their primitive cottages and hurried into the rye fields, where they brought all sorts of valuables, such as a sewing machine, for safekeeping.

5.7.41: *LEUTNANT* WALTER MELCHINGER (ARMY GROUP SOUTH)[59]

We've seen images among the most ghastly you could ever imagine. Mass murder of the Ukrainians, hundreds of corpses dreadfully worked over. The Jews have to dig these poor victims out of the mass graves with their bare hands, and then they're shot. That's just retribution. The poor Ukrainians know who the culprits are.

So, what do you think now of your Walter in all this murder and madness? The odor of the corpses is dreadfully strong. The Jews, who are being continuously shot, lie in piles.

As astonished as you must be, it all leaves me cold. What moves me the most is the rage against the murderers. Don't believe that war makes you brutal and unfeeling. It is simply a law of war to accept what has happened as done. It is an overwhelming necessity of life.

Death must be, because life must be. Our fallen comrades have given their lives for the lives of their wives and children. The Jews have given theirs for cleanness and decency [*Sauberkeit und Anständigkeit*], without which life is not possible. And the murdered Ukrainians? We're living in no paradise. Good and evil will always exist. Let us just be thankful that we're fighting for good, in order to eradicate evil. A new epoch is marching at our side.

6.7.41: *MAJOR* HANS MEIER-WELCKER (251 INFANTRY DIVISION, SIXTEENTH ARMY, ARMY GROUP NORTH)[60]

The artillery is causing us concerns, because the teams of horses can no longer manage the distances we're marching on these bad roads. It's shocking how many horses are dropping out. The problems began with the heavy artillery, and now the light battalions can hardly keep up.

6.7.41: FRANZL (OPERATIONS AREA OF ARMY GROUP SOUTH)[61]

I've just returned from viewing the bodies of our comrades from the *Luftwaffe* and the mountain troops who'd been captured by the Russians. I can't find the words to describe it. Our comrades were bound up; their ears, tongues, noses and genitals had been cut off. That's how we found them in the cellar of the courthouse at Tarnopol, and we also found 2,000 Ukrainians and ethnic Germans who had been similarly worked over. That is Russia and Jewry—the workers' paradise. If there is still a single Communist in Vienna, he should be beaten to death at once but not shot. We took our revenge right away.

Yesterday we and the SS acted mercifully, because each Jew that we nabbed was shot right away. Today it's different, because once again we found 60 mutilated comrades. Now the Jews have to carry the dead up out of the cellar and put them down nicely; then the hideous deeds are pointed out to them. After viewing the victims, they're beaten to death with clubs and spades. So far we've dispatched about 1,000 Jews, but that is far too few considering what they've done. The Ukrainians said that the Jews had held all the leading positions and had a great time of it with the Soviets, executing Germans and Ukrainians. I urge you, dear parents, to tell everyone, and father should let it be known to the local authorities [*NSDAP Ortsgruppe*], too. Should there be any doubt, we'll bring back photos. Then there'll be no doubt.

7.7.41: *GEFREITER* HANS CASPAR VON WIEDEBACH-NOSTITZ (20 PANZER DIVISION, 3 PANZER GROUP, ARMY GROUP CENTER)[62]

The crossing over the [Western Dvina] is to be forced today. Precisely at 1000 hours the Stukas[63] appear and the artillery starts up. Then the engineers launch a diversionary attack on another position with boats. Immediately a pontoon bridge is built and the advance detachment crosses over but encounters strong resistance. The situation here does not look favorable.

At midday we set off with the general [*Generalleutnant* Horst Stumpff, the division C-in-C]. In Ulla we bump into *Leutnant* Thomasius's reconnaissance squad where Pit is. I learn that *Hauptfeldwebel* K. has been killed. Then we cross on the pontoon bridge that bends lightly under the weight of our [vehicle]. And now we follow on after the advance detachment on an open stretch. *Oberst* von Bismarck, the commander of the advance detachment, who is everywhere when there is any shooting, has also here, with the tanks and infantry, broken the resistance. The Russians have withdrawn on the flanks and the advance detachment pushes forward almost to the gates of Vitebsk.[64] By evening we have also managed to advance about 60 kilometers.

7.7.41: ALBERT NEUHAUS (ARMY GROUP NORTH)[65]

Yesterday I heard the *Wehrmacht* report and was shocked to discover that Münster has been particularly heavily bombed.[66] Hopefully you and all loved ones are well, hopefully! When the name Münster was specially mentioned, I felt a dreadful sinking of my stomach. But our fate, yours and mine, is in higher hands and, I hope, quite safe. But you must write to me about the bombing. I am convinced that you are all in more danger than we are. We experience no danger at all anymore, the journey is almost like a modern package tour to us. . . .

The population up here[67] has breathed a sigh of relief, it must have suffered dreadfully under the Soviet oppression. Yesterday and today a comrade and I went to a small farm to acquire, if possible, butter and bacon. We soon got milk to drink, 1½ lbs butter, at least 2½ lbs bacon and even bread as well. Today, the woman saw the cord for my identity tag (I had my collar open) and she thought I was wearing a medallion. You wouldn't believe how delighted she was when I showed her a Madonna medallion my mother had sent me at the start of the war and I kept in my wallet. She quickly made clear to us that her pastor had also been shot dead by the Communists. And I'm convinced that the population is glad that German soldiers are now protecting them. And the defection of Russian soldiers really shows best how tired of their government the people are.

Right now we're lying in a little wood, very romantic. Only the horseflies and plagues of gnats are dreadful. My forehead looks like a range of mountains and valleys, one bite upon another. At home, we're annoyed when just 2 or 3 flies buzz around the bedroom. But if you go to the latrine, the whole business has to be completed in 3 or 4 seconds, or you risk not knowing where to begin scratching your most delicate body parts, because everything itches so much.

Now the war has been rolling on for 14 days and hopefully in another 14 days the verdict will be delivered. Victory is ours. Yesterday and the day before, we drove 200 km in all farther east. I'm curious about where we will end up.

7.7.41: *LEUTNANT* GEORG KREUTER (18 PANZER DIVISION, 2 PANZER GROUP, ARMY GROUP CENTER)[68]

We attempt to envelop and defeat the enemy on and along the highway. . . . We meet Red tanks everywhere. They appear to be very badly led. Many of them and a few trucks are destroyed. The enemy draws many forces into the encircled area. We are stuck in a forest area—the regiment with its staff, the 2nd Battalion, and I with my platoon headquarters group, with no guns. The commander of the panzer battalion (Teege) with 20 tanks is also with us. Who is encircling whom here??? That's the question!

We are cut off by tanks to the rear. Messengers can only get through occasionally. Russian tanks attack us! The second-heaviest type among them![69] Our Pak, even the 50mm, can only penetrate at the weakest points. One heavy and 4 light tanks are put out of action. One heavy tank has driven into our forest, another on the road around the forest. Since the antitank guns cannot reach them—and have no effect in any case—I receive the order from the regiment to destroy them. Our tanks were just as powerless and kept very quiet when they drove past, only a few meters away. I try it with hand grenades that I have adapted into concentrated charges. It's useless. Only a hand grenade down the barrel brought the interior to explode.

7.7.41: *OBERLEUTNANT* RICHARD D. (7 PANZER DIVISION, 3 PANZER GROUP, ARMY GROUP CENTER)[70]

Today the Russians attacked and fired into a village I had to go through. Our wagon barely managed to make its way over the potholes and we thought it might get stuck. After that there was the burning road, and because the houses are all of timber the flames were quite something, but we made it through despite the heat. The Russian farmers remove their caps and bow down to me; none of them even think of shooting at anyone. I think they're happy we're here, and that they can plunder the public offices of the Bolsheviks. They tear down the pictures of Lenin, Stalin, and Molotov, and go off with chairs, benches and other stuff. You don't see anyone running about without a bag of loot. Our soldiers are more interested in chickens, geese and pigs, and the ruckus that leads to is quite amusing.

7.7.41: *STABSFELDWEBEL* CHRISTOPH B. (*LUFTWAFFE* MOTOR TRANSPORT COLUMN 9/VII, OPERATIONS AREA OF ARMY GROUP SOUTH)[71]

I've been on Russian [occupied] soil for two days now, and tomorrow we'll likely be advancing farther to the east again. The signs of war are quite pronounced in some places. The population in most cities consists of 50–80% Jews. So you get an idea of the members of the chosen race. The Jews are also the ones who were the ringleaders in the atrocities [*Scheusslichkeiten*] committed against the Ukrainians. And many a German soldier has fallen victim to the deceitfulness of these dirty slobs [*Schmutzfinken*]. We Germans thus have no reason to spare these creatures. So right now, they don't even count as much as a dog to us. That's obvious to us soldiers.

8.7.41: *MAJOR* HANS MEIER-WELCKER (251 INFANTRY DIVISION, SIXTEENTH ARMY, ARMY GROUP NORTH)[72]

We have repeatedly observed that Russian officers will kill themselves rather than be taken prisoner. This behavior is partly due to the fact that the officers in Russia are told that they would be horribly mistreated by us.

But, aside from the English, *der Russe* is the toughest and bravest opponent that we've encountered in this war.

8.7.41: PETER SCH. (19 PANZER DIVISION, 3 PANZER GROUP, ARMY GROUP CENTER)[73]

The events here are rather overwhelming, and you lose any other frame of reference.... The entire affair here can only be described in strong soldierly vernacular but, still, human beings can become accustomed to anything! It certainly can't get any worse than it's been, and the weekly newsreel [*Wochenschau*] can no longer surprise me. So far we've been through just about everything—snipers, artillery [barrages] from two directions, and early today we were twice attacked by aircraft. Each time our tanks attack we leave more comrades and officers behind. For a few minutes sorrowful words are spoken, a grave is prepared, and the day rolls on.

8.7.41: *LEUTNANT* GEORG KREUTER (18 PANZER DIVISION, 2 PANZER GROUP, ARMY GROUP CENTER)[74]

The night was relatively peaceful. I had shoveled out a small hollow for myself under a tree, so I was somewhat protected from the artillery fire at the same time. My tank is burning out with lots of noise. An armored reconnaissance car belonging to the Reds is finished off. The artillery observer is no doubt sitting in a tank that is standing on the hill. But we can't destroy it. It's too risky for a raid [*Stosstruppunternehmen*], because the enemy infantry is too numerous. Our *Nebelwerfer* have taken serious losses. Their position is betrayed with every salvo by the huge smoke clouds from the rockets. Lt. Baumgärtel is wounded. The day before yesterday, Lt. Heicke and Lt. Scheer fell. Artillery is keeping us thoroughly pinned down again! . . . Great excitement in the evening, *der Russe* is attacking. Kober is badly wounded. The attack is repelled.

Our people have got very nervous. I am sent forward like an evangelist [*Wanderprediger*] by the regimental commander. Tell everyone I meet what the situation is and that it will be better tomorrow! When I return, my previous chief is just giving the regimental commander a report on the disposition of the battalion. Security is now established everywhere. He would check all the sentry posts himself. He asks if I would come along on the "evening stroll" as well, but I am tired, because I've just come from the front. A half hour later the message comes that he has been shot dead by a hidden sniper in our little wood!!

When I have to go forward again after all, I meet yet another one who doesn't react to my call; I finish him off with a hand grenade. Perhaps that was the fellow?

8.7.41: *UNTEROFFIZIER* HANS S. (ARMY GROUP NORTH)[75]

Now I've finally got around to writing. Otherwise, whenever we had no contact with the enemy, we had to get right on to cleaning the vehicles and to putting the guns and weapons in order. Clothes have to be cleaned and then, when you're done, you're dead tired. Right now we're driving through the eastern tip of Latvia. The day before yesterday we crossed over the Dvina. The troops ahead of us had the tough battles. Especially the SS. Pity that I can't speak Latvian. Now we've got through Lithuania, the former Poland, which the Russians had occupied, and now we're in Latvia. I really almost think that we will get a good way into Russia. The mail comes very sparsely at the moment now. But, if you all can, do send some *Treupel*,[76] cigarettes (as many as you can, we're 7 men attached to the gun and everything is shared now), and film. If you can get me some new heel protectors [*Fersenschoner*], that would be grand.

You can see that Latvia got a bit more culture than Lithuania. Where we come across manor houses, we can even detect that Germans lived and built there. By the way, Russian Poland is dreadfully judaicized [*verjudet*]. Out of 600 inhabitants, 500 Jews. That's what we encountered in one town.

Now, dear little mama, all my best wishes to you and everyone at home. So far I am well and, God willing, I will also come home safely.

9.7.41: *MAJOR* HANS MEIER-WELCKER (251 INFANTRY DIVISION, SIXTEENTH ARMY, ARMY GROUP NORTH)[77]

This morning I was sent as a liaison to a corps headquarters.[78] I used the opportunity to visit the grave of *Generalmajor* Lancelle[79] in K[raslau]; he had been killed in battle there several days before. He lies at a spot in front of the church, among [the graves of] various officers, NCOs, and enlisted personnel. A row of graves is being prepared by SS men, and the fresh dirt mounds are topped with the runes of death made of birchwood. The row of soldiers [graves] is marked with crosses. Two Latvian girls were kneeling before the general's grave and weeping. So there are still people who will do something simply for the sake of humanity!

9.7.41: *SOLDAT* H. (ARMY SIGNAL REGIMENT 501, EASTERN FRONT)[80]

We're deep inside Russia, in so-called paradise, as people call it. Russia is inviting our soldiers to desert into this paradise. Terrible poverty holds sway here, and for more than two decades the people have been subjected to the kind of oppression you can hardly imagine. We'd all prefer to die than to be a part of the squalor and the suffering that these people have endured. The day must come when all this comes to an end.

We've advanced quite a way today, nearly 90 kilometers. Once again the enemy lost an enormous amount of tanks and other war matériel. Many throw away their weapons and come over to us in large numbers. We often ask the Russian soldiers why they throw away their weapons and their answer is: "What exactly should we be fighting for? For the years of oppression and suffering that we had to go through?"

We hope soon to bring this terror state to its knees.

9.7.41: ALBERT NEUHAUS (ARMY GROUP NORTH)[81]

After we had spent 2 days in Latvia close by the Russian border, yesterday over the course of the afternoon we continued on and are now in actual Soviet Russia. In the worker's paradise, of which there has been so much prattle. We drove through Ostrov, a town that had to be fought over for 2 whole days and now lies in ash and rubble.[82] The heaviest Russian tanks lay along the roads again, burned out and in tatters. Unfortunately, yesterday we also saw a lot of German graves. Seeing these dreadfully heavy tanks lying there can give you a scare. Deepest shell craters to the right and left of our route of advance, a sign that a thorough job has been done here. The *Organisation Todt*[83] is working feverishly on repairing the roads, which have been ruined by the massive deployment of troops (on both sides). But the strange thing is that the bridges are all still in one piece. The Russians seem not to have had the time to blow them up. A few kilometers from Ostrov a very impressive bunker fortification [*ganz ansehnliche Bunkerbefestigung*] stretches along the border.[84] The bunkers had been struck quite respectably by our lot. . . . Our *Luftwaffe* really does rule the airspace. Yesterday morning I took a look at a damaged German fighter that had made an emergency landing. What magnificent machines they are! I'd like to fly one sometime. You become rather proud of our fighters.

9.7.41: SIEGBERT STEHMANN (163 INFANTRY DIVISION, GERMAN ARMY OF NORWAY)[85]

In the ancient Finnish forest.

I'm happy to be able to send you a sign of life right from the first bivouac. Yes, that was a long, long journey, one none of us would ever have dreamed of and one we, at our parting in Berlin, could never have imagined. But we are healthy and happy.

The eternal ancient forests and swamps in Suomi have taken us in. . . . It is midnight and yet almost as bright as day.

It is so peaceful here by the countless lakes close to the Finnish eastern border north of Lake Ladoga. Only the constant distant thunder of guns is a reminder of the burning proximity of the war that will soon take hold of us entirely. The Finns are fighting a heroic and desperate battle in the impenetrable jungle forests. May your prayers and your love be with us. In this struggle, which pits man against man, we need walls of prayer around us.

We have traveled around 1,500 km through Sweden right up to the farthest north, up to Lapland in the polar circle. This journey was a victory march [*Triumph-fahrt*] the like of which nobody could have foreseen. The sun in its high summer position beat down across Sweden's lush, rich meadows and villages. Wherever the train steamed through, the people streamed out of all the buildings to the railway stations, to the railway embankments, waving, tossing flowers into our hands. An unforgettable experience!

There by the Bothnian Sea, we finally reached the border of Suomi near Haparanda. Originally, we were supposed to go to the heavily contested northern front on the Arctic Ocean, toward Murmansk and the Kola Peninsula. But then we turned off toward the southeast and drove on in an endless journey right through Finland, the most impoverished country I have ever seen. Wilderness, forest thickets, swamps, destitute people, wretched wooden huts, emaciated livestock. Children and the elderly with guns and knives at the few railway stations. Then more women on the roads, timid as forest animals that only rarely see humans, immovable, with helpless and sorrowful eyes and with that marvelously inexplicable language, which will likely always remain a mystery to us.

And now, around midday, we have arrived close to the Russian border in the southeast, have set up our tents in the ancient forest, have taken an evening bath in one of the solitary lakes after the burning heat of the day, and now we await the things that are to come. They will surely come soon and will not be easy.

9.7.41: *GEFREITER* JEAN Z. (*NEBELWERFER* REGIMENT 51, 3 PANZER GROUP, ARMY GROUP CENTER)[86]

We're a good way into Russia now. Reached the Dvina River and bathed in it yesterday evening and today; after 14 days, that was an indulgence again. . . . We are *Heerestruppen* and are always being assigned to other divisions, where there are tough [enemy] units to combat. We were last in action on Monday [7 July], as the Dvina crossing had to be dealt with. While under enemy artillery fire, which, however, went past us to the left and right, we built up our firing position. By day, around 2:30 p.m., we began to fire. Six batteries were set up and fired off 1,080 rockets in 20 minutes. All high explosive shells [*Sprenggranaten*] weighing almost a hundredweight;[87] you can roughly imagine that everything was cleared up over there. . . . The panzers and engineers then went ahead and constructed a bridge over the Dvina, which we drove across yesterday. . . .

During the first days on the routes of advance there were always dangerous moments, the Russian bombers popped up everywhere, dropped bombs and let off machine-gun fire. But our fighter planes did a proper job, a very great many [Russian bombers] have been shot down now and now they're rarely to be seen. . . .[88]

Now we're sitting in a wood again, and it's off again in an hour. The war destroys so much, entire villages in rubble and ashes. The city of Minsk has also been badly shot up; we drove around it, as the streets weren't yet cleared. How long it's still going to take until we're in Moscow, that we don't know either.

9.7.41: *SOLDAT* JOSEF BECK (ARMY GROUP CENTER)[89]

We've been resting since midday today and I must make use of this time to write you a letter. . . . I imagine you are waiting eagerly for mail, just like I am. The last letter from you was from 19 June, so that was three weeks.

How are you all? My thoughts are often at home, with you. I picture how it could be if I were at home. By the way, that's a nice distraction during the march, especially at night, when you can almost fall asleep while marching. The hay harvest will be finished. My yearning to see you and our children again is too great. If I manage to survive this campaign, then I will come home again very soon.

You'll be curious about what it's like for us. We usually sleep in tents in the open, ten men to a tent. It's very cramped there and hard, too, especially if you don't find any straw. But we still sleep very well, because of course we're tired. Our time for sleeping lasts four to five hours, but sometimes less. If you get guard duty, that's two more hours knocked off. During the day I wear two pairs of socks and the boots, so you can imagine how warm my feet are. And the sun shines mercilessly from four in the morning until nine at night. I've not worn long underwear or a shirt for eight days now. The rough fabric was a bit itchy at first, but you get used to it. My coat sleeves are rolled up, my collar and one button are open. I also carry a gas mask, spade, bayonet, field bag, canteen, pistol, steel helmet and an assault pack [*Sturmgepäck*], which contains a shelter half, cooking utensils, cleaning equipment, soap, towel, shaving gear, repair kit and powder. The coat has three holes in it, but that's not noticeable now.[90]

I had it worse last year in France. There, I had to carry a carbine and 90 rounds. Now I'm a machine gunner. But when things get hot, I and a certain Wolf from Sommerhausen have to carry the machine gun and 600 rounds of ammunition. The machine gun weighs around 30 pounds.

When we're on the march and there are maybe just ten minutes rest, you lie down. Whether in a field or a ditch, doesn't matter. You're asleep within a minute. Many fall over with exhaustion, but that's not happened to me yet. You won't believe how we envy the motorized troops. Today, we're lying five to six kilometers in front of the Dvina River. The crossing has only been successful in a few places so far. Our engineers have been working on a bridge for two days now and it just isn't working. The river is fast-flowing and the Russians aren't resting either. You don't need to be afraid. There are usually motorized troops ahead of us. But you can never know. The Lord God will protect me. We've always been fortunate so far. But you can certainly pray for me, as often as you have time. I so seldomly get to pray. Sometimes you get to cursing, when the hardships [*Strapazen*] get too much. Sometimes you'd pay a [*Reichsmark*] just for a gulp of water. I will happily endure ten times that, if only the sun shines for the two of us again. And if it should turn out different, keep me in your memories.[91]

10.7.41: DR. HANS LIEROW (6 INFANTRY DIVISION, NINTH ARMY, ARMY GROUP CENTER)[92]

The heat is crazy. We march very early in the morning, setting out around 0300 hours. That means getting up at 0130 hours. But it's already hot at 0700 hours. We soon arrive at new quarters, then wash, eat, and sleep, as much as the mosquitoes and flies permit it. . . . My soldier's heart finds participating in the war as a doctor vulgar as well as unpleasant. Now I've got men with foot problems and weak hearts. I'm prohibiting unboiled water, and raw milk, bacon and ham as booty, and I'm still the man who can't make foot injuries better, or dyspeptics back to happy eaters fast enough.

11.7.41: *MAJOR* HANS SCH. (ENGINEER BATTALION 652, ARMY GROUP SOUTH)[93]

On 2.7.[1941] we took control in Luzk [Lutsk] of the equipment installed by our other bridging columns. . . . On this day in the old citadel 1,000 Jews were shot. It was an act of revenge [*Vergeltungsmassnahme*] for the 2,800 Ukrainians who were shot during Bolshevik times. 5,600 Russians have now paid for that with their lives. Two officers, whom I had dispatched to look for wire and other metalware, report that the Jews died without so much as uttering a sound. After this action—which although regrettable from a human point of view was absolutely necessary as a deterrent against the growing guerrilla warfare [*Freischärlertum*]—we saw how, the very next day, a large number of looters simply put their stolen goods out on the street.

11.7.41: *LEUTNANT* RUDOLF MAURER (251 INFANTRY DIVISION, SIXTEENTH ARMY, ARMY GROUP NORTH)[94]

In the morning I drive out to Daugavpils [Dünaburg].[95] The city is almost totally burned out. Who could have done that? The Jews? The Bolsheviks? The *Landser* say [it was] the Jews and that is their excuse for the fact that allegedly 800 Jews have been shot. I inspect the citadel, which is now a prison; it originated in Czarist times and is overflowing [with prisoners], among them a very large number of Jews, including women and children. It has a disgusting stench. There's not a thing to eat there. Next to the prison is a garden in which the Bolsheviks had shot reactionaries, whose corpses now have to be scraped out [of the ground] again by women prisoners. Utterly dreadful scenes.

11.7.41: ALBERT NEUHAUS (ARMY GROUP NORTH)[96]

Yesterday the Russian bombers actually wanted to plaster us. It's a strange feeling when a dozen or so of them are flying toward you and you see the bombs fall. They were overhead again last night, but nothing happened. And today our fighters dominate the entire field once again. A short time ago, one truck after another rolled by with Russian prisoners. Yesterday, we again passed a road junction where a violent tank battle had raged. There stood 20 of the heaviest Russian tanks, shot to pieces and burned out. The Russian leaders are now employing a method that is so sadistic it makes you shudder. As we've heard, the Russian tank drivers and crews are being locked in their tanks and, in that state, given orders to advance against us—that is, not against us, but against our tanks.[97] And our tanks simply mop up, and that's quite amusing.

Our tanks and aircraft are deciding our victory. We most likely won't have to wait much longer for the end.

11.7.41: KARL FUCHS (7 PANZER DIVISION, 3 PANZER GROUP, ARMY GROUP CENTER)[98]

Today our united forces captured the Russian city of Vitebsk.[99] It is a large city and has been totally destroyed. Most of the destruction, however, came at the hands of the Russians. Now we are only several hundred kilometers away from Moscow, and I'm certain that we will soon be in the enemy's capital. At any rate, these Russian dogs are now on the run. Sometimes I'm tempted to feel sorry for them because many of the soldiers are young boys, hardly sixteen or seventeen years old. But you can't afford to have pity on them.

For the time being I am in a safe spot. If I only had some water to wash myself! The dirt and dust causes my skin to itch and my beard is growing longer and longer. Wouldn't you like to kiss me now! I'm sure you can see the dirt on the paper on which I write.

11.7.41: *LEUTNANT* WILLIBALD G. (57 INFANTRY DIVISION, SIXTH ARMY, ARMY GROUP SOUTH)[100]

Since yesterday, I'm a battery officer, as Lt. Müller got a battery and yesterday our [technical sergeant] was made a *Leutnant* and will make observation post officer.

Since yesterday evening, we've been lying in front of a fortified line [the Stalin Line] and we've landed deep in the shit [*tief in die Scheisse geraten*]. By order of the regiment, we had to change our position at 7:00 a.m. and move into an open firing position [in view of the enemy]. Result: 2 dead, 8 wounded, of whom several will also die. The others will be cripples. Also, loss of 8 horses, which are almost indispensable here! The Russian artillery landed several direct hits when the guns were brought into position. The fellows shot devilishly well and are still keeping us constantly under fire.[101] We're shooting everything we've got from our guns and I'm writing you all this letter when there are breaks in the firing. Don't worry about me! I'm a tough old thing! I'm sitting in my foxhole and kept safe. After all, live rounds are used in war.

12.7.41: *GEFREITER* ALOIS SCHEUER (197 INFANTRY DIVISION, OKH RESERVE, ARMY GROUP CENTER)[102]

We have now marched approx. 400 km to the east already, along dusty, cross-country dirt roads, through forests, swamps, and marshes, past places where bitter battles were fought, littered with the remains of all kinds of material and countless dead. But we go on without pause, and take turns to sit up on our vehicles. Many are extremely foot-sore, some fall to the ground with exhaustion. Many horses are also dropping out, because the lack of water and the extreme heat and dust are really testing us. We haven't yet had to go hungry, but we have to endure all the more thirst; there are neither wells nor a water supply system, we take all our water from cisterns (draw wells). It is often dirty, but we drink it; after all, we're not sensitive to it anymore.[103]

13.7.41: *PANZER-OBERSCHÜTZE* ERICH HAGER (17 PANZER DIVISION, 2 PANZER GROUP, ARMY GROUP CENTER)[104]

Sunday. In the night an alert. The Russians tried to attack. Nothing came of it. Lots of fog. Lots of [Russian] deserters. . . . They've been so much fooled into thinking that we're going to cut off their hands and feet and all sorts. That's why they are so scared. A lot try to flee. They do not know that nothing will happen to them! They are cut down by our pilots.

In the village where we collect water we cleared out 3 military camps. The people fight over the things. Never seen anything like it. . . .

Orsha is on fire.[105]

13.7.41: *MAJOR* WERNER HEINEMANN (23 INFANTRY DIVISION, SECOND ARMY, ARMY GROUP CENTER)[106]

Unimaginable, that there should be water pipes anywhere in the world from which one could drink water, just like that, without contracting cholera! Bolshevism has undoubtedly been at work here and collectivized everything, i.e., the individual only has his house and his garden, everything else (fields, cattle, and agricultural machines) belongs to the village community. Even meals are taken by everyone together in the Party building.

The population is utterly stolid and opaque, but, where the lower classes are concerned, appears to have led a relatively content life. The people are unimaginably unambitious, and if they are not made to work, they do absolutely nothing.

In everything (e.g., road construction), you can somehow see the same general approach, which naturally should not be compared with our standards. Everything is incredibly crude and large and tastelessly primitive, but no doubt appropriate to this passive national character. It can be seen at every turn that, in this country, every individual manifestation of life has ceased completely.[107]

13.7.41: *GEFREITER* RUDOLF STÜTZEL (5 INFANTRY DIVISION, NINTH ARMY, ARMY GROUP CENTER)[108]

I am healthy and happy and full of cheer. The reason I haven't written for a few days is because I don't have any writing paper left. Hopefully, you've all sent some off. . . .

When I last wrote, we were in Zdiziol. There the Russians attempted to break out of their cauldron.[109] But we continued to hold the position. Several Pak guns and a few machine guns were positioned there. The Russians attacked in waves with dreadful cries of "Urrah" at 3:00 a.m. at night, but were all mown down. The ground was littered with thousands. We've had no enemy contact since that day. Our panzers' advance is just too fast. Today, we're in Ulla,[110] after being in Lida for several days. . . . There's a field airdrome next to us. I can tell you, that's quite a racket all day. Stuka Ju 87s are flying out against the enemy constantly. Up to five times a day. The front is around 70 kilometers away from us. . . .

Tonight I was on duty with three other men at the machine-gun position when a Russian plane dropped bombs on us. He actually wanted to hit the bridge. So, roughly six to seven bombs, two of them 100 and 70 meters away from us. The dirt and shrapnel near enough flew around our ears. One bomb right next to me; fortunately, it was a dud [*Blindgänger*].

13.7.41: DR. ADOLF B. (25 INFANTRY DIVISION [MOT.], 1 PANZER GROUP, ARMY GROUP SOUTH)[111]

The past five days were quite grim for us! We were exposed to both aerial assault and direct artillery fire that rained down on us for hours. The Reds try over and over again to attack us from the flank! And only after our tanks have broken through. The Bolsheviks stormed out of their hiding places in the woods and out of the cornfields in large swarms, and woe to the troops that are incapable of adequately defending themselves!

This war against the Bolsheviks is cruel and sinister [*grausam und unheimlich*]. Towns and cities that we've reached during the fighting are almost utterly in flames! The Reds set everything on fire and destroy anything of value, and only so nothing falls into German hands. During the last sudden artillery barrage of the Reds on our troops there were wounded and other "casualties." We all hope that this war will come to a swift and successful conclusion!

13.7.41: *SS-STURMMANN* HANS T. (SS BATTLE GROUP "NORTH," GERMAN ARMY OF NORWAY)[112]

You'll all have heard in the OKW report that Salla has now fallen, and so the Finns that had been evacuated can now return to their old home again. Father, it's a proud feeling for me to follow tradition, as it were, and to be able to participate in the struggle for the freedom of such a brave and patriotic people. Follow tradition insofar as in 1918, of course, you, too, as a German soldier, together with the soldiers of the Finns, who were striving for freedom, fought against the same enemy. Now, as then, we are fighting against the enemy: Bolshevism!

In the decisive days of the battle for the decision [*Entscheidung*], we had a lot to do. And it didn't go off without casualties in our platoon, but, thank God, we haven't had any fatalities yet! For our wounded comrades, it's naturally a disappointment, insofar as they can no longer take part in the fight, but we'll step in for them!

Now that peaceful days have returned again, our duties go on in the old way. It's gratifying every time, when the news comes through at 10:00 p.m. and so we can hear how hot things are being made for the Russian along the entire front! The Bolsheviks and their deceitful and cruel [*hinterlistig und gemein*] fighting have already earned the gruesome end that is being prepared for them by German soldiers and their allies! The peoples oppressed by Bolshevism have come to know the "Soviet Paradise" quite well enough!

14.7.41: *LEUTNANT* RUDOLF MAURER (251 INFANTRY DIVISION, SIXTEENTH ARMY, ARMY GROUP NORTH)[113]

I'm writing to you in the blazing heat and with a parched throat in the shade of a Russian farmhouse. I don't have much time. We are now advancing day and night. Now that we've had our first contact with the enemy the war's become more fun, even if the exertions have become greater. Yesterday . . . I was on my feet from 3.30 in the morning until 10.30 in the evening, and today I was on the move again at 5.30 in the morning. It's almost become more of a war against the difficulties of the terrain than a war against an armed adversary. At least that's how it is for us. So: Don't worry! . . .

Except for the thirst, which is always there, and my tiredness today because I got too little sleep, I'm doing quite well.

15.7.41: *MAJOR* HANS SCH. (ENGINEER BATTALION 652, ARMY GROUP SOUTH)[114]

The losses of our battalion, thank God, are still quite negligible. So far, I've had a very great deal of good fortune. *Der Russe* is more tenacious and brutal than the French.[115] Among the prisoners we took yesterday there were again many Ukrainians. All of them were in fear of their commissars, who had simply bumped off their men in front of the others. The Russians can only maintain discipline at the point of a gun. However, they are better equipped than we'd thought, stubborn and tenacious.

15.7.41: DIVISIONAL CATHOLIC PRIEST (18 PANZER DIVISION, 2 PANZER GROUP, ARMY GROUP CENTER)[116]

Ambulances [*Sankas*] come and go, unload their sad cargo, and disappear again in the direction of the front. I go from room to room. All words fail here. Quiet whispering and groaning, usually silence, large, wide open eyes. Only here and there a tired smile. Behind the building, in a shady corner, the dead: officers and men. The numbers ever increasing.[117] They are young people, barely come of age, for the division is, of course, comprised almost exclusively of active troops.

15.7.41: *GEFREITER* GERHARD BOPP (35 INFANTRY DIVISION, NINTH ARMY, ARMY GROUP CENTER)[118]

In the morning at 0300 hours we drive farther and, at 0500, we reach the detachment. At 1000 we continue the march. Along the entire route of advance there are [destroyed and damaged] tanks, automobiles, and the like. Bomb craters, toppled trees, burned-out underbrush—all bear witness to the destruction (our Stukas!). At midday we stop for a break, and begin our march again about 1700 hours. [Our route] always takes us through the forests. Some of our vehicles have to be towed through the deep sand, while the infantry simply passes us by. In the morning at 0200 we settle in just outside Lutschessa.

15.7.41: *SOLDAT* SEPP P. (*LUFTWAFFE* RESERVE FLAK BATTALION 717, EASTERN FRONT)[119]

Unfortunately, the flak is precisely the branch of our armed forces that has the least time. We must always be on our toes. The proverbial saying "The flak keeps watch day and night" [*Tag und Nacht hält die Flak Wacht*] is coming completely true for us. . . . I currently find myself approx. 700 km deep inside the Soviet empire. So far, we've been working in concert with the panzer troops at the forwardmost line the whole campaign, because we are also fully motorized. We come into contact with the enemy every day and have things dropped on and chucked at us by him every day. We are not only in action against enemy air targets, but also against tanks and armored vehicles. Yesterday at 1850 hours we had to repel a heavy air attack. Numerous shells of medium and heavy caliber churned up the ground right up to the area directly next to our position. The planes frequently shoot at us with their aircraft armaments or we get to feel the lash of the artillery.

What the life of a soldier who is on the advance is like, I'm sure you can't really imagine. Unfortunately, I don't have time for a description. That you have to endure many hardships and privations, that's unavoidable. One very unsatisfactory matter is sleep. We sleep on average 12–14 hours a week. For weeks now we have had no roof over us, instead we constantly camp outdoors. . . . I often wish that I could sleep properly in a nice bed, just once. Moreover, it's really unpleasant here, because frequently there's no water for many kilometers at a time, so that you can only wash yourself half the time. In short, I'll be happy if I get out of Russia healthy and sound. Even so, my morale isn't bad. I don't know when there'll be leave. Very probably it won't be for months.

16.7.41: WILLI F. (198 INFANTRY DIVISION, ELEVENTH ARMY, ARMY GROUP SOUTH)[120]

My feet are in good shape, and it seems my nerves have gotten used to quite a bit. We've had quite a few casualties as a result of nervous shock and whatnot, although in my view the situation was more than tolerable. But it's always been those who were the bigmouths [*grosse Mäuler*] back in the barracks.

16.7.41: *SOLDAT* RUDOLF B. (SUPPLY BATTALION 553, ARMY GROUP NORTH)[121]

You simply can't picture it, how it looks at many spots in Riga where the fighting took place. The city is on a large river [at the mouth of the Western Dvina] that is wider than the Rhein. On the opposite bank there are buildings, all of them badly shot up and burned out, and the only bridge is like the one in Breisach. The other bridges have all been blown up by the Russians. The Latvians are happy that the German soldiers are here. Under the Russians it wasn't good for them; if they even attempted to look out a window, they were shot at. Only now do they feel like human beings again. Riga is a very beautiful city. On Sunday, Russian aircraft had tried on a couple of occasions to attack the city, but they were driven off by our flak.

Today in the woods a wagon was discovered with dead children. Just imagine that—it was crammed full, and that despite the heat. Many people here were simply dragged off,[122] and no one knows anything of their fate.

16.7.41: *GEFREITER* PAUL B. (*LUFTWAFFE* FLAK SPECIAL EQUIPMENT WORKSHOP [*SONDERGERÄTE-WERKST.*] PLATOON 13, OPERATIONS AREA OF ARMY GROUP CENTER)[123]

Since my last letter of 22 June 1941, we've pushed forward hundreds of kilometers, along with the panzers. Day and night, with no regard for sleep. The road was our enemy, the swamps were our enemy, everything had to be overcome. The blazing Russian heat glared down onto the yellow, bottomless sand roads, the dust burned on our skin, eyes inflamed, lips cracked, tongues sticking to our gums. Animal carcasses have been tossed into the wells,[124] the water isn't even suitable for washing. And then don't get tired. Helmet on, hand grenades in your belt, pistol in the shaft of your boot.

Der Russe is lurking in the impenetrable forests on both sides of the road and attacks treacherously and perfidiously. The troops coming up behind are now combing through these huge sections of forest. In particular, female partisans [*Flintenweiber*] with red sashes shoot aimlessly, but anybody with a soldier who has any kind of ammunition or weapon with them is felled ruthlessly. If we give Russian peasants, who have been robbed of the corn on the stalks by the cursed *kolkhoz* system, a piece of bread, they kiss our hands. It is a struggle against all the elements that the Asiatic peoples, Judaism, Bolshevism, etc., could bring to bear. And the fact that our homeland and Europe is spared this is thanks to the *Führer* and the German soldiers.

And then the battle against the mosquitoes. They fall upon us in multitudinous swarms and large specimens; even with gloves on our fingers and turbans on our heads, the little beasts get through everywhere, and all of that in the immense heat. But everything's working: advance, fight, victory. If you ever hear names in the newsreels like Rozany, Slonim, Minsk, then you can think of me.

16.7.41: SIEGBERT STEHMANN (163 INFANTRY DIVISION, GERMAN ARMY OF NORWAY)[125]

We've advanced at a phenomenal pace. After resisting tenaciously to the last bullet the Russians have taken to their heels.

We've now reached, indeed we've crossed, the old Finnish-Russian border. We're still stationed in the woods and are making our marsh boots [*Sumpftreter*], so that we don't get stuck when the advance continues. We have no idea where we're headed to. Perhaps into the interior of Russia, and we'll advance east beyond Lake Ladoga. The lake is as long as the stretch from Berlin to Rügen. Which should give you sense of the distances involved.

Last night was agonizing. Anyone who's not been to Finland knows nothing about mosquitoes. Clouds of mosquitoes plunge right into our tents. Mosquito nets are quite useless. It's indescribable. And along with the [Russian] aircraft, which are constantly circling overhead, it's just one of the little extras of this summer in the primeval forest. The only thing we all long for is mail from home, but unfortunately our longing goes unfulfilled.

17.7.41: *LEUTNANT* RUDOLF MAURER (251 INFANTRY DIVISION, SIXTEENTH ARMY, ARMY GROUP NORTH)[126]

We're advancing farther to the N/NE. Inchowetschi and Bogomolovo are the next towns. There we find out that our antitank battalion has been encircled. On 13.7. our reconnaissance battalion had a similar experience;[127] [*Leutnant*] Eisenberg, from Dreihausen, District Marburg/L, was killed in action. Our 3rd Battalion of 471 IR managed to pry the antitank battalion loose. [*Oberleutnant*] Walter of Regiment 471 was killed by a Russian officer, despite the fact that he'd raised his hands [as if to surrender]. Our hopes of seeing action have been futile so far.

17.7.41: *MAJOR* WERNER HEINEMANN (23 INFANTRY DIVISION, SECOND ARMY, ARMY GROUP CENTER)[128]

How can those back home even begin to fathom how many countless sacrifices and how much sweat and deathly exhaustion of the infantry soldier make up such pursuit marches as these? The apathy of man and horse is often <u>so</u> great, that not even a kind word helps. . . . War is the toughest thing there is in life, and it is in the breathtaking tempo of our operations that the key to our rapid final victory lies. You have to have the courage to be tough, or else you can only conclude that you "can't go on!" Everything has to go on, and as fast as possible, but it's frequently bitterly difficult to have to demand everything and more, over and over again.

The poor horses suffer the worst. What they have to do with those heavy vehicles on the sand-covered roads is unimaginable. It breaks your heart to see how they fall away from day to day. Countless [numbers] of them collapse while still in harness, patiently allow the pistol to be placed at their ear for a mercy shot, and line the roads of our advance.[129]

17.7.41: KARL FUCHS (7 PANZER DIVISION, 3 PANZER GROUP, ARMY GROUP CENTER)[130]

Yesterday we moved past Smolensk on the city's northern fringe and are now heading toward Moscow. Russian opposition is weak and localized and wherever we meet them, they are forced to flee. Our Air Force, in particular the Stuka [divebombers], actively support our efforts. Our comrades from the Air Force are top-notch guys. . . .

Madi, a few words about Russia. All those who today still see any kind of salvation in Bolshevism should be led into this "paradise." To sum it up with one phrase: "It's terrible!" When I get back I will tell you endless horror stories about Russia. Yesterday, for instance, we saw our first women soldiers—Russian women, their hair shorn, in uniform! And these pigs fired on our decent German soldiers from ambush positions.

18.7.41: *OBERGEFREITER* G.B. (46 INFANTRY DIVISION, OKH RESERVE, ARMY GROUP SOUTH)[131]

Here the Jewish question [*Judenfrage*] is being resolved somewhat differently than by us [at home]. The Romanians round up all the Jews and shoot them dead—regardless if they're men, women, or children, because before it was the other way around.

19.7.41: AUGUST SAHM (ARMY GROUP SOUTH)[132]

We're dug in in the woods. Yesterday is a day I will never forget. It was the most difficult up to this point. All our commanders [*Führer*] have been wounded. I have also asked HIM that the cup pass me by, but HIS will be done, not mine. I want to try always to be ready to do HIS will. The Lord be with me and also with you.

19.7.41: *OBERFÄHNRICH* KLAUS B. (*LUFTWAFFE* ANTIAIRCRAFT SEARCHLIGHT UNIT [*FLAKSCHEINWERFER-EINHEIT*], OPERATIONS AREA OF ARMY GROUP CENTER)[133]

We've now advanced farther beyond Vitebsk in the direction of Smolensk. We went through Vitebsk on our march. It is supposed to have had around 200,000 inhabitants. In terms of area dimensions, it might be smaller than cities with this population size in Germany, because the Russians live [in] much more confined [spaces], but it at least still covered a considerable expanse. Now, there is not a single building in V. that isn't completely destroyed or ruined. The wooden buildings—these also dominate in Russian cities—have all been burned down; there's usually just a part of the chimney stack still standing. Insofar as the buildings are stone constructions, they are burned out and just a part of the fireproof walls remain standing. The war has really done a thorough job here [*hier hat der Krieg wirklich ganze Arbeit geleistet*].

Quite close to our position in Vitebsk there was also a prisoner assembly point [*Gefangenen-Sammelplatz*]. The fate of the prisoners in the first days is dreadful.[134] Around 5,000 men had been rounded up on an open square. They had been squatting there for days in the open, exposed to wind and weather, hardly anything decent to eat or drink and no adequate clothing. By now, it has got very cold—commensurate with the season, of course—we've also had rain repeatedly. Some try to slip away, which can succeed, since the number of guard details is extraordinarily low. Some of them are shot in the attempt, the guard details have no other option, of course. The prisoners are gradually being transported to the rear, as transport allows.

There are the wildest types among the Russians. The "Volga Germans"[135] are separated out, they naturally have to stay at the collection point, but aren't specially guarded, act as interpreters, and support the guard details in the supervision.

19.7.41: *SOLDAT* CARLHEINZ B. (SS-DIVISION "VIKING" [MOT.], 1 PANZER GROUP, ARMY GROUP SOUTH)[136]

For the past two days our survey battery [*Messbatterie*] was in action. We didn't sleep at all during the night, and washing was likewise a luxury. Yesterday morning we drove out with our vehicles to the forwardmost infantry and put in an attack under cover of a heavy machine gun. For hours the enemy artillery replied with strong harassing fire. We were right in the middle of the battle. Several days ago we had a heavy bombing attack. We huddled together in our foxholes while the bombs struck the ground all around us. Several of our best comrades were wounded.

For several days we've been foraging for ourselves. In every village we're now on the hunt for pigs and calves, which are then prepared by our field kitchens. We're also cooking up a few tasty morsels for ourselves each day around noon. For example, today we had fried potatoes with scrambled eggs and bacon. It tasted just like at home. The bacon and eggs were given to us as gifts by the Ukrainians; they're very friendly to us. We also get something from the Russian inhabitants, even if they're often unfriendly [*abweisend*] to us.

20.7.41: KARL FUCHS (7 PANZER DIVISION, 3 PANZER GROUP, ARMY GROUP CENTER)[137]

Today is Sunday and for a change the sun is shining. It had rained heavily in the last couple of days, but now in clear weather our Stuka dive bombers are once again on the prowl. These pilots are really something! Wherever they strike they create havoc and destruction.[138]

20.7.41: *SOLDAT* HANS OLTE (CORPS SIGNAL BATTALION 52, SECOND ARMY, ARMY GROUP CENTER)[139]

My dear parents! . . . Have also received the three little packages today and am truly grateful. Oh, German cigarettes are just too good. Just send cigarettes, tobacco, and cigarette papers. You have no idea how we crave cigarettes here. Buying cigarettes here in Russia is impossible [*ein Ding der Unmöglichkeit*].[140] In any case, I haven't been able to spend any money at all since I set foot on Russian soil, at the most occasionally for milk, eggs, or chickens.

20.7.41: *GEFREITER* FRITZ G. (101 LIGHT DIVISION, SEVENTEENTH ARMY, ARMY GROUP SOUTH)[141]

Since the last large-scale low-level Russian attack [*Tiefffliegerangriff*], we haven't been in any more significant action [that would have meant] having to make closer acquaintance with our "fine" enemy. The day before yesterday, some abundant rain put a quick stop to our advance, because apart from the prime movers, hardly any vehicle could get on. So, the whole of yesterday we had to stay put and wait until all the vehicles had caught up. So that we were also contributing, with the help of the male population enlisted [from the area], we made particularly impassable stretches of road more or less navigable. . . .

We've got the Russian in a tight fix again, and he's trying to break out in vain. There's something in the offing in this area, there are a lot of signs of it.

The day before, we had a sad incident. Our light telephone wagon, which was bringing an injured Russian back and coming a little later as a result, was attacked at halfway by some dispersed Russians and dragged back with them. They took with them one of our wounded telephone operators, who had received the Iron Cross, Second Class just two days before. They roughed up one of the motorcycle messengers from 1st Battalion, who was accompanying that very wagon, very badly. Our comrade very likely had it no better. So it is understandable that we shoot every one of these bestial fellows that falls into our hands and is somehow suspicious.

Since yesterday, the "roads" are more or less dry and navigable again, and our advance is moving.

21.7.41: *GEFREITER* HANS CASPAR VON WIEDEBACH-NOSTITZ (20 PANZER DIVISION, 3 PANZER GROUP, ARMY GROUP CENTER)[142]

Resupply, above all fuel and ammunition, were not getting forward; above all, the infantry was unable to fill the gaps that quickly and so close the *Kessel* [cauldron] that had been formed by the tank corps.[143] Our division had marched without a break, everywhere ruthlessly breaking the enemy resistance and covered this tremendous distance in 4 weeks, continually in battle. As a consequence, it had created an important precondition for the successful outcome of the Smolensk *Kessel* and had got there ahead of the Russians, who, coming from the north and east, wanted to prevent that. Now we had the mission to hold this position against numerically superior forces until we were relieved by the infantry.[144]

22.7.41: *MAJOR* HANS MEIER-WELCKER (251 INFANTRY DIVISION, SIXTEENTH ARMY, ARMY GROUP NORTH)[145]

We're now facing Siberian troops [*sibirische Truppen*] and they fight like lions [*schlagen sich wie die Löwen*].[146]

22.7.41: UNKNOWN SOLDIER (5 INFANTRY DIVISION, NINTH ARMY, ARMY GROUP CENTER)[147]

There have been tough battles here. Our infantry has had a few losses and two batteries of 5 Artillery Regiment have been completely wiped out. Only 4 horses and a few men remain from one battery. The enemy is fighting here with all available means. Even women are fighting in the front line. The Russian infantry has dug itself in, and they are not coming out of their foxholes. Every meter of ground has to be won in close combat. Our infantry is even fighting with fixed bayonets. The dead are usually stabbed with bayonets. The Russians still keep to their foxholes and are stabbed to death there.

You have to be very careful here. They may come out of one hole with their hands raised, while they shoot at you from another. . . . It's a great pity for every German soldier who falls victim here to this murdering gang. But, God willing, they will be exterminated in this war, and Europe will be freed from the bloodlust of Bolshevism.

22.7.41: *GEFREITER* HEINZ SCH. (ENGINEER REGIMENTAL STAFF 514 [FOR SPECIAL DUTIES], ARMY GROUP NORTH)[148]

If you read about or see the bridge over the Neman at Vilki (in German), or the bridge across the Dvina at Vandani, and also the bridge at Opotschka—those were built by our engineers, and we from the staff were there before our battalions. The terrain must first be scouted and a location found for building the bridge. Then comes the communication net and my vehicle. We can't worry about harassing fire from artillery, or about aircraft or tanks. On several occasions we've had to stop our vehicle and go into position with hand grenades and carbines. There's no safety anywhere in Russia! Just the poorest, most fearfully oppressed people—primitive human beings who are capable of anything. Whoever manages to get out of here in one piece has had good fortune. This is a cruel and insidious war. Woe be the driver who has to drop out of the column and gets stuck all alone. We've seen enough of that. You'll be able to see where we've been from the letters I'm sending back. So far it's been toward Leningrad! We won't be the last there!

22.7.41: *UNTEROFFIZIER* HEINZ H. (SUPPLY BATTALION 563, ARMY GROUP SOUTH)[149]

The Ukraine has the most fertile soil in all of Europe. Should there be a drought [*Trockenheit*] in the Reich, it won't affect our food supply at all, because Russia can not only supply Germany, but all of Europe, with grain. (Total world production of wheat amounts to 47 million tons, 20 million of that comes just from Russia.) If you've never seen them, you simply can't picture the enormous fields of grain. It's really a pleasure to see something like that.

23.7.41: *GEFREITER* M.F. (256 INFANTRY DIVISION, NINTH ARMY, ARMY GROUP CENTER)[150]

This war demands nerves of iron and real composure [*erfordert eiserne Nerven und Ruhe*]. The fact that our ration supply is often interrupted is due to the poor rail and road connections. Our rations are often very much in short supply, but we have to go on. At the moment, we have to get by with half a loaf of bread for the entire day, but we can't hang our heads. Oh how often I've longed for a proper meal, but always in vain.

23.7.41: SIEGBERT STEHMANN (163 INFANTRY DIVISION, GERMAN ARMY OF NORWAY)[151]

A quick letter here before the assault. We marched 275 km in one go. The history of this campaign will have to be written some time, it exceeds any standard measure! Daily 65-km march, day and night. No sleep. Barely a crust of bread. No supplies, no planes, tanks or heavy artillery with us, just wilderness, jungle, swamp, and desert sand, plus parching, blazing sun.

Exhausted to death, we stagger along behind the rattling covered wagon, a [walking] stick in our fists, loaded with baggage, nets around our heads to counter insects, no longer human, instead [we are] midnight ghosts [*Mitternachtsgespenster*] of filth and rags, who have forgotten time and the world. For hundreds of kilometers, no humans, no village, no house, not even any roads, just paths in whose desert sand the vehicles sink right up to their axles. The horses are exhausted and dropping dead. We are staggering with weariness, hunger, and exhaustion, a rabble of soldiers against a mighty opponent. The air is filled with the revolting, sweet stench of the decomposing corpses lying in the roads. It is ghastly. It's just strange how indifferent we are to it. Yesterday at midnight, I sat by a dead Russian by the side of the road to rest for a few minutes and ate my last piece of bread. The picture of war here is just like Goya's "Disasters of War"[152] shows it. Just now, while I've been writing, the heavy Russian shells are howling over us. I'll have to slip off.

23.7.41: UNKNOWN SOLDIER (5 INFANTRY DIVISION, NINTH ARMY, ARMY GROUP CENTER)[153]

The first salutation of the day is fierce artillery fire. Our division attacks. We have to press forward. The enemy is thrown back a way. In a small area, the Russian has ca. 60 dead, so the infantry reports to me. But our losses are also high—19 dead are taken away from the battlefield on a wagon. They are buried right next to our observation post. They are all from the 11./IR 56, including *Leutnant* Keller. Our infantry regiments have been seriously reduced in strength. One NCO from 75 Infantry Regiment reported to me that they had 83 fatalities and 240 wounded so far. The enemy on the opposing side is too strong. Our division is facing around 3 Russian divisions. The attack falters. We are now holding only the forward line.

24.7.41: *STABSFELDWEBEL* HELMUTH A. DITTRI (20 PANZER DIVISION, 3 PANZER GROUP, ARMY GROUP CENTER)[154]

Shortly after 2 o'clock the alarm sounded again—the Russians started a tank attack.[155] Again the shells came so thick and fast that you didn't know where to turn. Gradually we took in the situation and succeeded in concentrating our fire on the enemy. Our unit lost 2 machines and 6 men killed. . . .

One of our men approached a demolished Russian tank and was bumped off by its crew, which was lying hidden beneath it. We now took a close look at this juggernaut and discovered its commander, an officer. He blew his brains out and was holding the pistol when we arrived.

24.7.41: *LEUTNANT* WILLIBALD G. (57 INFANTRY DIVISION, SIXTH ARMY, ARMY GROUP SOUTH)[156]

The past few days have been fairly quiet and we've made serious progress. Since early this morning we're once again in position and taking part in a major encirclement battle.[157] The Russians are fighting doggedly [*verbissen*] and giving it all they've got to break loose from the iron ring. But they won't succeed in that and they're about at the end of their tether. Once they're out of ammunition and food the end will come quickly. Everyday prisoners are being taken, and they're clearly glad that for them the war is now over. For the most part they're a wretched lot. . . .

I'm curious how much longer the war's going to go on, and just how it will come to an end. I almost think that, in 14 days, it'll be all over except for the marching. It was amusing to see how our men reacted to the Soviet propaganda leaflets, which called upon them to desert and promised splendid treatment [*glänzende Behandlung*]. We kept one of the leaflets for documentation, while the others were used for more perfidious purposes, [and] our counter offer [*Gegenaufforderung*] is already much more successful.

24.7.41: AUGUST SAHM (ARMY GROUP SOUTH)[158]

My friend, I feel compelled to write to you. Today, I will try, although it pains me to do it.

So on 20 July, it happened. It was a Sunday. At 3:00 a.m. already we began our attack. The enemy fell back. Not a shot was fired. But around 10:00 a.m. he opened up with his artillery fire on us. Until 2:00 p.m. I lay in a ditch by the road close to a village. Then came the order to attack a wood around 4 kilometers away. Up to that point, just fields of corn, wheat and rye. The company deployed in open order.

Der Russe was shooting everything he had. I cannot describe to you what this fire was like. Shells landing simply everywhere and the cries of those who'd been hit. We got within a couple hundred meters of the wood, then nothing would get us further. We couldn't get off the ground, the enemy had us pinned down so tightly. From somewhere a voice shouted, "Dig in!"

I had just got hold of my spade when something struck close beside me. The air pressure threw me to the side and then I felt the pain in my right arm. I was very lucid and conscious all the while, inspected the hole in my sleeve, tried to move my arm. It worked, so couldn't be bad. Only then did I call for a medical orderly. He was close to me and bandaged me. I left my weapons and equipment there, took only my dispatch case with the letters and document and leapt to the rear. The firing continued unabated. But since I could no longer dig, it didn't matter whether I stayed put or raced to the rear.

After 2 kilometers I managed to get out of the zone of fire. But there was barrage and harassing fire ahead of me on the road and in the village I was trying to get to. So I stayed put in the cornfield until darkness. Then off I went back to the dressing station, got an injection for tetanus and an injection of opium for the pain. Then the ambulance came.

Every day we are moved further to the rear. It's slow progress, as all the roads are busy with traffic. A whole army of casualties moves to the west in this manner. All the things that I have had to see in these days. . . . So much for my report to you.

I don't really know what the purpose of telling this is. When I read back over it, I'm ashamed of it. The real, important thing [*das Eigentliche*] isn't there.

I prayed, Hermann.

25.7.41: *MAJOR* S. (20 PANZER DIVISION, 3 PANZER GROUP, ARMY GROUP CENTER)[159]

Gradually, a reaction of nervous tension made itself felt among us. Somewhat exhausted, we went a little way back along the road, up to a street attendant's cottage, where we sat down on a bench to rest. From there we had a good overview of the battlefield in the sunken ground. We saw both our own and enemy tanks that had been put out of action, but none combat ready from either party. About 100 meters away from us stood a burning T-34 that, as was later ascertained, had been shot into flames by the commander of 6th Company. Half an hour later it blew sky high with a dull crack, flinging the turret 30 meters away. Farther back at the forest edge we saw a T-34 that had rammed one of our Panzer IIs. It had even climbed up it and then not been able to free itself. From a distance it looked like the mating of two dinosaurs. This scene was later referred to in the regiment as the panzer wedding.

Of course some of my men had suffered a shock, as they were taken completely by surprise and attacked right up close by [enemy tanks] clearly superior in terms of weapons and armor plating. And even more so when they discovered that they had hardly any impact with their own little tank guns [*Kanönchen*]. Who could hold that against them? One noncommissioned officer drove back into the area of Combat Echelon B with his tank, which had been severely damaged in the fight. There, sinking down exhausted next to *Leutnant* K., he told the following about his experience:

"*Herr Leutnant*, it was terrible! One [of the Russian tanks] just advances up to me, I'm firing and firing, armor-piercing shells, high-explosive shells, with the machine gun. Hit after hit, but he doesn't notice any of it. And he's coming ever closer, his shots missing us by a hair's breadth. Shoots again, the shot tears the track shield from my tank. I can calculate when he will have the next huge shell in his barrel, then he will hit home. I'm only 30 meters away from him, and then another tank comes at me from the side, its barrel pointed at me. That's when my driver puts his foot down and we drive off between the two of them with gusto. They are better armored, better armed, and faster, what else could we have done? Look how I'm shaking! . . ."[160]

25.7.41: *OBERGEFREITER* KONRAD F. (1 INFANTRY DIVISION, 4 PANZER GROUP, ARMY GROUP NORTH)[161]

An awful lot of dead Russians are lying around here. There aren't enough prisoners to bury them. So the air is full of this disgusting smell. While I've been writing, heavy artillery has been shooting far above and beyond us and our fighters are flashing across the forests and finally keeping the Red bombers off our backs.

Could you get hold of a mosquito net to drape over the head and send it to me?

We are lying in a burned-out wood. It's a new tactic, setting the woods on fire with incendiary bombs so that we have no cover from air attacks.

An airdropped [propaganda] leaflet includes, among others, the message: "The German concentration camps [*KZ-Läger*] are full of Protestants and Catholics. Come to us: we guarantee you life and participation in the cultural institutions of the Soviet Union." It sounds like bitter mockery, and women have been saying that they can confess and receive communion about once a year, secretly, in barns. There are few priests here.

26.7.41: *GEFREITER* ALOIS SCHEUER (197 INFANTRY DIVISION, OKH RESERVE, ARMY GROUP CENTER)[162]

Dearest Friedchen!

I finally have a chance again to write a letter to you after 10 days.

I think we will march ourselves to death, we put 45 kilometers behind us nearly every day. We see and hear nothing of the enemy, the motorized units are always far ahead of us. Wherever we get through, the battles have always already taken place several days before. We march doggedly on, through destroyed villages, past fresh graves, always onward and onward.[163]

For the last few days I have had stomach problems for the first time, it must surely be because of the one-sided diet, because we're living very primitively. I also now have blisters and bleeding feet. Iodine and sticking plaster are the radical treatments for such troubles.

26.7.41: *STABSFELDWEBEL* HELMUTH A. DITTRI (20 PANZER DIVISION, 3 PANZER GROUP, ARMY GROUP CENTER)[164]

When you size up the Russians you are struck more and more by the fact—and you can't help admitting it—that they can take an enormous amount of punishment. For instance, despite the fact that their artillery received several direct hits today, the gun crews did not abandon their positions. Similarly, the Russian infantry shoots at the tanks at very short range and keeps on firing even though the whole area is already in our hands. We had a taste of this today, one of our mates being wounded. Our own tank has been hit several times in the last two days—once the turret, then the track, and besides one of its guns has been crippled.

The Russian artillery is never silent for a minute.

The whole day we had to stand the fire of one of their automatic riflemen whom we have not been able to spot, he's so well hidden. If you show him only your little finger he'll fire at it.

On taking stock of our regiment [21 Panzer Regiment] we are driven to the sad conclusion that there is very little left of it. . . . . There isn't enough to make a decent detachment. And our losses have been heavy, not only in men, but also in material.[165]

26.7.41: *GEFREITER* EBERHARD W. (5 INFANTRY DIVISION, NINTH ARMY, ARMY GROUP CENTER)[166]

We have been in action on the forwardmost line since the first day of the campaign against Russia. Right on the first day we also had the greatest losses so far. . . . . But on the first day the artillery fire was missing, to which we have now been subjected for four days and it rumbles on during the day. We've been participating in the encirclement of [several] Russian armies for four days, which are now attempting with all means to escape the deadly envelopment.[167] They try over and over again to break through, they even managed it in some sectors on the night of 24/25 July. Our regiment was in a horrible situation. We would have soon been encircled ourselves, and the ring [of encirclement] was getting very close. It had a diameter of roughly 4–5 kilometers! Luckily, on the following morning, 21 Stukas arrived and performed excellent work, if you want to use that word for mass murder. We have all dug ourselves in, because the Russian artillery fire lies on our positions for hours at a time. We hate the roaring noise in the air. And it's been going on for two days. We hope that the war will very soon come to an end and that we can then properly clean our clothes again. At any rate, I know war, I have seen enough dreadful and terrible things.

I've been in so-called Russian churches. Simply great! One is a cinema, another a theater, and yet another is a junk shop. With fixed bayonets [*mit aufgepflanztem Seitengewehr*], we tore the images of Stalin and his associates from the walls. And in the process of this activity I discovered the good core of this campaign and a certain personal mission that I am now carrying out. In this respect, this war is the most humane of all [wars] to date. Only today, from an escaped German soldier, we heard about a deed that is typical for this riffraff [*Gesindel*]. They had stabbed out the eyes of captured German soldiers and let them go.

26.7.41: *INGENIEUR* H.J. (GERMAN ARMY MISSION IN ROMANIA)[168]

Well, everything will be as it was and probably much nicer and better than we ever had it. Let's first bring the English and the Jewish pigs, that plague on the world, to the ground. At home in the Reich you could hardly meet a single Jew, but (here) there are plenty and to spare. There are gallows faces [*Galgengesichter*] among them, the like of which mean you can imagine what sort of villainies this "rabble" is capable of.

In Iassy, the Jews shot from the windows and roofs on the German and Romanian troops that were then marching through.[169] Well, our comrades made short shrift of them. I've seen pictures of it, so I can tell you what it looked like. Here with us, they've put the Jews in camps, but in Bucharest they are still walking around freely. Now and then, when we have to load something, we fetch Jews and then we teach them to work. I can tell you, they work like crazy as long as we're standing over them, because they're hugely frightened of us Germans. But as soon as we turn around and the Romanians take over supervision, it's back to the old ways, because the Romanians still have to learn how you have to deal with this scourge of humanity [mit diesen Geisseln der Menschheit]. Yes, I am experiencing all sorts and lots of new things.

28.7.41: *UNTEROFFIZIER* E.M. (17 PANZER DIVISION, ARMY GROUP GUDERIAN,[170] ARMY GROUP CENTER)[171]

You will have heard about the fighting around Smolensk on the radio. Those were my proud soldiers who achieved the breakthrough, the flag raised in victory. We are standing just outside Moscow, all units welded together into an iron chain, the like of which the world has never before seen. Only a short while still, and then that great event of world history will take place [dann wird das grosse Ereignis der Weltgeschichte sich ereignen].

28.7.41: *MAJOR* HANS MEIER-WELCKER (251 INFANTRY DIVISION, SIXTEENTH ARMY, ARMY GROUP NORTH)[172]

Delicate blue sky, green, rolling land. Meadows, cornfields, fallow land, birch trees, farmsteads, moors, forests, sand. Dusty roads, burned-out wooden bridges, shell craters, graves with crosses and helmets.

Humans and horses are performing feats on the deep, sandy roads. But even our motor vehicles are being tested hard. The mines that have been set out by the Russians in numerous places and in large numbers, which is easy to do in the light ground, are unpleasant. Every day, the Russian air force is increasingly making itself felt. Now the Red airplanes are even coming at night, with parachute flares. Recently, the Russians dropped ammunition and supplies into our cauldron as well. But the parachutes landed in our lines.

Burning villages and ones that have been untouched by the fire. In them, women who kneel crying in front of soldiers and beg, because the [soldiers] want to take their last calf or chicken from them. In another place, comrades are being buried, often whole rows of them; close by, other [soldiers] plunge upon a gaggle of geese. Soon the feathers are flying all over the place.

During the fighting, the population usually flees into the forests. When it's peaceful, they gradually reemerge. After a while they fetch the livestock, usually just a few, as the Bolshevik economy only permits the farmer a very small amount for himself. The large collective herds and holdings have, however, been moved to the interior of the empire by the Communists, in accordance with their plans. Once the population has begun to trust us a bit, they start to fetch their buried goods from the earth. Our *Landser* have already developed a good eye for these hiding places, too.

28.7.41: *UNTEROFFIZIER* HANS S. (ARMY GROUP NORTH)[173]

The Russian, or rather the Bolshevik, is an unusually hatred-filled and extraordinarily tough opponent. So far it has been the case that he has preferred death to captivity. His artillery shoots a lot, but usually from an open firing position, and when he's firing directly, he rarely has a forward observation post. In our sector, he doesn't really know how to deploy Pak or tanks. . . . We've also had very close contact with [their] planes. Heavy-caliber bombs and low-level attacks in close proximity. I've already written [to you] about it extensively. . . . He can handle small arms—machine guns, submachine guns, and the [new] automatic rifle [*Gewehr*]—superbly. Perhaps you've read about it in the propaganda company reports. The new type of rifle has a magazine with 10 rounds and works in principle like a pistol—i.e., it's a self-loader. You can achieve a high rate of fire with that. . . .

In our battalion's sector, he's already been firing with gas. Only the wind was unfavorable for shooting gas and the whole thing wasn't properly set up. Now he's taken on the appearance of 1812: Detonating bridges, setting villages ablaze, snatching up everything edible. Usually, he doesn't have any resupply himself and is dependent on the stores in the villages. Then he contrived all sorts of things that I don't want to write about yet.

So you see: it's an extremely hard struggle this time. People back at home shouldn't imagine it's so easy and make the mistake that I did when I underestimated the Russian. The *Wehrmachtbericht* of the last few days wrote that 11–12,000 Russians had surrendered at Nevel. We took part in that cauldron as well. We had established ourselves over several days in an area wooded with pines and repelled attempts to break out. He also shot with gas next to us.[174] It was an uneasy time [*war eine mulmige Zeit*].

28.7.41: *UNTEROFFIZIER* WILHELM WESSLER (6 INFANTRY DIVISION, NINTH ARMY, ARMY GROUP CENTER)[175]

The company was woken at 0800 hours. Our orders for the day's duties were clothing and weapons maintenance. Comrades gave me monies to be sent home and, at 1200 hours, I handed them over to the paymaster.[176] As a thrifty person, I put RM 80 into my savings account. It was a glorious sunny day; dressed only in swimming trunks, every man relaxed in his own way.[177]

Shortly after 1400 hours it was my turn to have my hair cut by our company barber, Fritz Gauseweg. While having my hair cut, Russian bombers suddenly thundered along over us. I heard the whistling of bombs and dashed literally head first into a pit. This leap saved my life, because at that very moment, there was an explosion. One of the bombs struck only a few meters away from my pit, right next to an ammunition truck that immediately caught fire.

Der Russe had done a pretty good job with those bomb drops; <u>the following result</u>:

The chair on which I had sat still stood there. Beside it lay Fritz Gauseweg, scissors and comb still in his hands. The bomb had ripped away the top of his skull.

<u>Those killed were</u>:

Schütze Schmelzer (my batman),

Schütze Specht,

Fritz Gauseweg—he lay so close to the ammo truck that his body had partially burned.

While the ammo truck burned, the ammunition blew up with a rattling crack. Everyone took to their heels, fearing a massive explosion. . . .

Suddenly I hear a scream; Rudi Roethemeier (our company shoemaker) is lying close to the ammo truck. With a bound, I'm next to him, blood spurting from a vein in his leg like a fountain. How I got hold of some underwear and a piece of wood, I don't know anymore. I fashioned a tourniquet on his leg with them. Although he had a small build, I only managed to get him away from the vicinity of the ammo truck with a great deal of effort.

29.7.41: *GEFREITER* VIKTOR CZERMAK (ARMY GROUP SOUTH)[178]

If I only knew that all of you were no longer worried about me, because it's really not necessary. Our Savior [*Heiland*] loves us still more than a mother loves her child, and also knows much better what is good and wholesome for his brothers and sisters. So we must really take solace in that. As He himself said: What is there for you to fear, you of little faith [*Kleingläubige*]. . . . May the Savior bless you! . . . I know that I'm in the hand of God, of the Lord. . . . I have given myself over to Him completely, to carry his light. . . . Yet should he desire that I suffer, then all praise and glory shall be His alone. For He helps others to eternal salvation.[179]

29.7.41: *LEUTNANT* RUDOLF MAURER (251 INFANTRY DIVISION, NINTH ARMY, ARMY GROUP CENTER)[180]

Around 1800 hours we start off toward Velikie Luki, which is still occupied by the Russians. It's a bad journey at night! *Der Russe* is defending himself tenaciously. His artillery plasters us constantly with fire. In addition, he's harassing our covering forces through armed reconnaissance; as a result, our 459 IR has losses. Among other things, the Russians have now given convicts [*Zuchthäusler*] from Moscow short-term training and sent them into action against us.

Our division stab is quartered in Nowosolkoljniki. Our neighboring division, the 253 ID, has been given the task of taking Velikie Luki. Thus, we've had to reinforce the 253 ID with our Infantry Regiments 459 and 471, our complete artillery regiment, and our engineer battalion. Velikie Luki occupies a key position between Leningrad and Moscow and is being defended quite vigorously by the Soviets. The capture of the city is not proceeding as rapidly as those "up above" had hoped. So they're looking for scapegoats. Rumor has it that our general is among them and, as a result, is going to be transferred.[181] We have a battalion commander with us who's been made a "scapegoat" because he had to retreat in the face of superior Soviet forces. Now he will face a court-martial.

29.7.41: ALBERT NEUHAUS (ARMY GROUP NORTH)[182]

The last 12 days have also been pretty demanding on us.[183] Not that we had to exert ourselves much physically, but during the day we perform reconnaissance and at night draw up plans again for the next position. Now it seems that the situation up here is also gradually becoming clear. When you're in action like that night and day, it does fray your nerves. I don't know whether we're going to be in action again in the next few days. You have to admit it, the Russians are defending themselves and shoot everything their guns can give. But yesterday our panzers went forward again, they'll certainly clear things up. We're barely bothered by Russian planes now. We don't see any bombs at all now. Just a few days ago, 6 Russian fighters came in low and strafed us with their machine guns. Thank God, our battery hasn't suffered any losses yet. . . .

Our major took a look at the Russian artillery positions that we had reconnoitered and shot in [eingeschossen]. One had been completely shot to pieces by us and a second had had its limber position and ammunition stores shot up. How must it have gone for the other batteries that we reconnoitered? The day before yesterday, for example, an enemy battery fired at us pretty heavily. They were still firing at us when we had located them with our equipment and soon our first greetings were zipping over to them. They received 40 rounds from our cannon, 40 from the howitzers and 20 from the heavy howitzers [Mörsern]. Not one of them let out a squeak after that. There's been many a daring exploit [Husarenstück] here. But you have to admit that every soldier has dug deep into his last reserves. At the start of this campaign we all thought we were already superfluous, but I've had to make a 100% correction to that opinion.

How do things look now in Münster? People must be working feverishly to mend the damage. This war will surely not last much longer,[184] and when our troops are then freed up here in the East and can be deployed in the West again, then God have mercy on England.

Dear Agnes, hopefully this letter will reach you. It may be that you've not received any number of greetings from me because our mail vehicle was ambushed.

30.7.41: *PANZER-OBERSCHÜTZE* ERICH HAGER (17 PANZER DIVISION, ARMY GROUP GUDERIAN, ARMY GROUP CENTER)[185]

Wednesday. After roll call we're going foraging. The same ones, back to where we were. Today there is a bigger hunt. We got 30 chickens and 10 ducks, worked out well with guns and rifles. Played football in the evening. The Russians attacked at night but didn't manage to succeed. They bombed the airfield heavily. Heavy flak was fired.

30.7.41: *SOLDAT* HEINZ SCH. (101 LIGHT DIVISION, SEVENTEENTH ARMY, ARMY GROUP SOUTH)[186]

This time we're staying longer in one spot. It's pretty dangerous, lots of unrest. We were attacked several times by [enemy] aircraft, and so forth. The ambulance drivers were lucky. They got off unscathed, but their vehicles are full of holes! They have to deal with quite a lot. Wounded men arrived throughout the night. I could hardly get any sleep. From 11:00 to 12:00 p.m. I was on guard duty, and then from 2.00 to 4.00 in the morning I guarded the infirmary [*Krankenwache*]. I was on duty in the operating room [until] 5:00 a.m.[187] It is simply dreadful what the men who've already been wounded have to go through again—fingers torn off, a foot removed. That latter case died (and three more as well). There were an awful lot of wounded, about 60 or 70, but I'm not exactly sure how many there were. Two nights ago I couldn't sleep much, because a wounded man couldn't stop his miserable groaning (a bullet through the lungs). And so you never really get any peace around here.

30.7.41: UNKNOWN SOLDIER (5 INFANTRY DIVISION, NINTH ARMY, ARMY GROUP CENTER)[188]

Our division is still in the middle of a heavy attack. The artillery is so far forward that it even has to seek cover from infantry fire. We are to the left of the highway that leads to Moscow. Change of position at midday. We go across the highway and into position on the right of it.

In the meantime, we make a little detour. I inquire whether Smolensk is clear of the enemy and discover that the city has been in German hands for some time already. Smolensk lies another 10 km farther [to the right] of the highway, and it is only a ¼ hour for our vehicle. We are there now, but it is simply not possible to describe how this city looks. It is a very large city, but not a single building is whole anymore. . . . Outside the city lies tank after tank, including German ones. Artillery and planes were deployed in huge numbers here, too. A lot of German blood has been spilled here, as the many graves testify. In the front garden of a larger building lie 60 soldiers of 7./IR 15 (mot.) [of 29 Infantry Division (mot.)].

30.7.41: *OBERGEFREITER* FERDI B. (197 INFANTRY DIVISION, ARMY GROUP GUDERIAN, ARMY GROUP CENTER)[189]

You cannot imagine the war here. Utterly incomparable to France. All towns, most of the villages burned down. The living conditions here, insofar as these "huts" are still standing, are simply catastrophic and completely unimaginable to us.

The advance [*Vormarsch*] continues. The division is now really getting into the battle at the forwardmost line. Until now, we have been endlessly marching hither and thither, around 1,200 km, and have cleared the forests of dispersed enemy troops. From Saturday to Sunday, I had to help outside of Mogilev. There was a dreadful battle raging. [Russian] machine gunners had been buried up to their chests in the earth, with the soil stamped down hard all round so that they couldn't move from the spot. The roads of Mogilev and the burning houses, too, full of the corpses of people and horses. An incredible stench of decay mixed with powder and smoke contaminated the air. The corpses were dreadfully mauled by the effects of our shells. That's where I saw and first came across female soldiers. Do you know the saying from Schiller's "[*Song of the*] *Bell*'?—"Then women to hyenas growing, do make with horror jester's art." We've already seen and experienced a lot in Poland. But what you have to partake in here is indescribable.

We can only overnight in tents here, because there are no houses anymore. The water, which in any case is scarce, is only drinkable once boiled. The half-decayed corpses of people and animals lie in the streams and rivers. Because *der Russe* doesn't bury his fallen. If water is nearby, dead people and animals are thrown in. Or else they are hastily buried in shell craters, so there is an awful stench of putrefaction everywhere, but we've already got used to it. Of course, there's a lot of insects here and all sorts of mosquitoes, so you've got to be careful not to get a bad case of blood poisoning. There are no roads here. Those that are shown on the map[190] are tracks that go right through field and forest and have raw edges to the verge. It's dreadfully dusty in this heat and after a short rainstorm everything is simply swamp and mud, through which our vehicles and motors can only work their way with difficulty. Everywhere, the roads are lined with destroyed tanks, artillery, etc. In the fields and forests everywhere, you come across the remains of shot-down planes.

I am happy to be able to be back with my dear old comrades, that I can be there where so many millions are fighting for the peace and happiness of our dear Fatherland. . . . We should always keep in mind that the *Führer* has called us to this struggle, this great sacrifice and heaviest of duties, for a better and more beautiful future. And the victories and sacrifices made so far, by which I mean the many young, hopeful lives that these victories have demanded of [so many] young Germans, they, most of all, place us under obligation. With these thoughts, we will continue to go our great, heavy, but promising path of destiny [*Schicksalsweg*] as good comrades.

30.7.41: *HAUPTMANN* FRIEDRICH M. (73 INFANTRY DIVISION, ELEVENTH ARMY, ARMY GROUP SOUTH)[191]

At 12 noon we reach our goal and 40 km of marching lie behind us. We find shelter in a brickyard behind the railway station in Tusova (7 km from Bessarabia's capital city Kischinev). . . .[192]

Then a messenger arrives and says that there's an officers' meeting at 5:00 p.m. in Kischinev. I don't have a vehicle yet. I drive with the head of 10th Column. We've soon reached the suburb. We look for the sign of the division's chief of communications, look for it all over town. So, unintentionally, we have the opportunity to see the raging destruction of the Bolsheviks. Kischinev was once a town; up and down the streets it is a picture of grim destruction. The shops burned out, all the floors collapsed, the apartment buildings in utter ruins. The fires had even been set right down into the cellars, and even today, seven days after its capture, we still encounter flames. The Red beasts did a thorough job here. Kischinev no longer stands, it has been more severely destroyed than any artillery or aerial attack could have destroyed or damaged it. Indeed, they didn't even leave the Germans the flowers in the parks; they, too, lie cut down, ripped up and dead in the grass. They had already begun their work of destruction the day before the [town's] capture; they set the buildings alight [and] detonated a large proportion of the public buildings so that they would under no circumstances fall undamaged into our hands. They even poured crude oil onto the streets to light it and so create a wall of fire to impede the German entry [into the town]. The water lines are destroyed and there is a great scarcity of water, the electricity plant has been blown up. Even the white dome of the cathedral shows severe burn marks. Kischinev is just one big pile of rubble [*Trummerhaufen*]. And wherever there's a building still standing, the owner was a Jew who had hoped to hold out through any shooting or bombardment in a well-equipped cellar furnished with every comfort. Now of course they have retreated with the Reds. . . .

We finally find the chief of division supply, and, when all the column leaders are together, the meeting starts. At the end, *Hauptmann* Balz explains the current situation to us and we hear for the first time about the achievements of our advance detachment. . . . On the return journey, we suddenly hear the bells pealing and on the wide, avenue-like road we meet a strange procession. Two men are carrying the image of the Romanian king Michael at the front. The Romanian national colors, the swastika banner, the Italian and Hungarian flags flash out in several places, on all the streets the ruins are lined by men and women, the latter often carrying burning candles. The main procession thus becomes bigger and bigger, whose path leads into a church for the thanksgiving service for the liberation from the yoke of Bolshevism. Never in my life will I forget this procession, these faces, flooded with grief, piety, and grateful joy.

30.7.41: *LEUTNANT* ERNST E. (13 PANZER DIVISION, 1 PANZER GROUP, ARMY GROUP SOUTH)[193]

In the last week, the main opponent on our advance, aside from the Russian, was the weather. The thunderstorms are incredibly violent; they're usually followed by a longer period of rain, which turns the black, fertile humus soil layer into a sticky, deep muck. Trying to make progress on these roads subsequently is almost impossible for wheeled vehicles—even in dry weather there are enough marshy spots—they demand the utmost effort from the panzers' motors. We recently had to sacrifice several valuable days in this manner. *Der Russe* withdrew much better and faster with his many horse-drawn units than we were able to advance.

Yesterday, we got right back on his heels and destroyed some of his rearguard—trucks, as well as horse-drawn vehicles and artillery. We were able to take a lot of prisoners. I am often astounded by the skillful conduct of the enemy rearguard. They plaster our routes of advance using just a few guns in perfectly camouflaged positions. Motorized or drawn by a team of six, they carry out one position change after another and can't be seen by ground observation, to try to apprehend them. As the *Wehrmachtbericht* quite correctly states, you notice that in spite of the strong local resistance there are currently no coherently led and complete units ahead of us.

31.7.41: ADELBERT-OTTHEINRICH RÜHLE (EASTERN FRONT)[194]

We are now on a motorized advance and have longer rest periods. We braise and fry potatoes with scrambled eggs, chickens, cherry soup, *Zuckerei* [a drink similar to eggnog], junket [*dicke Milch*], etc., all day long. Each of us knows something different from home, and so a proper spread is cooked up. I think fried potatoes only really taste good when you've dug up the potatoes yourself and been running around for hours, organizing eggs.[195] I'm sure I've already received a good pretraining to be a bachelor. Otherwise, we rest, even sleep under blankets for the first time in ages when the tarpaulin had to suffice. . . .

How long it goes on like this doesn't matter, it could change again any hour. Then I find my happiness in the feeling of being able to do something for the highest cause that there is for us on earth.

31.7.41: UNKNOWN SOLDIER (5 INFANTRY DIVISION, NINTH ARMY, ARMY GROUP CENTER)[196]

Our battery is in position from 0500 hours. This must have been the worst gun position. It was close to the front line, and bursts of Russian machine-gun fire and rifle bullets whistled out of the forest into our position. From time to time, we were even fired at by tanks. Despite this, everything went well, and we had no losses. We did not advance at all on this day. The Russian tried with all his strength to break through here. They stormed forward in huge numbers, but our infantry mowed them down, and in the night one could hear the loud screaming and groaning of the wounded.

CHAPTER 4

August 1941

Introduction

Facing fierce opposition to the end, Army Group Center did not complete the destruction of the Soviet armies trapped within the Smolensk pocket until 5 August. Once again, the result was a striking success for the Wehrmacht, *including another three hundred thousand prisoners along with thousands of Red Army tanks and guns destroyed or captured. GFM von Bock, in an order of the day to his men, characterized the cauldron battle (Kesselschlacht) as "another brilliant victory [glänzenden Sieg] for German arms and German fulfillment of duty. . . . This deed of yours, too, has become part of history!"[1]*

Meanwhile, in light of Hitler's directive of 30 July 1941 (see Chapter 3, p 56), ordering Army Group Center to halt its advance and assume the defensive, most of the Landser *along Bock's 700-kilometer (435-mile) front had already made the transition to positional warfare (Stellungskrieg), as the main action in the Eastern Campaign now moved to the flanks (sectors of Army Groups North and South).[2] In the weeks that followed, the army group's already weakened divisions conducted an improvised defense—often on unfavorable terrain—with dangerously extended divisional frontages and inexorably declining resources. Given the chronic shortage of combat infantry, the German defenses typically consisted of a string of strong points instead of a continuous front line in depth. Although the Red Army continued its aggressive offensive action, the German positions held firm despite local crises—at times the main battle line (Hauptkampflinie) could only be held by throwing in the final modest reserves—and dreadfully high attrition rates. Contributing to the German losses was the growing presence of Soviet artillery, whose barrages sometimes reminded older German veterans of their experiences in the Great War of 1914–1918.[3] And the bloodletting went on unabated throughout the month. Bock's divisions were, collectively, sustaining some three thousand casualties per day, including about seven hundred dead. Officer losses were alarmingly high, averaging about eighty per day through August 1941. In sum, by 31 August, the army group had suffered roughly 50,000 dead out of approximately 126,000 fatalities across the* Ostheer, *whose total losses (dead, wounded, missing) had climbed to several hundred thousand men. Combat strength of the infantry divisions in the East had plunged on average by 40 percent, that of the panzer units by fully 50 percent.[4]*

During the second week of August 1941, GFM von Leeb's Army Group North resumed its drive on Leningrad with a determined attack on the Luga River line, the city's
outermost defensive position. The offensive was to be supported by a joint Finnish-German
assault across the isthmus of Karelia (annexed by Stalin after Finland's defeat in 1940).
With the Stukas and medium bombers of General der Flieger (Air General) Wolfram
Freiherr von Richthofen's 8 Air Corps—recently transferred from Army Group Center—
providing effective air support, tank units of Hoepner's 4 Panzer Group, despite robust
Soviet resistance, broke out into the open country beyond the river line that lay just 100
kilometers (62 miles) from Leningrad. On 20 August, Leeb's right wing reached Chudovo,
severing the main rail line running southeast from Leningrad to Moscow; on 31 August, the
attackers cut the last rail link from Leningrad to the east at Mga. By now, the lead units of
General der Panzertruppe Rudolf Schmidt's 39 Panzer Corps—also detached from Bock's
army group—were barely twenty-five kilometers (sixteen miles) from the city. The noose
around Leningrad was beginning to tighten.[5]

Desperate to employ every possible armament in the defense of the city, the Soviets
brought the naval guns of the Neva Squadron into action against the Germans on 30
August; many naval guns were removed from their ships and mounted on land, and "even
the gun batteries of the 40-year-old cruiser Aurora, which had fired blanks on the Winter
Palace in November 1917, frightening the remnants of the Provisional Government into
surrendering to the Bolsheviks, were dismounted, and placed in position on the Pulkovo
heights."[6]

In the Ukraine, meanwhile, GFM von Rundstedt's Army Group South had also
been advancing. Following the reduction of the large Soviet pocket at Uman where, by
8 August, Kleist's 1 Panzer Group had destroyed two Soviet armies (over twenty Soviet
divisions) and bagged one hundred thousand prisoners (both army generals were captured),
along with nearly 1,200 guns and tanks, his panzer units pushed on toward Kirovo and
Krivoi Rog—the iron ore center of European Russia—capturing the latter on 14 August.
Exploiting Kleist's success, Rundstedt moved successfully to clear Red Army forces from the
entire western bank of the Dnepr River. By the end of August, the field marshal's infantry
armies and armored forces had put bridgeheads over the river at Cherson, Dnepropetrovsk,
Kremenchug, Cherkassy, and north of Kiev.[7]

While Rundstedt's forces widened their Dnepr bridgeheads, Guderian's 2 Panzer
Group (Army Group Center), had, by 25 August, begun to advance southward with two
panzer corps from positions northeast of Kiev. The dispatch of Guderian's tanks into the
Ukraine meant that five weeks of open conflict between Hitler and his General Staff over
the future direction of operations had finally come to an end. On 21 August, Hitler issued
new orders charting a clear course for the next phase of the campaign. Simply put, the
Führer opined that the "most important objective to be achieved before the onset of winter
is not the capture of Moscow"; rather, it was the occupation of the Crimea, the industry
and coal of the Donbas, and the isolation of the oil regions in the Caucasus, while in the
north Leningrad was to be encircled and a linkup with the Finns accomplished. In the next
paragraph, the document stated that the "uniquely favorable operational situation" resulting from Army Group Center having reached the line Gomel-Pochep was to be immediately exploited by a "concentric operation" involving the inner wings of both Army Groups
Center and South to effect the encirclement of Soviet forces in the area around Kiev. In

point of fact, the positions of the Soviet armies along the line of the Dnepr above and below Kiev were now dangerously exposed, creating a unique opportunity for a cauldron battle of unprecedented scope (a super Cannae) if the panzer forces of the two army groups—one driving north, the other pushing south—could succeed in joining up behind these Soviet armies and severing their line of retreat. The prospect posed an ineluctable opportunity that Hitler was now quick to seize—hence, as a first step, he had sent Guderian's tanks rumbling southward into the Ukraine.[8]

Yet despite the ongoing run of impressive victories across the eastern front, the nagging doubts that, in late July, had begun to assail Hitler and his General Staff as to the prospects for a successful outcome to the Russian campaign had continued to fester. Indeed, the increasingly tenacious and skillful Red Army resistance (including furious counteroffensives), the growing difficulties in supplying armies now hundreds of kilometers inside Soviet Russia, and the increasingly apparent shortcomings of a Barbarossa *force structure that simply lacked the resources—human and matériel—to meet its far-flung and burgeoning objectives, had, by early August 1941, only compounded the frustration and anxiety felt by the German dictator and his generals as they struggled to find a way to set their eastern armies on a path to victory.*

The climate of crisis that now enveloped the Army High Command's Mauerwald compound (just outside Hitler's East Prussian headquarters) was the subject of an alarming letter from Oberstleutnant *Hellmuth Stieff* *to his wife on 12 August:*

> *Sweetheart, you complain—and no doubt rightly so—that I write so little. But I am simply not in the mood for writing. This campaign is so utterly different [so ganz anders] to all the previous ones. A kind of tenseness and nervousness like never before hangs over all of us, such that you want to avoid everyone if you possibly can. It may in part have to do with the length of the war, which everyone is more than sick of. But the main thing is probably the oppressive feeling that, despite all the seemingly lovely successes, we're in the middle of a very acute crisis of which outsiders are, of course, unaware. The time up to the start of winter (start of October) is really preying on our minds, and we haven't yet achieved even half of what we need to in order not to end up in a war on two fronts.[10]*

Letters and Diary Entries (1–31 August 1941)

8.41 (EXACT DATE UNKNOWN): *MAJOR* S. (20 PANZER DIVISION, 3 PANZER GROUP, ARMY GROUP CENTER)[11]

The [peasant] houses are all built from tree trunks and, as a rule, contain one or two rooms. They all have a huge brick oven, which serves for both cooking and for heating. . . . There are not usually beds or cots. The family sleeps on benches, which are grouped round the big oven at night. Sheep skins, more or less infested with lice, serve as blankets. There is no cutlery or plates, a wooden spoon must suffice, they eat straight from the cooking pot. By way of furniture, there is a crudely constructed table, and that is all. Some cut-out pictures from newspapers might be stuck to the walls; that's the only interior décor. They are poor, unfortunate people, these Soviet villagers.

Their fields are usually as pitiful as they are miserably dressed. A consequence of the *Kolkhoz* economy [*Kolchoswirtschaft*].[12]

Our *Landser* are deeply sympathetic to these unfortunate and lowly peasant farmers. They think with gratitude about their own culture, their home, Germany. Nobody takes even the slightest thing from these unfortunates. Anytime an exchange is made for an egg, a cucumber, a tomato, or similar, the little Soviet peasant is always the one to get the better deal.

Seen as a whole, the people give an apathetic, joyless impression. After their bad experiences with the Soviet practices and their very dubious blessings, even the current war can no longer shock them.

1.8.41: FRITZ BELKE (6 INFANTRY DIVISION, NINTH ARMY, ARMY GROUP CENTER)[13]

Preparation of defensive positions is ordered. Construction of a HKL. . . .[14] We are confronted with this term, and with this activity, for the first time since the start of the campaign. We dig our foxhole in the hard, arid ground until late on into the night. Not funny, what is this all about? Ivan is finished, isn't he, the war is won!

The HKL: The length of the front to be covered by the company is determined. Contact with our neighbors on the right and left is secured, the infantry squads are allocated their sectors. Next, every rifleman digs his foxhole, then crawl trenches are dug from hole to hole, and these are quickly expanded into communication trenches. A trench system under construction. For an infantryman, the digging never stops. The gun pits are refined. Machine gun emplacements are expanded.

1.8.41: UNKNOWN SOLDIER (5 INFANTRY DIVISION, NINTH ARMY, ARMY GROUP CENTER)[15]

The next morning, a strong attack was mounted. Stukas and destroyer aircraft intervened in the battle on the ground. The Russians had to fall back in haste, and we made good forward progress. A large number of Russians beat a path into captivity. Women and civilians are constantly among them. In the evening, change of position.[16]

1.8.41: ALBERT NEUHAUS (ARMY GROUP NORTH)[17]

The noise of battle has subsided, only now and then in our sector is a shot fired. It seems to be the calm before the storm. Come what may, victory will be ours.

Today at noon our Major came by and expressed his recognition for the work we'd accomplished. He presented the wound badge [*Verwundetenabzeichen*] to an officer whose eardrums were burst by the air pressure of an exploding shell. This *Leutnant* had incredible luck; the shell exploded just 1 meter from his foxhole. Otherwise we still have nothing to complain about in our battery, and we hope that our luck will continue fair.

1.8.41: *SOLDAT* RUDOLF L. (EASTERN FRONT)[18]

There is no radio [in Russia] in our sense of it. There's just reception across a common network. Then the individual just has a loudspeaker. That means that everyone can only listen to the Moscow programming.

This is the only way to explain the incredible incitement [*Verhetzung*] and transformation of the people—even during peacetime. I even found schoolbooks that were nothing less than inflammatory texts against Germany. I will bring one back as documentary evidence. Some of the [Russian] soldiers were of the firm conviction that the Germans would make no prisoners. That explains the frequently extraordinary and useless resistance of encircled groups.

So overall, the Russian fights very tenaciously. We even experienced that on the Stalin line. His artillery, for example, can only be given a good report. The brutality that *der Russe* repeatedly exhibits, however, can only be explained by the incitement. This is a people that will need a long and good education process to become human. The character and nature of the Russians belong more to the Middle Ages than to the modern age. That's also why it isn't enough to give the Russian masses modern machines to fly and sophisticated tanks. They wouldn't know what to do with all that. The fields of wrecked tanks demonstrate that.

That's what it's like here. A landscape which is surely beautiful in peacetime, but which has too little useable water. In wartime dust, smoking buildings, scenes of destruction, dead horses and many refugees are added to this. And a scorching heat to top it all. No cultural things, no possibility of going shopping or stopping at an inn, or even of having film developed. Everything appears dreary and poor in our eyes. And this was supposed to be a paradise of the proletariat.

1–2.8.41: *LEUTNANT* RUDOLF MAURER (251 INFANTRY DIVISION, NINTH ARMY, ARMY GROUP CENTER)[19]

1.8. Up until today we were resting. Early in the morning we moved out and reached a point south of Velikie Luki. Once again it was a miserable drive through the darkness. In the morning, at dawn, I read Irene's birthday letter, which I have carried with me for days. *Der Russe* shelled us with artillery—a lovely start to my birthday. And the shelling only got worse in the evening. It was quite horrible [*Es ist ganz scheusslich*].

2.8. We couldn't catch a break the entire day. Artillery fire from morning to night. We crouched in the foxholes we had dug and waited, knowing a shell could strike us at any moment. That really strains the nerves. Toward evening there was also a Russian bombing attack. The wailing of the aircraft engines and the bombs still ring in my ears. Because of the artillery fire our infantry can make no further progress and takes evasive measures. The regiments are in disorder.[20]

1–7.8.41: *STABSFELDWEBEL* HELMUTH A. DITTRI (20 PANZER DIVISION, 3 PANZER GROUP, ARMY GROUP CENTER)[21]

1.8. Strong Russian artillery fire.

2.8. Strong Russian artillery fire.

5.8. Russian artillery fire.

7.8. We rejoined the remnants of our detachment located at our initial position a few miles behind our company. We were supposed to be relieved but we could not leave the spot as the Russians were sweeping the whole road with their blasted artillery.[22]

2.8.41: *OBERGEFREITER* HEINZ B. (23 INFANTRY DIVISION, ARMY GROUP GUDERIAN, ARMY GROUP CENTER)[23]

So we've survived that, too—our fourth attack in the East.[24] But this time it went badly for our company, which had 21 dead and wounded on the first day. My platoon is now short 25 men. One of the medical *Feldwebels*, whom I've already told you about, is wounded. Horrific scenes: Men without arms, legs, men with head shots, shots through the brain and chest.

I perform my work quite automatically now: dress the wounds; if there's no more purpose to it—identification tag, grave.

2.8.41: *GEFREITER* HEINZ B. (291 INFANTRY DIVISION, EIGHTEENTH ARMY, ARMY GROUP NORTH)[25]

Quite suddenly we were—and by that I mean our company [3./Pz.Jäg.Abt.291][26]—pulled out of the battalion and division and assigned to another division in another sector of the front. Nothing special has really taken place in the past few days. *Der Russe* is stuck in several cauldrons [*Kesseln*] that are now being systematically eliminated. Of course, that all takes time, and is made much more difficult by the immense forests, in which it's very easy to hide. So even though you believe they've all been cleared of the enemy, it's possible that enemy hordes will eventually emerge from these same forests. Because that's actually occurred, I believe it's best not to continue the advance until it's quite plain that all [the forested area] is clear of the enemy.

2.8.41: UNKNOWN SOLDIER (5 INFANTRY DIVISION, NINTH ARMY, ARMY GROUP CENTER)[27]

I do not want to describe in any more detail the images to be seen here on the battlefields and on the roads, because it is neither believable nor imaginable for somebody who has not seen or experienced it for themselves. Only now have we seen what a human being signifies. They lie around, in countless numbers. Body parts are torn away; some were only wounded, but then bled out as they dragged themselves forward a few meters in pools of their own blood. Others in turn are burned and charred. Horses are mutilated and full of holes, motor vehicles and tanks are burned down to their iron shells. With time, you get used to all these scenes; but the smell is unbearable and has such a powerful effect that one often has to put off meals.

2.8.41: *UNTEROFFIZIER* HEINZ B. (125 INFANTRY DIVISION, SEVENTEENTH ARMY, ARMY GROUP SOUTH)[28]

Nothing really new to report here, only that the fighting is pretty hard and bloody. Our division has already had to pay with its blood on many occasions, and we've now had the first fatality in our battery. One of our comrades, also an *Unteroffizier*, lost his life under tragic circumstances. . . . Otherwise things are moving along quite well, and the end won't be long in coming. The Russians are tough and treacherous, but that won't be enough to stop the German Army. The difficulties that have to be overcome here are enormous, but we always manage them. . . .

I can only say that the German people can never thank our magnificent *Führer* enough for all that he's done for Germany and, to be sure, for Europe. These beasts we're facing here have nothing at all to do with civilization. Whenever they get hold of German soldiers they murder them, smash in the heads of wounded soldiers, and other such things. If these hordes with their base instincts were ever to occupy our glorious cities - - - - - So, up and at the enemy!

3.8.41: *UNTEROFFIZIER* KARL SCHÖNFELD (ARMY GROUP CENTER)[29]

The *Kessel* at Smolensk is getting ever smaller, and for the Russians trapped there the situation is getting worse by the hour. This can be seen in the attacks up to Saturday morning, which 1st Company repelled. *Der Russe* wants to cross the Dnepr and is throwing everything at it in an effort to establish a crossing point as an exit out of the *Kessel*. But artillery and Stukas are ensuring the contrary. In the late afternoon another attack. Nighttime Russian raid [*Überfall*] on the Pak (Heiss fallen).

3.8.41: KARL FUCHS (7 PANZER DIVISION, 3 PANZER GROUP, ARMY GROUP CENTER)[30]

I've got some kind of rash. I'm continually scratching my entire body. That's how bad it is. I'm blaming the Russian drinking water for it. The water is hardly good enough to wash with, so I guess I really shouldn't drink it.[31] I can only tell you to be glad that you folks back home don't have to look at this "blessed" Soviet Russia. These scoundrels have been dropping idiotic pamphlets from their airplanes, asking us to surrender our arms and defect to their side. It really is laughable since those bums on the other side surely know that their time is up. All you have to do is look at the

Russian prisoners. Hardly ever do you see the face of a person who seems rational and intelligent. They all look emaciated and the wild, half-crazy look in their eyes makes them appear like imbeciles. And these scoundrels, led by Jews and criminals, want to imprint their stamp on Europe, indeed on the world. Thank God that our *Führer*, Adolf Hitler, is preventing this from happening! We're all of the opinion that it is merely a matter of weeks before these Russians will have to give up. Once they do, England will fall as well.

3.8.41: FRITZ KÖHLER (ARMY GROUP GUDERIAN, ARMY GROUP CENTER)[32]

The start of the attack has been set for 0630 hours, and thus we go forward at that time.[33] We advance along a broad front, a multitude of heavy weapons follows us. After about an hour, we receive the first rifle fire, and a Russian artillery piece has already taken us under direct fire. Our artillery responds, and once our heavy infantry weapons have also joined in, the Russian gun is soon reduced to silence. But one of our panzers also comes to grief and is shot up in flames. We push further forward and take around 150 Russians prisoner. In addition, we capture 12 to 15 modern flak guns (probably of American manufacture). . . . In the meantime, we have reached the edge of Roslavl'. White Very signal lights [*weisse Leuchtkugeln*] are flaring up to the right and left. Panzers and motorcycle riflemen have most likely already pushed into the enemy's flanks. We do not even experience any resistance and clean out the town. We find only isolated, scattered Russians. However, the Russians have set fire to the oil and gasoline supplies before they fled. Unfortunately, there is almost nothing to "organize" in this town. That sort of thing was better in France.

3.8.41: DR. ADOLF B. (25 INFANTRY DIVISION [MOT.], 1 PANZER GROUP, ARMY GROUP SOUTH)[34]

We would all be delighted if this Russia war could be victoriously concluded soon. The Russian is not capable of presenting truly serious resistance anywhere anymore—never mind staging an offensive somewhere! He is far too weakened for that and there can be no more talk of a unified strategic leadership among the Reds!

If only the weather would get better, dryer again soon, so that the advance can be continued to completion! Last night it rained like a deluge and that's very bad for our vehicles. We can't get out of the wet ground, which often has a 20- to 30-centimeter-deep mud and clay foundation. Sometimes we get stuck and occasionally even have to get ourselves towed out.

Der Russe would have been finished long ago if he hadn't been able to deploy these masses of people! But there will come a day, and a not too distant one, when we will be able to raise our victory flag over the Red plague. I hope the time for that is ripe by the end of August!

3.8.41: DR. HEINRICH HAAPE (6 INFANTRY DIVISION, NINTH ARMY, ARMY GROUP CENTER)[35]

I have never been so close to death as I was this morning at 0745. Except for a small shrapnel injury to my nose, which is so insignificant I didn't even need to bandage it, I was unhurt. It has been awful in the last few days [*Es war furchtbar in den letzten Tagen*], so awful that I don't want to speak of it. What should I say? A few brief words.

On 2 [August], after bloody combat in the evening, we had beaten back the Russians, who had broken through with strong forces.[36] The next morning we received heavy shell fire. I was with 10 people at the battalion command post. A shell struck 12 meters away from me; there were casualties. I called Dehorn, my orderly; we both got up, then a 2nd shell crashed into the ground 5 meters away from me. I was thrown to the ground by the immense air pressure. There were whimpering and screams all round me. After quickly regaining my composure, I immediately started to provide medical support for the soldiers and I found the following situation:

Dehorn's chest was torn open and his skull smashed, his brain lying next to his head (immediately dead). *Leutnant* Jakobi was lying with shrapnel lodged in his chest, shrapnel through the stomach, a shattered right knee, and his left foot was as good as shot off. He lived 1 hour longer and died. Both the legs of my driver, who was lying next to me, were smashed. Four others [were] severely wounded and one casualty with minor injuries. . . .

We are in the midst of a struggle of the utmost severity; we must not allow ourselves to harbor any delusions about this, whatever the magnitude of our successes. The days are filled with martial events that can only be endured with healthy nerves and the utmost commitment of all physical and psychological energies. The theater of war is sober, dirty, prosaic, and the enemy facing us of an Asiatic brutality and tenacity; it is war in its most terrible, archetypal form.

Yet the way in which the German soldier will fight this war, in which the leadership will surmount the unprecedented breadth of this theater of war with world-historical, unique operations and drive the enemy to its final destruction, that is surely the most phenomenal heroic drama, of such great dimensions, that the history of the war has to show to date.

3.8.41: *LEUTNANT* WILLIBALD G. (57 INFANTRY DIVISION, 1 PANZER GROUP, ARMY GROUP SOUTH)[37]

I am sitting on the cellar steps of a ruined and half-burned-out building and writing you all a few lines again. Outside, it has now been raining torrentially without interruption for several hours and we can't continue marching because the Reds have blown up yet another bridge. For 4 days now we've been on the march to a new operation. We're heading north now and we're already quite close to Kiev. These forced marches are very grueling [*aufreibend*] and I would much rather we were in position somewhere and at the enemy. At least then you don't have those pressing daily worries, like now, on the march. Right now we're marching through a rear area [*Etappengebiet*] that has been completely cleaned out of food. So now we have the daily worry of how to make sure 150 stomachs are full. There's no resupply coming from home and there's nothing here. The little that the Reds left behind was used up long ago. We haven't had any sugar for a long time. There's only Russian acorn coffee, which tastes revolting when unsweetened.

This would all be bearable. We always find a way. But the worst thing is that we have no oats for the horses. Their daily march performances are huge and now they are collapsing. Horses are falling by the wayside through exhaustion every day. How are the heavy artillery pieces and munitions vehicles to be brought forward now? The Russian *panje* horses[38] can't do it, and we don't want to leave army vehicles behind. These are the concerns of the officer, things about which the [ordinary soldier] doesn't worry his head, but which become more pressing on a daily basis. You really can't compare this war with any other!

4.8.41: *OBERGEFREITER* WERNER E. (73 INFANTRY DIVISION, ELEVENTH ARMY, ARMY GROUP SOUTH)[39]

Despite our hopes that we'd be transferred into the Reich and sent on leave, we're now in action in the East. Somewhere, on this very long front, we're doing our duty, proud of the fact that we're also taking part in this campaign against Bolshevism. So far, we haven't suffered any casualties,[40] despite being shelled by artillery and undergoing aerial attacks. Of course, others have given their lives here in the East, but the rumors, which are apparently circulating throughout the Reich, of enormous losses are all just a pack of lies. Of course the Russians have also dropped propaganda leaflets on us! They seem to think we're either awfully bad or stupid! The *Russkis* here will soon be finished off, and then we'll be marching and marching once again.

5.8.41: *GEFREITER* GU. (11 PANZER DIVISION, 1 PANZER GROUP, ARMY GROUP SOUTH)[41]

We come to a halt in a village. Two thousand prisoners pass by on the road like a mob of criminals [*Verbrecherhorden*]. And then more than 1,000 prisoners, among them female partisans [*Flintenweiber*] and adolescents. They bring their wounded along on *Panje* wagons; they also bring their own artillery back with them. Yesterday in the Uman *Kessel* (our sector) Cossacks put in an attack and were shot to pieces by our flak. Stukas are attacking in waves and destroying the encircled enemy. The number of prisoners is increasing constantly. Our flak downed a Russian reconnaissance aircraft, which disappeared in flames into the distance. The battle of annihilation [*Vernichtungsschlacht*] goes on throughout the night.

5.8.41: *SOLDAT* ALFRED V. (36 INFANTRY DIVISION [MOT.], 4 PANZER GROUP, ARMY GROUP NORTH)[42]

At the start, when the advance was going at such a furious pace, we all thought it would pass off quickly, and even I figured that by now we'd have been in B. for some time. But our commanders have slowed our progress for good reasons. . . . So now we wait until it all begins again, and we can get on with business like before. The kilometers will again rule our senses—woods, settlements, swamps and sand, bad roads, and so forth, will all pass before our eyes.

The culture of Bolshevism is quite evident in this country. We will see poverty and privation just as before. . . . So far I've seen a couple of churches, magnificent on the outside. At least you could see their earlier splendor. You could tell that they weren't being used because grass was growing all along the crevices of the steps and everywhere. In one corner there was <u>rusty</u> farm equipment from the collective; no pews inside, all the [religious] images shattered, the altar gone. In most cases there was no church bell; both the exterior and the interior plasterwork was crumbling away. And they're practically the only structures in larger settlements that are made of stone. That's Bolshevism. How different things are at home.

5.8.41: *OBERGEFREITER* MATTHIAS (6 INFANTRY DIVISION, NINTH ARMY, ARMY GROUP CENTER)[43]

I am dreadfully shaken. In 1st Platoon we now have only 25 men instead of 40. . . . We have lost the best comrades. In the meantime our patrols have found 11 of the missing comrades, all vilely mauled by the Soviets and killed by shots to the head. They were buried. We dug them up again and interred them with proper military honors. The [Catholic] divisional priest held a speech. It was very sad for us. . . . Now only 6 comrades are missing and they have probably fallen into captivity. According to statements by the local populace, the Soviets took them away in chains.

Yes, that is war! When the *Hauptfeldwebel* fell I was right next to him. Along with our medical NCO, I tried to bandage him up, but the Russians, who were armed with American-manufactured magazine-fed carbines, were already within 15–20 meters of us. We were the last of the company. If there had been no scrubland, it would have been too late. While the bullets whistled by and over me, I collapsed 5 or 6 times, but always pulled myself together with the thought: "You must not fall into the hands of the Russians!" A happy fate preserved me from that! I am grateful to my maker. . . .[44]

Today we heard the special report [*Sondermeldung*] about Smolensk. It's wonderful! Hopefully the advance will continue soon!

5.8.41: DR. HANS LIEROW (6 INFANTRY DIVISION, NINTH ARMY, ARMY GROUP CENTER)[45]

We are lying close to the Schutsche Lake and are waiting on our deployment. The cornfields are ripe, the ears of rye are already shedding their grains. The harvesters will be organized from tomorrow morning. It would be a scandal if the harvest were to spoil. The meadows are blooming so magnificently, the clover a summery violet, the daisies white, the cornflowers blue, and the hemp a delicate, fragrant blue. The whole sunny day the air hums with the sound of busy bees. . . .

A couple of [Russian] planes come during the night already. But they are only dropping very stupid propaganda leaflets, which cause nothing but hearty laughter among our soldiers. . . .

There is a lot of time to think about all sorts of things. So I do that and think about my past, my marriage, think about Gisela and the good fortune of having children.

5.8.41: *MAJOR* HANS MEIER-WELCKER (251 INFANTRY DIVISION, NINTH ARMY, ARMY GROUP CENTER)[46]

Once again we're not moving but conducting a war of position [*Stellungskrieg*], reminiscent of 1914/18. The Russian artillery is very active, shelling our positions and approach routes, anywhere they see movement or just dust rising. Russian aircraft appear early in the morning, around midday, and in the evening, dropping bombs and making low-level attacks with their aircraft armament. At night, the Russian infantry conduct aggressive patrols against our positions. The Russians are masters at exploiting the terrain, especially in the defense.

In addition, our infantry have been subjected to such heavy artillery fire by the Russians, that our troop commanders (World War I veterans) are saying that, during World War I, they hardly ever experienced such heavy fire during an *attack*, because back then you didn't attack before the enemy artillery had been effectively neutralized. But it wasn't possible to do this on 2.8., because the conditions for our observers were extremely unfavorable and our own artillery much too weak.

6.8.41: *SOLDAT* J.Z. (REGIONAL DEFENSE BATTALION [*LANDESSCHÜTZEN-BATAILLON*] 619, EASTERN FRONT)[47]

On Sunday we took in the city. The conditions that exist here you wouldn't find in any city in Germany. I can't describe to you what the Jewish quarters looks like, because you wouldn't believe it. Images of Jews, like those that have already appeared in *Stürmer*,[48] you can see here in the flesh [*in natura*] in droves. Dozens and dozens of them, draped in rags, which are mostly in tatters, roam about here. Those of us from the area around Main don't really have a clear understanding of Judaism. But here in the East you only need to look at the fellows and you know what kind of scoundrels you're dealing with, even without speaking to them. But a true German would hardly deign to speak to such rabble.

6.8.41: ALBERT NEUHAUS (ARMY GROUP NORTH)[49]

For the past two days it's been rather quiet on our side, but *der Russe* is still firing at us desperately, and yesterday really unloaded on our position. Like little mice we huddle in the trenches that we've dug. Yesterday a shell landed barely 3 meters from our commander's nose, but he was unscathed. The silence of our guns seems to be the great calm before the storm. . . .[50]

We've just got the *Sondermeldungen* about the dissolution and destruction of various cauldrons. The numbers are quite incredible. Almost a million prisoners and huge numbers of tanks, aircraft and guns.[51] If that continues, then the end will come quickly. We're all clinging to the thoughts of "stop it or end it," because we're really fed up with this shit. I really admire the veterans of the World War, who had to go through this hokum for four years.

6.8.41: *LUFTWAFFE* BOMBER CREW MEMBER (55 BOMBER WING [*KAMPFGESCHWADER 55*], CENTRAL FRONT)[52]

Just as we are flying along the edge of the Moscow cauldron, still rather hazy with cloud, dozens of powerful light sources flare up down below. Searchlights spin the Red capital into a gigantic net intended to ensnare our He 111. For several seconds, the white light, after restless searching, licks the belly of the bomber, but is unable to hang on to it.

The Red gunners put up an iron curtain barricade [*eisernen Sperrvorhang*] from a multitude of flak barrels. No matter! We penetrate it!

Now we are above the city precincts. Moscow has already received heavy blows. Three large fields of fire are the result of the first contingent of high-explosive and incendiary bombs that are to fall in their tens of thousands over the course of the night.

In one of these fields, eight large fires are raging. That was where the first heavy-caliber bombs struck. Direct hit to the center of the aircraft industry and to the support firms.

We can orientate ourselves well by the two large loops of the Moskva River, which comes from the southwest and reaches right up to the edge of the city. We now know where the Kremlin is.

So we circle, see barrage balloons like big, black ghost creatures swooping past us, lightning fast, observe the impact of incendiary and high-explosive bombs from other bomber aircraft in the air space above Moscow, until *Oberleutnant* Mylius has his target directly in his sights. Now our heavy bomb is also falling and the incendiary bombs follow immediately afterward, causing new destruction.

We turn back on a homeward course, but have to break through the heavy flak curtain again, which is directed at us, or perhaps even at the next wave of bombers.

7.8.41: *PANZER-OBERSCHÜTZE* ERICH HAGER (17 PANZER DIVISION, ARMY GROUP GUDERIAN, ARMY GROUP CENTER)[53]

Thursday. Go by car to the workshop 30 km back. The dust would have driven you mad! All day foot soldiers go forward, lots of them. In the workshops we have four Pz [IVs] that will be ready in a few days. Russian planes visit us again. Two of them were driven away by our fighter pilots. Grün is back from Warsaw, brought a lot of things with him. Today there are fried potatoes.

In the afternoon I go foraging. Get a calf. Also go swimming, drive on my own with an Opel [make of vehicle, probably the Opel "Blitz" 4×2 cargo truck]. There's mail again today, also for me. Thank God the battle for Smolensk is over. Some pals were attacked by armed civilians when they went to fetch water.

7.8.41: *LEUTNANT* RUDOLF MAURER (251 INFANTRY DIVISION, NINTH ARMY, ARMY GROUP CENTER)[54]

The *Sondermeldungen* from the OKW, which were released yesterday and spread through our ranks like a wildfire, have lifted our hopes that the campaign in the East will indeed come to an end in the near future. May God grant it. The Russian forces that are presently facing us are suffering from hunger. They had immediately confiscated and devoured the bread of a German soldier they had taken prisoner from the neighboring regiment; he managed to make his escape during a Stuka attack. On the other hand, it's an extraordinary achievement that we're getting our rations daily, and don't need to suffer from hunger. That's quite astonishing considering the bad roads and the enormous extent of the front.

8.8.41: *SOLDAT* HEINZ SCH. (101 LIGHT DIVISION, SEVENTEENTH ARMY, ARMY GROUP SOUTH)[55]

At the moment we're on alert [*Alarmbereitstellung*]. The Russians are basically encircled and the front is on two sides. Three days ago we were awakened at 2.00 in the morning. Fortunately, during the initial advance, we had nothing to fear; now we've been on this encirclement ring for three days.[56] We're taking prisoners every day. Yesterday we took 300 Russians prisoner, but 50 of them escaped because we were short of men [to guard them]. And how emaciated they are! The local inhabitants come and bring them food, and they're on it like animals. We're getting really deep in the muck, digging potatoes and beans out of the ground.

Our 101 Division is really run down [*schwer abgespannt*] and in need of relief. We're always being told that we're going to be relieved, but nothing happens.

Everything went much more rapidly in France. But Russia, this despicable place, is just so dreadfully large. I believe we'll still make it down to the Black Sea.

8.8.41: *UNTEROFFIZIER* HEINZ B. (125 INFANTRY DIVISION, SEVENTEENTH ARMY, ARMY GROUP SOUTH)[57]

My thoughts are always with you, and especially now, since I've heard on the radio that Karlsruhe was badly bombed by the English. I'm hoping that my worries are unfounded. I can't begin to imagine what I'd do if something happened to you. Let's just hope that all is okay.

Here in the Ukraine the battle is also nearing its end. Enormous numbers of prisoners pass by us each day. This morning we've already counted 9,000, and so it goes day after day. On the 6th we heard the tremendous *Sondermeldungen*. Only when you're in the middle of it all can you accurately gauge what those colossal figures really mean. *Der Russe* won't be able to go on much longer because his losses are irreplaceable.

8.8.41: *LEUTNANT* RUDOLF MAURER (251 INFANTRY DIVISION, NINTH ARMY, ARMY GROUP CENTER)[58]

The following entertaining experience of our Division Pastor Ufer during the first days of fighting near Newel[59] was making the rounds: Lying in a foxhole together with the judge advocate, the pair suddenly found themselves confronted with a Russian, who was followed by another 12. The startled judge advocate drew his defective pistol and the unarmed pastor his tobacco pipe, both aimed these weapons at the Russians and yelled, "Stoi!" The perplexed Russians surrendered and—with the pastor at the front and the judge advocate at the rear of this troupe of prisoners—were led off to [our] soldiers then hurrying up—surely a unique occurrence. But this example also shows that our enemies were not yet properly "set" for war. By contrast, the Soviets can obviously handle propaganda very well, because we are "informed" via dropped leaflets about the war situation and about our ammunition and supply shortages and encouraged to defect. In the evening, we advance and relieve our 471 IR. It's pouring rain. The holes in which we shelter are quickly full of water.

8.8.41: *LEUTNANT* WILLIBALD G. (57 INFANTRY DIVISION, 1 PANZER GROUP, ARMY GROUP SOUTH)[60]

We have been moving hither and thither for over a week now. We feel almost like a "flying division," even if we're not "flying" all that far. 30–40 km daily march is quite enough for us to keep the level of our equine losses within bearable margins. We haven't fired a single shot for 3 weeks and we'd think we were on maneuvers if it weren't for the Soviet air force providing some well-timed variety. We were attacked four times yesterday alone! Three times by 18 heavy bombers and once by 6 light biplanes, which are particularly vile [*ekelhaft*], because they drop so-called chain bombs [*Kettenbomben*]. They're bombs that are hung together in large numbers on a long chain and explode like they're being dragged on a string. Where must these fellows have got those aircraft? I think they're staking everything on one card and I'm convinced that, of the aircraft that attacked yesterday, very few are still operational today. Thanks to our tactic of dismounting straight away, leaping into the ditches by the road, and keeping the horses on a long rein, nothing has happened. Just that sometimes horses are lost and some of our vehicles have been pretty much shot full of holes. . . .

The *Sondermeldungen* from the day before yesterday were fantastic and they did us, who sometimes lose sight of the big issues amid the trifles of our daily worries, a lot of good. . . .

The Russian soldiers are strange people! In the campaigns before this, the troops always surrendered when they were hopelessly surrounded [*aussichtslos eingekreist*]. Here, they often fight to the last round of ammunition and to the last man! Even when it is entirely hopeless. Hence the Reds' vast losses. . . . A quick end [to this]!

9.8.41: *MAJOR* HANS MEIER-WELCKER (251 INFANTRY DIVISION, NINTH ARMY, ARMY GROUP CENTER)[61]

It's been raining for days. The rain batters against our tent. The storm is so intense that our tent is ballooning out and it's tearing at the pegs and the rope. But that doesn't bother you when you're sleeping. What's more uncomfortable is that the ground gets wetter and wetter. The moisture in the air makes all of our clothing and equipment quite cold and damp. We're eating our meals in a barn and the rain drips onto our utensils. The roads are in really bad shape and the motorcycle messengers [*Kradmelder*] can hardly get through. You can't get anywhere at all with a typical passenger car. The East is *beginning* to show its true face.

9.8.41: *LEUTNANT* ERNST E. (13 PANZER DIVISION, 1 PANZER GROUP, ARMY GROUP SOUTH)[62]

At the moment, my unit is 15 kilometers from the Dnepr.[63] During the past few weeks we haven't taken part in any significant action, but once we're beyond the Dnepr that will most likely change. In the area where we're currently stationed, the Russian administrative agencies [*Verwaltungsorgane*] are trying to get all the tractors, with the large harvester combines, and the herds of livestock across the Dnepr. But they don't seem to be succeeding with their plan the way they want, because all day yesterday we encountered long tractor columns with the harvesting machines and countless livestock—in each case hundreds of cattle—that were moving back into their original areas. I always find such scenes to be quite comforting, because it all helps to expand and secure the basis of the German food supply [*Ernährungsgrundlage*].

9.8.41: SIEGBERT STEHMANN (163 INFANTRY DIVISION, GERMAN ARMY OF NORWAY)[64]

For the last two weeks my five men and I have been lying in the primeval forest at the edge of a narrow swamp, eye to eye with the Russians. Beyond the swamp, so ca. 75–100 meters in front of us, *der Russe* has numerous bunkers in the forest. We can see him working, setting up posts, etc., and always have to be on our guard in case he comes visiting at night or in the fog; because he is numerically and materially enormously superior to us. Here in East Karelia, August is not a part of summer at all. It is cold and stormy, and it's been raining continuously for weeks. We're hunkered down, unprotected against shells and bullets and wretchedly poorly provisioned, cramped in a small tent. The swampy mossy ground is oozing wet, the shelter half has been leaky for some time, clothes are wet. And if, as happens at least once a day, the shells come screaming across from over there and crash all around us in a hellish roar, then you rather lose the desire to reach for a pencil. You reach for your steel helmet, pistol, and hand grenades, and lie down like a corpse in a wet ditch to protect yourself from the shrapnel. Yes, that's what it's like at the front. And yet, after the two assaults [*Sturmangriffen*], it all appears almost peaceful to us.

I am so grateful that I am still uninjured and healthy in body and soul, sitting in my tent, where I have your pictures and letters with me. How much can a person bear?! Had I ever been able to imagine that I could bear something like this for long? . . . In the winter, the temperature here is -50 to -51° [centigrade]. But the campaign with Russia can't go on for that much longer. Even the close of the summer is so lacking in all beauty here that you fervently wish for the end of war. You can only bear this country in the south and in the west, but not in the awful swamp and jungle of Karelia, between Lake Ladoga and Lake Onega. And, because of the war of position that's been going on for 14 days already, we're still 150–200 km away from our goal: Petrosawodsk near Lake Onega. Now we're sitting across from each other ca. 30 km from the old Russian border.

9/10.8.41: *LEUTNANT* RUDOLF MAURER (251 INFANTRY DIVISION, NINTH ARMY, ARMY GROUP CENTER)[65]

Several times each day *der Russe* shoots harassing fire with artillery and machine guns. When that happens we all disappear at once into our foxholes. The enemy fire has a major impact on morale. Late in the evening I go out to our positions right at the front. *Der Russe* is going to attack tomorrow. The ride is like a ghost ride [*Gespensterfahrt*].

10.8.41: *GEFREITER* RUDOLF STÜTZEL (5 INFANTRY DIVISION, NINTH ARMY, ARMY GROUP CENTER)[66]

During the cauldron of Smolensk, we spent a full week under the heaviest Russian artillery fire, the like of which had not yet been seen in this campaign. A field of 200 square meters was literally plowed up, the losses were also commensurate with that, although each one of us had dug his own foxhole. Often, it was simply no longer possible to bring food forward. Then there were also several tank assaults every day. Our company alone shot up 14 tanks during these assaults, some of them the heaviest tanks. My motorcycle was smashed by a tank shell during one such assault. Since then I've made do with all sorts of motorcycles, [but] since yesterday I have none at all.

A week ago now, we spent two days in infantry battles, assigned to an infantry regiment, deployed in the assault. The Russians really do fight until they collapse. Of course, they all think that there is no such thing as captivity with us. The majority shoot themselves when they see that there is no way out. That explains the prolonged sniper war [*Heckenschützenkrieg*] as well, because each of them defends himself to the last. All means are justified to him in fighting against his opponent. He frequently makes use of dreadful atrocities [*furchtbare Grausamkeiten*], although here not to the same degree as during [our] crossing of the border and in the first 14 days, when, in the main, we were having to do with Asiatic troops, who were capable of any atrocity. And in response, we no longer gave any quarter. We received the order to cease taking any prisoners. Of course, that's no longer the case, as it would be impossible.

Today we're once more at the ready and don't know when we'll get into battle, perhaps to the last battle, the strike against Moscow.

10.8.41: DR. ADOLF B. (25 INFANTRY DIVISION [MOT.], 1 PANZER GROUP, ARMY GROUP SOUTH)[67]

Today, Sunday morning, we had camp service [*Feldgottesdienst*] in the middle of a small wood. Shortly before and afterward, Red planes circled over us; these Red machines repeatedly try to rip holes in our ranks! Most casualties are currently the result of bombs and machine-gun fire! Shrapnel wounds are, some of them, quite dreadful. We often ask ourselves: "Where are our fighter planes?" But we do understand that those good flying marksmen can't be everywhere. Perhaps they are currently needed more urgently up there in Moscow than with us in the southeastern part of the vast Russian theater of war!

Now that the large cauldrons at Uman are "finished off"—you will have all heard of it on the radio—there is only minimal enemy resistance on our route of advance. *Der Russe* will presumably take up position again behind the great Dnepr River! But then that should be the end of Red enthusiasm for war. . . .

I frequently ask myself how this war in Russia will go on, whether we will occupy the whole of European Russia, whether our final objective will be Moscow, Khar'kov, Rostov, or Astrakhan in the south? We don't know! We don't know even one or two days beforehand if we must go on marching and where we're to go! We know and sense only this much: that everything is according to a grand plan and that we are only to be compared with mere "chess figures," which are urgently needed in some sort of operation here or there![68]

11.8.41: ALBERT NEUHAUS (ARMY GROUP NORTH)[69]

Yesterday our forces put in a rather big attack and as a result we've got some relief from our work. You simply can't imagine how tenaciously the Russians are defending themselves here. In our sector, we're facing the very best Russian artillery regiments, and they're firing at us with everything they've got. In addition, our engineers and infantry are having to fight their way through a dense line of bunkers, and unless you've done something like that you have no idea what it means to take a bunker line.[70] But the die has already been cast, and the Russians will be destroyed one way or another. Woe betide our beautiful Germany if these hordes were ever to have occupied our beautiful country. According to the latest *Wehrmacht* reports, our forces are striding from one success to another, and from the numbers of prisoners and the amount of booty you can get a picture of just what a threat we've faced here in the East. But our *Führer* was wide awake [to the danger] and soon we'll be making a clean sweep of it. Sometimes, it's hard to trust your own ears when you hear the numbers that are in the *Wehrmacht* reports.[71]

11.8.41: *GEFREITER* HANS B. (269 INFANTRY DIVISION, 4 PANZER GROUP, ARMY GROUP NORTH)[72]

Another day filled with rain has gone by. . . . Hopefully the rain will end soon, and the whole world will seem much better again. Otherwise it's all so miserable. . . .

Of course, that unfortunately plays a major role in all our combat actions. Our infantry is in an especially bad state—a large number of dead, many wounded and hardship after hardship [*Strapazen nach Strapazen*]. This war makes for a tough life. Yet despite all the difficulties, I'm still counting on a rapid and victorious end to the war. The divisions that are done for [*kaputt*] will simply be replaced by new ones and then they'll have the necessary impetus for the attack once again. In time, even the best units get worn down.

The enemy resistance is enormous. Bunkers in the woods and high-voltage wires [*Starkstromdrähte*] have also cost us lots of blood today. The enemy is also blowing up entire fields with mines. But we'll get it done, that's for sure.

11.8.41: *LEUTNANT* WILLIBALD G. (57 INFANTRY DIVISION, 1 PANZER GROUP, ARMY GROUP SOUTH)[73]

For the last 2½ days we've been in a new firing position and are securing it against a superior enemy. For a period, <u>we</u> were even "encircled," but since the cauldron of Uman has been finished off, we've got our backs free. So far, we haven't fired a shot, but the infantry has put severe forest battles behind it.

My word, the infantry! I'd gladly hand them the crown of the armed service branches. What they do is so incredibly grand [*ungeheuer grossartig*] that there are no words for it and every infantryman deserves the greatest respect! While we, backed up by the infantry, live here relatively comfortably still, laying on straw and in sleeping bags in our tent and sunning ourselves during the day, these poor fellows are out on guard day and night, from which, with the severely decimated units, they cannot be relieved, and must be alert day and night and ready for surprises. But it is precisely this that makes me glad that we have been working together with the List Regiment[74] since the start of the war, with whom you feel completely safe.

The situation here is strange. You can't really speak of a "front" at all. If earlier, during our exercises in Poland, we always smiled when we were told the enemy situation was: enemy all around or somewhere, well, that's become reality now. We belong to the *Panzergruppe* that is striking west of the Dnepr to the south and conducting "clearing-up operations" [*Aufräumungsarbeiten*]. That might seem rather nice, but the entire area is teeming with the remnants of smashed Russian divisions that must now all be surrounded and then squashed and worn down [*zerquetscht und zermürbt*]. That isn't easy, because these fellows defend themselves to the utmost, even when it is already entirely useless. Deserters report that the *Kommissare* shoot down anyone who wants to surrender. Otherwise the war would probably already be over!

13.8.41: *GEFREITER* RUDOLF STÜTZEL (5 INFANTRY DIVISION, NINTH ARMY, ARMY GROUP CENTER)[75]

First of all, please excuse me for the letter being so filthy, but we've been sitting in foxholes for two days now. Well, it's certainly not as bad now as it was on Hill 214 (from 22–30 July), [but] when Mother reads this—that we're sitting in foxholes at night—she's certain to think we're all going to catch cold.

Today we're stationed near Smolensk again and have taken up a defensive position, which we're going to hold for a while at any rate. . . . Even if every so often artillery shells scream by over our heads, or perhaps explode close to us, the Russians can't get at us because we're quite safe in our foxholes. But the Russian air force is something new for us. In our sector they have complete control of the air [*Luftherrschaft*],[76] but that's just because at the moment our planes are needed more urgently elsewhere. Again and again there are Russian bombers and fighters flying high above us, mostly in formations of up to 20 aircraft. Yesterday evening four Russian fighters made a low-level attack [*Tiefflug*] on one of our gun positions. At first we weren't sure what to do, as it was something totally new to us.

13.8.41: *GEFREITER* HANS B. (269 INFANTRY DIVISION, 4 PANZER GROUP, ARMY GROUP NORTH)[77]

Today there was another big attack, and I believe that this third attack has finally been crowned by success, [but] it is not yet fully certain that the great sacrifice in blood [*Blutopfer*] wasn't to no avail again. It began with the artillery firing 6,000 shells, supported by air forces and rocket launchers [*Nebelwaffe*],[78] and, finally, by the infantry with its weapons. So the battle took on the character of the World War.

These Russians are truly mad. Otherwise how could it be that an officer, for example, whose leg has been shot off, shoots down two Germans who are rushing to his aide. They've reinforced their bunkers with walls of wood that are a meter thick. Wood is resilient and is difficult to destroy. The Russian commissars with their submachine guns stand behind their troops and shoot down anyone who attempts to fall back or desert. The families of deserters are also shot. If it continues like this, Russia's best people will be forced to die in their millions. We're also suffering losses, and we're all hoping that the division will be pulled from the line. It simply can't continue like this. The fatal losses among officers we know are also high.

14.8.41: DR. HEINRICH HAAPE (6 INFANTRY DIVISION, NINTH ARMY, ARMY GROUP CENTER)[79]

I have just gone for a short ride past the front line, where our soldiers are in the middle of a defensive battle against the Russian divisions. We have been engaged in trench warfare for over 10 days now; we've built proper trenches and dugouts, and that's for operational reasons, so they say. It looks like another cauldron is being formed and then we'll storm eastward, on the heels of the enemy [*hart am Feind*].

At one point the Russian broke through, but we beat him back over the Mezha in a tough counterattack. Unfortunately, we also had losses, but that's the way things are—we're at war after all. Before every attack you think silently to yourself, who will be next? Never have so many bullets whistled about our ears as the last time; whistling and hissing in the air were the only things that could be heard. It was just our good luck that the Russians were too worked up and shot haphazardly. We captured a lot of weapons and ammunition. The Russian losses were heavy!

I also stood at the grave of my boy Dehorn again today. He was a good man; he died at my side in loyal fulfillment of his duties. It was like a stab through my heart to see him bleeding to death. He didn't speak a word; I had to take care of the other wounded. He was the dearest one to me of all those who die a soldier's death here.

At a fork in the road, in the forest, stands a simple birch cross with a steel helmet [*ein schlichtes Birkenkreuz mit Stahlhelm*].[80] A friendly fence, made of the same wood, embraces the tranquil spot of that final peace, decorated by simple means. The flowers, always fresh, bear witness to the love and remembrance of his comrades. Hanging inconspicuously on the cross is the Iron Cross Second Class [EK 2], which he received as an award for bravery and readiness for duty. . . .

The sight of his grave evokes a long series of memories—he was at my side at my every step. Christmas in France, shopping, packing boxes, experiences and work on the coast, then East Prussia, and the crazy war against Russia. All these images are shared experiences. He was a good comrade, that little Dehorn!

But life goes on here; we don't have time to stand still for too long, for the demands of the present are stronger than the past. We will continue unwaveringly along our road, no one wishes to miss it—fortunate is the soldier who can experience the great final victory of our beloved Fatherland, for which we will stake everything.

14.8.41: DR. KONRAD JARAUSCH (ARMY GROUP CENTER)[81]

Already on the way here I had kept my eyes open for signs of churches and crucifixes. . . . And so it was that on the morning after my arrival in Minsk[82] I noticed a church tower right next to the Lenin House in Minsk. It could have been located in one of the more modest neighborhoods in Berlin. The church was made of red brick and was Romanesque in style; it reminded me of the Kapernaum Church in the *Seestrasse* in Berlin-Wedding. Except that everything was more marked by poverty, and the tower was smaller. The church was likely built in the years before the World War. It wasn't damaged much on the outside. But there were no crosses or Christian iconography of any kind. Plastered on the fence posts outside were theater and cinema announce-ments. The main entry had been blocked off with a kind of glass wall that looked like a storefront window. A side entrance led me past a ticket counter. Inside, carpenters and others were at work. They were whitewashing the walls and refinishing the floor. A few men and women were standing around looking at what had already been ac-complished. So we started a conversation (I opened with a question in Polish). I could get the basic facts despite our problems in conversing—the Bolsheviks had converted this "beautiful, wonderful Kyrka [church]" into a movie theater. It is now supposed to be turned back into a church. It was clear that people were interested in it. Were they expressing some kind of religious sentiment? Who can say?

A few hours later I was standing in front of the "cathedral" on the market square. It is a modest building of the late baroque period; we've seen a number of such churches here in the East, some with old paintings. Here, the religious character of the building had already been reestablished. A crucifix made of pieces of birch stood on the altar, flanked by flowers. In front of it stood a smaller cross that had been saved through difficult times. One of the side chapels had also been restored. An old woman knelt at a pew. Otherwise only German soldiers were milling about. There were post-ers announcing both Catholic and Protestant field services.

As I was leaving (tired and with heavy feet), a siren sent people running from the market square: another planned explosion, this time right next to the church. I wonder if a new Christian spirit can rise up from the rubble? Or are the reopened churches yet another part of German war propaganda?[83]

15.8.41: *MAJOR* HANS MEIER-WELCKER (251 INFANTRY DIVISION, NINTH ARMY, ARMY GROUP CENTER)[84]

The Russians . . . bury their dead without any identification, which often makes it very difficult to determine how high the enemy losses are. The Russians sacrifice their people, and themselves, in ways that western Europeans can hardly fathom.

We also encounter young women among the Russian forces, however to this point we've only seen female doctors and female medical personnel.

15.8.41: *HAUPTMANN* FRIEDRICH M. (73 INFANTRY DIVISION, ELEVENTH ARMY, ARMY GROUP SOUTH)[85]

The Russian defends himself against us quite desperately (he is trapped in a cauldron). I was told yesterday that *Oberleutnant* Fischer, my ever cheerful friend, fell yesterday.

The minds of the Russians have been entirely dulled [*ganz verdummt*] and they have been persuaded that the Germans will slaughter all [their] prisoners. Yes, even the civilian population has been persuaded of that and they believed it, too. I talked with a *Volksdeutsche* woman,[86] whose husband had been murdered 20 years ago and whose 19-year-old daughter had been carried off by the Russians during the retreat to [help] dig trenches. She said that after the entry of the German troops, Russian women had come to her to get her to ask the German soldiers whether it was really true that they would now be slaughtered by the soldiers. And when the soldiers gave them, and even their children, something to eat, they, with amazed eyes, kept shaking their heads, over and over. An enormous fear of Bolshevik punishment still lives in them. When they were told that, for the coming year, they should stock themselves up with the fruits of the fields, that is, salvage the harvest, they didn't really want to get on with it, because they had been told that if they refused to repatriate the harvest after the withdrawal of the Russian troops, Russian planes would come and would shoot at them with machine guns or destroy the harvest with incendiary bombs. A poor, dull people, the object of exploitation for Jewish dominance. A sigh of relief is now passing through the Ukraine, the people are foreseeing, with sure instincts, their own property and better times.[87]

15.8.41: "HANS-OTTO" (268 INFANTRY DIVISION, ARMY GROUP GUDERIAN, ARMY GROUP CENTER)[88]

Our group can claim to have been the forwardmost boot of the German *Wehrmacht* for approximately 14 days. Since the end of last month we have been an irritating thorn in the pelt of the Russian bear, which he has been trying to attack with all his might. Despite all of his artillery, he does not succeed in removing this thorn, and his bloody infantry losses are unimaginable. The town [El'nia], which we surround, will one day be an important name in the history of this campaign.

Yes, these battles are tough, and in our ranks, too, death tears a hole in the ranks of our best every day. But in these battles, the soldier has now learned to become tough, too, and shown that he is also equal to "storms of steel," just like his fathers in the World War. The grandeur of many an expression from that time now becomes clear. The incessant metallic hammering of the artillery, the crashing explosions of the shells, and the zipping and humming of shrapnel makes its own music. And when that can be heard constantly from morning till night in any sector of the front, unending, without any indication that they are having to pause for breath over there, then you can put yourself in the position of the fighter in the World War.

But our guys have become tough in all this and have an admirable level of self-confidence, and if the Russian comes with infantry and tanks, then a bloody reception awaits him. And it matters not at all if one or two tanks break through the lines, because one of our Paks was destroyed and no other weapon can stop it. For then the infantryman leaps from his foxhole with hand grenade, Molotov cocktail, and a concentrated charge, and finishes it off as matter-of-factly as if he were conducting a peacetime demonstration.

Our *Ostmarkers* have particularly proved themselves here, defending a commanding elevation (125.6), which the Russian attacks again and again. And here is laid bare the spirit of the fighter in the current war, he who knows for what he fights and, if necessary, dies, in contrast to the stupid cannon fodder which is only whipped forward over and again by the Reds' pack of lies and a pistol or a machine gun.[89]

17.8.41: *SS-STURMMANN* EUGEN F. (SS INFANTRY REGIMENT 4, 2 SS-BRIGADE [MOT.], ARMY GROUP NORTH REAR AREA)[90]

Close to our camp there is a Russian prisoner of war camp. But the prisoners didn't seem to want to follow orders, so now we've shot 800 of them. Now they're quiet. They should be happy that they're still alive, because we know no mercy [*da kennen wir kein Erbarmen*]. They've had their first warning now, the damned dogs.

17.8.41: *SOLDAT* E.L. (1 MOUNTAIN DIVISION, SEVENTEENTH ARMY, ARMY GROUP SOUTH)[91]

The many hundreds of kilometers that we have now put behind us showed us the toughness and ferocity [*Härte und Grausamkeit*] of this struggle. I am not able to describe this all in detail, but this here really is a matter of being or not being [*Sein oder Nichtsein*]. The deeper we penetrated into Russia, the more frequently we met with Jews. The fellows are just as insolent as in [times of] deepest peace. Many more of these evil spawn really ought to be stood up against the wall than have been so far. The food conditions, here in the Ukraine as well, are so primitive that it is beyond the imagination of a normal European.

Our mountain division has been putting on a good show so far [*hat sich bisher grossartig geschlagen*]. The *Führer* himself awarded it special honors, since it has been able, albeit with considerable losses, to break resistance everywhere other units could no longer make progress. Our mountain antitank battalion has been resting for a few days; as an advance detachment it has had the greatest share in the successes to date. The whole lot is made up entirely of warriors, who have almost all already taken part in campaigns. Of course, we "young'uns" from the [replacement pool] feel quite small and pitiful in comparison. Last night we were distributed across various companies where the manpower losses have been not inconsiderable.[92]

17.8.41: *HAUPTMANN* FRIEDRICH M. (73 INFANTRY DIVISION, ELEVENTH ARMY, ARMY GROUP SOUTH)[93]

It is peaceful in the village itself. You see almost no people, only in the distance can you hear a few children playing; they are oblivious to the war passing by. . . .

From outside you can hear the muffled thunder of our guns, planes droning over us into enemy territory, and Red planes frequently come, too, trying to take out resupply columns with bombs and machine-gun fire.

One day is the same as another, just like the terrain and villages are all alike, as are the roads that we march along, a daily monotony [*Gleichklang*] where you can no longer differentiate the days of the week, you only know the date. How many will know that today is Sunday? That at home people in their Sunday best are resting from the working hours of the previous weekdays? And yet a good mood prevails among all the men; yesterday evening they sat around the man with the accordion and sang soldier songs into the quiet Russian night. Cracking jokes or one will rag another. That is how it must be. Nothing can get the German soldier down, and so we are certain of the final victory, however doggedly the Russian resists.

18.8.41: *LEUTNANT* OTTO SCH. (73 INFANTRY DIVISION, ELEVENTH ARMY, ARMY GROUP SOUTH)[94]

We're rattling around the mouth of a river with three letters, and perhaps we'll now have the opportunity to study the "successes" of the Red rulership [*Herrschaft*] in one of the most fertile countries on earth. Only in this campaign have we actually got to know what war really is. The most difficult thing is losing comrades you've become close to over the course of the war. The Reds defend themselves bitterly even in the most absurd situations; probably because they think we're just as cruel as their own countrymen, and so many more fall victim to their senseless resistance. Even in areas that have been in German hands for days already individual stragglers are holding out among the endless fields of sunflowers or in the cornfields and fighting to the last bullet.

18.8.41: *MAJOR* HANS R. (7 PANZER DIVISION, 3 PANZER GROUP, ARMY GROUP CENTER)[95]

You can't put into words what the Bolsheviks have done to this country. It is an intellectual and spiritual wasteland and an emptiness [*geistige und seelische Öde und Leere*] that you can only feel but hardly define. The impact of that is greatest on the people, who look on with a fixed and mindless gaze, and who exhibit a poverty and primitiveness that is frankly staggering. The complete absence of an intellectually somehow higher-status class is perhaps the most striking thing. Each person seems to be just as dumb and stubborn as the next. The villages, with their total uniformity, are exactly suited to the people. . . . It makes you shudder to think what these people would have done to us if they'd succeeded in coming to power [in Germany]. In any case, our soldiers are finally cured of any and all Bolshevik ideas.

18.8.41: *LEUTNANT* WILLIBALD G. (57 INFANTRY DIVISION, 1 PANZER GROUP, ARMY GROUP SOUTH)[96]

The infantry has made good progress and so today we are already in firing position, 7 km ahead of the Dnepr. The Russians have dug themselves in by the river, but they only have 2 heavy mortars and one light gun left. By contrast, early today, at the start of the assault, we fired 600 rounds in 1 minute. So you can imagine what sort of artillery there is here! The resupply [line] is quite extraordinary. The Russians would never manage that!

Early today, 18 Russian fighters and bombers again attacked in two waves and dropped bombs, without hitting anything. We are marvelously well camouflaged! Each and every gun has become a large bush. Two fighter planes are protecting us now, constantly circling above us. It's hot enough to boil your blood, but we prefer that to constant rain.

Yesterday was the 9th Sunday of the war already! A gypsy woman prophesied to us that the war would be over by the end of August. Let's see! Mail is supposed to come today. Hopefully there'll be something from you all there!

18.8.41: ALBERT NEUHAUS (ARMY GROUP NORTH)[97]

The mail's about to be leaving here again, so I want to quickly send you a brief, cheery greeting. . . . In your letter you asked what our rations are like. I can say that, recently, our rations have been excellent. There's butter, lard, canned fish, chocolate, candy, cigarettes, cigars, canned sausage; we've even got effervescent powder [*Brausepulver*] for mixing with water. Only we don't have an opportunity to prepare the powder, because in the woods here near Luga there's no good drinking water. We spread on the butter finger thick, since that's the best way to keep our badly strained nerves from failing us. We've been in action constantly for more than four weeks now, even if now and then there's a day in between that's a little quieter. Several days ago each of us received 1½ bottles of beer—the first beer we've had in nine weeks. Our supply line is also being put in order, because German armored trains are now reaching us. It's impossible to imagine how much work that took, because the entire Russian rail line had to be converted to the German gauge.[98] Here, like everywhere, lots of work has been done while in great danger. The latest reports are again most favorable for us, and we're hoping that the war will be over soon.

18.8.41: DR. HEINRICH HAAPE (6 INFANTRY DIVISION, NINTH ARMY, ARMY GROUP CENTER)[99]

Images from my memory waft unburdened through the bright day from the blue yonders of a happy time. It was a time when there was still peace, my heart was still young and saw life very differently; so I dream and forget the hardship of the present in this quiet hiatus. . . .

The consequence of battle is terrible right up to the final destruction . . . yet another bombing attack from the Russians. To our left the artillery booms, our neighboring regiment is in battle. Two reconnaissance patrols are running!

This is what we have become! None of this disturbs me. The constant pitiless deployment, the many dead and wounded comrades, the struggles, the readiness to die make you dull and indifferent to the moment. Where your own safety is concerned, you become fatalistic; the possibility of death barely fazes you. Soldierly duty and faith in victory give us strength and purpose. We carry in our hearts unconditional hopes of victory and the certainty of a happy future for our nation. For you all at home, for our beloved Germany, no sacrifice is too great for us!

Nobody believes how tough and yet how tender the soldier is. A typical incident comes to mind: during a counterattack, when we were driving the Russians back into the Mezha, I was crouching flat against the ground together with an *Oberleutnant* (Iron Cross First and Second Class, and Assault Badge). We couldn't go any farther, because the enemy machine-gun fire was too heavy and the bullets were whistling around our heads in an overly perilous way—then he suddenly and without warning pulled a letter secretively from his pocket and said: "Hey, Heinz, what do you think— [my girlfriend] wrote to me!" And then he read to me, dreamily, the loveliest and most elegant words from a young girl from France. He had forgotten the war.

Hell was all around us. The tanks were blasting from all barrels; enemy antitank guns pumped shells with steely determination ahead into the balconies of a wooden house. Village houses burned brightly—a firework display. Our artillery thundered resolutely into the nearby piece of woodland, causing fragments to fly up; in brief—all barrels were blazing, a tough, dogged battle, where "everything is at stake."

Such is the soldier who has come to terms with it all, a few minutes' contemplation are enough for him to wander off into a world of yearning, desires, and fantasies.

I am happy to be able to be here in this interesting world! The soldier, where death is so close, you feel so very much what life is!

19.8.41: SIEGBERT STEHMANN (163 INFANTRY DIVISION, GERMAN ARMY OF NORWAY)[100]

For a week now I haven't got any mail at all, and how I long for it in this dangerous wasteland [*Einöde*]. For weeks we've been getting by each day with just a half loaf of bread—which we devour dry because we don't have anything to spread on it—and with the thin, watery soup we get at midday. We're always famished and we're all getting thinner. The mere thought of a piece of bread with jam, or of some pudding, let alone meat, is like a fairy tale from the *Arabian Nights*. And now: Early today two more horses from our baggage train were torn apart by shellfire. So at least in the next few days we'll find a couple of bits of meat in our soup. Two days ago we were pulled off the forwardmost line, and we're now 2 kilometers behind the front with the heavy artillery.

19.8.41: *GEFREITER* HEINZ T. DEL B. (RESERVE HOSPITAL, OBORNIK/WARTHEGAU)[101]

Finally, after a never-ending train journey, we have arrived at our final destination. Now I will tell . . . everything . . . how everything has happened.

We were positioned 4 km south of Kiev and could see the first suburbs. The neighboring divisions to our right and left weren't up yet and so we were a wedge, pushed in deep and entirely on our own. On the first day we received such a heavy barrage, you might well have thought all hell had broken loose. From midday until dark, and any movement was to be avoided, because *der Russe* could see us. On the next morning, it continued unabated; it was railway guns and mortars. We attacked at midday and painstakingly, fighting for each meter, gained a better position.

On the following day, once again under the heaviest fire, there was not a single minute's quiet the entire day. Artillery, mortars, tanks, planes in constant rotation. During the night we changed position. The next day, on 11.8., the same, we couldn't move, sat in our narrow foxholes, waiting, waiting in a hail of projectiles and shrapnel. Sometime in the afternoon, a Russian counterattack was discovered, and since we were the reserve platoon, we came to reinforce 3rd Platoon, which lay ahead of us. The Russian attack was supported by mortars and Pak. Around 7:30 to 8 o'clock in the evening, they raked our line precisely and really dug around in it. I sat in my hole and was forever having to pull my head in.

Then there was suddenly an antitank shell, exploded on my shelter, 30 cm in front of me. I ducked down and really copped it. My glasses were smashed, mud flew into my face, I couldn't see anything. Only then did I feel something warm running down my arm. Bandaged up by the medical orderly, I waited until it was completely dark, went to the battalion command post, received a tetanus shot, and went back.

Ten comrades were injured along with me, one died. We reached the rear on automobiles, poor roads to the main dressing station [*Hauptverbandplatz*], and from there to Zhitomir, where, two days later, we rolled on to the west in freight cars. Rovno, Lublin, Warsaw, Łódź, Thorn, Posen, here. From Warsaw in a nice [rail] car; we traveled for four days. . . . I can't tell you how my arm looks, because it was last dressed six days ago.

19.8.41: *MAJOR* HANS SCH. (ENGINEER BATTALION 652, ARMY GROUP SOUTH)[102]

On 9.7. there was the shattering affair involving *Feldwebel* Schwarz. . . . Schwarz was put on trial by the court of Sixth Army for sentry duty offenses and for attempted rape and arson [*Notzucht und Brandstiftung*]. The court imposed the death penalty. In no way did this man have a perfect character. It was the first death sentence in the battalion, and it affects us more than anyone wants to admit. That said, I must admit that the sentence is a just one. But the fact that two others from my first company, after drinking too much vodka, killed a Ukrainian woman with a pistol shot, even though it was an accident—well that had me worked up for that entire day.[103]

20.8.41: DR. ADOLF B. (25 INFANTRY DIVISION [MOT.], 1 PANZER GROUP, ARMY GROUP SOUTH)[104]

73 days ago we stood together in front of Stuttgart Central Station and talked about the coming campaign! We didn't yet know back then that the struggle against Soviet Russia would break out, and we had no idea about the duration of the imminent

war, either! Today, we know that the struggle against the Soviets was unavoidable and urgently necessary. We can also already see that the military resistance will soon be broken! Anything that remains of the Russian forces will only be so-called gangs [*Banden*], which will wage a guerrilla war, carrying out ambushes in forest areas in particular. But even these gangs will be brought under control with the passage of time! We ourselves now know that our Fatherland has been threatened by an immense danger and that this has now been eliminated! That is why each of us does his soldierly duty gladly and willingly.

Horrible and bitter are only the Red bombing attacks, which are becoming more frequent—and by night now, as well! Our medical company has also had its own losses in dead and wounded. . . . If I could, I would request German fighter planes—more and more of them! Last Sunday we saw four Russian bombers come down in flames!

20.8.41: *LEUTNANT* ERNST E. (13 PANZER DIVISION, 1 PANZER GROUP, ARMY GROUP SOUTH)[105]

In my area of activity the war has taken a new turn in the past week.[106] While in the past we had to deal with the enemy on the ground and overhead, he's now also fighting against us underground with mines. Since I'm the engineer platoon leader in my battalion, that's my responsibility. Together with my men and equipment I've already dug up 135 mines.

What's striking at the moment is that the [enemy] troops facing us consist primarily of older age groups (Reserves). If it stays like that east of the Dnepr then it won't look good for the striking power [*Schlagkraft*] of the Russians. Yesterday in our attack sector we took around 1,000 prisoners. We're continuing to meet treacherous and dogged resistance. A Russian lifts up his gun to surrender, or does as if to do so. But after you let him approach he takes aim to fire. Another, acting in a similar manner, stabs one of our flak soldiers four times with his mounted bayonet until he's finally subdued. And still another stabs himself to death to avoid being taken prisoner.

20.8.41: *UNTEROFFIZIER* RUDOLF F. (267 INFANTRY DIVISION, SECOND ARMY, ARMY GROUP CENTER)[107]

In a triumphant breakthrough, our division forced the Dnepr just above the mouth of the Berezina and drove a wedge into the Bolshevik bulwark. Other German units thrust forward from the north to the south, and eventually a ring was formed in the area of Rogachev and Zhlobin.[108] Our regiments were occupied in difficult defensive battles against the desperate Russian attempts to break out. Of course, our victorious [advance detachment] was also deployed. The day before yesterday was the climax of these battles. The Russians had had nothing to eat for three days and were now storming toward the south with a last, desperate, and enormous force, [toward] the very point where we were positioned. I don't want to exaggerate, but it must have been several regiments that, in densely concentrated masses and with roars of "Urrah," ran into our machine-gun fire. I was lying in the forwardmost line with my equipment and was able to experience this dreadful battle up close. Pak and artillery shot directly into the attacking masses from a distance of 200 meters.

Then around 800 men broke through to our side and shot at us from the side and from behind. They got to around 100 meters from us, then I had orders to skedaddle with my valuable equipment and vehicle. But, thanks to the rapid action of a following reserve battalion, these elements that had broken through were soon finished off. Unfortunately, we also had relatively high losses, because it had come to some fierce hand-to-hand fighting.

20.8.41: *GEFREITER* FERDINAND M. (167 INFANTRY DIVISION, SECOND ARMY, ARMY GROUP CENTER)[109]

It all kicked off with this *Kessel* here eight days ago.[110] When I was finished with the letter to all of you, we got going right away. On the following day, we took over the lead position and from then on we were supported by tanks and assault guns. On 14 [August] our platoon suffered a severe blow. Our *Leutnant*, his driver—one of my friends—were severely wounded, one dispatch rider fell, and all of that from a single mortar shell. It was a sad scene, with them lying there in their blood.

Over the course of the following days, we also pressed forward to the south in the direction of Mogilev and now we are positioned outside Gomel.[111] The Russians have been constantly retreating in recent days. Yesterday we crossed a river and took a village without any difficulties. In the evening, however, the Russians began a counterattack with a ferocity the like of which we have never experienced before. We were just driving toward the village exit when all hell broke loose. There was such a droning and whistling that you couldn't hear or see. Then they began their assault, but were beaten back with bloody noses. The clouds from the flames towered up to the sky and combined with others to form a gigantic mass. But despite how awful it was, our company suffered no losses. . . . That's the thing: Yesterday it was awful but came off well, the other matter seemed harmless but came to a bad ending. If it's your time, then you're in for it.

20.8.41: *GEFREITER* ALOIS SCHEUER (197 INFANTRY DIVISION, ARMY GROUP GUDERIAN, ARMY GROUP CENTER)[112]

Right now, it's 10 o'clock in the morning. The sun is shining really warmly again and our stuff, soaked through in a heavy storm-filled night, is drying again. For several days now we have been in position on an elevation in the middle of a cornfield.[113] For the moment, we've settled into defensive positions. . . . The hours go past slowly, we lie in our foxholes and wait for further orders, wait for post from home. Now and then the silence of these hours is interrupted by the iron greetings of Russian artillery. If the impacts get dangerously close, we press our noses a bit deeper into the dirt. The spade has often proved itself to be a true lifesaver in such situations.

Our mode of life is extremely primitive. It is not at all unusual if we haven't washed or shaved for days. But the most unpleasant thing is that our rations are not completely adequate. Despite the turnips and carrots that we get from the gardens, we can't get rid of that constant sensation of hunger. We've even tried new potatoes, but they aren't ripe yet and our stomachs start to churn. . . .

I've met several comrades from St. Ingbert recently. . . . Each looks as scruffy as the next, and every one of them has only one desire: to get out of this country as fast as possible. There's many a loudmouth [*so manchen Maulheld*] still back home I'd like to see here just for 14 days, I think they'd soon be cured of that.

20.8.41: ALBERT NEUHAUS (ARMY GROUP NORTH)[114]

My dear Clemens![115]

My joyful thanks for your lines, which I received yesterday evening. . . . In this strange and dreadful country, one is twice, even three times happier to receive greetings from home. Hopefully, the time will soon come when we can turn our backs on this "workers' paradise."

No P.-K. Company[116] can portray to those at home the impressions that we gain here in the colors that we experience here.

I have seen East Prussia, Lithuania, and Latvia; in the latter two countries, poverty was certainly clear to see, but what you can see here, well, it cries out to heaven. The fact that they defend themselves like they do can only be chalked up to stupidity or to the Russians' organized hate.

During the first four weeks, the invasion seemed to us like a *K[raft] d[urch] F[reude]* excursion,[117] until we came up against dreadful resistance up here. And what the following four weeks meant for us, only those of us who experienced it can know. Day and night we sat, sketched, and worked, sometimes under heavy artillery fire, and for several days I was so on edge with my nerves that my heart raced if I only heard the whistling of a shell. A kindly fortune has preserved us from any significant damage so far, just a few vehicles have been shot up by shells and one comrade, who was posted at a particularly exposed position, had to have a leg amputated.

The extensive forests in which we have been living for weeks now are uncanny, it really is the sort of territory for waging war. But now the darkness that spread horror around us has begun to lift and we expect the victorious decision in a few days, at least for our sector. I can't write you more about it yet, perhaps the decision will already have fallen by the time you receive this letter. . . .

Be glad, Clemens, that you didn't have to join in with any of this rubbish [*Mist*] and you can perhaps understand how we all yearn to be back home. The way our boys from the infantry, from the engineers, from the panzers and the *Waffen SS* have bravely done their bit, no drama, no heroic epic [*Heldengedicht*] can describe. And we can be proud in the knowledge that we, with our reconnaissance work, cleared the path for those boys, for many, many an enemy battery has had to leave their lives behind thanks to our work. So, my dear Clemens, this was a modest personal report [*Erlebnisbericht*] [for you].

22.8.41: *UNTEROFFIZIER* W.F. (251 INFANTRY DIVISION, NINTH ARMY, ARMY GROUP CENTER)[118]

I've already had it up to here [*ich habe die Nase bereits gestrichen voll*] with this much-vaunted Soviet Union! The conditions here are prehistoric [*vorsintflutlich*]. Our propaganda definitely didn't exaggerate, more like didn't go far enough. At the moment, we're stuck outside a town between Petersburg [Leningrad] and Moscow and are keeping the Russians occupied. The losses in our regiment are pretty high, although in my unit they're normal. We're suffering a lot from artillery fire here, and we have to live day and night in foxholes for protection from shrapnel. The holes are full of water. Lice and other vermin creep in, too.

22.8.41: *LEUTNANT* WILLIBALD G. (57 INFANTRY DIVISION, SEVENTEENTH ARMY, ARMY GROUP SOUTH)[119]

Since an hour ago our assault troops have been driving into Cherkassy.[120] Today at 4:00 a.m. the Reds blew up the large railway bridge, which we had wanted to take in a surprise attack. What a shame! The division has lost out on a Knight's Cross as a result.

It's awfully busy in the air! Every couple of hours the Russians arrive with sheer masses [*hellen Haufen*] of bombers, fighters, and destroyers, and bombard and strafe everything with machine-gun fire for all they're worth. They haven't discovered us yet, because I've had a group of trees and bushes planted around all the guns [to mimic] the way they are scattered across the entire clearing here. That way they are completely invisible from above and we have shade in this extreme heat, which has lasted nearly 14 days now.

Four times a day, you could almost say: at specific times, 20 Stukas come with a fighter escort and bombard Cherkassy and the surrounding area until everything shakes. Unfortunately, except at these times, no German fighters are to be seen!

The evening before yesterday something jolly happened! I sent the fodderer, a noncommissioned officer, away to organize feed for the horses. After an hour he came back, but with 8 Russian prisoners instead of feed! He had been shot at from the forest, had galloped another 100 meters, then tied his horse to a tree, snuck up on the fellows from behind, and shot at them with his pistol. The result was that 8 little men tumbled out of the bush, threw away their guns, and surrendered to this lone man. Since we couldn't yet turn them over, they're now sitting with the field kitchen, peeling potatoes and making themselves useful. They have grown very confiding and are glad that for them the war is over and they've got something decent to eat again. . . .

We are repeatedly being told by prisoners that they are only forced at gunpoint by the commissars into this tough fight and usually useless resistance. When we catch a fellow like that, we make short shrift of him. One bullet, and goodbye![121]

23.8.41: *LEUTNANT* WILLIBALD G. (57 INFANTRY DIVISION, SEVENTEENTH ARMY, ARMY GROUP SOUTH)[122]

The evening meal is just marching up: liverwurst with black tea and mixed fruit compote. That's pretty good! In addition to that my telephone operators, among whom are some fine fellows, are making fried potatoes, and so I can't really complain. We have it pretty good in all, compared to the infantry, to whom I gladly award the crown of the armed service branches. The only stupid thing here is that, since of course we're with the firing position and all the "rear area services" of the battery here in the forest clearing (only the observation post is in a village 6 km from here, that's where the chief is, too), we have to get all the hay and grass for the horses from 6–7 km away, which, with our 150 horses, is no small task. Our *panje* wagons are on the road all day for this. We now have around 10 Russian *panje* wagons in the battery—small, maneuverable vehicles that we took from the Russians, complete with ponies. When an artillery battalion like that marches along, then it does look rather like a bunch of mercenaries. But this way we have at least been able to compensate some for our horse losses and taken the pressure off the heavy vehicles. So, but now that's enough about such things! The third [Russian] aerial attack in the hour in which I have been writing is just starting. We don't even bother looking up anymore! . . .

So, now it is almost dark and our daily friends, the mosquitoes, are filling the air with their humming. Soon we'll hit the tents and the magnificent feather sleeping bags. I think of you all when I see the Great Bear![123] Good night!

24.8.41: *PANZER-OBERSCHÜTZE* ERICH HAGER (17 PANZER DIVISION, 2 PANZER GROUP, ARMY GROUP CENTER)[124]

Sunday. Are dead tired as we couldn't sleep. Sch. . . . [illegible] and I seek out Kuscher. 6 o'clock fall in. Great SURPRISE, there are *Panzersturmabzeichen* [Panzer Assault Badges, awarded for three attacks on three different days].[125] Straight afterward red wine. Company is now together. Drinking and singing! Great mood! In a stupor Schross and I pitch a tent.

24.8.41: *OBERLEUTNANT* RICHARD D. (7 PANZER DIVISION, NINTH ARMY,[126] ARMY GROUP CENTER)[127]

Not much to report on what we're doing, because we're "enjoying" a veritable *Stellungskrieg*, and having to hold up to increased Russian pressure, while [our forces] make progress toward Petersburg in the north and south in the Ukraine. The enemy attacks are like those in the World War, with no concern for his losses, and the poor devils who have to ride them out are having no easy time of it. The division was sent into action as the corps reserve, and during a counterattack it lost 30 tanks and the regimental commander.[128] The cemeteries that are around the military hospital make for a gloomy scene. Each day the ministers, with whom I am billeted, are performing multiple burials.

We're really annoyed by the gaudy headlines in the newspaper—"Soviet Army is finally Beaten," or "Our Aircraft Dominate the Air Space"—because we notice very little of that here. But that's just in our sector; we soldiers don't see what's going on to the south and north.

24.8.41: SIEGBERT STEHMANN (163 INFANTRY DIVISION, GERMAN ARMY OF NORWAY)[129]

Suddenly, overnight, *der Russe* abandoned his fortifications in the woods, apparently in response to the overall situation and the heavy barrage of our guns. So we left our sanctuary in the swamp and moved up close to the old Russian border. We've been here for three days now. The little town here has burned down. Immense clouds of smoke rose up into the night sky, and the bloody glare of the fire gave everything an eerie look. We found living quarters and protection from the rain in several small, utterly demolished wood huts, which had been spared from the fire. We can heat up the oven to dry our clothes and get warm. We found fresh potatoes in a nearby potato field. That was a feast! We prepared fried potatoes, a real delicacy. What happens now, no one knows.

24.8.41: ALBERT NEUHAUS (ARMY GROUP NORTH)[130]

It can't really be any better for us at the moment; apart from alcohol, we have pretty much everything that the heart or stomach desires. And I think it's just a matter of hours or days until our job up here is completed or we have to be pulled farther forward, but I don't think that will happen. This morning the heavily laden German bombers flew past over us again and your heart leaps for joy in your chest when you see that. I am convinced of it, that no other service branch [*Truppengattung*] of the same type as us has had to master such difficult situations and I think we have achieved the most and most wonderful successes. Can you just imagine our chests swollen with pride? Just now the proudest message for us has arrived, which we've been waiting for since around 6 weeks: that Luga has fallen.[131] What that means for us—that, Agnes, can only be appreciated by those of us who have experienced it. Our chief has just picked up a submachine gun and is firing celebratory shots from it. Kid, you can probably imagine our joy and also our inner excitement. It is too wonderful! Luga, I will never forget this town and this name.

24.8.41: DR. HEINRICH HAAPE (6 INFANTRY DIVISION, NINTH ARMY, ARMY GROUP CENTER)[132]

Our division has to hold a line of 46 km against the constant attacks of the enemy, of which over 4 km have to be held by our battalion. A difficult task!

We have expanded our positions, proper field works with bunkers, trenches, etc.; let the Russian try his hand! He has been able to break through in two places—a stupid business, but after a few hours they were thrown out again with heavy losses. During our counterstroke, we found another 11 dead soldiers of our 1st Battalion, who, to a man, had stood firm with their machine guns and rifles when the Cossacks suddenly stormed our line with a blood-curdling "Urrah, Urrah!" They were finally overrun by the superior forces and cut down at their weapons in close combat.

At the moment, it is all peace and quiet here in the forest, where I sit beneath old pine trees and write. I do not only see the terrible war. In quiet hours I tear myself away and look at the smallest things in the forest—how the wood mouse blithely nibbles a small piece of bread that I have put down. Here, there are bright beetles of a size and peculiarity that I have never seen at home—and so many interesting things—you just have to keep your eyes peeled and be able to listen carefully to nature. . . .

It is all so very, very different here to home, a different world. Yet I find the old saying reaffirmed again and again: There is beauty in everything in the world! It's up to the individual to look for it and find it!

24.8.41: *MAJOR* HANS MEIER-WELCKER (251 INFANTRY DIVISION, NINTH ARMY, ARMY GROUP CENTER)[133]

The last hours on my straw mattress[134] were made more pleasant by the singing and dancing of the Russian girls in our little village. Because today is Sunday, and among the Russian population, as far as I know them so far, this day is full of celebration. Fifty paces in front of my open tent was a large circle of girls and soldiers. An old Russian, whom we had made mayor, played a dance tune on an accordion and the girls each danced in serene succession. Sometimes they utter singsong shouts. There was applause after every dance. After a little while, our people also sang a few good songs; two violins were produced and a musical duel gradually developed. Finally, our people were even dancing together with the Russian girls, which immediately caused great amusement. . . . And yet, 10 km farther east there is a front line at which several Russian divisions are being destroyed.[135] If a Russian plane comes, nobody pays it any attention, unless it is set for a low-level attack. There was only one interruption during this celebration, when several German Stukas appeared and, with curiosity, everyone watched their diving attack [*Sturzangriff*].

Naturally, the mood among the population wasn't the way I have just described it from the start. At first, the people were still intimidated and experienced a lot of suffering. As it happens, we set the boundaries of the clearance zone for the combat area so that our little village remained inhabited, so that we have a bit of life around us. Besides, I couldn't really stand by and watch the plundering anymore and took all possible measures with the *Feldgendarmerie* and military court to put an end to this nuisance, which exposes the population to death by starvation and injures all of us at the same time. . . . So the population is now gaining confidence [in us] and our little village is, of course, particularly protected. We are also working hard on bringing in the harvest. We have appointed a special officer who is solely responsible for it and now rules the area like a large-scale farmer.

24.8.41: *UNTEROFFIZIER* EDMUND M. (*LUFTWAFFE* FLAK REGIMENT 49, CENTRAL SECTOR, EASTERN FRONT)[136]

For days or even weeks, I really don't know anymore, we've been in a tough defensive battle against Russian attempts to break through. Somehow, the Reds have figured out that there's a weak spot in the front here, so they're making a major effort (there's talk of five divisions and two motorized divisions) to break through. So far they've yet to succeed. They've managed to push us back 7 kilometers, but only by suffering immense losses. But we've also lost many a brave comrade; two infantry regiments had to be pulled from the front due to losses and the never-ending hardships. In our sector, 22 heavy Russian batteries have been firing nonstop. Motorized forces have been hurriedly brought up to stop the Russians here, [and] now at least our rocket projector batteries, Stukas and 210mm [heavy howitzer] batteries have somewhat evened the score. We're living in the deep trenches we've dug, and I'm writing these lines to you from one of them.

24.8.41: DR. KONRAD JARAUSCH (ARMY GROUP CENTER)[137]

Keep this somewhere safe and do not copy.

Camp Kochanovo

(Partially based on my comrades' insights)

"Dulag" [*Durchgangslager*] is short for transit camp. Such camps serve to process prisoners once they've been removed from the battlefield and then to send them on. The camps thus follow on the heels of the fighting troops but lie beyond the battle zone. Depending on what's happening in the field, they can be filled quickly and then can become quiet again. . . .

The road here in K[ochanovo][138] winds its way through the village and then sinks and passes over a creek. The meadows on either side of this creek seemed to offer an ideal location for a camp. Everything was fine as long as the sun was shining. But then we had quite a downpour. The creek flooded and the meadows were covered in water. At the same time, we received some 10,000 to 12,000 prisoners. They had marched thirty to forty km from the front; they were soaked; they had gone days without food and had eaten green sheaves of grain. In an instant the meadow was transformed into a muddy morass, with the prisoners sprawled all about. Their hunger drove them to the kitchens. Shots were fired to keep them in order. Some (not many) were killed. Others rolled around in the mud, howling from their hunger pains. The next morning several corpses were pulled out of the mud; only their legs or heads stuck up out of the mess.

If you could see the camp now, eight days later, you wouldn't believe this had ever happened. Everything is so peaceful and orderly. There's a large, lofty building in between all the other buildings (they house two kitchens, the sentry post, storage rooms, quarters for captured officers), and thousands of men can find shelter there from the rain.

We have four kitchens set up. We hand out food in the morning, at noon, and in the evening: a liter of grits and 1,000 grams of dark bread; those at hard labor receive

1,700 grams. Prisoners serve in the kitchens, as overseers, and as medics. We don't see many Mongolian types anymore. When prisoners line up to eat by the hundreds, one sees mostly Eastern European farmers and workers. Some are really young boys with impish features; they're cheeky and trusting. Probably most of them are happy to be away from [the front] and that things are not worse.

25.8.41: *GEFREITER* RUDOLF STÜTZEL (5 INFANTRY DIVISION, NINTH ARMY, ARMY GROUP CENTER)[139]

I was injured on the 21st of this month during the fighting around L., but only slightly. My only injury is a small shrapnel wound in the right side of my chest. The fact that I have come so far back[140] is simply because all the dressing stations and military hospitals are overcrowded with severely wounded men, meaning that it's impossible to treat minor injuries. So, you can trust me completely, I have not kept anything secret from you all. Mother, in particular, doesn't believe in a light injury.

Two days before my injury, our company again successfully repelled a Russian tank attack. I was also actively involved in that, although I'm a motorcycle messenger. I shot up a tank during that attack. What's more, in my socks and with no steel helmet. There can't have been anything like it before. It went like this: . . .

I was just about to take off my shoes when suddenly the tank alarm sounded. In combat my position is beside that of the platoon leader. When the alarm was given, the first tank was already racing over the hill. Our gun didn't even have its barrel pointed in that direction when a hit tore through the protective shield and severely wounded Gunner 3. Everyone, even the platoon leader, immediately ran behind the reverse slope and left everything where it was standing. When I saw that the gun was standing there alone, I ran toward it. That's when the tank saw me and rushed toward me. At the last minute, I was able to find cover in the dug-out gun emplacement. A few meters behind our gun, the tank was shot up and burned. I jumped out to the gun; now I could use my knowledge of the Pak gun. Carrying out the activities of gunners 1–4 and the chief of section [*Geschützführer*] on my own, I shot at the next tank to charge over the hill. Behind me, I heard the shouts of my platoon leader: "Stützel! Fire!" The entire battle lasted just a few minutes. All the tanks shot up by us were finished off at a distance of less than 50 meters. There is among all the weapons no greater nervous tension than that of a Pak gunner. Believe me, I have now experienced it myself.

In the evening—the attack was at 5:10 p.m.—my company commander came and inspected the positions. Our gun had received three fist-sized impacts. He expressed his admiration to me. That's what a tank attack looks like.[141] Everything that can still move runs around frantically, infantry, artillery. Only, behind the little Pak guns, cramped together, close up against the protective shield, sit the brave antitank troops, waiting until they can let loose their first rounds. There is no braver soldier than our Pak gunners. Frequently, they have to fire 24 times until the tank comes to a standstill. (Height 214–52 ton tank.)

26.8.41: DR. HANS LIEROW (6 INFANTRY DIVISION, NINTH ARMY, ARMY GROUP CENTER)[142]

Our ranks are badly thinned out. . . . You can't even do your morning toilet in peace. Someone always needs to be with you. . . . Snipers . . . shoot into the dugout. The worst thing is that, at night, small enemy parachute detachments of approx. six men are dropped behind our front and conduct an independent sniper war [*Heckenschützenkrieg*]. . . . We have to continue to hold out. . . . Gradually, you become accustomed to this situation. I only fear that we will no longer be the first to make it into Moscow, even though we were once the forwardmost troops.

26.8.41: *LEUTNANT* WILLIBALD G. (57 INFANTRY DIVISION, SEVENTEENTH ARMY, ARMY GROUP SOUTH)[143]

We reemerged from the "hell of Cherkassy" again early this morning. The night before yesterday we changed position at the edge of the town of Ch[erkassy] and at daybreak moved into a firing position in a light acacia tree bosket, where the guns could be well camouflaged against aerial detection. The morning passed relatively peacefully, if you discount the many aerial attacks, which, however, didn't do us any damage.

Around 1300 the Reds began a murderously heavy barrage [*Trommelfeuer*], shooting everything they had with light and heavy batteries, as well as with railway and flak guns. That went on until 1700 and then the Russians began a counterattack, which, however, collapsed in our fire. Then we shot for a few hours, until it was evening. The Russians were intent on throwing our forwardmost elements back from the islands in the Dnepr (here, incl. backwaters and river branches, up to 7 km wide!), but they didn't succeed in that. They fired harassing fire the whole night with all calibers. By 2000 we had the ninth aerial attack behind us! We were so well camouflaged that they didn't find us. That was our good fortune! . . .

Early this morning we were then relieved by another division. We pulled back 6 km and now, during the day, we are lying in a lovely, bright oak forest. After the nervous tension of the last few days, the peace does us good and the thunder of the heavy artillery and the light crash of the flak just rolls over to us from a distance.

A strange phenomenon is the feeling of tiredness that has now come over everyone. Supposedly, that's the result of the constant jarring that comes from this incessant barrage fire. Today, at 2400 it's onward to the south, for 3 days to begin with. What happens then, we don't know yet. We don't ask, either, and a world without combat operations, without noise or marches and worries would seem very strange and unaccustomed to us at first. . . . But, despite it all, I can give you all reassurance at home by saying that still, today, every soldier knows why and for what he is fighting, and that even today everyone still holds to that watchword: come home victorious or not at all.

So, now we go to give our comrade, whom we brought back with us from the front, back to the earth. Another mother will cry, but the ultimate goal remains unalterable: Victory or death! We will choose victory, because the Fatherland still needs us!

26.8.41: *MAJOR* WERNER HEINEMANN (23 INFANTRY DIVISION, FOURTH ARMY, ARMY GROUP CENTER)[144]

What a desolate country this is here! The primitiveness and poverty of the population is, thanks to their exploitation by the Soviet authorities, so monstrous that it is not possible to conceive <u>how</u> the people can live at all. Yet the country is decidedly fertile, but then everything that they harvest is taken away from the people, and out of the proceeds of the party organization the huge armaments and the international propaganda are paid for.

So nothing remains but desolate, gray monotony in attitude, customs, clothing, and domestic economy, and, moreover, everyone is afraid of standing out from the rest of the colorless "human mass" in even the very slightest way (even if that is only by having a flower by the window or a neckerchief). The "commissars" keep the populace and military in constant fear for that little bit of miserable life in such unimaginable ways that any thought of protesting against this inhumane condition is extinguished right from the start.

That in such a country, across which, moreover, the war forged its bloody path, there was absolutely nothing more for us to obtain or buy in terms of goods should be evident. The term "to buy" is, in any case, utterly bourgeois, for that which the Soviet citizen "needs for life" is of course "allocated" to him by the state, and so a "shop" is nowhere to be seen. The pressure under which this country has been for the last 25 years still has an effect today where <u>we</u> are, and nothing is to be done with the population, either good or bad. Horrid!

27.8.41: DR. ADOLF B. (25 INFANTRY DIVISION [MOT.], 1 PANZER GROUP, ARMY GROUP SOUTH)[145]

It seems like the fighting in the East will be over in four to six weeks. Like many of my comrades and acquaintances, I would be delighted if our division were then allowed to return to Germany. And then never again to Russia! The activity at our main dressing station [*Hauptverbandplatz*] is still rather brisk, but should subside in the coming weeks. As soon as we've crossed the Dnepr, the pursuit will begin again, and there will be fewer casualties. How far will we still go to the east? We've already advanced farther east than any other unit (to the bend in the Dnepr, about 150 kilometers south of Dnepropetrovsk, which was captured yesterday).[146]

We've already passed by many German settlements (former Frisians and Dutch); they're Mennonites, who reject all oaths, military service and infant baptism. Tomorrow will be my third birthday in the field.

27.8.41: *LEUTNANT* RUDOLF MAURER (251 INFANTRY DIVISION, NINTH ARMY, ARMY GROUP CENTER)[147]

I have to reconnoiter a road northeast of Velikie Luki early in the morning. There, I saw the devastating effect of the German assault. The dead Russians lay like seed sown on the battlefield. In the afternoon, we begin the advance on the reconnoitered road. We discover that the event of Velikie Luki has been announced via *Sondermeldung*: 30,000 prisoners, 400 guns, 40,000 dead.[148]

While the army of prisoners was being led past us, 459 IR marching ahead of us and 471 IR following us were fired at by dispersed [enemy troops]. Four of these tenacious Russians were led close by us, amid angry shouts.

In the evening, rain set in. The night is dark. I drive ahead and instruct the regiment, an ungrateful task. Suddenly the regiment wasn't following anymore. It is 2300. The bicycle company and the remainder of my 14th Company thus remained alone. I sleep in the car, there's enough exhaustion to go round. And we're used to the "crouch position." Two years ago tomorrow, I joined the 14th Company of our 451 Infantry Regiment in Kassel.

27.8.41: KARL FUCHS (7 PANZER DIVISION, NINTH ARMY, ARMY GROUP CENTER)[149]

A few days ago the tanks were started up again and they rumbled toward the front. We shook hands with our comrades and off they went. Some [of] us, me included, are recuperating several kilometers behind the front line and are staying in one of these endless, monotonous Russian forests. It certainly is a strange feeling for me to be here and not in the midst of the fighting. But our company commander is of the opinion that, if possible, all members of the company should have the opportunity to fight at the front.[150]

Our losses so far have been minimal. This is due to excellent leadership and magnificent soldiering spirit. The Bolsheviks, however, who are under tremendous political pressure to win, are defending themselves desperately and their morale is low. Their losses are heavy. We're of the opinion that it's only a matter of weeks now until the final battles around St. Petersburg and in the Ukraine will be fought. . . . I'm convinced that the Russian army, decimated and beaten, will be destroyed by the end of this year.

27.8.41: *GEFREITER* HANS CASPAR VON WIEDEBACH-NOSTITZ (20 PANZER DIVISION, NINTH ARMY, ARMY GROUP CENTER)[151]

Any hopes of getting even a couple days' rest here are disappointed when the order comes at 0400 hours to get ready to move. Today we are supposed to be heading toward Urozel.[152] *Leutnant* Behr assumes command of the point reconnaissance troop and our reconnaissance troop assumes the lead of the advance guard and then things get moving. We drive on reasonably good roads, and then again through an area of forest. The road bends a lot and often crosses bridges. Everywhere we encounter Russian trenches and small bunkers. After we have covered about 20 kilometers we come upon the enemy, infantry, who soon scatter when they come under fire from our machine guns.

After a short while an advance reconnaissance troop comes back to us. They encountered the enemy in a village and managed to leave behind a Russian truck that they set ablaze. Now we move together toward the village. Most of the houses are on fire. Here one dare not get out of the vehicle. Snipers are everywhere, behind bushes and in the trees. Many Russians put up a heroic defense in their trenches. Grenades, thrown by our motorcyclists into their foxholes, are thrown back out by them again. Finally, they are flushed out. We only have 20 minutes for a midday halt. Meanwhile, the company has arrived but we are on the move again. *Leutnant* Behr who is once again at the head of the reconnaissance troop does not get far. The first vehicle is knocked out by a Russian antitank gun, the other two, which had almost been burned out, since the Russians had thrown Molotov cocktails at them, retreat. Two men are wounded.

Thereupon a major attack gets under way. We drive on the street, armored vehicles to the left and right beside us; behind them the motorcyclists on foot, led by Major Wolff. To our rear *Oberstleutnant* von Bismarck and *Oberleutnant* Kischnik are traveling in the *Kübelwagen*.[153] *Leutnant* Behr is also with them. We push through the wood to a village that is being set on fire by our combat vehicles, while resistance is being offered. The Russians have dug trenches everywhere along the streets from which they throw Molotov cocktails. Now things are not working out so well for them. They creep off into the woods, though a combat vehicle has started to burn and one man has been wounded who is now loaded onto our vehicle. We take him back a bit, to a military ambulance where the commander's armored command vehicle is also located.

There I see something dreadful. *Leutnant* Behr and *Unteroffizier* Wohlfeil are lying in the vehicle: they are both dead. That has finished me for today: I can't take any more. All of us were profoundly shaken. *Unteroffizier* Wohlfeil received a fatal shot to the stomach from a sniper shooting from the wood, and when *Leutnant* Behr was about to go to his assistance, he received a fatal shot to the head. At first, we can hardly grasp that this exemplary and daring soldier had been so suddenly torn away from us. He was always a selfless comrade, trusted by all. . . .

The combat vehicles and other vehicles turn around in order to get on the line of advance on the road that has now taken another course. We remain here for a while as security. . . . It starts to rain and we have to sleep bunched up in the vehicle. Only very slowly do my thoughts sort themselves out, thoughts that are still occupied with the horrendous events of the last few hours.

28.8.41: SIEGBERT STEHMANN (163 INFANTRY DIVISION, GERMAN ARMY OF NORWAY)[154]

Tomorrow we'll set out again, apparently into the Karelian Isthmus. It pains us to have to leave our huts, our warm oven, and all the lovely potatoes. The peace and quiet are over, and once again we're called to an unknown fate. But peace is within me, for today's biblical verse is: "I myself will search for my sheep and look after them." Ezekiel 34:11. And tomorrow's verse: "Look down from heaven, your holy dwelling place, and bless your people." Deuteronomy 26:15. And so now [we] commend [ourselves] to God! Dear Lord, protect and bless all of us henceforth.

29.8.41: DR. HEINRICH HAAPE (6 INFANTRY DIVISION, NINTH ARMY, ARMY GROUP CENTER)[155]

Parts of our battalion have been detailed to our neighboring regiment to provide support and help sweep the enemy out, who has broken through over there with two divisions. In the meantime we are holding our sector with weak forces! We don't like this trench warfare much. I hope and trust that in about a week we'll return to the attack—that suits us better!

I have just heard the result of the counterattack: the enemy beaten back with bloody losses; reached and restored the old battle line. Over 200 noncommissioned officers and soldiers fallen on the German side, plus [many] officers dead and 8 wounded.[156] The Russian losses incomparably higher as always! Time and again, he relentlessly throws reserves into battle, and our losses are not inconsiderable! Even the regimental commander has fallen; 4 days ago he had received the Knight's Cross [*Ritterkreuz*]. It is tragic.

However, I don't want always to be talking of the war, nor of the labors that the soldier has to undergo here, but instead say a few words about the poor possibilities for life in this Russian campaign: this is the land of vermin, head lice, crabs, insects, fleas, and clothes lice. They are common and omnipresent here, making an overnight stay in a house impossible! That is why I have been sleeping either outside in the fresh air, in my tent, or in my vehicle since the start of the war—because of possible surprise attacks at night, so we are always ready, we remove at most our field shirts and boots, but otherwise remain fully dressed—and beside us our guns, primed and ready to fire.

And this is a monotonous, uncultural, enslaved country [*ein eintöniges—unkulturelles, versklavtes Land*], this Russia! The only thing that is grown here is grain. No fruit, no vegetables—the people live in the most humble conditions.

Dysentery [*Ruhr*] is currently spreading widely among our soldiers,[157] transmitted principally through the millions of flies, which do not give us a moment's peace. We can hardly get away from the flies. I've also recovered from a slight dysentery infection, but I've been able to continue my service in every way. The days are hot and the nights cold—bloody battle in a country with no borders or culture!

30.8.41: *MAJOR* WERNER HEINEMANN (23 INFANTRY DIVISION, FOURTH ARMY, ARMY GROUP CENTER)[158]

When we, here at the position of the front projecting farthest to the east, will begin to advance again, nobody knows. Only that it must be, that we <u>have</u> to have Moscow this year, that's certain. The Russian is certainly shaken to his very core, but an increasing tenacity remains (he, after all, is fighting for "Russia," not for Bolshevism anymore) and an absurd number of men. Defectors arrive daily, but still he makes life most difficult for us, and the commissars above all know their trade, keeping the masses under pressure.

30.8.41: *OBERGEFREITER* FRANZ F. (12 PANZER DIVISION,[159] SIXTEENTH ARMY, ARMY GROUP NORTH)[160]

I can't write much to you, we're on the advance, and how. We're 10 kilometers from Petersburg and there's so much work to be done that we can't even wash up. We're in such a rush that I haven't been able to wash for eight days. Yesterday there were some big air battles, and four Russian bombers were shot down by our flak. That was great fun to watch. I fired my machine gun all day long, until the barrel turned red hot. The Russians are doing their best to defend Petersburg, but they don't have enough soldiers. [Those they do have] are old and young. Yesterday one of our men was wounded by two Russians—one was 53, the other 15 years old. Both of them had only been soldiers for three days. What a grand state of affairs.

30.8.41: *SOLDAT* WALDO P. (5 INFANTRY DIVISION, NINTH ARMY, ARMY GROUP CENTER)[161]

Here, you have no idea what the situation actually is. We lowly soldiers of course have no oversight over the great events that are occurring all over the place. At first, we were told we would have to hold the position here for three weeks so that the flanks to the right and left could catch up. In the meantime, our three-week *Stellungskrieg* has passed and once again we've been told that we'll be sitting here for at least as long again. So now we've constructed a dugout again for the fourth time.

In Smolensk barracks are already being unloaded for the winter. Yesterday, we requested winter clothing. On the other hand, we're always hearing that it must soon come to an end. Even if the boys have been at the front, they say the most contradictory things. . . . Be that as it may, everybody's wish is that the Soviets soon run out of gas and we can soon go home. There is, incidentally, a rumor of our imminent relief, but it is a rumor that is already pretty old.

30.8.41: *GEFREITER* RUDOLF STÜTZEL (5 INFANTRY DIVISION, NINTH ARMY, ARMY GROUP CENTER)[162]

Of course, how long I'm going to be in this military hospital, I don't know.[163] But I won't be back at the front so very soon, and even then, hopefully this dreadful battle will be over. Because this is not a battle like the ones in Poland, France, in the south or in Africa, this is no honorable battle, man against man. This is a dreadful, treacherous slaughter. That's why there are such heavy losses. It's a good thing that our people know nothing of these losses, that's fortunate. If you knew how many men a company, a battalion, a regiment still has, you would all shake your heads. For only then could you all comprehend how we have all been fighting and suffering. Fighting like lions, often. [At this point, several words have been made illegible by post censorship.] But this will soon come to an end. In the great, decisive blow new and fresh divisions will resoundingly defeat the enemy. There will be an annihilation [*Vernichtung*] the like of which history has never known. For there is no other way to bring these people to their senses except through utter annihilation.

31.8.41: *GEFREITER* MARTIN W. (52 INFANTRY DIVISION, FOURTH ARMY, ARMY GROUP CENTER)[164]

Once again we're resting far from the front and will be here for some time. Most likely we won't see action again, because we've already had lots of casualties. For 33 days I've seen action in the bloodiest and most tenacious battles in the forwardmost line. On the very first day, when we put in an attack, my company had 20 dead and more than 30 wounded. It was 16 July. And so it's gone on for more than a month, until the Russian resistance finally slackened. On 15 August we carried out a large and well-prepared attack. But we didn't find any Russians, because they'd already pulled back the night before. We took up the pursuit and captured more than 15,000 prisoners, as well as an enormous amount of war material. That was on 17 and 18 August. Then we were once again on the march for eight days behind the motorized forces; of course, we were far behind the front. We've now covered 1,000 kilometers marching through Russia.[165] That's about how far it is from Regensburg to Amsterdam. Just what we've gone through on the march can't be put into words.

31.8.41: *UNTEROFFIZIER* ROBERT RUPP (17 PANZER DIVISION, 2 PANZER GROUP, ARMY GROUP CENTER)[166]

I write to you in the crisp, early morning. So you see, the days and Sundays still—and always—belong to us. I can see you today, dressed in your Sunday best dress. Perhaps it's [time for] church in Wolkertshofen and you're singing and your voice doesn't quaver. . . . After this Sunday, our sunny month is to come, let's hope and pray. At the moment, there's such a material deployment [*Materialeinsatz*] at work that I believe firmly in September again. The war is being driven forward with such an urgency that on some days I don't get to writing. . . . I know you [are thinking of me] and [I know] of your loyal and brave suffering. You and Raini, you are my whole and only blessedness in this devil's world. God has been richly generous to us, so let us not be bitter toward the fate with which he has recently burdened us, nor toward the people who have the responsibility for this but do not bear it. Let's pray for a quick end, to the good fortune of everyone, and the healing of wounds in suffering borne.

31.8.41: ALBERT NEUHAUS (ARMY GROUP NORTH)[167]

We are now nicely back on the advance and are around 70 km outside Petersburg. You were quite right with your surmises about our travel destination. The last few days were, once again, full of all kinds of "enchantment." The changes of position made necessary by the advance always cause a lot of work for me and my comrades, but we do it gladly, since we know that we're making progress. *Der Russe* is going weak at the knees now and is beginning to take to his heels. We expect the decision here in the next few days or weeks now, too.

In recent days we have been driving along an asphalt road for the first time and it feels like sitting on a sofa! But the sideroads are dreadful. You often have to wonder how the vehicles can do it or cope with it. . . .

Now the Russians are deserting in large numbers; they have had nothing decent to eat for about 14 days and they are glad to have escaped the Russian hell. The prisoners are immediately put to repair work and to building bridges. Every bridge along the main road has been blown up and, in some areas, the terrain has been heavily mined. Of course the prisoners have to carry out this work under the supervision of our engineers. The Russians have either destroyed the railway tracks every 5 meters or taken the entire track with them. But all that matters little to the German advance. The day before yesterday Reval fell and that will naturally work out favorably for us.[168] It's just a shame that the weather is currently so unfavorable, with rain almost every day. It makes the roads so dreadfully boggy and the horse-drawn artillery sometimes has to harness a team of 12. Extraordinary demands are being made of man, beast, and equipment. But we will do it.

31.8.41: *GEFREITER* ALFONS L. (BRIDGE CONSTRUCTION BATTALION 159, ARMY GROUP SOUTH)[169]

We've been in the Ukraine now for two days. We're in action here to support the forces coming up from the south, and are attacking the enemy from behind. Due to the rapid advance, we're covering lots of ground in order to build bridges. For example, we constructed a bridge in four days that's 350 meters in length and 9 meters above the surface of the water. For this bridge we used 800 cubic meters of wood. So, you can work out for yourself how rapidly the work's getting done; also, the rivers have a depth of 4–6 meters.

There's no thought of rest here. Except for a period of eight days, we've constantly been in action—at times right at the front, then several kilometers behind the front. But never so far back that the enemy artillery couldn't reach us. Up to now, however, the Dnepr bridge has only been shelled once. We see lots of enemy planes; they're always trying to take out the bridge with bombs. Yesterday, two houses just 300 meters from us were blown sky high by aerial bombs. Not a day passes without them dropping their bombs here, but many of the planes are shot down. You become so indifferent [*abgestumpft*] to it all that you hardly pay attention any longer when the ground around you trembles, when the bombs fall. At the moment the front is just 8–10 kilometers away.

31.8.41: *LEUTNANT* RUDOLF MAURER (251 INFANTRY DIVISION, NINTH ARMY, ARMY GROUP CENTER)[170]

We have been constantly on the road again since the 28th and always in a northeasterly direction. We have crossed the Kun'ja and today we are lying outside Orka. The roads are very poor, especially since, till now, it has rained every day.

I have been forward several times to reconnoiter the roads, a not terribly easy task. Even if we don't always have a fighting opponent in front of us at the moment, nevertheless everywhere in this deep forest region there live dispersed enemy troops. Only yesterday, another *Unteroffizier* of 3rd Battalion, which was marching at the rear, was shot at. Moreover, our Russian maps are inaccurate. Every road usually has to be [reconnoitered] with the aid of an interpreter. After all, you risk driving over mines, because the Russians are masters at laying mines. And *last not least*—such assignments rob you of a goodly part of your night's sleep and there's not much of that anyway, since we usually only arrive in the area we've been ordered to late at night. And reconnaissance of the terrain starts again at daybreak, that is, before 5:00 a.m.

The population in this area close to Toropez is much friendlier to us than usual. Until now—apart from Lithuania—you might have got the impression that the people just apathetically let everything wash over them: one evil is just as great as another, we don't care whether the Germans or the Russians take up position by us, those are probably their thoughts. But here the inhabitants greet us. Yesterday I was the first German soldier to enter into several villages. The interpreter translated one woman saying, "I'm as happy as a child that the Germans are coming." And you can truly see the people's joy in their faces.

Photo Essay: Summer 1941

On the eve of the surprise attack on Soviet Russia, orders are read out to the men; perhaps he's reading Adolf Hitler's proclamation to the *"Soldaten der Ostfront."* (*Bundesarchiv, Bild 183-L25085, Foto: o.Ang., 21 June 1941*)

Troops of the elite 1 Mountain Division (Army Group South) cross the Russo-German frontier at dawn on 22 June 1941. (*Bundesarchiv, Bild 146-2007-0127, Foto: König*)

Hours later, General Hubert Lanz (C-in-C, 1 Mountain Division) honors his fallen comrades. Shortly after the picture was taken, Lanz, who had been injured by a shell splinter, collapsed due to loss of blood, but he would soon return to the battlefield.

At 0305 hours on 22 June 1941, German artillery, including 210mm heavy howitzers and *Nebelwerfer* rocket launchers, loosed a devastating barrage on Russian targets in and around the city of Tauroggen (Taurage) on the front of Army Group North. Despite the barrage, the Russians fought back tenaciously. (*RaBoe/Wikipedia, CC-BY-SA-3.0*)

German riflemen in action against the fortress of Brest-Litovsk. The cloth spread out in front of the men is most likely a recognition flag for the *Luftwaffe*. (*Pen & Sword*)

A German mortar crew in action against the fortress of Brest-Litovsk. The mostly Austrian 45 Infantry Division would sustain over three hundred dead assaulting the fortress on 22 June 1941—perhaps greater losses than those of any other division of the *Ostheer* on the first day of war. Organized resistance inside the citadel would not be broken until the end of the month. (*Pen & Sword*)

A self-propelled 150mm medium German infantry gun (s.I.G. 33 [sf]), most likely belonging to 1 Panzer Division of 4 Panzer Group (Army Group North), moves past an abandoned Soviet KV-2 heavy tank in late June 1941. (*Pen & Sword*)

German motorcycle troops on the move along a truck convoy shrouded in dust. (*Bundesarchiv, Bild 1011-265-0003-13A, Foto: Mossdorf, June–July 1941*)

The German advance in the opening weeks of the campaign was so swift that numerous Red Army units were overrun, even before they could deploy for action—as was the case with this trainload of Soviet light BT-7 tanks. (*Stackpole Books*)

German tanks of Army Group Center in the "fog of war" near Minsk (late June 1941). (*National Archives; hereafter cited as "NA"*)

Russian tanks destroyed by the *Luftwaffe* near Dubno, Poland, during the heavy tank combat on the front of Army Group South (*June 1941*).

Red Army troops taken prisoner in a forest in the Ukraine. At the start of the campaign, the often badly outnumbered and outgunned Soviet soldiers frequently fled to the relative safety of wooded areas, forcing the Germans to clear them out in difficult and costly combat. (*Bundesarchiv, Bild 101I-020-1268-10, Foto: Hähle, Johannes, June 1941*)

An example of the grinding poverty encountered by German troops in rural regions of the Soviet Union. Such images reinforced German impressions of the evils of Bolshevism and of the need to eradicate the Soviet state. (*Stackpole Books*)

A well-fed soldier was generally a soldier with good morale. In the idiom of the *Landser*, these field kitchen wagons were called "goulash cannons." (*Pen & Sword*)

Vormarsch through Latvia: Crews of two German assault guns (Stug IIIs) make a brief halt at the side of a road (July 1941). (*Bundesarchiv, Bild 1011-009–0882-04, Foto: Schröter, CC-BY-SA 3.0*)

An apocalyptic image of German troops of Army Group Center near the Beresina River with the woods on fire behind them (July 1941). (*Stackpole Books*)

A platoon of Germany infantry prepare to advance. The soldier in the foreground shoulders an MG 34 machine gun, while the man to the right is armed with an MP 40 submachine gun. (*Stackpole Books*)

An abandoned Russian artillery piece (most likely summer 1941). (*German War Graves Commission; hereafter cited as GWGC*)

A battery of German 150mm medium field howitzers (s.F.H. 18) on the southern front, supporting the attack on L'vov (Lemberg) (29 June 1941). The gun had a maximum range of 13,300 meters. (*NA*)

An impressive photograph of a 210mm heavy howitzer (21cm *Mörser* 18). The German Army's standard heavy artillery piece, it was an extremely accurate and devastating weapon with a range of 16,700 meters. These heavy howitzers were normally GHQ artillery and assigned to lower echelons on an as-needed basis. (*Stackpole Books*)

A German main dressing station (*Hauptverbandplatz*) somewhere behind the front (summer 1941). (*Pen & Sword*)

A German radio station in a ditch at the side of the road (July 1941). (*NA*)

General Hubert Lanz (far left) prepares his elite 1 Mountain Division (Army Group South) for an attack on the Stalin Line (15 July 1941).

German Waffen-SS soldiers inspect bunkers of the Stalin Line (summer 1941).

Exhausted German infantry of Army Group Center enjoy a short rest in Vitebsk on the Western Dvina River after a long march (23 July 1941). (NA)

A column of Panzer III tanks, loaded with extra equipment, advance toward the front, while supply trucks return to their depots. Although the standard German medium tank at the start of *Barbarossa*, the Panzer III was totally outclassed by the Soviet T-34. (*Stackpole Books*)

The legendary Ju 87 "Stuka" divebomber. Although the *Luft-waffe* began the eastern campaign with barely more than 350 operational Stukas (almost all of them assigned to Army Group Center), they proved to be a devastatingly effective close support aircraft. (*Stackpole Books*)

Soviet T-26 light tanks counterattacking during the heavy fighting near Smolensk in August 1941. (*Pen & Sword*)

Russian guns of all calibers and other war matériel captured by Army Group Center during the Smolensk cauldron (*Kessel*) battle in July–August 1941. (*NA*)

erman motorized and horse-drawn columns advancing
long the *Autobahn* between Minsk and Tolochino (13
July 1941). (*NA*)

hree German assault guns (Stug
IIs) move down a road past a
alted vehicle column. As the Rus-
an campaign progressed, the as-
ault gun became increasingly im-
ortant to the German infantry as
 highly effective support weapon
summer 1941). (*Pen & Sword*)

150mm medium field howitzer of 122 Infantry Division
Army Group North) in the summer of 1941. (*Andrea Lom-
ardi*)

Infantry of 122 Infantry Division (Army Group North) taking a short rest in the tall grass. (*Andrea Lombardi*)

German infantry of Army Group South, wearing their greatcoats, take up position inside a Soviet anti-tank ditch as they prepare to continue their advance on Kiev (late August 1941). (*Pen & Sword*)

The C-in-C of Army Group North, GFM Ritter von Leeb (at the telescope) and the C-in-C of Eighteenth Army, *Generaloberst* von Küchler at a forward observation post of the artillery (September 1941). (*Bundesarchiv, Bild 183-B12786, Foto: Schröter, CC-BY-SA 3.0*)

The Russian landscape was harsh, unforgiving, and mysterious. More than a few German soldiers responded with depression to this alien and forbidding country. (*Stackpole Books*)

CHAPTER 5

September 1941

Introduction

Throughout September 1941 the war of position [Stellungskrieg] continued along the expansive front of Army Group Center, taking its toll on German and Russian alike. On 5 September, from the Army High Command compound in East Prussia, Oberstleutnant Hellmuth Stieff commented darkly on the increasingly precarious predicament of Bock's army group: "The eastern front of [Army Group Center] has been involved in the heaviest defensive fighting on the scale of the World War (up to 300 enemy batteries in a single corps sector) for days, even weeks, during which there have been serious daily breaches [of the main battle line] and in the course of which the combat strength of our divisions has melted away like snow in the sun. The tragic thing in all this is that our troops are suffering chronic ammunition shortages due to transport issues. The situation there is on the razor's edge, because we have no more reserves. Hopefully the Russian will run out of steam first, otherwise there's the distinct danger of losing Smolensk."[1]

The Red Army maintained its furious counterstrokes against Army Group Center into the second week of September 1941, at which time they finally petered out. While these aggressive operations slowed and attrited German forces (e.g., as of 4 September, only 34 percent of the army group's tanks were considered combat-ready), they also ended in failure, the attacking Soviet forces sustaining enormous losses in personnel and equipment. The Soviets "congenitally overestimated" their own capabilities while underestimating those of their opponent. The "Soviet command cadre, in particular its senior officers . . . lacked the experience necessary to contend with the better led and more tactically and operationally proficient Wehrmacht."[2] *That duly noted, the Russian offensives did produce one noteworthy success: On 5 September, a Soviet rifle division stormed into the battered town of El'nia and, with the support of several more rifle divisions, seized the town the next day. For the Red Army, the victory at El'nia signified its first real victory of the war, modest though it was; in fact, it was the "first occasion when Soviet forces successfully penetrated prepared German defenses and regained a sizeable chuck of occupied territory."*[3]

On 6 September Hitler signed War Directive 35 ordering Army Group Center to prepare for another major offensive operation toward Moscow at the end of September.

Without addressing the considerable losses of the campaign so far or the run-down condition of the motorized and panzer divisions, Hitler's new directive called for Soviet forces on the road to Moscow to be "annihilated in the limited time that remains before the onset of winter weather."⁴ Hitler then envisaged a second and far more ambitious goal: "Only when Army Group Timoshenko has been defeated in . . . encircling operations of annihilation will our central army be able to begin the advance on Moscow."⁵ The perennial problem, however, remained supply. There was barely enough arriving at the front to meet the army group's immediate needs, to say nothing of building up stores for another major offensive farther east. As GFM Günther von Kluge, commanding the Fourth Army, complained in a report from 13 September: "With the growing distances the army is almost completely dependent on the railways. At the moment, the latter meet current consumption only. The transport situation [does] not allow the establishment of depots sufficiently large to enable the troops to receive what they need in accordance with the tactical situation. The army lives from hand to mouth, especially as regards the fuel situation."⁶

By early September, infantry forces of GFM von Leeb's Army Group North had cleared the Soviets from Estonia; while Leeb's right wing battled its way toward Tikhvin, panzer and motorized units fought their way into the suburbs of Leningrad. On 3 September, German long-range artillery opened fire on the city for the first time and, on 8 September, German forces seized Shlisselburg, on the shore of Lake Ladoga, depriving Leningrad of its last land link with the rest of the Soviet Union. The next day the Luftwaffe began to pound the city with around-the-clock bombing missions. On 10 September, German tanks penetrated Red Army defenses on the Dudergof height, barely 10 kilometers (6.2 miles) southeast of Leningrad. From this tactically vital patch of ground, the Germans could see the city spread out before them, with its gleaming golden cupolas and towers; warships were visible in the port, lobbing shells on German targets to their rear. But the attackers would get no farther, for Hitler had already decreed that most of Leeb's armor was to be transferred to Army Group Center to support the impending drive toward Moscow; soon Hoepner's 4 Panzer Group headquarters, three panzer corps headquarters, and several panzer divisions were on the move to join Bock's army group.⁷

Leeb's main offensive may have ended at Leningrad, but to the south Army Group North's advance continued under Generaloberst *Ernst Busch, commanding the Sixteenth Army, which drove toward Demyansk and the Valdai Hills. Logistical shortages and the boggy ground complicated Busch's advance, but he maneuvered to close a small encirclement that netted a further thirty-five thousand Soviet troops and 334 guns.⁸ At Leningrad the siege that would endure for nine hundred days had begun, but already on 22 September there were concentrated Soviet attacks south of Shlisselburg to relieve the city. The Soviet offensive was eventually repulsed, but only at heavy cost, and Leeb was reduced to desperate appeals to the High Command for more reinforcements.⁹*

In the Ukraine, GFM von Rundstedt's Army Group South pushed across the mighty Dnepr River and, in cooperation with strong mobile forces detached from Army Group Center (i.e., two panzer corps of Guderian's panzer group), began the envelopment of a half dozen Soviet armies east of Kiev. By 12 September, the converging spearheads of Kleist's and Guderian's panzer groups were barely 80 kilometers (50 miles) apart and closing fast. On the morning of 14 September, a small battlegroup from Guderian conducted a daring raid southward; hours later, white Very lights, which always signified a German presence, were exchanged between the battlegroup and a company of combat engineers belonging to Kleist's panzer group. The next morning (15 September), the lead elements of both panzer groups established "conclusive physical contact" at Lokhvitsa in the central Ukraine. Trapped inside their steel jaws, facing certain destruction, was the entire Soviet Southwestern Front. "The Battle at Kiev," Bock proclaimed triumphantly, "has thus become a dazzling success."[10] By 24 September, the fighting in the immense cauldron was over—fifty divisions had disappeared from the Red Army order of battle, the victorious German forces also capturing hundreds of thousands of Red Army prisoners and seizing thousands of tanks and guns. By any measure, it was one of the greatest military victories of all time.

The destruction of the Southwestern Front not only resulted in the capture of the central-northern Ukraine; it also left extremely little to counter Rundstedt's renewed advance. In late September his panzers attacked to the southeast along the Nogai Steppe toward the Sea of Azov, hoping to cut off two more Soviet armies. Yet while Germany's operational successes in September appeared almost flawless, the cumulative losses in manpower (dead, wounded, and missing in action) were taking a serious toll. Throughout the German Army in the East, casualties had reached 551,039 men, which equaled 16 percent of the total Barbarossa *invasion force.[11] On 26 September, Halder matter-of-factly noted in his diary that the* Ostheer *was short of two hundred thousand men and that these "could no longer be replaced." He also noted that the average daily loss of officers was running at a staggering 196.[12]*

Letters and Diary Entries (1–30 September 1941)

1.9.41: *SOLDAT* K.H.G. (13 PANZER DIVISION, 1 PANZER GROUP, ARMY GROUP SOUTH)[13]

It isn't exactly nice here. The place is teeming with Jews. I can't even begin to tell you what real specimens [*Muster*] you can see here. Thank God we no longer have to deal with any of that at home. Now you can really see just how beautiful our Fatherland is. But many still don't want to acknowledge that.

1.9.41: *OBERGEFREITER* MATTHIAS (6 INFANTRY DIVISION, NINTH ARMY, ARMY GROUP CENTER)[14]

A trench war has developed here, with communication trenches, "fox burrows," bunkers (in the earth), etc. It's bitterly cold and rainy. There's water in our positions, all the walls are collapsing, and the bunkers have become damp. Hopefully we'll be able to move on soon, too. The best thing would be a swift attack! To our right and left, the panzers have already pushed ahead and soon another cauldron will be complete. Leningrad is already encircled as well. According to rumors [*Latrinenparolen*], the same fate awaits Moscow, but I don't believe it, since nothing official has been announced about it. At any rate, the trap has to be sprung in September now or else it will soon be winter and the war will be up sh** creek!

1.9.41: MAJOR HANS MEIER-WELCKER (251 INFANTRY DIVISION, NINTH ARMY, ARMY GROUP CENTER)[15]

For days we've been in relentless pursuit [*rastloser Verfolgung*] of the enemy beaten at V[elikie] L[uki]. Our troops are giving everything they've got. There are units that for the past 2 or 3 days have been living off the land, without their field kitchens or normal rations. The "roads" are wretched, and it rains daily for several hours. Our motor vehicles are undergoing a trial that people in Germany wouldn't have thought possible. Of course, the number of vehicles that are still operational grows smaller by the day. Can any of you at home actually conceive of just what we're having to go through here? How boldly the men are being led; the responsibilities that we shoulder; how each day the men and the horses have to cover a large number of kilometers—fighting, bleeding, and dying while getting little in the way of food or shelter? We've having to fight on all sides—in front, in the flanks, and in the rear. But we're used to that now. We have to protect ourselves from potential attack from any direction. Otherwise we continue to advance.

1.9.41: *LEUTNANT* WILLIBALD G. (57 INFANTRY DIVISION, SEVENTEENTH ARMY, ARMY GROUP SOUTH)[16]

Tomorrow was supposed to be a rest day, but that has, as usual, fallen through, although we and the horses are in great need of it! It's just a good thing that we discovered 40 hundredweight [2,000 kilograms] of oats yesterday, so we can feed our horses properly for another few days! The population here is very nice and friendly. No combat operations have taken place here, so the *kolkhozes* are still full of livestock and horses and people are working hard on bringing in the rich harvest. It's a very reassuring feeling when you see that not a single straw goes astray under us, despite the campaign. All the municipalities have elected a mayor from among their own people, and in the larger towns a civil defense, equipped with sidearms, maintains peace and order. It's all very well organized.

A few days ago, we were quartered with a farmer, who acts as an animal doctor in a *kolkhoz* and so he had a bit more than his neighbors. The houses are all spick and span [*blitzsauber*] and all of them have a little flower garden, although just a little piece of land is the property of each farmer. The animal doctor was extremely hospitable. We were immediately given fried potatoes with sauerkraut and smoked bacon, as well as eggs. And then something very fine: little, white rolls sprinkled with poppyseeds and soaked in a honey sauce. It was delicious!

Later, there was 96% schnapps, which we could only drink diluted with water (the farmer and his wife drank it pure by the cup!) and pickled cucumbers, black bread and bacon. These little people really did give everything that they had. The man had been a prisoner of war in Rastatt for two years in the First World War and so could speak some German, which contributed significantly to our mutual understanding.

The whole country here is strangely peaceful. The train goes right up to the Dnepr, which was a great comfort to us in terms of resupply! Neither are there any

Russian planes to be seen here, although Stukas, Ju 88s, and fighters buzz and drone about all day. That, too, is very comforting, and has shown us that the Reds are deploying the few planes they still have in concentrated focal points. Hopefully, they will be shot down soon, too! Nothing is more fearsome than an air attack on the march. . . .

The Reds are firing a truly devilish ammunition from their armaments [*Bordwaffen*]: infantry bullets that, on firing, rip open into two parts ½ cm behind the tip, thereby creating a butterfly screw [*Flügelschraube*] that "drills" large wounds! Our 1st Battalion had a whole series of fatalities and casualties as a result.[17]

2.9.41: *OBERGEFREITER* M. H. (268 INFANTRY DIVISION, FOURTH ARMY, ARMY GROUP CENTER)[18]

We're experiencing grim times and heavy losses [*schlimme Zeiten und grosse Verluste*]. We've been stuck in the same place [the El'nia salient] for five weeks now and we're badly and constantly tormented by the Russian artillery. I just don't know how much longer our nerves can stand up to this. . . . I think we've already made enough heavy sacrifices. We're also constantly being promised that we'll be going back home, but it always comes to nothing.[19]

2.9.41: *GEFREITER* HEINZ B. (291 INFANTRY DIVISION, EIGHTEENTH ARMY, ARMY GROUP NORTH)[20]

In the past few days we've fought and advanced steadily and have closed the ring around Petersburg. *Der Russe* seems to have taken notice, because he's really letting us have it with his artillery. We spent the night huddled close together in an earthen bunker. Whenever it was time to relieve the guard, you practically had to be an acrobat to climb over the legs of your comrades. It's been raining now for several days. Anything you touch is moist and clammy and of course it's not possible to get any sleep in wet clothes. And to top it all off, now and then water drips through the earth and the pine logs that cover our bunker. Drops hit your nose, they run down your collar. My thoughts turn to home.

2.9.41: *LEUTNANT* JOCHEN HAHN (292 INFANTRY DIVISION, FOURTH ARMY, ARMY GROUP CENTER)[21]

We have been living in our dugout [in the El'nia salient] for over three weeks now— no sun, little daylight, constant shooting from the Russians. It could often drive you mad. But hopefully this, too, will all blow over. Another telephone operator was injured yesterday while locating a disturbance in the line. People are got like this almost every day, but only few replacements arrive. We now have 37 vacant posts. . . . You wrote recently about troop transfers to the west: we've also been hearing that watchword here, too, that we're to go west. . . . Keep your fingers crossed that we'll go to the west, since we've been here for three weeks in tough defensive combat. We horse-drawn artillery will never be considered for England, unless we were to be motorized. But at any rate, the main thing is to get out of this shit. It's a witch's brew out here.[22]

2.9.41: DR. HEINRICH HAAPE (6 INFANTRY DIVISION, NINTH ARMY, ARMY GROUP CENTER)[23]

You simply cannot imagine how we live here in such miserable conditions—in wet, damp, cold dugouts, foxholes, or temporarily in pitiful wooden lean-tos. No culture, not even the simplest contrivances of civilization can be found here. And we are constantly threatened by the enemy, by shell fire or attack. No variety, whether in life here or in the food. No vegetables, no fruit. Legumes for soup, potatoes with meat or canned food comprise, in the permanent, monotonous recurrence of the stew, our meals.

Please don't think that I'm moaning to you in writing this—if it came to it, I would gladly bear even more privations, but I want nothing more than sympathy for the wish list I'm going to write down now! There are no shops here, nothing to buy. Razor blades, comb, toothpaste, skin cream, soap, nail cleaner, writing paper, fountain pen, ink, *Frankfurter Zeitung*, *Koralle* [an illustrated magazine], card games, tobacco, all kinds of sweets, pocket handkerchiefs, etc.

2.9.41: *SOLDAT* HANS M. (262 INFANTRY DIVISION, SIXTH ARMY, ARMY GROUP SOUTH)[24]

Tonight we crossed over the Dnepr, to the south of our old location. Our neighboring regiment has established a bridgehead here. We're advancing through the most splendid chaos of vehicles of all types, and past the foul-smelling corpses of horses. Once, to the left of the road, [we saw] the dismembered body of a Russian and a mangled horse—both had stepped on a mine. Last night we slept in tents in the woods, but when morning came they were very cold inside. I also went through my first air attack on the battalion, and that was the first time I fired my weapon. Both yesterday and today our flak shot down a Russian plane. In general, the Russian aircraft are being a great nuisance [*belästigen uns sehr*].

3.9.41: DR. ADOLF B. (25 INFANTRY DIVISION [MOT.], 1 PANZER GROUP, ARMY GROUP SOUTH)[25]

The war here in the East should be moving slowly toward its end now, and we field gray soldiers might be allowed home by late fall.

Let's all hope that this Bolshevism will be totally finished off soon! You should have received all my letters regularly. It often takes three to four weeks for mail to reach us! We're already quite a long way from home; we're deep inside Russia and most likely will be advancing even farther to the east. But at some point the advance has to come to a stop, and I'm already looking forward to that! The war in Russia is much tougher and more remorseless than it was in France! We certainly hadn't expected to face such stubborn resistance from our Russian "brothers"! Now we only wish and hope that the battles still before us won't be so difficult or result in any more serious losses! And then: "Goodbye Russia forever!"

3.9.41: DR. KONRAD JARAUSCH (ARMY GROUP CENTER)[26]

The wood is crackling away in the oven, as if to prove that there is no end to the Russian forests. [The dog] Floki, our newest acquisition, is whimpering impatiently. He's bored here with me. I'm alone; this room is generally full of my comrades because they don't have any stoves in their rooms. No one can stand the cold there for long. And it's just the beginning of September! Hopefully it will get a little warmer for a while.

One can hear impatient cries from down in the camp.[27] Although they are covered from the rain and have some protection from the wind on one side, [the prisoners] must be freezing to death. We're having a hard time getting them any farther behind the front. The [troops] headed back usually don't have room, and if we were to use the trains to transport them we would need to post sentries, and we don't have the manpower. Hopefully we'll find a solution soon. Rumors are starting to fly again. It's hard for me to get enthusiastic about any given solution. I'm only really fully there when my job requires my attention.[28]

3.9.41: KARL FUCHS (7 PANZER DIVISION, NINTH ARMY, ARMY GROUP CENTER)[29]

In these last three weeks, a lot of things have happened and our comrades in the South, especially in the Ukraine, have experienced successes and have caught up with our push to the east. I wish you could have been here when we heard that Reval [a major naval base and Baltic seaport] had fallen. God, were we overjoyed! I guess the strength of the German soldier is unique and it seems that he is invincible. . . . I will never forget how the eyes of all my comrades lit up when, for the first time, orders for battle were given: Start the engines of your tanks! That's all we had been waiting for and once we started, we pursued and defeated the enemy wherever we met him. Not one of us thought of death in battle. Unfortunately, some of my best friends have been killed. Nevertheless, all of us have only one thought in mind—to defeat the enemy. I saw men weep who had lost their tanks in battle and I'll never forget how they attacked Russian tanks with small arms in their hands. A country such as ours that has men like these must live forever.

4.9.41: ALBERT NEUHAUS (ARMY GROUP NORTH)[30]

We've now moved up a bit again, and the front is directly before us once more. This morning there was quite an artillery duel and even now the front has yet to settle down. The rattle of the machine guns, infantry guns, antitank guns, even heavy artillery—they're all having their say quite forcefully. Hopefully the war will be over soon; over time it really makes you nervous. Furthermore, the weather is quite disagreeable, wet and cold. The night before last there was already hoarfrost and the frost has already turned the leaves on the potato plants completely black. It's quite fortunate that the advance [*Vormarsch*] has gone so well everywhere, and that in our sector the war has now entered a truly decisive phase. I'm thinking that in 10–14 days, P[etersburg] will likely have fallen; an iron ring is being placed around the city and the artillery that's moved up will do the rest! I'm sure you're following the reports of the *Wehrmacht* with great interest, and so you're also being kept up to date.

4.9.41: *LEUTNANT* WILLIBALD G. (57 INFANTRY DIVISION, SEVENTEENTH ARMY, ARMY GROUP SOUTH)[31]

Damn! Now I've been disturbed again by a couple of old Russian women, who complained that some soldiers dug up their potatoes. They're always scolding us something awful; you can hardly make out a word of it, though gradually you pick up bits and pieces. But it's always the same. I can't do a thing to help them either. And of course we're also not here for our amusement! [The weather] where we are is gradually turning to fall. The nights are getting cold and our horses (in Russian they're called "*Panje*" horses) will soon have their winter coats. Perhaps we'll even have to stay here during the winter, and that would hardly be pleasant. But we're soldiers and we must obey our orders.

4.9.41: *UNTEROFFIZIER* RUDOLF F. (267 INFANTRY DIVISION, FOURTH ARMY, ARMY GROUP CENTER)[32]

We were resting quite comfortably on the *Rollbahn*, far behind the front. We'd just slaughtered a chicken and set it on the fire, when suddenly the alarm was sounded. In a matter of hours we found ourselves in the middle of the worst sh**. . . . The Soviets had broken through with strong tank forces. As the advance detachment [*Vorausabteilung*] we were the first to be sent into action, northeast of Roslavl'. We had to hold the position for two days under heavy artillery fire, until the division had moved up. Then we attacked—this time reinforced with assault guns and tanks. I took part in the attack in the forwardmost line. There's no need to say more about it, just see the report of the propaganda company. After it was all over the battlefield was littered with burned-out Russian tanks. *Der Russe* has been forced back again now, and this cursed *Stellungskrieg* begins again, until the cauldron has been closed from behind. The same old story as at the Dnepr. At the moment, we've been pulled off the line for several days, but tomorrow we'll be going back into position. I'm slowly preparing myself for the Russian winter, for the moment at least inwardly.

4.9.41: *GEFREITER* ADOLF M. (260 INFANTRY DIVISION, SECOND ARMY, ARMY GROUP CENTER)[33]

Here in vast Russia everything is so different; here a letter from home means twice as much. Each day we're in combat, often quite tough, against a tenacious and numerically far superior enemy. Even today, once again I'm sitting in a foxhole in the forwardmost line—just 200 meters away from the Reds. They even tried to attack today, but our fire soon brought them to a standstill. Do <u>they</u> even have a clue what it means to attack! None of them get past us. On the 2nd we unexpectedly crossed over the Desna, a tributary of the Dnepr that's about 80 meters wide. That didn't suit the Russians at all, and they let us have it out of all barrels, but to no avail. German troops are now positioned to their rear, and soon they'll be totally destroyed. . . .

Each day we ask ourselves just how much longer this is likely to go on. The nights are already miserably cold, but we still always have to be outside. There's just so much pain, misery and poverty that we see here! Germany is a paradise [by comparison]. It really makes you realize what would have awaited us, if the Bolsheviks had succeeded in invading Germany. So it truly is worth the effort to fight with all we've got.

4.9.41: ALBERT M. (RAILROAD CONSTRUCTION BATTALION 511, ARMY GROUP SOUTH)[34]

Since the start of the campaign in the East I've been in southern Russia (Ukraine). We were given the task of converting the Russian railroad to the German gauge [*Spurweite*], and in this campaign that's of great importance[35] in order to ensure that the combat troops receive the supplies they need; because, given their condition, the roads can't meet the troops' requirements. We're always working from morning till night right behind the fighting troops, so we have to take advantage of every free minute to write a letter. The daily performance of a company is 8–9 kilometers, in addition to marching 15–20 kilometers or more. But we're getting it done and simply have to get it done, because without us it's not possible to advance this war along quickly.

The conditions in Russia are indescribable. The workers are truly impoverished in all respects, and I can hereby attest to the fact that the German newspapers have only written the truth. We must thank God that he appointed the *Führer* at just the right time to advance against this enemy and protect our homeland [*Heimat*]. It is hard enough when, each day, you have to pass by [the graves of] your dead comrades.

4.9.41: *LEUTNANT* ERNST E. (13 PANZER DIVISION, 1 PANZER GROUP, ARMY GROUP SOUTH)[36]

You'll already have found out from a letter to Rothenburg that we are currently, after Dnepropetrovsk was taken amid hard fighting, resting for several days. The new operations that are beginning in the coming days will certainly demand new vigor from us. Goals that have yet to be achieved this year are ahead of us.

Der Russe defended the important bridgehead at Dnepropetrovsk extremely tenaciously and with powerful forces. He had already had four antitank ditches set up in a radius of 50 km, which were almost exclusively excavated, through forced labor, by the women and girls from the rural population. From there on in, the terrain up to the city is traversed by undulations and gorges and so it offers ideal opportunities for defense. Extensive and modern industrial plants in the nearer and farther environs of this 500,000-strong city are of considerable importance for Russian iron ore smelting. But some weeks ago all the plants were destroyed by our *Luftwaffe* to such an extent that they could no longer contribute to Russian production. The bridges were blown up by the Russians; only one pontoon bridge fell into our hands, which, however, was damaged again while we were using it by constant Russian air attacks. Bridge-building columns are working on constructing a secure road bridge across the 800-meter-wide Dnepr.

6.9.41: DR. HANS LIEROW (6 INFANTRY DIVISION, NINTH ARMY, ARMY GROUP CENTER)[37]

A court-martial had to decide a dreadful case today. [A soldier] had robbed a fallen comrade: 1 wallet with 9 *Reichsmark*, a watch and a leather satchel. Sentence: Death by firing squad [*Tod durch Erschiessen*]!

6.9.41: *GEFREITER* HEINZ B. (291 INFANTRY DIVISION, EIGHTEENTH ARMY, ARMY GROUP NORTH)[38]

It almost looks like the cold and the incessant rain have slowed the tempo of the campaign, and that's certainly not what we had in mind, because we want to bring this to an end. We made our most recent attacks together with the infantry, but the roads were in such poor shape that our vehicles had to be left behind, and we were left struggling and straining to push and pull the guns through the muck and the mud.[39] Whenever we had worked our way up to [an enemy-occupied] village while moving through the woods, we were to defeat the enemy and clear out the village. And so, step by step, we slowly conquer the Soviet Union. And should it go on like this—step by step—and I see no means by which it could go more rapidly in these impassable woods, then the war with Russia will not come to an end this year [*dann ist der Krieg mit Russland in diesem Jahre nicht mehr zu Ende*].[40]

From one day to the next we continue to hope that mail will reach us. The waiting is miserable and quite depressing.

6.9.41: *UNTEROFFIZIER* MAX F. (256 INFANTRY DIVISION, NINTH ARMY, ARMY GROUP CENTER)[41]

Only, now it's getting cold where we are, won't be long now and then the winter will be here. I've got a lot of respect for it, because in the region where we are right now, the cold reaches as low as -40° [centigrade]. Hopefully the news that we are going back in the direction of home will come along soon. Next week, we will probably leave Nevel, in which direction is unknown, but in my view to Vel[ikie] Luki.

If anyone at home these days should grumble about anything, then he's welcome to come out to the much-vaunted Workers' Paradise. I imagined Russia to be poor, but the way it is, [I] never [imagined] that. The people even live on raw leaves and potatoes, which would never occur to us. Even in regard to the hardships of the soldier, I have to say that those of the West are clearly dwarfed. It's just a shame about the young fellows who lose their lives because of the Russian, very often in an underhanded way. But the German *Wehrmacht* will now clear up and stamp out the rabble here. Everything else can only be told firsthand [*kann man nur mündlich erzählen*], you must have read of the atrocities [*Greueltaten*] in the newspapers, and it's true, we can confirm that.

6.9.41: *UNTEROFFIZIER* RUDOLF F. (267 INFANTRY DIVISION, FOURTH ARMY, ARMY GROUP CENTER)[42]

Even when we're stationed 15 kilometers behind the front, we're reminded daily that there's a war on. Every day a couple of *Ratas*[43] buzz about and conduct low-level attacks that put us on notice. A moment ago three Russian bombers appeared and dropped several light bombs. Naturally, when the Russian planes come, a Me[sserschmidt] is nowhere to be seen, but otherwise you frequently hear their high-pitched hum [*hohes Singen*] that so distinguishes them from the coarse low growl and the bulging noses of the *Ratas*.

Well, even if we don't have the air superiority we'd like to have here, the *Russkies* don't do much. And we hit back three times as hard. Be on the alert—a couple more *Sondermeldungen* are coming soon, and they'll not just take our breath away, but Churchill's and Stalin's, too.

6.9.41: *LEUTNANT* WILLIBALD G. (57 INFANTRY DIVISION, SEVENTEENTH ARMY, ARMY GROUP SOUTH)[44]

We've been sitting here in the vicinity of Alexandrija for the fourth day now.[45] It's likely [we'll be] crossing the Dnepr in the next few days. We are marching up from behind and it almost looks like we're to be the occupation troops. Naturally, that doesn't suit us much. A winter in Russia won't be pleasant!

Unfortunately, our combat value [*Kampfwert*] isn't all that great anymore either, but we'd prefer a couple of weeks of fighting and then a winter at home to this solution. But, so far, it's all just supposition and it may turn out differently.

It's horrible, lying around like this and having nothing to do! No mail comes; 40 wagons of mail for the army are lying outside Lemberg [L'vov], having got stuck somewhere along the way. The newspapers and illustrated magazines have all long been read from cover to cover; the *Wehrmacht* [radio] receivers in the battalion are all broken and so we have nothing to do except eat and sleep. . . .

Today, the mood sank to freezing point when we three officers discovered that we, too, now have the pleasure of lice. The soldiers have had them for several weeks already, but we had always been able to avoid them.[46] Now, in addition to eating and sleeping, we can add a third activity: looking for lice every day. I changed all my clothes from head to toe and all the stuff will be boiled, but you can't get rid of them entirely. It's awful! [*Es ist scheusslich!*] What's it going to be like if we have to be here for the entire winter?

7.9.41: *LEUTNANT* RUDOLF MAURER (251 INFANTRY DIVISION, NINTH ARMY, ARMY GROUP CENTER)[47]

We've now reached the headwaters of the Dvina.[48] Last night into today, Sunday, was quite turbulent. The enemy attacked time and again. We have significant losses. The artillery fire that's near the regimental command post is too close for comfort. Due to the poor condition of the roads we haven't received any mail for almost 14 days. This damned Eastern Campaign!

7.9.41: *SOLDAT* MAX SCH. (17 INFANTRY DIVISION, SECOND ARMY, ARMY GROUP CENTER)[49]

After three rest days, the first we've had here since the start of the war, the bloody mess started up again yesterday. In the very first half hour my platoon leader was badly wounded. He was the ninth man to be wounded in my platoon. Who'll be the next? In our company we've had about 50 casualties, but that's manageable still. There are companies that no longer have the strength of a platoon, often just 20 men.[50] Now perhaps you can picture for yourself what the fighting is like here. We've now come down from the north, by way of Gomel, and have just about reached Tschernigow in the Ukraine. I hope that the *Kessel* will soon be disposed of, at least by the time you receive this letter. Then all will soon be over for us in the East.

7.9.41: KARL FUCHS (7 PANZER DIVISION, NINTH ARMY, ARMY GROUP CENTER)[51]

We've been camping out in this country now for eleven weeks and every day has brought something different: sometimes there are shouts of joy because of our mighty victories; at other times there is mourning because of our dead and wounded comrades—but always honest pride. All of us are guided by a beacon, and this guiding light is a belief in victory. Everything is possible with this belief in our hearts.[52] The actual experience of war is an overpowering one and your feelings during the battle are many-sided and unfathomable. I've tried to keep a diary and want to elaborate on them at a later date. . . . I know your love will protect me.

7.9.41: *PANZER-OBERSCHÜTZE* ERICH HAGER (17 PANZER DIVISION, 2 PANZER GROUP, ARMY GROUP CENTER)[53]

Sunday. Lovely morning greeting! 29 Russian bombers dropped their eggs. We got out of our tent and went for cover. Played Skat. More attacks. . . . Fighters, Russian, then bombers again.[54] The bombs fall ahead of us again. The Russians have broken through again beyond Potschep. There is fire. 7 bombers and 4 fighters are attacking us. Bombs fall ahead of us again. Not even any peace at lunch. 7 bombers come, chased away by our fighters. They hardly notice our fighters, they drop their bombs and skedaddle. Low-level attacks by Russians continue on us. Bomb attack again. Fall in the middle of town, immediately afterward a low-level attack by the Russians. *Feldwebel* goes to the Kfz.5 [light transport vehicle] makes a note on the chassis. We have to hand it over. The tanks are going into the army repair shop. Our regiment is heading south.[55] We can see that we are going to follow on. Have guard duty. A lonely experience. I saw a Russian funeral. The coffin open on a lorry. The family accompanies it in the already muddy ground. There's no cemetery anywhere. They are covered with earth like dogs at home.

7.9.41: *GEFREITER* EWALD M. (125 INFANTRY DIVISION, SEVENTEENTH ARMY, ARMY GROUP SOUTH)[56]

For several weeks now we've had no peace either day or night. The Russians are using what's left of their aircraft to try to do us as much damage as at all possible, and they don't seem to care much whether they drop a [five-hundred-kilogram] bomb on a single soldier or on a significant military target; but it's this very indifference that makes everyone nervous as soon as a Russian [plane] is spotted. To all appearances, they operate their machines and weapons badly. Our fighters shot down three bombers over us this morning and eight in total yesterday. These battles always put us into a state of high excitement, although any of us could be a candidate for death. Yesterday, ten men fell as the result of just one aerial attack. . . .

A few days ago, we crossed over the Dnepr at its narrowest point, 750 meters wide. We were barely back on solid ground with our column when Russian artillery and planes took us under fire. There followed a veritable death drive [*Todesfahrt*] of 7–8 km through swamp and ½-meter-deep sand. Vehicle after vehicle got stuck, and above us the Russians were circling and unleashing their fire on us from all barrels. The journey lasted for ten hours with automobiles and trucks, none of us will forget it.

Today is Sunday, but we don't notice any of it, because since 5:30 a.m. today the great battle of Kremenchug has been underway[57] and the firing of the artillery and aircraft hardly permits any quiet.

7.9.41: *SOLDAT* ALBRECHT B. (20 PANZER DIVISION,[58] SIXTEENTH ARMY, ARMY GROUP NORTH)[59]

Of course, there's always an injunction to maintain silence imposed on the question of the "where" of the soldier. And most especially during an operation itself. But my lip doesn't have to be completely buttoned, as I, along with a tank, have been cut off from the company, and, due to engine damage, I'm far behind. . . .

Only now, when I have been torn from the battle, have I fully, consciously felt how heavily this endless, monotonous Russian landscape has depressed me. Perhaps I have also only now become fully aware of it because we have had no sun for the entire week and it has been raining endlessly. Today, it is back again, after long and dark days, and dispensing its warmth. Ah, how good that is and how it lifts your heart at the same time! For without it, this endless land is so colorless, bleak, and empty that you can find nothing in it that could give you joy. The grim desolation [*trostlose Verwüstung*] and the deep poverty of this population make it all much more painful.

You know that my eyes have always hungered for beauty, color, and light! But how are they to be satisfied here! This [realization] penetrates deep into the soul and so deeply that it almost becomes a physical pain. It builds up in you and forces its way out into the open. Yet I can find no ear here that would hear my pain and my yearning.

This isn't some sort of homesickness, nor even weakness—it's not meant to be a complaint either—it is the deep longing and yearning for a future and for the things that you would like to achieve sometime! And so my thoughts, after all the battle-filled days, for which one could yet obtain joy and pleasure, frequently turn to you, for you are by all means included in my future. So I spend my days, which have become colorless and lightless, in the belief in this [future], in hope and memory (passing over the present).

8.9.41: *MAJOR* HANS MEIER-WELCKER (251 INFANTRY DIVISION, NINTH ARMY, ARMY GROUP CENTER)[60]

We have tough, difficult days behind us. The Russians attacked the Div[ision], which was in an exposed position, from the front and in its deep, open flank. The situation was critical. Exercising control over the battlefield was extremely difficult because, for the most part, we're fighting in swampland and in dense woods with little room to maneuver [*nur geringe Bewegungsfreiheit*]. Making matters worse is the truly ghastly condition of the roadways, so that units often require days to cover a distance that in Germany would only take a few hours. In such cases, the command must have strong nerves as well as patience at critical moments.

Since yesterday evening the situation has eased somewhat, even if it's still dangerous. We're waiting to be reinforced by artillery, and then *we'll* attack again. Of course, we'll only be able to conduct attacks with limited objectives, because the Russians facing us are too strong. Among other things, they've brought in a new Siberian Div[ision] that had yet to see action. The Russians prefer to fight at very close quarters [*aus nächste Entfernung*], so they often attack at night, in the woods, and in very difficult terrain. And when they do, they rush into battle with such ruthless disregard for their lives and with loud cries of "Urrah Stalin!"

8.9.41: WOLFGANG A. (1 INFANTRY DIVISION, EIGHTEENTH ARMY, ARMY GROUP NORTH)[61]

Today we were also able to admire an exciting aerial battle. Around midday, a few Russian planes appeared and dropped their bombs around the place indiscriminately. Close to us, too, a few of the things, accompanied by a concert of aircraft cannon, came down on our "hotel." Fortunately, everything was fine. Just one vehicle received a few small dents. And, then, all at once, our tried and true [Bf 109s] turned up. You could just see a couple of gun flashes, and then two "*Ratas*" corkscrewed, burning, to the ground. We were all astonished at our fighters' rapid victory, but delighted at the same time. But I think that won't be the last time that we'll be able to marvel at aerial battles. Our advance is now continuing at a brisk pace. And you'll have heard the *Sondermeldung* today about the capture of Schlüsselburg [Shlisselburg], too. Now the ring around Petersburg is being inexorably tightened. Hopefully it'll all soon be over here.

The weather is becoming markedly worse, as well—rain and cold. What'll it be like at [minus] 40°? But we don't let ourselves be disheartened. It's already been shown that the German soldier is superior to the Russian in every respect. We will yet be the victors.

9.9.41: *SOLDAT* HANS OLTE (CORPS SIGNAL BATTALION 52, FOURTH ARMY, ARMY GROUP CENTER)[62]

We're slowly going crazy here [*so langsam wird man hier blöde*]. Oh, you just cannot imagine (in fact, nobody who was not or is not here can imagine) the conditions prevailing here. You can't get anything here. And then everything's so filthy. Yes, that's what it's like here.

9.9.41: *GEFREITER* HANS CASPAR VON WIEDEBACH-NOSTITZ (20 PANZER DIVISION, SIXTEENTH ARMY, ARMY GROUP NORTH)[63]

Oberleutnant Kischnick comes to us and informs us that the company is to be disbanded. All that is left is a remnants echelon. The armored cars and trucks are to be allocated to the artillery and rifle regiment. We are off to the divisional headquarters. Then the *Oberleutnant* awards us the Tank Combat Badge certificate [*Panzerkampfabzeichenurkunde*]. Once again he summarizes all the shared experiences and provides an overview of the company's achievements. In the afternoon we drive off to the company. Our vehicle is attached to the Reconnaissance Squad B.[64]

9.9.41: *LEUTNANT* WILLIBALD G. (57 INFANTRY DIVISION, SEVENTEENTH ARMY, ARMY GROUP SOUTH)[65]

Yesterday we went over the Dnepr. The day before, the Russian had unleashed 28 air attacks on the bridge, but only lightly damaged it.[66] There's an awful lot of antiaircraft artillery concentrated here and our fighters are constantly on patrol. Lots of Russians have been shot down, too. . . . So now we're situated in the bridgehead, which is already rather extensive. . . . We're located right on the bank of the river. You can't hear anything of the "front" from here. Today, we had a rest day and made full use of it. We bathed in the Dnepr before eating and in the afternoon the artillery privates [*Kanoniere*] caught fish with hand grenades.[67] There are pikes up to 6 pounds in weight. So it's fish grilled on a stick in the evening! . . .

Today, the fighters shot down a Russian bomber quite close to us and it exploded while still in the air. It made quite a bang! The [Soviet] fighter machines made in America are particularly vile in low-level attacks.[68] They fire out of every rivet! But they're being mopped up in large numbers. And yet still they come, again and again.

Today, I'm sending you all another pamphlet. Their contents get increasingly idiotic! Don't for a moment think that any of it is true! Neither the "endless rows of graves" nor the "deserting comrades." It's an unforgettable impertinence for an army, which is constantly withdrawing and receiving devastating blows, to address the victor in this way. Today, a pamphlet arrived in which Marshal Budenny[69] himself calls the "Comrades, Officers and Soldiers" to a revolution against Hitler and Mussolini! Everybody is laughing at it, naturally.

9.9.41: ALBERT NEUHAUS (ARMY GROUP NORTH)[70]

My dear Agnes! Yesterday evening I had to stop writing, because work interrupted again. However, at this moment I'm in the right mood to tell you about our experiences early today. So, in short: major attack [*Grossangriff*] by our planes and our artillery. Around 5:30 a.m., we were woken by a strange rattle of engines, and before we could collect ourselves we had already taken cover. 8 Russian "*Ratas*," similar machines to our fighters, flew over our heads and fired with their M.G.s. Plus 3 Russian bombers. But nothing happened. Then a few German fighters appeared and the *Ruskis* were off. And then it kicked off.

The powerful hum of engines in the distance. Then the first German bombers emerged from the clouds—3, 6, 11, 17, 30, 40 of them, guarded by umpteen fighters. A magnificent scene! We were feverish with excitement. They swept over us in full glory toward the front. Then they opened their bomb racks and what tumbled out? They weren't rotten eggs, no, they were German bombs. And what do our excited eyes see coming from the side? Stukas, Stukas! Our hearts leapt for joy. Glorious, how they sought out their prey on the ground like hawks. They circle and circle and, there, the first tilts, the second, third tilt, and so on. Elegantly, the machines pull back up. A shuddering goes through the ground; the bombs have done their work.

This accompanied by the unearthly thundering of the unleashed artillery. Now and then the Russian flak interrupts with a crash, but they are just tiny droplets compared to the elemental force [*Urgewalt*] that is pushing forward from the German side against the cauldron. Rolling attacks! My dear sirs! Let us speak plainly. Just now there was another major attack by our planes, the Stukas' howling cuts through marrow and bone. Agnes, I wish you could have seen it, that magnificent scene. There's an atmosphere now that could not be more wonderful or excited. The belt of fortifications around Petersburg is being cut to pieces. And the weather is superb. Big, fat, gleaming white clouds above us and on the horizon. A scene, unspeakably beautiful. We haven't seen anything like this so far; we've always longed for it and now it's here. How our artillery flashed in among it! As if all hell had been let loose. . . . I don't believe you could imagine my mood. You have to have seen something like that; you have to have experienced something like that; you have to have been there.

11.9.41: DR. HEINRICH HAAPE (6 INFANTRY DIVISION, NINTH ARMY, ARMY GROUP CENTER)[71]

Today was another hot day with great successes for us; we even took over 100 prisoners when the Russians attacked, but we had fatalities and casualties, too. This war is dreadful [*furchtbar*], but we will triumph, even though the road is long and difficult! This is not to say that, what with the difficult things we have to experience, the thought arises: why are we at war with Russia? War with R. had to come, and the fact that it has now come—we should be grateful for that, because it is the only way to success! This dreadful war is the fate of our nation! [*das Schicksal unseres Volkes!*]

12.9.41: *LEUTNANT* WILLIBALD G. (57 INFANTRY DIVISION, SEVENTEENTH ARMY, ARMY GROUP SOUTH)[72]

Yesterday at daybreak in the pouring rain, we pushed forward another 8 km into the bridgehead. . . . We are still army reserves and not yet in action. But around us all sorts of things are happening. Day and night [you hear] the impacts of the German shells crashing down and the sky is fairly bustling with activity.

In our previous quarters on the river bank, I spoke with the Ukrainian mayor, who could speak German well. He told me a number of interesting things. . . . He said that the [Soviet] troops located here did not want to fight, but they were driven into battle at gunpoint by the commissars. The results proved it! So far, 12,000 prisoners have been made in a few days. All men between 40 to 50 and 16 to 18 years old, who had been soldiers for just 3 days and didn't know how to handle their weapons. Their uniforms still had fresh creases as they began the "march to Berlin."

The day before yesterday, the Reds launched a tank assault with 60 heavy tanks, of which 48 were shot up.[73] The remaining ones were bombed by the Stukas yesterday. The tank crews were drunk. The colonel of the armored unit surrendered. He stated that Stalin had given the order to reduce the bridgehead with all means and that the tanks should instigate it. And now this Comrade Colonel feared for his head and preferred to surrender to the barbarian Germans. Yesterday, around evening, there was a lot of activity in the sky. Around 35 Stukas in 2 groups simultaneously bombed the enemy positions. Then bombers arrived and then our panzers attacked, the infantry behind them. So the bridgehead made good progress and we will soon be in Khar'kov! . . . Everywhere, there's vigorous forward progress and I am convinced that this business here will be at an end before the start of winter.

12.9.41: *UNTEROFFIZIER* WILHELM PRÜLLER (9 PANZER DIVISION, 1 PANZER GROUP, ARMY GROUP SOUTH)[74]

After a few more stops and starts we finally arrive at Petrovo to spend the night. It's 12:15 a.m. and it's taken us 20 hours to go 60 kilometers! It's almost unbelievable!

We take up quarters in a house but don't go in yet because it's not certain whether we're to go on in the evening or not. When the orders come through that we shall apparently move on in the early morning, we set up night quarters in the stinking hole. As in all peasant houses, there's no window that you can open here either. We break two small window panes, which will probably be described as barbarous. Imagine people being able to *stand* it?

On the wall hangs a map of Russia. That it hangs upside down they don't even know. After all, it's supposed to show their education and their interest in the great Soviet empire. Some pictures, colored, with glittering junk, are what you see in every house. Perhaps it's a custom; is this supposed to represent enthusiasm for the fine arts?

There is no electric light, no toilet, no running water, etc.—but there's a loudspeaker. There is one wireless apparatus for the whole village, and from it everyone hears the blessings of their paradise. I think, however, that the real reason is that the people aren't supposed to listen to foreign broadcasts.

At every step you find new proofs that it's foolish people living here. If I had a choice they would have to drag me to Russia with wild horses, I find the place so revolting.

14.9.41: *GEFREITER* HEINZ SCH. (ENGINEER REGIMENTAL STAFF 514 [FOR SPECIAL DUTIES], ARMY GROUP NORTH)[75]

It is a heavy blow to find out that plans are already in the works for the construction and organization of winter quarters. That would be bad. Just when and where we'll have to halt our advance will depend on the arrival of winter. Of course, then we'll be able to count on taking <u>leave</u>. But not a single one of us would ever want to return again to this horrifying country [*grauenerregenden Land*]. We're still hoping on the quiet that our divisions, which have gone through a lot, will be relieved and perhaps even return to Germany.

We're in position east of Lake Il'men', having crossed both the Lovat' and Pola rivers quite some time ago! But we're advancing more slowly now, the obstacles are becoming greater, the terrain stands defiantly in our way! Oh, may we soon live to see that every meter of earth we set foot on leads us farther <u>away</u> from this wretched land [*Elendslande*].

14.9.41: *GEFREITER* HANS F. (FLAK INSTRUCTIONAL [*LEHR*] REGIMENT, ARMY GROUP NORTH)[76]

I had another really close call just now; barely managed to escape with my life. All of my things have been burned up, even my gun and ammunition pouches with the ammunition. I just got away with what I had on my person—all my letters, photos, writing paper, everything [gone]. The Russians had hit us with artillery fire. An ammunition wagon was hit, caught fire, and immediately went up in flames—it had just taken on shells close to our gun. But we only suffered one fatality and seven wounded, so despite the heavy shelling we were really quite lucky. As I always say—everything can be replaced, except for the lives [of our men]. We're now in the Valdai Hills and are defending ourselves, but only until it's all over in Petersburg. Then we'll begin to advance again. *Der Russe* is shooting at us day and night, but we're holding firm as a rock.

14.9.41: ALBERT NEUHAUS (ARMY GROUP NORTH)[77]

We have moved another stretch forward and now we're lying around 30 km outside Petersburg. We have come through forest regions in which the war has raged with all its merciless severity, and much stalwart *Soldatenblut* has been spilled here for the homeland. But the advance continues and the cauldron is getting tighter and tighter. It's just a question of days now until we will have reached our goal and the city will fall.[78] With assaults like those that the German *Wehrmacht* has carried out, there can be no halting them. . . . Everything is hammering away together—the armored reconnaissance vehicles, the light and heavy panzers, the infantry with its various weaponry, the light and heavy artillery, the [*Nebelwerfer*], the far-reaching long-range guns, and above all of this sweeps the proud *Luftwaffe*. Good Lord, what music! And how *der Russe* did dig and burrow against it. We came through forest regions where foxhole followed upon foxhole; one bunker was more secure than the next, linked by underground communication trenches [*Laufgräben*]. You can't picture it. Our Stukas and panzers cracked those things open and every infantryman really has earned the Knight's Cross here. Compared to the infantry, we have it damned easy. We have our work, too, but compared to those boys, we have it good. . . .

This morning we even saw captured Russian *Flintenweiber* being washed . . . , not at all bad. Now it may be that our male eyes have suffered somewhat this last quarter year and so we saw with aroused eyes what little femininity there was in these beasts. Kid, kid, when you see something like that, and you can call a lovely, dear German woman your own, then our shaggy men's chests puff with pride and gratitude. My dear girl! That will have to be enough of a *Wehrmachtbericht* from your husband for today; as for the other things that interest you, I'd ask you "to see them from the daily newspapers." The newsreels, etc., do present things in a pretty unadorned fashion.

14.9.41: *LEUTNANT* WILLIBALD G. (57 INFANTRY DIVISION, SEVENTEENTH ARMY, ARMY GROUP SOUTH)[79]

Today is a hugely unlucky day! We've been back in action since early this morning, alongside the division with the black grouse feather[80] and many other units. There is more artillery amassed by us in a huge arc here than I have ever seen brought together before.

And it's necessary, because *der Russe* has again thrown everything that he's still got at us. At first, only old reservists were here, of which a whole division was captured in short order; and there was no artillery here, but now, after that, a lot of batteries have been brought into position, there are also railway guns and the advance of our infantry will be hampered by numerous mines. The Reds have learned from our artillery. They now also fire in sudden concentrations [*Feuerüberfälle*] and heavy barrages [*Trommelfeuer*] the way we do, although without even nearly the same effect, because the tactics are lacking.

I'm writing to you all from our firing position and it's taking me a lot of effort to show my people a happy and confident face all the time. Sometimes I do think it will never work. But it <u>must</u>, and it's my duty to be a good example! Our superiors, the old men, sometimes lose their nerve and then we young ones have to leap in and hold up our heads.

15.9.41: DR. HEINRICH HAAPE (6 INFANTRY DIVISION, NINTH ARMY, ARMY GROUP CENTER)[81]

Brief word on the situation: the war with Russia will not come to an end this year. We are currently in the middle of the toughest defensive battle here, and the greatest demands are being made on efforts, commitment, and blood, so that the battles in the north can be ended all the more successfully and those in the Ukraine, the breadbasket of Europe, can be continued victoriously. So the war will not be brought to an end in this year. We are currently (in fact, since 28 July) standing, in a relatively thinly occupied line, against an enemy with far superior numbers. The broad countryside lies gray ahead of us, and the cold Russian winter!

15.9.41: *UNTEROFFIZIER* RUDOLF F. (267 INFANTRY DIVISION, FOURTH ARMY, ARMY GROUP CENTER)[82]

What will the coming weeks bring? I believe it's going to start up again with a vengeance, also on our sector of the front. *Der Russe* must be totally worn down before winter arrives, above all we need his armaments industry around Moscow and Tula to do it. Well, we'll see what fall will bring us (besides mud and cold). . . .

We also witnessed a terrific German air assault at the front. The Reds had broken through in the neighboring sector with tanks and were then thrown back with air support. Six "Ju 88s" made a low-level assault on the Russian tank and infantry positions. The crash of the bombs and the rattle of the machine guns were tremendous. Our *Landser* leaped out of their cover for sheer joy and watched. Everything remained quiet over there.

Something like that really lifts battle morale enormously, because of course the *Landser* are not as enthusiastic as they were at the start of this campaign. In almost uninterrupted action since the start, then the not inconsiderable losses, numerous battles of position in very poor terrain—none of all that is easy, so the infantryman becomes apathetic.

15.9.41: *LEUTNANT* GEORG KREUTER (18 PANZER DIVISION, 2 PANZER GROUP, ARMY GROUP CENTER)[83]

Haven't received any mail for 4 weeks! . . . I've also taken over the headquarters company. For some time now we've been all together in the headquarters building. . . . We're already preparing for the winter and gathering firewood. . . . Whenever a new film is being shown in our improvised movie theater in S[molensk], we're always there. We've also seen some traveling theater here at the front, but so far without any female performers. Today we saw the "White Ravens." It was really nice. The only disturbance was caused by enemy bombers, which flew past us overhead at low level before making a "lovely" attack on the airfield. But the performance went on! When we left the theater, the ammunition depot on the airfield was lit up in flames. There were some casualties, and throughout the night flak ammunition was exploding and shooting up into the sky.

15.9.41: GEO. S. (ARTILLERY REGIMENT 70, ARMY GROUP NORTH)[84]

For several days now we have no longer been where we were at the start, in Golpino near Leningrad, when we came to the north, but rather somewhat more to the east, to the south of Schlüsselburg [Shlisselburg]. We usually station our command post in buildings now, which has the advantage that we are at least warm and dry. One disadvantage, however, is that when towns are shelled, the troops there are rather more at risk, and what with the unclean conditions of the Russian housing, we often find vermin on us, like fleas and bugs.[85] So let's hope that we can get out of this Russia soon, which is the epitome of poverty to us. Because even if it might be just about all right in the summer, over winter it will certainly be almost unbearable.

Shoes are unfortunately a lost cause. Similarly fabrics. I am definitely of the opinion that many of you have entirely false ideas about the conditions in Russia. First of all, endless expanses of land in which now and then a completely impoverished farmstead or village of just a few houses appears. There are no medium-sized towns or larger villages to speak of at all. If we do arrive in a town, it is almost always utterly destroyed. The fault for that lies in the fact that the entire street that has been evacuated by the populace burns down if just one house begins to burn and can't be extinguished immediately. If by chance you do find something, it's usually some useless thing, because other objects have, firstly, been taken away by the Russians or destroyed; or, secondly, looted by the civilian population, which behaves like animals. . . .

As we have just discovered, our sojourn here in Russia will probably be a longer one. So, please, in addition, do all send me a scarf, a pair of gloves, a pair of wrist warmers, and head protection.

16.9.41: A. V. (36 INFANTRY DIVISION, 3 PANZER GROUP, ARMY GROUP CENTER)[86]

Yesterday, we also transported prisoners. Many old men over 40 years old, and there are young, 15-year-old women with them as well. Mongolians, Chinese, Asiatics, a mix in the true sense of the word.[87] Most of them happy that, for them, the war is over. Sometimes you see a hanged man. They are men who have committed an offence against army property or soldiers dressed in civilian clothes skulking about the woods and carrying out acts of terrorism. They are left hanging there for two to three days, as a deterrent.

16.9.41: ALBERT NEUHAUS (ARMY GROUP NORTH)[88]

The terrain that we drove through yesterday was battleground in the truest sense of the word. And the traces of all the battle action were clearly visible. The *Ruski* dead lay like they had been sown for harvest. It's a chilling sight. The Russians had no more time here to take the dead with them. Despite the severe battles in the last months, we've seen really very few dead Russians lying around; either they are buried immediately or taken away by their comrades. But now in recent days it's been much worse. It can almost make you retch when you see these corpses, shot about and lacerated.

16.9.41: SIEGBERT STEHMANN (163 INFANTRY DIVISION, GERMAN ARMY OF NORWAY)[89]

The advance has been unstoppable. The degree of our exertions and privations has meant that I couldn't write for 8 days. Just think: We have over 500 km march behind us, under conditions that can't be described. You just find yourself incapable of writing or thinking. Well, that's the war from the perspective of the infantryman. We're down close to the mouth of the Svir River on Lake Ladoga.

The physical exertions for us have increased, immensely so. 4 a.m. start, arrival 24 hours later, and in between a 20 km stretch in desert sands with full baggage and ammunition box. At night it rains, too—icily cold. Ah, it is so lonely, in me and around me. I must lie down and sleep away a little of the night.

16.9.41: DR. KONRAD JARAUSCH (ARMY GROUP CENTER)[90]

It's disgusting how intimately our soldiers interact with the Russians; they do so despite all the rules against it and both sides benefit from it. In the end things are the same here as they were in Amiens, despite the differences. Everyone is on the lookout for "booty."[91] It's hard to believe the things that can be found here to trade: butter by the kilo; honey, but also tarps, boot shafts that can be made into gloves, boots from dead Russians that can be traded for good riding boots, etc. It's hard to say how this will turn out in the future. . . . I worry that the result will be a Europe that is entirely consumed with the need to restore the destroyed foundations of the material existence. We've been able to survive because we've had new possibilities: first 1940 in Western Europe and then 1941 in the Ukraine. We are living at the expense of these people and are sucking them dry. What should we expect, other than bitterness and an abiding desire to overthrow this foreign rule? This is the great moral advantage the British and Americans possess. Our relationship to the occupied areas resembles that of the British in India or now in Persia. I don't understand how we can expect anything good to come of such circumstances.

16.9.41: LEOPOLD ARTNER (EASTERN FRONT)[92]

I have been in the East since the start of the war, so deployed on the Russian front since 22 June, and always in the front line. Experienced, then, right on the Russian border, that solemn and significant moment when, on the first day of war, at the designated time, the first shot heralded the day of judgment for Bolshevism and immediately we had navigated the border, the Bug River, and there experienced a baptism of fire. Ever since, we have been continually in action and always in the first wave. Long, exhausting marches, days of battles of position against the enemy, with heavy artillery fire that often lasts nine hours at a time, then heavy assault again, alternating continuously. We have melted away to a small cluster of individuals in these deployments, which last for weeks, as many comrades fell and others lie wounded in hospital.

How much misery and human suffering must one experience here! If you look back on what has happened, you just don't understand how it is possible to have survived so many great dangers and cannot thank God enough for the undeserved mercy [*unverdiente Gnade*]. Despite the difficult time that is now behind us, it is strange how quickly even the blackest days fade into the background and you are always looking to the future with renewed confidence and hope.

17.9.41: FRITZ PABST (SIXTH ARMY, ARMY GROUP SOUTH)[93]

There's still a lot of fruit and potatoes still standing in the fields in the Ukraine, but the captured Ukrainians are now being released and have to rescue the harvest. A Ukrainian self-defense group has been formed, and they are really tidying up among the Jews and commissars [*diese räumen unter den Juden und Kommissaren*] so that soon we won't see any more of these beasts, for they are nothing other than that, I can confirm that, even in the short time that I have been here. . . .[94]

For myself, I feel considerably better than in Greece. Now we're hungry again and there's no shortage of food here. There's certainly enough meat. A cow or a steer costs 10 RM; you'd hardly believe it possible, but it's true.

17.9.41: R. B. (31 INFANTRY DIVISION, FOURTH ARMY, ARMY GROUP CENTER)[95]

While all the other groups out there are on road construction like every day, we are sitting inside and can rest from our not-so-everyday work. Our group had the following assignment: hang 3 civilian bandits who had attacked one of our battalion's ambulance vehicles a few days before. So that was sorted out this morning and now there's a body dangling by each of the entrances to the village. A warning and a deterrent for the inhabitants. A commissar was also shot. This war brings one to the most dreadful actions, ones that seem almost medieval.[96]

17.9.41: *GEFREITER* HANS ROTH (299 INFANTRY DIVISION, SIXTH ARMY, ARMY GROUP SOUTH)[97]

Budenny's swallows[98] appear by surprise around noon. However, the situation is different than the last time in Terempki. Flaks, calibers of 8.8 and 2cm, have been arranged in masses to maintain the attack. The scenes that follow are awesome.

The Bolsheviks perform two laps of honor. Our Flaks don't fire a single shot. Great! The Russians, who were unable to see our camouflage antiaircraft cannons, feel like they own the sky. They return with just as much force as they did in the initial days of August. And then it starts: the tack-tack-tack of the 2cm Flaks and the tinny sounds of the 8.8cm. Eighteen Martin bombers crash to the ground in flames within the next 20 minutes. Well, now it's really serious, Father Budenny!

18.9.41: *LEUTNANT* RUDOLF MAURER (251 INFANTRY DIVISION, NINTH ARMY, ARMY GROUP CENTER)[99]

My dear Karl-Wilhelm!

I am going to write you a birthday letter on the writing paper that your dear mother sent me. You will soon be 7 years old. This will be your first birthday as a schoolboy. . . . Now you will hear what I am experiencing in Russia so far away from Halsdorf (you have to drive 60 times from Halsdorf to Marburg to travel the same distance that I am away from you dear ones) = $20 \times 60 = 1200$ km. You should know the main point of this right at the start: It is much nicer in Germany, and above all in Halsdorf. You cannot find a village as nice as Halsdorf in all of Russia. The houses are all built out of planks. They are small. And in many houses there are also chickens in the parlor. And then the roads in the villages! They all look like huge mud puddles! And even great, strong horses have difficulty getting through it. And the people are as filthy as the buildings and the roads. There's no difference between men, women, or children in that. If any boy or girl in Germany (or maybe even in the parsonage in Halsdorf) should not be cleanly washed, people would have to tell them: you are like a Russian! And none of you want to be like that. And the towns are as filthy as the villages. There is no beautiful town like Marburg, with a palace and beautiful churches, in Russia either. And many Russians don't believe in the dear Lord Jesus. And the mayors in Russia have stormed the churches and chased away the ministers. So that is why we hope that God will help our soldiers to victory, so that these godless Russians don't win.

I am writing to you in a building that the soldiers built into the earth in a large forest, where there are still real wolves. We all carpentered everything ourselves, the building, the benches, the table and even the stove. I do believe you would like to be here with me. But you can well believe that it is nicer in Halsdorf. The roads are so poor that I don't drive with my car, I ride on a horse. Yesterday, I had a skittish horse that was very wild and wanted to throw me off. But I was able to get it to obey. Perhaps you and Reinhard and Elisabeth have been wondering why I haven't written to the three of you for so long. I hadn't forgotten you all and I am always thinking about you. But I have to look after more than 100 soldiers, have to order them, and tell them where and how to shoot at our enemy, have to make sure that they get hot food every day, that the wounded men are tended to, and much, much more.

Our army postal service has a lot to do. That's also a reason why I can't write to you more frequently.

18.9.41: KARL NÜNNIGHOFF (16 PANZER DIVISION, 1 PANZER GROUP, ARMY GROUP SOUTH)[100]

Our advance is very extensive again at the moment. The amount of prisoners and booty is never-ending. This morning a procession of prisoners passed by us and it took almost half an hour before they had all marched past us. There were at most ten German soldiers accompanying these endless rows as an escort party. All the different faces and caricatures to be seen there would make a mockery of any [attempt at] description. We can assume that it [the war] will soon be done, let us hope for the best.

18.9.41: *GEFREITER* HANS ROTH (299 INFANTRY DIVISION, SIXTH ARMY, ARMY GROUP SOUTH)[101]

Our 21 and 30.5cm cannons have been firing onto the Russian defense lines around the outskirts of the city [of Kiev] for the last 24 hours. There are rolling attacks from our Stukas. A dark, black cloud hangs over the city after a few hours. These guys deliver precision work. According to orders, the residential neighborhoods of the city are not to be attacked. They are to attack the fortress, the train stations, ammunition depots, and the Dnepr bridges. Orders for the general attack arrive in the afternoon. Tomorrow is the day. Guys, prepare for the mass grave! You can live out your hatred against the city that has been right in front of your faces for weeks, though as of yet unattainable. Tomorrow—finally, finally!!!!

19.9.41: *UNTEROFFIZIER* WILHELM PRÜLLER (9 PANZER DIVISION, 1 PANZER GROUP, ARMY GROUP SOUTH)[102]

In the morning I accompany the C.O. [commanding officer] in the town [Piryatin]; although it is forbidden to enter and this order is being checked by the M.P.s [military police], we manage to get in. I can't describe how the enemy vehicles in the town look, and how many there are—at least 2,000. In a curve they were standing four abreast, apparently knocked out by our Stukas. Hundreds of skeleton vehicles were standing there, burned out right down to the iron frame.

I grab one of the intact cars and intend to drive it in our company. The M.P. won't let me out of the town with it though, so I sneak out with the car, using side streets.

20.9.41: DR. KONRAD JARAUSCH (ARMY GROUP CENTER)[103]

The world is so barren without God both here and at the other side of the front. I have often thought so when watching yet another one of our prisoners lie dying. No priestly words. Carried out like a corpse. Such deaths occur by the millions. This is truly the work of the devil.

20.9.41: *UNTEROFFIZIER* ROBERT RUPP (17 PANZER DIVISION, 2 PANZER GROUP, ARMY GROUP CENTER)[104]

We'll be in Russia one more month at most, according to the latest promises. The boss says he's heard from the top that the tasks of the motorized troops have to be complete by 20 October: Leningrad, Moscow, Kiev, Khar'kov. I had always reckoned with September.

20.9.41: *UNTEROFFIZIER* WILHELM PRÜLLER (9 PANZER DIVISION, 1 PANZER GROUP, ARMY GROUP SOUTH)[105]

A Russian regiment is supposed to be fleeing toward the south. According to the prisoners we've taken, several groups of staff officers are in this three-rivers region—they are supposed to have got away from the battle of Kiev. That lures us on, of course. The C.O. and battalion decide to chase the enemy regiments at once.

After passing through the first village, we spread out over the fields. Beforehand we are assigned some tanks, and now we've spread out the tanks and other vehicles in a broad formation over the fields and are charging into the fleeing Russians. The order of the companies and other units has got a bit mixed up in the intoxication of this fabulous chase, but it's wonderful to watch the vehicles tearing ahead. There ought to be some newsreel men here; there would be incomparable picture material! Tanks and armored cars, the men sitting on them, encrusted with a thick coating of dirt, heady with the excitement of the attack—haystacks set on fire by our tanks' cannons, running Russians, hiding, surrendering! It's a marvelous sight!

We take a few prisoners: most of them have to be dragged out from under haystacks or flushed out of the furrows. Shy, unbelieving, filled with terror, they come. Many a Bolshevik has to lay down his life here—his stupid pigheadedness and his fear (drilled into him) have to be paid for by his death.

21.9.41: *GEFREITER* HANS CASPAR VON WIEDEBACH-NOSTITZ (20 PANZER DIVISION, SIXTEENTH ARMY, ARMY GROUP NORTH)[106]

Getting on midday we get going in a shaky, clapped-out 6-cylinder Renault truck. We have only made 200 meters and we stop. The driver works away for half an hour, then the journey resumes perhaps for another 500 meters or so. The engine is working on four cylinders and the vehicle gets stuck in every puddle. Then of course everyone has to get out and push. When the vehicle gets going again the driver drives like a madman so that those of us in the back of the vehicle fly about half a meter in the air every time the vehicle goes over a hole. The journey continues like this until evening.

21.9.41: *HAUPTWACHTMEISTER* H. S. (255 INFANTRY DIVISION, NINTH ARMY, ARMY GROUP CENTER)[107]

All of us out here are only interested in one question now, namely whether we will bring the war to a victorious conclusion before the start of winter. Kiev has been taken, one very large forward city, and Petersburg is the next big step that is now being taken. The general assumption is that the third step will be toward Moscow. God preserve us from a winter campaign in the East. Even now it's already very cold here and it rains almost daily. The roads are dreadful. You can simply never imagine how poor and primitive the Red paradise is. And you'd have to read the leaflets which he has been dropping upon us here recently. Clumsy and stupid.[108] By contrast, our leaflets have been a remarkable success.[109] I have also currently employed a couple of Ukrainians as workers, who are jolly glad to have escaped the Reds.

21.9.41: ALBERT NEUHAUS (ARMY GROUP NORTH)[110]

Hopefully the decision will soon be made for us up here. You get sick of it pretty quickly. This afternoon the Russians dropped leaflets: we should surrender. Such clumsy propaganda makes even the most elderly boiler hens laugh. The whole sheet read like the desperate cry of a devilish power doomed to death.

22.9.41: WERNER BEERMANN (NINTH ARMY, ARMY GROUP CENTER)[111]

At home, at every opportunity, people are told, yes, we're short of this and that because our soldiers have to be taken care of first and foremost. On that basis, people at home must assume that we get everything in copious amounts. But that's not true. . . .

It's a wide, treeless, and bushless terrain with lots of large, flat hollows. Anybody new here can hardly believe, can hardly see that there are soldiers here. Yes, we live like cavemen. Deep in the hillside of the hollow facing away from the enemy (partially meadow, clover and cornfield), we have dug ourselves deep into the clay soil, always three, four men in an earthen bunker. The neighboring village almost disappeared from the earth; all the buildings were broken up, bit by bit, to obtain beams and planks for the bunker construction. . . . I built a stove out of vertical bricks in the communications section's bunker and it heats superbly. . . .

Ever since Smolensk we've been lying in defense in the new positions. It's a war of position that can hold its own against the World War in terms of severity. The past orders of the day always state that Army Group Center must endure the self-sacrificing defense situation until the time is ripe, which probably means until the north and south wings have advanced more. . . . Here, it's been peaceful all the time, the enemy just thundered about the place [der Feind hat nur in der Umgebung gedonnert]. I've been able to recover well during these weeks of not marching.

22.9.41: KARL FUCHS (7 PANZER DIVISION, 3 PANZER GROUP, ARMY GROUP CENTER)[112]

Our German proverb, "different people have different customs," does not apply to this endless, monotonous country of Russia. I suppose this proverb may be applicable to many countries on earth, but not here. This country, like its people, seems to be eternally gray and monotonous. Everywhere you look there is nothing but poverty and wretched misfortune. Poverty looks at you from every corner, and certainly the men, women and children are terribly poor. Can you imagine that human beings grow up to live like animals? That seems to be the case here. Just the other day I mentioned to one of my comrades that even a little flower in God's wonderful nature grows up with more sunshine during its lifetime and enjoys more care and happiness than these people here. It would be inconceivable for me to have our child live in such an environment! I suppose it is just as impossible to ask a Russian to think of something beautiful and noble.

If you only knew under what arduous conditions our victories were fought and won. Sometimes it was incredible, fighting on muddy Russian roads or in rainy weather that seemed to have no end. Time and space are suspended. Once that last battle is over, peace will return to Germany and Europe. We out here on the front carry this belief in our hearts. You back home should have the same belief and hope as we do. Due to this common belief and hope, the front and the homeland are united in the real sense of the word. This point of view should play an important part in the schools of today. You as teachers who are able to mold and educate the youth of our great country should, in this difficult and proud time, let our children participate in the heroism of their brothers and fathers.

22.9.41: FRITZ KÖHLER (ARMY GROUP CENTER)[113]

[Köhler was stationed near Lochwica holding the eastern perimeter of the Kiev encirclement.] We are an advance detachment and have the task of stopping the withdrawal of the encircled Russians and preventing attempts to break out. Around 10:00 a.m. we had contact with the enemy. We were recognized and, after we'd dismounted, could hardly dig ourselves in. Suddenly, half a dozen Russian tanks appear. Our 37mm antitank guns, 105mm field howitzers are pulled up for direct fire and machine guns for defense. But they can't do anything against the heavily armored T-34. The shells just slide right off them. But the tanks with their guns put one artillery gun after another out of action and, just to be safe, they even drive over the finished guns and light prime movers. They drive very close, some of them right beside our holes, and those are very unpleasant minutes for us to experience. One even trundles along about 5 meters from my hole, even coming to a stop occasionally. I make myself very small and curl up and hardly dare to breathe. Finally, the tank drives on, but I will certainly never forget those moments.

A hundred meters behind us the tanks come to a stop and shoot at us from behind. After a while, though, they drive back. Not long after, there's a second assault and we have no heavy weapons anymore. Those of our battalion are all destroyed and of the six field howitzers, five are finished. It takes hours for the antitank weaponry to reach us. Finally, 88mm antitank guns, heavy antiaircraft guns, and artillery arrive and our engineers lay mine defense across the road. . . . Fortunately, the Russian infantry weren't sitting on the tanks, because otherwise it's likely that few of us would have lived to see the evening. They follow behind the tanks at some distance and could be kept down.

22.9.41: H. K. (72 INFANTRY DIVISION, ELEVENTH ARMY, ARMY GROUP SOUTH)[114]

Three months ago today the campaign against Russia began. Everybody supposed at the time that the Bolsheviks would be ripe for capitulation within no more than eight to ten weeks. That assumption, however, was based on a widespread ignorance of the Russian war matériel. But not just that. We have been spoiled by the previous blitzkriegs and thought it was certain to go just as quickly as it had done in, e.g., France. But once we'd had a glimpse of the Russian array of men and matériel, and also of terrain, we had to realize that the campaign would take as long again as the French campaign. Just this morning we happened to hear that, for example near Kiev, 600 guns and 150,000 men were captured. What kind of figures are those! Russia is almost inexhaustible.

Neither do I believe that it will ever come to a ceasefire with Russia. We will succeed in beating the Russian army. But Stalin and his comrades will keep organizing new resistance, regardless of the sacrifices or the utter futility.

23.9.41: ERNST GUICKING (52 INFANTRY DIVISION, SECOND ARMY, ARMY GROUP CENTER)[115]

In your letter of 23.8. you ask whether we carry guns. But, Bobi, what do you think? What do you really think? Do you think we're throwing stones out here? Of course every soldier has his gun. And even a pistol as well. Don't worry. . . .

And now I'll tell you a bit about our work. You wanted to know what we do. This was the day before yesterday. We had the task of storming the village occupied by the enemy, taking prisoners, and getting back unharmed if at all possible. So it all kicked off at 2:30 a.m. I took another two men from the section with me, because during the attack we were always laying a telephone line so that we could stay connected with the front behind us. A railway line goes through the middle of the village. The same one runs from our section to the Russian front. So 40 men advance on the left, 40 men on the right of the railway line. At 4:20 a.m. our artillery begins hammering. At 5:00 a.m. the last shell falls. Now the path is clear for us. During the darkness, we have come, unnoticed, to within 200 meters of the first buildings. With our telephone. Now the machine guns and our mortars were barking. The infantry race for cover in the first buildings. Shooting begins. There's whistling and shooting all round our heads. The Russians are shooting wildly about the place. They were very rudely awakened from sleep. They don't know where they should run to and even less where they should be shooting.

You see, surprise attack, that is a particular strength. You should have seen their stupid faces. A surprise like that must be dreadful. That's nothing new for us. We don't notice it anymore. But this fear, this stubborn blockheadedness [*sture Verbohrtheit*], that we're going to shoot them, it just makes us shake our heads. Well, that's Soviet propaganda. The poor people get told, if you are captured, then the Germans will shoot you. You see, my little Bobel, at 7:00 a.m. we had finished our work. There was death there, too. We immediately set about our withdrawal. So that we wouldn't immediately attract the attention of the Russian artillery. Just on the short way back that the three of us took, we counted 90 dead Russians. The Russian lost 150 prisoners and just as many dead on this party. An antitank gun went the same way. On our side there were one fatality and seven casualties. The three of us now had to roll the telephone line back up unnoticed. He had placed the mortars very close here. And everything else left us cold. At 8:00 a.m. we were back sitting in our bunker and really enjoying the hot ground coffee.

23.9.41: *GEFREITER* HANS ROTH (299 INFANTRY DIVISION, SIXTH ARMY, ARMY GROUP SOUTH)[116]

Early on September 19 we penetrated the heavily armed outer ring of the city. The enemy, by far not as strong as we had assumed, was defeated in bloody, close combat, and by 0900 hours we had already reached the western part of the city. The Reds have quit their attempts at heavy street fighting. At the same time strong assault parities attacked the citadel from the direction of Lysa-Hora, and by 1100 hours Nazi swastikas were raised there.

By noon we are in the center of the city, no shots are heard; the wide streets and squares are abandoned. It is eerie. The silence is making us nervous, for it is hardly believable that such a large city has fallen into our hands in such a short amount of time. . . . What does this western defense line, which Budenny depended upon just like the French did with the Maginot Line, look like? It's not a common line of bunkers; no, it is a collection of diabolic resources, which can only be conceived by the brain of a paranoiac. I will try and describe some of these horrific death zones that we passed through while intensely fighting on September 17, 18 and 19:

To the rear of Gatnoje, there are fields of cooperatives, vast vegetable farms. They lie there harmlessly in the sun. Who would believe that hiding among those plants is the most horrific death: a high-voltage current! Atop the vegetation is a webbing of fine-caliber wire the length of several kilometers. This rests on thin, isolated metal poles, which are all painted green; a deadly net of high current, which is run by a power plant in a bunker. It is so well camouflaged that we recognize it unfortunately much too late, only after continued accumulation of losses.

Then there are the devil's ditches, lined up in great depth, several hundred meters long. They are mined, and when a single land mine is tripped, entire fields, which are connected underground by detonation channels, explode. At the same time, water pipes explode and rapidly flood the area two meters deep.

There are even a few more goodies that happen to be just lying around, seeming random objects that are interesting to every soldier: watches, packs of cigarettes, pieces of soap, etc. Each of these objects is connected to a hidden detonator. If the soldier picks any of these objects up, he starts the ignition and detonates a mine or an entire minefield.

In this category also belong well-hidden trip wires, which cause contact mines to explode. These monsters jump up ¾ of a meter and explode. . . . There are other areas where hidden among trip wires are thousands of knife-sharp steel spikes, which are poisoned and cause the injured to die a horrible death ten minutes later. All of the defensive belts are littered with automatic flamethrowers, which are activated by pressure.

Well—just imagine, among all these devilish things there are still normal battle installations: two-story bunkers, automatic weapons stands, ditches, kilometers of barbed wire, tank barriers, in addition to the average mined streets and paths. Add to that infantry mines, booby traps, ban mines, vehicles mines. And now, just imagine this whole hellish apparatus during combat; this is their defense against our attack. . . .

Mine dogs: we shot about a dozen of these German shepherds alone near Schul-jany. The animals carry a device with explosives on their back. According to a prisoner who has trained these dogs, they are made to attack tanks and other vehicles with their load of 3 kilos of ammunition.

23.9.41: *LEUTNANT* SOEFFKER (6 INFANTRY DIVISION, NINTH ARMY, ARMY GROUP CENTER)[117]

Our Army Group Center is on the verge of great, decisive operations. In a few days the major offensive on Moscow will begin for us. Until now, our march direction was always Moscow. Our greatest wish is to hold to this direction and to be there when Moscow is stormed. We have been here on the defensive for weeks. This has caused an unfair internal readjustment for our men, but soon what will count for us is that word again: Attack!

23.9.41: HELMUT VON HARNACK (ARMY GROUP CENTER)[118]

Just why does it pull you back here so soon, to the troops at the front? It's not just ambition or personal impatience by a long shot, it's the feeling of duty that you must help your comrades, who are standing in the muck, the feeling that you simply belong there, that you can't escape because out here feels very much like home [*weil man sich hier draußen fest heimisch fühlt*].

23–24.9.41: *GEFREITER* HANS CASPAR VON WIEDEBACH-NOSTITZ (20 PANZER DIVISION, SIXTEENTH ARMY, ARMY GROUP NORTH)[119]

As a consequence of the great loss of vehicles which the 20 Panzer Division had suf-fered from the constant operations and most recently the bad roads toward Demiansk, the division had to set aside a great part of its men who were brought together in the remnants echelon. At this present time the Panzer regiment alone had only 30 to 40 of its original 200 vehicles. . . . Why the 19 and 20 Panzer Divisions took the route to Cholm and Demiansk was not clear to anyone. At the very least they lost several vehicles. These two divisions now set off via Vitebsk to the central sector. We stayed in the remnants echelon at Toropez. On Monday after we had luckily reached the company, we managed to set ourselves up rather comfortably in a house.

23–24.9.41: ADOLF B. (2 PANZER GROUP, ARMY GROUP CENTER)[120]

Hard days of battle and many fearful hours lay behind us! We took part in the great battle of Kiev! That was a crack and a thunder of cannons and other weapons from every nook and cranny. Often one did not know who was encircled, the Bolsheviks or us! Luckily we had the better strategy, the better weapons, and the also the better soldiers. Now the Kiev pocket must be cleared. The radio broadcast delivered the *Sondermeldung* of the largest battle of encirclement and pincer movement of all time this morning. So far, 380 thousand prisoners have been brought in, etc.!! For hours the beaten, miserable and degenerate-looking criminal masses of *Bolshewiki* marched past us! . . . The losses on our side are also quite high.

24.9.41: *UNTEROFFIZIER* H. G. (79 INFANTRY DIVISION, SIXTH ARMY, ARMY GROUP SOUTH)[121]

Have survived the cauldron battle east of Kiev well. I had assumed that we would be pulled out after this battle, but unfortunately it's out of the question, even though we have shrunk to a particularly small group. We're now marching to the next cauldron around Khar'kov. Whether there it is an end to Russia this year I doubt very much. The [Soviet] military might is indeed broken, but the country is too big, and capitulation is not an option for the Russians. It's simply not a battle of country against country, but rather between two fundamentally different worldviews. Because two men are fighting about their ideas, millions of people must bleed to death.

24.9.4: DR. (NAME UNKNOWN) (3 PANZER DIVISION, 2 PANZER GROUP, ARMY GROUP CENTER)[122]

A chaotic scene remained [as the cauldron battle of Kiev came to an end]. Hundreds of lorries and troop carriers with tanks in between are strewn across the landscape. Those sitting inside were often caught by the flames as they attempted to dismount, and were burned, hanging from turrets like black mummies. Around the vehicles lay thousands of dead.

24.9.41: *GEFREITER* ALOIS SCHEUER (197 INFANTRY DIVISION, ARMY GROUP CENTER)[123]

We know that we are standing before great decisions that could end the war here in the East. It's about time too as the cold already makes everything very uncomfortable.

25.9.41: *GEFREITER* HANS ROTH (299 INFANTRY DIVISION, SIXTH ARMY, ARMY GROUP SOUTH)[124]

Early this morning I drove with 3 other guys to Terempki. It was a most sensitive undertaking. The whole area is still full of landmines. . . . Even now, days after the fighting, the empty positions reach out for our lives. . . . Everything here is sinister, still fresh the traces of the terrible battle but there is no shrieking or whistling in the air here, or thunders of detonations. . . .

My God what a sight! Along the total length of the high forest of Terempki, friend and enemy are still lying there, exactly how they died 6 weeks ago. Yes, this Terempki forest, which once was a magnificent forest, but now there are only ripped tree trunks and in between the horror assaults you! Damned me, a soldier should not stroll as a pedestrian on those battlefields which have not completely absorbed all the blood, where within the barbed wires there are hanging things, which were worn by soldiers once during battle. . . .

Then we reach a huge pile of rubble: Terempki. All around us a landscape of moon craters. There were our battle positions. Then we are standing at the spot where we buried the dead comrades. The earth has been tilled many times. Nothing is discernable anymore; there, where we laid them to their final rest, are now huge funnels at the bottom of which we can see murky groundwater. How fortunate that the young women, mothers, and brides know nothing about all this! . . .

We are driving back, nobody is speaking, silently each on his own with his thoughts. Farewell to Terempki, from all these dear comrades. The memory of this piece of earth is heavy. How can anybody in his lifetime forget these zones of horror? . . . When will this horrible war find its end? . . . Everybody is telling me I am seeing the world all black in an alarmist way—no comrades, to the contrary, I see white, I am seeing white snowy areas and many, many of you all dead.

26.9.41: KARL FUCHS (7 PANZER DIVISION, 3 PANZER GROUP, ARMY GROUP CENTER)[125]

My dear father,

It seems that you are now stationed much farther away from me than I had initially assumed. I have not heard a word from you in weeks. Perhaps you were participating in the monumental battle of encirclement around Kiev and thus were unable to write. If you were there, I assure you that our tank battalion will vie with you for this glory. Yes, thank God, I have a new tank and am waiting for my orders. My tank crew and I are eager to move out and we're itching to prove ourselves once more in battle. Once the last battle is fought and won out here on the Russian front, those fellows on the other side of the English Channel will really get worried. We can hear them already, lying foaming at the mouth, and inciting others against us. None of that will help those British scoundrels. Once our German sword strikes, they will be hurting for sure.

My God, you cannot believe how proud we are of our Fatherland and how often we long to be back in our homeland, to see its forests and meadows, its lakes and mountains. Let me greet you with Germany, Sieg Heil!

26.9.41: *UNTEROFFIZIER* WILHELM PRÜLLER (9 PANZER DIVISION, 1 PANZER GROUP, ARMY GROUP SOUTH)[126]

You should see the act the civilians put on when we make it clear to them that we intend to use their sties to sleep in. A weeping and yelling begins, as if their throats were being cut, until we chuck them out. Whether young or old, man or wife, they stand in their rags and tatters on the doorstep and can't be persuaded to go to their neighbors or to the empty houses. When we finally threaten them at pistol point, they disappear for a few minutes, only to return again yelling even more loudly.

26.9.41: *GEFREITER* HANS ROTH (299 INFANTRY DIVISION, SIXTH ARMY, ARMY GROUP SOUTH)[127]

[In Kiev] the SS special commando is extremely busy. Interrogations and executions nonstop. Somewhat suspicious individuals are simply shot in the street and their bodies remain right where they fell down. Men, women, and children are walking by, talking and laughing: "*nitschewo*," this is nothing special, a dead person, not much! . . .

The *Einsatzkommandos* of the Waffen-SS are very busy as well.[128] All Jews without exception had until noon of the 25th to report. Sure, only half of them show up, but nobody will evade us, for a tight belt of outposts surround the city. That very day the revenge for our comrades who lost their lives in the mine attacks is beginning.[129] Now 24 hours later, already 2000 Hebrews have been sent to Jehovah!

I have a long conversation with a young SS soldier of this "kill commando." They "freed" all the larger cities which were touched by our advance of the Jewish population. They understand their butcher job well; their boys are experienced killers, I am astonished. We soldiers in the first attack wave have never thought about the stuff that happens behind us in the cities we leave, as we're chasing farther after the enemy.[130]

First I cannot speak at all. This young man talks about it as if he was on a casual pheasant hunt. I cannot believe all this and tell him so. He laughs and says I should have a look. We are riding our bikes to the outskirts of the city, to a steep gorge. I will cut this short; the food in my stomach is curiously loose. What I see there is terrible, this horrible picture I will never forget in my entire life. At the edge of the gorge there are Jews standing, the machine guns are whipping into them, they fall over the edge, 50 meters. . . .

My God, my God. Without a word I turn and run more than walk back to the city.

27.9.41: HANS SIMON (12 INFANTRY DIVISION, SIXTEENTH ARMY, ARMY GROUP NORTH)[131]

Don't let the gossipers at home fill your ears, they are hardly worth the bullets to shoot them. It's a shame that we can never get our hands on someone like that here at the front. Better to wait for my mail and not listen to criminals like that, who only scare our mothers, wives, and relations and want to stir up fear. How strange that these people can never be found out here, where it counts. But it's easier to tell cock-and-bull stories at home than it is to be out here with us, facing the enemy. It's really a shame that you can never get your hands on people like that. Right now, we've been spending some time facing the enemy with the SS, who used to guard the concentration camp Dachau. There was trouble again. The Russians did try to break through here. And in doing so a gunner, one from our antitank battalion, shot 16 tanks down in 2 days. They stuck through all sorts of things, the SS. Now we're back by Demiansk and not Moscow.

You would hardly believe how Communism has changed the Russian people. One thing first. The countryside here, bleak, monotonous, has a dulling effect on people, as we are experiencing ourselves. You become a piece of clay. A beautiful building sticks out, doesn't fit here at all. Everything is rotten and so the landscape contains this closed character within it, too. So that explains the Russian dullness and stubbornness. Now, Stalin's system of People's Commissars is worked out in such fine detail that, truly, you'd never believe it, a father cannot trust his son. Anybody could be a GPU spy.[132] So now perhaps on the one hand you can understand a little of the tenacity of the struggle. I know very well that you find it difficult in this regard to change your old understanding and experiences of the Russians. At that time, perhaps you knew the cruelty that is typical of the Asiatic.

To return to the commissars. In the scattered groups you only really find resistance where you also have just one commissar. These 20 years have had a terrible effect in this regard. And I would wish that you didn't see Russians now. You would feel deep heartache at what has happened to that good core of the people. If you can't get anything done with Russian civilians through threats and pull out a pistol, you won't achieve anything more by it, because it is nothing new for the Russians. If you properly understand what I have outlined on this sheet of paper, then you can draw yourself a picture of the current state of the soul of the Russian people.

27.9.41: DR. HEINRICH HAAPE (6 INFANTRY DIVISION, NINTH ARMY, ARMY GROUP CENTER)[133]

The war of position [*Stellungskrieg*] has reached its zenith! Some of our trenches are 80 meters away from the Russian positions. Everything has holed itself up in the ground. Provisions, ammunition, and other necessities are only brought up at night. We lead the life of a veritable military mole. The shells crash down all day around our little homemade dugouts. Next to my sleeping bunker a medical aid bunker has also been built, where I can shelter the wounded during the day and provide medical care; then they are taken back to the main dressing station at night. It is our justifiable hope that this boring and yet dangerous crap will soon come to an end.

I am well as always, our dear God has so far had his protecting hand over me in the most miraculous way, even in the most dangerous and difficult hours; and I hope that he will continue to bless my path!

The fact that I have come closer to God here on the battlefields of Russia is not due to fear and anxiety; I really do not feel those anymore and I am prepared to walk any path, even through the darkest gates of death [*dunkelsten Todespforten*] if it must be! We look all dangers straight in the eye with clarity and calmness, just as we took an oath to do! No! Here reigns deep solemnity; here you are more directly confronted with all causal things; here God speaks to us at a close proximity, and I am not alone in hearing this speech!

They are not empty words I speak when I say: "*Mit Gott, Führer und Vaterland!*"

27.9.41: *LEUTNANT* SOEFFKER (6 INFANTRY DIVISION, NINTH ARMY, ARMY GROUP CENTER)[134]

This morning at 0800 hours I was riding with 2 noncommissioned officers and 2 men to reconnoiter the road. . . . As I'm riding my bicycle on the return journey through Prechistaya, I run into a Russian low-level attack. 3 bombers and 2 fighters are flying at lowest altitude over the road. The bombers drop [about] 20 fragmentation bombs, while the fighters blanket the march route with machine-gun fire. I leap from my bicycle and seek cover behind a house. There's a lot of confusion. The drivers shamefully and irresponsibly leave their vehicles and horses in the lurch. Horses run whinnying all over the road. Motor vehicle drivers leap from their vehicles and abandon them with engines still running.

To my right, 6 bombs land in a garden. The shrapnel whizzes over the road, smashing windowpanes and house roofs. Some houses immediately go up in flames. The civilian population suffers considerable losses. Several severely injured Russians are carried out of one house, some of them are missing arms and legs. Beside me, a sobbing woman carries a small, naked child covered in blood out of the house. I myself have been enormously lucky, that was the first proper low-level attack [*Tiefangriff*] that I have ever experienced. Now I can finally picture what it must be like when German fighters and bombers attack Russian march columns.

28.9.41: ERNST GUICKING (52 INFANTRY DIVISION, SECOND ARMY, ARMY GROUP CENTER)[135]

Yes, the blasted war. Yesterday, the wife of one of our fallen soldiers wrote. What should I write to the woman? Report the truth? And make her suffering even greater. She would like to know her husband's last wish. You can do that, if you close your eyes in a feather bed or in a hospital. But not in war. For example, there's a clap of thunder and a flash of lightning and then there's nothing left of a little person like that. Well, I'll have to try to reassure her. It's just the way it is. The war demands its sacrifices. . . . [*Der Krieg erfordert seine Opfer.* . . .] Why get dejected about it? You don't win a war that way. I can't do anything about it.

28.9.41: HANS-ALBERT GIESE (NINTH ARMY, ARMY GROUP CENTER)[136]

In the next few days we will again march somewhat farther. We look forward to it because the quicker we advance, the earlier we come home to Germany again. The news of the past few days was again really big. These Bolsheviks will not last too much longer.

28.9.41: *GEFREITER* ALOIS SCHEUER (197 INFANTRY DIVISION, ARMY GROUP CENTER)[137]

What I have experienced and lived through in this quarter of a year in Russia I cannot put into words. There is much I would like to forget and never be reminded of again. I always, however, try not to lose hope and courage, but there are hours in which the loneliness and desertion are almost unbearable. . . . September is coming to an end, maybe October will bring a change because the longer this now lasts the worse everything will get. We hope for the best.

28.9.41: *GEFREITER* L. B. (269 INFANTRY DIVISION, SIXTEENTH ARMY, ARMY GROUP NORTH)[138]

We are not deployed right now. I do not think that we will get to it again. But even so, it's still dangerous everywhere because of the many mines that have been set. In Kiev, for example, there was one explosion after another because of mines. The city has been burning for eight days already, the Jews are doing it all [*alles machen die Juden*]. So the Jews between 14 and 60 years old were shot, and even the Jews' women are shot, or else there'd never be an end to it.[139]

28.9.41: WERNER BEERMANN (NINTH ARMY, ARMY GROUP CENTER)[140]

In the evenings in our bunker we often contemplate how the upcoming advance might turn out for us. This time it will be the motorized troops that advance and then we come. We won't have to torture ourselves with excessive heat, dust, mosquitoes, and a great deal of what lies behind us, almost like a dream. But when these tribulations, too, have passed, the fall season will produce new ones. It's mellowing and quite frequently here getting chilly at night and that is why we will likely suffer with the cold a lot. . . .

A few minutes ago, just like yesterday, a Russian plane carried out a low-level attack using machine guns. Shooting at our regiment's position: but it can't achieve anything by that, because for that short time everything has got under cover. A few days ago, I saw how Russian bombers with a fighter escort attempted to fly into the occupied hinterland. But here there's a lot of our antiaircraft artillery, which lets loose a terrific amount of fire. Right away, a bomber was shot in flames, three airmen ejected with parachutes and the smoking bird crashed with a great bang. The crew immediately scattered to the four winds, all the planes turned and fled hurriedly in the direction of home. They had quickly lost their appetite. For the last few days, wave upon wave of our planes have been flying with bombs in the direction of Moscow.

I'm listening to the *Wehrmachtbericht* at the moment.[141] Another load of ships belonging to the English has been sunk; and, finally, there's a report on the battle of Kiev as well. It's really good that I can now listen to some radio now and again. It means I always know the latest news and some nice music around midday or in the evening prevents you from getting too dull.

29.9.41: ERNST GUICKING (52 INFANTRY DIVISION, SECOND ARMY, ARMY GROUP CENTER)[142]

Bobi, don't be cross if, from tomorrow, I can't write to you every day; I did already write you that things will get rolling again soon. The second push is starting. Hopefully, it's the last one. The prisoners that we took last night come from the Urals. So things must look pretty dire on the other side. It looks like these are their last reserves. And so now it's off right into the middle of things. Kiev is over. Now it's Center's turn again. The grand finale will soon be played in the East. We are placing all our hopes on the coming four weeks.

29.9.41: HEINZ RAHE (13 PANZER DIVISION, 1 PANZER GROUP, ARMY GROUP SOUTH)[143]

Early yesterday morning I drove with *Hauptmann Graf* Münster along the roads that I had reconnoitered. Traffic slowed down at the bridge over the river St. But everything funneled across in the end. Below, by the bridge, lay two burned-out vehicles with a number of still recognizable Russian corpses, some of them were partially burned, others intact. They had wanted to take possession of the bridge and had been shot up. It was still smoldering a bit, but otherwise multitudes of supply columns were crossing over and the war machine rolled on. Then it was off over country tracks, where we took our chances, followed the sun and a poor map to look for the division headquarters and we found them. I drove back again, and on the way you could see the traces of the battles, numerous stinking horses and Russians, several tanks, and a dozen graves of German soldiers. It was quite lively on the advance road, a number of Russian bombers above us dropped their bombs, but essentially hit nothing. There was a lot going on at the front with the division headquarters, and at the same time there was a sandstorm to presage a coming storm.

When we moved into a few farmsteads, the inhabitants left their homes, with a packed bundle. Around evening, I drove into R. with a paymaster official. A captured city like that is a terrible picture. Incalculable columns of vehicles went through it, a lot of buildings in the center have been completely destroyed by our planes or burned out. The stores . . . have barred their windows and doors, but entrance to the interior has been found in most cases, everything has been ransacked and is strewn around. The impoverished population that has not fled takes its pickings and, loaded with bundles, keeps to its quarters. We first drove to the railway station, which has been very severely damaged, and some wagons were still burning. There, we found a storehouse with eggs, tomato paste, and mineral water. Otherwise, there's very little to find. While we were looking some more, I met various people from my company. They described the battles: two noncommissioned officers fallen, *Feldwebel* Haase and others wounded. One newly promoted *Feldwebel* from my platoon is also dead.

You wouldn't believe how deeply it affects me. Ruins all around, plundered buildings, rabble, and then this news as well. The boys have had to undergo some difficult things. I'm going to drive over to them. Like all of us today, they are resting. There's currently a lot of activity in the air. Now our planes are there and will undoubtedly clean up. Yesterday evening I also made rather a haul. We were looking for appropriate quarters for us to occupy and came across a garden nursery. There were fragrant begonias and roses. I took one of them with me. I don't want to look at anything else. By contrast to the West, I am disgusted by things here. I don't know why. I hope that Moscow has been reached in 14 to 20 days—although not by us—and that this disastrous campaign is thus ended [*dieser unselige Feldzug beendet ist*]. The Russians have lost a lot of tanks in our section, but it's not come to an actual retreat yet. Now we are more restrained, as we evidently advanced too rapidly. Stupendous tactics! Naturally, we're enjoying the breathing space. I may be sitting primitively on the ground in the barracks area, but I have been able to shave in peace, have got my dyed linen jacket on, and am listening to the first *Sondermeldungen* in between times.

I met the general earlier. He spoke about his very floral reception by the population. So far, I have only seen one triumphal arch erected for us. But once we've advanced more, that'll increase. The Soviets are supposed to have murdered numerous Ukrainians, like in 1919! That's why every functionary is shot. Hopefully, there'll be a just order here. May God help this country!

29.9.41: GEORG FULDE (LUFTWAFFE, ARMY GROUP NORTH)[144]

I thought I'd send another sign of life so you all aren't left completely without news. You all may already know that I am a pilot and commander with a bomber squadron in Russia. I've been here 8 weeks now, have carried out around 30 sorties and dropped my bombs over Russia on many a night.

I'm going to receive the Iron Cross 1st and 2nd Class and the Front Flying Clasp [*Frontflugspange*] for bomber pilots soon. I have had to fight bitterly in many a sortie for these medals. They have been handed in for me! My time here is supposed to be up on 1.10. But my squadron commander insisted on keeping me and now I've been transferred here. I'm hugely delighted about it, because it's fun. So I'll take part in the war until the end with the squadron and won't return now to Tutow.

Many a night I've been in the brightest searchlights and antiaircraft fire with my good old Heinkel 111. But my bombs have never missed their mark. Many a Russian railway station has been blown to pieces. But sometimes my machine was shot up as well. I can always get home. Recently, at 6 o'clock in the morning, after I had blown up a large barracks outside Leningrad, 3 enemy fighter planes attacked me. I wasn't doing so well. A fighter put a gun shot through my left cabin window from behind, 10 cm from my head. He was finally shot down by one of our fighters: it was a great air attack. Your machine may frequently be shot to pieces, but you've got to be lucky and that's what I've been every time, I can hardly believe it myself.

14 days ago, on Saturday night, after 1:00 a.m., I received a direct hit to my right engine while flying over Leningrad. It started to burn. But I still got the machine back home in one piece. That's often how it goes. But it's so exciting when all these colorful things fly toward you and then explode that you almost fly from your seat yourself. Last night I blew up a gasometer in Leningrad, the detonation was indescribable! There were tremendous fires. Yesterday was Sunday as well. I started off with the setting sun at 6:00 p.m. So that was my sunset flight. There's no such thing as a weekend here. You often don't know how you're living. Tonight, we'll be off 2x for Leningrad, then the city will soon be finished. We only attack militarily significant targets. Not like the Tommy, who chucks his bombs onto houses and then skedaddles as quickly as possible. For myself, I even drop a parachute flare after bomb release to see whether my bombs have hit their mark. Once Leningrad has fallen, it's onward to Moscow. I've already bombed that city once in August. It's extremely lively there. Around 700–1,000 searchlights and a lot of antiaircraft artillery. But by constantly feinting, you can mess around with the Russians so much that they always shoot and miss. Of course, a deal of experience is needed for that.

I have a superb crew. We get on. Once we've dropped our bombs, on the flight back home the first cigarette is smoked and we listen to news and dance music using the direction finder set. That's some relaxation. When we get home, there's hot soup, ground coffee, eggs, etc. We want for nothing. But you don't half need it. Because when we attacked Moscow the first times, we flew there from Königsberg with 40-weight bombs. Start time was 7 o'clock in the evening and we landed back again at 5 o'clock in the morning. Always 10 hours. Probably none of you can imagine what a 10-hour sortie means! We were utterly spent! It was like that every night. When the airfields in Russia got better, we moved.

Russia is a miserable desert. No human can imagine it. And added to that this rotten, brutish people and the muck. I don't want to know what would have happened to all of you and to Germany if the Bolsheviks had got into the Reich, as had been planned. But, thank God, it turned out the other way round. If the Russian had been a bit more humane, not so infinitely filled with hate, the war would already be over. These simply aren't people, they are utterly bestialized. [*Das sind ja gar keine Menschen, sie sind völlig vertiert.*] But everyone can depend upon it, we are giving it to them, wherever they are.

These rascals are torching everything, the dwellings of their own fellow humans. It's a daily sight. It's a grisly beautiful scene when you fly over the actual front at night. The front is burning for hundreds of kilometers on the Russian side, entire towns and villages. The sky is fiery red. Below us rage desperate battles. But we fly deep into enemy territory. When you then come back from the sortie in the morning and drive back to quarters in the car, you have to be prepared for a ground fight with scattered Russians. Every night there are still shootouts in the hinterland. Drivers have been shot down and murdered on lonely country roads, cars shot at. You can only go to the toilet with a submachine gun, similarly going to sleep. When we were shot at recently when returning home in the morning, I had us halt and then we laid 5 of those thugs flat. I finished 3 of them off with a submachine gun when they tried to throw hand grenades at our feet during their capture. But that's nothing new anymore. It's just war. And here it will soon be over. We airmen will make sure of that.

29.9.41: *UNTEROFFIZIER* WILHELM PRÜLLER (9 PANZER DIVISION, 1 PANZER GROUP, ARMY GROUP SOUTH)[145]

In the early morning we make a campfire out of haystacks, but it only warms the side you turn toward the fire, while the other goes on freezing. The summer really is finished. The rain is depressingly regular. The roads, which are mad anyway, will be quite impassable. And what these mean for an armored division, anyone can see. If we all had tank tracks, or at least four-wheel drive, we could make the grade. But the way it is, the wheels just spin in the deep mud and you can't even get the vehicles started.

30.9.41: ERICH DOHL (SIXTEENTH ARMY, ARMY GROUP NORTH)[146]

Recent days have been great. We can be very grateful to our Lord God that we come away from it all so well, despite the many attacks. At any rate, I was always happy when it was evening, although I never had the feeling that anything could happen at all. Anyhow, I have done my duty, nothing more can be demanded. . . .

Hopefully, the end isn't all too far off. However, it looks like it will go on for another few years, at least if you look at the map. The Russian system is exactly like ours. Here it's *Kommissar*, for us it's *Blockwalter* [block administrator]. Anyone who rebels is neutralized. In Russia, neutralized means "shot dead." The government won't be brought down all that easily, anyhow. But we don't want to see these things too gloomily [*allzu schwarz sehen*]. Dear God will help us. . . .

The rumor is going round here again that we'll be pulled out. While some claim to know that we'll be out of here on the 10th, others maintain that we'll be shipped off 14 days before Christmas. I don't believe the latter at all, because if we're still here then, we'll be staying here for the rest of winter. I'm curious to see whether we'll receive our winter clothing. Everything depends on that. Apparently, it's been denied to a number of units, which means so much as our return to Germany or France. Normally there's some truth to every rumor, so let's hope that's also true in our case. . . .

I can't imagine that there'll be any leave at all coming from Russia. The few trains that are available are far more important for other purposes. If there's snow lying on the ground, then it's off all together. Perhaps we'll not get any rations sometimes. At any rate, I imagine the winter in Russia to be dreadful. . . . Experiences of the front are being told around the table just now. Grisly, I can tell you. It's all passed off well now. Dear God will continue to protect me like before.

CHAPTER 6

October 1941

Introduction

On 2 October, Army Group Center's great fall offensive, code named Typhoon, burst forth along the central part of the Eastern Front spearheaded by three reinforced panzer groups. In the south, Guderian's tanks attacked toward the northeast, creating an encirclement around Briansk that eliminated up to one hundred thousand Soviet troops. Yet it was in the north, on the road to Moscow, that the greatest encirclement after the Kiev pocket was closed. The combined panzer groups of Hoepner and Generaloberst Hans-Georg Reinhardt (who had replaced Hoth)[1] closed on the town of Viaz'ma, trapping well over half a million Soviet troops.[2]

Coming so soon after the victory in the Ukraine, Nazi propaganda declared that the last remnants of the Red Army before Moscow were now caught in two steel rings. On 10 October, the Völkische Beobachter, a Nazi daily newspaper, carried banner headlines extolling the news: "The Great Hour Has Struck!" "Campaign in the East Decided!" "The Military End of the Bolsheviks."[3] Not everyone in the German High Command was so convinced, and, as the letters below reflect, even some of the soldiers struggled to reconcile the claims of their propaganda with what they themselves were experiencing.

At the eastern edge of the Briansk and Viaz'ma pockets, carnage ensued as Soviet command and control broke down and masses of Soviet men attempted to smash their way through the German encirclement front. General der Flieger Wolfram von Richthofen, commanding the VIII Air Corps, gained perhaps the most striking impression of the sheer volume of the killing when he flew over the pocket at Viaz'ma: "There are horrific scenes of destruction in the places where the Red Army soldiers have made unsuccessful attempts to break out. The Russians have suffered a total bloodbath. Piles of bodies, heaps of abandoned equipment, and guns are strewn everywhere."[4]

After the elimination of the pockets at Viaz'ma and Briansk, Army Group Center attempted to exploit the breakthrough in all directions. Not only was there an advance on Moscow in the center, but in the north major formations drove on Kalinin, while some 600 kilometers (373 miles) to the south, Kursk was the objective. Only an estimated ninety thousand Soviet troops now guarded the direct approaches to Moscow, but by the middle of the month Bock's army group was confronting a new enemy—the rain and mud of the Russian Rasputitsa or "quagmire season."[5] This presented the German motorized columns with an unprecedented topographical challenge, denying them their much-prized "shock" and rapid maneuver. It also compounded the already desperate logistical situation, slowing all movement and seriously limiting Army Group Center's exploitation of its early victories. Writing of the October conditions, the chief of staff of the Fourth Army, Generalmajor Günther Blumentritt, explained,

> We had anticipated this [the Rasputitsa] of course, for we had read about it in our studies of Russian conditions. But the reality far exceeded our worst expectations. . . . It is hard to convey a picture of what it was like to anybody who had not actually experienced it. . . . The infantryman slithers in the mud, while many teams of horses are needed to drag each gun forward. All wheeled vehicles sink up to their axles in the slime. Even tractors can only move with great difficulty. A large proportion of our heavy artillery was soon stuck fast and was therefore unavailable for the Moscow battle. The quality of the mud may be understood when it is realized that even tanks and other tracked vehicles could only just get along and were frequently and repeatedly mired. The strain that all this caused our already exhausted troops can perhaps be imagined.[6]

Throughout the second half of October, Bock's army group fought desperately against these conditions as well as against the Red Army's unceasing resistance, yet at the end of the month Army Group Center was halted to await the first frosts of winter, which would allow the advance to resume on solid ground.

Just as GFM von Bock's panzer groups were wreaking havoc in the center of the front, in the south Rundstedt's sole panzer group under Generaloberst von Kleist began driving to the Sea of Azov. The aim was to cut off two Soviet armies of the Southern Front, which by 11 October was successfully achieved with another hundred thousand Soviet troops captured.[7] Thereafter the road into the resource-rich Donbas region was open, and the panzers raced eastward to complete their conquest of the Ukraine. Meanwhile, General der Infanterie Erich von Manstein's Eleventh Army was turning south to attack into the Crimea, which Hitler regarded as a vital objective to prevent Soviet bombers from threatening the Romanian oilfields at Ploesti. Manstein's task was complicated by the Red Army's evacuation of the port city of Odessa, which had been under siege by Romanian forces for two and a half months. These additional Soviet troops reinforced the Crimea, and Manstein was only able to decisively break through the Soviet lines on 28 October.[8] Farther north, Army Group South was also seeking to advance, but as Rundstedt wrote to his wife on 14 October, "the weather frustrates all plans."[9] GFM Walter von Reichenau's Sixth Army was driving on the great industrial city of Khar'kov, while Hoth's Seventeenth Army was attempting to cover its southern flank all the way to the Donets River. Yet simply moving men and supplies was a huge task, complicated by the fact that the army group had no real concentration of effort. In the aftermath of the victory at Kiev, Army Group South was attempting to attack in all directions, and by the end of October its men were exhausted and its vehicles in need of major overhauls.

At Army Group North, German documents make clear that Leningrad was to be "worn down by terror and hunger," which was a strategy that would impact the defending

Soviet troops as well as the civilian population.[10] *To ruthlessly maintain the pressure, any attempt by starving civilians to leave the city was to be prevented; as* Generalmajor *Eduard Wagner explained, "What do we do with a city of 3.5 million people, which is just reliant on our supply bases? There is no room for sentiment there." Indeed, German plans for the anticipated capture of the city would see the city's inhabitants interned in ghetto-like settlements and the city razed to the ground.*[11] *While Army Group North was stalled in front of Leningrad, to the south Busch's Sixteenth Army was preparing to launch a wildly ambitious offensive to forge a junction with the Finnish army east of Lake Ladoga. Leeb was attempting to conduct a 250-kilometer (155-mile) advance to reach the Svir River, but the operation, which only began in the middle of the month, suffered from rain, mud, ice, and snow. The advance slowed to a crawl, and even Hitler considered breaking off the attack, but Leeb argued against this, and the attack continued.*[12]

Letters and Diary Entries (1–31 October 1941)

1.10.41: DR. HEINRICH HAAPE (6 INFANTRY DIVISION, NINTH ARMY, ARMY GROUP CENTER)[13]

Things are finally moving onward; the war of position came to an end for us. At dawn we will be assaulting the Russian positions. At the moment, we are making ready, just like the first day on 22.6.[1941]. We will now be advancing on Moscow through the wet and cold to break the Russians' spine. The long-awaited decisive battle is finally looming and however tough it will be, I am happy that the wretched war of position is over.

Even if I don't look it, I am always calm and detached, but the constant shellfire does get on your nerves over time. We were bombarded with the heaviest shells on a daily basis and you would wait for a direct hit on your dugout, which would tear you apart, as happened to many a soldier. Heavy shells also struck close to my dugout. We held our positions, sometimes under the toughest circumstances, repulsed attacks, made counterattacks, endured bombing and attacks from low-flying aircraft. We held out and were master of our task, and were thus party to the successes in the south and the north. We are full of fighting courage and are storming ahead to the final battle. We all know that the road will be difficult, but an end is in sight!

1.10.41: WILLY (ARMY GROUP NORTH)[14]

When our fighting in the Waldai heights had ended, we began a brisk march back to the rear. . . . The train ride was very comfortable, but we arrived in Vitebsk today. On this trip we met several transports from the Spanish and Ukrainian as well as from the Dutch volunteers.[15] I was particularly astonished by the "Blue Division,"[16] because these fighters against Bolshevism cannot be distinguished from German soldiers either by the uniform or their arms. Their beautiful sad, but also melancholy songs of home, reveal their origins.

2.10.41: *GEFREITHER G.* (11 PANZER DIVISION, PANZER GROUP 4, ARMY GROUP CENTER)[17]

A magnificent day breaks. At 5:30 a.m. the German artillery opens fire and keeps up a heavy barrage for three hours. Our panzers attack. Our own attack is carried out, supported by Stukas, which, in rolling deployments, fight the retreating enemy with bombs. There are also Heinkel and Do [Dornier] aircraft. The roar of the engines never ceases for a minute. Me 109s keep the air clear. At 4:00 p.m. we advance. Everything is pushing forward [*Alles drängt nach vorn*]. In the distance, Stukas bomb a fortified village into flames. A more wonderful combination of weapons, *Luftwaffe*, army has hardly been seen. It continues early into the night.[18]

2.10.41: ALBERT NEUHAUS (ARMY GROUP CENTER)[19]

That's when, around 500 m away, I see 2 bombers flying toward us, right over the runway. The construction of the machines seems odd to me and barely have I grasped the notion that it could be Russian bombers than the explosions hit. The soil sprays up to the right and left of us, there can be no thought of a proper search for cover now. I crouch down behind our vehicle. A wild shooting [*Eine wüste Schießerei*] begins, directed at us and our vehicles. . . . These are eerie seconds for us and they seem to us like a small eternity. Perhaps it's more the dreadful crashing of the aircraft guns than the impact of the bullets into the earth that agitates us. Finally, the two machines roared off around 60–80 m over us and approx. 50–100 m behind us, they let a couple more bombs drop, which, however, only explode sometime later. Everything has come off well, nothing, but absolutely nothing has happened. A good guardian angel or a lucky star has watched over us. Now, once the danger has passed, everyone has a certain visible reaction and this is completely understandable.

3.10.41: *UNTEROFFIZIER* WILHELM PRÜLLER (9 PANZER DIVISION, 1 PANZER GROUP, ARMY GROUP SOUTH)[20]

When we set up quarters for the night, we set up our wireless set as usual, which only takes a few minutes; and we nearly fall flat on our faces when we realize that the *Führer* is about to speak. I've been a soldier now for quite a while—a battle soldier, too. And I really know what our men prefer, if they could choose between mail from home—letters and parcels—or a quiet, undisturbed night, or listening to one of the *Führer*'s speeches. No one knows what this beloved voice means to us—how our cheeks glow, our eyes sparkle, when the *Führer* takes the war criminals to task. What a lift his words give us, as we crowd round the wireless set, not wanting to miss a single word! Is there a finer reward after a day of battle than to hear the *Führer*? Never! We all of us thank him!

3.10.41: ALBERT NEUHAUS (ARMY GROUP CENTER)[21]

When you drive like this, day and night, then you really become aware of the vastness and the bleakness [*die Weite und die Trostlosigkeit*] of the Russian landscape. Endless distances that one could well term steppe. When German organizational spirit and German intellect arrive here later, a blossoming country will emerge. Shame that the towns had to be so bombarded and shot up. I do believe that a decade's work could not restore the towns that now lie so desolated.

4.10.41: *OBERGEFREITER* JOSEPH B. (2 PANZER DIVISION, 4 PANZER GROUP, ARMY GROUP CENTER)[22]

The night passed quietly. We can sleep fairly free of disturbance, although the fireworks of the previous night were very unpleasant. . . . The Stukas are aiding our advance a great deal and visit us frequently. You can deduce the resistance from that. We haven't yet any losses in our unit, but there have been in the battalion. . . .[23]

Despite sunshine, a sharp wind whistles across the fields. We could really use gloves. I have already ordered some from Aunt A. When it gets really bad, we pull socks over our hands. You have to know how to help yourself. There is nothing to obtain here [*Zu organisieren gibt es hier gar nichts*]. Above all, nothing to eat. Sometimes we boil or fry some potatoes from the fields. Otherwise, turnips at most. The people here are content with little. We simply can't imagine it. If you compare the Russian soldiers with our earlier opponents, you can only be happy that, e.g., the Greeks were no Russians. We had to make many sacrifices. I don't know if everything can be put down to their intractability and stupidity.

Yesterday the *Führer* spoke of big decisions. I wasn't able to hear his speech myself. But I can confirm to you, if that is at all necessary, that the successes in the *Wehrmachtbericht* are successes in reality.

5.10.41: FRITZ PABST (SIXTH ARMY, ARMY GROUP SOUTH)[24]

I have driven through the city [Kiev] with the car several times by now and got to know it better. There are wonderful buildings to see, but many of them were destroyed by the large fire that raged for four days last week. The sight here is harrowing, almost the entire center has been destroyed or burned out by it. The fire was caused by the Jews' sabotage, who have all now received their punishment for it [*Entstanden ist diese Feuer durch Sabotage der Juden die ja nun auch alle ihre Strafe dafür bekommen haben. . . .*][25] You'll all have to be satisfied with the sultanas, because there is nothing else here now, the Bolsheviks have utterly destroyed everything. I have seen horrific scenes of destruction and can only tell you to thank our *Führer* that he has freed us from this threat.[26] There are beasts among them who eat each other up. [*Es gibt Bestien unter ihnen, die sich gegenseitig auffressen.*] These aren't illusions but facts which I have seen for myself.

5.10.41: DR. HEINRICH HAAPE (6 INFANTRY DIVISION, NINTH ARMY, ARMY GROUP CENTER)[27]

3 days ago saw the start of the great battle for Moscow and we are in the middle of it! You cannot imagine how hard this fight is. Since 3 [October] we have hardly slept a wink; the challenges are relentless. I have been able to help a lot and have looked death in the eye all too frequently. I have remained true to myself and our dear God has always miraculously protected me. On the first day we had 12 dead and 25 wounded in the attack on the well-prepared Russian positions. We broke through and are in action day and night. Today will be the first night in which I can stretch out on a straw bed in a barn. How I am looking forward to that—I am dog-tired! Tomorrow we will continue to pursue the enemy and however great the resistance, he will be beaten!

Deep sorrow runs through my heart. I am so sad for the bleeding and dying of my comrades. It is too dreadful! Such dear men have fallen and with such self-sacrifice. It is a holy war, for you all, for Germany. In quiet hours, it chills me how little fear I have when it comes down to it! I am very tired, good night!

5.10.41: *GEFREITER* H. J. (ARMY GROUP NORTH)[28]

That the Jews are stopped there for work, I think is very correct. In Riga, the Jewish "ladies," marked on their chest and back with their star, had to sweep the street! And yet still those insolent faces!!

6.10.41: FRITZ SIGEL (ARMY GROUP CENTER)[29]

Yesterday evening our lieutenant asked for fifteen men with strong nerves. Naturally I immediately volunteered. We did not know what it was for. We were to report at five this morning in front of the company office with helmet and receive three hundred rounds per man. We waited with great excitement for the morning. At five exactly we reported and our lieutenant explained to us what we had to do. There were about one thousand Jews in the village of Krupka, and they all had to be shot today. One platoon was detailed to us as a guard. They had to make sure no one escaped. At exactly seven the Jews were to report at the main square—men, women and children. The list was read and then the whole formation marched off in the direction of the nearest swamp. The execution squad, to which I belonged, marched ahead and the guard detail marched to the left and right. It was a rainy day and the sky had just one heavy cloud like in Blei. The Jews were told that they would be sent to Germany so that they could work there. Yet as we crossed the railroad tracks and continued on toward the swamp, most of the Jews suspected what was coming. A panic broke out and the guards had their hands full trying to control the crowd. When they got to the swamp they all had to sit down, facing the direction from which we came. Fifteen meters away was a deep ditch full of water. The first ten had to stand before the ditch and undress down to the waist, then they had to get into the water so that the shooting squad, that is us, stood over them. One lieutenant and one noncommissioned officer were with us. Ten shots, ten dead Jews. That continued until all of them were dead. Only very few kept their composure. Women held onto their men and children onto their mothers. It was a spectacle that one does not soon forget.[30]

6.10.41: DR. KONRAD JARAUSCH (ARMY GROUP CENTER)[31]

Many people hope that when Russia is finished, England will be ready to sue for peace. That would be the best outcome. But we can't place our hopes on that. If that were the case, how willing we'd all be to stick it out here until Christmas, or even longer! We often talk about how it will be impossible to get furlough once the snow arrives.

7.10.41: *LEUTNANT* HANS-JOACHIM BREITENBACH (SIXTEENTH ARMY, ARMY GROUP NORTH)[32]

But now it has become a bit quieter, even if all kinds of things do frequently come our way; in the first days it was still around 1,000–1,500 shells daily. Almost every square meter here has been plowed up. During the day it is impossible [to be outside]. . . . It is dreadful to have to lie here and just be shot up like this.

The food, ammunition, and mail only get to the front at night; the food is usually sour, and in any case always cold; often, only the bottoms of the pans are covered, the rest has tipped out as a result of constantly being put down while under fire. And that means going dog-hungry again. We're all pretty low.

I was at the front for 17 days before I was relieved for a few days. But what that means, to be at the front in this hell for 17 days, nobody can imagine! 17 days of no hot food—if any provisions got to the front at all. 17 days of almost no sleep, 17 days of icy cold, lots of rain, damp things, wet feet, no blankets. 17 days unwashed, unshaven, always thirsty—some drank the dirty muddy water that collected in the foxholes—and constantly artillery, aircraft bombs, mortars, tanks, heavy machine guns, sharpshooters; fire from forward, from the left, from the right, from half to the right, below and above! You've got to have nerves like barbed wire! . . . [*Da muss man Nerven wie Drahtseile haben!*]

There were lots of fatalities and casualties. . . . What I saw for the first time here as well was nervous breakdowns of all levels of severity right through to imbecility. My platoon leader, an old *Oberfeldwebel* [master sergeant] also suffered such a severe shock to his nerves that he had to be transported by plane back to Germany. . . . The young soldiers who had come as reserves, fresh from home, were so done in that they cried and screamed. I had to bring them back to the artillery individually. They near enough clung to me and didn't want to leave me, as if it was safer with me. And then you're supposed to keep your nerves together as well.

7.10.41: *UNTEROFFIZIER* WILHELM PRÜLLER (9 PANZER DIVISION, 1 PANZER ARMY, ARMY GROUP SOUTH)[33]

Tonight we had the first real Russian snowstorm. The snow didn't stay on the ground, but the wind whistled through every nook and cranny of our hut, and we expected the straw roof to take off at any moment. A nice foretaste of the coming winter. That can be a real mess! (Personally I think we'll have to be pulled out of action this month.) We've not much more petrol, and none will come for quite a while because our tankers are standing way back and it'll take a long time to get through all the mud.

Tomorrow we're to storm the town of Dmitriyev, 5 km in front of us. Everyone is saying that this is to be our last job, and that the division will rendezvous in D. It would be the best thing, too, for all the companies are thoroughly beaten up, and many of the vehicles are already knocked out. If it really does get on, though, it would be better to create a battalion out of the regiment; then it could be properly equipped with men and machines and would be ready for battle.

8.10.41: SIEGBERT STEHMANN (163 INFANTRY DIVISION, GERMAN ARMY OF NORWAY)[34]

It's pouring, the air is icy and stormy. But it is wonderfully warm and cozy in my foxhole. . . . Although, it's not really a foxhole we're sitting in anymore, but a wonderful bunker deep in the earth, protecting against shells and shrapnel. We're five to a room (the *Feldwebel*, two noncommissioned officers, and two gun commanders [*Gewehrführer*]), which is 3.5 by 3 m large. It's lined all around with tree trunks, large timbers support the beam ceiling at the sides, and another layer of sand 1 m deep lies on that. A little stove stands in the corner. The bed with deep straw is ½ m high and takes up the largest proportion of the building. We sit next to each other on the edge of the bed. The total height of the room is 1.50 m, you get down to the depths via a covered passageway. We built all of that for ourselves out of 120 tree trunks in two days' work. There is nothing to see of the building above the earth. You could even overwinter here, if necessary. Unfortunately, we have to economize on light.

8.10.41: ERNST GUICKING (52 INFANTRY DIVISION, SECOND ARMY, ARMY GROUP CENTER)[35]

My dear, things are becoming increasingly interesting with the Russian now. . . . They themselves are to follow in order to rescue the capital city. They get rid of their commissars and come over to us in groups of ten, twenty men. They tell of the useless activity of their constant movement [*den unnützen Tun ihres dauernden Laufens*]. They want to topple Stalin and the craziest thing is that they know nothing of Germany, they know nothing of France.[36] The only world that exists for them is the Worker's Paradise. They know nothing of Europe. So, just imagine the intellectual level of Russia proper, they have been kept extraordinarily stupid. . . . Wait! 19 Russians are just marching past again. They look cheerily over to us. These bandits, it's always the same. The brutalities that they have done to our comrades, you forget them far too quickly.[37]

8.10.41: *UNTEROFFIZIER* E. T. (ARMY GROUP SOUTH)[38]

Hopefully the ongoing decisive blow will bring us the desired conclusion in the East. Yesterday, we had the first snow here. Thank God, it was just a cheeky harbinger of winter. Today, it is warmer again and the wind has dried almost everything. We aren't adjusting the railway tracks to the German width here anymore, but instead repairing them for Russian trains instead. In contrast to the Ukraine, where we avoided dropping bombs on the railways wherever possible, here, farther into the interior—we are southeast of Kiev—it is different. Our pilots have done a splendid precision job. Here, we have a 30-km-long stretch to work on, on which, among other things, there are also approx. 300 destroyed wagons. Our task is to remove these and restore the railway lines. In between times, we've made detours into neighboring unoccupied villages. Russians are still prowling around the forests and extorting food from the civilian population. We were able to capture a few of these bandits. We knocked off one Jew, who was still carrying a pistol, on the spot. So duties are currently very varied, like the weather.

8.10.41: DR. HELMUT MACHEMER (1 PANZER ARMY, ARMY GROUP SOUTH)[39]

What this war demands of its soldiers can only be judged by somebody who has served with them for days and nights on the open fields of Russia and lain alongside them in the foxholes. In snow drifts and icy wind, freezing and hungry, expecting attack at any moment. Keeping guard through the nights, half asleep, and marching, driving, fighting at daybreak. . . . The greatest demands on each man. We bear it, because each of us knows that it matters now. . . . It is a trial of will, a tougher one is hardly imaginable. We know: We are cut off [*Wir wissen: Wir sind abgeschnitten*], no connections to the rear, none to the flanks. All around: the enemy, who desperately tries to break through, to get out, to rescue his army or at least his own bare life. . . .

Impossible to form a closed line. . . . Worst of all is the night. In the evening we move into the hills and form a kind of hedgehog. Riflemen and machine gun nests all around, vehicles in the center as best as possible, protected from the bullets of enemy MGs. From here, the columns that are passing by are fired upon. Some cars go up in flames and illuminate the field, so that further passage is no longer possible. But a few cars still manage to escape. . . .

The field is dotted with dead horses and Russians. A herd of individual horses grazing in the fields. This is the real destruction of an army! . . . No one cares about the corpses of the Russians and their wounded. . . .

When light came, we found comrades at the front stabbed, some dead or seriously wounded. Apparently, they had fallen asleep from fatigue, been surprised and attacked by the Russians. The bitterness of our comrades is great. We catch some Russians in the area in the morning, they are hit with rifle butts and then shot.

8.10.41: *UNTEROFFIZIER* WILHELM PRÜLLER (9 PANZER DIVISION, 1 PANZER ARMY, ARMY GROUP SOUTH)[40]

Some enemy positions are still blocking the eastern entry to D[mitriyev], but using hand grenades and pistols we get the Russians out of their caves and foxholes. They must be thoroughly impressed by our fire; their eyes are filled with fear, and they certainly can't understand why we aren't mowing them down right away. "Stalin kaput": with these words they are taken off to the prison camps. It's a better life for them than under the whips of the commissars. For them, the war's finished. . . .

A wrecked Russian armored scouting car is sitting on the street, and as we look inside it, a Russian climbs out. He was the driver, and was anxiously awaiting our arrival though he was afraid we'd shoot him. But his common sense won. Someone explains to him in Russian that nothing will happen to him, whereupon he wants to embrace all of us, and is quite willing to give us information about everything.

When we've established our security units, we go and look for a house near the bridge. The one we picked is the best I've ever seen in Russia. With real furniture, proper rooms—a real treat for us. The people there were very afraid at the beginning, they were especially terrified that we would shoot their 17-year-old son. But when we've assured them nothing will happen, they become friendly and bring us milk, butter, honey, warm some water for us and serve us hand and foot. Is it respect on their part, or is it fear of the German soldier?

9.10.41: *UNTEROFFIZIER* EGON N. (6 INFANTRY DIVISION, NINTH ARMY, ARMY GROUP CENTER)[41]

Just now we have learned that there was a *Sondermeldung* on the radio, whereby the encirclement of the three remaining combat-worthy armies of Mr. Timoshenko . . . means the final victory over the Soviet army. Hopefully someone all too eager didn't exaggerate this report. And if it really has been stated on the radio, then everything is absolutely all right. . . . When we attacked on 2 October, we made a decisive contribution to the progress of eastern operations in the center. The Russian was aware of the significance of this attack as well, because he defended himself vigorously.

Yesterday, we had the first snow. Of course, it was mostly rain, which on the other hand has the disadvantage that the roads get sodden. The mud is dreadful. How fortunate that this matter can't last much longer.

9.10.41: ANTON BÖHRER (294 INFANTRY DIVISION, SIXTH ARMY, ARMY GROUP SOUTH)[42]

The *Führer* recently issued a great proclamation, stating that the war against Russia will come to an end sometime this year.[43] According to the latest reports, the front outside Moscow has now eased and as soon as the capital city has fallen, it can be assumed that of course Stalin, along with those of his generals who have not yet been done in with a shot through the back of the head, will make off to America and so then the country will be free again and soon we won't need to fight anymore.

9.10.41: KARL FUCHS (7 PANZER DIVISION, 3 PANZER GROUP, ARMY GROUP CENTER)[44]

I am sure that you must have heard the special radio announcements about our battle achievements. Yes, you can find me somewhere on this front near Moscow! The Russians didn't believe that we would attack at this time of the year when the cold weather was setting in. They probably thought that we would give them a recuperative period until next year. The last hour of Bolshevism is near and that means that Old England's destruction is imminent.

9.10.41: HANS-ALBERT GIESE (NINTH ARMY, ARMY GROUP CENTER)[45]

At any rate, the third part of this campaign here began for us with our breakthrough of the Russian positions on 2 October, together with our panzers. It was 6.00 in the morning. The sun smiled down from the sky and our hearts all beat faster as the first shell flew toward the enemy. For me, it was wonderful to be able to experience this attack up close [*Es was für mich ganz herrlich, daß ich diesen Angriff aus nächster Nähe miterleben durfte*]. A banging and rattling erupted along the entire front, because our guns were sending their greetings to the *Russkis*. Then our bombers and Stukas arrived and when they had done their work, our panzers and the other troops came along. You can't imagine how happy we all were. After our initial rapid advance, we now had several weeks of position warfare behind us, which had been anything other than pleasant. Now we've pushed forward quite a bit again. Slowly but surely toward Moscow. In a few weeks no doubt all sorts of things will have been accomplished, so it won't take much longer here. It's already got pretty cold here. At night it's freezing and during the day there's sometimes snow. But that can't rattle us anymore.

10.10.41: JAKOB GEIMER (ARMY GROUP SOUTH)[46]

Now that the battle of annihilation around Kiev has ended, we are back on the advance, going farther, in the direction of the east. . . . Only he who knows the endless distances of Russia, and has taken part in it all from the start, can understand the many hardships of this. The misery, the dirt, and the wretched huts that exist here have already been amply described. How fortunate that we don't experience anything like this in Germany and everyone can only be grateful to the *Führer* that the danger has now been averted.[47] In his speech, the *Führer* praised our achievements in particular. And above all "the German infantryman," now we're particularly proud of that [*darauf sind wir nun besonders stolz*]. When I'm back home again, we can talk about it better.

10.10.41: *OBERGEFREITER* JOSEPH B. (2 PANZER DIVISION, 4 PANZER GROUP, ARMY GROUP CENTER)[48]

Yesterday, we shot off more, far more [ammunition] than in the entire campaign in Greece. You heard the *Sondermeldung* about the encirclement of Viaz'ma, too. The Russians are embittered. But a lot are deserting as well. You can often see them in small bands with one of the passes that have been dropped by our pilots.[49] It's a shame I don't have a camera with me. There are enough subjects. The villages almost all look the same. Nothing but Russian wooden houses or wreckage. The destruction is immense [*Das Vernichtungswerk ist ungeheuer*]. You can't even always determine the direction from which the villages, gasoline, or ammunition stores have been destroyed. It's beyond doubt that our Stukas and panzers and even the artillery played a large part in it.

10.10.41: DR. HELMUT MACHEMER (1 PANZER ARMY, ARMY GROUP SOUTH)[50]

Long columns of Russian prisoners are still arriving. They come without any escort. But you have to be cautious. Just yesterday it happened that, when one of our armored reconnaissance vehicles took a group of prisoners and prepared to drive back, one of the prisoners suddenly reached into his bag, pulled out a hand grenade, and threw it through the turret hatch into the reconnaissance vehicle. One officer was severely wounded, the reconnaissance vehicle burned out. The Russian's combat methods are insidious [*Die Kampfweise des Russen ist hinterlistig*].

10.10.41: *GEFREITER* JOSEF B. (23 INFANTRY DIVISION, SECOND ARMY, ARMY GROUP CENTER)[51]

We've been merrily advancing since 2 October, after we had merely been holding the front for almost two months. But now it's onward again and at a double-quick pace, even if the Russian does doggedly try to defend himself, morale is so low that yesterday alone our battalion took 1,200 prisoners. You can tell what things are like here simply from the fact that I have not been able to wash or shave since 2 October. During the weeks before 2 October, we still saw Russian bombers and fighter planes, but now it's as if they've been blown away by the wind. Either they're scared or there are no more of them and the gentlemen in the Kremlin need the few remaining ones to abscond. Our gut tells us that it'll soon be through with the Russian resistance. The only things that will still be fighting then will be scattered remnants and we'll soon be done with that.

10.10.41: DR. ADOLF B. (25 INFANTRY DIVISION [MOT.], 1 PANZER ARMY, ARMY GROUP SOUTH)[52]

With delight yesterday evening we heard the *Sondermeldung* about the defeat of the Soviet army: "The Russian armies, still fighting, have been completely encircled by Viaz'ma and Briansk and are facing their own destruction! Thus, the decision has been made in the East." Now let's hope that the weather stays all right, that is to say, dry, so that the concluding battles can take place soon! Perhaps we "motorized" can anticipate being relieved by infantry divisions in four to six weeks!

10.10.41: *GEFREITER* HANS ROTH (299 INFANTRY DIVISION, SIXTH ARMY, ARMY GROUP SOUTH)[53]

On the radio we heard news of the victorious encirclement battle near Viaz'ma and Briansk. The Eastern Campaign has been practically decided. The remnants of the Red Army are one step away from annihilation; the Bolshevik leaders have fled from Moscow. Is the end in sight for the East? We hear this and even more over the loudspeakers; surely this will be the headline in the daily papers at home. I grab my head; how is this possible, has our leadership gone mad overnight? All of this is not true, it cannot be true; all of us here see too clearly what is going on. Do these gentlemen have blindfolds over their eyes!?!

What is the homeland supposed to think? Our wives, our mothers, and brides will go crazy with happiness when they hear this news; they will cry tears of joy that the horrible bloodshed will be over in a few days, and will expect their men and sons home by Christmas at the latest.

For heaven's sake, the reality is totally different. The eastern armies are encountering the ultimate test of nerves. We Germans are not used to winter combat in freezing temperatures and all of this mud. Is it really necessary to employ such devices, such poisonous stuff? At home, there will be a terrible awakening from these happy illusions. In a few weeks the newspapers will be full of black crosses like never before.

11.10.41: KLAUS K. (ARMY GROUP CENTER)[54]

We've had snow and frost for two days . . . it's gradually getting unpleasant here. The roads are in an unimaginable state. No structured foundations and the vehicles can barely get through. You simply can't write or describe it. You have to have seen it.

You're just happy to have a roof over your head at night. But now it's full steam ahead toward the enemy. So that we can still have Christmas at home. Hopefully something will come of it.

I'm sitting in a farmhouse. We're here with our telephone equipment. The guns have just been driven into position. We're to lay a line to the observation post. There's a huge cauldron here. Our planes are constantly dropping leaflets so that they'll surrender. Another few hundred prisoners are just going by. Now we're to shoot at the enemy with our guns employed for ground fire [*Erdbeschuß*]. No grass grows anywhere that heavy flak has been used in ground fire. The infantry here have come to appreciate flak used in direct fire, as well as panzers. Some of our panzers would not even attack without our guns.

11.10.41: HANS ALBRING (EASTERN FRONT)[55]

You know, the new division of humans into Jews and Aryans does have its benefits. The Jews are behaving miserably. Old men here servilely doff their caps to us young snappers. Urgh, it's spineless. . . .[56]

Rumor has it that German troops are outside Moscow. Can it be true? We hear and see nothing, absolutely nothing, and at night we sleep with a pistol by the bed, safety catch off. There are a very great many partisans here and so the atmosphere is uneasy.[57]

The people we are quartered with are fabulous beasts: she, as strong as two men of medium strength, plays guitar [*Klampfe*], balalaika, sings like a girl, cooks well, and paints, naively, but not at all badly and with pleasure. In addition, she has raised her children well and works hard—he is also full of music, works incredibly hard, trusting, but clever and very jolly. I am quite well liked here, am called "Wanja," "Wonka" by the children, and she—she is not quick to be tender, but when she is, then it has a certain charm—she sometimes even calls me "Wanuschka"—that really means something. We make music almost every evening—she loves to hear a little love song that is always falsely attributed to Bach, in the music book for his wife it says, Giovannini's Aria, "Will you give me your heart," I'll have to play it for her sometime.

11.10.41: FRANZ SIEBELER (14 PANZER DIVISION, 1 PANZER ARMY, ARMY GROUP SOUTH)[58]

After the conclusion of the encirclement, in which we played a magnificent part, we have advanced a good bit farther toward the sea.[59] We'll quite likely reach the shores of the Sea of Asov today. The weather is still quite good. The cold wind has become routine. Yesterday afternoon, we motorcyclists raced forward to avoid the rain and the resulting mud. We were lucky and arrived at our night quarters at the last minute by the skin of our teeth. Then, everything was sludge. A strong wind blew all through the night so early this morning everything is dry again. Thank God, because now we can drive on again. The war can't last much longer. The day before yesterday we brought in a few thousand prisoners, including female partisans [*Flintenweiber*].[60] Utterly abject figures. The enemy had been entirely encircled and hundreds of dead Russians lay about the battlefield. Horrifying devastation! Everything tangled and broken!

11.10.41: ALBERT NEUHAUS (ARMY GROUP CENTER)[61]

And the signs of the Russian armies' collapse are becoming more obvious every day. When we advance like this, every few meters along the way we are approached by Russian soldiers and they are unescorted, they just don't carry any weapons on them anymore. And it's like that from morning to evening.

11.10.41: *GEFREITER* HANS ROTH (299 INFANTRY DIVISION, SIXTH ARMY, ARMY GROUP SOUTH)[62]

Again, a powerful snowstorm. All of a sudden there is a deep freeze, 7°C below zero! The roads are frozen solid. We would be able to advance if, yes if, there was any fuel! Gas and supply trucks are still far behind, somewhere hopelessly sunk into the mud. About 60% of the cars are somewhere hopelessly sunk into the mud. That's right; this is what a victorious march forward looks like! And the muddy season has only just begun, and already after two days of rain we have these losses. All of this does not fit quite well with yesterday's victory fanfare![63]

11.10.41: DR. HELMUT MACHEMER (1 PANZER ARMY, ARMY GROUP SOUTH)[64]

Everywhere where there was something to be earned, especially in the administration, sit the Jews. They were the first to flee with great clamor. That is how the inhabitants knew the Germans were coming.

One had told the people that the German soldiers would burn and shoot everything. That is why the population were afraid and hid when we came. The people believed what they had been told. But after we had been here a few hours they—even the Russians—were trustful. The women wash our clothes and cook and bake, as long as they have something. . . . But they cannot yet believe that we don't have any bad intentions for them.

12.10.41: HARALD HENRY (ARMY GROUP CENTER)[65]

I'll try to tell [you] quickly about the overwhelming impressions of the last few days. It was really tremendous. The advance in the evening light, through steeply descending ravines, across streams on bottomless paths, was tremendous; traversing rivers on logs, in drifts of snow was tremendous; digging trenches again, and for the first time with the front to the west, was tremendous. The encirclement is closed, we move into defensive position in the holes hollowed out by the Russians behind their front, so as to intercept them. I accompany the lieutenant, we search bunkers, pull out a Russian, make contact with the neighboring battalion, which is still fighting—and all at a speed that cannot be described. We are positioned on a steep hillside, looking down into the cauldron, by the time the villages go up in flames. This night is terrible, but still nothing in comparison with that which follows. The frost is excruciating, it prevents the pus-filled wounds on my hands from healing.

On the road, a horse lies wounded, thrashing about, somebody shoots it to put it out of its misery, it leaps up again, another fires from the next panzer, the horse is still fighting for its life, many shoot, but the rifle shots don't close the horse's dying eyes very quickly. It's over. In general, the horses are ripped up by shells, petrified, eyes popped out of empty, red sockets, standing and trembling, bleeding, bleeding out slowly, but ceaselessly out of a small hole in the chest—that's how we've been seeing them for months now. It's almost worse than the faces of the humans, ripped away, the burned, half-charred corpses with bloody, open rib cages, worse than the narrow stripes of blood behind the ear of somebody who has collapsed onto their face.

12.10.41: KARL FUCHS (7 PANZER DIVISION, 3 PANZER GROUP, ARMY GROUP CENTER)[66]

For days now the enemy has tried to break out of our iron encirclement, but their efforts have been in vain. Wherever there is a hot spot, we appear like ghosts and engage the enemy in battle. Yesterday must have been our company's proudest day in this campaign. The alarm sounded and our tanks moved out! Russian tanks reinforced with support troops wanted to break out of our ring. My unit (and I'm its temporary commander) was assigned the task of scouting the opposition. Visibility was low because of ground fog. We moved four tanks into an advantageous position. Suddenly three heavy Russian tanks, big as battleships, appeared out of the fog to the right of us. We opened fire immediately, but these tanks had enormous armor plating. If they had known that only four tiny scout tanks were opposing them! But here as well, courage and audacity brought us victory. Two of their tanks were burning and the third pulled away. Once the fog lifted from the valley, we really let them have it with every barrel. Tanks, antiaircraft guns, trucks and the infantry fired on everything in sight. Once the main body of our company arrived, our comrades destroyed their remaining forces. Proud and satisfied, our company commander smiled at us while our eyes were still flashing. We had no losses at all. My cap, though, had a five-centimeter tear in it, due to a splinter.

12.10.41: DR. KONRAD JARAUSCH (ARMY GROUP CENTER)[67]

I received four Russian psalms from the Martin Luther Bund in the mail today. I gave one of the pamphlets to our prisoner, who is a good, honest soul. A few days ago he showed me a handwritten prayer book that he had hidden from the commissars. They took away the Bibles from all the soldiers. It's understandable that he's not especially fond of the Bolsheviks. They all are hoping they'll be released after the fall of Moscow. Many of them will be disappointed.

This afternoon the first of 2,000 men[68] from the October battles arrived. We could give them some warm food and put them in some covered shelters. But we've already almost filled all the adequate space we have. The others are going to have to freeze. . . .

For hours now Vassily has been sitting ramrod straight in the hallway, reading the psalms by the light of the oil lamp that I gave him this afternoon. How pathetic we are in comparison, with all of our intellectual pretensions! Vassily refuses all of the extra rations that we offer him. Sometimes he'll accept some bread and eat whatever is left over from our lunches. The simplicity of the Russian soul is not a literary invention. . . .

I may need to travel a great deal over the next few days to secure some supplies. But it's pretty quiet. The SS are cleaning out [the area] in terrible fashion.[69]

13.10.41: EDGAR STEUERWALD (ARMY GROUP SOUTH)[70]

I am, I can confidently say, very well. My wound has already healed. I have no pain anymore. Now I'll tell you all how I got here: On 7 October our company carried out an attack. The first squadron, in which I am, was initially in reserve. To our right lay 1st Company—and to our left 3rd Company. The natural boundary to the left between our company, that is, the 2nd, and the 3rd Company was a railroad embankment. All at once, we saw, to our great amazement, that the Russian was marching calmly along a causeway that lay ahead of us. He had horse-drawn artillery and antitank guns with him. We had only been assigned a 37mm antitank gun and a light panzer. Our antitank gunners received the order to fire at the marching column. And almost every shot hit home, since it was a distance of only approx. 400 meters. At that, the Russian immediately made a counterattack. He was many times superior to us in numbers [*Zahlenmäßig war er uns um ein Vielfaches überlegen*]. We received heavy machine-gun fire from the front, as the Russian had brought a heavy tank into position. There were apparently several tanks over there. At that, the 1st + 3rd Comp. pulled back to the left and right of us. But initially, our comp. chief didn't give us the order, as he was still hoping for a good outcome in our favor. But the Russian thrust forward to the right and left against our retreating troops, and we received heavy fire from the front, right and left. 1st Platoon was pulled to the left and had to cover the embankment. When our comp. leader realized that things were getting dicey, he gave the order to go back. So the entire company pulled back. In the process I received a ricochet shot to my left shin. At first, I was in a lot of pain, but that subsided considerably after medical treatment. Now the wound, which isn't all that big, has already healed up. I can even already walk perfectly again. Well, my dear parents, 7 October was really sh** for everyone. I don't want to write of the losses at all.

14.10.41: HEINRICH WITT (EASTERN FRONT)[71]

Column after column passes us by, all in the direction of Moscow. Everywhere you hear the same amazement that the fighting should be over by 18 October. Quite possible, if you consider the huge amounts that have been deployed here. The day before yesterday, Stukas were flying the whole day, the whole day in rolling, continuous deployment to the east. Fighters are continuously zooming over the road to prevent any enemy attack.

14.10.41: *UNTEROFFIZIER* H. H. (6 INFANTRY DIVISION, NINTH ARMY, ARMY GROUP CENTER)[72]

We are resting, and there's not much to be seen or heard of the bad enemy anymore. It almost seems to us that the war is already over. I assume that by the time this letter is in your hands the bells across all the German country will have proclaimed the victory over the mightiest enemy of civilization. For it cannot last much longer now and the *Führer*'s words are gospel to us [*und für uns sind die Führerworte ein Evangelium*]. Now we're trying to guess what is going to be done with us here. Will we go to Germany or will we stay here as occupying troops?

14.10.41: DR. HELMUT MACHEMER (1 PANZER ARMY, ARMY GROUP SOUTH)[73]

Almost 300 kilometers to the east in the last three days! We're at the head of the division as an advance detachment. . . . And the towns always present the same picture: very disparate residential areas with straw-roofed mud huts, squalid and frequently falling apart. . . . Burning haystacks, factories in the American style, looking like foreign bodies in the landscape, usually destroyed, bombed railroad lines and bridges. And, finally, always the same inhabitants, impoverished, raggedy, slave-like.

15.10.41: WALTER NEUSER (ARMY GROUP CENTER)[74]

Fifteen days' deployment have passed. You can imagine what that means in this cold. Since we haven't received winter clothing, every soldier is improvising in his own way. So they've found fabric or fur, or taken gloves from prisoners. Anybody who hasn't done that yet has to reckon with frozen bones [*Wer das noch nicht getan hat, muß mit erfrorenen Knochen rechnen*].[75] The first snow arrived on the 6th of the month. Since then, it's nothing new for us anymore.

The attack began at dawn on 2.X. [2 October], initiated successfully once again with immense force from the heavy weaponry. Here, again, the impeccable work of the Russians prompted amazement and admiration. The Russian is a master of constructing field positions and camouflage, and he doesn't make it easy for us to achieve success after success. They arrive in droves on the first day. Day in, day out, the same scene and yet still there's resistance. The forests are still full of Russians, so that involuntarily remaining behind usually means death. Reports of ambushes come in every day. Security detachments are positioned everywhere, so that, gradually, Very signal flares go up everywhere and then go out. Early in the morning on 2.X. the proclamation of the *Führer* was read to us. We had wonderful weather from the 2nd–4th. The weather is particularly significant when combat operations are resumed. . . . Stukas are the embodiment of dread. We knew from our instructions and from word of mouth that our opponent had mined the area thoroughly. So everyone stayed nicely in line with the vehicle tracks from morning to night, because anything else could mean death. Wooden box mines are a fantastic weapon, because they lack metal and so are virtually undetectable. . . .

The roads are catastrophic. The frost does have an upside: the muddy tracks are hard. Furthermore, hunger and cold forces the Russians out of the forests. On the 7th we marched a few kms on the highway and afterward we looked like we'd been dusted with cinnamon. The mud dust creates a lot of work. I also looked at a church in which the Russians had installed a workshop. It looked devastating. On the 8th the general informed us that the cauldron was closed and there were 300,000 men inside it. Every day we now see them marching past us in multitudes. We spent the night from 8th–9th in the bush again. It wasn't pleasant. . . . Horses run around in great masses, but they're just *panjes*, shaggy little horses, and our own exhausted horses.

We lived through the night from 10th–11th in a meadow. It was hellishly cold. On the morning of the 11th we fired direct shots into the forest. Then you could just see them coming. Around evening, we took up new positions. We could move into this village, in which I am also writing this letter. At first, we didn't see any of the population, but they gradually emerged from their bunkers. They were extremely scared that we would set their houses on fire. Only women and children. You have to see what such a household is like. It's utterly lousy. Only half the village is still standing. Of course, that makes our situation and that of the local population much worse. Every day, we're 35–40 men to a room that is roughly as large as my bedroom. It works because it has to work. The cold forces everyone inside.

Early today we made a nice catch [*netten Fang gemacht*]: a medical noncommissioned officer and a commissar, whom we immediately signed over, of course. . . . During the night from 12th–13th [October], our command post was attacked. *Uffz.* Pfeifer happened to be there, distinguished himself during the defense, and was promoted from commander to technical sergeant [*Wachtmeister*] that same night. *Obltn.* Mielke, *Lt.* Eggers, 2 telephonists and 2 drivers fell. Several others were wounded. Russians are still hiding everywhere, but the infantry is clearing them out day and night.

15.10.41: KARL FUCHS (7 PANZER DIVISION, 3 PANZER GROUP, ARMY GROUP CENTER)[76]

My brave young friend Roland just died of severe wounds. Why did he have to give his life now, with the end practically in sight? We hardhearted soldiers have no time to bemoan his fate. We tie down our helmets and think of revenge, revenge for our dead comrades. The battle of Viaz'ma is over and the last elite troops of the Bolsheviks have been destroyed. I will never forget my impressions of this destruction. From now on, their opposition will not be comparable to previous encounters. All we have to do now is roll on, for the opposition will be minor. . . . What all of us fear most now is the snow and the accompanying cold temperatures, but we will get used to it. It will not last much longer. Right now our activities are about as dangerous as if we were on a mere expedition.

15.10.41: DR. KONRAD JARAUSCH (ARMY GROUP CENTER)[77]

We now have 7,000 of the prisoners who were captured during the October campaigns. Because of the poor external conditions here they are quite a lot of work. Everything is spread out and in different places. We have to scamper from one place to the next. No one is here who has a clear sense of the whole situation and who can allot forces accordingly. Everything is improvised in a makeshift fashion. . . .

When I passed by the dark rows [of prisoners] last night, I was reminded how I had been so occupied before the war with the idea of the "Christianity" and historical "reality" of the miracle of the loaves. Feeding the hungry is truly a miracle that only God can perform. When one sees a man crying because a comrade who was supposed to share his portion of soup had already eaten it, one can see how redemption in the afterlife must overcome even this misery. . . .

There were many wounded among the prisoners; much suffering and pain. Up until now we've only been able to give them warm food twice. If the transports continue [at this pace], that won't be possible. . . . And then we had the most terrible autumn weather. Everything is soaked through—and now at 8:45 p.m. 2,000 more men are arriving in the dark of the night, escorted by only four Germans! Things are absolutely chaotic.

16.10.41: HANS-HEINRICH LUDWIG (ARMY GROUP NORTH)[78]

Breakthrough of our divisions over the Volkhov River with the "Blue Division." Spaniards! Fantastic daredevils [*Tolle Draufgänger*]! Fighting to destruction before winter, certainly. Now it's already here! It is very tough. Unfortunately, hardly a bite to eat. Likely not tomorrow and the day after tomorrow either. I have seen dreadful things again so far on the journey. I have become very earnest. Once you've had dying men in your arms, it is unavoidable.

16.10.41: GEERT-ULRICH MUTZENBECHER (ARMY GROUP CENTER)[79]

Prisoners are constantly driving past. They are traveling in open goods wagons in these snowstorms. I just saw a women's battalion among the Russians. You can't imagine their treatment. What Dwinger tells in his books about the treatment of captured Germans is nothing compared to our measures. Perhaps it has to be like that, . . . but none of you should get to see too many of these images.

Minsk was already quite destroyed, but here in Smolensk it really is dismal. Can you all imagine what it means to see a national capital lying in ashes?[80] In the face of these scenes you might lose faith in humanity, but it doesn't seem to work any other way in the Russian battles.

16.10.41: EDGAR STEUERWALD (ARMY GROUP SOUTH)[81]

Well, my dear parents, the letter number in my previous letter meant to show the number of fatalities we had in the battle on 7 October (54). A considerable number, don't you think? It is a pity about those boys. Many of them were only wounded and were murdered by the Russians. But we took no uncertain revenge. We took almost no prisoners during a subsequent attack with heavy panzers, everything was coldly, brutally, ruthlessly shot down. We didn't stint on the ammunition. Every shot was a hit [*Jeder Schuß war ein Treffer*]. The Russians should learn what they get for their murdering ways.[82]

16.10.41: DR. HELMUT MACHEMER (1 PANZER ARMY, ARMY GROUP SOUTH)[83]

I am well. We have battles almost daily, but our losses are low. Apparently, only very recently trained armies are available to the Russian, which fight very bravely, but they're not very practiced. This morning they tried to prevent our advance south of the industrial area with a powerful assault, also involving cavalry. What with the heavy weaponry we are carrying with us, the attack was unsuccessful and caused them severe losses. Only the pilots are still numerous, but the quality is sinking. Recently, there have been a few Americans among them, but they don't make any difference [*machen die Suppe auch nicht fett*].[84] We are reckoning with an imminent end to the war, at least as far as Russia is concerned.

16.10.41: *LEUTNANT* WILL THOMAS (NINTH ARMY, ARMY GROUP CENTER)[85]

Where should I start to explain? Actually, I can say nothing. My heart is still so full of all the horrors and difficulties of the last days and hours. . . . We broke through a line of bunkers made from concrete and steel and experienced the war in all its severity and ruthlessness. In addition to many others, this day took a particularly dear comrade from me. . . . His laugh and his uniquely fierce handshake are still constantly with me. . . . We were making good forward progress until all at once we received fire from three sides and were in danger of being encircled by the Russians. We gave our utmost

[*Da galt es nun das Letzte*]. The battle raged back and forth until around midday we finally did it and had averted the greatest danger. Until night drew, we lay fifty meters across from the enemy and had to withstand a great deal there, too. Again and again comrades fall left and right, that I often believed I was left alone in the field. But it all went well after all. Once, a bullet made a glancing impact with my steel helmet, making me roll onto my side for a moment and *Feldwebel* Klein, who was lying next to me, called out: "Now our lieutenant is dead as well!" But it wasn't so bad. A small splinter just grazed the skin on my left eye. . . .

We were completely soaked through from all the crawling around in the snow. There could be no hope of rations arriving, of course. And so night came. It was one of the most terrible that I have ever experienced. How frozen we were there, indescribable. Once we had recovered our dead and wounded, we huddled in our foxholes and tried to keep each other warm. Around morning more snow fell and so the frost got a little milder. But the bleakness of our situation fortunately came to an end, as the enemy, as he had often done when he'd received a bloody nose, had withdrawn.

17.10.41: HARALD HENRY (ARMY GROUP CENTER)[86]

If one believed every time to have survived the worst it is not so. There always comes more. Since I last wrote you I have lived through hell. . . . That I survived 15 October, the most terrible day of my life, seems a wonder. How sick my whole body is, but I will certainly not be allowed into the hospital. . . . I am too miserable to write more. Later I will tell of these days, what can be said. I wish everything would end. What have we been through! Oh God!

17.10.41: ERNST GUICKING (52 INFANTRY DIVISION, SECOND ARMY, ARMY GROUP CENTER)[87]

The Russian is being squeezed on all sides and is trying to break through here. We are tripping all over fallen Russians here. It is truly a horror [*Es ist das wahre Grauen*]. Yesterday, 3,000 prisoners, a never-ending number of fatalities. Many women among them. No battlefield can look worse. It has become a habit for us in the last ten days. We have got used to this horror. Fighting here together with the *Groß Deutschland* regiment. And wherever these men are, the forest roars. We are positioned in buildings with them here. We relieve each other every day. Our successes are great. But our losses are also bitter and painful. Such dear and brave comrades lie here in the Russian soil. Fate has been merciful to us so far. Yesterday we buried two bearers of the Knight's Cross. They were from the *Groß Deutschland* regiment. I can't say anything about the bigger picture. . . .

The Russian would rather freeze in his foxholes than surrender. . . . We have been deployed with a special assignment since 2 October and so far there has been not a single day without battle. . . . Our task in all this will soon be done. The cauldron is just about to burst. . . . Well, it will come to an end sometime soon. It can't be much longer.

17.10.41: KLAUS K. (ARMY GROUP CENTER)[88]

You will all be wondering why I'm writing again already. We are still in a resting position. Carrying out maintenance the whole day, off-duty at 4:00 [p.m.]. So you're always bored. Have written 10 letters to all relations in recent days. My three roommates are playing constant rounds of Skat the whole day.[89] We live well here, and warm, so everything we could need, except cigarettes. . . .

The roads will soon be impassable for vehicles. . . . Unless it's vehicles with cross-country mobility, the others can't get through at all. We have a few captured Russian vehicles. They are completely useless on these roads. The Russian also abandoned 300 vehicles and 2 52-ton tanks here.[90] They had all sunk into the ground. So he's not getting any farther in this weather, either. . . .

You can always find 15–17-year-old boys and women among the prisoners now.[91] So it can't be far off for the Russian. They're only still fighting because they've been told that the Germans don't make any prisoners, then they're forced to attack at gunpoint by the commissars.[92] During one operation, there was a river between us and the Russians, they were hounded into attacking through the river, 30–40 got across and 200 drowned. So that, too, is finished. I think we can judge that best over here. . . . Our losses are very low in contrast to the Russian. If you think about how many thousand airplanes + tanks have been destroyed. We can certainly thank the *Führer* for stealing a march on the Russian. I think we would all have been lost otherwise. And they would certainly have butchered everyone [*alles niedergemetzelt*].[93]

17.10.41: DR. ADOLF B. (25 INFANTRY DIVISION [MOT.], 1 PANZER ARMY, ARMY GROUP SOUTH)[94]

The last *Sondermeldungen* sound extremely positive: Odessa taken, Petersburg and Moscow encircled, the Red Army beaten to destruction everywhere and more similar news of victory! You might think that the war in the East will soon be over. I wish it were so, because now I would like to get out of this cold, louse-infested Russia. At the moment, it's minus seven degrees and there's twenty-centimeter-high snow lying outside. Vehicles can barely drive anymore, because the country roads are so muddy that you get stuck everywhere. . . . Oh, how fine it would be if we were soon to go in the direction of home and not in the direction of Moscow!

18.10.41: DR. HELMUT MACHEMER (1 PANZER ARMY, ARMY GROUP SOUTH)[95]

Suddenly, a [mounted] Russian infantry troop appeared over the hill that bordered the left side, riding in to attack our center, brandishing their sabers. A beautiful scene, really. You could see the details through field glasses.

It was reminiscent of battle scenes from the war of the 1870s.[96] But what a folly, this attack [*Aber welch ein Unsinn, diese Attacke*]! We may have been rather weakly protected by riflemen and I had taken my submachine gun out of the car just in case—but the panzers! They turned just a little, cool as you please, to the left, a few bursts from the machine guns, and in a few seconds the ranks [of soldiers] had crumbled away. The riders fell from the horses and only a confused cluster fled on foot back over the hill. But even without the panzers, the few machine guns would have stopped the riders. We found the remaining horses later, grazing in the area. After two hours of battle, the Russians saw that they could do nothing and pulled back. They had to leave many dead and wounded behind.

As we found out from prisoners, these were newly established regiments that had just received their baptism of fire, just two months at arms. They received a bloody nose straight off. But we had losses that are hardly worth mentioning, just a few casualties. Our company even came through it unscathed. We conclude that the Russian no longer has command over any better troops. We also hear that the Russian is already beginning to carry out demolitions in the industrial region. So he's already half admitting defeat. The next few days will prove it.

18.10.41: HARALD HENRY (ARMY GROUP CENTER)[97]

From 5:45 a.m. until 2:00 a.m. at night, with a short break, we were out in the snowstorm. Our things slowly got wet through, our coats froze stiff on our bodies. Everything dripped and jangled. We were immeasurably sick to our stomachs and guts. The cold soon exceeded every measure. Lice! The frost took hold in festering fingers. . . . Our company . . . went into the woods until we were over our knees in snow, which filled our boots. Across frozen marshes that broke open so that icy water ran into our boots. My gloves were so wet that I could not bear them any longer. I wound a towel around my ruined hands. . . . My face was contorted from tears, but I was already in a sort of trance. I stamped forward with closed eyes, mumbled senseless words and thought that I was experiencing everything only in a sleep as a dream. It was all like madness. . . . Agony without end. . . . We are all more or less sick. Every fiber of me is broken [*Ich bin zerbrochen in jeder Faser*], but I will no doubt have to continue with everyone when the advance begins again tomorrow morning.

18.10.41: HANS ALBRING (EASTERN FRONT)[98]

It's not safe here at the moment. 22 murdered comrades in one day—I'm sure you can see clear as day [*geht Dir nicht eine Stallaterne auf*] how unsafe we consider ourselves—yesterday, in broad daylight, 2 bullets whistled past my head. I suspected the worst only when a whole group were set to search. At night we sleep with a gun, safety catch off, close by. While new partisans are dangling from the gallows. It'll soon be 4 weeks since there's been any mail, but tomorrow there's to be mass again. Otherwise no news.

18.10.41: JOHANNES HUEBNER (ARMY GROUP CENTER)[99]

It has now been almost four months and the "holiday trip" in the Soviet paradise has surely meant a lot to everyone. For me personally I feel quite well among the Russian people. Their simple lifestyle is attractive and admirable. The Russian makes his house himself, with all its contents, the implements and tools, in a not inadept way, if rather primitively. Everything that he wears on his back has been spun and woven by his wife in laborious work on long winter evenings.

18.10.41: WILLY (ARMY GROUP NORTH)[100]

Today, this Sunday morning, my thoughts run to you again, indeed this is the only opportunity not to go mad here. At least we have now moved into solid quarters, as we've gone over to a rest position. We have set ourselves up domestically in a Russian school. The main thing is that we've got a warm room when it's snowing outside and there are temperatures of minus 15 degrees.

We are always reminded of the slogan: "Urrah, we've gone mad!" [*Urrah, wir sind verblödet!*] We don't get any mail, any newspapers, any radio, just card games from morning till night. All day, you hear nothing but "Fifty RM [*Reichsmark*] stick" and "Twenty, twenty-one draw!" . . . By contrast, we Bavarians are more restrained, we play a civilized game of *Schafkopf*[101] and keep our money, just in case we do get to come home.

In general, our situation is, to put it mildly, bleak. But nevertheless we mustn't complain, if we consider that the soldiers who are fighting at the front and scoring great victories in this inhuman cold do not have the privileges that we do. Even so, even this war will come to an end, and if we are so fortunate [*wenn es uns vergönnt sein sollte*], a new life will begin.

18–20.10.41: HANS-HEINRICH LUDWIG (ARMY GROUP NORTH)[102]

Clear icy sky. Superior Russian air activity. Unpleasant corner here at the bridge. Constant traffic blockages. Burned-out barracks. Fresh traces of the war. Dead bodies. Mines. Finally, we advance as well, offensive fire, nothing to eat. Cold feet. Went into firing position in the evening. Back on prime movers at night. We receive artillery fire for the first time in a while. I immediately leave the prime mover, when I return, I find a large piece of shrapnel in my seat. A cathartic moment sets in. We have to give our gun in for repair and come back to the limber position. A wooden hut with stove and hay—and we are the happiest people in the world.

19.10.41: GERHARD KUNDE (68 INFANTRY DIVISION, SEVENTEENTH ARMY, ARMY GROUP SOUTH)[103]

Today, we have been living in this lauded land for 17 weeks, but I'd be lying if I said that we've been able to see any good sides to it. On the contrary, our yearning for central European culture is taking ever clearer shape. What 2 *Landser*, who had been acquiring vehicle replacement parts in Germany, told us about the homeland was not especially pleasing, however.[104] Above all, what I found very ugly was that they had been told by many, ["]What, you want to buy that away from us as well, you've got more of it than we do.["] Now people are even begrudging *Landser* a couple of cigarettes and a bit of schnapps. That's not good.

20.10.41: HARALD HENRY (ARMY GROUP CENTER)[105]

Hell bubbles in all cauldrons. What we are currently witnessing of the misery of the prisoners, the population, and ultimately also experiencing ourselves, borders on the grimmest visions of a fevered imagination. I am too miserable and too tired to describe everything. The weather is so bad that we are resting, because there is no way of advancing on the roads anymore. Our quarters are getting worse almost by the day, usually 30 men lying on the floor of a farmhouse room. The air gets dreadful. There, in the middle of the night, even the children, pushed around outside in the cold all day, get diarrhea, [relieve themselves in] the middle of the room, trickling between our blankets and packs. We've all got diarrhea and stomach pains ourselves. The amount of awfulness and sadness that such a war can muster isn't usually heaped on us tortured humans even by the [passage of many] years.

How long is that going to take? There must finally be an end or at least some relief for us. In all the major battles of the Army Group Center, Belostok, Minsk, Mogilev, Roslavl', Desna, Viaz'ma, and Briansk, we were outstanding and took heavy losses. Finally one must also let us get some rest. It cannot be endured much longer.[106]

20.10.41: KARL FUCHS (7 PANZER DIVISION, 3 PANZER GROUP, ARMY GROUP CENTER)[107]

Looking outside you would think that I was writing this letter in the middle of the night, but when I look at the clock I see that it is only 8:30 pm. It has been dark for hours because in the winter months darkness comes early to these regions. Furthermore, it has been raining again and an unexpected thaw has set in. The formerly white cover of snow has turned dirty brown and mud and slush are everywhere. We drive our vehicles across the fields and leave deep furrows behind. Frequently the vehicles slip and slide and even get stuck. We have lost all sense of time and don't know what day it is or what time it is. . . . The landscape is so bleak and desolate. If we weren't here to fight and were only here to live—I mean to exist here—we would become complete imbeciles. Now that we have been here for some time and have had a chance to become acquainted with this land, we all of a sudden understand why it was an easy thing for the Communist agitators to systematically poison these people.

When we had the first real cold spell, the people were still walking around barefooted. Most of them have no shoes, but only rags that they wrap around their feet. They do this no matter if it is dry or wet and now in this muddy weather, they are walking around with incredibly dirty rags around their feet. Hygiene is something totally foreign to these people. You folks back home in our beautiful Fatherland cannot imagine what it is like. These people here live together with the animals, indeed they live like animals. If they could only once see a German living room. That would be paradise for them, a paradise that these Communist scoundrels, Jews and criminals have denied them. We have seen the true face of Bolshevism, have gotten to know it and experienced it, and will know how to deal with it in the future.

20.10.41: *UNTEROFFIZIER* WILHELM PRÜLLER (9 PANZER DIVISION, 1 PANZER ARMY, ARMY GROUP SOUTH)[108]

Who brings the rumors, and who thinks them up, you never know. All at once everyone's saying: winter quarters in Russia. If it weren't so ridiculous, one might believe it. But here's the situation: we as an armored division, which is used to driving into the enemy and pushing him in front of us, whose name is only mentioned by the Russians as "terror of the Ukraine" or "the yellow SS," we with our vehicles are supposed to spend the icy winter in Russia, especially when we've been way up front since the very beginning; we whose successes have been so numerous, *we* are supposed to spend the winter in Russia. Impossible! Is all I have to say to that.

Unfortunately three things happened in the companies that can only be thoroughly condemned. One lieutenant, a platoon leader, apparently lost his nerve during a Russian attack and fled with his men, without informing his neighbors. Incidentally, there weren't any Russians at all where the platoon was stationed and they never showed up afterward either. Rather comic.

Two noncoms are known to have shot themselves in the hand. Out of fear for their personal safety and hoping in this way to be able to lead a quieter and less dangerous life. They are the only three such occurrences in this war I know of; but regrettably, they did happen. It's scandalous, not only for themselves, but for the companies. What do they think? What makes them different from the Russians? I shall never understand it. Let's hope they get punished properly.

21.10.41: DR. HEINRICH HAAPE (6 INFANTRY DIVISION, NINTH ARMY, ARMY GROUP CENTER)[109]

The weather has been very bad in recent days. We are marching through frost and snowdrifts. Today we will cross the Volga for the second time. The most severe demands are being made of man and horse. Hopefully the war will come to an end for us this year, which would mean that our division will not have to overwinter here in Russia.

I am convinced that the main Russian forces are most likely being destroyed, but that the war will still go on in the next year. The path that we Germans must go is tough, but we will prevail! We are ready to continue to endure everything that is necessary. I will tell you another time of the difficult battles we have had. . . . I haven't received any mail since 1 October.

21.10.41: KLAUS BECKER (ARMY GROUP CENTER)[110]

We're currently stuck here. There's been milder weather and rain for two days now. In its fundaments, the ground is still frozen, but at the top there's dreadful mud, so that the roads are near impassable, at least for our heavy vehicles. So we will probably stay here a while until the road conditions have improved. Of course, everything is suffering under these road conditions, not just the motorized units but all the mounted troops and the reserves as well.[111] But somehow the advance will be managed. There are few enemy aircraft at the front, so we're hardly required; so for that reason, we stay here. Otherwise we'd have to get farther forward in spite of the worst road conditions. We'd manage it. But otherwise we just churn up and block the roads unnecessarily. Of course, that's really boring for us. With this dismal weather—it's weather like we frequently get in November—it's already dark at 5:00 p.m. The solution is sleep and yet more sleep. But of course you can't sleep all the time.

There is nothing cheerful here, either. It's always the same scenes in Russia: dilapidated buildings, dirty villages, impoverished people, and no joy or sunshine anywhere. But then there is absolutely nothing here that could give joy. Even with the *Wochenschau*, you can't imagine how dreary life is for the Russian. Many buildings have thus already been abandoned by their inhabitants before the campaign without anyone caring about it. They are even more dilapidated than the inhabited buildings. The same old scenes are repeated here as well: farmers with no animals and hardly the barest necessary food and drink for themselves. This is what true Communism looks like. . . .[112]

We can barely really imagine a civilian life anymore. To put on properly clean underclothing, just once, after you've bathed, to be able to sleep in a white bed, to sit at a well-laid table, to have a warm room and decent accommodation, these are all things that are just dreams for us right now. It's just a good thing that we have gradually got accustomed to our current life. First the barracks, then the cabins, then the barn, then the tent, but in summer, and then gradually wet and cold and darkness on top of that. If things are now getting more adverse by the day, we hardly notice it anymore. You slowly become indifferent to everything. After military duties, only eating and drinking and sleeping are important. It's not all that easy for anyone who comes to us now, straight out of the barracks, to get used to. I'd really wish a life like this on many a bigmouth at home, grandstanding about National Socialism and love of the Fatherland, all from behind a warm hearth and a well-laid table. Here, you learn to despise those resounding words and their originators, insofar as that isn't already the case anyway.[113] Everyone silently does their duty without making a fuss of it [*Jeder tut schweigend seine Pflicht, ohne Aufheben davon zu Machen*]. May others then be still too.

21.10.41: KURT MARLOW (68 INFANTRY DIVISION, SEVENTEENTH ARMY, ARMY GROUP SOUTH)[114]

Everything you write to me about the many foreigners and the Jews, I've heard it here from many others.[115] Apparently the Italians behave quite incredibly everywhere, at work they are miserably lazy and then some. A woman who has anything to do with such riffraff deserves a hiding and yet another hiding. What on earth is the matter with these cadets, everywhere they go, they bring one defeat after another, then the Germans have the honor of reconquering the lost territories. There's a nation that's all mouth and nothing more. It's the same with the Romanians, the Czechs, the Poles, etc., we've got to know them plenty, a German's a German and that's that.[116] I'd like to see what would have happened to these countries if they'd had an enemy like England, never mind one like Russia. It is simply a constant puzzle how the simple German soldier managed to defeat such an opponent, who had endless supplies of weaponry. If that massive army had got going, Germany would have been smashed to smithereens, but fate looked favorably again. Poor England will literally blow its top [*der Hut hochgehen*] when the German infantry marches into its own country, there'll not be a dry eye, let me tell you. Let's not even speak of the Jews, because everybody is fed up with that sort of person. The mention of "Lemberg" is enough for me.[117]

22.10.41: *WACHTMEISTER* JOSEF L. (129 INFANTRY DIVISION, ARMY GROUP CENTER)[118]

I haven't had the slightest chance to write for more than 14 days. . . . Difficult days lie behind us. Telling you all the hardships that we endured is impossible. We marched day in, day out, from early morning until late at night, through cold, snow, rain, and wind, slept a few hours in farmhouse rooms, and then carried on. A whole infantry division forged its way through enemy-free territories. We've put 320 km behind us since 2 October. After we crossed the upper reaches of the Dnjepr, we traced a large arc via the town of Gzhatsk and arrived yesterday afternoon in Kalinin by the Volga, after overcoming the most difficult terrain, and took up our positions in a suburb. On it inexorably went, alone, in the middle of enemy territory, no supplies, for weeks with no bread or any sort of provisions.

23.10.41: DR. KONRAD JARAUSCH (ARMY GROUP CENTER)[119]

I have to take care of more than 11,000 [Soviet POWs]. Fortunately, 4,000 of them are to leave tomorrow morning. Hopefully then our number will stay low. It's not the work feeding the prisoners that weighs on me—although we're had some difficulties on that front. We've not been able to get any provisions because the locomotives are broken and no trains are running. . . .

Our superiors are now making appearances in odd ways. But the most important thing is that responsibility for the running of the camp has fallen in large part on me. . . . Either everything would go to pieces or brute force would decide everything. So the work had fallen on me, or rather, on the prisoners. . . . I'm trying to do what I can. It's not much in the face of the worst suffering I've encountered in my life. But perhaps I can prevent further calamities. The Russians are helping me. There are a few experienced men among them. . . .

On Sunday one of the Russians said to me: "This is hell." Now at least we have some semblance of order. But we achieved it with blood and tears. And next to the loud [death] is this quiet dying from exhaustion and illness.

23.10.41: *WACHTMEISTER* A. R. (EASTERN FRONT)[120]

Your idea of the war here is too simple! You think that we only came here as occupying troops. There I have to contradict you and maintain the opposite, because since our arrival here we have been involved in the great operations in the East that the *Führer* mentioned in his speech. Above all, we have to deal with bandits and guerrilla war. Only yesterday, in a neighboring area, a German officer was shot by Russians in civilian clothing. For that, the entire village was set ablaze [*Dafür wurde aber dann das ganze Dorf in Brand gesteckt*]. There's a lot that's different in this Eastern Campaign compared to the Western Campaign.

23.10.41: HANS-ALBERT GIESE (NINTH ARMY, ARMY GROUP CENTER)[121]

We've been located in and around the area of Kalinin for some time. It's a city of a few hundred thousand inhabitants, located around 150 km northwest of Moscow. There are large stone buildings here, but in the main the huts here are just the same as in the villages, utterly pitiful wooden buildings. We've furnished one of those huts for ourselves, more or less, and feel quite well. The last few days were relentless for us. By contrast, we only notice the Russian here by his bombers or by the greetings sent by his artillery, although he only sporadically sends those over here.

23.10.41: *LEUTNANT* RUDOLF MAURER (251 INFANTRY DIVISION, NINTH ARMY, ARMY GROUP CENTER)[122]

Today, after the constant battles of recent days, there's "rest." I haven't got to see much of it. But, to mark the day, I have finally washed myself thoroughly, shaved properly, and fitted myself out with a clean shirt and I feel reborn. Since I also slept right through without interruption last night for the first time in many days, I lack very little to complete my happiness. . . .

By the way, I have had to scale back my aesthetic feelings. I have to accept a lot of things that would otherwise have seemed impossible to me. In recent days, we've all had a lot to do. The Russian had been thrown out of his well-constructed positions on the Volga by a, for him, surprise attack. In the following night he attempted to win back the old positions and made one counterattack after another. His attacks were repelled under bloody losses. Our antitank artillery made an important contribution to that. During that night I had the task of leading an ammunition section to the front. The drive across the Volga in the middle of the dark night, in the firelight of burning villages, was very strange and unforgettable. And what I then experienced with my antitank squad and with the battalion was memorable. Two nights later, I was assigned the defense of the bridgehead. Over the Volga again. The Russian was not so bad. But the night went better and was quieter than I had initially assumed it would be. The following day we attacked again and threw the Russians back. . . .

Yesterday afternoon, a Volga German came to me. His great-grandparents had emigrated to the Volga region. His father had been a teacher and things had gone well for them in czarist Russia. Their time of suffering began with Bolshevism. "You simply can't imagine everything we've gone through," he kept saying. "Everyone dead, everyone buried, butchered by those pigs." Now he'd like to fight with the German Army and after the war he wants to go to the Reich as a settler. "Then life will really begin." You can't imagine his happiness at the German successes. . . . Continuation: 27 October: We're back on the advance. Very bad weather, rain, filth, everything unimaginable. We tried without success, for hours in the pouring rain, to get the vehicles going and were completely soaked through.

23.10.41: DR. HEINRICH HAAPE (6 INFANTRY DIVISION, NINTH ARMY, ARMY GROUP CENTER)[123]

Tomorrow we attack! The objective: a larger town northwest of Kalinin. We now fight against the enemy pushing forward from the north.

Now I can tell you something very special: I was awarded the Iron Cross First Class today! At risk of my life I was able to save the lives of many comrades or considerably reduce their suffering! I have remained true to myself. I have taken part in every attack at the very front line. We are in God's hands. My hour has not yet come. Now I firmly believe that I will survive the Russian campaign. I have often thought when things were going crazy, that I would never see you again. I do believe the hardest has been achieved!

23.10.41: HELLMUTH H. (50 INFANTRY DIVISION, ELEVENTH ARMY, ARMY GROUP SOUTH)[124]

We've been back at the front for a few days now, on the isthmus of a large island or a peninsula. There's fighting with all the trimmings, planes are being deployed in full by the Russian side in particular. Tanks also appeared, one just in front of us, but it turned away when I fired at it with my 3 antitank rifles.

By the way, there were all sorts of losses yesterday; I know of 3 fatalities and 20 casualties. . . . More and more of the old boys from the company are falling. Hopefully, it will all soon be over at the southern front [*Hoffentlich ist die Sache vorn südwärts bald ausgestanden*]. The Russians are defecting in droves, but they shoot a lot beforehand, have good artillery, all kinds of weapons that we don't have or know, 25–30 bombers and fighters over us every hour; like I said, everything is in the game and you have to wonder that nothing more happens. Yesterday, somebody said sarcastically: Less than 10 years and we'll have the Russians' weapons, too![125] If you are worked up about my harmless wound, that's very illogical, because in that moment, of course, every danger was banished for a time, and so from your perspective you ought to be entirely reassured now.

By the way, I forgot to say that a lively paper war has flared up between us and the Russians; from the Russian side, e.g., it's raining "News from Home," "News from Abroad,"[126] even "News from the Front," communist poems about the "oath of allegiance," "Graveside conversation between two fallen *Landser*, disappointed by the *Führer*," historical parallels and statements from German military persons from Stein to List on the German-Russian relationship, "Suffering and diseases of the German soldier," etc., etc. All these with passes to the Reds; there is absolutely no hope that anyone falls for it, the Russian seems to have no idea of crowd psychology or rather psychology at all.[127]

24.10.41: KURT MIETHKE (ARMY GROUP SOUTH)[128]

I'm on guard duty again today and got a post where there are many graves, there are around 2,000 lying in them.[129] That'd be something for you. You wouldn't stay 10 minutes. But that can't shock us anymore, you get used to it [*Aber uns kann das nicht mehr erschüttern man gewöhnt sich daran*]. It's just the rain and cold that disturb us.

Were the planes there again?[130] There are none to be seen near us. I often think of you when I'm standing watch at night and you are already lying in your warm little bed. Well, perhaps it won't be all that much longer before we can be back together again. I think the war will be over in late spring. Because the Russians can go on for another 4–5 weeks at most, then they're through. You'll say, he's got a sense of humor, well, you can't lose that here, nor hope either.

25.10.41: *LEUTNANT* JOACHIM H. (131 INFANTRY DIVISION, SECOND ARMY, ARMY GROUP CENTER)[131]

The Urrah patriotism of home, as it's expressed sometimes on the radio and in the press, is felt by us to be less wonderful. With some radio plays or propaganda company reports, all you can do is shake your head. Such bad roads can't rob us of our good mood, but even so we don't feel like singing. All there is here is rutty field roads on which you can't keep step at all, instead you have to help pull or push the vehicles. Equally, it is also wrong to portray the Russian soldier as an easily defeated opponent. The Russian is actually a dogged fighter [*zäher Kämpfer*] and would rather be chopped into pieces than give in, never even mind his good weaponry, which meets all modern requirements.

The lifestyle, clothing, accommodation, etc., of the population stands entirely in contrast to that. This primitiveness defies all description. There is no measure with which to compare it. For us, it is a very strange feeling to hear dance music on the radio (assuming we have the opportunity for it). Then you remember, good Lord, of course there is also music, dancing, theater, and here . . . only filth and dereliction—that's the Soviet paradise.

25.10.41: *UNTEROFFIZIER* WILHELM PRÜLLER (9 PANZER DIVISION, 1 PANZER ARMY, ARMY GROUP SOUTH)[132]

At 09.30 we push off toward Shdanovo, which is only a few km away; but the mud is knee high and won't allow us to get to S. before evening. Even getting out of Linez is a real problem for our routine drivers, but what goes on along the march route defies description. Many vehicles get stuck after the first few meters and can only be freed with the combined assistance of everyone present. Our drivers have now had experience in four campaigns. They mastered the ploughed fields of Poland, the swift tempo of Holland, the breathless chase in France, the mountains of the Balkans; they drive in pitch darkness, without lights, as safely as if it were bright sunshine. But the worst of the lot is undoubtedly the Soviet Union; and yet they master that, too—many of them with the last drop of petrol. They are worthy to stand side by side with the brave fighters in battle.

25.10.41: DR. KONRAD JARAUSCH (ARMY GROUP CENTER)[133]

The days have become somewhat less stressful since I last wrote. Friday morning we sent a few thousand prisoners off on a march. And it's a lot easier to handle 6,000 than 12,000. I no longer have to play the policeman and don't need to beat anyone down with a nightstick or have them shot. Still, things are harrowing enough. . . . We try daily to meet the demand [to feed the prisoners]. But we have so few means [at our disposal]. Luckily the older officers still have human qualities of the traditional sort, so that I have some support and can make things happen (like having two meals a day) against the will of the "bureaucrats" and many of my comrades, who don't comprehend what I'm doing. There is some room for humanity here. I listened to an opera singer from Moscow yesterday, who sang a Russian folk song for the major and then some Mozart and Wagner.

I had just come back from a walk to the uppermost floor of the factory, where we had to ascertain if it were true that the Russians had stolen a corpse in order to cut the flesh off of it. We didn't find that corpse, but we did find others (fully clothed) that had been there for days.

26.10.41: FRITZ PABST (SIXTH ARMY, ARMY GROUP SOUTH)[134]

Now it's turning to winter and so you, my dear, can go to the cinema more often, that'll give you a change and you'll also see what's happening in the East, of course you don't see everything by a long shot and can't have an inkling of the volumes of blood that have flowed here, i.e. on the Bolshevik side, of course, and mainly the Jews; there aren't any of them anymore wherever Germans are [*hauptsächlich der Juden, die gibt es ja hier wo Deutsche sind, nicht mehr*].[135]

But we've seen nothing of battle itself here and probably won't get to the front now, because the war here will likely be over sometime soon. Then, hopefully, we'll also get our long-deserved holiday leave.

26.10.41: *LEUTNANT* JOACHIM H. (131 INFANTRY DIVISION, SECOND ARMY, ARMY GROUP CENTER)[136]

Who would have believed half a year ago that they'd eventually end up here. By and large, this war is anything other than pleasing in comparison with the campaign in the west. Since 22 June, we have been constantly deployed with our division or at least on the march: We crossed over the 2,000-km-limit long ago. . . . Unfortunately, the weather has brought us considerable difficulties in the last ten days. That concerns provisioning above all. What with the sodden clay roads, simply no vehicle can get through anymore. It's just a good thing that the enemy resistance is already so weak that almost no artillery ammunition is necessary, otherwise we could get into the tightest of spots. For six days now, neither rations, nor fuel, nor mail has arrived. Just as little mail leaves. . . . So we have to "feed ourselves from the land," as our orders so nicely put it. When there's nothing to find, those are golden words. At least a large-scale cull of hens, ducks, and geese has begun already, and some *Kolchos* (farms) still provide honey, oats, flour, etc., so that we can even bake bread ourselves. Hopefully, there'll be a frost soon so that these provisioning difficulties stop.

26.10.41: *WACHTMEISTER* JOSEF L. (129 INFANTRY DIVISION, ARMY GROUP CENTER)[137]

Our daily conversation revolves solely around the end of this campaign. In eight weeks, Christmas will be over, in nine weeks New Year. Will we see home or at least Germany again by then? . . .

Even if the participants in the World War were at the front longer than we have been, they didn't have to cover these vast distances in the Russian region like we have. They usually lived in positional warfare, while we have fought on the move. In recent weeks, we've been advancing without stopping or resting. Can you imagine what it means to slog for over 20 hours in a sodden hollow, to drag, in teams of men, vehicle after vehicle through the half-meter-deep muck? Wet boots and socks, face and clothing full of muck, the horses can get no grip in the mud, [they] fall and thrash themselves ever deeper into it. The individual man must do everything, engine power is no use here, praying and cursing is no help. Always setting off so as to get forward, so as not to fall away from the other troops. For everywhere there is the Russian, death lies in wait in the bushes and in the forests. [Those at] home do not know what is, and has to be done, at the front, especially during an advance.

26.10.41: KARL FUCHS (7 PANZER DIVISION, 3 PANZER GROUP, ARMY GROUP CENTER)[138]

A great friendship binds us German soldiers together out here. It is this camaraderie and the support that we are able to give each other that is, in my opinion, the secret behind our incredible successes and victories. This loyalty and devotion to the cause again and again was the decisive factor in many a battle and I tell you, this comradeship has been one of the most magnificent experiences out here. This loyalty is the essence of the German fighting spirit. We can depend on each other unconditionally. Each one of us sets an example for the other and that makes us strong. I have always known of this loyalty, but today it burns in me like a holy flame. Let this loyalty which I have experienced out here in comradeship be the foundation of our future life.

27.10.41: ALBERT NEUHAUS (ARMY GROUP CENTER)[139]

For a short time, as a result of the dreadful transport difficulties, ammunition got scarce for us and the Russian used this time thoroughly and peppered us with artillery so much that on both days we were close to losing our hearing and sight. It was the first time in the whole campaign, and, God willing, the last time, that we had to move into an alternate position. I can't tell you how hard both sides are fighting here. At the moment we have Moscow young communists, a Russian elite group, in front of us. But fate is taking its inexorable course and German leadership will soon also master this [*Aber das Schicksal nimmt unerbittlich seinen Lauf und die deutsche Führung wird auch dies bald meistern*]. There has never been a battle like that being fought out here and those comrades, who have already taken part in the previous campaigns, say that the earlier campaigns were child's play compared to this battle. Sadly, sadly, the weather has been very unfavorable for us recently and we all currently look like pigs. . . . You often have to wade through mud that goes up to your knees, and then you have to imagine the vehicles and especially the very heavy vehicles. Well, hopefully the homeland will later be grateful to its soldiers for everything that they are now doing in manly fulfilment of duty.

28.10.41: HEINZ RAHE (13 PANZER DIVISION, 1 PANZER ARMY, ARMY GROUP SOUTH)[140]

My love! I will once again write to you the kind of endless epistles on things and thoughts that may not interest you much. Yesterday, N. read me a sentence from a letter that a girl had written him: "You are my sweet, little, tubby, lovely Fritzerl!" Something like that. That made me realize again how very sober in fact my letters, or even our mutual letter correspondence is—at least compared to that. And yet! What does that girl find out from her "sweet Fritzerl" apart from a few smoochy phrases, naturally nonbinding on both sides? I always try to bring you into my way of think-ing, because I hope that through that we will both best stay bonded with each other, much more than if the letters were filled with all sorts of promises. You know, the word love is such cheap coinage today that I don't want to use it for us, at least not in the manner of current speech. I would much rather be with you to forget everything I have heard and seen and to leave everything untrue and impure behind me, as if I had never found out about it.[141]

28.10.41: DR. KONRAD JARAUSCH (ARMY GROUP CENTER)[142]

The prisoners are asking me daily as I make the rounds of the camp, "Moscow kaput?" Everyone wants this campaign to be over. The educated Russians don't think the Bolsheviks will ever give up. . . . "The Russians have always suffered; that is nothing new," one of the men said to me during our time together on Sunday. Because I have these wonderful opportunities to converse with the Russians, [my reading] will have to take a back seat. . . . We're starting to get to know the communist Russia about which we once theorized. These people are people just like us. Being with them is good and awakens thoughts and feelings that in the end lead me back to you and our child.

28.10.41: SIEGBERT STEHMANN (163 INFANTRY DIVISION, GERMAN ARMY OF NORWAY)[143]

Elk came past today. We shot one of them for ourselves so just for once there'd be a tasty morsel in the kitchen, because of course the weather is hindering provisioning in the ancient forest. Above all, socks! . . .

The Russians are sitting in thick furs and we have nothing. If we only knew what was to happen with us on the northern front. No prospect of an end to the war before the start of winter, no prospect of leave, and eternal uncertainty of [our] fate. But we are grateful for every day that we remain healthy.

29.10.41: DR. HEINRICH HAAPE (6 INFANTRY DIVISION, NINTH ARMY, ARMY GROUP CENTER)[144]

The war has now taken on the kind of shape that means we are very nearly finished with it. Yesterday, Russian tanks broke through to our rear and occupied the division's only communication road. We have been living from the land for 14 days. We have had dead and wounded daily. At the moment, it is one German for every 10 dead Russians. We are taking a lot of prisoners. It's a desperate struggle of extraordinary severity that the Russians are carrying out. All the Russian bravery and courage will not help—they will be destroyed!

29.10.41: *UNTEROFFIZIER* L. K. (183 INFANTRY DIVISION, FOURTH ARMY, ARMY GROUP CENTER)[145]

Now we, too, are also part of the last great battle outside Moscow. Hopefully, it will succeed in defeating the Bolshevik capital city before the great chill breaks out. The war here in Russia is a completely different one to other states. These aren't humans anymore, but wild hordes and beasts [*Das sind keine Menschen mehr, sondern wilde Horden und Bestien*], who have been bred like this by Bolshevism over the last 20 years. You can't permit any sympathy for these people to arise, because they are all very cowardly and deceitful.

29.10.41: HEINZ RAHE (13 PANZER DIVISION, 1 PANZER ARMY, ARMY GROUP SOUTH)[146]

Now the conditions in the East are currently in flux. As soon as national states, such as the Ukraine, Belarus, Russia, and Georgia have formed here, it will be difficult to undertake a correction in our favor and to their disadvantage. You may perhaps wonder, dear wife, that I take such a strong position in these questions. You will certainly also be able to perceive a reversal and a contradiction to my first letters from this campaign. That is certainly the case. But back then I did not yet know what mismanagement the Soviets had delivered. Moreover, I saw this campaign much more as destiny rather than a promising opportunity for great new tasks. If you have spent as much time as I have as V.O. [*Verbindungsoffizier*—liaison officer], then of course you think a lot about the sense of this campaign and the prospects that might justify the sacrifices being made for it. The only map I own shows the eastern European regions from the [General] *Gouvernement* [in Poland] to the Ural Mountains. So central Europe falls to the back of our thoughts and I daily ask myself the question how much farther will we have to march and what will we make of this endless region?[147] Mariupol is located at the eastern exit of the Ukraine—but it is halfway to Baku. I can hardly imagine that we will reach the Caucasus before winter. The road conditions are too bad for that. We are still over 200 km away from the nearest railway station, which is so very important for our supplies of ammunition and fuel. It's still a long way on bottomless roads from Dnepropetrovsk to here. Moreover, the nights are getting longer and driving at night is a suicidal undertaking [*Selbstmordunternehmen*]. . . .

In the meantime it had rained heavily. That's not just a disadvantage for field post, although of course that's hopelessly stuck for the time being. You absolutely cannot imagine the detrimental influence a single rain shower has. There are no solid roads in the European sense here. It all depends on the weather. So far, we've had tolerably good weather. And even so!—some of the roads were bad and even worse!

30.10.41: WALTER NEUSER (ARMY GROUP CENTER)[148]

It's storming heavily outside again. This is a region with difficulties that are just crazy. Now I can really say I'd be happy if there were frost.[149] Then at least the mud would stop. It's hardly possible to get boots dry. . . .

The [local Russian] men have all been drafted [by the Red Army]. Captured, dead, perhaps still with the fighting troops or wandering around in the area. We must have 20 men standing guard here every night. There's something going on every day. You'd think that the forests are empty. But there are still a few roaming around who feel the itch to carry out guerrilla war. There are shots in broad daylight. Anything that's captured certainly doesn't escape righteous justice [*entgeht bestimmt nicht der gerechten Strafe*]. It's war, but these rough fellows have certainly come to the right address with us. . . .[150]

It's fantastic that you all sent me the illustrated magazines. We hadn't had any newspapers or illustrateds in our possession for a long time. And so for once another world other than this Russia opens up for us.[151]

We think about winter. It'll bring us a few surprises yet. But in the World War the soldier withstood 3 winters in Russia, so we can certainly manage one winter.

30.10.41: JAKOB GEIMER (ARMY GROUP SOUTH)[152]

The Russian who fights honorably and fair is respected as an opponent, with the others, well, there we know only one phrase "kill." Don't worry about that, at the moment we're just marching, but if we are deployed again, we do our work well. . . .

[W]e've already put around 3,000 km behind us, and still we go onward. You can check on a map sometime. Then these dreadful roads, nothing but thick mud and filth, you can hardly move forward. That's why it takes so long with the mail. The vehicles get stuck, cars and everything can't get forward, or only with difficulty, and human and animal are subjected to the greatest hardships. Despite it all, the goal will still be reached, even if food only follows slowly. It's just the way it is, and everyone has to put up with it. The quicker the war is over, the better. We will likely stay in the south, Petersburg, Moscow, and so on will hopefully also fall soon.

30.10.41: DR. ADOLF B. (25 INFANTRY DIVISION [MOT.], 1 PANZER ARMY, ARMY GROUP SOUTH)[153]

The plague of flies (malaria, etc.) is no longer so severe; but there are still hordes of mice and lice! I haven't yet been able to find a louse on me with absolute certainty. Just because you feel a bite somewhere doesn't mean it's a louse by a long shot! The hygiene conditions in the Soviet paradise are extremely wanting; France was superb in comparison. . . .

In general, a certain halt has occurred in our section of the front (center: Orel). The most important centers still to deal with are just the industrial regions around Rostov, Moscow, and around Leningrad. . . .

As long as we are stuck to the spot because of the bad weather, we'll just have to wait and spend our time reading and playing chess; militarily, the war is already decided [*der Krieg ist ja militärisch schon entschieden*] and it's questionable whether we'll be deployed again. If we had always had good weather, we would have been beyond Orel long before now! We probably won't be part of the encirclement of the Moscow cauldron now. We learned soon enough how dangerous such an encirclement is at the formation of the Kiev cauldron.

CHAPTER 7

November 1941

Introduction

At the beginning of November, Army Group Center was halted eighty kilometers (fifty miles) from Moscow, awaiting the hard frosts of early winter and desperately trying to bring up enough men, equipment, and supplies to sustain another offensive push. The Soviet defensive efforts had focused on the so-called Mozhaisk Defensive Line, which sought to block the main approaches to Moscow at the four main approaches to the Soviet capital: Volokolamsk, Mozhaisk, Maloiaroslavets, and Kaluga. In October Bock's panzer and motorized divisions had taken each of these four defensive bastions, but the fighting had exhausted the combat formations and depleted their ranks. In fact, the pause in German operations to recover strength and await the winter frosts was of greater benefit to the Red Army, which was much closer to sources of supply and aided by better infrastructure. Helmuth James von Moltke, the great-grandnephew of the celebrated German commander Moltke the Elder, wrote in a letter on 18 November:

> *The war looks bad. There is a joke going around here: "Eastern Campaign extended by a month owing to great success." A bitter remark. I don't think that we can still make significant progress before the new year. . . . The unfortunate millions of troops who now freeze out there, are wet, and die! A comparison with the World War 14/18 is impossible, for then fewer people were involved, and could therefore be better looked after, and there were houses in which they could stay. The present situation is different in both respects. What will the army that we meet again in March be like? With no leave worth mentioning, insufficient supplies, no quarters, no adequate clothing, no military success?[1]*

Contemporary observers often question why the German command did not adopt winter quarters once it became clear that Operation Typhoon had ground to a halt and the dreaded Russian winter beckoned. Yet few of the principal German commanders entertained any such notion of assuming winter positions while still short of Moscow. Understanding this has a lot to do with the Wehrmacht's own offensive ethos, which itself had deep roots in German military culture but was sharpened by the dominant memory of the

"Miracle of the Marne" from 1914.[2] Here the great German offensive sweeping through northern France was halted, and trench warfare soon resulted. To German generals directing Operation Typhoon, however, the stalemate on the Western Front in the Great War was the result of excessive caution and a failure to press the attack on Paris with every means possible. Now that Moscow was the objective, pressing the attack with everything available appeared to be the lesson of 1914. Accordingly, Army Group Center resumed the advance in the middle of November, but there was no rapid envelopment on the flanks of the Red Army; rather it was a grinding, costly frontal attack. The Red Army was being pushed back but not destroyed. In fact, unbeknown to the Germans, in the last week of November the Soviet High Command began transporting five new reserve armies, formed behind the Volga River, to the front lines.[3] Three of these took up positions east of Moscow, while the remaining two were sent south.[4] Army Group Center's November offensive, for which Bock believed "the last battalion that can be thrown in will be decisive," was a farce.[5] The Red Army was not being destroyed on the road to Moscow; in fact it was fighting with one hand behind its back, awaiting the moment to switch from the defense to the offense.

Already in November, Soviet offensive strength was capitalizing on Army Group South's overextension. Kleist's panzer army finally seized Rostov on 20 November but the very next day concluded that a withdrawal would be necessary if reinforcements could not be provided.[6] A Soviet offensive from the north and northwest threatened to cut off Kleist's advanced divisions, and a flurry of dispatches ensued to secure a withdrawal that Hitler never granted. By the end of November, the profound danger of the situation forced Rundstedt to authorize Kleist to fall back on the Mius River, which saved his panzer group but at the cost of the field marshal's command. Army Group South's new commander, GFM von Reichenau, quickly agreed that the retreat to the Mius had been correct.

In the Crimea, Manstein's Eleventh Army had broken through the defensive positions at Ishun and was now pursuing the remaining Soviet forces. Three German Army corps advanced—one toward Sevastopol, one to the south coast, and the third toward the Kerch peninsula. The advance in the east was slowed by Soviet resistance, but once this collapsed in the middle of the month the Crimea was fully occupied aside from the fortress of Sevastopol, which came under siege and held out until the middle of 1942.

At Army Group North, the drive to link up with the Finnish army was reinforced in early November by one motorized and two panzer divisions, ensuring the capture of Tikhvin on 8 November. It was a significant achievement in itself—some twenty thousand Soviet POWs were captured—but Busch's Sixteenth Army was still well short of its planned objective.[7] More critically, mud, ice, and snow had drastically reduced all movement, while Soviet resistance north of the town stiffened notably. With barely enough supplies to meet immediate needs and no prospect of further reinforcement, Tikhvin became the high water mark of Army Group North's last offensive of the year.[8]

At Leningrad the Eighteenth Army's siege was already having its desired effect with hunger stalking the city, while German artillery and aircraft battered the city and its morale. On 12 November, one resident wrote in his diary: "Now hunger is not merely knocking at the door, but has come right inside on its bony legs. The food situation in Leningrad is precarious. . . . The Germans intend to starve us out. Will the Leningraders, nearly three million of them, be able to endure this immense ordeal? But it is not just a question of *starvation. It was good flying weather today and there were five alerts in the course of the day. . . . So we have hunger, cold, bombing, and shells whistling over our heads."*

Letters and Diary Entries (1–30 November 1941)

1.11.41: KARL NÜNNIGHOFF (16 PANZER DIVISION, 1 PANZER ARMY, ARMY GROUP SOUTH)[10]

I already mentioned in my previous letter that I've sent off another two packages, each with 2 rubber aprons, hopefully they'll arrive. I see that there are rumors going round at home that the troops are to be pulled out of the East. Dear parents, this rumor has been going around here for a long time already, but we've not yet seen anything of it. When, some time ago, we were resting for 14 days, we were supposed to start our march to the rear, but quite the opposite, it was off to the front; I, personally, don't believe any such tales at all anymore.[11]

1.11.41: RUDOLF OEHUS (ARMY GROUP SOUTH)[12]

You can't imagine the muck on the roads here at the moment, and despite it all we carried on, although we sat out 1–2 days in between, but then on we'd go again. With our telephone wagon [*Fernsprechwagen*] we still got through everywhere; by contrast, the guns and ammunition wagons frequently got stuck fast, often arrived at their day's destination at midnight and then it was onward the following morning. Last week, I and a couple of comrades had to do around 75 km in one day and one night with our horses, [we] had to fetch an ammunition wagon that had fallen behind, so we did our [usual] daily march 3 times. But gradually you come to be at ease with it all, because you are used to it already. We've been up against the enemy all this time, but he has only been fighting with weak forces, he has often retreated without putting up a fight, we've only really had losses from the planes, 4 fatalities and several casualties in all.

1.11.41: *UNTEROFFIZIER* WILHELM PRÜLLER (9 PANZER DIVISION, SECOND ARMY, ARMY GROUP CENTER)[13]

At 12.00 the attack on Kursk begins. The major, energetic as ever and (as in every battle) up in front, with an encouraging word for every one of us, says: "Squeeze that tube, boys there are quarters waiting for us in Kursk." And brother, do we squeeze that tube! We all want to get to a real bed.

In quick march, preceded by the tanks, we move up far enough to have the city lying in front of us. To the left we see ssome enemy positions which probably won't be dangerous for us, but the tanks fire at them anyway. The Russians leave their trenches and run like rabbits. We avoid a minefield, marking it as we go past, and then we're in front of the northeast side of Kursk. All over the place you can see trenches, MG installations and foxholes, but the Russians have preferred to disappear. Better for them, better for us.

Is it the wish to be the first man in Kursk? Or is it the hope of a bed? Or is it that we want to get out of the enemy artillery line of fire? Anyway, running like a bunch of pigs, we reach the first houses of Kursk. Night is already upon us. We find ourselves in a street in a suburb of Kursk—lots of small, hideous huts. To look for a decent house is pointless. There aren't any. Moreover, our artillery has broken every pane of glass in town. Now we can curse them—there's not a room in town without draughts! Despite it all, we lie down and sleep the sleep of the just.

1.11.41: DR. HELMUT MACHEMER (1 PANZER ARMY, ARMY GROUP SOUTH)[14]

The German soldier is cautious in defense but daring in offense, sometimes reckless, simply unstoppable. So it was this time. The group had worked itself well forward when a Russian truck that had remained behind appeared around 200 meters ahead of them. One noncommissioned officer followed the truck on his motorcycle, two other motorcycle riders followed him—a wild chase [*eine wilde Jagd*]! Attempts to call them off were in vain. The chase went on and on into the Russian positions. . . . We heard nothing more of the foremost drivers. Will they still be able to break through to us? They've probably been murdered by the Russians. We're very low: they're four of our best people. And the loss was unnecessary!

1.11.41: DR. KONRAD JARAUSCH (ARMY GROUP CENTER)[15]

Every day we have to end work a little earlier. The world sinks into the foggy gray dusk of autumn at 5 p.m. I'm so exhausted every night I can't use the free time very well, and I don't have the energy to write letters. I'm in the camp at 6:45 in the morning. We are faced with the same misery during the hours that lie between. One becomes rather numb to things. Because I now have to oversee the provision of 17,000 to 18,000 warm meals and 9,000 servings of bread, the sheer effort is so overwhelming that I can hardly concern myself with details. Every time I leave the vicinity of the kitchens I'm surrounded by such cries—"*pan, pan!*" ["Sir, Sir!"]—I can barely tend to any one person's needs: food, bread, shoes, illness, work, release, theft—I'm supposed to help with all of that. Since most of the silent dying occurs in the barracks, where the sick are assembled, it remains out of sight. We only see horribly emaciated corpses lying before us. . . . In the middle of all this—the rags, the stench, and disease—we have to keep our heads up and act like we're superior [to them] and then every now and then play a more human and empathetic role.

2.11.41: *UNTEROFFIZIER* X. M. (707 INFANTRY DIVISION, ARMY GROUP CENTER)[16]

It seems that two buildings here were once churches. In 1925 an electricity works was already built in one, so one Russian told me when I was viewing it from the inside. And the other one may have been a Jewish synagogue well into this war. Only the walls of this sturdy building, which was constructed in 1664 and shows signs of considerable dimensions, are still standing. I think that the Jews in this country will soon no longer need any prayer house. I've already described to you why. It's really the only right solution for these abominable creatures [*gräuliche Kreaturen*].

2.11.41: *UNTEROFFIZIER* WILHELM PRÜLLER (9 PANZER DIVISION, SECOND ARMY, ARMY GROUP CENTER)[17]

At 9:00 we start to take over the city [Kursk]. Civilians inform us that the streets are full of barricades and that a lot of mines have been laid to hinder our progress. The Red Army has cleared out, but armed a lot of partisans beforehand. This can be tricky. Of the 120,000 inhabitants, 30,000 are said to have fled to Voronezh. Like yesterday, many buildings were burning during the night. Blown-up bridges and railway installations bear witness to the destructive fury of the Soviets.

The first minutes go fine. Distrustful, we look into all the side streets, into all the windows—partisans can be hidden anywhere, and they want to slit our throats. In front of a church the C.O. orders a halt. With a connoisseur's glance, he takes in the curious mixture of clay and wooden huts and houses, and after curt orders to the platoons, we move on swiftly. And not a bit too soon. A few minutes later, as the regimental battle headquarters reached the church, the partisans' bullets were whistling round the tower. And from this moment, our unopposed advance is at an end. Every second a bullet wings past us. You never know where it comes from. Pressed flat against the house walls, bent down, your gun ready to shoot, your grenade in the other hand, you creep along.

Several times we shoot at suspicious-looking places, straight from the hip with our MG; all round you can hear the dull thuds of hand grenades exploding. Some civilians, who despite our order don't stand still, are shot down. We get to a street crossing, which some partisans are raking with excellently placed and well-aimed fire. Some of our men get across; the fifth meets up with a bullet and rolls down a short incline. To go on across this square would only mean unnecessary losses, and some of our men have grasped the situation at once and turn left, without waiting for any orders. Then we get to the first barricades. The MGs set up and rake them, and the platoons go ahead.

"Watch out for mines," yells the C.O., and not a second too soon: the first men were about to trot right over a mine. Left and right of the barricade they left a small passage open which was strewn with mines. One hundred meters farther on we hit a main street. Shots come from all over. Some civilians whisk into a house and at that moment we have another wounded man on our hands.[18] Armed civilians and suspicious characters on the one hand, wounded on the other—who can wonder if we mow down everything in our path. . . . It's not long before some of the accursed partisans turn tail and run. After knocking off a few more civilians, we get almost as far as the city limits.

3.11.41: DR. HELMUT MACHEMER (1 PANZER ARMY, ARMY GROUP SOUTH)[19]

We have moved into quarters in a small town. Cramped. We lie alongside each other, barely finding space on the ground. But much preferable to be here in this little shack than with the majority of the division in the town behind us. They're really suffering under the airborne attacks there. During the day the Russians come and at night the English with their large, low-flying night bombers.[20] These planes are the only thing that the Russians can show in considerable numbers. Whole squadrons fly over us. Yesterday this went on almost uninterrupted through the entire day. The rows of columns of smoke that rise high into the sky mark the impacts of the heavy calibers, even here the earth shudders with the explosions. A wild rattling and shooting answers from the depths. We see four planes fall, but new ones always come. Good thing that they aim poorly, the losses are relatively low. During the night the attack is continued, first they drop parachute flares and then their bombs. It went on like that through almost the whole night. We stood outside our hut and watched the spectacle, almost like watching fireworks when the chain of tracer bullets goes up on all sides. Good thing that we're out of that fire show [*Feuerzauber*].

4.11.41: SIEGFRIED ROEMER (1 PANZER ARMY, ARMY GROUP SOUTH)[21]

We've ended up in places that we would never have allowed ourselves to dream we'd ever see. Now we have conquered them. The Donez region is securely in our hands, the Caucasus, Volga, and Caspian Sea are all coming into view. But always the secret, almost furtive glances into the [Russian] interior and backward. Like children, we are looking through the locked gate into the garden of home and at brightly lit Christmas displays behind glass windows. But these are not children's eyes looking into your beautiful, peaceful homes, not children's hands that want to touch you and caress you, not children's hearts that often cry themselves to sleep to forget their wishes as they take shape and as they fade, but rather men, looking steadfastly into the distance to what is firmly theirs, wanting to keep secure that which is their only and most holy thing, and ascending with their longings through every night and day as if through difficult, endless mountain terrain. It's not death that lies in wait for them, not fatigue and despondency that accompany them; they are instead facing cold, dark eternity, daily, hourly, in order to win from her a limited little piece of finitude, in which their longing and love have a meaning and purpose, beginning and end. But what can our little hearts achieve in this great war of peoples!

4.11.41: FRITZ PABST (SIXTH ARMY, ARMY GROUP SOUTH)[22]

Yesterday I received another three letters dated 30 August! 10 and 16 October, for which, my dear little Mott, I thank you warmly. The one from 30 August was opened officially, almost all the letters that were transported with it carried that mark.[23] There wasn't anything of significance in it anyway, for me sure, but not for others.[24]

There's been all kinds of things going on again in recent days, various large buildings have burned out and many of the beautiful, large buildings will soon be destroyed.[25] It's all sabotage and the consequence of that is the shooting of many hundred civilians [*die Folge davon Erschießungen vieler hundert Zivilisten*].[26] You can all tell Uncle Karl that there is a large field of rubble around one square kilometer in the middle of the town; that was on 23 Sept. when it began to burn, I had just arrived here, then there were a number of explosions and then it burned for 4 days. Almost all the large buildings have been loaded with explosives by the Bolsheviks and are caused to detonate via a timed ignition. So that's Bolshevism: destruction and devastation and, not least, murder.

4.11.41: KURT MIETHKE (ARMY GROUP SOUTH)[27]

Yes, the Russians may be as wild as they like, but we don't allow ourselves to be shaken and if there's no other way, then things bang. We're getting another 10,000, up to 1,200 arrived already today. Around 20–30 die every day.[28]

4.11.41: HANS MARTIN STÄHLIN (EASTERN FRONT)[29]

I firmly believe that even the soldier's death is not an arbitrary end to a life destined for other things, but rather the conclusion of an individual fate fulfilled. A man is burdened with it as their fate and their fellow man [is burdened with it] as a test. In death, the realms of God and man adjoin and the question of death is the question of God, just as one only asks about a door if one wants to know something about the room behind it. Soldiers know this. Can you understand when I say that how we think of our dead is not irrelevant? I believe they are still so close to us that our thoughts reach them. It isn't empty talk when people say that the dead are still with us. But it is important that they are glad to be with us.[30]

5.11.41: OBERFELDWEBEL E. K. (260TH INFANTRY DIVISION, FOURTH ARMY, ARMY GROUP CENTER)[31]

Until now we have forty-nine dead and ninety-one wounded in the company. I think one can see that we certainly were in battle. The company is at the foremost line in every battle. But chin up at all times, even if it's hard. We will destroy the Russian sometime. We are positioned 80 km south of Moscow. The Russians are now at the stage that the *Kommissars* have to force the soldiers forward at the point of a gun, otherwise they wouldn't fight at all.

5.11.41: KLAUS BECKER (ARMY GROUP CENTER)[32]

We're gradually becoming free of that humanitarian rubbish. First comes food and drink and a warm bed for the soldiers, and only then is it the civilian population's turn. Of course, there's no other way if you want to wage war. That's hard to do at first, but, in your own interests, you get used to it. . . .[33] Here, you can hardly imagine what life without war looks like. We're now even at the point that we're telling ourselves 1 year or 2 years or even longer, it doesn't matter. The war will come to an end at some point.

5.11.41: *OBERSTLEUTNANT* HELLMUTH STIEFF (FOURTH ARMY, ARMY GROUP CENTER)[34]

Since yesterday—thank God—frost (4–5 C) has set in, so the worst of the mud has stopped. But until a period of prolonged frost has set in there can be no notion of continuing the assault. First we have to join up with our vehicles, which we had to leave all over the place and put the provisioning on a proper footing. It's just rotten that we had to get stuck in the muck such a short distance—barely 60 km—from Moscow. But essentially that doesn't change anything about the fact that we, at the mercy of a lunatic, will have to sit in precisely this lousy country [*Lauseland*] for years to come. I am heartily sick of it! . . . I'm just always sorry for these decent people here at the front who have to suffer such unspeakable things because of it. But it is precisely for their sakes that you can't wish for the end of this tyranny soon enough. Because otherwise it will bring us to the same misery that we see daily with our own eyes.[35]

I am filled with a bottomless hatred! My knowledge from my role to date (group leader, operational section, High Command of the Army) in conjunction with what I've experienced in the last 6 weeks (Ia [operations officer] AOK 4 [Fourth Army Command]) has given it a solid foundation! Because here you are helplessly exposed to an inhuman fate. Since 2 October our divisions have almost bled more than in the months before, because we constantly assumed conditions for the enemy that were incorrect. But that didn't lead to any sort of realization—on the contrary, the demands are becoming increasingly extreme. They will have the effect of leading to self-destruction.[36] It is appalling to have to witness this with fully functioning senses, for I no longer believe in miracles.

6.11.41: GÜNTER VON SCHEVEN (ARMY GROUP CENTER)[37]

Of joy in this world I do not expect much. I have distanced myself to a great extent from what otherwise fulfils people. It is not yet time to speak about it. Horror and death are still too close. I must first get out of the gloomy atmosphere.

6.11.41: *GEFREITER* ALOIS SCHEUER (197 INFANTRY DIVISION, ARMY GROUP CENTER)[38]

The war here in Russia in all its forms is terrible, all human thought and feeling you have to turn off. In addition to the enemy, with whom we have a life-and-death struggle, there is now cold and hunger too. But we have to endure as hard as it may be. Blessed be the man who survives this happy and healthy. I would like to do my duty as best I can, though it is often unspeakably difficult.

6.11.41: KURT VOGELER (ARMY GROUP NORTH)[39]

We are marching another 50 kilometers further into the Donez basin so as to set up winter quarters there, currently the destination of our long, military trek through a thousand plains and across innumerable rivers. The front is stagnating in our sector. The general direction of the thrust is southeasterly, toward Rostov and the Sea of Asov.

Dear Mother, I am happy to write to you even when the fatigue of the march and the thought of our nation's fate dulls the mood. But believe me I am nearer to God than usual. The mystery of the light is greater than the darkness.[40]

6.11.41: HELMUT NICK (EASTERN FRONT)[41]

Well, it's not yet over here. The Russian was simply better armed than we could have known. I do believe that another great effort will come and then the Russian will be pretty much done with. The war is decided here, but just not yet over. The Russian fights with other methods than the Frenchman did. It really is the case that the Russian doesn't mind about dying[42] and is tenacious. Today, we killed another 20 of the partisans, not one of them would have buckled [*zusammengeknickt*] any earlier. For them, this death is just as natural as any other.[43]

6.11.41: *DIVISIONSPFARRER* (DIVISIONAL PRIEST) JOSEF EICKHOFF (EASTERN FRONT)[44]

One would like to know a dear person is in the comfort and safety of the parental home for as long as possible. I see, more than any other in the division, the concentrated suffering of a war in the clearing stations. During the month of October alone I cared for over one thousand casualties. And if I didn't get so much joy from the pastoral work with the boys here—my nerves would be put to too great a test.

6.11.41: *MAJOR* HANS RIEDERER (ARMY GROUP CENTER)[45]

A deserter reported and claimed that a completely fresh Russian cavalry division comprising active regiments arrived here last night and is located with a regiment in

Osheikina. So we've landed nicely in a wasp's nest. But the attack can't be stopped now. It's already on the roll. Soon the first reports arrive from (*Leutnant*) Fürstenberg: flanking fire from the left flank. I send an armored reconnaissance car section there as a covering party. The first casualties return, on prime movers and motorcycles. Increasingly loud calls for help from Fürstenberg, ongoing casualty transports. The attack comes to a halt. The engineer platoon, with a few reconnaissance cars, is led forward by Dobmeyer to relieve the right flank of the motorcycle riflemen, the left flank is reinforced with another reconnaissance patrol. But now I have nothing more available; the staff is deployed for self-defense. I request urgent relief from the division through an attack to the flank and rear of the enemy. The casualty transports continually increase. The picture is depressing. Everywhere, casualties totter toward you, others are supported or carried by their comrades. You come across scattered groups of uninjured soldiers. But nowhere a complete troop. I gather the scattered parts and lead them to the most threatened spot, the left flank. I meet Fürstenberg amid the remnants of his company, a handful of perhaps 20 men. I am deeply shaken by the condition of my proud motorcycle rifles company. But one mustn't let anyone notice.

7.11.41: WILHELM BORGER (ARMY GROUP SOUTH)[46]

I haven't had any mail for 14 days now, and now even worse we've got stuck with our vehicle and are completely cut off from the company, so we have to provision ourselves, we're living like gypsies. You'd all have to see the conditions, sometimes it's enough to make you want to run off. . . . My entire throat is full of ulcers and [I've got] a severe cold and nobody here who can give me something for it, because we're now too far away from the unit. . . . I'm used to quite a lot, but I'll pray 100 "Our Fathers" if we get out of Russia.

7.11.41: DR. HELMUT MACHEMER (1 PANZER ARMY, ARMY GROUP SOUTH)[47]

While our troops in the south are already fighting just outside Rostov, we are gathering to carry out a bold push to the east and south and surround this city from the east, and then take it together with those troops. We know that this whole area is still defended with considerable forces and so there are serious battles ahead. . . .

When our battalion started off in the early morning, a dense autumn fog lay over the countryside. Good for us, because the enemy couldn't see any of our approach. When the fog rose and formed clouds, our German Stukas came in proud flight and circled over us to tell us that they were there. A sight like that has a bracing and heartening effect. At the same time, our panzers moved forward in an endless chain on the horizon, a defiant silhouette. At exactly 7, at the designated time, the neighboring troops began the attack, recognizable from the distant noise of battle. Although the Russian, as we heard from prisoners, had expected our attack, he was still taken by surprise. Hardly an hour had passed and the hill had been taken. Now we pushed forward, and soon the long chain of vehicles and motorcycles snaked through the hilly terrain, at the front our armored reconnaissance vehicle. The panzers followed behind us, occasionally driving a few hundred meters into the terrain to the sides in order to dig out any fortified enemy positions. That's how the advance of a division is carried out. To our right and left the neighboring troops marched at intervals of a few kilometers. So we created a broad breach that infantry following to the sides secured against flanking attacks by the enemy. What preparation, what discipline is required to launch such a planned attack!

8.11.41: SIEGBERT STEHMANN (163 INFANTRY DIVISION, GERMAN ARMY OF NORWAY)[48]

The snow lies deep, around ½ m high. It's cold. At 4:00 a.m. it's dark. We sit warm in our dugout and are glad of every day that keeps us away from the emergency. The Finns go invisible in white clothing and on skis. By contrast, we are near incapable of action [*aktionsunfähig*]. The Russian war remains unpredictable and with it the return home. When will we see each other again? My longing for music is immense. Not a note of music for over 4 months, just the thunder of cannon and complaint.

8.11.41: ELMAR LIEB (2 PANZER ARMY, ARMY CENTER)[49]

In our current quarters, which even possesses electrical light—albeit somewhat dim, but which one can write by—I even found a playable grand piano and much-thumbed score book. After the first few beats, the motif seemed very familiar to me. I read the Cyrillic title more carefully: it was pieces by a German master: a prelude by Bach, a gavotte by Handel, sonatas or excerpts thereof by Mozart, Beethoven and Haydn.[50]

9.11.41: KURT MIETHKE (ARMY GROUP SOUTH)[51]

Our [POW] camp is getting fuller by the day. We were just about to clean our things when the alarm sounded and another 1,500 Russians arrived. They were figures of absolute misery. Our security is also taken care of, because we've now got several machine gun towers and woe betide anyone who acts up, because it hails blue beans. . . . Winter has started quite nicely here, because it snows every day. It is very unhealthy weather. But I always keep myself nice and warm and so we will survive it.

9.11.41: DR. HELMUT MACHEMER (1 PANZER ARMY, ARMY GROUP SOUTH)[52]

[To his children.] This letter will require a long time to reach you. Many Sundays will pass, because it has a very long journey to make. If Daddy was allowed to drive to you in a car he would have to drive for a week to be with you. That is how far Russia is from Stadtlohn. But Daddy is not allowed to leave here because not all the Russians have been killed or captured. But it surely will not be too much longer.

Here there are very many German soldiers and we have many cannons, tanks, and planes. When Daddy is again with you, he will tell you a lot and show many nice pictures and films. . . . You must be very well-behaved so that Daddy does not have to worry about you. You can be proud of your father because he is in the field, but Daddy also wants to be proud of you.[53]

10–12.11.41: HANS-HEINRICH LUDWIG (ARMY GROUP NORTH)[54]

Firing position in the evening, safely found the bunker, there on the road. The cold comes at night. Minus 35 degrees! Standing sentry almost drives you to despair, you don't know what to do with your feet. But our large bunker makes it all right, was evidently equipped with iron bedframes by Comrade Commissar. . . . Change of position at 3:00 a.m. at night under a starry sky. Deep snow. Many vehicle losses. Tanks slide off the road and freeze. We are done. There are constant slogans about relief, but it goes on. The mood is indescribably low. Russian bombers by day, no accommodation by night. Frozen bread, sausage and butter.

10.11.41: DR. HEINRICH HAAPE (6 INFANTRY DIVISION, NINTH ARMY, ARMY GROUP CENTER)[55]

Yesterday I wrote a postcard, which I sent with an *Oberleutnant* who was severely ill and transported by airplane. How much I would have liked to fly with him to be back at home, to have a few hours' peace. Since 22 June we have been nearly constantly at the enemy, constantly in battle, on the attack or on the defense. The holes in our lines torn by death or injury are deep!

Yes, it's possible to dream that you are in a happy, now almost strange atmosphere, in another world, but when the shells scream down or the Red tanks attack, then the music of our reality penetrates our ears. Then everyone silently does his duty. We are true to the oath that we gave to the *Führer*. We carry on.

How hard are the challenges of our time and how wonderful it would be to live in peace, but we do not want to think of that—the thought would make you go half crazy. Physically and mentally I am bearing up, in contrast to the many who are already physically and mentally coming apart from the strains.

There can be no thought of leave for the moment. The railways are so overburdened by the most varied requirements;[56] for the moment every man is needed here. I will certainly be spending Christmas in the distant East!

10.11.41: DR. HELMUT MACHEMER (1 PANZER ARMY, ARMY GROUP SOUTH)[57]

While we lie waiting in our quarters day after day and not knowing how we are to pass the time for boredom, we can imagine what a winter in Russia would look like. Meager quarters, in which one fights a running battle with vermin, in which one's comrades are penned in together with too few duties and too much free time, nothing to read, no radio. There's no main electricity and batteries are even rarer. Only here and there one of the pitiful captured Russian gramophones with rough Russian records, each worse than the next, making a noise—it can't be termed music—out of which only with much trouble and goodwill can a melody be discerned. Worse than our oldest gramophone models! You find mountains of records, dance music in the German and English style, probably copies, operetta music, and above all: always endless speeches by Stalin in dozens of record series. What's more, the Russian winter holds other surprises. We're expecting the cold and snow in the next few days.

And in spite of this we will also take all of this upon ourselves, if necessary, just as our fathers had to bear it. Nobody who has fought here in Russia can doubt that this war was necessary and unavoidable. And that it is being fought out here is a constant good fortune for our people [*unendliches Glück für unser Volk*]. We will gladly take the afflictions of this country upon ourselves, as the home country is preserved from the terrors of this war. There is only one opinion on this in the entire German Army.

10.11.41: *OBERGEFREITER* JOSEPH B. (2 PANZER DIVISION, 4 PANZER GROUP, ARMY GROUP CENTER)[58]

We haven't marched yet either. Weather and supplies. You can't do anything against higher powers. You just have to accept it. . . . It looks dreadful to the rear. The so-called automobile express highways or taxiways, hole after hole. You all might think, well, once our troops have reached the first highway, then it's forwards and then there'll finally be an end to it. But you can't speak of highways in our sense of them! Country tracks at home are better!

11.11.41: L. B. (EASTERN FRONT)[59]

One just cannot understand why we have not received winter things. If it goes on like this it will be Napoleonic and untold numbers will freeze. I think in 1812 they were better equipped than we are. Almost everyone has ruined socks and no ear muffs (only those who own them privately). This is the same in other units too. This is how little they provide for us! In the year 1941! (Not 1812!)

They can't know that at the top, or they would certainly take care of it. In the army, a portion will have to croak before anyone does even the most essential thing for the troops. The reality is after all rather different than the radio presentations on the billeting and provision of the troops. If I was not in the military and someone said something like that to me, I would flatly reply, I don't believe it. But [I've] seen and experienced [it] myself in 1941!

11.11.41: *UNTEROFFIZIER* WILHELM PRÜLLER (9 PANZER DIVISION, SECOND ARMY, ARMY GROUP CENTER)[60]

Unfortunately we still have to put up with some partisan stupidities—one dead, one wounded in our ranks. Although a house round the corner from us was mined, and it was forbidden to go into it, two of our people couldn't resist searching it. They climbed in through a window and got into one of the rooms through an open door. In there was a desk—the place had been the "House of the Red Army"—and one of the drawers was half open, so that you could see a little pistol inside. One of them opened the drawer, and the next moment there was a frightful explosion. A leg and an arm torn off, the other with light wounds: he could drag himself out. We couldn't save the one who was badly wounded, for in five minutes the house was in flames from attic to cellar. He burned in there. The engineers are busily clearing the whole city [Kursk] of mines, but of course they can't be everywhere at the same time.

11.11.41: KARL NÜNNIGHOFF (16 PANZER DIVISION, 1 PANZER ARMY, ARMY GROUP SOUTH)[61]

On 9 November, so the day before yesterday, the Russian pilots wanted to show that they were still there. Bombers and fighters flew over our positions in a quarter-hourly sequence and beat upon us with bombs and armaments. The consequence was that two of the bombers constantly attacking were shot down by our fighter planes, just in our area, who knows how many Russians went under the ground [*noch eine Etage tiefer mußten*]? The beasts frequently came over us, low-flying, and "strafed" us with their machine guns and aircraft cannon. In their excitement, because they were constantly being chased by our fighters, they all shot off target; we've now had to go through that often, we don't mind it much anymore, we've become as cold-blooded as anything now. . . .

You all know that I am happy to be out here, but I wouldn't want to come to Russia a second time, the conditions that prevail here are just unbelievable for a modern person. If anybody ever says it's nice in Russia, like in a paradise, I'll immediately declare them to be completely mad, because I know where it's nicer. This life here borders on utter drudgery [*Verblödung*], if we were here a few years, we'd be as dull-minded as a cow. If anyone in Germany ever claims things aren't good for him, then he ought to be sent to Russia; it can't be as miserable for anyone in Germany as it is for the people here in Russia.

11.11.41: *UNTEROFFIZIER* KARL R. (5 PANZER DIVISION, 4 PANZER GROUP, ARMY GROUP CENTER)[62]

It's pretty cold where we are now, around about 8 (degrees [centigrade]) cold during the day, snow on the ground as well, so a proper start to winter. It has been colder, so our panzer, which had sunk into the ground, is properly frozen to the spot and we couldn't move away under our own steam. We're increasingly having to reconcile ourselves to the idea that we'll have to spend the winter in R. We're just annoyed when we read in the newspapers from around mid-October, which we're now gradually getting, that the war here has been finally decided and no more resistance is possible, etc. The reality looks rather different.[63] Our 2nd Battalion was deployed these last few days in order to advance a bit farther on the taxiway. During this attack over 20 panzers were lost [*gingen flöten*]. And if we overwinter here and it starts all over again in spring, there's certainly very strong resistance to be expected again.

11.11.41: DR. KONRAD JARAUSCH (ARMY GROUP CENTER)[64]

We still have about 10,000 prisoners in our camp. . . . It's not easy to keep one's nerves with the stress. Every day we see the same thing: the same sallow, haggard faces, the same rags, especially for those hundreds of prisoners we find in the woods without papers and among whom the partisans try to hide themselves (most of them don't look like they're physically capable of any independent action). It's pleasing to see our policemen, their stomachs almost filled, march off singing a lovely Russian marching song. They sing much better and with more feeling [than we do]. Their songs aren't like the brutal rhythmic yelling of our marching songs. And their singing creates a sense of freedom. One can forget the barbed wire for a while. Otherwise, it seems that every new group [of prisoners] is more miserable and haggard than the previous one. The first Russian prisoners I saw were still glowing with the tension of battle as well as with the ravenousness of days of hunger. Now exhaustion and weakness show on every face. It's understandable that the mortality rates are on the rise in the camps in the West.[65]

12.11.41: *WACHTMEISTER* JOSEF L. (129 INFANTRY DIVISION, ARMY GROUP CENTER)[66]

Last night there was no sleep for us. The Russian is trying to break through our positions using well-prepared artillery fire. . . . We stood by the artillery the entire night and sent our salvos over at the right moment. Wonderful fireworks lit up over the snow-covered ground for hours until morning dawned. The temperatures are more than 15 [degrees Celsius] below zero. Cutting wind penetrates all our limbs. The earth is covered with around 5 cm of snow. As long as you're moving, you don't mind the extreme cold, but if you have to stand or sit still for hours, like we have had to do at the telescope frequently in recent days, that's something quite different. Great care is necessary to ensure that ears, nose, chin, and feet don't freeze. You will have found out that Kalinin is situated about 160 km northwest of Moscow. Our advanced position reaches like a nose into the enemy territory. A significant railway hub is thus in German hands, and it's easy to understand that the Russian is trying with all available means and force to bring this strategically important spot back into his own hands.

We have been here since 22 October and have been holding this important position successfully with relatively weak forces.

12.11.41: *GEFREITER* HANS JOACHIM C. (23 INFANTRY DIVISION, SECOND ARMY, ARMY GROUP CENTER)[67]

The day after tomorrow we will load up onto wide-gauge goods wagons and be moved just beyond Viaz'ma. From there it should only be a day's march to the front. I can't imagine that we'll live in trenches there, because it's bitterly cold now. But it has to be, because the Russian is still very active around Moscow. Apparently, [the Russian] still has around 80 airfields in the surrounding area. So what lies ahead of us is immense [*unermesslich*]. That's when one sings the praises of this dark shack here, in which 200 people will soon live in a space of 250 square meters. At least it's more or less warm. . . . The wretched Russian prisoners, who do not dare to believe in anything anymore, simply lie down outside in the nighttime cold so that they won't wake up the following morning.

13.11.41: H. D. (16 PANZER DIVISION, 1 PANZER ARMY, ARMY GROUP SOUTH)[68]

I'm still well. I've moved a bit farther on with my lot. But I've managed to get some pretty good accommodation. These little people have a little girl of 2 years old, a really very attractive, charming child (or it would be, if it was washed a couple of times every day and dressed according to our standards). The little worm [*Das kleine Würmchen*] just runs around barefoot on the tamped mud floor, and yet since yesterday it has been so cold outside that everything crackles. But she evidently feels fine.

We've already shown the people here photographs of home with houses and "dressed" people; they look at these pictures like things from another world. Earlier, I showed the mother of the little child your picture and she went quite quiet with awe. . . .

Do you think, darling, that you can imagine the conditions under which the people here live? Listen up! You're standing at the front door to my place. First, you come into the outer room: inventory = two cows, 1 calf, 1 sheep, 1 piglet, 1 breeding sow with 4 babies, 15 chickens, and all sorts of greens and turnips all higgledy piggledy in the smallest space. And inside there are also a couple of boxes, in 1 corner a pile of fuel for the fire reaching up to the ceiling = dried cow dung mixed with straw. So when you enter my "hall" you have to wend your way carefully between cow's tails, etc. Care has to be taken in the dark in particular, because otherwise you step on the piglet's or the sheep's toes or elsewhere you land on something "soft." As you can see, despite the war and marching, I haven't lost my connection to the "country." But would you believe, coming through the stable into the dwelling, that's as normal here as electrical light is at home.

13.11.41: ALFONS HAAS (EASTERN FRONT)[69]

Dear Brother! . . .

The feelings that you may have when you go to the front I know very well. I have set off many times and a special guardian angel was always with me. . . . True, life at war is hard, often very bitterly hard. But for us of course the suffering has a purpose. Furthermore, you even said to me once: "What doesn't kill you makes you stronger!" So come back after the war, spiritually young and very strong!

13.11.41: DR. HELMUT MACHEMER (1 PANZER ARMY, ARMY GROUP SOUTH)[70]

Winter has broken. We can say broken, because it got icily cold overnight here. Right on time, as predicted—the *Volksdeutsche* [ethnic Germans] told us: between 12 and 15 November. It cleared up around evening and got so cold that the mud froze. . . . The thermometer is showing -17 degrees. Such sudden temperature changes make you feel the cold twice as keenly. We are now busy getting our winter things in order. Unfortunately, I don't have any woolen underclothing and only thin shirts.

Who would've thought there'd be war right into winter? . . . Well, we provide for ourselves as best we can, and anything that's missing we requisition. Some of our comrades can hardly be told apart from Russians: fur hat, Russian quilted coats, overpants and felt boots.[71]

14.11.41: DR. KONRAD JARAUSCH (ARMY GROUP CENTER)[72]

The dull dying around us is just so terrible. I often ask myself what would have happened to me if I had been sent to the front. Our days are somewhat quieter now. The cement factory is housing a little more than 2,000 prisoners. This camp is to be closed completely on Sunday. But twenty-five prisoners die there daily. In the larger camps farther west, in which tens of thousands are being held, the numbers of the dead are correspondingly in the hundreds. One tries to help. When they come to get their food and are frozen stiff from the cold (it's twelve below today and yesterday it was fifteen below during the day) they stagger, fall over, and expire right at our feet. We discovered another case of cannibalism today. Yet the corpses, when they are carried without clothes to the graves, are scrawny like late gothic figures of Christ, frozen stiff. The soldiers look somewhat better because they have their uniforms. There are civilians among the prisoners, many who are just in shirtsleeves—especially the Jews. It would really be the most merciful thing if they would be taken out into the forest and bumped off, as the experts put it.[73] But the whole thing is already more murder than war.

15.11.41: DR. HELMUT MACHEMER (1 PANZER ARMY, ARMY GROUP SOUTH)[74]

[While out on patrol a German *Sonderführer* met a group of Russians.] At a road crossing he met a squad of 20 Russian soldiers led by a noncommissioned officer. Both were equally as surprised by the encounter as the other. He got out—note: in German uniform—[and] approached the Russian officer and asked in Russian: "Where are you going, then?"

The man answered: "The devil knows, I'm looking for the front!" "Then you need to go that way!" he called over, got into his car and drove on. The still fully armed Russians set off in the opposite direction. A strange war! [*Ein merkwürdiger Krieg!*] Truly, most of the time you don't know what's up and what's down.[75]

16.11.41: ANTON BÖHRER (294 INFANTRY DIVISION, SIXTH ARMY, ARMY GROUP SOUTH)[76]

Our mail does now seem to be trickling in, because everything has frozen and now the trucks can drive unhindered across the normally terrible mire. One part of the mail seems still to be missing. . . . In general, morale is excellent again. Thanks to the late arrival of the mail some young fathers are often finding out about the arrival of a boy or a daughter rather late, but the happiness is now all the greater. . . .

Otherwise, we're now very busy with the maintenance of our "war material." There's work galore and you wouldn't believe that one could repair everything so well. . . .

Now and then yet another building goes up because somebody set mines in it, but then a number of Jews or other riffraff [*oder sonstiges Gesindel*] are hanged for it. It's the only punishment that has any effect here anymore. You have to be ruthlessly strict and trust nobody, no matter how nice-looking a person. You are in enemy territory, which, after all, we have conquered and not the Russians. There's work going on again in some factories and it's a good thing if the rabble disappears from the street. . . .

On 9 November the *Führer* made another big speech that the English at any rate won't be able to believe their ears and eyes in the coming years when we appear with our special weapons. The Americans can't deliver much more to the Russians, either, because over time all the harbors have frozen over. We've taken iron and coal as well as aluminum from the Russians and now it ought to be difficult for them to manufacture things.[77]

16.11.41: JOHANNES HAMM (1 PANZER ARMY, ARMY GROUP SOUTH)[78]

The day before yesterday I had guard duty on a lighthouse on the sea [of Asov]. I was compensated for the barbaric cold on the platform with the magnificent starry sky over the freezing sea and the red sickle of the rising moon. Everything was quiet, just ground signals now and then in the distance, a few rifle shots from the outguards. Russian war ships, destroyers and gunboats, which now and then fire too short into the harbors, weren't to be seen and I could indulge my own thoughts. . . .

Before night had fallen I had drunk a lot of *Sekt* [sparkling white wine]. Yes, now you're surprised. My battery chief had captured this *Sekt* as loot from a raid. He went out for a ride with a motorboat outside the harbor, broke down, flagged down a passing steamboat by shooting his pistol and going aboard. There he found 28 drunken Bolsheviks who had *Sekt* and other good things on board. He directed the ship into the harbor and now the *Sekt* is being "discharged" [*gelöscht*] here. . . .

There'll be an attack tomorrow for sure, but we're not part of it. It's a certain comfort to me that we are part of an armored command here. Of course, I can't name names, I'm not even allowed to say the sea, the coast of which we are currently safeguarding, but it doesn't take much to guess its name.

How can we thank God that he has preserved Germany, that he has preserved all of you and everyone else at home from the horrors of the war and from these subhuman Bolsheviks [*bolschewistischen Untermenschen*]. Everything beautiful in Russia has died. I saw something beautiful just one single time. A bronze statue of Peter the Great, erected on the cliff coast at the Sea of Asov. The inscription on the marble baroque pedestal had been chipped away. Half to the right in front of it there was an old gun barrel and a pyramid of cannon balls, so he stood there and gazed, a bold conqueror, across the sea. Perhaps he annexed this part of Russia into his empire, perhaps he founded the harbor, I don't know.[79] But he doesn't stand in the middle of lovely grounds, but on a kind of village green, miserable fishing huts in the background. . . . This monument stood on a magnificently situated spot and was in itself very beautiful, but so that nobody should know who it was, the inscription had been removed. It was like that everywhere in Russia. Wherever you discovered traces of former beauty, everything was removed to leave nothing that identified it as from the times of the tsars.

17.11.41: *UNTEROFFIZIER* W. F. (251 INFANTRY DIVISION, NINTH ARMY, ARMY GROUP CENTER)[80]

Our front here has become fixed. At least it seems so. We'll likely have to spend the winter here. Now and then the Russian artillery forces us into our foxholes. Otherwise we live in louse-ridden Russian shacks. We can't stand it outside any longer. We had minus 20 degrees at 11.00 in the morning today. Standing in a foxhole in this weather is not particularly fun. I don't know how the thing is going to continue. Here the general opinion is that it'll be onward to the Urals next spring. They probably don't want to leave things half done. Complete destruction is necessary simply in order to give the wretched Russian people better living conditions. Nobody who hasn't seen it can picture it at all.

17.11.41: WERNER BEERMANN (NINTH ARMY, ARMY GROUP CENTER)[81]

Yesterday evening I . . . arrived in Kalinin on the Volga. There was still fighting at the edge of the city. The city has only been fully in German hands for a few days; three times the Russians had pushed back in again, and then had to be thrown back in tough street fighting. Now Stalin will just have to accept the loss of the city. K. is a large city of nearly 300,000 inhabitants who have almost all remained in the city. You can see traces of the battles everywhere, especially in the industrial areas.

The general opinion is that our division has done enough and is among those divisions that will soon, or around spring, go back to Germany for resting. But of course all kinds of rumors and gossip make the rounds in the military, few of which turn out to be true. But for the moment we're all hoping for it. Just a few weeks and then even the severity of the Russian winter will force the operations to stop, unless the Russian capitulates beforehand.

18.11.41: *UNTEROFFIZIER* WILHELM PRÜLLER (9 PANZER DIVISION, SECOND ARMY, ARMY GROUP CENTER)[82]

At 1400 our C.O. was ordered to report to the regimental aide-de-camp. I thought he was going to get the German Cross in Gold, or was ordered there for some other reason. I thought of innumerable possibilities, but neither I nor anyone else guessed the right one. We almost fell over. We innocent angels thought we had in front of us some pleasant weeks which we would spend next to nice warm stoves; we hadn't a clue what our superiors had in store for us. All those dire prophecies had something to them. Now they've caught up with us: we are to advance in the direction of Voronezh [130 miles east of Kursk]! But now comes the most interesting part: we are to *on foot!* We've become infantry! How fatuous!

I don't get angry, though. An old soldier's proverb says: "Don't be angry; just marvel." And all you can do the whole time you serve is to marvel. So I laughed, and laughed heartily, out of malicious joy at my own misfortune.

18.11.41: *UNTEROFFIZIER* ROBERT RUPP (17 PANZER DIVISION, 2 PANZER ARMY, ARMY GROUP CENTER)[83]

Very rarely have I cried. Crying is a way out as long as one is in the midst of things. Only once I am back with you all, resting and overcoming things, will we have to cry a lot and then you will understand your husband. Here, crying at even the saddest scenes makes no sense, and "sympathy" is cruel when it substitutes for aid and action. The sense of human poverty and human guilt, which is rooted in everyone, grows. A deep shame is growing. Sometimes I am even ashamed that I am loved. You understand that, don't you, Maria. There are such poor people that you can only be ashamed of your wealth. . . . You know it because you live it, too. It's not possible to describe it better. O, things are happening in the world!

18.11.41: *GEFREITER* HANS ROTH (299 INFANTRY DIVISION, SIXTH ARMY, ARMY GROUP SOUTH)[84]

Lebedyn, by Russian standards, is a pretty country town and paradise for us after the lice-infested *Panje* huts of Krawino. The Soviets have erected here large, administrative buildings; on the outskirts of the town are airfields and barracks. Nothing but Potemkin villages![85] From afar they are imposing, with their whitewashed chalk facades. But what a great disappointment when you're standing right in front of them, or when you even enter them. Meter-long cracks in the ceiling and walls, doors that hang crooked on their hinges, which neither open nor close; staircases that are bent out of shape, swollen window frames, and uneven floors are the least of the problems, all of which astonish us.

None of the buildings is older than five or six years. One thing strikes me here again: nowhere in this workers' paradise have we encountered an electrical line under the stucco ceiling! The wiring is always done in the form of a twisted extension cord along the wall and the ceiling. They are not even familiar with insulated lead pipes, which are mandatory in our country. It is always the same; even in the cities we find shocking primitivism and poverty. . . .

Immediately within the first few days, a militia was formed of trustworthy Ukrainians who have proven themselves to be faithful and brave comrades during these crucial hours over the upcoming weeks.

A partisan group of 2,000 men has been reported. We deploy our men and encounter initial exchanges with these well-armed gangs. They possess machine guns, mortars, PAKs, and even infantry weapons. As these *Schweine* are beginning to seriously threaten Lebedyn, we acquire reinforcements from Achtyrka. At one point, we even have to flee, leaving our dead and injured men behind, whom we later find mutilated like animals. In the town itself, insecurity is mounting. A petty officer is mugged; the culprit is hanged from the gallows on the very same day. The next evening I was attacked by two thugs. It was pitch dark out, and they were both able to escape into the labyrinth of housing nearby. One of them must have been badly injured, for during our sweep of the area the next morning we noticed traces of blood all over the place. Nevertheless, we have not been able to apprehend the perpetrators.

During the afternoon, ten hostages were shot dead. We are now acting with an iron fist; the gallows in the town square is always busy. Executions are the daily norm. It has to be this way.

19.11.41: ANONYMOUS (EASTERN FRONT)[86]

Why do the Russians fight to utter destruction, we ask ourselves. Why are there so many martyrs for the Bolshevik idea among them, which exerts such enormous power?

There is something diabolical about it. Why do thousands allow themselves to be driven to their death as if they were going to a feast? Why do neither humanity nor culture nor social justice exist here? Questions elicit no satisfactory answer. These facts just have to be accepted as given, we can't change anything about it. We can research into the causes as for every history event, why this had to happen, we don't know.

19.11.41: *OBERSTLEUTNANT* HELLMUTH STIEFF (FOURTH ARMY, ARMY GROUP CENTER)[87]

Our winter clothing is only trickling in—a few gloves, woolen vests, and hats. God knows when the rest will come! The supply situation should have been resolved weeks ago. It is an extraordinary mess, and we are supposed to be "the best armed forces in the world." At the same time, the other clothing, especially boots and pants, are so tattered that some people are walking around in just lace-up shoes and putting on overalls [*Drillichhosen*] over the other rags so that they have some protection. . . .[88] One's heart nigh-on bleeds when you see, by contrast, the impeccable winter equipment of the Russian Far Eastern divisions now coming, fresh, into battle with us (fur hats, quilted coats and pants, high-shafted felt boots). But we just make sure to help ourselves and take the felt boots that are standard here and quilted items of clothing away from the *Panjes* for our people. Better that the [local] population starves and freezes than us.[89] One becomes dreadfully brutish, for a good 95% of the population is decent and trusting. But for us this is about our bare survival. A large part of our troops, in battle now for 5 months, are simply at the end of their physical strength. The majority of officers and noncommissioned officers have fallen or been wounded. As a result, we have units who simply run away at the first appearance of a Russian tank. You can't yourself rely on active divisions anymore! . . .

I don't have any reserves anymore, replacements won't get through before spring. . . . Our only salvation is snow, soon and lots of it, so that the larger battle operations stop completely and our units can get some rest. Otherwise there'll be a catastrophe here. . . .

The rail restrictions have nothing to do with us, just the woeful state of the railroad at home. . . . But the railroads are still adequate enough to send a train full of Jews from the Reich to Minsk every two days and then deliver them to their fate there [*und sie dann dort ihrem Schicksal preiszugeben*]. That is unworthy of a supposed cultural nation, just like the Jewish star in Berlin, which I saw there in September! There will be a revenge taken upon us for all this in time—and rightly! It is brazen, for the sake of a few scoundrels [*Halunken*] such a good people is being driven to misfortune.

19.11.41: ERICH DOHL (SIXTEENTH ARMY, ARMY GROUP NORTH)[90]

The Russian air force is still very strong. Yesterday and today as well another one was shot down by our battery. Whether we'll be credited with the machines is a different thing. There's too much antiaircraft artillery around here. There's such a banging and crashing during an assault that you'd think hell has broken loose. But they don't seem to be coming quite as frequently now. Nevertheless, the Russians are bold pilots, too. They'll fly over our heads, barely 20 m up, and shooting with everything they've got. But they hit just as little as we do. A good thing, too, because otherwise things would be going pretty badly for us. Hopefully the whole war will come to an end soon. It'll be unbearable in the long run.

20.11.41: *WACHTMEISTER* ARTUR W. (129 INFANTRY DIVISION, NINTH ARMY, ARMY GROUP CENTER)[91]

After all sorts of possible and impossible rumors, we've now landed up in Kalinin after all. Firing position in a large cabbage field. . . . We don't need to fire yet, it's become very quiet after the last attack. However, the planes visit us a few times every day. As usual, in quiet positions you have twice as much work. [Lt.] Wittmer [orders us to] dig the guns into the ground right up to the barrel, sort out the camouflage. . . . Apparently, we are to spend the winter here. It's just sad that you can't even ferret out a potato in this city anymore. What I have seen today I never thought possible. The civilians were hacking pieces of flesh out of old horse cadavers with axes. They queue in front of the division butcher for the scraps like guts, tripe [*Pansen*], etc. They'll do any work for a piece of bread. So far we have been in villages, you didn't see anything like that there. There was just one wish there: get out of this misery.

Latest rumor: Vacation from 1 December. The train goes to Staritza, 70 km from here. Our chief has had a nervous collapse and will likely also leave soon.

20.11.41: DR. KONRAD JARAUSCH (ARMY GROUP CENTER)[92]

The past few weeks at the end of last month and the beginning of this one belong to the most difficult ones of my life. There is infinite suffering here among the prisoners, and it wears one down and makes one weak. Now there's quiet at least outside. Most [everyone] has been sent farther west. And we're too far back for the battles that are now raging. We'll probably remain here with a few thousand prisoners who will keep the streets and the rail lines free of snow. . . . Given the smaller number of prisoners it's also possible to have somewhat more humane conditions.

21.11.41: *OBERGEFREITER* FRITZ N. (35 INFANTRY DIVISION, NINTH ARMY, ARMY GROUP CENTER)[93]

Our thoughts always drift homeward. We often sit there for minutes without one or the other of us saying a word, it's like that for everyone. The war in the East is just lasting too long for us. Since 22 June there have been very few rest days allowed us. Don't understand my letter as a complaint or moaning, you know that I don't do that, and if others aren't happy with it, I'm still content with it for a while. But at the moment the newspapers from 15–25 October are reaching us and we're repeatedly having to read that the war is nearly over and it's all being downplayed. All the while, in recent days we've had to take part in battles that do not pale in comparison with Smolensk. Yes, the war in the East is decided and Bolshevism is as good as beaten, but even so it still isn't completely finished. But we don't break our heads over all these questions, war is war and we will fight until total victory is achieved [*bis uns der totale Sieg winkt*]. We're just not particularly happy about the time. All too often we sit together in the evenings and talk about later, what it will be like then.

In the evening here it's already nighttime at 4 o'clock. Outside it's always very cold and so we've got too much time during the long winter evenings to think about such things. Sometimes we don't know what to do and playing cards doesn't keep you content in the long run, and so we inevitably end up talking about things that are otherwise never touched upon. Everyone has undergone a very big change thanks to this war, I can feel it in me. For example, I can't be as cheerful and cocky in my letters like before. We sense that life, due to the fact that we have, as it were, repeatedly rescued it, has become much more valuable to us than it was before. . . . As a result of the miserable living conditions, for our part, too, you come to recognize what life means and what purpose it has. Anyone who doesn't pass unheeding past the milestones of this war in Russia will draw many a sober lesson and truly recognize the value of a normal life, which is really only made up of small things.

21.11.41: DR. HELMUT MACHEMER (1 PANZER ARMY, ARMY GROUP SOUTH)[94]

War tactics are not only familiar with the advance and the attack; evasion and withdrawal are also important tools and, correctly carried out, require just as much skill and luck. They are even partly decisive for success. However, the German soldier finds this art unattractive, at least. It is unknown to us so far. But today we became familiar with it for the first time. . . .[95]

Can we rely on our people? We have now spent several nights outdoors, are tired and frozen through with this icy cold. Will they hold their nerve? And what can we do against heavy tanks? Hope that they don't come!

21.11.41: *UNTEROFFIZIER* E. K. (98 INFANTRY DIVISION, FOURTH ARMY, ARMY GROUP CENTER)[96]

We are currently located in a defensive position around 80 kilometers north of Moscow. I am writing this letter in a foxhole, which is particularly unpleasant now in winter. My feet are already half frozen. We few remaining soldiers of our division crave so badly the forlorn hope of replacement. On 26 October there were still 20 men in our company. Since almost as few are left in every regiment of our division, one battalion in every regiment has been dissolved. So now each regiment has two battalions and every battalion has two rifle companies, 65 men strong.

22.11.41: HELLMUTH H. (50 INFANTRY DIVISION, ELEVENTH ARMY, ARMY GROUP SOUTH)[97]

1. Several details tell us how hard the fighting is at the entrance to the Crimea: Our Stukas have been blowing long, narrow rows of bomb craters into the enemy-free foothills ahead of the Tatar Ditch to create cover in the coverless terrain for the advance of our own infantry.

   The Russian planes didn't just drop bombs, but also artillery ammunition, indeed even scrap, pieces of iron, chains, etc.

2. 5 men, on the way from the hospital to the front, made a fire during the cold days of last week at a rest point by the railroad embankment not far from here; unfortunately right on top of a mine. Result: 2 dead, 3 casualties. And so the enemy is still fighting in the hinterlands.

3. In this area at the same time, a train with 2,000 prisoners and an 8-man guard got stuck for several days. Starving, the Russians scratched the potatoes from the frozen ground and collected the grains from the cornricks. Even so, every day a number of them died from exhaustion and cold. Not easy days for those 8 men. So the Russian winter effects the Russians themselves.

4. 2–3 km away from the house, in the vast steppe, the [former] battlefield begins, lying there strangely dormant and untouched for a month. The [dead] Russians lie with their guns and weapons, in foxholes, in positions or on the surface, just as death mowed them down, disfigured and changed, just as the cool season alters the dead. Neither friend nor foe has time for burial, as everyone has to prepare for winter! . . .

5. In the adjoining room a Russian lies with an infected lung shot. Yesterday night I heard him through the wall, continually calling with Slavic lack of restraint [*slawischer Hemmungslosigkeit*]: *w domi, w domi!* Home, home! It's the instinct of the suffering creature, the longing of the human being wounded in body or soul, here, there, and everywhere. *W domi*, home!

6. When one company had taken numerous prisoners, the company chief ordered an outstanding noncommissioned officer, without any good reason, to shoot one of the prisoners. The noncom refused, replying that he was a soldier not an executioner. At that, the company chief shot the prisoner himself. 2 days later he fell. Can the ordinary man's sense of right be blamed when he tries to find a higher justice in these events? . . .

Not all too long ago, a general visited a field hospital, greeted each casualty individually, and said at the end: "Now I have something that will make you all very happy; each of you will receive from me the Iron Cross II!" and placed one on each of their beds. Among the casualties, however, was a man from the reserves whose foot had been run over by a car. He didn't dare say anything, but when he returned to the company he turned in the Iron Cross [saying] he didn't want to make himself ridiculous. How many others would have preferred to accept the curse of being ridiculous!

23.11.41: EDGAR STEUERWALD (ARMY GROUP SOUTH)[98]

I can't imagine how the Russians are keeping their heads above water. In my view, the Russians must die of starvation sooner or later because the food situation is so bad.[99] And now it's extremely cold here. On average -16 degrees [to] -20 degrees cold. Hopefully we'll soon get to another region.

23.11.41: FRANZ SIEBELER (14 PANZER DIVISION, 1 PANZER ARMY, ARMY GROUP SOUTH)[100]

One day passes just like another in this joyless isolation. One day is as relentless as the next! For us in the last few days there was at least the happy news that Rostov, bitterly fought over, has fallen.[101] With that, we have broken the final railroad link between the Caucasus and central Russia. What is still very important is the following fact: The two bridges over the Don, several kilometers long, have fallen undamaged into our hands. . . . Our lot is also now out of the city, as we've been deployed somewhere else.

That's just what's so varied about the soldier's life. Here today—tomorrow there. But one thing is always the same: miserable shacks and indescribable poverty. Repeatedly, one word springs to my mind: Workers' Paradise! Never in humanity has that word been such a deception. May all our wars so far be whatever they want, just or unjust, may they be the machinations of diplomats, one thing is certain: this war against the criminal work of Bolshevism is the struggle for a just cause. . . .

In one month now it'll be Christmas. Christmas, celebration of peace! But humans know nothing about peace, there is only war in every [written] line. Where will we celebrate it this year?

23.11.41: HEINZ RAHE (13 PANZER DIVISION, 1 PANZER ARMY, ARMY GROUP SOUTH)[102]

The military and political tasks, with which our nation finds itself faced, are great. May God grant that they do not overextend the energies of our nation. The successes at Tula and by the Volga, as well as the capture of Rostov, allow us to hope for a favorable continuation of operations before the heavy snowfall despite the vigorous resistance of the Russians. Without question, the winter will present quite enough special tasks. For some time now, the picture that the political New Order in the East is to bring about is taking clearer shape. Ever since the establishment of the Reich Commissariat *Ostland* and Ukraine there can be no more doubt that we consider large parts of the conquered regions to be colonies. I hoped so for "*Ostland*," feared it for the Ukraine.[103] It opens a whole new period of history for our nation; the Bismarckian nation-state will become a European imperium with Czechs, Poles, Ukrainians, and Baltic [Germans], who will initially maintain the balance with our nation, but thanks to their rapid growth will soon far outstrip ours. That is the principal danger I see, which may place all the successes of today into doubt within just one generation. . . . When one considers that, then one asks oneself if the current successes will not exceed our energies after all and whether, after 1–2 generations, we will have to begin the retreat. Then today's successes would be a pyrrhic victory.

24.11.41: KLAUS BECKER (ARMY GROUP CENTER)[104]

It looks like I'll be writing to you from this position for the last time. Because tomorrow it's all go again. Of course, we regret it very much, we're unlikely to have it as good again as we've had it here for the last 10 days. But even Lisa, our host [*Quartierwirtin*], regrets our leaving. For a start, she found it quite entertaining with us and it seems to have helped her get over sad thoughts; because her husband and her eldest son are soldiers and her daughter is sitting in Moscow. Her liking for us also had a pragmatic basis, though. As long as we are in the building, no other soldiers will come who will take away the pigs and sheep that she has in the stable. . . . When the soldiers are hungry, of course they take the very last animals away from the population. . . . Because the population will cop it first before the troops starve. The Russians are like children in their feelings. Lisa frequently cries when she thinks of her family members; she is especially worried about her daughter, because naturally she knows that Moscow is being heavily attacked by our *Luftwaffe*. Then she seeks reassurance from Müller, who points out to her that our planes are only attacking military targets.[105] And soon she's laughing again and wanting to drink tea with me. But it's only heated water, as there's no tea. Of course I am happy to pass up the brew, make a few jokes that she doesn't understand and she responds in a way equally incomprehensible to me. . . . But it's off in the direction of Moscow—Volokolamsk—Klin, all big places that are marked on the big map of Russia. So we're entering the region north of Moscow. Whether we're then to go farther eastward and take part in the encircling of Moscow in that way, of course we don't know. . . .

I don't need to tell you how much I would like to be at home and how much I miss the Christmas joy of home. It will be very difficult for us, particularly over the festive days, having to be here in vast Russia and many a melancholy hour awaits us when the days are getting ever shorter and the dark time of the day gets so much longer. But we can cope with it much easier in a group of comrades.

24.11.41: ERICH DOHL (SIXTEENTH ARMY, ARMY GROUP NORTH)[106]

Evening has fallen, the hour for writing has come. . . . How awful it must be for those who cannot read or write. My dear, don't say something like that hardly exists anymore. We recently received a new lot of soldiers from Upper Silesia, none of whom can write.[107] There's one here at the gun as well. Comrades write this poor devil's letters for him. He says his wife can read and write. Now just imagine how he gets teased when a letter comes from home and there are a few intimate things in it. I do hope that it doesn't get too bad, but it must be dreadfully awkward. . . .

A bitter battle is still raging around Tikhvin. Russian 52-ton tanks are already rolling out into the town, so we are told. . . . Hopefully they won't send us out to the front for the final battle on top of all that. With our 20mm we can't do anything against tanks at all. We are just far too cumbersome. Thank God, though, reinforcements are coming forward every day. It's a bad sector here in Tikhvin. There's still shooting everywhere, right and left and forward. Planes were here again today. We are right happy about it because if it gets any quieter here they'll soon send us forward. So you always have to balance one evil with another. . . .

But the war will have to end sometime. Our successes must be very great around Moscow. However, there's nothing to see of success around us. But new troops are advancing. If they don't arrive soon we'll have to pull back.

Now, how is it with you all, my darling? Hopefully, you are all still healthy and happy for me. Do the English still come frequently? They must be in Kassel very frequently, according to what someone from Kassel told me yesterday evening. I'd be happy if I knew you were out of danger in this regard. But the dear Lord will surely protect you all. Nevertheless, every alarm costs nerves [*Allerdings kostet jeder Alarm Nerven*]. You, my darling, and above all things the children will certainly be suffering from it, if you are being torn from sleep so often. I can still remember the last war very well, even though I was such a little chap still. Back then the airplane visits were quite harmless compared to today. It really would be a welcome thing if it would all finally decide to end.

24.11.41: *OBERSTLEUTNANT* HELLMUTH STIEFF (FOURTH ARMY, ARMY GROUP CENTER)[108]

For I lost any enjoyment of my job long ago. . . . I do my duty without any passion! . . . I feel forced, not at all willing or even happy, to be a tool of a despotic will to destruction, which ignores all rules of humanity and of the simplest decency. . . . I have become so immeasurably bitter! None of that changes even if the situation has currently relaxed and we were able to carry out a successful attack to the north wing. . . . Even so, we have had the "pleasure" of a war against God and the entire world thanks to a madman! I don't wish to speak of it any longer!

24.11.41: DR. HELMUT MACHEMER (1 PANZER ARMY, ARMY GROUP SOUTH)[109]

This here wasn't a matter of a local push, but rather a large-scale offensive by the Russians that stretched across the entire sector. . . . The aim is nothing less than to free Rostov, which has just been captured, and to cut off all parts of the German Army positioned in these regions. . . .

It was important to continue defending the town until the engineers' work was done. That was a sad task. The entire town, principally comprising thatched buildings, was set on fire. Already in the evening the flames were leaping from the buildings at the edge of the town and lit up the road for us for kilometers. Now it was just a single sea of flames. The smoke stood in dense plumes over the area. A building like that burned down in a few minutes. What wouldn't burn was blown up, other buildings were set with mines so that they would blow to pieces as soon as somebody set foot in them. . . .

No question, the war is now showing its brutal face. It is strategically important for us that this place doesn't become an assembly point for enemy troops. . . . But for the population this measure is unprecedentedly cruel. . . . We have no sympathy for the Russians, but this scene of misery did touch our hearts. But as a soldier you have to be hard.[110]

25.11.41: ALOIS DWENGER (ELEVENTH ARMY, ARMY GROUP SOUTH)[111]

We recently arrived in an entirely enclosed Tartar village for the first time; before then we had only passed by small, scattered settlements. The men are tall, well built, and evidently also intellectually able, their faces are frequently oval, hair and beards very dark, heavy Russian influences in their clothing. The women are handsome, with smooth, dark hair usually parted in the center, with large, shining, dark eyes like Turkish women. But we also see faces with typical Mongol features, with prominent cheekbones and slit eyes. We were given a vivid reminder of the Mongol period some little time ago when we came past the tomb of an ancient Mongolian king, which was supposed to date from the time of the conquest of the Crimea by the nephew of the great Genghis Khan Temüjin and was therefore thought to be 700 years old.

The misery in the villages with their colorful mix of peoples, of Russians, Ukrainians, Tartars, Greeks, and Bulgarians, especially when the battle rages through, is frequently terrible. Many of the buildings are in flames, on the streets are dead or wounded women and children, who can sometimes only be taken care of after days. Always the same scenes: the troops approach with their advanced lines and despite the firing the inhabitants are busy plundering the *kolkhoz* storehouses, which had until then been guarded by some *Politruks* or other. So only rarely is there any success in obtaining any comestible booty. How often have we had the experience of following hard on the heels of the enemy only to find the inhabitants drunkenly staggering to meet us.

25.11.41: *OBERLEUTNANT* AUGUST D. (131 INFANTRY DIVISION, FOURTH ARMY, ARMY GROUP CENTER)[112]

We're currently positioned south of Alexin. We will attack the town in the coming days. Everywhere, everything is moving forward at a pace so we are in good spirits and hopeful. When the encirclement of Moscow is finished then that will finally be an end to it. We are currently fighting against well-trained and equipped Siberian troops who, like all Russians, fight extraordinarily bravely [*ausserordentlich tapfer kämpfen*]. Unfortunately, the newspapers don't acknowledge that. Unfortunately, in this great cold, the war is very difficult, with many losses. We have companies that are already on their ninth [company] leader. In my old regiment 18 out of 43 officers have fallen.

25.11.41: RUDOLF OEHUS (ARMY GROUP SOUTH)[113]

Dear parents, nobody thought at the start of the war in Russia that we would still be here over the winter, since everybody believed it would all pass quickly, but the Russian just has too much material and human power, we should thank God if it's all over next year. We live blindly during this time in this war, don't hear any news and receive no information at all about what is going on at the front and anything else that is happening. Well, just let them, they won't be able to keep the final victory quiet from us.

26.11.41: *OBERGEFREITER* JOSEPH B. (2 PANZER DIVISION, 4 PANZER GROUP, ARMY GROUP CENTER)[114]

We have also already put on our "winter dress." Not warm pieces of clothing, but our vehicles have come into contact with white paint. Meanwhile, there's been good progress and there have been new experiences, even if they can't touch those of 20 November. We were supposed to shoot up a tank platoon. But our panzers finished them off. They are really "on the ball" [*auf Draht*]. I recently saw how they shot up three Russians. They burned immediately. And one of them carried on driving, right straight over an antitank gun. Yesterday they shot up English tanks here, constructed in 1941.[115]

Apart from artillery, the airplanes on the Russian side are very active. . . . The gloomy days are the most propitious for the Russian pilots. Our fighters and our antiaircraft can't do much then. But then they stick it to them all the more when the weather is clear. Yesterday, even the heavy transport machines (Ju 52) were deployed here as bombers.

26.11.41: FRITZ (ARMY GROUP CENTER)[116]

The day before yesterday I took part in an attack on two villages, like it was 1870. We stormed it at double quick time, I covered the next place from a standing position and then it all gets stuck in. The Russian is defending himself with a new automatic gun, the remaining tanks, and light artillery. Until yesterday that made us the soldiers who were closest to Moscow. Yesterday panzers arrived as well and of course they've taken our place in that race. . . . When we fall in again we'll have to creep farther through the forest until just outside Moscow. But then we'll have reached it.

We have also captured enough good Russian winter clothing. A very special kind of warfare has developed here. Heavy weapons can only [come] later. . . . All machines on *panje* carts and sleds.

26.11.41: ERICH DOHL (SIXTEENTH ARMY, ARMY GROUP NORTH)[117]

There's another icy wind blowing here. The thermometer must be sliding down to -20° [centigrade] again. The cold seems to be setting in again. So long as we're not changing position that's not so bad. It is lovely and warm in our bunker. We've even let the fire go out. In the evening you can't sleep for heat. But then it is bitterly cold in the early morning. Well, thank God, Russia isn't lacking in firewood. . . . I don't think there is a single person here who isn't sick of the war and in particular of Russia.

27.11.41: SIEGBERT STEHMANN (163 INFANTRY DIVISION, GERMAN ARMY OF NORWAY)[118]

The general says he knows it all and even understands the difficulties with leave, mail, provisioning, but can't change anything about it. And as long as we can sit here in a warm dugout, busy with nothing other than night duty at the machine gun, we still feel exceptionally good, not least because we've now received fur hats, fur jackets, and white snow coats. And it's not cold at all. Just a few degrees below zero with a moderate wind.

27.11.41: DR. HEINRICH HAAPE (6 INFANTRY DIVISION, NINTH ARMY, ARMY GROUP CENTER)[119]

Something very special, happy, has suddenly entered into my soldier's life, which I would not have thought was even a possibility in recent times, what with the difficult enemy situation and the operations of our troops. Even though we are still in battle, I have been permitted, as the first medical officer of the regiment, to take leave, and I hope to be able to start my journey to Germany in roughly 8–14 days.

Could this be true? I can't believe it yet! Christmas at home! We will see each other at home!!

So if it comes true, if no particular unforeseen circumstances intervene—we will even celebrate our engagement then. I would like to set the celebrations for Sunday, 28 December 1941. Please make sure everything is in place for it. Cross your fingers that nothing else gets in the way at the last minute.[120]

28.11.41: *GEFREITER* H. T. (EASTERN FRONT)[121]

New reports arrive daily of German soldiers and officers found murdered [*ermordet*], they were cut to pieces [*zerschnitten*] or shot in their vehicles. A colonel with two good engineers as well. Anything that is wandering around at night or spending the night in the forests or on the road without credentials [*ohne Ausweis*] from the responsible authorities will be. . . .[122] The *Wehrmacht* is only permitted to frequent the busiest roads.

28.11.41: *OBERGEFREITER* H. S. (131 INFANTRY DIVISION, SECOND ARMY, ARMY GROUP CENTER)[123]

I have found the most incredible fellows among the Russians. Soldiers who die with their weapon in their hands and [soldiers] who have stormed us with cries of "Urra" and then, just meters from us, thrown away their weapons and put their hands up. A single fanatical Bolshevik keeps a group of Russians together right up to the end. I have seen how a *Kommissar* fell who was standing and fighting at the most dangerous spot. Hours later I came upon him again and, in spite of myself, had to stand there. He looked at me out of open, vivid blue eyes, with an indescribably happy smile. Never have I seen such a beautiful corpse. His face was transfigured, like that of the unknown woman of the Seine.[124] This experience is unforgettable to me. Unforgettable, because I have rarely seen any other humans among the enemy, really almost exclusively only degenerate subjects, fellows the like of which we simply don't see in Germany. Asiatics, beasts. I have seen the power of an inoculated worldview, no matter that it was a destructive power like the Soviet one. One fanatical believer holds many followers, even opponents of his ideas, together. The Russian's methods of leading people are just as brutal as his mode of warfare. He is ruthless with himself and his comrades, and so also with his enemy. We had to become that. [*Wir mussten es erst werden.*] We are stronger than he is. Our morals, our confidence, our belief, and the power of our weapons.

Every member of the German nation who does not have a son or a husband in Russia should be given the opportunity to walk just 1,000 km through Russia without any enemy intervention. They would, just like we did and are still having to do now, look for their own roof over their heads and their own food themselves. After a week, they'd be cured for life. Then the home front would become a front with no holes in it, one on which the soldier can rely. You all wouldn't believe how petty the concerns of many a civilian seem to us. Here we measure things against a different yardstick, and it's true! Let's not speak of our fighting and victory, which keep the home country safe from unspeakable suffering. So many at home have just got it far too good. I can well imagine the thoughts and unspoken worries that the new clothing ration card has brought with it. I wish that this restriction had been introduced immediately upon mobilization. Then many a person would have seen the war somewhat more vividly. The filthy infantryman in position has concerns quite other than when he's going to get a new coat. And God knows he needs one! Here out in Russia we soldiers at the front are the poorest sons of Germany, but also its most loyal.

29.11.41: DR. HELMUT MACHEMER (1 PANZER ARMY, ARMY GROUP SOUTH)[125]

The Fatherland truly demands a lot from me. Here I am again, sitting at the forwardmost line, I guess I can say that, enduring hardships, hunger, and cold, the dangers that threaten us all around here, taking it all upon myself for my homeland and my people. And at the same time [I] am persecuted and humiliated by that homeland. Because it is nothing other than that when they have been denying my promotion for two years and, as I have been told, there is no prospect of that changing. And so sometimes I find it damned hard to participate here. . . . I don't complain about it, even if I do find it hard sometimes to take part, to follow with them, to freeze with them, to be hungry with them. Do I wish things were different for me? No! I always come to the same conclusion, that my place is here at the front. . . .

But how will it go if it should ever be my turn to go? Who will then defend my children? It is them, ultimately, that all of this is for. Will there be anyone who will look after them? Will they be given the right to life that has been denied their father? Or will they be defenseless, left to rely on their own resources, perish sooner or later? That is the great worry that fills me.

30.11.41: *GEFREITER* ALOIS SCHEUER (197 INFANTRY DIVISION, ARMY GROUP CENTER)[126]

We've moved into another new position since yesterday evening (60 km outside Moscow). I'm sitting with my comrades in the semidarkness in a dugout. You can't imagine how filthy and louse-ridden we all look and how much of a torture this life has become to me. This can't be described in words anymore. I only have one thought anymore: When do I get out of this hell?

Yesterday I received three letters from you. My morale has sunk so low that I can barely be happy about it. But it's certainly not malice on my part. It was and is still simply too much for me, everything that I have to do here. One is slowly ruined by it. [*Man geht langsam dabei zugrunde.*] In addition to my pain and misery, the worry and suffering that you have to bear also weighs extremely heavy on me. Your letters are witness to your pain. I feel with you and cannot help you or me. I often ask myself: is there any happiness for us still, is there still joy in this life or would it be better to be released from it all? Yet, we must live, we have two children. That is why we must not despair, must endure and do our duty, however hard it may be.

30.11.41: ERICH DOHL (SIXTEENTH ARMY, ARMY GROUP NORTH)[127]

The weather is properly like winter. It snowed the entire day. If it carries on like this we'll be snowed in tomorrow morning. At any rate, the Russian winter now seems to be starting. . . . Lt. Büchele leaves us alone. So we lay about the whole day. The latest thing is that we play cards. But over time that gets boring as well. Now we've put November behind us, because today is the last [day of the month]. I'm interested to see whether we get out of here this December or not. One is tempted to assume the latter. There's an order lying in the orderly room, according to which there are to be 20 days' leave for the troops. However, it also says that first the infantry may go and later the motorized [troops]. At any rate, we don't yet have any expectations of leave. We've not heard anything of a change of position, either. I'd be for it, but not for forward, but backward instead. I'd have nothing against having to stay in Russia, if we can at least stay in a town like Staraia Russa or Velikie Luki. There at least there are solid buildings, a bath, and even movie theaters. But it would be even better if we could go home to Germany. . . . You, my little darling, can surely best understand me, that I am so feverish to get out of this miserable country. Even so, you will hardly be able to imagine how we live in this wasteland. Wherever you look there is forest and snow. Even the stillness soon gets on my nerves. . . . How long will this terrible war carry on? We shouldn't have gone into the war with Russia, then maybe there would be peace now. But what use are ifs and buts to us now. For us it means enduring and hanging on.

Photo Essay: Fall 1941

The devastating effects of German SD-10 fragmentation bombs on Soviet forces withdrawing near Kiev in the sector of Army Group South.

A small fraction of the hundreds of thousands of Red Army soldiers made prisoner in the encirclement battle of Kiev deep in the Ukraine in September 1941.

A German sentinel in the citadel of Kiev (ca. 20 September 1941) looking down on the city and the burning Dnepr River bridge. (*Bundesarchiv, Bild 183-L20208, Foto: Schmidt, CC-BY-SA 3.0*)

Soviet POWs packed into railroad freight cars en route to Germany (October 1941). Over the course of the war, more than half of the Soviet soldiers taken prisoner—as many as 3.3 million—would perish in German captivity.

2 October 1941: A 150mm medium howitzer in action, as Army Group Center finally begins Operation "Typhoon" and advances toward Moscow. (*H. Sohn*)

2 October 1941: Low to the ground, German Ju 87 Stuka divebombers head east at the start of "Typhoon." (*H. Sohn*)

A Soviet bunker position near the Desna River, about thirty kilometers northeast of Roslavl', captured by the 197 Infantry Division (2 October 1941). (*NA*)

A Soviet T-34 tank, destroyed after it had broken through the lines of 18 Infantry Regiment (6 ID) in October 1941. (*Haape Family Archive; hereafter cited as "HFA"*)

The burning village of Kasilovo in the sector of Army Group Center (7 October 1941). (*H. Sohn*)

Troop carriers of 9 Panzer Division advancing toward the front. Note the "K" for Kleist's 1 Panzer Group of Army Group South on the rear of the vehicle on the lower right.

A German column northeast of Ivanovka (sector of Army Group North) after it had been ambushed by a Soviet KV-1 heavy tank on 9 October 1941. The burning 88mm flak gun and its prime mover were destroyed before they were able to deploy. (*Pen & Sword*)

Oil refineries and installations on the Black Sea coast go up in flames after German air attacks (*n.d.*).

German supply truck stuck in the mud. By early October 1941, the heavy rains of the *Rasputitsa* (literally, "the time without roads") were transforming Russian "roads" into a miasma of mud and goo; the mud produced by just a few hours of rain was enough to transform a typical Russian road into a quagmire, significantly slowing the advance of Army Group Center toward Moscow. (*H. Wijers*)

German draft horses suffered terribly during the Russian rainy season, many collapsing and dying in their harnesses (fall 1941). (*K.-F. Hoyer*)

The burning town of Orel, captured in a coup-de-main by tank forces of Guderian's 2 Panzer Group on 3 October. (*D. Garden and K. Andrew*)

A German light self-propelled AT gun entering the strategically important city of Rostov-on-the-Don in the operations area of Army Group South (*November 1941*).

German Ju 87 Stuka divebombers being transferred to Army Group North, where they would support the drive on Leningrad (*n.d.*).

Infantry of Army Group North, supported by a Panzer 38(t), advance through a birch wood in October 1941. (*Bundesarchiv, Bild 101I-213-0267-13, Foto: Gebauer, CC-BY-SA 3.0*)

German infantry advance through a blazing suburb of Leningrad (*November 1941*).

Thousands of artillery shells have disfigured the terrain south of Leningrad, bearing mute testimony to the intensity of the fighting there (*n.d.*).

Elements of 129 Infantry Division advance in open order toward the Volga reservoir in -15°C temperatures and without winter clothing (15 November 1941). (*H. Boucsein*)

A column of German Panzer III tanks on the march somewhere on the eastern front; these tanks are all outfitted with the 50mm L/42 main armament, which was incapable of destroying the T-34 or KV-1 frontally. (*Stackpole Books*)

A column of German infantry and vehicles (including a Stug III assault gun) advancing on the central front (fall 1941).

Vehicles of Guderian's 2 Panzer Army (note the "G" on the motorcycle) spread across a vast frozen field. By November 1941, the advance of Guderian's badly attrited forces had slowed to a crawl due to weather and increasingly effective Soviet resistance. (*Pen & Sword*)

A battery of 105mm light field how-itzers (l.F.H. 18) deployed in open firing positions. This artillery piece had a maximum range of 10,700 meters; a typical 1941 German in-antry division was equipped with thirty-six of these guns. (*Stackpole Books*)

Soldier with an MG 34 heavy ma-chine gun mounted on a tripod for air defense (n.d.) The MG 34 was also a devastating weapon against enemy infantry. (*Pen & Sword*)

A soldier of the Waffen-SS, somewhere on the east-
ern front, wearing makeshift winter clothing (n.d.).
In general, Waffen-SS soldiers were provided with a
winter clothing suite superior to that of their regular
Wehrmacht counterparts during winter 1941/42. (*Pen
& Sword*)

A destroyed Soviet BM-13 "*Katyusha*" ("Little Kate") multiple
rocket launcher. The weapon was first employed on the eastern
front in July 1941 and, by the fall, was regularly encountered by
German forces. The Germans dreaded the massed fire of the
"Stalin Organ," as they christened it, with its infernal and distinc-
tive scream. (*GWGC*)

A battery of artillery of 35 Infantry Division in position northwest of Moscow (2 December 1941).

German tanks on the move on the central front (14 December 1941). (*H. Sohn*)

Panje sleds taking on loads of supplies from Ju 52 transport aircraft (winter 1941).

A decimated infantry battalion of 6 Infantry Division (Army Group Center) on the retreat from Moscow. GFM von Bock's army group would lose a thousand horses a day during the winter of 1941-1942 (December 1941). (*H. Bruenger*)

A signal unit of 35 Infantry Division retreating through a vast Russian wasteland near Volokolamsk (mid-December 1941). (*H. Sohn*)

Mountain soldiers have assembled two MG 34 machine guns on tripods (most likely in the sector of Army Group South). (*Stackpole Books*)

A German military cemetery of Dr. Heinrich Haape's 6 Infantry Division (winter 1941-1942). *(HFA)*

The identification tag *(Erkennungsmarke)* of a German soldier killed in Russia. He belonged to 5 Company, Signal Replacement Battalion 16. By the end of December 1941, more than three hundred thousand German soldiers and airmen had been killed on the eastern front. *(C. Luther)*

CHAPTER 8

December 1941

Introduction

Army Group Center's offensive toward Moscow continued until 5 December, when the utter exhaustion of its last attacking formations forestalled any prospect of capturing the city. A small number of German forces were undoubtedly close to Moscow, but the city was heavily fortified by December 1941 and could not have been seriously contested by a handful of understrength divisions. More importantly, the German High Command had no idea that a major Soviet winter offensive was about to strike their overextended lines. At the focal point of Soviet attention, north of Moscow, the Red Army held a 2.5:1 superiority in manpower.[1] Moreover, many of the Soviet formations committed to the new offensive had not taken part in the grueling fighting on the approaches to Moscow. In fact, German intelligence did not even know that Stalin had multiple reserve armies with which to attack.[2] Illustrative of the depths to which Army Group Center had sunk were the comments of Heinrici, the commander of the 43 Army Corps, who wrote home on 6 December, "The army has not been able to reach the desired success. And it did not help that the strength of the remaining units had dwindled to such a ridiculous level and that the men were mentally and physically extremely exhausted after five months of offensive warfare, while the Russian was sending more and more troops against us. . . . We have nothing like that. Our victories have brought us to the end of our tether."[3]

Not surprisingly, when the Red Army hit Army Group Center on 6 December, it sent the panzer forces reeling back. Soon the limited scope of the offensive, which had begun against Reinhardt's panzer group north of Moscow, spread to Guderian's panzer army and the Second Army in the south. Later it hit the Ninth Army near Kalinin and Fourth Army in the center of GFM von Bock's front. The crisis was not just limited to Soviet attacks; it also meant that poorly equipped German soldiers were forced out of their occupied houses and bunkers and sent into long retreats from which thousands of cases of frostbite resulted. By 12 December, Hoepner, commanding 4 Panzer Group, wrote to his wife, "One only gets bad news. . . . The mass of Russians is crushing us. . . . Losses from frostbite are almost as numerous as those from battle. Our situation has despairing similarities with Napoleon in 1812. . . . The commanding generals scream for help."[4]

On 7 December, Japan attacked Pearl Harbor, which days later led to Hitler declaring war on the United States, making the war truly global. For Germany, the sudden attention directed toward the war in the Far East was not enough to disguise the fact that the Wehrmacht *was suffering serious reversals on the Eastern Front. Yet the Red Army's success came at a staggering cost with as many as 552,000 casualties for the month of December alone. Indeed, over the course of the first winter the attacking Soviets suffered 1.6 million losses, which was six times those of the* Ostheer.[5] *Army Group Center may have been in retreat, but it fought with an experience and skill that the many raw Soviet recruits and their green officers could not hope to match.*

Army Group North's attempt to link up with the Finnish army east of Lake Ladoga had reached Tikhvin and then stalled. The cold weather, which on 5 December dropped to -35° centigrade, and Soviet counterattacks to cut off the German spearhead not only prevented any further progress but also demanded a withdrawal. Hitler was adamant that Tikhvin be held and that a relief attack south of Lake Ladoga be mounted, but there were few substantive reserves immediately available, and their transportation typically undercut every timetable. By early December the crisis at Tikhvin demanded a response, and GFM von Leeb pleaded unsuccessfully with Hitler for a retreat. Yet as disaster beckoned, and with the OKH's support, Leeb ordered the withdrawal on 7 December, and Hitler reluctantly gave his consent the following day.[6] It was not the last time Leeb would need to take bold action to save his formations from destruction. On 15 December, Leeb was again desperately seeking Hitler's permission to pull back his endangered forces east of the Volkhov River, but when no decision was forthcoming, the commander of Army Group North took the decision himself, without informing anyone in the High Command.[7]

In besieged Leningrad, the bitter reality of being cut off from any road or rail supply led to anywhere between eight hundred thousand and one million deaths in the winter of 1941–1942.[8] Indeed, by early December, mass starvation was openly anticipated and discussed. As Geori Kniazev wrote in his diary on 8 December, "The blessings of civilization have come to an end. . . . My wife said: 'If it's going to go on like this, we are bound to die of starvation in January or February.' She said this unemotionally and added: 'But since death by starvation is extremely agonizing, we ought to find some other way to die. You will kill me, and then yourself as well.'"[9]

Since late November, Army Group South had already been dealing with a major Soviet counterattack, which had forced GFM von Rundstedt into an unauthorized withdrawal from Rostov, leading to his replacement by Reichenau. The problem for Hitler was that Reichenau was reporting that a halt of the withdrawal east of the Mius River was simply not feasible and that any forces committed to this would simply have to be "written off." In other words, GFM von Reichenau was backing Rundstedt's original order despite the clear fate of his predecessor. Accordingly, Hitler opted to fly to Army Group South on 2 December to gain a clearer picture of events and was treated to an unvarnished set of reports, including from the commander of SS Leibstandarte, who Hitler trusted more than any of the army commanders.[10] When Hitler finally confronted Rundstedt, it was clear that the field marshal had been convinced of the decision to withdraw from Rostov and, while the Führer *could not bring himself to admit any fault and did not reverse his decision to relieve Rundstedt of command, he promised to reinstate him in a new command after a period of rest.[11]*

Letters and Diary Entries (1–15 December 1941)

12.41 (EXACT DAY UNKNOWN): KURT VOGELER (ARMY GROUP NORTH)[12]

The world has seen many great, even grand wars. But there has probably never been a war in its history, which can measure up to the present in Eastern Europe. This is true both of its size, which stretches for many hundreds of kilometers of active front, the vast spaces that host battles with million-man armies of opposing nations, but also by the method and manner of the fighting itself. I do not intend to go into more detail on this. I am neither a member of the General Staff nor a military man who sees the war solely through the eyes of a tactician, rather I am a human being who has experienced and [continues to] experience the war as a human being.

What misery we encounter, day in, day out. For example, a Russian came to us, wanting to sell us a homemade German-Russian vocabulary primer, that is to say swap it for bread. We were in the middle of eating and gave him some. He fell on it like a wolf and gobbled it up. A sight that you don't forget. The man was 58 years old and spoke English, French, and Japanese in addition to his mother tongue. When we asked him his profession, he told us that he had been ill a great deal and earns his living by making crosses to be worn around the neck. The crosses were touching in their primitiveness and demonstrated the deep piety of the Russian people. I have not seen a single house where there was no image of a saint. The Russian people are going through a time of suffering. . . .

Poor, unhappy Russian people! Who can refuse to feel compassion? Is it not still the same people that brought us the great Russian poets and writers—that became dear to us because of the depth of its soul. Its distress is unspeakable and its misery heart-rending. Can no committee in "highly cultivated" Europe, which looks down upon the Russians with such great arrogance, bring—from sheer humanity—aid, rouse the conscience of the world, so that the human being is treated as human? [But] I forget: the age has become a different one and wishes to know nothing of humanity. Brutal violence is the hallmark of our century and so we will also have to suffer with our Russian brothers and sisters, all of us for whom justice, humanity, and human kindness is an obligation of our faith. Suffering—above all because we are prevented from helping, because we see hundreds of thousands, indeed millions of people suffering and starving and have no recourse to be able to intervene in this misery either through words or actions. What a deplorable war is this killing of humans in Eastern Europe! A crime against humanity!

1.12.41: HELMUT GÄDEKE (ARMY GROUP CENTER)[13]

All our activity here has gained the utmost seriousness. Any errors that are made are paid for in blood, and responsibility weighs all the more heavily on any commands. Every day that God continues to give us we will receive gratefully from His gracious Father and joyously make the most of. But at home, too, everyone should understand that it is a particular mercy and reason for joy if we return home. But sacrifice is natural for every soldier who sets out to go to war. Furthermore, the Christian knows that he is secure in God's love in life and in death.

1–3.12.41: HARALD HENRY (ARMY GROUP CENTER)[14]

This shall be my Christmas letter for you, written from the deepest bitterness of a life that has become abysmal. The last few days were again so terrible, the nights so agonizing that they were like the old days when it was said that people turned gray in a single night. . . . I am going to be spending this celebration differently from you all, perhaps in a foxhole shattered and wounded by this terrible cold. . . . Maybe I am lucky, at least for a few moments, the happiness to think of you all. So many beloved, wonderful years, so many lovely Christmas celebrations. . . . Probably I will just be lethargic and sad and think of something edible. Oh, this Christmas!

Now we're positioned even farther forward, right up close, and a war of position, which probably no German has experienced like *this*, awaits us. God have mercy on us! There is nothing that can be taken for granted now: It can no longer be taken for granted that we have a roof over our heads, food, mail, that we'll spend the winter nights in heated buildings—all of this is a special grace, a gift, a Christmas gift one could call it. . . .

But you all mustn't view all this through the shimmering illumination of Christmas candles, but rather through the deep disorder and destruction to which we are now subjected. To a dreadful disease, an error of human nature. It seems increasingly doubtful to me that a cure is possible at all.

1.12.41: *UNTEROFFIZIER* WILHELM PRÜLLER (9 PANZER DIVISION, SECOND ARMY, ARMY GROUP CENTER)[15]

At 7.00 we're off. It's snowing hard and a strong wind is up. Terrible weather for marching: many in the companies have foot trouble already. We've got a lot of characters with flat feet, fallen arches, etc.—not at all suitable as foot soldiers.

We're supposed to find shelter in a village some 6 km to the north, but when we get there, we find the entire village consists of exactly two huts—scarcely room for a single group. So we have to go on another 8 km or so. The other companies roll past us, often with a sarcastic smile for us poor limping chaps. We slowly limp into the next place, where we are assigned 3 small huts and 3 so-called Russian houses—one room for a platoon of 39 men. They can barely stand up inside, and that's where they are supposed to spend the night. I can't stand that idea, so I go and fetch the aide-de-camp so he can see our plight for himself. This isn't war anymore but a fight for billets.

1.12.41: HANS-HEINRICH LUDWIG (ARMY GROUP NORTH)[16]

We soon had to leave our lovely bunkers. To another spot, where the Russian was attacking like mad. Very unfavorable terrain, all dense forest. As artillery, we got quite far forward. It was another 200 to 300 meters to the front, I heard the wild choral cries of the storming Russians' "Urrah" and our lot recently returned the cry "Urrah."

These were desperate battles. What our gunners had to withstand can't ever be measured! And being on the watch at night in the snow. . . . None of you can imagine it.

2.12.41: ANTON BÖHRER (294 INFANTRY DIVISION, SIXTH ARMY, ARMY GROUP SOUTH)[17]

Yesterday we were in the cinema. I made sure that it really did happen, because we hadn't been to a movie since June or even May. There was a nearly new *Wochenschau* about Orel and the tank advance at Mariupol, all very interesting, but when you've been fighting in it yourself, it's very different. The dirt on the roads, for example, was much more intense for us outside Khar'kov. . . . The trucks just spun around as if on ice. Many vehicles got stuck and sank, others slid off and had to be put to right with prime movers. Well, now, if everything were presented as it [really] happened, then the moviegoers would end up going home with faces covered in tears, since they haven't become quite so hardened as the fighters at the front. . . .

In Russia, you really do see properly what advantages we enjoy in Germany. Today, you can't buy anything at all in Khar'kov, much less go into a café or even just buy a box of matches, for example. The Bolsheviks have simply destroyed everything or taken it all with them. I saw the only merchant yesterday, who was selling a pair of shoelaces on a large square. By the way, several partisans, who had been conducting explosions or other such mischief, had recently been hanged from balconies on precisely this square. It's a radical way [of doing things], but it certainly makes the greatest impression on the Russians when they see their comrades dangling from a rope. It was very restless here at the beginning, because you could often hear detonations, usually as if coming from explosions, although you never knew exactly where they were, but it has got quieter again now.

2.12.41: DR. HERMANN TÜRK (3 PANZER DIVISION, 2 PANZER ARMY, ARMY GROUP CENTER)[18]

Wind storms and snow. We can scarcely imagine that a reasonable [military] operation is still feasible. Things are very bad. How are we supposed to advance? And yet: we take Romanova. I move my vehicles forward. Motorcycle driver Ebel drives in front of us to show us the way. When we reach the high ground at Romanova there is suddenly a bang, a shock with a powerful blast wave. The motorcycle is blown into a thousand pieces. The individual pieces fall slowly from the sky. Miraculously Ebel is lying on the ground. I approach cautiously. There is not much more to do. I would like to give him morphine, but it's impossible. It doesn't work. I carry the morphine in my pants pocket to keep it warm, but just as I am about to inject it, the morphine freezes in the cannula. In cold like this there is virtually nothing I can do. It is terrible for us. Our fingers are freezing.

We take a closer look around [for the cause of the explosion]. In front of our car there is a large mine barrier. There are two mines just 1.5 meters away, directly in front of my front wheels. Again I have been saved by a miracle. A few seconds later and we would have had it. While we are busy recovering the wounded and turning our vehicles, we come under heavy mortar fire from a nearby wood. A round lands 20 meters to the right, the next 20 meters to the left. Time to get out of here. At that moment an explosion where my vehicle had been seconds earlier. Fragments whiz about our ears. Now I try to get [to Romanova] by another route. Outside Romanova there is a ravine with a river. It was dammed. The Russians have now opened the dam and the ice sags. There is only one place to cross and it is under continuous, accurate artillery fire. Several vehicles try to get across. One direct hit after another. Fourteen vehicles knocked out in short order. There are many killed and wounded. I have to leave the ambulance behind. The wounded are carried across the ice. The entire area is under mortar fire. Division ambulances also come. One is hit. II Battalion's ambulance is also destroyed by a direct hit. There is pure chaos. One's nerves are not what they were in the beginning. The regiment has 47 casualties.

2.12.41: *OBERGEFREITER* JOSEPH B. (2 PANZER DIVISION, 4 PANZER GROUP, ARMY GROUP CENTER)[19]

There's lovely, clear weather today. The [Soviet] planes are very lively. We can hardly move. Shooting almost always only at night. Moscow is very close now [*Moskau ist schon sehr nahe*], but the road is certainly long and tough. We still don't know whether we'll really stay here the whole winter. We all hope! Right now Russian planes (*Ratas*) are thundering overhead and the light antiaircraft gun is firing. Usually it just holds the planes off or attracts their attention.

3.12.41: SIEGBERT STEHMANN (163 INFANTRY DIVISION, GERMAN ARMY OF NORWAY)[20]

Every now and then it happens that bitterness intrudes uninvited into the conversation of we homeless and distant wanderers [*Heimatlosen und Fernewanderern*]. But don't worry. There's no going forward or back, and it looks like we're stuck here for the longer duration. You're surprised that we're back at the front. We've been in the front line for five months, because there's nobody behind us who could relieve us. In any case, it's best at the front. You do your sentry duty, throw yourself into trenches and foxholes when there's mortar fire, but otherwise you've got enough peace and quiet during the day for your own thoughts and ponderings. Just that there isn't any possibility of vacation in this wintry "quiet." Many haven't been home for 1½ years. Perhaps it will even end up being 2 years. Our division is in a remote corner of the world.

3.12.41: ERICH DOHL (SIXTEENTH ARMY, ARMY GROUP NORTH)[21]

I finally have the chance to send you all a sign of life. . . . It was damned hard and we have a lot of fatalities and casualties. In 4th Platoon 3 men are dead and 10 wounded. Now, however, the danger has passed. The Russian was hard on our heels. . . . I finished off many Russians. How easily it might have been different. Gläser, Federl, and Trendt are the only uninjured [men] in 4th Platoon. . . . At any rate, I can be happy that I am no longer in 4th Platoon. . . . We don't yet know how we're to be deployed with the 5 guns that we've still got. Certainly not in ground attack anymore, however, because our vehicles are all broken down.[22] Perhaps we'll get out of this country yet. At any rate, we've escaped the hell of Tikhvin, thank God.

3.12.41: *LEUTNANT* GERHARD S. (29 INFANTRY DIVISION [MOT.], 2 PANZER ARMY, ARMY GROUP CENTER)[23]

For myself, I quartered myself and two people from my section group in a very clean *panje* hut, the like of which we've not found in a long time. . . . On the following morning we met the town's schoolmaster, a Sudeten German,[24] who had, however, been living in this area for a long time and received the paltry salary of 400 rubles a month. He reported how the Germans had very unexpectedly taken the town of Orel. The Russians had expected the attack of the German panzers to come from the west and were astounded when suddenly the first panzers rolled into the town from the east. As a result, the town fell almost undamaged into German hands. In his haste, the Russian was only able to set fire to individual buildings, including a shoe factory and a few grain stores. . . .

The village schoolteacher also reported that the Russian population fears less the German soldiers than the returning Russian ones, should the Germans ever not be in the country anymore. They particularly fear acts of violence on the part of the commissars, because they have not carried out Stalin's order to burn down all the villages and to follow the retreating Russians, along with all their animals.

3.12.41: JOHANNES HAMM (1 PANZER ARMY, ARMY GROUP SOUTH)[25]

I myself, since I had already had a sore throat for several days, had to lie down the following day and on the day after that I reported sick, with 40 [degree] fever. So I experienced the first day of Advent as an infirmary case with the *Oberstabsarzt*. It's festering tonsillitis, but it's already receding. I was very embarrassed that I had to go to the rear in such critical days, but it occurred against my will. As you heard on the radio, the first of Advent was a black day in other respects. I experienced something for the first time that has never entered my soldierly existence until now—"retreat." So I've not had any rest either, never mind relaxation. I've been fasting for 5 days and now am beginning to eat a little again, swallowing was impossible before now. On said critical day, by the way, I immediately went back to the front so as to be able to take part somehow if necessary. The battalion commander gave me a dreadful dressing down for it and the *Oberstabsarzt* was very annoyed. But those gentlemen had forgotten that they had sent me away with no medications and no food, and nor had they said when I should come back. What's more, I had no blanket, no washing things, and anything else one needs. . . .

Now I'd like to say something of my inner self, that I have so far, quite unjustly, considered myself to be an "old warrior." I keep noticing that, still, every shell that is announced by its whistling and every bomb that falls in my vicinity gets on my nerves and affects my stomach. I cannot yet call that imperturbability of the old World War soldier, of which literature so gushes, my own. I am also initially so unsettled by the suffering of a comrade that I feel I'm going to be sick [*es mir heiß hoch kommt*]. I think that I can hide it. But my comrade *Leutnant* Lehdenich told me that I kept going very pale. I hope I will be able to overcome this, too. My chief recently made a scornful comment to another that I went very pale when the bomb hit our signal vehicle. . . .

Don't pass this letter on, on account of the word "retreat." Some people will make up unfounded rumors with it. I think today the matter will come to a standstill and the tables will turn so that the final victory will lie with us. The Russian has so far lost 50% of his attacking troops in 3 days. Let him attack another 3 days! I am writing it only because of course these letters are supposed to be my diary. . . .

A letter like this is the only thing with which one can give one's heart a little air to breathe. I haven't got any comrades here like with Rifle Regiment 3. Even if they were all simple people, we were all close to each other, like brothers, because we had exercised, marched, and fought shoulder to shoulder long enough. That's why back then I didn't need to share [my thoughts] so much. The company was my second family. But now I only have you, so please don't take it so hard if I keep pouring out my heart to you.

3.12.41: ERICH DOHL (SIXTEENTH ARMY, ARMY GROUP NORTH)[26]

Now, I have something unpleasant to tell you. Last night we changed our position to Tikhvin. What I had always suspected has now come true. They've dropped us in the sh** again. At any rate, we're back very close to the enemy and he's hitting us with all the artillery fire he's got. During the day, you can't let yourself be seen in the open because of all the impacts. However, it is a bit quieter at night. . . .

I would have liked to spare you this new worry that I'm burdening you with, but I can't bring myself to simply not write. I have not lied to you so far and I hope that I will never do so, regardless of the matter. The dear Lord will continue to keep me in his protection.

We receive our food at night. Yesterday, it was 1:00 a.m. when we received the first food in 25 hours. It hasn't come yet for today, either, although it is already 8:00 p.m. . . .

Our bunker, a Russian bunker, is very solidly constructed. 4 layers of wood are layered up over one another, that'll withstand quite a bit. So a light shell will most likely not touch us. Admittedly, I don't want to test that out. I don't know if you can imagine a war like this. Probably not, because there is nothing worse in the world. . . .

A young comrade of mine, Willi Braun, ran off yesterday evening and he is not back yet. Seems to have gone mad. When they find him, he'll probably be shot. Everyone, without exception, is scared for their life [*Angst um sein Leben hat jeder ohne Ausnahme*] but, with the right trust in God, it's all right. . . . Hopefully, we'll be pulled out of here very soon, otherwise our nerves will be completely wrecked.

4.12.41: DR. HELMUT MACHEMER (1 PANZER ARMY, ARMY GROUP SOUTH)[27]

It became ever clearer, even for us soldiers, that we have little insight into the wider events of the war at the front, because we each of us only have a small sector of the front before us. It was soon clear that the Russians' attacks were part of a larger offensive. When this fact was realized, then our advance was also stopped at once, and that explains why we were inactive for almost three weeks.

Then, when the Russians arrived, in large numbers and with new weapons, our task force initially retreated behind the Tuslov [River], determined to hold this position. And it would have been held, too, if the Russian hadn't sent, almost simultaneously, even more troops into battle east of Rostov. . . . It may be that the second Russian thrust from the east surprised us, because it's being said that we had to leave some war material behind in Rostov. There was apparently not enough gasoline available to drive all the vehicles back. . . .

We took up positions a further two times, a further two times we let the Russian get right up close to us, only to turn the situation round when he was right in front of our noses. A test of our nerves. But all went well. With no serious losses [and] seven light casualties we arrived at the Mius [River] in the evening, where the bridge, already set with mines, was waiting for us to get us across. When, at a late hour, we passed by our—meanwhile well-constructed—positions and took up warm quarters in a safe location, our hearts felt rather lighter.

4.12.41: AUTHOR UNKNOWN (ARMY GROUP CENTER)[28]

Today it's our first day at rest again, whether it's onward again tomorrow, we don't know; sometimes it's off to the rear, because there's the devil going on here near Moscow, the Russians are deploying everything here, there are also a lot of Russian planes coming now, they're giving us a hard fight, they're shooting the horses away from vehicles, and one co-driver is dead and one wounded. And tanks are also now coming from the Russians and running everything down, they're so powerful that our [antitank gun] can't do anything, they drive right over our [antitank] guns, only our artillery and heavy antiaircraft guns shoot them up.

Today we're positioned in a village, it looks a mess, everything all over the place, our antiaircraft guns have really shot the Russians up, there are piles of horses and vehicles and cars and people, and some of ours also fell, a lieutenant and an acting corporal in our company, and two noncommissioned officers wounded, and 5 soldiers. If only this war would finally come to an end, and we could get home healthy; it's just indescribable how things are here, the second battalion here was just run over by the tanks, I wouldn't have wanted to be there, hopefully dear God will carry on protecting me, so that we can see each other again at home. . . .

We are 40 kilometers from Moscow and are holding the front steady from the north so that they can't get to the ring around Moscow, although whether Moscow will fall, nobody knows, if it would just fall for Christmas, that'd be the nicest Christmas present for us. Our lieutenant, on the same day that he fell, he destroyed a tank that was standing in the forest and the crew was sleeping in it and he threw a hand grenade in and they died, and on the same day he received a shot to the head, when they were taking a village.

4.12.41: *GEFREITER* HANS JOACHIM C. (23 INFANTRY DIVISION, SECOND ARMY, ARMY GROUP CENTER)[29]

We reached the company just as it was being prevented from continuing its march by the Russians. That meant being on watch duty day and night. I can't describe to you what that's like. First, the dreadful cold, snow storm, feet that are wet through and through—*boots never dry and mustn't be taken off*—and, second, this *test of nerves* from the Russians. . . . We've now been placed under direct command of a panzer division. Special duties! That means crazy amounts of marching and being right at the front with the enemy. *Everyone is thinking of the end. . . .* I write these details to you, but ask that you keep them from my parents to prevent unnecessary agitation.[30]

5.12.41: DR. HERMANN TÜRK (3 PANZER DIVISION, 2 PANZER ARMY, ARMY GROUP CENTER)[31]

It is minus 39 degrees. It is unbelievable what the troops have to do. This can't go on for long . . . the 17 Pz. Div. has been beaten back. It is already again twenty kilometers south of Kashira. We are supposed to go to its aid, but almost none of our vehicles are functional because of the frightful cold. In the tanks of the first company [6 Pz. Rgt.] boiling water is poured in above, by the time it reaches the radiator it is already ice. The oil is solid too. The transmission no longer turns. In almost all the tanks even the steering is frozen. The road to Moscow has also been abandoned again.

The 4 Pz. Div. has had to face the most powerful attacks by fresh Siberian troops with tanks. Cavalry too. As they can't get their vehicles going, many of them have had to be blown up. The men don't understand what is happening. The Siberians are terrible. Now they have nailed a German officer to a board and thrown him into a hole in the river. One can't describe this bestiality. It seems our operations here are through for the winter. The battalion is to be sent into action again tonight at 0200 . . . suddenly someone pounding on the door of our shack. It is an officer, who came through the village on a motorcycle and saw my vehicle. The Russians are already at the edge of the village. It's high time for us to go. . . . But we are about to get away before the leading troops can catch us. Then we drive cross-country, navigating by compass alone.

5.12.41: *LEUTNANT* GERHARDT LINKE (87 INFANTRY DIVISION, 4 PANZER GROUP, ARMY GROUP CENTER)[32]

I went to the fringe of the forest to find out what the situation was. A yellow cloud of smoke was rising over Palizi. Flames were burning many buildings. The earth was in constant tremor from the detonations of high-explosive shells. Some heavy [Soviet] tanks were already skirting the village. We were impotent against these juggernauts. Many wagons and horses were burned today. . . . The day cost us another 11 killed and 39 wounded. Nineteen soldiers are badly frostbitten. Casualties among the officers are considerable. . . .

It's enough to drive anybody to despair. Not one of the sick or wounded sent to the rear ever comes back. One might as well forget about ever receiving fully trained replacements and there is no end in view to our stay here. We are beginning to calculate how long it will be before there is no one left to man the guns. Special crews, as for instance those for heavy machine guns and grenade guns, have become so few that with further losses guns will be left without crews. Already during the December 1st offensive some of these guns had to be left with their supply trains in Ruza for lack of personnel.

The snow, driven by an icy wind, stings our faces. A thick crust forms round our helmet cloths from our breath. We have to watch each other's faces and signal frostbite symptoms. Some parts of the face very quickly become white and frostbite may set in a few minutes after stepping into the open. Our equipment stands no comparison with the winter outfits of the Russians. The enemy is provided with quilted trousers and jackets. He has felt boots and fur caps. . . . Our footwear affords inadequate protection against the cold climate, particularly with boots and socks in the condition in which they now are.

6.12.41: *GEFREITER* FRITZ SIGEL (ARMY GROUP CENTER)[33]

[Minus] 32 degrees. My God, I've never experienced anything like it. Almost everybody has come in for their share of it. One has had his entire hands frozen, had to go to the hospital immediately, almost everyone has frozen fingertips, I have a frozen left thumb. . . . We are deployed in battle around the town of Tula. . . . As long as it's this cold, no attack can take place, because the infantry would freeze in the process.

My God, what will this Russia yet bring us! [*Mein Gott, was bringt dieses Rußland uns noch alles!*] This warfare has to stop sometime; otherwise we'll all perish in this situation.

7.12.41: *LEUTNANT* H. H. (258 INFANTRY DIVISION, FOURTH ARMY, ARMY GROUP CENTER)[34]

On the Russian side there were new, battle-ready Siberian divisions. . . . In addition, the Russians had established a wide area of defensive positions with mines and fortifications, which first had to be broken through. . . . The unfavorable weather canceled a planned strike by the *Luftwaffe* before we even got underway. An icy snowstorm swept across the landscape limiting visibility. The ground was so slippery that our horses had difficulty keeping upright. The machine guns did not work in the cold.

Despite all these disadvantages, the attack went ahead and the spearhead of our regiment (the one from Colonel Wolff) came within thirty kilometers of Moscow, which is proof of the heroic courage, preparedness, and endurance of our troops. Of course, such an operation has its victims. . . . When, in the end, the attack could not be capitalized upon . . . the effect was that in the night of 3 December we returned to the starting positions. In places, there were only small remnants of once strong companies.

7.12.41: *WACHTMEISTER* JOSEPH L. (129 INFANTRY DIVISION, NINTH ARMY, ARMY GROUP CENTER)[35]

We are in battle against mighty enemies. A strong will, good ideas, courage, and strength will defeat the enemies, wherever [they] show themselves. Imagine if the Russians had succeeded in overrunning our beautiful Germany. We would have been helplessly subjected to grim days. But we are close to the final victory. What do weeks and months signify when the good of a nation for a thousand years is at stake. Every day in the East demands sacrifices [*Jeder Tag im Osten fordert Opfer*], much suffering and tears at home. . . . But we must stay here for now. The front is so endlessly vast, we must not let up, allow the Russian any breathing space, otherwise the sacrifices will be greater. I have reconciled myself to the thought that I will not be coming home very soon. Millions of comrades carry this burden, just like I do. We here at the front know what is at stake.

7.12.41: *OBERSTLEUTNANT* HELLMUTH STIEFF (FOURTH ARMY, ARMY GROUP CENTER)[36]

I'm not taking your curtain lecture [*Gardinenpredigt*] personally, but it damn reeks of homeland patriotism [*Heimatpatriotismus*]. . . . But you all seem to be clueless about how things here really look. . . . Forgive me if I have become bitter! But you simply cannot understand it. It is entirely different to how the unbelievable propaganda describes it to you all. We are standing on a knife-edge every day here. That is why we feel so betrayed. . . . We don't care a fig about any crusade, we are fighting for our bare lives here, every day and every hour, against an opponent who is a great deal more superior to us in all areas on the ground and in the air. We are being sent nothing from the rear, on the contrary, 3 divisions . . . were pulled away prematurely, the *Luftwaffe* is pulling almost everything away, and our "winter equipment" is a joke in the current conditions. And the opposing side has brought in 10 new divisions from Siberia in one week . . . , and the superiority [of the Russians] in the air is legion (Hobe and I lie flat on the ground often enough every day when the bombs are howling [around us]). I'll stop. You don't understand me anyway.

9.12.41: WERNER BEERMANN (NINTH ARMY, ARMY GROUP CENTER)[37]

I can well imagine that you, like many in the homeland, have a very hazy picture of what is happening here. According to the newspapers, radio announcements, and newsreels everything is crystal clear: "The war in the East is decided! All preparations for overwintering are being made around us. Looks like larger-scale assaults will only be possible in late spring. For us that means another few months of a war of position. The Russian is located so close to the outer city boundary that he is still able to shoot proficiently into the city area. Russian planes also visit us frequently. . . .

The 5th of the month was Stalin's Constitution Day and so we already suspected beforehand that the Russians would attack. And so it was: he ran up against our positions with great force the whole day. On that day around 600 Russian fatalities were counted in front of our regiment's sector.[38] We had only 3 dead and 20 casualties. It's constantly amazing what our soldiers achieve in the forward lines. Even though they have been deployed all these months without interruption. . . .

The weather here is still very changeable, hard frost alternates with sudden thaws. Yesterday it was still [minus] 30° cold and today the water is dripping from the roofs. Lying in a trench in such low temperatures must be a tough thing. There have already been individual cases of hands, feet, noses, and ears freezing. The cold frequently impacts on the weapons, causing the mechanisms to block and during a Russian attack this situation can have fatal consequences. The Russian must have a lot of ammunition stored, he frequently fires his guns and machine guns just to keep the weapons warm.

Japan and America are now also in the war.[39] We hope that it all develops to Germany's favor.

9.12.41: *UNTEROFFIZIER* KARL R. (5 PANZER DIVISION, 4 PANZER GROUP, ARMY GROUP CENTER)[40]

As you can see from the letter written in ink, we have once again got away from the foremost line. That is, our entire division is in the process of moving approx. 25 km back because we were too far forward in relation to [our] right and left. In some spots we were just 25 km from the center of Moscow. As a result, the main Russian resistance concentrated itself against us, setting extremely elite troops and the heaviest tanks against us. Since we were only attacking with relatively weak forces, there hadn't been real forward movement recently.

In the last few days we were then sitting at the outermost tip of the front, together with a rifle company (or what was still left of the company) and held a village against Russian counterattacks. It was a dumb situation, the village surrounded by forest, enemy in front, right, and left. The bunkers were at most 200 to 250 m away from us, we were constantly under machine-gun fire, as well as artillery and shells, as well as that blasted rocket launcher [known as the Stalin organs]. We were relieved from this situation the day before yesterday. The village in question will only hold until this evening anyway, then everything will pull back a bit. We were in dire need of it, because ever since 15 November we have been at the enemy day in, day out and night in, night out, first on the attack and then back in defense.

Despite the cold (the inner walls of the panzer were covered in centimeter-thick ice), we barely got out of the panzer, even for one night. The food, sausage, bread, and cheese, were usually frozen, so we often couldn't eat anything. The field kitchen frequently couldn't get forward to us—well, to sum it up, it was often really sh**. . . . Today, we're now sitting at the Istra emplacement, a large dam that we took only around 14 days ago. We are to go even farther back for rest. The winter position will likely be held somewhere near here, unfortunately now a large number of comrades lie buried in the region, which is now to become no-man's land. There was even one who we couldn't get out of the shot-up panzer. So for us the war could be over by spring. I'm afraid we'll spend the winter here; some may be hoping that we'll be freshened up in Germany. I'm just hoping that we'll have different panzers by spring, because our guns can't even penetrate at 150–200 m, while the Russian tanks can shoot us down at 600–800 m. Thank God they haven't shot as accurately as us in general.

9.12.41: *OBERSTLEUTNANT* HELLMUTH STIEFF (FOURTH ARMY, ARMY GROUP CENTER)[41]

Unfortunately, no easing of the tension has taken place in our position. . . . The situation is particularly critical for Hoepner's armored group, which had to be taken back to Istra-Klin because north of there, between Klin and the Volga reservoirs, near Reinhardt's armored group, the Russian had taken fresh forces and penetrated deeply. . . .[42] The bitter accusation that has to be cast at our highest leadership is that, despite constant serious indications, they, apparently impressed by their own propaganda, brought out 3 divisions before the decision had really been made—not because of heavy losses, but instead because of reorganization for the distant goals of next year! And furthermore they are never clear about the true conditions because they are sitting too far from the shooting. They are playing at geometry in an appalling way! . . . We even had to take the most grave decisions in that way, without knowing the overall situation. . . .

And in addition to all this, the really dreadful worries about providing the things necessary for life! . . . The roads are navigable, but 75% of the vehicles are broken, replacement parts can't get through, and new vehicles at home are blocked off for restructuring. We are to help ourselves by cannibalizing the broken vehicles. But it's usually always the same things that break. Cannibalizing doesn't help there.[43] It's impossible! We feel so dreadfully abandoned. . . . [*Wir fühlen uns so entsetzlich verlassen.* . . .]

Oh, darling, it is so difficult! I was and still am always an optimist. But for weeks there has been nothing but difficulties, worries, now one piece of bad news after the other, you soon don't know where to turn, because if a miracle doesn't happen soon, we'll be looking at another 1812 here.

11.12.41: *LEUTNANT* GERHARDT LINKE (87 INFANTRY DIVISION, 4 PANZER GROUP, ARMY GROUP CENTER)[44]

The whole unit is busy building new defenses. There are not enough tools. Entrenching tools are lacking altogether. There is no chance of having a supply of indispensable items brought up now. According to orders, rear detachments are to break away from the enemy and set the abandoned villages on fire. Numerous big fires light up the nocturnal sky.

11.12.41: HEINZ POSTENRIEDER (137 INFANTRY DIVISIONS, SECOND ARMY, ARMY GROUP CENTER)[45]

The squadron is in Shatilovo. The Russians are pushing us closer and closer together. The division gives way, more and masses of troops come into the small village. A snowstorm rages. During the night, soldiers, artillery, and horses have to stay in the street. I have duty at night. At 2:30 the radio connection breaks. Shatilovo has been overrun.

12.12.41: *UNTEROFFIZIER* WILHELM PRÜLLER (9 PANZER DIVISION, SECOND ARMY, ARMY GROUP CENTER)[46]

Yesterday we learned that the names of two worthy and deserving men in each company are to be turned in by tomorrow for home leave. I'm one of the two. Urrah! To be home on Christmas Eve? That would be the loveliest Christmas present.

I feel a bit like a coward, a deserter, who leaves his *Kameraden* sitting out on the limb. Moreover, I never thought of going before Christmas, but now that the possibility exists, I can barely wait. Private First-Class Möslinger was to have gone with me. Father of 6 children. This afternoon he fell, a splinter from a Russian shell got him. Isn't that tragic?[47]

12.12.41: DR. HELMUT MACHEMER (1 PANZER ARMY, ARMY GROUP SOUTH)[48]

Reports are that *der Russe* is still bringing in more forces from the Caucasus [region] across Rostov. They are in part entirely new, as yet undeployed divisions, in part those from the remnants of older armies, all thrown together. Their weaponry and their fighting spirit are accordingly different, but it would be wrong to underestimate them.

Of course, this is a troubling situation, in which the only possible thought can be a defense. But we will master even this situation. . . . Even though the Russian people have had more than enough of the war, the *Kommissare* keep the armies together with an iron fist and drive them into battle with no regard for losses and using the most brutal methods. As long as the Russian is within his own sphere of influence, he fights and he fights well. He only defects if there is an opportunity to defect without danger. [There can be] no doubt: The back of the main Russian body has been broken, it won't be able to recover from this blow now. But there are still hard struggles ahead before this war will be over. The decisive question will be whether the Russian can adequately replace the lost war material over the course of the winter. It will be a race for industry. For the battles ahead will also be battles of material, and the better material—in addition to the art of warfare—will be decisive.[49] The Russian has developed the most important devices and brought them, together with foremen and specialized workers, to the East. It's just a question of whether he can establish an industry that is the same or even remotely the same there. Because devices and devices alone, even raw materials, do not make a functioning industry. There is so much more to it, not least transport routes and organizations of all kinds, so it's doubtful whether even a better organized nation in a more favorable environment could succeed in mastering this staggering task.

And now, in addition to that, the Russian will have to stand alone in his armor in the future, now that America and England have got their own worries in the Far East. There really ought to be no doubt about how the scales of victory will tip in the more distant future. But for now no decisive battles are expected until our own rundown armory of vehicles, guns, planes, and tanks is restocked again or replaced from home. For us it is ultimately just a question of transport, which, however, will become easier to solve with every month that passes here at rest. That's how I see the current situation. The thing to do for now is just to stop here.

In the spring, which here means March already, it will very quickly come to decisive blows with fresh forces, who will rapidly make short work of the remnants of the Russian army.

13.12.41: HEINZ POSTENRIEDER (137 INFANTRY DIVISION, SECOND ARMY, ARMY GROUP CENTER)[50]

Early 5 o'clock alarm. The Russians are here. We take our stuff and scram. Antitank gun fires. Tracer bullets whistle through the night. . . . The general is with us.

14.12.41: KLAUS BECKER (ARMY GROUP CENTER)[51]

You will have heard from the *Wehrmachtbericht* that, as a consequence of the winter, the battles here in the East are only very localized now. So both sides are now increasingly concentrating on defense. Everything that lies between the battle lines is thus removed, if possible, so as to ensure no surprises. So at night you see many examples of firelight from villages that are being burned down, some likely by us, others by the Russians. However, in some places the Russian is still pressing quite hard, but that, too, will only be of short duration and then the winter combat lull [*winterliche Kampfruhe*] will set in, apart from aircraft activity, which, here, looks like it will never rest. So Moscow looks like a no-show now this winter. Of course, we don't know where we will finally end up. For the moment, we're going back a bit because of lack of quarters.

14.12.41: SOLDIER UNKNOWN (FOURTH ARMY, ARMY GROUP CENTER)[52]

We are now in the large encirclement outside Moscow. I've just got 40–50 kilometers more to get to Moscow. So, here's just a little bit about our war in Russia: The combat operations around us have quietened down a bit ahead of Moscow. We all thought we would be done with Russia this year and would come back to Germany, to our home, but the winter started too early here. So now there's a war of position for us over the winter. We've a great many tough battles behind us already and there are more tough, many tough battles to come until the time comes for Russia to be thrown to the ground. The Russian is a very good, tough soldier. None of us estimated the Russian to be as good as he is. He is as strong as us with weaponry, he's just lacking leadership. We broke the strongest weapons he had. It cost us a lot of blood, too.

14.12.41: SIEGBERT STEHMANN (163 INFANTRY DIVISION, GERMAN ARMY OF NORWAY)[53]

I know that it's difficult, and for many a man it is too difficult, because the night of mundane things holds him hostage. And, in any case, anyone who has never been out [here] doesn't know how dreadful it is, especially here in the swampy forests. A world separates our thinking from that of the rearmost communications zone. Anyone who has experienced the storm of steel knows that you have to be very tough. He knows that better than any friends at home.

14.12.41: *LEUTNANT* GERHARDT LINKE (87 INFANTRY DIVISION, 4 PANZER GROUP, ARMY GROUP CENTER)[54]

We did not succeed in sealing the breach in our lines. The danger is increasing. . . . Orders have been issued to leave our positions tomorrow. How painful it is! We are practicing the kind of military operations that we have never been taught. With incredible difficulty and absolutely inadequate means we dug up the ground (we literally scraped it with our fingernails!) and fixed up what is still but an apology for a shelter. We spent out last building materials on it. The engineers haven't a nail left, not the least bit of wire. And now we are to give it all up, surrender to the enemy all this territory that we had won in our victorious offensive. Oh my God, what crimes have we committed that we deserve such punishment?

We marched all night. . . . We did not know what the position was. All telephone lines were out of order. Had the enemy cut us off?[55] The icy ground caused us much trouble. It took tremendous effort to drag the machines up the steep inclines. But the [artillery was] too much for us, try as we would. I subsequently learned that one of these constantly skidding guns was blown up. Nothing is known of what happened to the other one.

Soon the road became congested as other regiments used it simultaneously for their retreat. . . . We could hew our way through only by casting aside all pretense of civility.

14.12.41: HEINZ POSTENRIEDER (137 INFANTRY DIVISION, SECOND ARMY, ARMY GROUP CENTER)[56]

It is barely light and all hell breaks loose. All around from the heights the Russians shoot into the middle of the dense columns. Horses rear, tumble and fall, or race over the field. In a wild panic everybody flees to the left. The explosions of the "Stalin organ" hit everywhere. Herbert lies with a shattered head. Kubitzki dead. I partake in an infantry counterattack, machine gun whistles, bullets whiz by like bumble bees, low-flying Russian airplanes attack the fleeing columns, mow down horses, cars burn. I lie pressed to the ground, shoot and have given up hope of seeing home or my Christl again. Again airplanes roar. I look and could scream with joy. Finally! They are German destroyers.[57] We are not yet forgotten and given up. They are now spitting fire on the Russians. Again and again the four birds circle the "kettle" and attack. Steeply they dive and pull up again like swallows. Slowly it is getting quiet. But our general has been torn apart by the "Stalin organ" and comrades are dead. I look up. Our infantry is already moving over the gorge. But the horror of the war lies over the field. Torn-apart people, torn-apart horses. The suffering of the innocent animals bothers me the most. Fatally wounded, they try to get up one more time and fall down again. Whole hitches lie in bloody heaps. One horse is still standing, but blood drips from its flanks. The cruel, merciless winter night will hide everything, and extinguish the last life. We collect ourselves to the left at a *Kolchos* for the breakthrough. Cars start roaring, a fantastic chase. Bullets whistle, soldiers hang on every car. We get through. . . . Many dead Russians on the road.

15.12.41: *UNTEROFFIZIER* GOTTFRIED KUCHENBROD (ARMY GROUP CENTER)[58]

Since the middle of October we have been iron, marching infantry again. . . . At an average [minus] 25 to 30 degrees, we now scuttle along on the country road and presumably into another sector of the front. In the evening you can barely find a more or less adequate "quarters." . . . The Russian conditions have become around eighty percent worse compared with the summer. At other times you would have argued over a tree where you could pitch your tent for the night, now you fight for a nook "behind the stove!" . . . Yes, we have become poor devils [*Ja, wir sind arme Schweine geworden*].

15.12.41: WILLY (ARMY GROUP NORTH)[59]

But this campaign has changed us both outside and in. By that I don't mean to say that I am now a mature man. No, quite the opposite, but the zip of bullets and the thundering of the guns has hardened our souls and made our hearts more receptive to the stirrings of love. . . .

Now, my dear, back to raw reality. There is no news, since, as is well known, the German Army has moved into positions for winter. . . . We have set ourselves up for overwintering twice and now we may have to move on again. The soldier's life brings a lot of variety with it.

15.12.41: *LEUTNANT* GEORG KREUTER (18 PANZER DIVISION, 2 PANZER ARMY, ARMY GROUP CENTER)[60]

At 0400 I take over the rearguard [*Nachhut*]. It consists of two companies in the forward line and a battery of light field howitzers. I attempt to establish wire communications with the companies, but at 0500 I give up, because everything is destroyed. Elements of the regiment are moving through the village; to be sure, [they're moving through] much later than ordered, because the icy roads are making the withdrawal terribly difficult. 3 Panzer IIs have to be blown up, as they're no longer march worthy. In some instances, they're only short a battery. In addition, at least 10 motor vehicles are set on fire. Nothing must be allowed to fall into the hands of the enemy! But it's really a shame that so much of value has to be destroyed. . . . I have covering parties [*Sicherungen*] set up and send out a patrol to make contact with the company on the left. At 0900 the 4th battery also arrives. But still elements of the battalion are stuck here, it's enough to drive one to despair [*es ist zum Verzweifeln*]. There are more horses laying down than are standing. At 1000 1st Company reports that it is pulling back under considerable enemy pressure. . . . The last elements of the battalion abandon their horse-drawn vehicles, burn them, and fall back on foot. . . . In the night I nearly lost my way. It's quite difficult to find your bearings. Everywhere it's burning.

Appendix 1

Equivalent Military Ranks[1]

GERMAN / AMERICAN

Officer Ranks:
Generalfeldmarschall	Field Marshal
Generaloberst	General
General (der Infanterie, etc.)	Lieutenant General
Generalleutnant	Major General
Generalmajor	Brigadier General
Oberst	Colonel
Oberstleutnant	Lieutenant Colonel
Major	Major
Hauptmann or Rittmeister	Captain
Oberleutnant	First Lieutenant
Leutnant	Second Lieutenant

Non-Commissioned Officers (NCOs):
Stabsfeldwebel	Sergeant Major
Oberfeldwebel	Master Sergeant
Feldwebel	Technical Sergeant
Unterfeldwebel	Staff Sergeant
Unteroffizier	Noncommissioned Officer

Enlisted Men:
Stabsgefreiter	Administrative Corporal
Obergefreiter	Corporal
Gefreiter	Lance Corporal
Obersoldat	Private 1st Class
Soldat (Schütze)	Private (Rifleman)

Medical Ranks:

Oberstarzt	Colonel (med.)
Oberfeldarzt	Lt.Col (med.)
Oberstabsarzt	Major (med.)
Stabsarzt	Captain (med.)
Oberarzt	First Lt. (med.)
Assistenzarzt	Second Lt. (med.)
Unterarzt	NCO (med.)

Appendix 2

Order of Battle of Germany's Eastern Army (*Ostheer*)[1] (22 June 1941)

ARMY GROUP NORTH

GFM Ritter von Leeb

ARMY GROUP RESERVE

206 Infantry Division
251 Infantry Division
254 Infantry Division

OKH RESERVE (AT ARMY GROUP NORTH)

86 Infantry Division (in transport)
SS "Police" Infantry Division (in transport)

REAR ARMY AREA 101[2]

207 Security Division
281 Security Division
285 Security Division

SIXTEENTH ARMY

Generaloberst Ernst Busch
253 Infantry Division (army reserve)
2 Army Corps
  12 Infantry Division
  32 Infantry Division
  121 Infantry Division
10 Army Corps
  30 Infantry Division
  126 Infantry Division
28 Army Corps
  122 Infantry Division
  123 Infantry Division

4 PANZER GROUP

Generaloberst Erich Hoepner
SS *"Totenkopf"* Infantry Division (mot.) (group reserve)
41 Panzer Corps
  1 Panzer Division
  6 Panzer Division
  36 Infantry Division (mot.)
  269 Infantry Division
56 Panzer Corps
  8 Panzer Division
  3 Infantry Division (mot.)
  290 Infantry Division

EIGHTEENTH ARMY

Generaloberst Georg von Küchler
1 Army Corps
  1 Infantry Division
  11 Infantry Division
  21 Infantry Division
26 Army Corps
  61 Infantry Division
  217 Infantry Division
  291 Infantry Division
38 Army Corps
  58 Infantry Division

ARMY GROUP CENTER

GFM Fedor von Bock

ARMY GROUP RESERVE

293 Infantry Division

OKH RESERVE (AT ARMY GROUP CENTER)

15 Infantry Division (in transport)
52 Infantry Division (in transport)
106 Infantry Division (in transport)
110 Infantry Division (in transport)
112 Infantry Division (in transport)
197 Infantry Division (in transport)
900 Instructional ("*Lehr*") Brigade (mot.)

REAR ARMY AREA 102

221 Security Division
286 Security Division
403 Security Division

2 PANZER GROUP

Generaloberst Heinz Guderian
255 Infantry Division (group reserve)
12 Army Corps
   31 Infantry Division
   34 Infantry Division
   45 Infantry Division
24 Panzer Corps
   3 Panzer Division
   4 Panzer Division
   10 Infantry Division (mot.)
   267 Infantry Division
   1 Cavalry Division
46 Panzer Corps
   10 Panzer Division
   SS "*Das Reich*" Infantry Division (mot.)

Infantry Regiment "*Grossdeutschland*" (mot.)
47 Panzer Corps
  17 Panzer Division
  18 Panzer Division
  29 Infantry Division (mot.)
  167 Infantry Division

FOURTH ARMY

GFM Günther von Kluge
7 Army Corps
  7 Infantry Division
  23 Infantry Division
  258 Infantry Division
  268 Infantry Division
9 Army Corps
  137 Infantry Division
  263 Infantry Division
  292 Infantry Division
13 Army Corps
  17 Infantry Division
  78 Infantry Division
43 Army Corps
  131 Infantry Division
  134 Infantry Division
  252 Infantry Division

NINTH ARMY

Generaloberst Adolf Strauss
8 Army Corps
  8 Infantry Division
  28 Infantry Division
  161 Infantry Division
20 Army Corps
  162 Infantry Division
  256 Infantry Division
42 Army Corps
  87 Infantry Division
  102 Infantry Division
  129 Infantry Division

3 PANZER GROUP

Generaloberst Hermann Hoth
5 Army Corps
  5 Infantry Division
  35 Infantry Division
6 Army Corps
  6 Infantry Division
  26 Infantry Division
39 Panzer Corps
  7 Panzer Division
  20 Panzer Division
  14 Infantry Division (mot.)
  20 Infantry Division (mot.)
57 Panzer Corps
  12 Panzer Division
  19 Panzer Division
  18 Infantry Division (mot.)

ARMY GROUP SOUTH

GFM Gerd von Rundstedt

ARMY GROUP RESERVE

99 Light ("*Jäger*") Division

OKH RESERVE (AT ARMY GROUP SOUTH)

4 Mountain Division
79 Infantry Division (in transport)
95 Infantry Division (in transport)
113 Infantry Division (in transport)
125 Infantry Division
132 Infantry Division (in transport)

REAR ARMY AREA 103

213 Security Division
444 Security Division
454 Security Division

ELEVENTH ARMY

Generaloberst Eugen *Ritter* von Schobert
22 Infantry Division (army reserve)
72 Infantry Division (German Army Mission Romania)
11 Army Corps
  76 Infantry Division
  239 Infantry Division
30 Army Corps
  198 Infantry Division
54 Army Corps
  50 Infantry Division
  170 Infantry Division

SEVENTEENTH ARMY

General der Infanterie Carl-Heinrich von Stülpnagel
97 Light Division (army reserve)
100 Light Division (army reserve)
4 Army Corps
  24 Infantry Division
  71 Infantry Division
  262 Infantry Division
  295 Infantry Division
  296 Infantry Division
49 Mountain Corps
  1 Mountain Division
  68 Infantry Division
  257 Infantry Division
52 Army Corps
  101 Light Division

SIXTH ARMY

GFM Walter von Reichenau[3]
168 Infantry Divison (army reserve)
17 Army Corps
  56 Infantry Division
  62 Infantry Division
44 Army Corps
  9 Infantry Division
  297 Infantry Division

1 PANZER GROUP

Generaloberst Ewald von Kleist
13 Panzer Division (group reserve)
16 Infantry Division (mot.) (group reserve)
25 Infantry Division (mot.) (group reserve)
SS *"Adolf Hitler"* Infantry Division (mot.) (group reserve)
3 Panzer Corps
  14 Panzer Division
  44 Infantry Division
  298 Infantry Division
14 Panzer Corps
  9 Panzer Division
  16 Panzer Division
SS *"Wiking"* Infantry Division (mot.)
48 Panzer Corps
  11 Panzer Division
  57 Infantry Division
  75 Infantry Division
29 Army Corps
  111 Infantry Division
  299 Infantry Division

Appendix 3

Order of Battle of German Army Group Center[1] (2 October 1941)

ARMY GROUP RESERVE

19 Panzer Division
Infantry Regiment "*Grossdeutschland*" (mot.)
900 Brigade (mot.)

COMMANDER, REAR ARMY AREA CENTER

221 Security Division
286 Security Division
403 Security Division
454 Security Division[2]
339 Infantry Division
707 Infantry Division
SS Cavalry Brigade

2 PANZER GROUP

Generaloberst Heinz Guderian
34 Army Corps
   45 Infantry Division
   134 Infantry Division
35 Army Corps
   1 Cavalry Division
   95 Infantry Division

262 Infantry Division
293 Infantry Division
296 Infantry Division
24 Panzer Corps
  3 Panzer Division
  4 Panzer Division
  10 Infantry Division (mot.)
47 Panzer Corps
  17 Panzer Division
  18 Panzer Division
  29 Infantry Division (mot.)
48 Panzer Corps
  9 Panzer Division
  16 Infantry Division (mot.)
  25 Infantry Division (mot.)

SECOND ARMY

Generaloberst Maximilian *Freiherr* von Weichs
  112 Infantry Division (army reserve)
13 Army Corps
  17 Infantry Division
  260 Infantry Division
43 Army Corps
  52 Infantry Division
  131 Infantry Division
53 Army Corps
  31 Infantry Division
  56 Infantry Division
  167 Infantry Division

4 PANZER GROUP

Generaloberst Erich Hoepner
12 Army Corps
  34 Infantry Division
  98 Infantry Division
40 Panzer Corps
  2 Panzer Division
  10 Panzer Division
  258 Infantry Division
46 Panzer Corps
  5 Panzer Division

11 Panzer Division
252 Infantry Division
57 Panzer Corps
20 Panzer Division
3 Infantry Division (mot.)
SS *"Das Reich"* Infantry Division (mot.)

FOURTH ARMY

GFM Günther von Kluge
7 Army Corps
7 Infantry Division
23 Infantry Division
197 Infantry Division
267 Infantry Division
9 Army Corps
137 Infantry Division
183 Infantry Division
263 Infantry Division
292 Infantry Division
20 Army Corps
15 Infantry Division
78 Infantry Division
268 Infantry Division

NINTH ARMY

Generaloberst Adolf Strauss
161 Infantry Division (army reserve)
8 Army Corps
8 Infantry Division
28 Infantry Division
87 Infantry Division
23 Army Corps
102 Infantry Division
206 Infantry Division
251 Infantry Division
256 Infantry Division
27 Army Corps
86 Infantry Division
162 Infantry Division
255 Infantry Division

3 PANZER GROUP

Generaloberst Hermann Hoth
5 Army Corps
  5 Infantry Division
  35 Infantry Division
  106 Infantry Division
6 Army Corps
  26 Infantry Division
  110 Infantry Division
41 Panzer Corps
  1 Panzer Division
  6 Infantry Division
  36 Infantry Division (mot.)
56 Panzer Corps
  6 Panzer Division
  7 Panzer Division
  14 Infantry Division (mot.)
  129 Infantry Division

Appendix 4

Soldiers of *Barbarossa*—Names, Ranks, and Units of German Soldiers Whose Field Post Letters and Diary Entries Are Cited in the Narrative

Note: While the vast majority of the soldiers whose letters and diary entries fill this volume are now deceased, protecting their privacy—and, more to the point, the privacy of their still surviving family members—remains important to many scholars and to institutions such as the Library for Contemporary History (*Bibliothek für Zeitgeschichte*), Stuttgart, Germany. As a result, a slight majority of the surnames of the German soldiers used in this collection are incomplete (e.g., "Paul R." or "Gefr. Franz B."); in several cases, the soldiers remain anonymous, and once or twice pseudonyms are in play. In most cases, the soldiers' ranks could be readily determined; however, this was sometimes not possible (unit designations were much easier to ascertain). While the organization of the names below may, at first glance, appear unorthodox, given the great diversity in how the names are presented, it seemed to make sense to first list the minority of soldiers for whom no rank was found and to follow that with an alphabetical listing by both rank (or professional title) and first names (which are mostly complete). What this organizational template reveals is that enlisted personnel and NCOs make up the majority of the contributors, while officers (2nd Lt. to Major with just one rank of Lt.Col.) are a distinct minority—hardly surprising given that the former outnumbered the latter by a wide margin in the German Army. And perhaps it goes without saying that it is these men—enlisted ranks, NCOs, and lower-ranking officers—who are the real "Soldiers of *Barbarossa*," and, perforce, have the most graphic and compelling stories to tell of the most deadly, destructive, and genocidal military campaign the world has ever witnessed.

Adelbert-Ottheinrich Rühle (Ostfront)
Albert M. (H.Gr.Süd)
Albert Neuhaus (H.Gr.Nord)
Alexander Cohrs (H.Gr.Süd)
Alfons Haas (Ostfront)
Alois Dwenger (11 Armee)
Anon. (H.Gr.Mitte)
Anon. (K.G. 55)
Anon. (5 ID)
Anon. (18 PD)
Anon. (20 PD)
Anon. (45 ID)
Anon. (45 ID)
Anton Böhrer (294 ID)
August Sahm (H.Gr.Süd)
A.V. (36 ID)
Edgar Steuerwald (H.Gr.Süd)
Elmar Lieb (2 PzGr)
Erich Dohl (16 Armee)
Erich Kuby (3 ID [mot.])
Ernst Guicking (52 ID)
Friedrich G. (Z.G. 26)
Franzl (H.Gr.Süd)
Franz Siebeler (14 PD)
Fritz (H.Gr.Mitte)
Fritz Belke (6 ID)
Fritz Köhler (H.Gr.Mitte)
Fritz Pabst (6 Armee)
Fritz Sigel (H.Gr.Mitte)
Geert-Ulrich Mutzenbecher
    (H.Gr.Mitte)
Georg Fulde (Luftwaffe)
Geo. S. (H.Gr.Nord)
Gerd Habedanck (Kriegsberichter)
Gerhard Kunde (68 ID)
Günter von Scheven (H.Gr.Mitte)
Hans-Albert Giese (9 Armee)
Hans Albring (Ostfront)
Hans-Heinrich Ludwig (H.Gr.Nord)
Hans Martin Stählin (Ostfront)
Hans-Otto (268 ID)
Hans Simon (12 ID)
Harald Henry (H.Gr.Mitte)
H.D. (16 PD)
Heinrich Witt (Ostfront)

Heinz Postenrieder (137 ID)
Heinz Rahe (13 PD)
Hellmuth H. (50 ID)
Helmut Gädeke (H.Gr.Mitte)
Helmut Nick (Ostfront)
Helmut von Harnack (H.Gr.Mitte)
Hermann Stracke (Ostfront)
H.K. (72 ID)
H.T. (Ostfront)
Jakob Geimer (H.Gr.Süd)
Johannes Hamm (1PzGr)
Johannes Huebner (H.Gr.Mitte)
Josef Eickhoff (Ostfront)
Karl Fuchs (7 PD)
Karl-Gottfried Vierkorn (23 ID)
Karl Nünnighoff (16 PD)
Klaus K. (H.Gr.Mitte)
Kurt Marlow (68 ID)
Kurt Miethke (H.Gr.Süd)
Kurt Vogeler (H.Gr.Nord)
L.B. (Ostfront)
Leopold Artner (Ostfront)
Paul R. (44 ID)
Peter Sch. (19 PD)
R.B. (31 ID)
Rudolf Oehus (H.Gr.Süd)
Siegbert Stehmann (163 ID)
Siegfried Roemer (1 PzGr)
Walter Neuser (H.Gr.Mitte)
Walther Loos (45 ID)
Werner Beermann (9 Armee)
Werner R. (8 PD)
Wilhelm Borger (H.Gr.Süd)
Willi F. (198 ID)
Wolfgang A. (1 ID)
Dr. Adolf B. (25 ID [mot.])
Dr. Hans Lierow (6 ID)
Dr. Heinrich Haape (6 ID)
Dr. Helmut Machemer (1 PzGr)
Dr. Hermann Türk (3 PD)
Dr. Konrad Jarausch (H.Gr.Mitte)
Fw. Hans M. (79 ID)
Fw. Heinz R. (H.Gr.Süd)
Fw. Herbert E. (SS "DR")
Gefr. Adolf M. (260 ID)

Gefr. Alfons L. (H.Gr.Süd)

Gefr. Alois Scheuer (197 ID)

Gefr. Eberhard W. (5 ID)

Gefr. Ewald M. (125 ID)

Gefr. Ferdinand B. (125 ID)

Gefr. Ferdinand M. (167 ID)

Gefr. Franz B. (198 ID)

Gefr. Fritz G. (101 le.Inf.Div.)

Gefr. G. (11 PD)

Gefr. Gerhard Bopp (35)

Gefr. Gu. (11 PD)

Gefr. Hans B. (269 ID)

Gefr. Hans Caspar von Wiedebach-
Nostitz (20 PD)

Gefr. Hans Efferbergen (H.Gr.Süd)

Gefr. Hans F. (Flak-Lehr-Rgt.)

Gefr. Hans Joachim C. (23 ID)

Gefr. Hans Roth (299 ID)

Gefr. Heinz B. (23 ID)

Gefr. Heinz B. (291 ID)

Gefr. Heinz Sch. (H.Gr.Nord)

Gefr. Heinz T. del B. (Res.Laz.
Obornik/Warthegau)

Gefr. Herbert R. (45 ID)

Gefr. H.J. (Hr.Gr.Nord)

Gefr. Hubert Hegele (1 MD)

Gefr. Jean Z. (Nb.Werf.Rgt. 51)

Gefr. Josef B. (23 ID)

Gefr. L.B. (269 ID)

Gefr. Ludwig B. (296 ID)

Gefr. Martin W. (52 ID)

Gefr. M.F. (256 ID)

Gefr. Otto St. (H.Gr.Nord)

Gefr. Paul B. (Luftwaffe Flak-
Sondergeräte-Werkst.Zug 13)

Gefr. Röder (H.Gr.Nord)

Gefr. Rudolf Stützel (5 ID)

Gefr. Viktor Czermak (H.Gr.Süd)

Gefr. W. (137 ID)

Gefr. Werner R. (Zug Art.M.P.L.715)

Gefr. Wilhelm H. (Bau-Btl.46)

Hptm. Friedrich M. (73 ID)

Hptm. Herbert Pabst (77 St.K.G.)

Hpt.Wm. H. S. (255 ID)

Ing. H.J. (Dt. Heeresmission Rumänien)

Lt. Arnold Döring (53 K.G.)

Lt. Ernst E. (13 PD)

Lt. Ernst-Martin Rhein (6 ID)

Lt. Georg Kreuter (18 PD)

Lt. Gerhardt Linke (87 ID)

Lt. Gerhard S. (29 ID [mot.])

Lt. H.-J. Breitenbach (16 Armee)

Lt. Heinz Döll (18 PD)

Lt. Helmut D. (4 MD)

Lt. Helmut H. (258 ID)

Lt. H.H. (258 ID)

Lt. H.J. Schmidt (H.Gr.Mitte)

Lt. Joachim H. (131 ID)

Lt. Jochen Hahn (292 ID)

Lt. Otto Sch. (73 ID)

Lt. Pohl (18 PD)

Lt. Rudolf Maurer (251 ID)

Lt. Walter Melchinger (H.Gr.Süd)

Lt. Willibald G. (57 ID)

Lt. Will Thomas (9 Armee)

Mj. Hans Meier-Welcker (251 ID)

Mj. Hans R. (7 PD)

Mj. Hans Riederer (H.Gr.Mitte)

Mj. Hans Sch. (H.G.Süd)

Mj. S. (20 PD)

Mj. Werner Heinemann (23 ID)

Oblt. August D. (131 ID)

Oblt. Fabich (IR "GD") [mot.])

Oblt. Juerg von Kalckreuth (6 ID)

Oblt. K. (20 PD)

Oblt. Richard D. (7 PD)

Obstlt. Hellmuth Stieff (4 Armee)

O.Fähnr. Klaus B. (Luftwaffe
Flakscheinwerfer-Einheit)

Offz. Hans Hertel (3 PzGr.)

Offz. Leo Tilgner (H.Gr.Nord)

Offz. Martin Steglich (H.Gr.Nord)

Offz. Udo von Alvensleben (16 PD)

O.Fw. E.K. (260 ID)

O.Gefr. Ferdi B. (197 ID)

O.Gefr. Franz F. (12 PD)

O.Gefr. Fritz N. (35 ID)

O.Gefr. G.B. (46 ID)

O.Gefr. Heinz B. (23 ID)

O.Gefr. H.S. (131 ID)

O.Gefr. Joseph B. (2 PD)
O.Gefr. Konrad F. (1 ID)
O.Gefr. Matthias (6 ID)
O.Gefr. M.H. (268 ID)
O.Gefr. Werner E. (73 ID)
Pz.-O.Sch. Erich Hager (17 ID)
Sold. Albrecht B. (20 PD)
Sold. Alfred V. (36 ID [mot.])
Sold. Carlheinz B. (SS-Div. "Wiking"
    [mot.])
Sold. E.L. (1 MD)
Sold. H. (Armee-Nachr.Rgt. 501)
Sold. Hans M. (262 ID)
Sold. Hans Olte (H.Gr.Mitte)
Sold. Heinz Sch. (101 le.ID)
Sold. Josef Beck (H.Gr.Mitte)
Sold. J.Z. (Landesschützen-Bataillon
    619)
Sold. K.H.G. (13 PD)
Sold. Manfred V. (32 ID)
Sold. Max Sch. (17 ID)
Sold. Rudolf B. (H.Gr.Nord)
Sold. Rudolf L. (Ostfront)
Sold. Sepp P. (l.Res.Flak-Abt. 717)
Sold. S.K. (78 ID)
Sold. Waldo P. (5 ID)
Sold. Werner F. (Fla.M.G.Btl. [schw.]
    mot. Z 52)
SS-Sturmm. Eugen F. (2. SS-Brigade
    [mot.])
SS-Sturmm. Hans T. (SS-Kampf-
    gruppe "Nord")

St.Fw. Christoph B. (Trsp.
    Kol.d.Lw.9/VII)
St.Fw. Helmuth A. Dittri (20 PD)
Uffz. Edmund M. (Luftwaffe
    Flak-Rgt. 49)
Uffz. Egon N. (6 ID)
Uffz. E.J. (Bau-Btl. 44)
Uffz. E.K. (98 ID)
Uffz. E.M. (17 PD)
Uffz. E.T. (H.Gr.Süd)
Uffz. Fritz Hübner (H.Gr.Mitte)
Uffz. Gottfried Kuchenbrod
    (H.Gr.Mitte)
Uffz. Hans S. (H.Gr.Nord)
Uffz. Heinz B. (125 ID)
Uffz. Heinz H. (6 ID)
Uffz. Heinz H. (H.Gr.Süd)
Uffz. H. G. (79 ID)
Uffz. H.H. (6 ID)
Uffz. Karl R. (5 PD)
Uffz. Karl Schönfeld (H.Gr.Mitte)
Uffz. L.K. (183 ID)
Uffz. Max F. (256 ID)
Uffz. Robert Rupp (17 PD)
Uffz. Rudolf F. (267 ID)
Uffz. W.F. (251 ID)
Uffz. Wilhelm Prüller (9 PD)
Uffz. Wilhelm Wessler (6 ID)
Uffz. Willy P. (167 ID)
Uffz. X.M. (707 ID)
Wm. A.R. (Ostfront)
Wm. Artur W. (129 ID)
Wm. Josef L. (129 ID)

KEY TO ABBREVIATIONS:

Fw. = Feldwebel
Gefr. = Gefreiter
Hptm. = Hauptmann
Hpt.Wm. = Hauptwachtmeister
Ing. = Ingenieur
Lt. = Leutnant
Mj. = Major
Oblt. = Oberleutnant
Obstlt. = Oberstleutnant

O.Fähnr. = Oberfähnrich
O.Fw. = Oberfeldwebel
Offz. = Offizier
O.Gefr. = Obergefreiter
Pz.-O.Sch. = Panzer-Oberschütze
Sold. = Soldat
St.Fw. = Stabsfeldwebel
Uffz. = Unteroffizier
Wm. = Wachtmeister

Notes

CHAPTER 1

1. Mühleisen (ed.), *Hellmuth Stieff Briefe*, 140.

2. Buchbender and Sterz (eds.), *Das andere Gesicht des Krieges. Deutsche Feldpostbriefe 1939–1945*, 13–14.

3. Fröhlich (ed.), *Die Tagebücher von Joseph Goebbels, Teil II: Diktate 1941–1945, Band 2: Oktober-Dezember 1941*, 476 (11 December 1941).

4. Buchbender and Sterz (eds.), *Das andere Gesicht des Krieges. Deutsche Feldpostbriefe 1939–1945*, 13–14.

5. BA-MA RH 27-2/22, KTB 2. Pz.-Div., 31.1.42.

6. BA-MA RH 27-1/58, KTB 1. Pz.-Div., Fol. 45, 9.11.41.

7. Ibid. Fol. 47, 12.11.41.

8. Luther, *Barbarossa Unleashed. The German Blitzkrieg through Central Russia to the Gates of Moscow. June-December 1941*, 345.

9. Lubbeck, *At Leningrad's Gates. The Story of a Soldier with Army Group North*, 118–119.

10. Nünnighoff, *Museumsstiftung Post und Telekommunikation* (MPT), 3.2008.1388 (26 November 1941).

11. Adamczyk, *Feuer! An Artilleryman's Life on the Eastern Front*, 159.

12. All examples as cited in Vaizey, *Surviving Hitler's War. Family Life in Germany, 1939–48*, 57.

13. Beak (ed.), *Feldpostbriefe eines Landsers 1939–1943*, 55 (30 December 1941).

14. Fritz, *Frontsoldaten. The German Soldier in World War II*; Latzel, *Deutsche Soldaten—nationalsozialistischer Krieg? Kriegserlebnis—Kriegserfahrung 1939–1945*; Humburg, *Das Gesicht des Krieges. Feldpostbriefe von Wehrmachtssoldaten aus der Sowjetunion 1941–1944*; Müller, *Deutsche Soldaten und ihre Feinde. Nationalismus an Front und Heimatfront im Zweiten Weltkrieg*; Neitzel and Welzer, *Soldaten. On Fighting, Killing and Dying: The Secret World War II Tapes of German POWs*.

15. Buchbender and Sterz (eds.), *Das andere Gesicht des Krieges. Deutsche Feldpostbriefe 1939–1945*, 13.

16. On the many issues associated with field post as a historical source see Latzel, "Feldpostbriefe: Überlegungen zur Aussagekraft einer Quelle," in Hartmann, Hürter and Jureit (eds.), *Verbrechen der Wehrmacht. Bilanz einer Debatte*, 171–181.

17. As cited in Vaizey, *Surviving Hitler's War. Family Life in Germany, 1939–48*, 11.

18. Buchbender and Sterz (eds.), *Das andere Gesicht des Krieges. Deutsche Feldpostbriefe 1939–1945*, 13.

19. http://www.lexikon-der-wehrmacht.de/Soldat/Feldpost-R.htm

20. Buchbender and Sterz (eds.), *Das andere Gesicht des Krieges. Deutsche Feldpostbriefe 1939–1945*, 14 and 24.

21. Latzel, *Deutsche Soldaten—nationalsozialistischer Krieg? Kriegserlebnis—Kriegserfahrung 1939–1945*, 26–28.

22. Humburg, "Die Bedeutung der Feldpost für die Soldaten in Stalingrad," in Wette and Ueberschär (eds.), *Stalingrad. Mythos und Wirklichkeit einer Schlacht*, 72.

23. Latzel, *Deutsche Soldaten—nationalsozialistischer Krieg? Kriegserlebnis—Kriegserfahrung 1939–1945*, 26–28.

24. Kilian, "Postal Censorship from 1939 to 1945," at http://www.feldpost-archiv.de/english/e11-zensur.html.

25. Buchbender and Sterz (eds.), *Das andere Gesicht des Krieges. Deutsche Feldpostbriefe 1939–1945*, 15.

26. Kilian, "Postal Censorship from 1939 to 1945," at http://www.feldpost-archiv.de/english/e11-zensur.html.

27. Bremer, *Die verlorene Jugend. Jahrgang 1923. Geschriebene und gezeichnete Skizzen über den 2. Weltkrieg und dessen Vorbereitungen*, 25.

28. Vaizey, *Surviving Hitler's War*, 55.

29. Similar restrictions were imposed on Finnish field post in 1941, but as Sonja Hagelstam noted, "Sometimes it seemed more important to the soldiers to give utterance to different topics than to follow the regulations by the letter." Hagelstam, "Families, Separation and Emotional Coping in War: Bridging Letters Between Home and Front, 1941–44," in Kinnunen and Kivimäki (eds.), *Finland in World War II. History, Memory, Interpretations*, 283.

30. Ehrenburg, *Russia at War*, 106.

31. Humburg, *Das Gesicht des Krieges*, 170–171. See also, Kilian, "Moods in Wartime: The Emotions Expressed in Forces Mail," in Echternkamp (ed.), *Germany and the Second World War*. Volume IX/II, *German Wartime Society 1939–1945: Exploitation, Interpretations, Exclusion*, 284–285.

32. Pabst, *The Outermost Frontier: A German Soldier in the Russian Campaign*, 35.

33. Bähr and Bähr (eds.), *Kriegsbriefe Gefallener Studenten, 1939–1945*, 83 (20 October 1941).

34. Domarus, *Hitler. Speeches and Proclamations 1932–1945: The Chronicle of a Dictatorship. Volume IV. The Years 1941 to 1945*, 2497 (9 October 1941).

35. Piekalkiewicz, *Moscow 1941. The Frozen Offensive*, 113.

36. Sebastian, *Journal, 1935–1944*, 425 (10 October 1941).

37. Fröhlich (ed.), *Die Tagebücher von Joseph Goebbels, Teil II: Diktate 1941–1945, Band 2: Oktober–Dezember 1941*, 87–88 (10 October 1941).

38. Buchbender and Sterz (eds.), *Das andere Gesicht des Krieges. Deutsche Feldpostbriefe 1939–1945*, 86 (11 November 1941).

39. Beermann (ed.), *Soldat Werner Beermann Feldpostbriefe 1941–1942*, 181 (9 December 1941).

40. Fröhlich (ed.), *Die Tagebücher von Joseph Goebbels, Teil II: Band 2*, 483 (12 December 1941).

41. Steinert, *Hitler's War and the Germans. Public Mood and Attitude during the Second World War*, 152.

42. By early 1942, Goebbels's lack of success would convince him to change how the war was represented to the German people in order to better manage expectations. Welch, *The Third Reich: Politics and Propaganda*, 102–103.

43. *Gefr.* Hans Joachim C. (06 742 C), Collection *Bibliothek für Zeitgeschichte* (hereafter cited as "Collection BfZ").

44. Ehrenburg, *Russia at War*, 106.

45. Vaizey, *Surviving Hitler's War. Family Life in Germany, 1939–48*, 12.

46. Reddemann (ed.), *Zwischen Front und Heimat. Der Briefwechsel des münsterischen Ehepaares Agnes und Albert Neuhaus 1940–1944*, 222–223 (25 June 1941).

47. Fuchs Richardson (ed.), *Your Loyal and Loving Son. The Letters of Tank Gunner Karl Fuchs, 1937–41*, 112.

48. Ltr., Dr. Heinrich Haape, to his fiancée, 22.6.41.

49. Kempowski (ed.), *Das Echolot. Barbarossa '41. Ein kollektives Tagebuch*, 192–193.

50. Sahm (ed.), *Verzweiflung und Glaube. Briefe aus dem Krieg 1939–1942*, 40–41.

51. Wette, *The Wehrmacht. History, Myth, Reality*, 180.

52. All quotations gleaned from Hannes Heer, "How Amorality Became Normality: Reflections on the Mentality of German Soldiers on the Eastern Front," in Heer and Naumann (eds.), *War of Extermination. The German Military in World War II 1941–1944*, 331–332. See also, Latzel, *Deutsche Soldaten—nationalsozialistischer Krieg? Kriegserlebnis—Kriegserfahrung 1939–1945*, 315–316.

53. Lubbeck, *At Leningrad's Gates. The Story of a Soldier with Army Group North*, 112.

54. Reese, *A Stranger to Myself*, 182.

55. Rutherford and Wettstein, *The German Army on the Eastern Front. An Inner View of the Ostheer's Experiences of War*, 169.

56. Stargardt, *The German War. A Nation under Arms, 1939–1945*, 211.

57. Heer, "How Amorality Became Normality: Reflections on the Mentality of German Soldiers on the Eastern Front," 329–344.

58. Fritze is writing in relation to National Socialists, and, although only a small minority of German soldiers were party members, the analysis may be applied more generally. Fritze, "Did the National Socialists Have a Different Morality?" in Bialas and Fritze (eds.), *Nazi Ideology and Ethics*, 59, 65.

59. Pine, *Hitler's "National Community." Society and Culture in Nazi Germany*, 93.

60. Thanks to Dr. David Harrisville for advance access to his forthcoming study.

61. Kühne, "Guppenkohäsion und Kameradschaftsmythos in der Wehrmacht," in Müller and Volkmann (eds.), *Die Wehrmacht: Mythos und Realität*, 539.

62. Bidermann, *In Deadly Combat. A German Soldier's Memoir of the Eastern Front*, 70.

63. Günther, *Hot Motors, Cold Feet. A Memoir of Service with the Motorcycle Battalion of SS-Division "Reich" 1940–1941*, 207.

64. Pöppel, *Heaven and Hell. The War Diary of a German Paratrooper*, 71.

65. Fuchs Richardson (ed.), *Sieg Heil! War Letters of Tank Gunner Karl Fuchs 1937–1941*, 117 (1 July 1941).

66. Rutherford, *Combat and Genocide on the Eastern Front. The German Infantry's War, 1941–1944*.

67. Neitzel and Welzer, *Soldaten. On Fighting, Killing and Dying*, 238.

68. Ibid, 5.

69. "Gegen Kritik immun," interview by Spörl and Wiegrefe, in *Der Spiegel*, 23/1999, 62.

70. Hartmann, *Wehrmacht im Ostkrieg. Front und militärisches Hinterland 1941/42*, 802.

71. Pohl, *Die Herrschaft der Wehrmacht. Deutsche Militärbesatzung und einheimische Bevölkerung in der Sowjetunion 1941–1944*, 348–349.

72. Wiegrefe, "Abrechnung mit Hitlers Generälen," in *Spiegel Online*, 27 November 2001.

73. See Kay and Stahel, "Reconceiving Criminality in the German Army on the Eastern Front," in Kay and Stahel (eds.), *Mass Violence in Nazi-Occupied Europe*, 173–194.

74. Diary entry recorded on 30 March 1942 in the village of Burtsevo. The diary remains unpublished and was made available by the family to Dr. Oleg Beyda. I am grateful to Oleg for supplying this excerpt.

75. Shils and Janowitz, "Cohesion and Disintegration in the Wehrmacht in World War II," in *Public Opinion Quarterly*, Vol. 12, No. 2, 1948, 280–315.

76. Bartov, *The Eastern Front, 1941–45, German Troops and the Barbarisation of Warfare*; Bartov, *Hitler's Army. Soldiers, Nazis, and War in the Third Reich*. A highly critical perspective on Bartov's use of field post is provided by Latzel, "Wehrmachtsoldaten zwischen 'Normalität' und NS-Ideologie, oder: Was sucht die Forschung in der Feldpost?" in Müller and Volkmann (eds.), *Die Wehrmacht. Mythos und Realität*, 577–580. Challenging Omer Bartov's claim that the primary groups were largely destroyed in 1941 is Christoph Rass's study of the 253 Infantry Division. Rass, "Menschenmaterial." *Deutsche Soldaten an der Ostfront. Innenansichten einer Infanteriedivision 1939–1945*.

77. *True to Type. A Selection from Letters and Diaries of German Soldiers and Civilians Collected on the Soviet-German Front*, 32 (5 January 1942).

78. Kühne, "Male Bonding and Shame Culture: Hitler's Soldiers and the Moral Basis of Genocidal Warfare," in Jensen and Szejnmann (eds.), *Ordinary People as Mass Murderers. Perpetrators in Comparative Perspectives*, 64.

79. Hillgruber, "The German Military Leaders' View of Russia Prior to the Attack on the Soviet Union," in Wegner (ed.), *From Peace to War. Germany, Soviet Russia and the World, 1939–1941*, 169–170.

80. Förster, "Zum Russlandbild der Militärs 1941–1945," in Volkmann (ed.), *Das Russlandbild im Dritten Reich*, 141–163; Wette, "Juden, Bolschewisten, Slawen. Rassenideologische Rußland-Feindbilder Hitlers und der Wehrmachtgeneräle," in Pietrow-Ennker (ed.), *Präventivkrieg? Der deutsche Angriff auf die Sowjetunion*, 40–58.

81. Kipp, *Großreinemachen im Osten. Feindbilder in deutschen Feldpostbriefen im Zweiten Weltkrieg*. In addition, as Peter Fritzsche observed, "In World War II as in World War I, soldiers classified friends and foes in terms of relative cleanliness, but in this conflict they were much more apt to make sweeping judgments about the population and to rank people according to rigid biological hierarchies. Even the ordinary infantryman adopted a racialized point of view, so that 'the Russians' the German fought in 1914–1918 were transformed into an undifferentiated peril, 'the Russian,' regarded as 'dull,' 'dumb,' 'stupid,' or 'depraved' and 'barely humanlike.'" Fritzsche, *Life and Death in the Third Reich*, 148.

82. For a comprehensive list see http://www.feldpost-archiv.de/english/e5-literatur.html.

CHAPTER 2

1. Four divisions committed to Operation *Barbarossa* (sixty-seven thousand men) were posted in Finland and assigned to the German Army of Norway (*Armeeoberkommando Norwegen*). Ziemke and Bauer, *Moscow to Stalingrad: Decision in the East*, 7.

2. The tank force embraced 281 Pz I (a light tank, already obsolete, armed with two 7.92mm machine guns); 743 Pz IIs (another light tank, also out of date, most with a main armament of one 20mm gun L/55 while a small number were flamethrower tanks); 979 Pz IIIs (a medium tank, and the German Army's main battle tank, most outfitted with the "upgunned" 50mm L/42 gun, the remainder with a 37mm cannon); 444 Pz IVs (main armament a short-barreled

75mm L/24 cannon); 157 Pz 35(t)s (originally a Czech tank, with a 37mm main armament); and 651 Pz 38(t)s (also of Czech design and equipped with a 37mm gun). There were also 250 assault guns (*Sturmgeschützen*) designed for close infantry support and equipped with the 75mm L/24 gun mounted on the chassis of a Pz III tank. Boog et al., *Germany and the Second World War*, Vol. IV: *The Attack on the Soviet Union*, 219.

3. Combat-ready aircraft along the main battle front included (in rounded numbers): 750 bombers, 325 divebombers, 725 fighters, 60 destroyers, and 175 transport aircraft. Ibid., 364.

4. Unlike the *Luftwaffe*, the Red Air Force (*Voenno-vozdushnikh sil*, or VVS) was not an independent air arm but was part of the Red Army.

5. Because sunrise occurred minutes earlier on the left (northern) wing of the German attack, Army Group North and the left wing of Army Group Center began their artillery barrage at 0305 hours, while the right wing of Army Group Center and Army Group South began their preparatory barrage at 0315 hours.

6. Halder, *The Halder War Diary, 1939–1942*, Burdick and Jacobsen (eds.), 410.

7. NKVD: People's Commissariat of Internal Affairs (Soviet Secret Police).

8. Pleshakov, *Stalin's Folly. The Tragic First Ten Days of WWII on the Eastern Front*, 144.

9. Panzer generals Erich von Manstein (56 Panzer Corps, Army Group North) and Heinz Guderian (2 Panzer Group, Army Group Center), "who were to win Hitler his greatest eastern victories, descended from landowners of those parts." Keegan, *The Second World War*, 182.

10. Glantz, *Barbarossa. Hitler's Invasion of Russia 1941*, 50.

11. The fierce armored counterthrusts by the Red Army in the Ukraine, while ultimately a costly failure, succeeded in holding up the progress of Rundstedt's Army Group South "for at least a week." Ibid., 51.

12. In fact, "a generation of Communist rule and propaganda had prepared the Red Army soldier *psychologically* for war in a way the czars could have but envied." Luther, *The First Day on the Eastern Front: Germany Invades the Soviet Union, June 22, 1941*, xxx.

13. *Gefr.* Hans B. (38 051), Collection BfZ.

14. Wm. Josef L. (22 633 C), Collection BfZ.

15. Hartmann, *Wehrmacht im Ostkrieg: Front und militärisches Hinterland 1941/42*, 248.

16. *Gefr.* Hans B. (38 051), Collection BfZ.

17. *Gefr.* Heinz B. (26 391), Collection BfZ.

18. Werner R. (N97.3), Collection BfZ.

19. To support the initial breakthrough on 22 June, Ninth Army's 6 ID was temporarily assigned to Hoth's 3 Panzer Group; the division then reverted back to control of Ninth Army.

20. Ltr., Dr. Heinrich Haape, to his fiancée, 21.6.41.

21. Dollinger (ed.), *Kain, wo ist dein Bruder? Was der Mensch im Zweiten Weltkrieg erleiden musste—dokumentiert in Tagebüchern und Briefen*, 78–79. *Leutnant* Schmidt was killed in Russia in 1942.

22. Given his location at the "Suwalki tip," *Leutnant* Schmidt was most likely assigned to either 3 Panzer Group or Ninth Army.

23. Ellis, *Barbarossa 1941. Reframing Hitler's Invasion of Stalin's Soviet Empire*, 314. *Gefreiter* von Wiedebach-Nostitz served in 20 PD's reconnaissance battalion (Pz.AA 92); he would be wounded in January 1942 and spend thirteen months in a military hospital. Ibid., 311.

24. Kaltenegger, *Die Stammdivision der deutschen Gebirgstruppe. Weg und Kampf der 1. Gebirgs-Division 1935–1945*, 202–203.

25. To support the initial breakthrough on 22 June, Fourth Army's 45 ID was temporarily assigned to Guderian's 2 Panzer Group; the division then reverted back to control of Fourth Army.

26. Habedanck, "Bei Brest-Litovsk über die Grenze," *Die Wehrmacht, 1941,* 233 (cited in Kershaw, *War Without Garlands. Operation Barbarossa 1941/42,* 29).

27. *Oberleutnant* Kalckreuth was on the staff of 18 Infantry Regiment (6 ID). The first paragraph is from a letter to his wife, Gisela; the second was gleaned from his personal diary. D 107/56 Nr. 4, "Aus Briefen des Adjutanten Inf. Rgt. 18, Oberleutnant Juerg von Kalckreuth," Staats- und Personenstandsarchiv Detmold.

28. Bähr and Bähr (eds.), *Kriegsbriefe Gefallener Studenten, 1939–1945,* 51–52.

29. As his letter reveals, the twenty-two-year-old Hermann Stracke—like many of the *Landser* on the Eastern Front—willingly embraced war with Russia as an opportunity to prove one's manhood in the hard and merciless crucible of combat. Stracke was killed in action on 29 September 1941. Ibid., 51.

30. Kaltenegger, *Die Stammdivision der deutschen Gebirgstruppe. Weg und Kampf der 1. Gebirgs-Division 1935–1945,* 206–207.

31. *Fw.* Hans M. (28 193 B), Collection BfZ. On 22 June, 79 ID was an OKH reserve division still in transport to Army Group South.

32. Prüller, *Diary of a German Soldier,* Landon and Leitner (eds.), 63.

33. In his diary (22 June), Prüller noted that he and his comrades did not hear until 6.00 in the morning that Germany was at war with the Soviet Union. Is it possible they were not privy to Hitler's dramatic proclamation ("To the Soldiers of the Eastern Front"), read out by German officers up and down the line only hours before? If that is indeed the case, perhaps it is because 9 PD was still well back from the Russo-German frontier on 22 June and would not cross the border until 29 June 1941. Ibid., 63–65.

34. *Lt.* Helmut D. (04 255 C), Collection BfZ. On 22 June, 4 Mountain Division, though in position directly behind the front, was still an OKH reserve division in Army Group South; an order of battle for 27 June 1941 shows the division attached to the army group's Seventeenth Army. Boog et al., *Germany and the Second World War,* Vol. IV: *The Attack on the Soviet Union,* 550.

35. Kempowski (ed.), *Das Echolot. Barbarossa '41. Ein kollektives Tagebuch,* 23.

36. At 0443 hours, eighty "submarine" tanks (*Tauchpanzer*) of 18 PD (Pz IIIs and Pz IVs) began to ford the Bug by wading directly through the river. The special tanks, originally intended for Operation *Sealion* (the canceled invasion of Britain), had all openings sealed and were outfitted with air intakes and exhaust snorkel pipes. The specter of "swimming" tanks caused something of a sensation and, at least as far as *Lt.* Döll was concerned, more than a little skepticism. BA-MA RH 27-18/20, *KTB 18. Pz.-Div.,* 22.6.41.

37. Herbert R. (N11.15), Collection BfZ.

38. At no point on the Eastern Front was the opening barrage more intense, more devastating, than against the fortress of Brest-Litovsk, where the Germans unleashed a veritable whirlwind of fire—the progressive stages of the concentrated fire plan given the names of flowers: "Anemone," "Crocus," "Narcissus," etc. For a detailed account of the German assault on the fortress on 22 June, see Luther, *The First Day on the Eastern Front: Germany Invades the Soviet Union, June 22, 1941,* 168–173.

39. Aliev, *The Siege of Brest 1941. The Red Army's Stand against the Germans during Operation Barbarossa,* 64–65.

40. Hammer and Nieden (eds.), *Sehr selten habe ich geweint. Briefe und Tagebücher aus dem Zweiten Weltkrieg von Menschen aus Berlin,* 226–227.

41. To support the initial breakthrough on 22 June, Ninth Army's 35 ID was temporarily assigned to Hoth's 3 Panzer Group; the division then reverted back to control of Ninth Army.

42. Bopp, *Kriegstagebuch. Aufzeichnungen während des II. Weltkrieges, 1940–1943,* 72.

43. Kempowski (ed.), *Das Echolot. Barbarossa '41. Ein kollektives Tagebuch,* 24–25.

44. The initial German assault in *Unteroffizier* Hübner's front sector took place opposite the Soviet town of Belostok; the artillery preparation had most likely commenced at 0315 hours.

45. *Oblt.* Richard D. (35 232), Collection BfZ.

46. Garden and Andrew (eds.), *The War Diaries of a Panzer Soldier. Erich Hager with the 17th Panzer Division on the Russian Front 1941–1945*, 31. Hager would serve on the Eastern Front with 17 PD until finally captured by the Russians in early 1945. He passed away in 2003. Ibid., 4–5.

47. To support the initial breakthrough on 22 June, Sixth Army's 57 ID was temporarily assigned to Kleist's 1 Panzer Group; the division then reverted back to Sixth Army control.

48. *Lt.* Willibald G. (N02.5), Collection BfZ.

49. Before the Russian campaign, the Germans introduced several effective new weapons. One of them was the "*Nebelwerfer 41*," a six-barreled 150mm rocket launcher that hurled a high-explosive shell some seven thousand meters with devastating effect. Also available in 1941 was another version of the *Nebelwerfer* that fired 280mm (high-explosive) or 320mm (incendiary) rockets; this devastating weapon, christened "*Stuka zu Fuss*" (Stuka on foot) by the troops, had a range of about two thousand meters. Most of the *Nebelwerfer* in service with the German Army in June 1941 were the 150mm weapons; however, each panzer division had a platoon in its armored combat engineer battalion equipped with the 280/320 rockets, which were fired from crates mounted on the sides of an armored personnel carrier (APC). Luther, *The First Day on the Eastern Front: Germany Invades the Soviet Union, June 22, 1941*, 398n8; see also, US War Department, Technical Manual TM-E 30-451, *Handbook on German Military Forces*, 395–401.

50. *Sold.* Werner F. (34 911), Collection BfZ. This soldier's letter indicates that he was in occupied Poland (near the Russo-German frontier), that the general offensive began at 0305 hours, and that he observed large numbers of Stuka divebombers; thus, his unit was positioned somewhere on the left wing of Army Group Center.

51. To support the initial breakthrough on 22 June, Sixth Army's 299 ID was temporarily assigned to Kleist's 1 Panzer Group; the division then reverted back to Sixth Army control.

52. Alexander and Kunze (eds.), *Eastern Inferno: The Journals of a German Panzerjäger on the Eastern Front, 1941–43*, 26–27.

53. Bergström and Mikhailov, *Black Cross Red Star. Air War over the Eastern Front*. Vol. I: *Operation Barbarossa 1941*, 32. *Leutnant* Döring was a Heinkel He 111 pilot in *Kampfgeschwader 53* of GFM Albert Kesselring's 2 Air Fleet, supporting Army Group Center. The account is gleaned from Döring's diary and describes his wing's initial raid on a major Soviet airfield at Dolubovo (south of Belostok).

54. *Tagebuch, Lt.* Rudolf Maurer, 22.6.41. The 251 Infantry Division was one of three infantry divisions held in reserve by Army Group North on 22 June 1941. Its arsenal of weapons was largely typical of a standard German infantry division and included the following: 12,558 bolt-action rifles (*Karabiner 98K*), 405 light machine guns (le.MG), 112 heavy machine guns (s.MG), 87 light mortars (le.Gr.Wr. 36), 54 medium mortars (s.Gr.W. 34), 67 37mm Pak, 6 47 mm Pak (French), 20 75mm light infantry guns (le.IG 18), 6 150mm medium infantry guns (s.IG 33), 36 105mm light field howitzers (le.F.H. 18), and 12 150mm medium field howitzers (s.F.H. 18). Meier-Welcker, *Aufzeichnungen eines Generalstabsoffiziers 1939–1942*, 212.

55. Meyer-Detring, *Die 137. Infanterie-Division im Mittelabschnitt der Ostfront*, 20–21.

56. *Gefr.* Ludwig B. (04 650), Collection BfZ.

57. To support the initial breakthrough on 22 June, Sixth Army's 44 ID was temporarily assigned to Kleist's 1 Panzer Group; the division then reverted back to Sixth Army control.

58. Paul R. (NO2.1), Collection BfZ.

59. "Die ersten acht Tage," in *Kampf gegen die Sowjets. Berichte und Bilder vom Beginn des Ostfeldzuges bis zum Frühjahr 1942*, OKW (ed.), 37–38. The task of seizing the fortress of Brest-Litovsk, and protecting the inner flanks of Guderian's panzer corps (which began their attacks on either side of the citadel), was assigned to *Generalmajor* Fritz Schlieper's 45 Infantry Division.

60. The fortress sat at the confluence of the Bug and Muchaviec rivers, whose waters formed four partly natural and partly artificial islands. The center island (Citadel Island), the smallest of the four, was the heart of the fortress and was ringed by the other three islands; together, they formed the four fortified blocks of the massive citadel. The islands were studded with strong points of all kinds—hundreds of casemate and cellar positions, armored cupolas, dug-in tanks, bastions or old casement forts complete with towers, etc.—with many of the fortifications concealed by thick undergrowth and clumps of tall trees. For an in-depth account of the attack on the fortress on 22 June, see Luther, *The First Day on the Eastern Front: Germany Invades the Soviet Union, June 22, 1941*, 168–173.

61. The savage and bloody fighting for the fortress on 22 June cost 45 ID 311 dead—21 officers and 290 NCOs and enlisted men—perhaps greater losses than those sustained by any other German division on this first day of the war. Organized Soviet resistance inside the citadel would not be broken until the end of the month, by which time 45 ID had suffered 482 dead and 1,000 wounded. Ibid., 173.

62. Kaltenegger, *Die Stammdivision der deutschen Gebirgstruppe. Weg und Kampf der 1. Gebirgs-Division 1935–1945*, 212.

63. There is an eighteenth-century composition (*Lied*) by Conradin Kreutzer and Nikolaus Lenau called "Zauber der Nacht" and also a poem by Joseph von Eichendorff called "Nacht-zauber." So this is most likely a reference to German romanticism.

64. The final entry in the war diary of *Generalmajor* Hubert Lanz's 1 Mountain Division on 22 June was a sobering one: "After the experiences and practices of the campaigns in France and Yugoslavia, the troops will have to get used to such a tough and skillful enemy [*zähen und gewandten Feind*] as the Russian has turned out to be." Luther, *The First Day on the Eastern Front: Germany Invades the Soviet Union, June 22, 1941*, 254.

65. Ltr., Dr. Heinrich Haape, to his fiancée, 22.6.41.

66. For 22 June 1941, the war diary of Dr. Haape's 18 Infantry Regiment recorded a total loss of thirty-one KIA (two officers and twenty-nine NCOs and men) and fifty-four wounded.

67. *Gefr.* Franz B. (17 736), Collection BfZ. Franz B. was in a bakery company (*Bäckerei-kompanie*) in 198 ID. As he was not a combat soldier, his initial thoughts on the outbreak of war (e.g., pocketing extra front pay, no opportunity for leave) appear—in part at least—rather more parochial in nature. Moreover, Eleventh Army, operating out of Romania, would not cross the Russo-German frontier until 2 July 1941. Jacobsen (ed.). *Kriegstagebuch des OKW (WFSt.), Bd. I: 1. August 1940—31. Dezember 1941*, 425.

68. *Gefr.* Otto St. (46 010), Collection BfZ. The author of this letter worked in the ration supply office of the construction staff (Verpfl.Amt./Oberbaustab 5, Gumbinnen).

69. Pabst commanded a Ju 87 Stuka squadron operating in the sector of 2 Panzer Group. *Hauptmann* Herbert Pabst, "Berichte aus Russland Sommer 1941," AFHRA, Maxwell AFB, AL.

70. *Tagebuch*, Dr. Hans Lierow, 23.6.41

71. In a reorganization of the German Army's rear services prior to the start of *Barbarossa*, the three army groups, to boost the capacity of their large motor transport pools (each army group controlled one), had stripped the foot infantry divisions of all but their most essential motor transport. (The motor transport pools were responsible for moving supplies from the railheads to the divisions at the front.) The loss of motorization in the infantry divisions was

"made good" by the addition of some fifteen thousand Polish *"Panje"* horse-drawn wagons. For more details, see Stahel, *Operation Barbarossa and Germany's Defeat in the East*, 128–133.

72. *Fw.* Herbert E. (07 874), Collection BfZ.

73. Ltr., Dr. Heinrich Haape, to his fiancée, 23.6.41.

74. Kempowski (ed.), *Das Echolot. Barbarossa '41. Ein kollektives Tagebuch*, 65–66.

75. Ibid., 59.

76. Buchbender and Sterz (eds.), *Das Andere Gesicht des Krieges. Deutsche Feldpostbriefe 1939–1945*, 72.

77. On 23 August 1939, Germany and Soviet Russia, in one of the slickest diplomatic démarches in history, had shocked contemporaries by signing a nonaggression pact. The pact had freed Hitler to attack and destroy Poland in September 1939 and then to move against the western powers, England and France, without fear of danger on his eastern flank. Many Germans, however, having absorbed the vehement anti-Soviet propaganda of the Nazi regime, adjusted with difficulty to this tactical alliance with the USSR that had opened the war and, when it came to an abrupt end on 22 June 1941, reacted with a certain relief. As one German woman remarked on that day, "I don't think anybody really took the friendship between the USSR and the German Reich very seriously. We all had our doubts about whether this would go well and we didn't trust the Russians." Ibid., 70.

78. *Tagebuch, Lt.* Rudolf Maurer, 24.6.41.

79. Rhein, *Das Rheinisch-Westfälische Infanterie-/Grenadier-Regiment 18 1921–1945*, 55. *Leutnant* Rhein was a company commander in 18 IR of 6 ID.

80. *Tagebuch*, Dr. Hans Lierow, 24.6.41.

81. Garden and Andrew (eds.), *The War Diaries of a Panzer Soldier. Erich Hager with the 17th Panzer Division on the Russian Front 1941–1945*, 32.

82. The use of so-called dum-dum and explosive bullets by the Red Army was reported by German troops from the very outset of the invasion. These bullets caused terrible wounds and were proscribed under international law. While the accounts of German soldiers must be viewed with caution (it was not uncommon for German soldiers, who had been badly wounded by rifle or MG fire, to attribute their wounds to such illegal projectiles), cases involving the use of such ammunition by the Russians were recorded by the German War Crimes Bureau, along with the repeated seizure of dum-dum and explosive bullets by German units. The bureau's findings do not indicate if the German government ever lodged a formal protest with the Soviet Union about the use of such projectiles. Luther, *Barbarossa Unleashed. The German Blitzkrieg through Central Russia to the Gates of Moscow. June–December 1941*, 469–472.

83. *Uffz.* Willy P. (19 279 D), Collection BfZ. On 22 June, 167 ID had been temporarily assigned to 2 Panzer Group to assist with the initial breakthrough; however, Army Group Center quickly took back control of the division and, by 4 July, it had been assigned to Second Army. Boog et al., *Germany and the Second World War*, Vol. IV: *The Attack on the Soviet Union*, 528–529.

84. *Tagebuch, Lt.* Georg Kreuter, 24.6.41.

85. On the night of 24/25 June, the forward CP of 18 Panzer Division, located not far from the town of Slonim, suddenly found itself isolated and enmeshed in a wild and violent skirmish that can only be characterized as surreal. *Leutnant* Kreuter described the unsettling incident in his diary (his account continues below, on 25 June).

86. Ltr., Werner Heinemann, 25.6.41. Major Heinemann was a battalion commander in 23 ID. As his candid remarks reveal, he had quickly come to realize that the Red Army soldier was a more than worthy opponent. Indeed, *"der Russe,"* as the Germans often labeled their adversary, was unlike any other enemy the *Landser* had hitherto encountered—in addition to being

dogged, brave, and cunning (as noted by Heinemann), he could also be brutal and, at times, even bestial in his behavior. (See also Heinemann letter of 30 June 1941.)

87. Kempowski (ed.), *Das Echolot. Barbarossa '41. Ein kollektives Tagebuch*, 98.

88. *Tagebuch, Lt.* Georg Kreuter, 25.6.41. *Leutnant* Kreuter also wrote, "Everywhere there is skirmishing, primarily at night. Russian vehicles often join our marching column. Whoever detects the presence of the other first tosses a hand grenade into their vehicle. On occasion, when we've challenged a Bolshevik vehicle, they answered: 'Don't shoot, we're transporting German wounded!'"

89. Ltr., Karl-Gottfried Vierkorn, 25.6.41.

90. Woche, *Zwischen Pflicht und Gewissen. Generaloberst Rudolf Schmidt 1886–1957*, 104.

91. The tanks of Schmidt's 39 Panzer Corps were driving southeast from Vilnius toward Minsk. Thies, *Der Zweite Weltkrieg im Kartenbild*, Bd. 5: Teil 1:1: *Der Ostfeldzug Heeresgruppe Mitte 21.6.1941–6.12.1941. Ein Lageatlas der Operationsabteilung des Generalstabes des Heeres*, "Lage am 25.6.1941 abds., Heeresgruppe Mitte" (hereafter cited as Thies, *Der Ostfeldzug—Ein Lageatlas*).

92. From 22 June onward, the pace of operations was remorseless, the panzer generals pushing their men, tanks, and vehicles, and often themselves, to the limits of human endurance. Moreover, like General Schmidt, the panzer generals led from the front lines, even accompanying their spearheads into battle. As a result, close calls with the enemy were common. In this case, Schmidt and his small party—ambushed and surrounded in a wooded area near Molodechno—were soon fighting for their lives; under cover of darkness, they somehow managed to extricate themselves from their existential predicament and, early the next morning, linked up with friendly troops. (Woche, *Zwischen Pflicht und Gewissen. Generaloberst Rudolf Schmidt 1886–1957*, 105–106.) The day before (24 June), *Generaloberst* Guderian (C-in-C 2 Panzer Group) had survived a harrowing encounter with Russian tanks on the outskirts of Slonim. For his graphic account, see Guderian, *Panzer Leader*, 154–156.

93. Sold. S.K. (16 120 C), Collection BfZ.

94. Similar to the marching infantry, great demands were placed on the German Army's horses during the *Vormarsch* (advance) through Russia, and they suffered accordingly. The horses, too, were adversely affected by the extreme heat and the poor sanding tracks over which they endlessly toiled. Horse losses began to mount early in the campaign; most severely affected were the heavy draft horses used to haul the light and medium artillery. For the vital role played by horses in the German Army, see Richard L. DiNardo, *Mechanized Juggernaut or Military Anachronism? Horses and the German Army of World War II* (New York, 1991).

95. Reddemann (ed.), *Zwischen Front und Heimat. Der Briefwechsel des münsterischen Ehepaares Agnes and Albert Neuhaus 1940–1944*, 221.

96. On the morning of 22 June, artillery and *Nebelwerfer* of 4 Panzer Group had subjected Tauroggen to a horrific bombardment—what the panzer group commander called an "enormous fireworks." Luther, *The First Day on the Eastern Front: Germany Invades the Soviet Union, June 22, 1941*, 125.

97. Reddemann (ed.), *Zwischen Front und Heimat. Der Briefwechsel des münsterischen Ehepaares Agnes and Albert Neuhaus 1940–1944*, 222–223.

98. Johanna Schuppert, his older sister.

99. Albert Neuhaus could hardly have known that the first mass shooting of Jews in Lithuania had already occurred. Near Tauroggen the day before, in the border village of Garsden, 201 Jews (among them children and the elderly) and persons suspected of being Communists ("*kommunistenverdächtige Litauer*") were liquidated by an alarm unit (*Alarmzug*) of the Memel' municipal police (*Schutzpolizei Memel*). The killings were instigated by the *Einsatzkommando Tilsit* formed by the Gestapo and the SD. Systematic mass killings of Jews and other "undesir-

ables" would begin in late June 1941, following the arrival of *Einsatzgruppe A* in Army Group North's area of operations. Reddemann (ed.), *Zwischen Front und Heimat. Der Briefwechsel des münsterischen Ehepaares Agnes and Albert Neuhaus 1940–1944*, 222–223n7.

100. Kempowski (ed.), *Das Echolot. Barbarossa '41. Ein kollektives Tagebuch*, 95–97.

101. In their letters and diaries, German soldiers often conveyed their impressions of the Russian landscape through which they marched. While most were not as lyrical as *Offizier* von Alvensleben in their observations, they were, almost to a man, overwhelmed by the vastness of the country, which they found to be oppressive and which induced a certain melancholy in many. While many also found the terrain to be tiresome in its sameness, others were fascinated by the natural beauty—the diversity of the flora and fauna—they encountered.

102. The 16 PD was in action west of Dubno, having advanced more than sixty kilometers from the Russo-German frontier. Glantz, *Atlas and Operational Summary. The Border Battles 22 June–1 July 1941*, "Lutsk-Rovno Axis, Situation, 2300 hrs 25 June 1941."

103. *Uffz.* Egon N. (06 209 E), Collection BfZ.

104. *True to Type. A Selection from Letters and Diaries of German Soldiers and Civilians Collected on the Soviet-German Front*, 8.

105. There were many instances in the initial days of the war when Red Army soldiers, stunned by the *force majeure* of the German attack, fled to the forests or swamps (or to other hiding places), discarded their uniforms, and changed into civilian clothes; while some eventually gave up (due to hunger, if nothing else), others continued the fight behind the front, using guerrilla tactics and helping form a basis for the Soviet partisan movement.

106. Kempowski (ed.), *Das Echolot. Barbarossa '41. Ein kollektives Tagebuch*, 111–112.

107. Stützel, *Feldpost. Briefe und Aufzeichnungen eines 17-Jährigen 1940–1945*, 33–34. Stützel served in an antitank (*Panzerjäger*) company in 5 ID.

108. Moutier (ed.), "Liebste Schwester, wir müssen hier sterben oder siegen," *Briefe deutscher Wehrmachtssoldaten 1939–45*, 123–126. This is a long yet insightful selection, with *Feldwebel* Heinz R. discussing challenges faced by the German invaders that were universal along the Eastern Front in the summer of 1941—the poor, often primitive condition of roadways and bridges, which slowed the German advance to a crawl; the perpetual struggle to flush out and neutralize Soviet stragglers (and the seemingly ubiquitous and deadly snipers) who had fled to the forests, marshes, and other hiding places, from where they ambushed German supply columns, motorcycle messengers, isolated individuals, or small groups of soldiers; and, of course, the remorseless dialectic of atrocity and reprisal that would result in ever-increasing cycles of violence and death.

109. The summer in this region of the Ukraine was hot and dry but short.

110. Sahm (ed.), *Verzweiflung und Glaube. Briefe aus dem Krieg 1939–1942*, 40–41.

111. Wm. Josef L. (22 633 C), Collection BfZ.

112. *Uffz.* E.J. (00 700), cited in Manoschek (ed.), *"Es gibt nur eines für das Judentum: Vernichtung." Das Judenbild in deutschen Soldatenbriefen 1939–1944*, 29.

113. Kempowski (ed.), *Das Echolot. Barbarossa '41. Ein kollektives Tagebuch*, 121–122.

114. Reddemann (ed.), *Zwischen Front und Heimat. Der Briefwechsel des münsterischen Ehepaares Agnes and Albert Neuhaus 1940–1944*, 224–225.

115. The reference is to two revolutionary Soviet tank models that were only beginning to be introduced into service: the KV-1 and KV-2. The KV-1 weighed roughly forty-six tons and mounted a 76mm main armament; the KV-2 weighed ca. fifty-two tons and mounted a massive 152mm howitzer (for destroying bunkers) in a bulky, slab-sided turret (the Soviets, however, produced only a small number of KV-2s, as they were difficult to manufacture and there was only a limited need for the heavy projectile). "Clumsily handled by inexperienced crews," observed historian Dennis E. Showalter, "they nevertheless shocked the Germans by their virtual

invulnerability to existing tank and antitank guns at ranges as short as fifty to a hundred yards. To knock them out it was necessary to maneuver to their flank or rear, taking advantage of the thin armor there." Historical Commentary by Dennis E. Showalter in Fuchs Richardson (ed.), *Your Loyal and Loving Son. The Letters of Tank Gunner Karl Fuchs, 1937–41*, 123.

116. The reference is to the German 88mm antiaircraft gun, a battery of which helped to blunt the Soviet attack by immobilizing several of their heavy tanks. The German "88" was one of the most successful weapons of the war produced by any belligerent. Several versions of the weapon were built for use against air, ground, or sea targets. (Field Marshal Erwin Rommel's use of the "88" as an antitank gun in North Africa is legendary.) The gun possessed a rapid rate of fire (fifteen to twenty rounds/minute), long range, and high muzzle velocity (2,690 feet/ second). In the summer of 1941 (and beyond), it was often the only weapon that could reliably destroy the heavy Soviet KV and T-34 tanks, about which the Germans knew almost nothing prior to the start of the Eastern Campaign. For more details on the German 88mm gun, see US War Department, Technical Manual TM-E 30-451, *Handbook on German Military Forces*, 349–350.

117. On 24 June, a large Soviet mechanized force (tanks and infantry) furiously counterat-tacked elements of Hoepner's 4 Panzer Group east of Raseinai. The attacking Red Army forces, among them large numbers of the new T-34 and KV tanks, initially stunned the German de-fenders (elements of 6 Panzer Division), driving them back with serious losses to the outskirts of the town. Yet "after the Soviets failed to exploit their success, German sappers systematically destroyed the Soviet tanks with explosive charges. Later they learned that the Soviet tanks ran out of fuel and had orders to 'ram' the German tanks, since the T-34s and KVs had not been bore-sighted and thus could not fire a round. Within 24 hours after the engagement, German forces bypassed, encircled and destroyed the immobile Soviet tank [forces]." Glantz, *Barbarossa. Hitler's Invasion of Russia 1941*, 217n24.

118. Rhein, *Das Rheinisch-Westfälische Infanterie-/Grenadier-Regiment 18 1921–1945*, 58.

119. Unlike earlier entries in Pabst's account, no date is given here. From the context, how-ever, it is most likely 27 June 1941. *Hauptmann* Herbert Pabst, "Berichte aus Russland Sommer 1941," AFHRA, Maxwell AFB, AL.

120. From *Hauptmann* Pabst's account, it is easy to understand why "friendly fire" incidents involving aircraft and ground troops were so common.

121. *Lt.* Willibald G. (N02.5), Collection BfZ.

122. Ralph Ross would perish in an unfortunate act of nature on 9 July, when the lake in which he was bathing was hit by a lightning strike; stunned by the lightning, he drowned. Ross had celebrated his eighteenth birthday just a few days before. Willibald G. (N02.5), Collection BfZ.

123. This is most likely a reference to the Soviet T-34 medium tank, which weighed about thirty tons.

124. Kempowski (ed.), *Das Echolot. Barbarossa '41. Ein kollektives Tagebuch*, 136.

125. Promoted to *Oberleutnant*, Melchinger would go missing at Stalingrad in 1943.

126. Garden and Andrew (eds.), *The War Diaries of a Panzer Soldier. Erich Hager with the 17th Panzer Division on the Russian Front 1941–1945*, 33–34.

127. Note from the book's editors: "Erich often refers to an individual whom he calls 'Gef.' We believe this to be his company commander due to the respect he gives him and the com-mand function of the individual." Ibid., 5.

128. *Gefr.* Ewald M. (01 137), Collection BfZ.

129. On Sunday, 29 June, beginning at 11.00 in the morning, the OKW broadcast twelve "special announcements" (*Sondermeldungen*); one after the other—and each introduced by the new Russian fanfare, based on Liszt's "Hungarian Rhapsody"—they trumpeted the capture of

this or that city, the securing of this or that objective. If the public reception was less enthusiastic than hoped—people soon tired of the special announcements and suspected they were colored by propaganda—the *Führer* was scenting victory. Kershaw, *Hitler 1936–1945: Nemesis*, 398.

130. Hinze, *Hitze, Frost und Pulverdampf: Der Schicksalsweg der 20. Panzer-Division*, 32. On 28 June 1941, soon after 12 Panzer Division had done so, advance elements of 20 PD entered Minsk, where they fought fierce street battles in the southern part of the city.

131. Observed historian Frank Ellis, "Even allowing for the impact of Nazi indoctrination, [the perspective of the German soldier on] Soviet society was far from flattering." Ellis, *Barbarossa 1941. Reframing Hitler's Invasion of Stalin's Soviet Empire*, 307.

132. Ellis, *Barbarossa 1941. Reframing Hitler's Invasion of Stalin's Soviet Empire*, 317–318.

133. German aerial bombing of the city of Minsk in the first days of the Eastern Campaign was savage and unremitting. Observed historian Constantine Pleshakov, "Even the parks were in flames. The capital of Belorussia was shrouded in smoke, and blasts shook the air. One wave of German bombers after another rolled over the city, turning it into rubble. Thousands of refugees streamed east, only to be massacred by German pilots on blocked roads. . . . German pilots looked at Minsk as one huge target and dropped bombs indiscriminately, making no distinction between Western Front headquarters and a grocery store." (Pleshakov, *Stalin's Folly. The Tragic First Ten Days of WWII on the Eastern Front*, 144–145.) Reaching Minsk in early July 1941, days after the fighting there had ceased, soldiers of 137 ID marveled at the destruction wrought by the *Luftwaffe* on this important road and rail junction: "In the city center, smoke-blackened chimneys revealed that wooden houses had stood there. . . . It looked particularly bad in the area around the train station. Here, the Stukas had virtually ploughed the ground over; burned-out trains, ripped-up rail carriages, and chaotically twisted rails jutting up into the air embodied a picture of total destruction. Mighty iron posts of the rail system had snapped like matchsticks. In multitudes the civilian population migrated into the countryside. A sack slung over the shoulder contained all the possessions that these people had been able to retrieve from the chaos." Meyer-Detring, *Die 137. Infanterie-Division im Mittelabschnitt der Ostfront*, 32.

134. *Gefr.* Wilhelm H. (13 063), Collection BfZ.

135. In the German occupation zone of Poland, the western provinces (Silesia; Pomorze; Poznań; most of Łódź; and parts of Warsaw, Cracow, and Kielce provinces), had been annexed to the Reich by a decree of October 1939 and were known as the Wartheland; they amounted to ca. 90,000 sq.km. (35,000 sq.mi.) and about 9.5 million of Poland's prewar population. In the remaining territory that came under German control, the Nazis had established a "General Government," which was envisaged as a labor colony for the Reich; it comprised some 96,000 sq.km. (37,000 sq.mi.) of territory—including the cities of Warsaw, Cracow, and Lublin—along with twelve million inhabitants. Dear (ed.), *The Oxford Guide to World War II*, 696.

136. Friedrich G. (L 29 759), Collection BfZ.

137. Dollinger (ed.), *Kain, wo ist dein Bruder? Was der Mensch im Zweiten Weltkrieg erleiden musste—dokumentiert in Tagebüchern und Briefen*, 83–84.

138. Kempowski (ed.), *Das Echolot. Barbarossa '41. Ein kollektives Tagebuch*, 160.

139. What is striking about this short letter is how casually—and abruptly—the letter writer shifts topics from the largely trivial to the deadly serious. In doing so, he betrays a callous indifference to the suffering of the Jews at the hands of the local civilians. His attitude also evokes the thought that such incidents were, only nine days into the campaign, beginning to become commonplace.

140. Bähr and Bähr (eds.), *Kriegsbriefe Gefallener Studenten, 1939–1945*, 69–70.

141. Ltr., Werner Heinemann, 30.6.41.

142. On 29 June 1941, the tanks of *Generalmajor* Walther K. Nehring's 18 Panzer Division (2 Panzer Group), racing up to Minsk from the south, linked up with elements of 3 Panzer Group. The outer wall of the encirclement ring around the Soviet Western Front was now complete. Thus, by the end of June, the remnants of four Soviet armies (3, 4, 10, 13) were trapped in several pockets stretching from Belostok through Novogrodek to Minsk. Luther, *Barbarossa Unleashed. The German Blitzkrieg through Central Russia to the Gates of Moscow. June–December 1941*, 272–273.

143. *Uffz.* Heinz B. (29 524 C), Collection BfZ.

CHAPTER 3

1. Halder, *The Halder War Diary, 1939–1942*, Burdick and Jacobsen (eds.), 446.

2. Kershaw, *Hitler 1936–45: Nemesis*, 405.

3. As historian Dennis E. Showalter has argued, one can make the case that the "relative tactical and operational superiority" of the German Army's mobile forces over their opponents "was never greater than in the first half of July 1941, on the high road to Moscow. Guderian spoke of attacks going in like training exercises." Showalter, *Hitler's Panzers. The Lightning Attacks that Revolutionized Warfare*, 170–171.

4. Thies, *Der Ostfeldzug—Ein Lageatlas*, "Lage am 15.7.1941 abds., Heeresgruppe Mitte."

5. Ibid., "Lage am 30.7.1941 abds., Heeresgruppe Mitte."

6. As chief of the Army General Staff, Halder noted in his diary on 8 July 1941, "It is the *Führer's* firm decision to level Moscow and Leningrad, and make them uninhabitable, so as to relieve us of the necessity of having to feed the populations through the winter. The cities will be razed by air force. Tanks must not be used for the purpose." Halder, *The Halder War Diary, 1939–1942*, Burdick and Jacobsen (eds.), 458.

7. Total German fatal casualties in the East in July 1941 amounted to 63,099. Overmans, *Deutsche militärische Verluste im Zweiten Weltkrieg*, 277. As early as 11 July 1941, General Walther K. Nehring, sounding the alarm on the dangerous attrition of men and tanks in his 18 Panzer Division (Army Group Center), had warned that the high loss rates should not be allowed to continue, "if we do not intend to victor ourselves to death" (*wenn wir uns nicht totsiegen wollen*). Luther, *Barbarossa Unleashed. The German Blitzkrieg through Central Russia to the Gates of Moscow. June–December 1941*, 365.

8. Trevor-Roper (ed.), *Hitler's War Directives 1939–1945*, 91.

9. *Tagebuch, Oblt.* K., cited in Andres, "Panzersoldaten im Russlandfeldzug 1941 bis 1945. Tagebuchaufzeichnungen und Erlebnisberichte," 7–9.

10. The German soldiers of the *Ostheer* responded to the poverty, deplorable conditions, and human misery they encountered in different ways. As a general observation, it can be stated that they developed (at best) highly ambivalent attitudes toward the Russian people and their predicament. For many *Landser*, what they observed, or experienced directly, served only to reinforce deeply ingrained racial prejudices against the Slavic peoples as a less than fully human life form, an *Untermensch*. Despite such prejudice, some German soldiers responded compassionately to the poverty and human suffering that swirled about them.

11. Kempowski (ed.), *Das Echolot. Barbarossa '41. Ein kollektives Tagebuch*, 174.

12. *Lt.* Helmut H. (39 057), Collection BfZ.

13. The reference is to Frederick II, the king of Prussia from 1740 to 1786, the longest reign of any of the Hohenzollern kings. Prussia rose to a major military power in Europe during his rule. He became known as Frederick the Great, with the sobriquet *Der Alte Fritz* ("The Old Fritz").

14. Ltr., *Lt.* Rudolf Maurer, to his wife, Irene, 1.7.41.

15. Halsdorf is a small village in Hesse (not far from Marburg, a university town in Hesse). The Maurer family moved there from Hermannrode in October 1938. Maurer, *Die hessisch-thüringische 251. Infanterie-Division: wird im Zweiten Weltkrieg vom Jäger zum Gejagten*, 105.

16. Prüller, *Diary of a German Soldier*, Landon and Leitner (eds.), 67–69.

17. Reddemann (ed.), *Zwischen Front und Heimat. Der Briefwechsel des münsterischen Ehepaares Agnes and Albert Neuhaus 1940–1944*, 228–229.

18. In their letters, German soldiers often sought to still the anxieties and fears of their loved ones at home; doing so was not a difficult task in the opening days and weeks of the campaign, when most Germans (soldiers and civilians alike) believed the war would be over in a matter of weeks.

19. Ltr., Dr. Heinrich Haape, to his fiancée, 2.7.41.

20. After its initial contact with Soviet forces at the frontier on 22/23 June, Dr. Haape's 6 Infantry Division would march for several weeks with virtually no contact with the enemy, as it sought to catch up with the mobile units of 3 Panzer Group ranging far to the east.

21. Meier-Welcker, *Aufzeichnungen eines Generalstabsoffiziers 1939–1942*, 121.

22. *Gefr.* Ferdinand M. (22 200), Collection BfZ. By 4 July 1941, 167 ID was in the order of battle of the newly activated Second Army of Army Group Center. Boog et al., *Germany and the Second World War*, Vol. IV: *The Attack on the Soviet Union*, 529.

23. The German General Staff map for 2 July shows the 167 ID directly southeast of Pruzhany. Thies, *Der Ostfeldzug—Ein Lageatlas*, "Lage am 2.7.1941 abds., Heeresgruppe Mitte."

24. Sahm (ed.), *Verzweiflung und Glaube. Briefe aus dem Krieg 1939–1942*, 41.

25. *Gefr.* Hans B. (38 051), Collection BfZ.

26. Kempowski (ed.), *Das Echolot. Barbarossa '41. Ein kollektives Tagebuch*, 192–193.

27. *General der Panzertruppe* Werner Kempff, C-in-C 48 Panzer Corps.

28. *Generalmajor* Hans Hube, C-in-C 16 Panzer Division.

29. *Sold.* Manfred V. (02 544), Collection BfZ.

30. *Die Deutsche Wochenschau* (The German Weekly Review) was the official newsreel of the German government from 1940 until the end of World War II. Released in cinemas throughout Germany, it was a vital instrument for the mass distribution of Nazi propaganda. Many German women—millions of whom had sons, fiancés, husbands, or brothers fighting in the East—were deeply disturbed by what they witnessed in the *Wochenschauen*, even though the newsreels offered highly sanitized depictions of events.

31. *Gefr.* Heinz B. (05 854), Collection BfZ.

32. The Russian soldier quickly became—begrudgingly, to be sure—an object of respect to the German soldier, who admired his adversary's toughness, resilience, and individual fighting qualities, while deploring the enemy's often brutal methods. Moreover, the *Landser* were often astonished by the excellent quality of much of the Soviet arsenal of weapons and equipment. In a letter on 2 July 1941, an unknown soldier registered his surprise at the "splendid matériel" (*tadelloses Material*) of the Red Army. Kempowski, *Das Echolot. Barbarossa '41. Ein kollektives Tagebuch*, 183.

33. *Tagebuch, Lt.* Rudolf Maurer, 3.7.41.

34. Kempowski (ed.), *Das Echolot. Barbarossa '41. Ein kollektives Tagebuch*, 200–201.

35. Paul, *Geschichte der 18. Panzer-Division 1940–1943*, 29.

36. A medium tank, the T-34 weighed about thirty tons, was operated by a crew of four, carried a high-velocity 76mm main armament, had armor protection from 45–52mm, and an excellent top speed of 55 k/h. The tank's 60 percent sloping armor was revolutionary, offering significantly enhanced protection against flat trajectory antitank shells, which often failed to penetrate and simply ricocheted away (the standard 37mm and 50mm AT guns of the German

Army of 1941 were virtually useless against the T-34). Most historians of the Second World War rate the T-34 among the top two or three tanks produced by any combatant during the war, if not the very best.

37. *Gefr.* Ferdinand B. (19 685), cited in Manoschek (ed.), *"Es gibt nur eines für das Judentum: Vernichtung." Das Judenbild in deutschen Soldatenbriefen 1939–1944*, 31.

38. Just days after the German invasion, the Soviet Secret Police (NKVD) executed some five thousand inmates in a number of provisional prisons in L'vov. Methods employed to exterminate the prisoners included shooting them in their cells, tossing hand grenades into their cells, or simply bayoneting them to death. Dear (ed.). *The Oxford Guide to World War II*, 549.

39. In contemporary German accounts—field post letters, personal diaries, war diaries—a word began to appear almost at once with disturbing frequency—*Heckenschütze*, or sniper. Indeed, from the very first hours of the war, the *Landser* faced a cunning and deadly adversary who was to torment him mercilessly throughout the war—the Red Army sniper, often outfitted with an excellent automatic rifle with telescopic sights. According to statistics from 1944, 43 percent of German soldiers who died on the battlefield (i.e., were buried without ever having made it to a field hospital for care) were killed by headshots—a favorite tactic of snipers everywhere. Schneider-Janessen, *Arzt im Krieg. Wie deutsche und russische Ärzte den zweiten Weltkrieg erlebten*, 423.

40. *Gefr.* Ferdinand B. served in a medical company (*Sanitätskompanie*) in 125 ID.

41. Prüller, *Diary of a German Soldier*, Landon and Leitner (eds.), 73–74.

42. Although Prüller doesn't specify, the tank in question is most likely a Soviet KV-1.

43. *Tagebuch*, Dr. Hans Lierow, 3.-8.7.41.

44. Bähr and Bähr (eds.), *Kriegsbriefe Gefallener Studenten, 1939–1945*, 70–71.

45. The brutal pace of the *Vormarsch*, the unholy trinity of heat, dust, and thirst, forced the *Landser*, particularly the marching infantry, into a daily existence that often approached—even surpassed—what seemed humanly endurable. Marching on foot, thirty, forty, even fifty kilometers a day on primitive roadways; often carrying a full pack; desperately short of sleep; hungry, thirsty, tormented by dust, heat, and insects—man (and beast) was pushed to the brink of exhaustion and beyond.

46. *True to Type. A Selection from Letters and Diaries of German Soldiers and Civilians Collected on the Soviet-German Front*, 14–15.

47. On 20 June 1941, *Stabsfeldwebel* Dittri had jotted in his diary, "The great moment is at hand. . . . We have been preparing long enough for this day. Russia, too, does not frighten us." Yet barely two weeks into the campaign, it was becoming clear to him—and to his comrades as well—that "the Russian" was a more than formidable adversary. On 10 July he would write, "We still could not move forward any farther. The Russian resistance was indescribable and our troops remained stationary in the vicinity of Vitebsk. We were again in front as our vanguard was unable to withstand the fierce opposition of the Russians." Ibid., 14–15.

48. *Lt.* Willibald G. (N02.5), Collection BfZ.

49. *Uffz.* Heinz H. (19 836), Collection BfZ.

50. At this point in the campaign, 6 ID was on the march some 150 kilometers behind the spearheads of Hoth's 3 Panzer Group; hence, it was not a priority for the Russian air force (VVS).

51. Fuchs Richardson (ed.), *Your Loyal and Loving Son. The Letters of Tank Gunner Karl Fuchs, 1937–41*, 112.

52. This soldier's reaction, common to so many German soldiers on the Eastern Front, "contributed significantly to the *Wehrmacht's* complicity in the Nazi war of conquest and extermination. The high-riding *Landser* felt little common humanity toward the peasants whose fields and villages they overran—a pattern dating to September 1939." Historical Commentary

by Dennis E. Showalter in Fuchs Richardson (ed.), *Your Loyal and Loving Son. The Letters of Tank Gunner Karl Fuchs, 1937–41*, 113.

53. Karl Fuchs was killed in action near the town of Klin, northwest of Moscow, on 21 November 1941. Ibid., 3.

54. This grim encounter described by *Oblt.* Fabich of the elite Infantry Regiment "*Grossdeutschland*" (mot.) took place near Stolpce, on the southern perimeter of the Minsk pocket. Spaeter, *Die Geschichte des Panzerkorps Grossdeutschland*, Bd. I, 267.

55. *Rollbahn:* A road designated by the Germans as a main axis of motorized transportation, from which all marching columns and animal transport were normally barred.

56. For the attack on Russia, the Germans were to make the first large-scale use of a highly effective new weapon—the StuG III (*Sturmgeschütz*) assault gun. On 1 June 1941, the German Army possessed 377 StuG IIIs, 250 of which were committed to the Eastern Campaign in eleven battalions and five separate batteries. Its main armament was a short-barreled 75mm L24 gun mounted on the chassis of a Panzer III tank. Because the weapon system had no turret (the 75mm gun was built directly into the hull), it had a low silhouette, enhancing its survivability. The assault gun provided close armor support to the infantry and also performed an antitank role. Those infantry divisions fortunate enough to be assigned a battery or company of assault guns would come to deeply appreciate the weapon; the Russians would come to fear it. Luther, *Barbarossa Unleashed. The German Blitzkrieg through Central Russia to the Gates of Moscow. June–December 1941*, 118; Boog et al., *Germany and the Second World War*, Vol. IV: *The Attack on the Soviet Union*, 219.

57. *Gefr.* Werner R. (37 717), Collection BfZ.

58. The German military leadership genuinely feared the prospect of the Red Army unleashing gas—as well as other chemical and/or biological contaminants—on their troops. For example, the OKH deployment directive for Operation *Barbarossa* (31 January 1941) indicated that the troops must be prepared for the Russians to use chemical weapons and that such weapons might even be dropped from the air. In general, they expected the Russians to react with brutality and excess far exceeding earlier campaigns, and, in the initial days and weeks of *Barbarossa*—as revealed in many contemporary accounts—the Germans experienced more than a few false alarms about the use of chemical agents by their Russian adversary. Ironically, while the Soviet Union did not adhere to either the Hague Conventions of 1907 or the Geneva Conventions of 1929, it had signed the 1925 Geneva Protocol banning the use of poison gas and bacteriological warfare. Bellamy, *Absolute War. Soviet Russia in the Second World War*, 20; also, Luther, *Barbarossa Unleashed. The German Blitzkrieg through Central Russia to the Gates of Moscow. June–December 1941*, 97.

59. Kempowski (ed.), *Das Echolot. Barbarossa '41. Ein kollektives Tagebuch*, 245.

60. Meier-Welcker, *Aufzeichnungen eines Generalstabsoffiziers 1939–1942*, 121.

61. Manoschek (ed.), *"Es gibt nur eines für das Judentum: Vernichtung." Das Judenbild in deutschen Soldatenbriefen 1939–1944*, 33. Beyond his first name ("Franzl"), no further identification (e.g., no field post number) is provided by the editor.

62. Ellis, *Barbarossa 1941. Reframing Hitler's Invasion of Stalin's Soviet Empire*, 320.

63. Hoth's 3 Panzer Group was brilliantly supported by the bombers, fighters, destroyers, and Stuka divebombers of *General der Flieger* (Air General) Wolfram *Freiherr* von Richthofen's 8 Air Corps—the only dedicated close air support (CAS) formation in the *Luftwaffe*.

64. Despite furious Soviet counterattacks, by late 9 July the battlegroup of *Oberst* von Bismarck, together with infantry of *Generalmajor* Hans Zorn's 20 Infantry Division (mot.), had seized the flaming city of Vitebsk, which had been set on fire by the Russians before they withdrew. Demolition squads were still setting off charges as the Germans entered the city. (Luther, *Barbarossa Unleashed. The German Blitzkrieg through Central Russia to the Gates of*

Moscow. June–December 1941, 317–320.) The systematic destruction of Vitebsk is illustrative of the fact that, from the very start of the German invasion, the Red Army conducted a ruthless scorched-earth campaign, destroying anything—crops, livestock, food, factories, etc.—that could not be taken back as it withdrew.

65. Reddemann (ed.), *Zwischen Front und Heimat. Der Briefwechsel des münsterischen Ehepaares Agnes and Albert Neuhaus 1940–1944*, 231–232.

66. On the night of 5 July, the British RAF struck cities in western Germany; most badly hit were Münster and Bielefeld (Neuhaus's wife, Agnes, was at their home in Münster). British bombers would again strike Münster just days later, causing Neuhaus additional worry about his wife and their home.

67. Neuhaus's unit was in Gauri (Gavry), a town in Latvia about seven kilometers from the 1939 Latvian-Russian border and on the main highway leading from Rezekne (Rositten) to Ostrov.

68. *Tagebuch, Lt.* Georg Kreuter, 7.7.41. The engagement described here took place some fifty kilometers west of Orsha, along the main highway (*Rollbahn*) to Moscow.

69. The reference here is most likely to a Soviet KV-1. In an after-action report submitted by *Leutnant* Kreuter on 11 July 1941, he referred to the tank he eventually neutralized as weighing forty-two tons. "Bericht, Kreuter, Lt. u. Kp.-Führer, 11.7.41," in *Tagebuch, Lt.* Georg Kreuter.

70. *Oblt.* Richard D. (35 232), Collection BfZ.

71. *St.Fw.* Christoph B. (L 34 215), Collection BfZ.

72. Meier-Welcker, *Aufzeichnungen eines Generalstabsoffiziers 1939–1942*, 122.

73. Peter Sch. (18 055), Collection, BfZ.

74. Kempowski (ed.), *Das Echolot. Barbarossa '41. Ein kollektives Tagebuch*, 291–292.

75. Moutier (ed.), "Liebste Schwester, wir müssen hier sterben oder siegen," *Briefe deutscher Wehrmachtssoldaten 1939–45*, 130–131.

76. Tablets for treatment of pain and fever due to cold-related illnesses.

77. Meier-Welcker, *Aufzeichnungen eines Generalstabsoffiziers 1939–1942*, 122.

78. Major Meier-Welcker was the chief operations officer (Ia) on the staff of 251 ID.

79. *Generalmajor* Otto Lancelle, C-in-C 121 ID, had been killed on 3 July in the fighting at the Krāslava bridgehead at the Western Dvina River. Website at www.lexikon-der-wehrmacht.de.

80. Buchbender and Sterz (eds.), *Das Andere Gesicht des Krieges. Deutsche Feldpostbriefe 1939–1945*, 73–74.

81. Reddemann (ed.), *Zwischen Front und Heimat. Der Briefwechsel des münsterischen Ehepaares Agnes and Albert Neuhaus 1940–1944*, 232–233.

82. Neuhaus's unit was still far behind the front. Spearheads of *Generaloberst* Erich Hoepner's 4 Panzer Group had captured Ostrov on 4 July 1941.

83. Headed by Fritz Todt, the eponymous Organization Todt (OT) carried out construction tasks vital to the German war effort. Simply put, it built fortifications and built and repaired bridges, roads, railways, dams, and other essential infrastructure for the *Wehrmacht*. The OT's "greatest task" came in June 1941, with the start of Operation *Barbarossa*, for "the military construction battalions alone were incapable of building the necessary railway links, bridges, and repair facilities in the vast expanses of the USSR." Todt himself perished in a mysterious air accident in February 1942; his successor as head of the OT was Albert Speer. Dear (ed.), *The Oxford Guide to World War II*, 870.

84. Before 1939, the Red Army had built strong defensive positions along and behind the Soviet Union's old border, fortifications the Germans christened the "Stalin Line." The Stalin Line was, for the most part, not a line at all but a system of fortified regions (*ukreplennyi raion*— UR), each with bunkers, light artillery, machine-gun positions, and tank traps. Following the Soviet occupation of eastern Poland, the Baltic States, and Bessarabia in 1939–1940, much of

the Stalin Line was dismantled to provide weapons and matériel for new fortified zones along the new border with Germany. The result was predictable: when the Germans struck the Stalin Line had been seriously compromised, while not nearly enough had been done to create fortified zones along the new frontier.

85. Stehmann (Sprenger, ed.), *Die Bitternis verschweigen wir. Feldpostbriefe 1940–1945*, 111–112. For a detailed account of Finnish-German operations in the far north, see Ueberschär, "Strategy and Policy in Northern Europe," 941–1020, in Boog et al., *Germany and the Second World War*, Vol. IV: *The Attack on the Soviet Union.*

86. *Gefr.* Jean Z. (25 130), Collection BfZ.

87. The German term for "hundredweight" is *"Zentner."* One "hundredweight" amounts to fifty kilograms.

88. In the initial days of the Eastern Campaign, waves of Russian medium bombers, manned by inexperienced crews and attacking in rigid tactical formations without fighter cover, were repeatedly decimated by German fighter aircraft or flak artillery. GFM Albert Kesselring, the C-in-C of 2 Air Fleet (supporting Army Group Center), who observed the slaughter firsthand, called it "sheer 'infanticide'" (*der reinste "Kindermord"*), while German soldiers watched in awe and fascination as the Soviet bombers tumbled slowly out of the sky. Indeed, the hopelessly one-sided aerial battles that filled the battlespace above them convinced many a *Landser* that victory would be easily come by. Kesselring, *Soldat Bis Zum Letzen Tag,* 120.

89. *Letzte Lebenszeichen. Briefe aus dem Krieg* (published by the German War Graves Commission), 28–29.

90. For a detailed discussion of the equipment, clothing, and diet of the German infantry in Russia in the summer of 1941, see Luther, *Barbarossa Unleashed. The German Blitzkrieg through Central Russia to the Gates of Moscow. June–December 1941,* 368–376.

91. This was *Soldat* Beck's last letter to his wife, Elisa; he was killed in action on 13 July 1941. *Letzte Lebenszeichen. Briefe aus dem Krieg,* 28.

92. *Tagebuch,* Dr. Hans Lierow, 10.7.41.

93. *Mj.* Hans Sch. (33 691), Collection BfZ.

94. *Tagebuch, Lt.* Rudolf Maurer, 11.7.41.

95. On 26 June 1941, after a spectacular advance of 300 kilometers ("as the crow flies") from their starting point on the East Prussian frontier, Manstein's 56 Panzer Corps (4 Panzer Group) had captured Daugavpils (southern Latvia) and seized intact the bridges there over the Western Dvina. Jacobsen (ed.), *Kriegstagebuch des OKW (WFSt.), Bd. I: 1. August 1940–31. Dezember 1941,* 420; Manstein, *Verlorene Siege,* 182–183.

96. Reddemann (ed.), *Zwischen Front und Heimat. Der Briefwechsel des münsterischen Ehepaares Agnes and Albert Neuhaus 1940–1944,* 236.

97. It is far from a simple matter to discern fact from fiction when evaluating some of the more remarkable claims made by German soldiers in the East vis-à-vis their Russian adversary. This editor (C.W.H.L.) has also read contemporary German accounts of Russian soldiers being locked in their bunkers or chained to their machine guns. Given the fanaticism of many Red Army commissars, such stories cannot be dismissed out of hand. What is no doubt true is that it was not uncommon for *Rotarmisten* who fell back in combat (without orders to do so) to be shot by their commissars.

98. Fuchs Richardson (ed.), *Your Loyal and Loving Son. The Letters of Tank Gunner Karl Fuchs, 1937–41,* 113.

99. Karl Fuchs is slightly mistaken here—hardly surprising for, as a simple soldier, he had little knowledge of events beyond his own immediate area of concern. The city of Vitebsk had actually been seized by forces of 3 Panzer Group two days earlier, on 9 July 1941.

100. *Lt.* Willibald G. (N02.5), Collection BfZ.

101. Throughout the Russo-German War, the Soviets would rely more on their artillery than any other major combatant; moreover, since Czarist times, the Russians had a deserved reputation for producing excellent guns and soldiers who knew how to use them. The Soviet artillery park comprised a mix of guns and howitzers—some obsolete, some modern types—in 76mm, 107mm, 122mm, and 152mm calibers. Like the German artillery, most of it was horse-drawn in 1941, while very few of the tracked artillery pieces could operate off the roads. Mawdsley, *Thunder in the East. The Nazi-Soviet War 1941–1945,* 26.

102. Scheuer (ed.), *Briefe aus Russland. Feldpostbriefe des Gefreiten Alois Scheuer 1941–1942,* 23.

103. David M. Glantz: "One of the most serious problems for the [German] infantrymen was the lack of water since, although the shallow wells in the villages sustained the local population, they were wholly inadequate to quench the thirst of a million and a half men [of Army Group Center] and hundreds of thousands of horses. Nor was the water safe to drink without first boiling it and then purifying it with chlorine." Of course, Glantz's observations were applicable across the entire Eastern Front. Glantz, *Barbarossa Derailed. The Battle for Smolensk 10 July–10 September 1941,* Vol. I: *The German Advance to Smolensk, the Encirclement Battle, and the First and Second Soviet Counteroffensives, 10 July–24 August 1941,* 62.

104. Garden and Andrew (eds.), *The War Diaries of a Panzer Soldier. Erich Hager with the 17th Panzer Division on the Russian Front 1941–1945,* 38.

105. Hager's 17 PD had reached the Dnepr River at Orsha. The division commander, *Generalmajor* Karl Ritter von Weber, was badly wounded near Smolensk on 19 July and died the next day. Weber was the 17 PD's third commander since the start of the Russian campaign. Dinglreiter, *Die Vierziger. Chronik des Regiments,* 47; website at www.lexikon-der-wehrmacht.de.

106. Ltr., Werner Heinemann, to his wife, 13.7.41.

107. "Contempt for alien ways seems virtually a universal characteristic of armies—particularly in the combat units, which are not usually manned by cosmopolitan intellectuals. For the *Wehrmacht's* rank and file, a vague, centuries-old, sense of defending the West from Slavic barbarism was reinforced by direct experience of a culture that seemed at once incomprehensibly alien and overwhelmingly threatening to Germans whose provincialism had been fostered and reinforced by National Socialism." Historical Commentary by Dennis E. Showalter in Fuchs Richardson (ed.), *Your Loyal and Loving Son. The Letters of Tank Gunner Karl Fuchs, 1937–41,* 121–122.

108. Stützel, *Feldpost. Briefe und Aufzeichnungen eines 17-Jährigen 1940–1945,* 37–38.

109. Stützel's 5 ID took part in the destruction of the Belostok-Minsk pocket through early July 1941. By 6 July, the division had begun to drive east toward the Western Dvina River. Thies, *Der Ostfeldzug—Ein Lageatlas,* "Lage am 6.7.1941 abds., Heeresgruppe Mitte."

110. Ulla—a town on the Western Dvina, some sixty-five kilometers west of Vitebsk.

111. Stader (ed.), *Ihr daheim und wir hier draussen. Ein Briefwechsel zwischen Ostfront und Heimat, Juni 1941–März 1943,* 21.

112. SS-Sturmm. Hans T. (47 888), Collection BfZ. On 22 June, the SS Battle Group "North" (*SS-Kampfgruppe "Nord"*) was deployed in northern Finland, close to the Russian border town of Salla.

113. Ltr., *Lt.* Rudolf Maurer, to his wife, Irene, 14.7.41.

114. *Mj.* Hans Sch. (33 691), Collection BfZ.

115. As more than a few of the preceding field post letters have made abundantly clear, the *Landser* were often shocked by the tenacity, toughness—even fanaticism—of the Red Army fighting man; such comparisons to the campaign in France of 1940 were quite common.

116. Risse, "Das IR 101 und der 2. Weltkrieg." The date for this entry is approximate.

117. Despite the *Ostheer*'s heavy losses of troops and tanks, few replacements were reaching the front. 18 PD, for example, was soon down to twelve operational tanks, while, in general, the armored forces of Army Group Center were declining rapidly in strength. Luther, *Barbarossa Unleashed. The German Blitzkrieg through Central Russia to the Gates of Moscow. June–December 1941*, 492.

118. Bopp, *Kriegstagebuch. Aufzeichnungen während des II. Weltkrieges 1940–1943*, 90–91.

119. *Sold.* Sepp P. (L 34 818), Collection BfZ.

120. Willi F. (10 273 E), Collection BfZ.

121. *Sold.* Rudolf B. (20 149), Collection BfZ.

122. This appears to be a reference to the actions of Soviet authorities after they had occupied the Baltic States in June 1940; many putative enemies of the USSR were deported, never to be seen again.

123. *Gefr.* Paul B. (L 46 281), Collection BfZ.

124. In the letters of German soldiers and in official unit war diaries are more than a few references to the wells (of towns and villages) being poisoned or otherwise rendered unusable by withdrawing Red Army troops. For example, the war diary (*Kriegstagebuch*) of 7 Panzer Division recorded on the morning of 24 June that troops were to be alerted at once because the local wells had all been poisoned (*vergiftet*). BA-MA RH 27-7/46, *KTB 7. Pz.-Div.*, 24.6.41.

125. Stehmann, *Die Bitternis verschweigen wir. Feldpostbriefe 1940–1945*, 113.

126. *Tagebuch, Lt.* Rudolf Maurer, 17.7.41.

127. In the summer of 1941, German forces—particularly the mobile forces—due in part to the often furious pace of the advance, sometimes found themselves cut off or surrounded by Soviet forces. While this occasionally resulted in their annihilation, in most cases the surrounded German forces were able to leverage their superior training, tactics, and experience to extricate themselves from such unpleasant situations.

128. Ltr., Werner Heinemann, to his wife, 17.7.41.

129. Many German soldiers were deeply moved by the suffering of their horses—which the men could do little to ameliorate—as they struggled ceaselessly through the deep sand and the searing heat, pulling the heavy guns and the supply and ammunition wagons.

130. Fuchs Richardson (ed.), *Your Loyal and Loving Son. The Letters of Tank Gunner Karl Fuchs, 1937–41*, 115.

131. *O.Gefr.* G.B., cited in Manoschek (ed.), *"Es gibt nur eines für das Judentum: Vernichtung." Das Judenbild in deutschen Soldatenbriefen 1939–1944*, 36.

132. Sahm (ed.), *Verzweiflung und Glaube. Briefe aus dem Krieg 1939–1942*, 43.

133. Moutier (ed.), *"Liebste Schwester, wir müssen hier sterben oder siegen," Briefe deutscher Wehrmachtssoldaten 1939–45*, 133–134.

134. The total figure of *Rotarmisten* captured during the war is 5.7 million. Of these, between 55 and 60 percent perished in German captivity, or as many as 3.3 million. When, in mid-September 1941, Admiral Wilhelm Canaris, the chief of military intelligence (*Abwehr*), protested the treatment of Soviet POWs and the ongoing liquidation of "politically undesirable" prisoners—both in crass violation of international law—he elicited a sharp rebuke from the chief of OKW, *Generalfeldmarschall* Keitel: "Your misgivings reflect the soldierly conceptions of a chivalrous war. At issue here is the annihilation of a *Weltanschauung!* For that reason I approve of the measures and support them." Ueberschär and Wette (eds.), *"Unternehmen Barbarossa," Der deutsche Überfall auf die Sowjetunion 1941*, 21; see also, Streit, "Soviet Prisoners of War in the Hands of the Wehrmacht," in *War of Extermination. The German Military in World War II, 1941–1944*, Heer and Naumann (eds.), 80–81.

135. The Volga Germans were the descendants of German settlers who had immigrated to Russia in the eighteenth century during the reign of Czar Catherine II and settled along the

Volga River. (In general, during the NS period, all communities of German-speaking minorities living outside the Reich were characterized as "Volksdeutsche" [ethnic Germans]. They were often used by the *Wehrmacht* as interpreters.) Following the German invasion, about a half-million Volga Germans were exiled to Siberia and Kazakhstan, where both men and women were forced to do labor in the forests and mines. The expulsion of the Volga Germans was completed by end of September 1941.

136. *Sold.* Carlheinz B. (25 328), Collection BfZ.

137. Fuchs Richardson (ed.), *Your Loyal and Loving Son. The Letters of Tank Gunner Karl Fuchs, 1937–41*, 116. On 21 July, 7 PD reported a combat strength of 118 tanks, with 96 others under repair. To maintain combat effectiveness, the division temporarily broke up one of its three tank battalions to keep the remaining two at effective strength. The division had begun *Barbarossa* with 265 tanks. Jentz (ed.), *Panzer Truppen. The Complete Guide to the Creation & Combat Employment of Germany's Tank Force, 1933–1942*, 190.

138. "The Stukas' success resulted in large part from the absence of effective fighter or antiaircraft opposition. The vulnerability of the dive bomber, first demonstrated in the Battle of Britain and proved again and again in the Mediterranean, nevertheless did not prevent the *Luftwaffe* from using Stukas effectively against the Russians throughout the war, after 1943 more as a tank buster than a strike aircraft." Historical Commentary by Dennis E. Showalter in Fuchs Richardson (ed.), *Your Loyal and Loving Son. The Letters of Tank Gunner Karl Fuchs, 1937–41*, 116.

139. Latzel, *Deutsche Soldaten—nationalsozialistischer Krieg? Kriegserlebnis—Kriegserfahrung 1939–1945*, 50. "Olte" is a pseudonym used by the author.

140. On the eve of Operation *Barbarossa*, cigarettes and chocolates were distributed to troops across the Eastern Front. A careful reading of soldiers' field post letters and diaries makes clear that smoking was a commonly shared activity—a perspective supported by numerous photographs of the period.

141. *Gefr.* Fritz G. (19 768 B), Collection BfZ.

142. Ellis, *Barbarossa 1941. Reframing Hitler's Invasion of Stalin's Soviet Empire*, 324.

143. By mid-July 1941, Hermann Hoth's 3 Panzer Group had breached Soviet defenses along the Western Dvina River and fanned out rapidly to the east along a broad front of roughly two hundred kilometers. On the panzer group's right wing, *Generalmajor* Hans *Freiherr* von Funck's 7 Panzer Division (39 Panzer Corps) had captured the town of Iartsevo on 15 July, blocking the *Autobahn* leading from Smolensk to Moscow and, in conjunction with the drive of Guderian's panzers from the south, creating the conditions for another great battle of encirclement—this time around Smolensk. Yet despite 3 Panzer Group's rapid progress, Red Army resistance had begun to stiffen beyond the Dvina River, as the Soviet conduct of the battle gradually became more energetic, coherent, and effective. Luther, *Barbarossa Unleashed. The German Blitzkrieg through Central Russia to the Gates of Moscow. June–December 1941*, 515.

144. The panzer and motorized divisions had been designed for fire and maneuver, not for static defense. Yet because the foot infantry habitually lagged so far behind the mobile units, the latter typically had no choice but to man the encirclement rings for days at a time. Always short of motorized infantry, their defensive perimeters often consisted of little more than thin picket lines, and they were sometimes badly mauled trying to contain Soviet forces desperately seeking to escape, until eventually relieved by the infantry divisions. Because in both the Minsk and Smolensk cauldron battles major components of 2 and 3 Panzer Groups were immobilized for days in a static defensive roll, the timetable of the German advance was disrupted and the momentum of the blitzkrieg blunted.

145. Meier-Welcker, *Aufzeichnungen eines Generalstabsoffiziers 1939–1942*, 123.

146. The first major battle in which Meier-Welcker's 251 ID took part was on 20–24 July and involved the encirclement and destruction of several Soviet divisions just west of Nevel. The trapped Red Army forces sought desperately to escape from the pocket and inflicted serious losses on 251 ID, its 451 IR alone sustaining 563 men KIA and wounded (including 33 officers), while 78 men went missing in the fighting. Ibid., 123; also, Jacobsen (ed.), *Kriegstagebuch des OKW (WFSt.), Bd. I: 1. August 1940—31. Dezember 1941*, 536.

147. *Tagebuch* (author unknown), cited in *Gefallen! . . . und umsonst—Erlebnisberichte deutscher Soldaten im Russlandkrieg 1941–1943*, Duesel (ed.), 20. The 5 ID, in position along the northern shoulder of the Smolensk pocket, played a significant role in the pocket's reduction into early August. Thies, *Der Ostfeldzug—Ein Lageatlas*, "Lage am 22.7.1941 abds., Heeresgruppe Mitte."

148. *Gefr.* Heinz Sch. (20 158), Collection BfZ.

149. *Uffz.* Heinz H. (28 743), Collection BfZ.

150. *Gefr.* M.F. (38 088 D), cited in Manoschek (ed.), *"Es gibt nur eines für das Judentum: Vernichtung." Das Judenbild in deutschen Soldatenbriefen 1939–1944*, 37.

151. Stehmann, *Die Bitternis verschweigen wir. Feldpostbriefe 1940–1945*, 116.

152. The "Disasters of War" is a series of eighty-two prints created between 1810 and 1820 by the Spanish romantic painter and printmaker Francisco Goya (1746–1828).

153. *Tagebuch* (author unknown), cited in *Gefallen! . . . und umsonst—Erlebnisberichte deutscher Soldaten im Russlandkrieg 1941–1943*, Duesel (ed.), 20.

154. *True to Type. A Selection from Letters and Diaries of German Soldiers and Civilians Collected on the Soviet-German Front*, 15.

155. Beginning on 23 July and continuing through the first week of August, the Red Army launched fierce assaults on German positions stretching from Belyi in the north to Roslavl' in the south in an effort to relieve Soviet forces trapped in the Smolensk region. While Army Group Center successfully repelled each Soviet attack, the "cumulative effect of these poorly coordinated Soviet actions was to deprive the Germans of operational flexibility, erode their offensive strength, and convince the German leadership of the wisdom of halting direct offensive action along the Moscow axis in favor of a thrust into the seemingly more vulnerable Ukraine." Glantz, *Forgotten Battles of the German-Soviet War (1941–1945)*. Vol. I: *The Summer-Fall Campaign (22 June–4 December 1941)*, 47–51. For an account of the Soviet Smolensk counteroffensive, see Luther, *Barbarossa Unleashed. The German Blitzkrieg through Central Russia to the Gates of Moscow. June–December 1941*, 520–524.

156. *Lt.* Willibald G. (N02.5), Collection BfZ.

157. By late July 1941, the armor of Kleist's 1 Panzer Group—supported by infantry units of Army Group South—was effecting the encirclement of Soviet 6 and 12 Armies (some twenty-four divisions in all) deep in the Ukraine west of the Dnepr River near Uman'.

158. Sahm (ed.), *Verzweiflung und Glaube. Briefe aus dem Krieg 1939–1942*, 43–44.

159. *Tagebuch*, Major S., 25.7.41, cited in Andres, "Panzersoldaten im Russlandfeldzug 1941 bis 1945. Tagebuchaufzeichnungen und Erlebnisberichte," 24–25. In his personal diary, Major S. vividly described the visceral shock of his unit's encounter with Soviet T-34 and KV tanks. On this day, he and his battalion took part in a harrowing engagement against a heavy Soviet tank brigade. After expending their armor-piercing rounds on a KV-1, to no effect, the major and his crew discovered that their tank's engine would no longer turn over. Immobilized and out of shells, they abandoned their machine. Evading the Russian tank's machine-gun fire in a desperate "cat and mouse" game, they managed their escape.

160. If the tank crews of this heavy Soviet tank brigade had been well led and trained, the destruction of Major S.'s battalion would most likely have been assured. That it managed to

survive a nearly hopeless situation was due to the superior training, better marksmanship, and quicker responses of the German *Panzermänner.*

161. *O.Gefr.* Konrad F. (09 624 A), Collection BfZ.

162. Scheuer (ed.), *Briefe aus Russland. Feldpostbriefe des Gefreiten Alois Scheuer 1941–1942,* 26.

163. The German infantry did two things in the summer of 1941—they marched and they fought. However, after the initial frontier battles, which came to an end about 9 July, they mostly marched, from dawn to dusk, until they caught up to the mobile units ranging far to the east. In the sector of Army Group Center, the infantry, after a series of brutal forced marches through the "vast oppressiveness of Belorussia," finally reached the forward edge of battle in mid- to late July 1941. See situation maps of the German Army General Staff (Operations Branch) for 15–31 July 1941, in Thies, *Der Ostfeldzug—Ein Lageatlas.*

164. *True to Type. A Selection from Letters and Diaries of German Soldiers and Civilians Collected on the Soviet-German Front,* 15–16.

165. What had begun on 22 June 1941 as a strategic war of movement had gradually withered into an unremitting war of attrition. By late July, the losses of both personnel and armored fighting vehicles in Hoth's 3 Panzer Group had become alarming. For example, the panzer regiment of 20 Panzer Division was reduced to about thirty operational tanks by 31 July 1941, roughly equivalent to the authorized strength (*Sollstärke*) of one-and-a-half tank companies. Hinze, *Hitze, Frost und Pulverdampf: Der Schicksalsweg der 20. Panzer-Division,* 56.

166. *Gefr.* Eberhard W. (06 323 E), Collection BfZ.

167. As noted, *Generalmajor* Karl Allmendinger's 5 ID was making a major contribution to the reduction of the Smolensk pocket while experiencing savage Russian breakout attempts; the division was now holding a position on the northwest shoulder of the Smolensk encirclement ring. Thies, *Der Ostfeldzug—Ein Lageatlas,* "Lage am 26.7.1941 abds., Heeresgruppe Mitte."

168. *Ing.* H.J. (10 900), cited in Manoschek (ed.), *"Es gibt nur eines für das Judentum: Vernichtung." Das Judenbild in deutschen Soldatenbriefen 1939–1944,* 38.

169. Is it conceivable that a number of Jews (civilians?) acted together to make war on German and Romanian soldiers as they began their advance across the German-Soviet frontier? In fact, it strains credulity to think that this is anything but a wild rumor; after all, spreading rumors has been a pastime practiced by soldiers in all armies throughout history, and the *Wehrmacht* was no exception. In any case, this editor (C.W.H.L.) knows of no instance of coordinated armed resistance by Jews in the initial days or weeks of Operation *Barbarossa.*

170. On 28 July, Guderian's 2 Panzer Group was reinforced with several infantry divisions to support its impending attack on Roslavl' (a major road junction and communications node), where powerful Soviet forces threatened the right flank of the panzer group; Guderian's significantly enlarged command was elevated in status to that of a full army group (*Armeegruppe* Guderian), although it remained subordinate to Army Group Center. The new command arrangement would remain in place until 21 August. Jacobsen (ed.), *Kriegstagebuch des OKW (WFSt.), Bd. I: 1. August 1940—31. Dezember 1941,* 543, 583; also, Guderian, *Panzer Leader,* 183.

171. Buchbender and Sterz (eds.), *Das Andere Gesicht des Krieges. Deutsche Feldpostbriefe 1939–1945,* 75.

172. Meier-Welcker, *Aufzeichnungen eines Generalstabsoffiziers 1939–1942,* 123–124.

173. Moutier (ed.), "Liebste Schwester, wir müssen hier sterben oder siegen," *Briefe deutscher Wehrmachtssoldaten 1939–45,* 136–137.

174. Twice in this letter to his father *Unteroffizier* S. makes the remarkable claim that the Red Army was using gas—and one can only assume the reference is mistaken. There is no evidence that the Red Army ever made use of chemical weapons (or biological weapons) during World War II.

175. *Tagebuch*, Wilhelm Wessler, 28.7.41.

176. Wessler was the accountant and pay NCO (*Rechnungsführer*) in his battalion.

177. After days of exhausting marches, 28 July had been set aside as a rare day of rest for Wessler's company, a time normally used for cleaning weapons, doing maintenance on vehicles, resting overworked horses, and catching up on personal hygiene.

178. König (ed.), *Ganz in Gottes Hand. Briefe Gefallener und Hingerichteter Katholiken 1939–1945*, 27–29.

179. These are excerpts from *Gefreiter* Czermak's last letter to his parents; he was killed in battle (*gefallen*) near Kiev three days later. Ibid., 28.

180. *Tagebuch*, *Lt.* Rudolf Maurer, 29.7.41. On 29 July, 50 AK (251 and 253 ID), hitherto attached to Sixteenth Army on the extreme right wing of Army Group North, was posted to Ninth Army, Army Group Center. Thies, *Der Ostfeldzug—Ein Lageatlas*, "Lage am 29.7.1941 abds., Heeresgruppe Mitte"; also, Jacobsen (ed.), *Kriegstagebuch des OKW (WFSt.), Bd. I: 1. August 1940—31. Dezember 1941*, 446.

181. The commander of 251 ID, *Generalleutnant* Hans Kratzert, who had led the division since August 1939, was indeed replaced as division commander by 6 August 1941.

182. Reddemann (ed.), *Zwischen Front und Heimat. Der Briefwechsel des münsterischen Ehepaares Agnes and Albert Neuhaus 1940–1944*, 259.

183. Neuhaus's artillery unit had reached the front in the Luga River region about 18 July. Now that he is finally in combat, one detects a not-so-subtle change in attitude (see, for example, his letter of 7 July above).

184. Two days later (31 July), Neuhaus wrote to his wife: "Surely the collapse of the Russian armies can't be long in coming. Hopefully, it will all be over in a couple of weeks. But one has to admit—the Russians have made a very bold stand [*wehren sich verdammt tapfer*]." Reddemann (ed.), *Zwischen Front und Heimat. Der Briefwechsel des münsterischen Ehepaares Agnes and Albert Neuhaus 1940–1944*, 260.

185. Garden and Andrew (eds.), *The War Diaries of a Panzer Soldier. Erich Hager with the 17th Panzer Division on the Russian Front 1941–1945*, 45.

186. *Sold.* Heinz Sch. (41 455), Collection BfZ.

187. *Soldat* Heinz Sch. was in a medical company (*Sanitätskompanie*) in the division.

188. *Tagebuch* (author unknown), cited in *Gefallen! . . . und umsonst—Erlebnisberichte deutscher Soldaten im Russlandkrieg 1941–1943*, Duesel (ed.), 22.

189. *O.Gefr.* Ferdi B. (05 261), Collection BfZ. The 197 ID was in position along the defensive front of Bock's army group, some fifty-plus kilometers south of Smolensk. Thies, *Der Ostfeldzug—Ein Lageatlas*, "Lage am 30.7.1941 abds., Heeresgruppe Mitte."

190. Poor, even inaccurate, maps posed a nearly universal problem for the Germans in the opening stages of the Russian campaign. Recalled Panzer General Hermann Hoth, "Only gradually, beginning in January 1941, did the army and corps commanders become familiar with their tasks in the Eastern Campaign. . . . Only now were military-geographic descriptions of the terrain and maps prepared. These were based, in part, on meticulous work done in the years before World War I and were now outdated and insufficient. From the maps we were given we could only seldom determine which roads and bridges were useable for motor vehicles and tanks. Frequently, roads had to be assigned without knowing if they were actually passable, leaving it up to the units themselves to deal with whatever problems arose." Hoth, *Panzer-Operationen. Die Panzergruppe 3 und der operative Gedanke der deutschen Führung Sommer 1941*, 44.

191. *Hptm.* Friedrich M. (20 305), Collection BfZ.

192. Bessarabia and Northern Bukovina had been seized from Romania by the Red Army in the summer of 1940; following their incorporation into the Soviet Union, somewhere be-

tween one hundred thousand and half a million Romanians were deported from Bessarabia to Central Asia—to work in the factories and collective farms as replacements for Russians being drafted into the army. The deportations were interrupted by the German invasion and, by late July, German and Romanian forces had reoccupied the lost provinces. During their retreat—as *Hauptmann* M.'s letter graphically illustrates—the Soviets made use of scorched-earth tactics, destroying towns and infrastructure and transporting movable goods to Russia by rail. Dear (ed.), *The Oxford Guide to World War II*, 101.

193. *Lt.* Ernst E. (05 714), Collection BfZ.

194. Rühle (ed.), *Die Feldpostbriefe des Adelbert-Ottheinrich Rühle 1939 bis 1942*, 42.

195. The ration requirements of German forces in Russia were enormous. For example, the daily ration of food for 6 Infantry Division (at full strength) amounted to some thirty tons; other divisions, no doubt, had similar needs. The precampaign planning of German logisticians had envisaged the *Ostheer* subsisting off the land to the fullest extent possible (even if this meant a death sentence to millions of Russian civilians by starvation). However, obtaining grains, livestock, foodstuffs, and forage for horses in requisite quantities from local sources often proved to be a challenge, in no small part due to Soviet scorched-earth policies, as the retreating Red Army burned large quantities of grain and destroyed many farm implements while also seizing grain and most of the cattle from the collective farms. Yet during the summer of 1941, the German invaders did manage to secure much of their food supply from local sources and to acquire part of the fodder for their horses as well. A regular pastime of *Landser* across the Eastern Front was scouring the countryside and local villages—singly, or in small groups—for eggs, milk, poultry, livestock, and other foodstuffs with which to supplement their often spartan diet. The German soldiers even had a widely used slang term to describe these foraging expeditions—"to organize" (*organisieren*).

196. *Tagebuch* (author unknown), cited in: *Gefallen! . . . und umsonst—Erlebnisberichte deutscher Soldaten im Russlandkrieg 1941–1943*, Duesel (ed.), 23.

CHAPTER 4

1. Bock, *Generalfeldmarschall Fedor von Bock. The War Diary 1939–1945*, Gerbet (ed.), 273–274.

2. The line of Army Group Center stretched from just south of Velikie Luki in the north, eastward in a great bulging arc around Smolensk, until curling back in a southwesterly direction to the Dnepr (opposite Rogachev–Shlobin) and, from there, to the northern edge of the Pripiat Marshes. Thies, *Der Ostfeldzug—Ein Lageatlas*, "Lage am 1.8.1941 abds., Heeresgruppe Mitte."

3. In field post letters (*Feldpostbriefe*) from the front to family and friends, more than a few soldiers of Army Group Center began to remark that they were now undergoing many of the same experiences as had their fathers in the trenches of World War I. For a detailed discussion (including case studies) of the positional warfare along the front of Army Group Center, see Luther, *Barbarossa Unleashed. The German Blitzkrieg through Central Russia to the Gates of Moscow. June–December 1941*, 557–578, 626–634.

4. Ibid., 620. See also, Overmans, *Deutsche militärische Verluste im Zweiten Weltkrieg*, 277.

5. Luther, *Barbarossa Unleashed. The German Blitzkrieg through Central Russia to the Gates of Moscow. June–December 1941*, 636; Boog et al., *Germany and the Second World War*, Vol. IV: *The Attack on the Soviet Union*, 635–637; Mawdsley, *Thunder in the East. The Nazi-Soviet War 1941–1945*, 84.

6. Gilbert, *Second World War*, 228.

7. Jacobsen (ed.), *Kriegstagebuch des OKW (WFSt.), Bd. I: 1. August 1940—31. Dezember 1941*, 560; Boog et al., *Germany and the Second World War*, Vol. IV: *The Attack on the Soviet Union*, 597; Mawdsley, *Thunder in the East. The Nazi-Soviet War 1941–1945*, 78.

8. Luther, *Barbarossa Unleashed. The German Blitzkrieg through Central Russia to the Gates of Moscow. June–December 1941*, 610, 637; see also, "Wehrmachts-Führungsstab/L, Nr. 441412/41 g.Kdos. Chef, 21. August 1941," in Jacobsen (ed.), *Kriegstagebuch des OKW (WFSt.), Bd. I: 1. August 1940—31. Dezember 1941*, 1062–1063.

9. *Oberstleutnant* Stieff was serving in the OKH Operations Branch at Mauerwald in the summer of 1941.

10. Mühleisen (ed.), *Hellmuth Stieff Briefe*, 119.

11. *Tagebuch*, Major S., cited in Andres, "Panzersoldaten im Russlandfeldzug 1941 bis 1945. Tagebuchaufzeichnungen und Erlebnisberichte," 10.

12. This is a reference to the collective farms that dominated the Soviet agricultural economy. Under Stalin's leadership, the Soviet Union had implemented collectivization of its agricultural sector beginning in 1927. In the early 1930s, despite fierce resistance from the Russian peasantry, over 90 percent of agricultural land was collectivized. The collectivization era resulted in several famines (among them famines that were the direct outcome of official government policy in a successful effort to break the back of any opposition), resulting in the deaths of millions.

13. Belke, *Infanterist*, 35–36. The date is approximate.

14. HKL = *Hauptkampflinie*, or main battle line. The line now held by 6 ID extended for forty kilometers, a length that was considered "an impossibility at the time," at least from a prewar perspective. In Russia, however, due to the persistent shortage of infantry, such vast defensive frontages would almost become commonplace in the years ahead. BA-MA RH 26-6/8, *KTB 6. Inf.-Div.*, 30.7.41; also, Grossmann, *Die Geschichte der rheinisch-westfälischen 6. Infanterie-Division 1939–1945*, 56.

15. *Tagebuch* (author unknown), cited in *Gefallen! . . . und umsonst—Erlebnisberichte deutscher Soldaten im Russlandkrieg 1941–1943*, Duesel (ed.), 23.

16. *Generalmajor* Karl Allmendinger's 5 ID was still playing a major role in the destruction of the Smolensk pocket, which had by now been reduced to a small area due east of the city. Thies, *Der Ostfeldzug—Ein Lageatlas*, "Lage am 1.8.1941 abds., Heeresgruppe Mitte."

17. Reddemann (ed.), *Zwischen Front und Heimat. Der Briefwechsel des münsterischen Ehepaares Agnes and Albert Neuhaus 1940–1944*, 263, 265.

18. *Sold.* Rudolf L. (L 35 512), Collection BfZ.

19. *Tagebuch*, *Lt.* Rudolf Maurer, 1–2.8.41.

20. On 7 August, *Leutnant* Maurer recorded in his diary, "During the past four days it was 'quiet,' quiet in theory, [but] for all practical purposes there was unrest due to constant artillery fire and air attacks." Ibid.

21. *True to Type. A Selection from Letters and Diaries of German Soldiers and Civilians Collected on the Soviet-German Front*, 16–17. The 20 PD was posted to the front of Army Group Center south of Belyi, where for days it was subjected to violent Soviet attacks. On 1 August, the division noted in its war diary that its rifle regiments were "severely exhausted" due to the "unceasing battles," while officer casualties had reached 50 percent. (BA-MA RH 27-20/2, *KTB 20. Pz.-Div.*, 1.8.41, cited in Stahel, *Operation Barbarossa and Germany's Defeat in the East*, 326.) On 8 August, 20 PD was withdrawn from the front for a brief period of technical refitting of tanks and vehicles and well-deserved rest for its men. Thies, *Der Ostfeldzug—Ein Lageatlas*, "Lage am 8.8.1941 abds., Heeresgruppe Mitte."

22. Under the conditions of positional (static) warfare now taking shape, the excellent Soviet artillery arm began to make itself increasingly felt. During the first phase of the war, Soviet artillery

had played a relatively minor role; as one German report noted, "During the days of the war of movement [*Bewegungskrieg*] the Soviet artillery had a negligible impact [*geringe Wirkung*]"; as a result, "sizeable losses did not occur." In their foxholes and bunkers, however, the *Landser* were now frequently outgunned by longer-range Soviet artillery with seemingly inexhaustible stockpiles of shells, leading the report to conclude that "the powerful impact of artillery fire on our own troops is now becoming clear. . . . As a final judgment and consideration of the relative advantages and disadvantages [of German and Soviet artillery], it is clear that the German artillery is far superior [in every respect]. That said, with regard to the enemy's artillery, the German troops 'have also met their toughest opponent.'" Yet even if the Germans' artillery arm was better led and more technically proficient, that hardly mattered if their guns couldn't shoot. For it was during this period that the flow of munitions to the front, over the badly overstretched arteries of supply, often slowed to a trickle, denying the Germans the ability to respond effectively to the hail of shells raining down on them. For the detailed report (cited here) on the Germans' initial experiences with Soviet artillery, see BA-MA RH 26-6/16, "Erfahrungsbericht über russische Artillerie," *Artillerie Regiment 78*, 29.8.1941, in *Anlagenband 1 zum KTB Nr. 5 der 6. Inf.-Div., Ia.*

23. *O.Gefr.* Heinz B. (05 854), Collection BfZ.

24. The 23 ID was taking part in the attack of Guderian's group on Roslavl'. See below, Fritz Köhler (3.8.41), and the supporting annotation.

25. *Gefr.* Heinz B. (26 391), Collection BfZ.

26. 3./Pz.Jäg.Abt.291= 3rd Company, Antitank Battalion 291.

27. *Tagebuch* (author unknown), cited in *Gefallen! . . . und umsonst—Erlebnisberichte deutscher Soldaten im Russlandkrieg 1941–1943*, Duesel (ed.), 23–24.

28. *Uffz.* Heinz B. (29 524 C), Collection BfZ.

29. Dollinger (ed.), *Kain, wo ist dein Bruder? Was der Mensch im Zweiten Weltkrieg erleiden musste—dokumentiert in Tagebüchern und Briefen*, 92. *Unteroffizier* Schönfeld would be killed fighting with Army Group North in late September 1941. Ibid., 98.

30. Fuchs Richardson (ed.), *Your Loyal and Loving Son. The Letters of Tank Gunner Karl Fuchs, 1937–41*, 118.

31. "Skin diseases were an increasingly common affliction among tank crews in the summer of 1941—products of water shortages, crowded conditions, dust laden with unfamiliar bacteria, and, more obviously, insects. Karl was almost certainly lousy by this time." Historical Commentary by Dennis E. Showalter in Fuchs Richardson (ed.), *Your Loyal and Loving Son. The Letters of Tank Gunner Karl Fuchs, 1937–41*, 118–119.

32. Dollinger (ed.), *Kain, wo ist dein Bruder? Was der Mensch im Zweiten Weltkrieg erleiden musste—dokumentiert in Tagebüchern und Briefen*, 92.

33. Guderian's army group, reinforced with several infantry divisions, attacked at Roslavl' on 1 August in a successful effort to clear its right flank of strong Soviet forces. The city was stormed and captured by the vanguard of 4 PD on 3 August. Soviet forces trapped directly north of the city were systematically sealed off and liquidated over the next two days; 38,561 Russians were herded into captivity, the victorious German forces also capturing or destroying 250 tanks and tracked vehicles and 613 guns of all types. Jacobsen (ed.), *Kriegstagebuch des OKW (WFSt.), Bd. I: 1. August 1940—31. Dezember 1941*, 553, 561.

34. Stader (ed.), *Ihr daheim und wir hier draussen. Ein Briefwechsel zwischen Ostfront und Heimat, Juni 1941–März 1943*, 23–24.

35. Ltr., Dr. Heinrich Haape, to his fiancée, 3.8.41.

36. The 6 ID was now holding a front some forty kilometers in length in the Mezha River sector, one hundred or more kilometers north of Smolensk. The division's thinly held lines (a series of strong points, not a continuous front) were suddenly attacked by two well-equipped

Soviet cavalry divisions on 2 August, precipitating a local crisis. While the crisis was soon overcome, it cost the division sixty-five casualties, including twenty-five dead and missing. The Russian cavalry divisions left behind three hundred dead. For Dr. Haape's dramatic account, see the new edition of his iconic Eastern Front memoir, *Moscow Tram Stop. A Doctor's Experiences with the German Spearhead in Russia* (Stackpole Books, 2020, C. W. H. Luther, ed.), 65–67; also, Luther, *Barbarossa Unleashed. The German Blitzkrieg through Central Russia to the Gates of Moscow. June–December 1941*, 559–564.

37. *Lt.* Willibald G. (N02.5), Collection BfZ.

38. The *panje* horses—the small native breed of Eastern Europe—exhibited great endurance while being easy to feed, handle, and stable; thus, they were quickly drafted into service by the German Army. The hardy little horses were appreciated by rank-and-file soldiers and generals alike. In early 1942, *General der Panzertruppe* Joachim Lemelsen (47 Panzer Corps) jotted in his diary, "These *panje* horses are certainly tough animals. It is almost frightful [*ungeheuerlich*] what can be demanded of them, and they get by with just a little hay as feed and require no care." (BA-MA MSg 1/1148, *Tagebuch Lemelsen*, 14.2.42) Despite their renowned toughness, the *panje* horses were far too light and small for hauling artillery and, in many cases, horse-drawn vehicles.

39. *O.Gefr.* Werner E. (21 389), Collection BfZ.

40. The 73 ID was an OKH reserve division at the beginning of the Russian campaign; it had been assigned to Eleventh Army but was still "unloading" as of late July. (Boog et al., *Germany and the Second World War*, Vol. IV: *The Attack on the Soviet Union*, 555.) A German General Staff situation map for 1 August shows the division in the front lines. Website at www .lexikon-der-wehrmacht.de.

41. *Gefr.* Gu. (13 517 A), Collection BfZ.

42. *Sold.* Alfred V. (42 616), Collection BfZ.

43. Rhein, *Das Rheinisch-Westfälische Infanterie-/Grenadier-Regiment 18 1921–1945*, 75–76.

44. As noted above (see entry for Dr. Heinrich Haape, 3.8.41, and supporting annotation), the first major crisis for 6 ID in its defensive battles along the Mezha River line (northeast of Velizh) had come on 2 August, when Russian cavalry forces attacked in far superior numbers; among the German casualties that day were nineteen soldiers who had been brutally massacred by the attacking Soviet forces.

45. *Tagebuch*, Dr. Hans Lierow, 5.8.41.

46. Meier-Welcker, *Aufzeichnungen eines Generalstabsoffiziers 1939–1942*, 126.

47. *Soldat* J.Z. (20 355 D), cited in Manoschek (ed.), *"Es gibt nur eines für das Judentum: Vernichtung." Das Judenbild in deutschen Soldatenbriefen 1939–1944*, 40.

48. *Der Stürmer* was a weekly German newspaper (tabloid format) published by Julius Streicher, the *Gauleiter* (district leader) of the NSDAP for Franconia. The newspaper was a significant National Socialist propaganda organ throughout the war and vehemently anti-Semitic.

49. Reddemann (ed.), *Zwischen Front und Heimat. Der Briefwechsel des münsterischen Ehepaares Agnes and Albert Neuhaus 1940–1944*, 272–273.

50. Between 8 and 10 August, Army Group North would resume its advance on Leningrad, with tanks and infantry of Hoepner's 4 Panzer Group striking the city's outermost defenses stretching from Novgorod northwest across the Luga River line to Narva.

51. On 6 August 1941, German Armed Forces High Command (OKW) released several special reports (*Sondermeldungen*), noting victories achieved by Army Group North, the final dissolution of the Smolensk cauldron on the central front, and the capture of nearly nine hundred thousand Red Army soldiers since 22 June. Reddemann (ed.), *Zwischen Front und Heimat. Der Briefwechsel des münsterischen Ehepaares Agnes and Albert Neuhaus 1940–1944*, 272n80.

52. Kurowski, *Balkenkreuz und Roter Stern. Der Luftkrieg über Russland 1941–1944*, 103. The *Luftwaffe* bomber offensive against Moscow had begun on the evening of 21–22 July 1941, with 127 bombers disgorging 104 tons of high explosive (HE) and 46,000 incendiary bombs on the city; the next two nights, raids were again carried out with more than one hundred bombers on each occasion. In the weeks and months that followed, however, the raids became smaller, with fewer bombers taking part. All told, the *Luftwaffe* flew thirty-five raids between 21 July and 30 September 1941; of these, only nine involved fifty or more bombers, while twenty-one were conducted with fewer than fifteen aircraft. Although the bombing would continue (albeit irregularly) into April 1942, the results of the *Luftwaffe*'s attempt to wage a strategic air campaign against the Soviet capital—given the relatively small number of bombers committed as well as their decidedly limited capabilities—were highly disappointing. Hermann Plocher, "Einsatz gegen Moskau im Jahre 1941." For an in-depth account of the raids on Moscow, see Luther, *Barbarossa Unleashed. The German Blitzkrieg through Central Russia to the Gates of Moscow. June–December 1941*, 530–537.

53. Garden and Andrew (eds.), *The War Diaries of a Panzer Soldier. Erich Hager with the 17th Panzer Division on the Russian Front 1941–1945*, 45.

54. Ltr., *Lt.* Rudolf Maurer, to his wife, Irene, 7.8.41.

55. *Sold.* Heinz Sch. (41 455), Collection BfZ.

56. The 101 Light (*Jäger*) Division took part in the Uman cauldron battle (as described in the chapter introduction).

57. *Uffz.* Heinz B. (29 524 C), Collection BfZ.

58. *Tagebuch, Lt.* Rudolf Maurer, 8.8.41.

59. The 251 ID (C-in-C *Generalmajor* Karl Burdach) was still in position on the extreme left flank of Army Group Center, just southwest of the town of Velikie Luki. Thies, *Der Ostfeldzug—Ein Lageatlas*, "Lage am 8.8.1941 abds., Heeresgruppe Mitte."

60. *Lt.* Willibald G. (N02.5), Collection BfZ.

61. Meier-Welcker, *Aufzeichnungen eines Generalstabsoffiziers 1939–1942*, 127.

62. *Lt.* Ernst E. (05 714), Collection BfZ.

63. A German General Staff situation map (1.8.41) showed 13 PD just west of Cherkassy and the Dnepr River. Website at www.lexikon-der-wehrmacht.de.

64. Stehmann, *Die Bitternis verschweigen wir. Feldpostbriefe 1940–1945*, 117–119.

65. *Tagebuch, Lt.* Rudolf Maurer, 9./10.8.41.

66. Stützel, *Feldpost. Briefe und Aufzeichnungen eines 17-Jährigen 1940–1945*, 40–41.

67. Stader (ed.), *Ihr daheim und wir hier draussen. Ein Briefwechsel zwischen Ostfront und Heimat, Juni 1941–März 1943*, 25–26.

68. Like the vast majority of German soldiers on the Eastern Front, Dr. Adolf B. has complete faith in his *Führer* and the High Command. Certainly, everything must be unfolding according to a well-designed master plan! Of course, he could not know that Hitler and his General Staff—aware that the initial hammer blows of the *Wehrmacht* had failed to meet their objective of shattering the Red Army and the Soviet state—were beset by indecision and fundamental differences of opinion as they sought to recalibrate the campaign and bring it to a successful conclusion. As noted in the chapter introduction, Hitler would not reach a final decision on the future course of operations until 21 August.

69. Reddemann (ed.), *Zwischen Front und Heimat. Der Briefwechsel des münsterischen Ehepaares Agnes and Albert Neuhaus 1940–1944*, 281-82.

70. War diary of OKW on 14 August: "In difficult battles, 4 Panzer Group's 56 Panzer Corps broke through the first and second lines of the deeply echeloned [Soviet] Luga bridgehead and took ca. 100 bunkers; 13 tanks were destroyed, 11 guns and many pieces of equip-

ment captured." Jacobsen (ed.), *Kriegstagebuch des OKW (WFSt.), Bd. I: 1. August 1940—31. Dezember 1941*, 571.

71. In a letter to his wife on 2 August, *Oberstleutnant* Hellmuth Stieff, who served in the Army General Staff's Operations Branch in summer 1941, wrote bitterly, "The *Wehrmacht* reports are no longer anything more than a means of political propaganda [*Mittel der politischen Propaganda*], are drawn up only by him [i.e., Hitler] personally with no concern for the impact, impressed on him often enough, on the mood and expectations of the combat forces, for whom they are the only means of briefing on the overall progress of the battles. What is more, they exaggerate purported successes in such an abhorrent way and are anything but sober reports of the facts. Their truth content can justifiably be doubted." (Mühleisen [ed.], *Hellmuth Stieff Briefe*, 115.) While Stieff's assertion that Hitler personally prepared the reports is highly doubtful—although Hitler may have intervened from time to time in their preparation—his damning critique of the reports is certainly accurate!

72. *Gefr.* Hans B. (38 051), Collection BfZ.

73. *Lt.* Willibald G. (N02.5), Collection BfZ.

74. In September 1939, the division's 199 Infantry Regiment was renamed the "List" regiment in honor of the Bavarian regiment Adolf Hitler had fought with in World War I. Many of the fateful decisions made by Hitler between 1939 and 1945 were shaped by his experiences in the List Regiment between 1914 and 1918. Nafziger, *The German Order of Battle. Infantry in World War II*, 103.

75. Stützel, *Feldpost. Briefe und Aufzeichnungen eines 17-Jährigen 1940–1945*, 41–42.

76. Although the Soviet Air Force (VVS) was largely eviscerated in the first few days of Operation *Barbarossa*, it made a surprisingly rapid recovery in the weeks and months that followed. A contributing factor was that the *Luftwaffe*, with inadequate resources and operating over much too broad a front, was unable to maintain requisite pressure on Soviet air forces (the air superiority mission) while simultaneously meeting the growing demands of the armored spearheads as they advanced farther eastward. As early as July 1941, the VVS was even gaining local air superiority over certain sectors of the front. Luther, *Barbarossa Unleashed. The German Blitzkrieg through Central Russia to the Gates of Moscow. June–December 1941*, 307–308; also, Boog et al., *Germany and the Second World War*, Vol. IV: *The Attack on the Soviet Union*, 804–805.

77. *Gefr.* Hans B. (38 051), Collection BfZ.

78. Reference is most likely to the "*Nebelwerfer 41*" 150mm rocket launcher. For more details on this devastating weapon, see Chapter 2, entry for "*Leutnant* Willibald G." (22.6.41).

79. Ltr., Dr. Heinrich Haape, to his fiancée, 14.8.41.

80. As revealed by photographs too many to count, the "simple birch cross" of which Dr. Haape writes signifies an iconic image of the fate of the German soldier in Russia; such crosses lined the route of the German advance throughout the summer of 1941.

81. Jarausch (ed.), *Reluctant Accomplice. A Wehrmacht Soldier's Letters from the Eastern Front*, 250–251.

82. Dr. Jarausch had just arrived in Russia, after transport by train from Warsaw via Brest-Litovsk to Minsk; he served behind the front in a reserve battalion. He would die of typhoid in 1942.

83. Following the capture of towns and cities, one of the first acts of German military authorities was often to open the mostly orthodox Christian churches for use by the local population. These churches had been closed to the public for years and, in many cases, diverted by the Communists to other purposes (e.g., cinemas, market places, grain storage facilities, even breweries and horse stalls). In his "recollections," General Maximilian *Freiherr* von Weichs, who, in the summer of 1941 commanded German Second Army, registered his disgust at the Soviet desecration of Christian churches while also noting that a generation of Communism

had failed to eradicate the deep faith of the Russian people. As Weichs also indicated, Hitler's decree governing use of churches in the East was, on occasion at least, flouted: "The return of religious freedom could have been an important way of fostering a good relationship with the Russian population. Hitler, however, sought to limit these efforts. It was, by decree, permissible to open the churches for the use of local residents, but it was forbidden to use the churches for military services or to help the people in re-establishing the churches. Since the last mentioned activity had brought particularly good results, this proscription was not adhered to strictly. The population was grateful and filled the reclaimed places of worship. The old Russian church songs resounded in the church services. Often, masses of young people came to be baptized. But baptism of Polish or Russian people by German Army chaplains [*Feldgeistliche*] was forbidden by Hitler." BA-MA N 19/9, *Nachlass von Weichs. Erinnerungen, Ost-Feldzug bis Frühjahr 1942.*

84. Meier-Welcker, *Aufzeichnungen eines Generalstabsoffiziers 1939–1942*, 127.

85. *Hptm.* Friedrich M. (20 305), Collection BfZ.

86. The *Volksdeutsche* were ethnic Germans who were citizens of other countries.

87. "The dearest hope of these peasants was for an end to Soviet power. In September 1941, though, they learned that the Germans had ordered that the collective farms should stay. Like the prewar Soviet authorities, the conquerors cared only for the ease with which the peasants' grain could be collected and shipped off. It was an irreversible mistake." Merridale, *Ivan's War. Life and Death in the Red Army, 1939–1945*, 133–134.

88. *Feldpost*, "Hans-Otto," 15.8.41. The surname of this soldier is unknown.

89. Since the end of July, 268 ID had been committed to the El'nia salient. The town of El'nia had been captured by 10 PD after bitter fighting on 19 July. The German bridgehead there dominated the outermost approaches to Moscow, and, thus, it offered a vital foothold from which to continue the all-important drive on the Soviet capital. Indeed, for both Germans and Russians alike, El'nia and its environs was what Sun Tzu had called "desperate ground"— terrain that had to be defended or captured. The German divisions in the salient would be badly attrited by Red Army counterattacks until the town was finally evacuated in early September.

90. *SS-Sturmm.* Eugen F. (09 239), Collection BfZ.

91. *Soldat* E.L. (24 768), cited in Manoschek (ed.), *"Es gibt nur eines für das Judentum: Vernichtung." Das Judenbild in deutschen Soldatenbriefen 1939–1944*, 41.

92. In general, replacement personnel were only reaching the front in driblets and, thus, were wholly inadequate to make good the high attrition rates (particularly among the combat infantry). The Replacement Army in Germany had begun the Russian campaign with a pool of only three hundred thousand to four hundred thousand replacement personnel and, by the end of the summer, practically all these men had been dispatched to the front. As chief of the Army General Staff, Franz Halder observed on 26 August 1941, "After 1 Oct. we shall have exhausted practically all our replacements." On 1 September, the German Army High Command (OKH) stated that "at the moment there is such a shortage of men that it is no longer possible to offset casualties." Both cited in Reinhardt, *Moscow—The Turning Point. The Failure of Hitler's Strategy in the Winter of 1941–42*, 66–67n26.

93. *Hptm.* Friedrich M. (20 305), Collection BfZ.

94. *Lt.* Otto Sch. (22 353 D), Collection BfZ.

95. *Mj.* Hans R. (21 688), Collection BfZ.

96. *Lt.* Willibald G. (N02.5), Collection BfZ.

97. Reddemann (ed.), *Zwischen Front und Heimat. Der Briefwechsel des münsterischen Ehepaares Agnes und Albert Neuhaus 1940–1944*, 287.

98. The poor rail infrastructure (like the poor roads) inside Soviet Russia posed a truly staggering problem that seriously complicated the movement and supply of Germany's armies fighting in the vast depths of the country. The entire USSR possessed only eighty-two thousand

kilometers of railroads—all of a slightly wider gauge (1528mm, a legacy of the Czarist era) than those in Germany, Western Europe, and German-occupied Poland—and they had to be converted to the standard gauge (1435mm), a time-consuming and labor-intensive process to which the Germans committed wholly inadequate resources (both human and material). Luther, *Barbarossa Unleashed. The German Blitzkrieg through Central Russia to the Gates of Moscow. June–December 1941*, 65, 69n165.

99. Ltr., Dr. Heinrich Haape, to his fiancée, 18.8.41.

100. Stehmann, *Die Bitternis verschweigen wir. Feldpostbriefe 1940–1945*, 122.

101. *Gefr.* Heinz T. del B. (11 320 B), Collection BfZ.

102. *Mj.* Hans Sch. (33 691), Collection BfZ.

103. Discipline in the *Wehrmacht* during World War II was extremely harsh. As many as twenty-two thousand German soldiers were executed during the war, while the Imperial German Army of 1914–1918 condemned fewer than fifty men to death. Observed historian Dr. S. Hart et al., "The German Army maintained order, discipline and combat effectiveness through a draconian system of military justice in which even minor offenses could meet with severe punishment." Dr. S. Hart et al., *The German Soldier in World War II*, 11.

104. Stader (ed.), *Ihr daheim und wir hier draussen. Ein Briefwechsel zwischen Ostfront und Heimat, Juni 1941–März 1943*, 26–27.

105. *Lt.* Ernst E. (05 714), Collection BfZ.

106. As of 1 September, the bulk of 13 PD was in refurbishment (*in Auffrischung*) west of Dnepropetrovsk, while elements of the division were already in the Dnepr bridgehead just beyond the city. Website at www.lexikon-der-wehrmacht.de (German General Staff situation map).

107. *Uffz.* Rudolf F. (10 203), Collection BfZ.

108. In mid-August, Second Army encircled and destroyed elements of a half-dozen Soviet rifle divisions southeast of Rogachev. See Jacobsen (ed.), *Kriegstagebuch des OKW (WFSt.), Bd. I: 1. August 1940—31. Dezember 1941*, 575; Thies, *Der Ostfeldzug—Ein Lageatlas*, "Lage am 15.8.1941 abds., Heeresgruppe Mitte." For a detailed account of this little-known *Kessel* battle, see Glantz, *Barbarossa Derailed. The Battle for Smolensk 10 July–10 September 1941*, Vol. I: *The German Advance to Smolensk, the Encirclement Battle, and the First and Second Soviet Counteroffensives, 10 July–24 August 1941*, 387–392.

109. *Gefr.* Ferdinand M. (22 200), Collection BfZ.

110. The reference is to Second Army's encirclement battle southeast of Rogachev.

111. Second Army captured Gomel on 19 August. Jacobsen (ed.), *Kriegstagebuch des OKW (WFSt.), Bd. I: 1. August 1940—31. Dezember 1941*, 579.

112. Scheuer (ed.), *Briefe aus Russland. Feldpostbriefe des Gefreiten Alois Scheuer 1941–1942*, 32–33.

113. *Gefreiter* Scheuer's 197 ID was defending positions along the Desna River, northeast of Roslavl'. Thies, *Der Ostfeldzug—Ein Lageatlas*, "Lage am 20.8.1941 abds., Heeresgruppe Mitte."

114. Reddemann (ed.), *Zwischen Front und Heimat. Der Briefwechsel des münsterischen Ehepaares Agnes and Albert Neuhaus 1940–1944*, 288–289.

115. This is a letter to Albert Neuhaus's brother-in-law.

116. Propaganda company.

117. *Kraft durch Freude* (Strength through Joy)—a National Socialist recreational organization whose purpose was to stimulate morale among workers. Established in imitation of a similar Italian organization founded by Mussolini, *KdF* was "the carrot that was to lead the German workers to greater productivity. . . . Participants in a new form of mass tourism, *KdF* holiday makers cruised on luxury liners and traveled by train to the Alps, Venice, Naples, and

Lisbon. There were also many tourist trips to Norway. . . . The *KdF* program also included subsidized theater performances, concerts, exhibitions, sports, hiking, folk dancing, and adult education courses." With the outbreak of war, holiday travel was stopped. Snyder, *Encyclopedia of the Third Reich*, 199.

118. Buchbender and Sterz (eds.), *Das andere Gesicht des Krieges. Deutsche Feldpostbriefe 1939–1945*, 79.

119. *Lt.* Willibald G. (N02.5), Collection BfZ.

120. Infantry of Seventeenth Army (to which *Leutnant* Willibald's 57 ID was now attached) seized Cherkassy on 22 August, after the Russians abandoned their bridgehead there; the withdrawing Soviets, however, managed to blow up the bridges over the Dnepr before the Germans could secure them. Jacobsen (ed.), *Kriegstagebuch des OKW (WFSt.), Bd. I: 1. August 1940—31. Dezember 1941*, 584.

121. The notorious Commissar Order ("Guidelines for the Treatment of Political Commissars") had been promulgated by the OKW on 6 June 1941. Simply put, it authorized summary extrajudicial execution of Soviet political officers, who were uniformed members of the Soviet military and thus fully covered by the protections of the international laws of war. The Germans considered the commissars—responsible for the political indoctrination of Red Army troops—to be the "core of the Communist military system and the 'originators of barbaric Asiatic fighting methods.'" As a result, they were to be shot immediately upon capture by front-line German troops—a war crime of the first order. While some German commanders were hostile to the order, which contradicted all soldierly traditions, many carried it out with enthusiasm. Megargee, *War of Annihilation. Combat and Genocide on the Eastern Front, 1941*, 38–39. See also Römer, "The Wehrmacht in the War of Ideologies: The Army and Hitler's Criminal Orders on the Eastern Front," in Kay, Rutherford and Stahel (eds.), *Nazi Policy on the Eastern Front, 1941. Total War, Genocide and Radicalization*, 73–100; Römer, *Der Kommissarbefehl. Wehrmacht und NS-Verbrechen an der Ostfront 1941/42*.

122. *Lt.* Willibald G. (N02.5), Collection BfZ.

123. The Great Bear (Ursa Major) is a constellation in the northern sky; its name distinguishes it from the nearby Little Bear (Ursa Minor).

124. Garden and Andrew (eds.), *The War Diaries of a Panzer Soldier. Erich Hager with the 17th Panzer Division on the Russian Front 1941–1945*, 47.

125. Note: From the photograph of the award document, it is clear that Hager's actual award was for the Tank Combat Badge in Silver (*Panzerkampfabzeichen im Silber*); however, eligibility for this decoration was the same—a minimum of three tank battles on three separate days. The award document is dated 18 August 1941 and is signed by the division commander, *Generalmajor* Wilhelm Ritter von Thoma. Ibid., 47.

126. In late August, 7 PD (hitherto a component of 3 Panzer Group) was temporarily assigned to 8 Army Corps of Ninth Army; however, it would soon rejoin Hoth's panzer group and, beginning in mid-September, enjoy a brief period to rest and refit. Website at www. lexikon-der-wehrmacht.de; Glantz, *Barbarossa Derailed. The Battle for Smolensk 10 July–10 September 1941*, Vol. I: *The German Advance to Smolensk, the Encirclement Battle, and the First and Second Soviet Counteroffensives, 10 July–24 August 1941*, 382; Thies, *Der Ostfeldzug—Ein Lageatlas*, "Lage 15.-29.9.1941 abds., Heeresgruppe Mitte."

127. *Obtl.* Richard D. (35 232), Collection BfZ.

128. On 17 August, the Red Army had launched another major counteroffensive against Army Group Center. The Germans responded by counterattacking as often and aggressively as their limited resources allowed to patch up holes in the main battle line (HKL). Such was standard German practice, and while the practice was effective, it could also be costly. The 20 August counterstroke by *Generalmajor* Hans *Freiherr* von Funck's 7 PD immediately lapsed

into a two-day slugging match, during which the panzers were ensnared in a "deadly web of dug-in tanks, interlocking infantry and antitank strongholds and under a hail of Soviet artillery and mortar fire." About two-thirds of 7 PD's tanks were destroyed and the remainder forced to withdraw. The Russian victory signified the first time in the war the Red Army had stopped a major German armored thrust, and stopped it dead in its tracks. Glantz, *Barbarossa Derailed. The Battle for Smolensk 10 July–10 September 1941*, Vol. I: *The German Advance to Smolensk, the Encirclement Battle, and the First and Second Soviet Counteroffensives, 10 July–24 August 1941*, 485, 528.

129. Stehmann, *Die Bitternis verschweigen wir. Feldpostbriefe 1940–1945*, 123.

130. Reddemann (ed.), *Zwischen Front und Heimat. Der Briefwechsel des münsterischen Ehepaares Agnes and Albert Neuhaus 1940–1944*, 292.

131. Strong panzer and infantry elements of Army Group North had finally broken through the Luga Line, capturing Shimsk (12 August), Novgorod (16 August), Chudovo (20 August), and Luga (24 August). The army group's offensive reached the Volkhov River, severing the Moscow-Leningrad railroad line—as well as vital Red Army communications—and inflicting devastating losses on defending Soviet forces. Glantz, *Barbarossa. Hitler's Invasion of Russia 1941*, 104.

132. Ltr., Dr. Heinrich Haape, to his fiancée, 24.8.41.

133. Meier-Welcker, *Aufzeichnungen eines Generalstabsoffiziers 1939–1942*, 128–129.

134. Meier-Welcker, the division operations officer (Ia), had suffered for several days from a high fever due to an infection; however, he continued to perform his duties.

135. The reference is to the fighting at Velikie Luki, where large Soviet forces were encircled and being destroyed; Meier-Welcker's division took part in the reduction of the pocket.

136. *Uffz.* Edmund M. (L 09 244), Collection BfZ.

137. Jarausch (ed.), *Reluctant Accomplice. A Wehrmacht Soldier's Letters from the Eastern Front*, 261–263. The date for this entry is approximate.

138. The town of Kochanovo was about twenty kilometers west of Orsha, a larger city and railroad hub more than one hundred kilometers southwest of Smolensk. The POW camp was *Durchgangslager 203*.

139. Stützel, *Feldpost. Briefe und Aufzeichnungen eines 17-Jährigen 1940–1945*, 43–44.

140. Stützel was sent back to a hospital in Leipzig, Germany. Ibid., 50.

141. The Russian tank attack described by Stützel took place near the town of Asarinki (5 ID was holding defensive positions about seventy-five kilometers northeast of Smolensk). For his heroism, he was awarded the Iron Cross on 2 September by his division commander, *Generalmajor* Karl Allmendinger; barely eighteen years of age, Stützel was, no doubt, one of the youngest soldiers of the *Wehrmacht* to have been awarded the medal. Ibid., 57.

142. *Tagebuch*, Dr. Hans Lierow, 26.8.41.

143. *Lt.* Willibald G. (N02.5), Collection BfZ.

144. *Feldpost*, Werner Heinemann, 26.8.41.

145. Stader (ed.), *Ihr daheim und wir hier draussen. Ein Briefwechsel zwischen Ostfront und Heimat, Juni 1941–März 1943*, 28.

146. The OKW war diary 25 August 1941: "The enemy, on the entire front of [Army Group South] east of Kiev, has been thrown back across the Dnepr. . . . After a difficult battle, 1 Panzer Group has taken Dnepropetrovsk and—driving across the Dnepr behind the fleeing enemy—established a bridgehead on the northern bank." Jacobsen (ed.), *Kriegstagebuch des OKW (WFSt.), Bd. I: 1. August 1940—31. Dezember 1941*, 589–590.

147. *Tagebuch, Lt.* Rudolf Maurer, 27.8.41.

148. A *Wehrmachtbericht* announced the results of the operation: "After several days of difficult battles the mass of the Soviet 22 Army was encircled and destroyed east of Velikie Luki.

More than 30,000 prisoners were taken and 400 guns captured. That the losses of the enemy were unusually high is confirmed by the identification of more than 40,000 dead." (Hinze, *19. Infanterie- und Panzer-Division. Divisionsgeschichte aus der Sicht eines Artilleristen*, 185.) The war diarist of Ninth Army exulted that the results "greatly surpass our expectations. . . . One can indeed declare without exaggeration, that this victory is unique [*einzigartig*] in both the dispatch with which it occurred and in its completeness." Contributing decisively to the outcome was the "immortal spirit of attack [*unsterbliche Angriffsgeist*] of the German soldier." BA-MA RH 20-9/16, *KTB AOK 9*, 26.8.41.

149. Fuchs Richardson (ed.), *Your Loyal and Loving Son. The Letters of Tank Gunner Karl Fuchs, 1937–41*, 125–126. As noted above (see entry for *Oblt.* Richard D., 24.8.41), the 7 PD had come under temporary command of Ninth Army in late August.

150. Fuchs's 7 PD was now posted directly behind the front north of Smolensk (near the town of Dukhovshchina). Roughly ten days before, the rest of 39 Panzer Corps (to which 7 PD had belonged) had been transferred to Army Group North to assist with the drive on Leningrad; by early September, 3 Panzer Group's other panzer corps (57 Panzer Corps) would also be on its way to Army Group North. Thies, *Der Ostfeldzug—Ein Lageatlas*, "Lage am 19.8.1941 abds., Heeresgruppe Mitte" and "Lage am 7.9.1941 abds., Heeresgruppe Mitte."

151. Ellis, *Barbarossa 1941. Reframing Hitler's Invasion of Stalin's Soviet Empire*, 332–333. The 20 PD had also recently been transferred from 3 Panzer Group to Ninth Army. The OKW war diary (27 August) shows that it was in the order of battle of Ninth Army's 40 Panzer Corps at this time. Jacobsen (ed.), *Kriegstagebuch des OKW (WFSt.), Bd. I: 1. August 1940—31. Dezember 1941*, 595.

152. The 20 PD had played a major part in the (now completed) reduction of the *Kessel* at Velikie Luki and, late on 26 August, was in position due east of the town. Thies, *Der Ostfeldzug—Ein Lageatlas*, "Lage am 26.8.1941 abds., Heeresgruppe Mitte."

153. The four-seat *Kübelwagen* was the German equivalent of the American jeep. It's ease of operation and ability to perform in all types of terrain made it a favorite of German troops everywhere. However, according to the US War Department's detailed study of the German military and its equipment (first published in March 1945), the *Kübelwagen* was "inferior in every way" to the US jeep, "except in the comfort of its seating accommodations." See US War Department, Technical Manual TM-E 30-451, *Handbook on German Military Forces*, 416–418.

154. Stehmann, *Die Bitternis verschweigen wir. Feldpostbriefe 1940–1945*, 125.

155. Ltr., Dr. Heinrich Haape, to his fiancée, 29.8.41

156. Before dawn on 27 August, two Russian cavalry divisions, suddenly and without warning, struck the overextended and sparsely held line of 6 ID's 37 Infantry Regiment; achieving a rapid breakthrough, they advanced as far as the regimental command post. As was nearly always the case in such crisis situations, the Germans put in an effective counterstroke, which embraced elements of Dr. Haape's 18 Infantry Regiment; by 1800 hours, the original main battle line had been restored. The 37 IR alone on this day sustained 348 casualties: 10 officers and 162 NCOs and men KIA; 13 officers and 127 NCOs and men wounded; 36 NCOs and men MIA. While some 400 Russian dead blanketed the battlefield, the savage and bloody melee of 27 August was yet another example of how severe and unremitting attrition was ominously reducing the combat strength of Army Group Center. Luther, *Barbarossa Unleashed. The German Blitzkrieg through Central Russia to the Gates of Moscow. June–December 1941*, 567–569.

157. From the outset of the Russian campaign, stomach and bowel problems resulting from contaminated food or water, or the lack of proper hygiene, were not uncommon, while in marshy regions isolated cases of malaria occurred. The most common ailment was bacterial dysentery (*Ruhr*), which soon flared up in some units. *Oberleutnant* Kurt Kummer, an artillery

officer in 18 Panzer Division, recorded in his diary on 24 August that half his battery was suffering from diarrhea, resulting in some hospitalizations. *Tagebuch, Oblt.* Kurt Kummer, 24.8.41.

158. Ltr., Werner Heinemann, to his wife, 30.8.41.

159. 12 PD was also one of the divisions of 3 Panzer Group transferred from Army Group Center to Army Group North to support the assault on Leningrad.

160. O.Gefr. Franz F. (01 096), Collection BfZ.

161. *Sold.* Waldo P. (11 668), Collection BfZ.

162. Stützel, *Feldpost. Briefe und Aufzeichnungen eines 17-Jährigen 1940–1945*, 59.

163. *Gefreiter* Stützel was lightly wounded on 21 August and sent back to a hospital in Germany (see entry for Stützel, 25 August 1941).

164. *Gefr.* Martin W. (09 378 B), Collection BfZ.

165. By late summer, for a German foot infantry division to have covered a thousand kilometers since the start of the Russian campaign was hardly uncommon. Indeed, as early as the end of July, more than a few infantry divisions had already reached this milestone.

166. Dollinger (ed.), *Kain, wo ist dein Bruder? Was der Mensch im Zweiten Weltkrieg erleiden musste—dokumentiert in Tagebüchern und Briefen*, 95.

167. Reddemann (ed.), *Zwischen Front und Heimat. Der Briefwechsel des münsterischen Ehepaares Agnes and Albert Neuhaus 1940–1944*, 296–298.

168. Reval (Tallinn), a major naval base and Baltic port on the northern coast of Estonia (opposite the Gulf of Finland), was in the hands of German Eighteenth Army by 29 August 1941. Jacobsen (ed.), *Kriegstagebuch des OKW (WFSt.), Bd. I: 1. August 1940—31. Dezember 1941*, 598–600.

169. *Gefr.* Alfons L. (29 549), Collection BfZ.

170. *Tagebuch, Lt.* Rudolf Maurer, 31.8.41.

CHAPTER 5

1. Mühleisen (ed.), *Hellmuth Stieff Briefe*, 128.

2. The Soviet High Command "would not understand this reality until mid-1942." Glantz, *Forgotten Battles of the Soviet-German War (1941–1945)*. Vol. I: *The Summer-Fall Campaign (22 June–4 December 1941)*, 104.

3. Glantz, *Barbarossa. Hitler's Invasion of Russia 1941*, 90. For a detailed account of the German defense of the El'nia salient, see Luther, *Barbarossa Unleashed. The German Blitzkrieg through Central Russia to the Gates of Moscow. June–December 1941*, 631–634.

4. Trevor-Roper (ed.), *Hitler's War Directives 1939–1945*, 96.

5. Ibid., 97.

6. Van Creveld, *Supplying War. Logistics from Wallenstein to Patton*, 170–171.

7. Luther, *Barbarossa Unleashed. The German Blitzkrieg through Central Russia to the Gates of Moscow. June–December 1941*, 636–637.

8. Kirchubel, *Operation Barbarossa 1941 (2). Army Group North*, 65.

9. Boog et al., *Germany and the Second World War*, Vol. IV: *The Attack on the Soviet Union*, 644.

10. Thies, *Der Ostfeldzug—Ein Lageatlas*, "Lage am 12.9.1941, abds., Schlacht bei Kiew"; Luther, *Barbarossa Unleashed. The German Blitzkrieg through Central Russia to the Gates of Moscow. June–December 1941*, 638; Bock, *Generalfeldmarschall Fedor von Bock. The War Diary 1939–1945*, Gerbet (ed.), 313.

11. Halder, *Kriegstagebuch: Tägliche Aufzeichnungen des Chefs des Generalstabes des Heeres 1939–1942*. Bd. III: *Der Russlandfeldzug bis zum Marsch auf Stalingrad (22.6.1941–24.9.1942)*, Jacobsen and Philippi (eds.), 266.

12. Ibid., 254.

13. *Soldat* K.H.G. (39 274 D), cited in Manoschek (ed.), *"Es gibt nur eines für das Judentum: Vernichtung." Das Judenbild in deutschen Soldatenbriefen 1939–1944*, 43.

14. Rhein, *Das Rheinisch-Westfälische Infanterie-/Grenadier-Regiment 18 1921–1945*, 82–83. The date is approximate. The letter was written by *Obergefreiter* Matthias to his family at the start of September. Like most of the *Landser*, he was disappointed by the slowdown of the war on the central front and longed for the front to be in motion again.

15. Meier-Welcker, *Aufzeichnungen eines Generalstabsoffiziers 1939–1942*, 130–131.

16. *Lt.* Willibald G. (N02.5), Collection BfZ. On 1 September, 57 and 295 ID were the reserve divisions of Seventeenth Army. On the same day, 57 ID was located southwest of Kremenchug. Jacobsen (ed.), *Kriegstagebuch des OKW (WFSt.), Bd. I: 1. August 1940—31. Dezember 1941*, 605; also, German General Staff situation map for 125 ID (1.9.41) at website www.lexikon-der-wehrmacht.de.

17. The reference is to the putative use by the Red Army of so-called dum-dum bullets, which were proscribed under international law. See Chapter 2, entry for *Panzer-Oberschütze* Erich Hager (24.6.41).

18. Buchbender and Sterz (eds.), *Das Andere Gesicht des Krieges. Deutsche Feldpostbriefe 1939–1945*, 79–80.

19. The same day (2 September) GFM von Bock noted that his divisions within the El'nia salient were simply being "bled white," and, after several conversations with GFM von Kluge (C-in-C Fourth Army), Bock decided the time had come to abandon it. As always, his eyes were riveted on Moscow, and he explained his decision by noting that "the attack to the east cannot begin until the last third of September at the earliest! Until then it is vital to preserve and save our strength, for only two fresh divisions . . . are being sent to the army group from the rear." Bock, *Generalfeldmarschall Fedor von Bock. The War Diary 1939–1945*, Gerbet (ed.), 302.

20. *Gefr.* Heinz B. (26 391), Collection BfZ.

21. Ltr., Lt. Jochen Hahn, 2.9.41.

22. *Leutnant* Hahn can be forgiven for hoping to make a sudden escape from the Russian Front. After all, after three weeks in the meat grinder of the El'nia salient, the prospect of fighting against the "Tommies" must have seemed like a salvation of sorts in comparison. Yet, alas, it was not to be. It was simply a rumor. And like so many rumors that swirled through the ranks of the *Landser* on the Eastern Front, it soon faded away and was forgotten.

23. Ltr., Dr. Heinrich Haape, to his fiancée, 2.9.41.

24. *Sold.* Hans M. (21 999 B), Collection BfZ.

25. Stader (ed.), *Ihr daheim und wir hier draussen. Ein Briefwechsel zwischen Ostfront und Heimat, Juni 1941–März 1943*, 31.

26. Jarausch (ed.), *Reluctant Accomplice. A Wehrmacht Soldier's Letters from the Eastern Front*, 275.

27. Dr. Jarausch was posted at a POW transit camp near Orsha (see entry for 24 August 1941).

28. German treatment of Soviet prisoners of war signified one of the worst—and, yet, largely forgotten—war crimes of World War II. Even the efforts of well-meaning men, like Dr. Jarausch, meant little when the German military authorities—due to a lack of concern, a lack of resources, or both—failed to furnish what was necessary to provide the prisoners with adequate food, shelter, and medical care. As a result, by September 1941, the signs of an impending catastrophe in the POW camps "were already unmistakable. Documents exist showing that in a

number of camps desperate prisoners were driven by hunger to eat grass, leaves, or tree bark. In some camps in the East, epidemics caused by hunger were already claiming thousands of lives." Cases of cannibalism among the starving Russian soldiers in the camps were also recorded. Streit, "Soviet Prisoners of War in the Hands of the Wehrmacht," in *War of Extermination. The German Military in World War II*, Heer and Naumann (eds.), 82.

29. Fuchs Richardson (ed.), *Your Loyal and Loving Son. The Letters of Tank Gunner Karl Fuchs, 1937–41*, 128–129.

30. Reddemann (ed.), *Zwischen Front und Heimat. Der Briefwechsel des münsterischen Ehepaares Agnes and Albert Neuhaus 1940–1944*, 299–300.

31. *Lt.* Willibald G. (N02.5), Collection BfZ.

32. *Uffz.* Rudolf F. (10 203), Collection BfZ.

33. *Gefr.* Adolf M. (05 905 D), Collection BfZ.

34. Albert M. (05 042), Collection BfZ.

35. See entry for Albert Neuhaus (18.8.41), and supporting annotation, in Chapter 4.

36. *Lt.* Ernst E. (05 714), Collection BfZ.

37. *Tagebuch*, Dr. Hans Lierow, 6.9.41.

38. *Gefr.* Heinz B. (26 391), Collection BfZ.

39. *Gefreiter* Heinz B. served in the division's antitank battalion (*Pz.Jäg.Abt.291*).

40. By later summer, as revealed in many field post letters, the *Landser* were slowly beginning to realize what Hitler and his High Command already knew—that Operation *Barbarossa* had failed to deliver a knock-out blow and that the war in the East would continue unabated into 1942.

41. *Uffz.* Max F. (38 088 C), Collection BfZ.

42. *Uffz.* Rudolf F. (10 203), Collection BfZ.

43. The Polikarpov I-16 "*Rata*" single-engine, single-seat fighter. While slow and outdated by 1941, the I-16 would remain in VVS service in relatively robust numbers through 1942. With its excellent maneuverability, the "*Rata*" was often a worthy adversary for even the faster Messerschmidt Bf 109.

44. *Lt.* Willibald G. (N02.5), Collection BfZ.

45. The town of Alexandrija was southwest of Kremenchug, where Seventeenth Army had established a bridgehead over the Dnepr River.

46. As the temperatures began to fall, the problem with lice grew accordingly. As one historian observed, "Lice were the scourge of the Eastern Front, an irritant contributing to ill-health and cumulative psychological depression. Painstakingly picked off the body, they could only be killed with certainty by cracking them between fingernail and thumb after they were gorged with blood." (Kershaw, *War Without Garlands. Operation Barbarossa 1941/42*, 189.) A former German artillery officer recalled, "The lice were a torment that was to stay with us for months. . . . We scratched arms, legs, stomach, the small of the back, and it was a constant burning in the armpits. It was worst at night, and the men would thrash restlessly in their blankets." Knappe, *Soldat. Reflections of a German Soldier, 1936–1949*, 218.

47. *Tagebuch, Lt.* Rudolf Maurer, 7.9.41.

48. *Leutnant* Maurer's 251 ID had now advanced more than one hundred kilometers beyond Velikie Luki and had reached the Dvina River just west of the town of Andreapol. Thies, *Der Ostfeldzug—Ein Lageatlas*, "Lage am 7.9.1941 abds., Heeresgruppe Mitte."

49. *Sold.* Max Sch. (09 390 E), Collection BfZ.

50. German fatalities in the East (all combat arms) would be even higher in September (51,033) than they had been in August (46,066). Of these fatal losses about 94 percent were sustained by the ground forces (army 90 percent, *Waffen-SS* 4 percent), and these fell dis-

proportionately on the combat infantry. Overmans, *Deutsche militärische Verluste im Zweiten Weltkrieg*, 277.

51. Fuchs Richardson (ed.), *Your Loyal and Loving Son. The Letters of Tank Gunner Karl Fuchs, 1937–41*, 130.

52. "This attitude so often repeated in Karl's letters is more than abstract rhetoric or youthful enthusiasm. The *Wehrmacht* was permeated from top to bottom by a kind of military vitalism, stressing morale factors, as opposed to physical and material considerations. It antedated the Nazi era, being in large part a product of World War I and its aftermath—a period in which German military doctrine stressed the importance of intangibles. . . . But, while morale factors may considerably enhance fighting power, they will not make their possessors bulletproof and cannot compensate entirely for numerical or technical inferiority. Far too often, even in the early stages of *Barbarossa*, Germany's commanders put an almost mystical faith in the ability of the man on the front line to surmount any difficulty by ingenuity and force of will." Historical Commentary by Dennis E. Showalter in Fuchs Richardson (ed.), *Your Loyal and Loving Son. The Letters of Tank Gunner Karl Fuchs, 1937–41*, 130.

53. Garden and Andrew (eds.), *The War Diaries of a Panzer Soldier. Erich Hager with the 17th Panzer Division on the Russian Front 1941–1945*, 50.

54. Hager's diary entries record unremitting Soviet air attacks beginning in late August and continuing into September. On 31 August he wrote, "More air attacks. That's really getting on our nerves! . . . 6 bombs fell near us, so that everything is covered in dust." Ibid., 48.

55. Hager's 17 PD—including its 39 Panzer Regiment (to which he belonged)—along with the bulk of Guderian's 2 Panzer Group, was now driving south into the Ukraine, beginning the encirclement of the Soviet Southwestern Front east of Kiev in cooperation with Kleist's 1 Panzer Group of Army Group South.

56. *Gefr.* Ewald M. (01 137), Collection BfZ.

57. The OKW war diary records that, on this day (7 September), Seventeenth Army launched major attacks in a successful effort to expand its bridgehead across the Dnepr at Kremenchug to the north and west. Jacobsen (ed.), *Kriegstagebuch des OKW (WFSt.), Bd. I: 1. August 1940—31. Dezember 1941*, 617.

58. The 19 and 20 PD (57 Panzer Corps) had just departed the left wing of Army Group Center and were now arriving in the operational area of Army Group North, where they were assigned to the Sixteenth Army. See Jacobsen (ed.), *Kriegstagebuch des OKW (WFSt.), Bd. I: 1. August 1940—31. Dezember 1941*, 612; also, Thies, *Der Ostfeldzug—Ein Lageatlas*, "Lage am 7.9.1941 abds., Heeresgruppe Mitte."

59. *Sold.* Albrecht B. (19 997), Collection BfZ.

60. Meier-Welcker, *Aufzeichnungen eines Generalstabsoffiziers 1939–1942*, 131–132.

61. Wolfgang A. (04 089), Collection BfZ.

62. Latzel, *Deutsche Soldaten—nationalsozialistischer Krieg? Kriegserlebnis—Kriegserfahrung 1939–1945*, 53. "Olte" is a pseudonym used by the author.

63. Ellis, *Barbarossa 1941. Reframing Hitler's Invasion of Stalin's Soviet Empire*, 335.

64. By late summer/fall 1941, given the relentless ongoing attrition of personnel and matériel, it was not uncommon to see (mostly smaller) units disbanded or the remnants of badly depleted units assigned to other formations. The losses among both infantry and armored forces had been alarmingly high, with few replacements provided to make good those losses. On 4 September, just 47 percent of the tanks on the Eastern Front (four panzer groups) were rated combat-ready; among the panzer divisions of Army Group Center, however, only 34 percent of the tanks were operational, and this at the time when Guderian's panzer group had already begun its advance into the Ukraine. On 5 September, *Oberstleutnant* Stieff, an officer in the Army General Staff, noted in a letter to his wife that personnel losses would soon "require

the disbandment [*Auflösung*] of about 15 divisions to bring the others back up to strength." Like the ground forces, the *Luftwaffe* had also experienced frightful attrition throughout the summer of 1941. Müller-Hillebrand, *Das Heer 1933–1945*, Bd. III: *Der Zweifrontenkrieg. Das Heer vom Beginn des Feldzuges gegen die Sowjetunion bis zum Kriegsende*, 20, 205; also, Boog et al., *Germany and the Second World War*, Vol. IV: *The Attack on the Soviet Union*, 1128–1129; Mühleisen (ed.), *Hellmuth Stieff Briefe*, 126–127.

65. *Lt.* Willibald G. (N02.5), Collection BfZ.

66. The Russian air force (VVS) sought desperately to strike bridges and other crossing points over the Dnepr in an effort to disrupt the German advance. For example, on 8 September, the VVS conducted twenty-two separate attacks (*heftige Luftangriffe*), each with six to eight bombers and fighters, against bridges, ferrying operations, and the German forward lines near Dnepropetrovsk (in sector of 1 Panzer Group). Jacobsen (ed.), *Kriegstagebuch des OKW (WFSt.), Bd. I: 1. August 1940—31. Dezember 1941*, 620.

67. "Fishing" in lakes and rivers with hand grenades appears to have been a fairly common pastime of German troops in Russia.

68. By the fall of 1941, references to Anglo-American equipment (airplanes, tanks, trucks, etc.) in service of the Red Army begin to appear in letters of German soldiers. While one can question the accuracy of individual German accounts, British aid to Russia had begun as early as August 1941, and, in October 1941, the United States and Great Britain signed the Lend-Lease Agreement with the USSR. By 31 December 1941, Lend-Lease had provided the Soviets with hundreds of tanks and combat aircraft, helping to make up for shortfalls in Soviet production. Glantz, *Barbarossa. Hitler's Invasion of Russia 1941*, 228n2; also, Winchester, *Hitler's War on Russia*, 136.

69. Marshal of the Soviet Union S. M. Budenny, the "legendary hero" of the Russian civil war. "In 1941, as first deputy defense commissar and a member of the Stavka, Stalin's general headquarters committee, he coordinated the Southwestern and South *fronts* (army groups) during the encirclement of Kiev (August-September)." Dear (ed.), *The Oxford Guide to World War II*, 132.

70. Reddemann (ed.), *Zwischen Front und Heimat. Der Briefwechsel des münsterischen Ehepaares Agnes and Albert Neuhaus 1940–1944*, 304–305. On this day, Albert Neuhaus bore witness to the beginning of the *Luftwaffe*'s massive assault on Leningrad—an event that he described with absolute awe and wonderment. In the days ahead, German bombers would pound the city around the clock.

71. Ltr., Dr. Heinrich Haape, to his fiancée, 11.9.41.

72. *Lt.* Willibald G. (N02.5), Collection BfZ.

73. The OKW war diary (10 September) recorded that the Soviets had brought up reinforcements to contest the bridgehead of Seventeenth Army at Kremenchug; moreover, a major Red Army armored thrust, despite a minor penetration, was smashed by the German defenders, resulting in the loss of sixty-eight tanks. Jacobsen (ed.), *Kriegstagebuch des OKW (WFSt.), Bd. I: 1. August 1940—31. Dezember 1941*, 624.

74. Prüller, *Diary of a German Soldier*, Landon and Leitner (eds.), 104–105.

75. *Gefr.* Heinz Sch. (20 158), Collection BfZ.

76. *Gefr.* Hans F. (07 735), Collection BfZ.

77. Reddemann (ed.), *Zwischen Front und Heimat. Der Briefwechsel des münsterischen Ehepaares Agnes and Albert Neuhaus 1940–1944*, 307–308.

78. As noted in the introduction to Chapter 3, Hitler had decreed as early as July that Leningrad (like Moscow) was not to be attacked directly by ground forces (other than artillery); rather, it was to be tightly sealed off, bombed, and starved into submission. Thus commenced

the horrific—albeit from the Soviet perspective, clearly heroic—nine-hundred-day siege of Leningrad that would not be lifted until January 1944.

79. *Lt.* Willibald G. (N02.5), Collection BfZ.

80. The reference is to the 97 Light Infantry Division.

81. Ltr., Dr. Heinrich Haape, to his fiancée, 15.9.41.

82. *Uffz.* Rudolf F. (10 203), Collection BfZ.

83. *Tagebuch, Lt.* Georg Kreuter, 15.9.41.

84. Geo. S. (18 719 A), Collection BfZ.

85. During the summer campaign, German troops had, for the most part, assiduously avoided quartering in villages and towns for the very reasons noted by this soldier, preferring to camp in their tents in the outdoors. In the fall, and, of course, in the winter, German soldiers sought refuge in the peasant dwellings to avoid the arctic cold, for which they were largely unprepared; the result was a significant increase in soldiers plagued by lice and other pests, coupled with a concomitant increase in sickness and disease.

86. Buchbender and Sterz (eds.), *Das andere Gesicht des Krieges. Deutsche Feldpostbriefe 1939–1945*, 80.

87. There were no Chinese soldiers in the Red Army; this is almost certainly a mistaken reference to recruits from Central Asian Soviet republics.

88. Reddemann (ed.), *Zwischen Front und Heimat. Der Briefwechsel des münsterischen Ehepaares Agnes und Albert Neuhaus 1940–1944*, 309.

89. Stehmann, *Die Bitternis verschweigen wir. Feldpostbriefe 1940–1945*, 128–129.

90. Jarausch (ed.), *Reluctant Accomplice. A Wehrmacht Soldier's Letters from the Eastern Front*, 287.

91. On the implications of German soldiers seeking "booty" in the East, see Kay and Stahel, "Reconceiving Criminality in the German Army on the Eastern Front, 1941–1942," in Kay and Stahel (eds.), *Mass Violence in Nazi Occupied Europe*, 173–194.

92. König (ed.), *Ganz in Gottes Hand. Briefe gefallener und hingerichteter Katholiken 1939–1945*, 69.

93. Fritz Pabst, Museumsstiftung Post und Telekommunikation, Berlin, 3.2002.0306.

94. For more on the Ukrainian nationalists that conducted these operations, see Beyda and Petrov, "The Soviet Union," in *Joining Hitler's Crusade. European Nations and the Invasion of the Soviet Union, 1941*, 411–418.

95. R. B., Museumsstiftung Post und Telekommunikation, Berlin, 3.2002.7227.

96. For an excellent set of essays charting the barbarization of warfare, including a number focused on the Eastern Front of the Second World War, see Kassimeris (ed.), *The Barbarization of Warfare*.

97. Alexander and Kunze (eds.), *Eastern Inferno. The Journals of a German Panzerjäger on the Eastern Front, 1941–43*, 97.

98. This is a reference to Soviet Marshal S. M. Budenny. By "swallows" he means Soviet planes.

99. Ltr., *Lt.* Rudolf Maurer, to his son, 18.9.41.

100. Karl Nünnighoff, Museumsstiftung Post und Telekommunikation, Berlin, 3.2008.1388.

101. Alexander and Kunze (eds.), *Eastern Inferno. The Journals of a German Panzerjäger on the Eastern Front, 1941–43*, 97.

102. Prüller, *Diary of a German Soldier*, Landon and Leitner (eds.), 106.

103. Jarausch (ed.), *Reluctant Accomplice. A Wehrmacht Soldier's Letters from the Eastern Front*, 291.

104. Hammer and Nieden (eds.), *Sehr selten habe ich geweint. Briefe und Tagebücher aus dem Zweiten Weltkrieg von Menschen aus Berlin*, 251.

105. Prüller, *Diary of a German Soldier*, Landon and Leitner (eds.), 106–107.

106. Ellis, *Barbarossa 1941. Reframing Hitler's Invasion of Stalin's Soviet Empire*, 337.

107. Buchbender and Sterz (eds.), *Das andere Gesicht des Krieges*, 80–81.

108. Airdropped Soviet leaflets, for example, emphasized a fictitious level of destruction carried out by British bombing. One leaflet claimed that the German newspapers were withholding the true scale of the British aerial offensive, which included one thousand tons of bombs being dropped on Cologne over a six-day period in July 1941, five hundred tons of bombs being dropped on Bremen, and over two thousand tons dropped on the industrial area of the Ruhr. "The bombardment will kill your parents, your wives, your children. The human victims are countless." Another leaflet described abysmal working conditions for German women, who were said to be working for just 40 percent of a man's income while putting in ten- to twelve-hour days. German children were reported to be going hungry, and therefore youth crime was rising rapidly along with instances of child sexual exploitation and child prostitution. "What is happening with your family?," the leaflet asked. See the *Württembergische Landesbibliothek Stuttgart Flugblattpropaganda im 2. Weltkrieg (1941)*, Mappe 92-26 and 92-22.

109. For an excellent, if dated, study of German propaganda to Soviet soldiers, see Buchbender, *Das tönende Erz. Deutsche Propaganda gegen die Rote Armee im Zweiten Weltkrieg.*

110. Reddemann (ed.), *Zwischen Front und Heimat. Der Briefwechsel des münsterischen Ehepaares Agnes und Albert Neuhaus 1940–1944*, 314.

111. Beermann (ed.), *Soldat Werner Beermann Feldpostbriefe 1941–1942*, 137–138.

112. Fuchs Richardson (ed.), *Your Loyal and Loving Son. The Letters of Tank Gunner Karl Fuchs, 1937–41*, 134–135.

113. Dollinger (ed.), *Kain, wo ist dein Bruder? Was der Mensch im Zweiten Weltkrieg erleiden musste—dokumentiert in Tagebüchern und Briefen*, 97–98.

114. Buchbender and Sterz (eds.), *Das andere Gesicht des Krieges*, 81.

115. Kleindienst (ed.), *Sei tausendmal gegrüßt. Briefwechsel Irene und Ernst Guicking 1937–1945*. Accompanying this book is a CD-ROM with some 1,600 letters, mostly unpublished in the book. This letter appears only on the CD-ROM and can be located by its date (23 September 1941).

116. Alexander and Kunze (eds.), *Eastern Inferno. The Journals of a German Panzerjäger on the Eastern Front, 1941–43*, 103–106.

117. *Tagebuch*, Lt. Soeffker, 23.9.41, in *Rundbrief Nr. 50 (Traditionsverband Inf.Rgt. 37/184/474)*, 15–16.

118. Bähr and Bähr (eds.), *Kriegsbriefe Gefallener Studenten, 1939–1945*, 90–91.

119. Ellis, *Barbarossa 1941. Reframing Hitler's Invasion of Stalin's Soviet Empire*, 338.

120. Stader (ed.), *Ihr daheim und wir hier draußen. Ein Briefwechsel zwischen Ostfront und Heimat Juni 1941–März 1943*, 34.

121. Buchbender and Sterz (eds.), *Das andere Gesicht des Krieges*, 82.

122. Kershaw, *War Without Garlands. Operation Barbarossa 1941/42*, 162. This date is approximate.

123. Scheuer (ed.), *Briefe aus Russland. Feldpostbriefe des Gefreiten Alois Scheuer 1941–1942*, 41.

124. Alexander and Kunze (eds.), *Eastern Inferno. The Journals of a German Panzerjäger on the Eastern Front, 1941–43*, 109–110.

125. Fuchs Richardson (ed.), *Your Loyal and Loving Son. The Letters of Tank Gunner Karl Fuchs, 1937–41*, 135.

126. Prüller, *Diary of a German Soldier*, Landon and Leitner (eds.), 108.

127. Alexander and Kunze (eds.), *Eastern Inferno. The Journals of a German Panzerjäger on the Eastern Front, 1941–43*, 111–112.

128. The *Einsatzgruppen*, to which the *Einsatzkommandos* belonged, did not belong to the Waffen-SS but rather to the SD (*Sicherheitsdienst*, or Security Service).

129. On 24 September, five days after the Germans had captured Kiev and firmly established themselves in its many buildings, a series of explosions rocked the city, including at the Grand Hotel, where numerous high-ranking German officers were quartered. An estimated two hundred Germans were killed in either the initial explosions or the resulting fires, including *Oberst Freiherr* von Seidlitz und Gohlau of the Army General Staff. Civilian losses were much harder to estimate as tens of thousands of people had fled the city with the Red Army. See Stahel, *Kiev 1941. Hitler's Battle for Supremacy in the East*, 257–259; Berkhoff, *Harvest of Despair. Life and Death in Ukraine under Nazi Rule*, 30–31.

130. While such wholesale campaigns of murder against all Jews were by no means absent from the early weeks of the campaign, these were part of the radicalization from below—in which local SS commanders ordered such "actions" on their own authority. The planned murder of all Soviet Jews was not part of the original plan but quickly developed over the summer of 1941. These tasks were entrusted to *Reichsführer-SS* Heinrich Himmler, who in turn charged his deputy *Obergruppenführer* Reinhard Heydrich, the chief of the Reich Security Main Office (RSHA = *Reichssicherheitshauptamt*), with organizing mobile killing squads known as the *Einsatzgruppen* (action groups). The total strength of the *Einsatzgruppen* came to only about three thousand men organized into four battalion-sized groups, designated A, B, C, and D. *Einsatzgruppe A* was to operate behind Army Group North, *Einsatzgruppe B* was to follow Bock's Army Group Center, *Einsatzgruppe C* was assigned to the northern elements of Army Group South, and *Einsatzgruppe D* was to operate in the extreme south of Ukraine with the German Eleventh Army. Given the vast size of the operational areas, the individual *Einsatzgruppen* operated in smaller company-sized groups known as *Einsatzkommandos* or *Sonderkommandos*, which fanned out over the newly occupied territories in search of victims. Mallmann, Angrick, Matthäus, and Cüppers (eds.), *Die "Ereignismeldung UdSSR" 1941: Dokumente der Einsatzgruppen in der Sowjetunion*; Klein (ed.), *Die Einsatzgruppen in der besetzten Sowjetunion 1941/42. Die Tätigkeits- und Lageberichte des Chefs der Sicherheitspolizei und des SD*.

131. Hans Simon, Museumsstiftung Post und Telekommunikation, Berlin, 3.2002.1288.

132. GPU = State Political Directorate of the Soviet Union.

133. Ltr., Dr. Heinrich Haape, to his fiancée, 27.9.41.

134. *Tagebuch, Lt.* Soeffker, 27.9.41, in *Rundbrief Nr. 50 (Traditionsverband Inf.Rgt. 37/184/474)*, 18.

135. Kleindienst (ed.), *Sei tausendmal gegrüßt.* This letter appears only on the CD-ROM within the book and can be located by its date (28 September 1941).

136. Elmshäuser and Lokers (eds.), "Man muß hier nur hart sein," *Kriegsbriefe und Bilder einer Familie (1934–1945)*, 141.

137. Scheuer (ed.), *Briefe aus Russland. Feldpostbriefe des Gefreiten Alois Scheuer 1941–1942*, 41–42.

138. *Gefr.* L.B. (04 650), cited in Manoschek (ed.), *"Es gibt nur eines für das Judentum: Vernichtung." Das Judenbild in deutschen Soldatenbriefen 1939–1944*, 45.

139. Because partisan warfare had been openly declared by Stalin, justifying in the Nazi view operations against civilian targets, there existed the possibility for large-scale "actions" against Jews under the pretext of combating partisans. Indeed, in many German orders, Jews were equated with partisans and were also to be dealt with in the same way. As one order to a police battalion operating in the East read, "Where there is a partisan there is a Jew and where there is a Jew there is a partisan." Himmler himself said on 9 July during an inspection tour

at Grodno that "all Jews are to be regarded as partisans, without exception." With Soviet Jews now marked as hostile elements and indistinguishable from partisans, German "actions" against Jewish settlements needed no evidence to justify their elimination. Longerich, *The Unwritten Order. Hitler's Role in the Final Solution*, 113.

140. Beermann (ed.), *Soldat Werner Beermann Feldpostbriefe 1941–1942*, 141–142.

141. These reports can be located in a three-volume publication: *Die Wehrmachtberichte 1939–1945. Bands 1–3.*

142. Kleindienst (ed.), *Sei tausendmal gegrüßt*. This letter appears only on the CD-ROM within the book and can be located by its date (29 September 1941).

143. Heinz Rahe, Museumsstiftung Post und Telekommunikation, Berlin, 3.2002.0985.

144. Georg Fulde, Museumsstiftung Post und Telekommunikation, Berlin, 3.2002.0202.

145. Prüller, *Diary of a German Soldier*, Landon and Leitner (eds.), 109.

146. Erich Dohl, Museumsstiftung Post und Telekommunikation, Berlin, 3.2009.1998.

CHAPTER 6

1. Hoth, the former commander of 3 Panzer Group, had been promoted to command of Seventeenth Army in Army Group South. Reinhardt took over on 9 October 1941.

2. Stahel, *Operation Typhoon. Hitler's March on Moscow, October 1941.*

3. Piekalkiewicz, *Moscow 1941. The Frozen Offensive*, 113.

4. Cited in Jones, *The Retreat. Hitler's First Defeat*, 32.

5. Glantz, *Barbarossa. Hitler's Invasion of Russia 1941*, 154.

6. Blumentritt, "Moscow," in William Richardson and Seymour Freidin (eds.), *The Fatal Decisions*, 55–56.

7. Jacobsen (ed.), *Kriegstagebuch des OKW (WFSt.), Bd. II: 1. August 1940-31. Dezember 1941*, 693.

8. Boog et al., *Germany and the Second World War*, Vol. IV: *The Attack on the Soviet Union*, 613.

9. Messenger, *The Last Prussian. A Biography of Field Marshal Gerd von Rundstedt*, 153.

10. Boog et al., *Germany and the Second World War*, Vol. IV: *The Attack on the Soviet Union*, 647.

11. Shepherd, *Hitler's Soldiers. The German Army in the Third Reich*, 180.

12. Boog et al., *Germany and the Second World War*, Vol. IV: *The Attack on the Soviet Union*, 650.

13. Ltr., Dr. Heinrich Haape, to his fiancée, 1.10.41.

14. Ulrike Meyer-Timpe (ed.), "Träume recht süß von mir," *Eine deutsche Freundschaft in Briefen 1940–1943*, 100–101.

15. For more on why foreign volunteers were prepared to serve on the Eastern Front, see Stahel (ed.), *Joining Hitler's Crusade. European Nations and the Invasion of the Soviet Union, 1941.*

16. The Spanish 250 Infantry Division, known as the "Blue Division" (*Division Azul*), was dispatched to the Eastern Front by Spain's chief of state, General Franco, as his country's contribution to the so-called European crusade against Soviet Russia. Attached to Sixteenth Army, the division—composed of volunteers who swore their allegiance to Adolf Hitler (though the wording was modified to make clear that it applied only to the "battle against Bolshevism")— first saw action in Russia in October 1941. Pressure from the Allies, and changes in Spanish policy, would result in the division's return to Spain in late 1943.

17. *Gefr.* G. (13 517 A), Collection BfZ.

18. This is the beginning of Operation *Typhoon*; for recent literature on this battle, see David Stahel, *Operation Typhoon*; Lev Lopukhovsky, *The Viaz'ma Catastrophe, 1941. The Red Army's Disastrous Stand against Operation Typhoon*; Michael Filippenkov, *Konev's Golgotha. Operation Typhoon Strikes the Soviet Western Front, October 1941.*

19. Previously Neuhaus's unit belonged to Army Group North, but at the end of September it was sent to Army Group Center to support Operation *Typhoon*. Reddemann (ed.), *Zwischen Front und Heimat. Der Briefwechsel des münsterischen Ehepaares Agnes und Albert Neuhaus 1940–1944*, 322, see also 324–325.

20. Prüller, *Diary of a German Soldier*, Landon and Leitner (eds.), 110.

21. Reddemann (ed.), *Zwischen Front und Heimat. Der Briefwechsel des münsterischen Ehepaares Agnes und Albert Neuhaus 1940–1944*, 324.

22. *O'Gefr.* Joseph B. (25 341), Collection BfZ.

23. The 2 PD (and the 5 PD) only arrived on the Eastern Front in late September, shortly before Operation *Typhoon* began. They had been the spearheads of the Balkan campaign (April 1941) and then spent much of the summer being refitted in Germany.

24. Fritz Pabst, Museumsstiftung Post und Telekommunikation, Berlin, 3.2002.0306.

25. Pabst appears to have been well aware of the murder of the city's Jewish population. Posters had been plastered all around the city that at eight o'clock in the morning on 29 September all Jews in the city and its environs were to report to the corners of Mielnikovskaja and Dokhturovskaja streets. Any Jews failing to appear would be shot. The Jews crammed into the streets near the assembly point and from there were led to the Babi Yar ravine just outside of the city. Here the killing continued for two days until 33,771 Jews were dead. Klee, Dressen and Riess (eds.), *"The Good Old Days." The Holocaust as Seen by Its Perpetrators and Bystanders*, 66–67; Gilbert, *The Holocaust. The Jewish Tragedy*, 202–205.

26. For the representation of Bolshevism within National Socialist Germany, see Kallis, *Nazi Propaganda and the Second World War*, 76–79.

27. Ltr., Dr. Heinrich Haape, to his fiancée, 5.10.41.

28. *Gefr.* H. J. (23 140), cited in Manoschek (ed.), *"Es gibt nur eines für das Judentum: Vernichtung." Das Judenbild in deutschen Soldatenbriefen 1939–1944*, 46.

29. Dollinger (ed.), *Kain, wo ist dein Bruder? Was der Mensch im Zweiten Weltkrieg erleiden musste—dokumentiert in Tagebüchern und Briefen*, 100–101.

30. A few days later the same soldier wrote of participating in another massacre with a similar number of Jews. There are numerous reports of German soldiers taking part in the mass killing of Jews. As one member of the *Einsatzgruppen* stated after the war, "on some occasions members of the *Wehrmacht* took the carbines out of our hands and took our place in the firing squad." As cited in Fritz, *Frontsoldaten: The German Soldier in World War II*, 59. For more firsthand accounts on the *Wehrmacht*'s role in the Holocaust, see Rubenstein and Altman (eds.), *The Unknown Black Book. The Holocaust in the German-Occupied Soviet Territories.*

31. Jarausch (ed.), *Reluctant Accomplice. A Wehrmacht Soldier's Letters from the Eastern Front*, 302.

32. *Letzte Lebenszeichen. Briefe aus dem Krieg.* Published by the German War Graves Commission (*Volksbund Deutsche Kriegsgräberfürsorge e.V.*), 36–37.

33. Prüller, *Diary of a German Soldier*, Landon and Leitner (eds.), 111–112. Kleist's 1 Panzer Group was redesignated 1 Panzer Army on 6 October 1941.

34. Stehmann, *Die Bitternis verschweigen wir. Feldpostbriefe 1940–1945*, 134.

35. Kleindienst (ed.), *Sei tausendmal gegrüßt.* This letter appears only on the CD-ROM within the book and can be located by its date (8 October 1941).

36. For a more comprehensive insight into the varied motivations of Soviet defectors, see Edele, *Stalin's Defectors. How Red Army Soldiers Became Hitler's Collaborators, 1941–1945*, Chapter 6.

37. While there certainly were numerous atrocities committed by the Red Army, there was no explicit order or policy to murder all German POWs. In the autumn of 1941, however, Stalin radicalized the war against Germany by encouraging openly hateful propaganda, which led to the increased killing of captive Germans. Yet as Mark Edele has explained, it was "the interaction of signals from above and reactions on the ground, a dynamic specific to the way the Stalinist dictatorship worked in practice," that accounted for a sharp increase in the killing of German POWs in this period. Edele, "Take (No) Prisoners! The Red Army and German POWs 1941–1943," in *The Journal of Modern History*, no. 88 (June 2016), 348 and 356. See also, Weiner, "Something to Die for, a Lot to Kill For: The Soviet System and the Barbarisation of Warfare, 1939–1945," in Kassimeris (ed.), *The Barbarization of Warfare*, 113.

38. *Uffz*. E.T. (26 029), cited in Manoschek (ed.), *"Es gibt nur eines für das Judentum: Vernichtung." Das Judenbild in deutschen Soldatenbriefen 1939–1944*, 47.

39. Machemer and Hardinghaus (eds.), *Wofür es lohnte, das Leben zu wagen. Briefe, Fotos und Dokumente eines Truppenarztes von der Ostfront 1941/42*, 44–47.

40. Prüller, *Diary of a German Soldier*, Landon and Leitner (eds.), 112–113.

41. *Uffz*. Egon N. (06 209 E), Collection BfZ.

42. Anton Böhrer, Museumsstiftung Post und Telekommunikation, Berlin, 3.2002.0889.

43. When the German press chief Dr. Otto Dietrich visited Hitler on 9 October, the dictator was convinced the Soviet Union was stricken and would never rise again. With Hitler's hubris soaring and Dietrich keen to indulge the spotlight, the stage was set for an announcement that would strike the German people and the wider world with astonishment. Dietrich appeared grinning before the German and international press. Behind him were red velvet curtains, which were then drawn to reveal a vast map of the Soviet Union. Dietrich then began to explain the strategic situation. The last remnants of the Soviet armies opposite Moscow were now caught in two steel rings that were being destroyed by the *Wehrmacht*. To the east, Dietrich assured his audience, was simply undefended space. "The campaign in the East has been decided by the smashing of Army Group Timoshenko," Dietrich proclaimed. Neutral journalists looked on as those from Germany and the Axis nations cheered and raised their arms in the Nazi salute. See Stahel, *Operation Typhoon*, 100–101; Domarus, *Hitler: Speeches and Proclamations 1932–1945. The Chronicle of a Dictatorship. Volume IV. The Years 1941 to 1945*, 2497; Overy, *Russia's War*, 95.

44. Fuchs Richardson (ed.), *Your Loyal and Loving Son. The Letters of Tank Gunner Karl Fuchs, 1937–41*, 136.

45. Elmshäuser and Lokers (eds.), *"Man muß hier nur hart sein." Kriegsbriefe und Bilder einer Familie (1934–1945)*, 150–151.

46. Jakob Geimer, Museumsstiftung Post und Telekommunikation, Berlin, 3.2002.0894.

47. The Nazi regime was the first to present Operation *Barbarossa* as a preemptive war to thwart an imminent Soviet attack in 1941, which some of the German generals further propagated in their postwar memoirs. Debate later resurfaced in the late 1980s, with a number of sensationalist historians claiming to present "new evidence" in support of such claims. The first-rate studies produced to rebut these pseudo-academic apologists' works not only revealed their yawning lack of credibility but have contributed greatly to clarifying the prewar motivations and political maneuvering of Stalin and Hitler. For the best recent surveys of the debate, see Pietrow-Ennker (ed.) *Präventivkrieg? Der deutsche Angriff auf die Sowjetunion*; Ueberschär and Bezymenskij (eds.), *Der deutsche Angriff auf die Sowjetunion 1941. Die Kontroverse um die Präventivkriegsthese*; Gorodetsky, *Grand Delusion: Stalin and the German Invasion of Russia*. A

guide to the many publications in this debate can be found in the latest edition of Müller and Ueberschär, *Hitler's War in the East 1941–1945. A Critical Assessment.*

48. *O'Gefr.* Joseph B. (25 341), Collection BfZ.

49. Some of *Fliegerkorps II's Heinkel* units, and even on occasion scarce divebomber formations, dropped millions of propaganda leaflets (244,000 on 5.10.41 alone) along the Smolensk-Moscow highway. See Muller, *The German Air War in Russia*, 58–59.

50. Machemer and Hardinghaus (eds.), *Wofür es lohnte, das Leben zu wagen. Briefe, Fotos und Dokumente eines Truppenarztes von der Ostfront 1941/42*, 50.

51. *Gefr.* Josef B. (25 144 C), Collection BfZ.

52. Stader (ed.), *Ihr daheim und wir hier draussen. Ein Briefwechsel zwischen Ostfront und Heimat, Juni 1941–März 1943*, 41.

53. Alexander and Kunze (ed.), *Eastern Inferno. The Journals of a German Panzerjäger on the Eastern Front, 1941–43*, 1181–1119.

54. Klaus K., Museumsstiftung Post und Telekommunikation, Berlin, 3.2002.0817.

55. Hans Albring, Museumsstiftung Post und Telekommunikation, Berlin, 3.2002.0211.

56. For a more comprehensive assessment of soldiers' attitudes toward Jews, see Fritz, *Frontsoldaten*, 195–200.

57. The multiple Soviet armies destroyed in the October fighting was a calamity for the Red Army, but it also left countless numbers of Red Army men who had slipped through the German encirclements to carry on the fight in Army Group Center's rear. Whether or not these men were, strictly speaking, "partisans" in the eyes of most German soldiers, they were referred to and treated as such. Slepyan, *Stalin's Guerrillas. Soviet Partisans in World War II*, 29.

58. Franz Siebeler, Museumsstiftung Post und Telekommunikation, Berlin, 3.2002.1285.

59. Siebeler is referring to the battle on the Sea of Azov (17 September to 7 October) in which 106,000 Soviet POWs, 212 tanks, and 766 guns were captured by the Germans. There is no specific study of this battle, but a good overview is provided in Kirchubel, *Atlas of the Eastern Front 1941–45*, 52–53.

60. The People's Commissariat of Defense conscripted 5,594 women in 1941, but on 7 March 1942 the Red Army announced the regular mobilization of women for military service. By 1 January 1945, 490,000 women had been conscripted, of whom some 463,503 were serving in combat and support capacities. Reese, *Why Stalin's Soldiers Fought*, 283–284. See also, Markwick and Cardona, *Soviet Women on the Frontline in the Second World War*; Krylova, *Soviet Women in Combat. A History of Violence on the Eastern Front*; Pennington, "Offensive Women: Women in Combat in the Red Army in the Second World War," in *The Journal of Military History*, vol. 74, no. 3 (July 2010), 775–820; Pennington, "Women," in Stone (ed.), *The Soviet Union at War 1941–1945*, 93–120.

61. Reddemann (ed.), *Zwischen Front und Heimat. Der Briefwechsel des münsterischen Ehepaares Agnes und Albert Neuhaus 1940–1944*, 327.

62. Alexander and Kunze (ed.), *Eastern Inferno. The Journals of a German Panzerjäger on the Eastern Front, 1941–43*, 119.

63. This is a reference to the German *Sondermeldungen* (special news bulletins) that announced with great ceremony the encirclements by Bock's Army Group Center.

64. Machemer and Hardinghaus (eds.), *Wofür es lohnte, das Leben zu wagen. Briefe, Fotos und Dokumente eines Truppenarztes von der Ostfront 1941/42*, 50.

65. Bähr and Bähr (eds.), *Kriegsbriefe Gefallener Studenten, 1939–1945*, 78–79.

66. Fuchs Richardson (ed.), *Your Loyal and Loving Son. The Letters of Tank Gunner Karl Fuchs, 1937–41*, 137.

67. Jarausch (ed.), *Reluctant Accomplice. A Wehrmacht Soldier's Letters from the Eastern Front*, 304–306.

68. The reference is to Soviet POWs.

69. In November and December 1941, 1,213 Jews were murdered by mobile killing squads in Kritschew. See Currilla, *Die deutsche Ordnungspolizei und der Holocaust im Baltikum in Weißrußland*, 443.

70. Edgar Steuerwald, Museumsstiftung Post und Telekommunikation, Berlin, 3.2002.1234.

71. Bähr and Bähr (eds.), *Kriegsbriefe Gefallener Studenten, 1939–1945*, 63.

72. Buchbender and Sterz (eds.), *Das andere Gesicht des Krieges*, 84.

73. Machemer and Hardinghaus (eds.), *Wofür es lohnte, das Leben zu wagen. Briefe, Fotos und Dokumente eines Truppenarztes von der Ostfront 1941/42*, 55–56.

74. Walter Neuser, Museumsstiftung Post und Telekommunikation, Berlin, 3.2002.0947.

75. Much has been written about the absence of winter clothing for German soldiers. Jeff Rutherford has written at length on the concept of "military necessity," whereby German behavior in the East is largely determined by the needs of the army to maintain its effectiveness. In this sense, many actions were determined less by ideology, which functions more as a facilitator, than by the strict requirements of the military. In this instance, Soviet POWs were stripped of their own protection against the cold to provide for German soldiers, while the matter-of-fact description of the event points to both its general acceptance as well as the lack of concern for the POWs themselves. On military necessity, see Rutherford, *Combat and Genocide on the Eastern Front. The German Infantry's War, 1941–1944*. On the treatment of Soviet POWs, see Streit, *Keine Kameraden. Die Wehrmacht und die sowjetischen Kriegsgefangenen 1941–1945*.

76. Fuchs Richardson (ed.), *Your Loyal and Loving Son. The Letters of Tank Gunner Karl Fuchs, 1937–41*, 138.

77. Jarausch (ed.), *Reluctant Accomplice. A Wehrmacht Soldier's Letters from the Eastern Front*, 306–307.

78. Bähr and Bähr (eds.), *Kriegsbriefe Gefallener Studenten, 1939–1945*, 66.

79. Mutzenbecher, *Feldpostbriefe an meine Eltern: 1941–1945*, 34.

80. Minsk was the capital of the Belorussian Soviet Socialist Republic, but Smolensk was only a regional capital within the Russian Soviet Socialist Republic.

81. Edgar Steuerwald, Museumsstiftung Post und Telekommunikation, Berlin, 3.2002.1234.

82. There are no reliable figures for the extent of such immediate killings, but according to Christian Streit, a five- or possibly even a six-figure number are thought to have been shot by the *Wehrmacht* on the battlefield or en route to the camps. Streit, *Keine Kameraden. Die Wehrmacht und die sowjetischen Kriegsgefangenen, 1941–1945*, 106. David Glantz claims that, during the course of the whole war, anywhere between 250,000 and 1 million Soviet POWs died en route to the camps. Glantz, *Colossus Reborn. The Red Army at War, 1941–1943*, 622. See also, Krivosheev (ed.), *Soviet Casualties and Combat Losses in the Twentieth Century*, 236.

83. Machemer and Hardinghaus (eds.), *Wofür es lohnte, das Leben zu wagen. Briefe, Fotos und Dokumente eines Truppenarztes von der Ostfront 1941/42*, 60.

84. No American pilots served in the Soviet Union in 1941, although by the end of the year a small number of American Tomahawk fighters had been shipped to the Soviet Union as part of the Lend-Lease deal. For figures on these, see Hill, *The Great Patriotic War of the Soviet Union, 1941–45*, 171, Document 118. American pilots did, however, later serve in the Soviet Union during Operation Frantic—a series of shuttle bombing operations conducted by American aircraft in 1944. See Conversino, *Fighting with the Soviets: The Failure of Operation Frantic*.

85. Bähr and Bähr (eds.), *Kriegsbriefe Gefallener Studenten, 1939–1945*, 97–98.

86. Bähr and Bähr (eds.), *Die Stimme des Menschen. Briefe und Aufzeichnungen aus der ganzen Welt. 1939–1945*, 113–114.

87. Kleindienst (ed.), *Sei tausendmal gegrüßt*. This letter appears only on the CD-ROM within the book and can be located by its date (17 October 1941).

88. Klaus K., Museumsstiftung Post und Telekommunikation, Berlin, 3.2002.0817.

89. Skat was a popular German card game.

90. The fifty-two-ton Soviet tanks were either KV-1s or KV-2s, which were also almost invulnerable to German defensive fire. Yet in 1941, their battlefield prowess was dramatically undercut by a common lack of support services such as fuel and munitions or inexperienced crews and poor tactical employment by commanders. See Forczyk, *Panzerjäger vs KV-1. Eastern Front 1941–43*.

91. On Soviet youth participation in the war, see deGraffenried, *Sacrificing Childhood. Children and the Soviet State in the Great Patriotic War*.

92. While there can be no doubt that extreme methods of coercion existed within the Red Army, Roger Reese's important study warns against generalizing such measures to the Red Army as a whole or overestimating their effectiveness. Reese, *Why Stalin's Soldiers Fought*, 158–175.

93. Klaus K. was twenty-one years old in 1941 and, like many of his fellow German soldiers, had come of age under National Socialism. For representations of Russia in Nazi Germany's school system, which help explain the views of soldiers in 1941, see Volkmann, "Das Rußlandbild in der Schule des Dritten Reiches," in Volkmann (ed.), *Das Russlandbild im Dritten Reich*, 231–244.

94. Stader (ed.), *Ihr daheim und wir hier draussen. Ein Briefwechsel zwischen Ostfront und Heimat, Juni 1941–März 1943*, 42.

95. Machemer and Hardinghaus (ed.), *Wofür es lohnte, das Leben zu wagen. Briefe, Fotos und Dokumente eines Truppenarztes von der Ostfront 1941/42*, 60–63.

96. This is a reference to the Franco-Prussian War in 1870–1871.

97. Bähr and Bähr (eds.), *Kriegsbriefe Gefallener Studenten, 1939–1945*, 81–82.

98. Hans Albring, Museumsstiftung Post und Telekommunikation, Berlin, 3.2002.0211.

99. Bähr and Bähr (eds.), *Kriegsbriefe Gefallener Studenten, 1939–1945*, 179.

100. Meyer-Timpe (ed.), *"Träume recht süß von mir." Eine deutsche Freundschaft in Briefen 1940–1943*, 113–114.

101. A card game similar to *Skat* and particular to Bavaria.

102. Bähr and Bähr (eds.), *Kriegsbriefe Gefallener Studenten, 1939–1945*, 66.

103. Gerhard Kunde, Museumsstiftung Post und Telekommunikation, Berlin, 3.2002.1941.

104. It was by no means exceptional for formations to independently dispatch vehicles to Germany to directly obtain items in short supply. In one such case, a truck was sent all the way back to Spandau in Berlin to bring back sausage production machinery. "Kriegstagebuch 19.Panzer-Division Abt.Ib für die Zeit vom 1.6.1941 – 31.12.1942," BA-MA RH 27-19/23. Fol. 84 (7 December 1941).

105. Bähr and Bähr (eds.), *Kriegsbriefe Gefallener Studenten, 1939–1945*, 82–83.

106. With incontestable evidence linking the *Wehrmacht*'s top leadership to the Nazi cause and its ideals (as research into the war of annihilation has shown), one may well begin to enquire just how far the Nazi worldview informed the generals' judgments in strictly military matters. In other words, if National Socialist thinking had already convinced the generals to partake in blatantly criminal matters, how far did this same corrupting phenomenon influence their direction of military campaigns? Certainly, there are no easy answers, but already in 1941, one can identify central tenants of the Nazi worldview impacting military decisions. Emphasizing the primacy of "will" in the achievement of objectives would be one example, just as the ardent adherence to an *Endsieg* or "final victory" would be another. In spite of the prevailing circumstances, which seemed to demand a cessation of the attack, the refusal to halt the offensive and concede some measure of failure was never discussed by the High Command. The generals simply sought to maintain the prospect of victory by refusing to accept that *Barbarossa*

had failed in its central objective. For more on this see Stahel, "The Wehrmacht and National Socialist Military Thinking," in *War in History*, vol. 24 (2017), 336–361.

107. Fuchs Richardson (ed.), *Your Loyal and Loving Son. The Letters of Tank Gunner Karl Fuchs, 1937–41*, 140–141.

108. Prüller, *Diary of a German Soldier*, Landon and Leitner (eds.), 115–116.

109. Ltr., Dr. Heinrich Haape, to his fiancée, 21.10.41.

110. Klaus Becker, Museumsstiftung Post und Telekommunikation, Berlin, 3.2002.0224.

111. By 20 October the army quartermaster-general, Major-General Eduard Wagner, could not deny the effects of the autumn rains. "It can no longer be concealed," Wagner wrote, "we are hung up in the muck, in the purest sense." Wagner (ed.), *Der Generalquartiermeister. Briefe und Tagebuchaufzeichnungen des Generalquartiermeisters des Heeres General der Artillerie Eduard Wagner*, 207 (20 October 1941).

112. As Thomas Kühne noted, "The poor living conditions of the Slavic peoples the Germans faced in the East seemed in fact to confirm the propaganda they had long been fed about the absence of culture and civilization in the East." Kühne, *The Rise and Fall of Comradeship. Hitler's Soldiers, Male Bonding and Mass Violence in the Twentieth Century*, 140.

113. As Aristotle A. Kallis observed of the early period of the war, "Goebbels complained in private how fragile and superficial the Germans' loyalty to their regime and their faith in the 'leadership' still were after many years of indoctrination. On the other hand, widespread war-weariness was leading more and more people to 'switch-off' from the propaganda and ignore the propaganda media." Echternkamp et al., *Germany and the Second World War*, IX/II *German Wartime Society 1939–1945: Exploitation, Interpretations, Exclusion*, 226.

114. Kurt Marlow, Museumsstiftung Post und Telekommunikation, Berlin, 3.2002.0884.

115. Germany was actively recruiting foreigners to work in its armament and agricultural sectors. See Herbert, *Hitler's Foreign Workers. Enforced Foreign Labor in Germany under the Third Reich*.

116. The condescending view of German allies was also shared by the Nazi leadership and undercut any prospect of a coordinated Axis strategy. Stahel (ed.), *Joining Hitler's Crusade. European Nations and the Invasion of the Soviet Union*, 9–12.

117. Lemberg (L'vov) in western Ukraine was annexed by the Soviet Union in September 1939 (the town was known as Lwow in Polish). Marlow is probably referring to one of the most notorious massacres of the Soviet retreat, which took place in the town and was blamed on the Jews by German propaganda in early July 1941. See Fröhlich (ed.), *Die Tagebücher von Joseph Goebbels, Teil I: Aufzeichnungen 1923–1941*, Band 9, 6–8 July 1941.

118. *Wm.* Josef L. (22 633 C), Collection BfZ.

119. Jarausch (ed.), *Reluctant Accomplice. A Wehrmacht Soldier's Letters from the Eastern Front*, 307–308.

120. Buchbender and Sterz (eds.), *Das andere Gesicht des Krieges*, 84–85.

121. Elmshäuser and Lokers (eds.), *"Man muß hier nur hart sein." Kriegsbriefe und Bilder einer Familie (1934–1945)*, 152–153.

122. Ltr., *Lt.* Rudolf Maurer, to his wife, Irene, 23.10.41.

123. Ltr., Dr. Heinrich Haape, to his fiancée, 23.10.41.

124. Hellmuth H., Museumsstiftung Post und Telekommunikation, Berlin, 3.2002.7139.

125. *Generaloberst* Ewald von Kleist, who later rose to the rank of field marshal and remained on the Eastern Front until March 1944, stated after the war, "[The Soviet] equipment was very good even in 1941, especially the tanks. Their artillery was excellent, and also most of the infantry weapons—their rifles were more modern than ours, and had a more rapid rate of fire." Liddell Hart, *The Other Side of the Hill*, 330. See also, Raus, "Russian Combat Methods

in World War II," in Tsouras (ed.), *Fighting in Hell. The German Ordeal on the Eastern Front*, 35–36.

126. Each leaflet included a series of short articles, such as "America Helps the USSR," "Uprising in Yugoslavia," "Romanian Oilfields in Flames," "Czechoslovakian and Romanian Hospitals Overflowing with German Wounded," "Peru Cuts Ties to Germany," and "Hopkins Is Impressed on His Trip to Moscow." *Württembergische Landesbiblithek* Stuttgart, *Flugblattpropaganda im 2. Weltkrieg (1941)*, Mappe 92-32 and Mappe 92-36.

127. Walter Tilemann insisted that "no one dared to trust the 'safe-conduct passes.'" However, he then added, "This changed only when new daily rumours and terrible news made the rounds." Tilemann, *Ich, das Soldatenkind*, 160. Likewise, Helmut Günther recalled, "We may well have had a few 'safe-conduct passes' in our pocket. The 'comrade' promised us a lot in this scrap of paper: Good treatment, first-class food, immediate release after the end of the war and many more wonders. It was a friendly offer that almost elicited tears of emotion. But we knew better!" Günther, *Hot Motors, Cold Feet. A Memoir of Service with the Motorcycle Battalion of SS-Division "Reich" 1940–1941*, 234. For the only major study of German desertion, see Koch, *Fahnenfluchten. Deserteure der Wehrmacht in Zweiten Weltkrieg—Lebenswege und Entscheidungen.*

128. Kurt Miethke, Museumsstiftung Post und Telekommunikation, Berlin, 3.2002.0912.

129. Miethke is referring to a mass grave of Soviet POWs at a camp he is guarding.

130. Although British bombing of German cities in 1941 was still terribly inaccurate and inflicted relatively little damage, it nevertheless constituted a disproportionate level of concern for German soldiers at the front. A statistical analysis completed in August 1941 by D. M. B. Butt of the British War Cabinet Secretariat revealed that a staggering 80 percent of bombers did not reach their designated target area, which was broadly defined as seventy-five square miles around the target. Richard Overy, "Statistics," in Dear and Foot (eds.), *The Oxford Companion of the Second World War*, 1060.

131. *Lt.* Joachim H. (18 967), Collection BfZ.

132. Prüller, *Diary of a German Soldier*, Landon and Leitner (eds.), 116–117.

133. Jarausch (ed.), *Reluctant Accomplice. A Wehrmacht Soldier's Letters from the Eastern Front*, 310–311.

134. Fritz Pabst, Museumsstiftung Post und Telekommunikation, Berlin, 3.2002.0306.

135. Such comments show not only a knowledge of the mass murder of Soviet Jews but also a willingness to share the information. This suggests that the taboo around such killings was by no means universal and that at least a part of the German civilian population did indeed have some idea of what was happening in the East. For more on this, see also Johnson and Reuband, *What We Knew. Terror, Mass Murder, and Everyday Life in Nazi Germany.*

136. *Lt.* Joachim H. (18 967), Collection BfZ.

137. *Wm.* Josef L. (22 633 C), Collection BfZ.

138. Fuchs Richardson (ed.), *Your Loyal and Loving Son. The Letters of Tank Gunner Karl Fuchs, 1937–41*, 142.

139. Reddemann (ed.), *Zwischen Front und Heimat. Der Briefwechsel des münsterischen Ehepaares Agnes und Albert Neuhaus 1940–1944*, 334–335.

140. Heinz Rahe, Museumsstiftung Post und Telekommunikation, Berlin, 3.2002.0985.

141. Rahe's attitude reflects the difficulties of expressing intimacy on paper and how some men questioned the appropriateness of writing anything that might be construed as being of a sexual nature. Such content is relatively restrained in most of the letters addressed to wives or girlfriends, which may be explained by the more conservative view of such topics in the 1940s and was by no means unique to Germany. Most National Socialist views of sexuality also frowned upon open displays of emotional or sexual need, although some in the party attacked

this concept as being a result of medieval Christianity and "Eager clerical 'moralists.'" See Dagmar Herzog, "Hubris and Hypocrisy, Incitement and Disavowal: Sexuality and German Fascism," in Dagmar Herzog (ed.), *Sexuality and German Fascism*, 9–11.

142. Jarausch (ed.), *Reluctant Accomplice. A Wehrmacht Soldier's Letters from the Eastern Front*, 311–313.

143. Stehmann, *Die Bitternis verschweigen wir. Feldpostbriefe 1940–1945*, 139.

144. Ltr., Dr. Heinrich Haape, to his fiancée, 29.10.41.

145. Buchbender and Sterz (eds.), *Das andere Gesicht des Krieges*, 85.

146. Heinz Rahe, Museumsstiftung Post und Telekommunikation, Berlin, 3.2002.0985.

147. Such a casual observation struck many Germans who studied maps of the Soviet Union and wondered how much further Germany could hope to extend itself into the "endless" space in the East. To no small extent, Germans underestimated the megalomaniac ambitions and utopian plans of the Nazi leadership, which largely doomed their military campaign (Operation *Barbarossa*) and occupation policy (General Plan East).

148. Walter Neuser, Museumsstiftung Post und Telekommunikation, Berlin, 3.2002.0947.

149. In fact, Army Group Center's operations toward Moscow halted at the end of October in the hope that the coming frosts would harden the roads and allow one last drive on the Soviet capital.

150. On German antipartisan warfare in Army Group Center, see Shepherd, *War in the Wild East. The German Army and Soviet Partisans*.

151. There was a dearth of reading material available on the Eastern Front for two main reasons: first, the shortage of paper for German newspapers and, second, the absence of transport capacity to the East. Books were somewhat unaffected by the paper shortage since public collections throughout the war yielded over forty-three million titles. Deciding which of these were best suited for the front, there was a concerted effort to satisfy the wishes of the soldiers, and in the winter of 1941–1942 it was determined that the most popular titles were light reads in genres such as adventure, romance, crime, and almost anything from Karl May (who was best known for novels set in the American wild west). Hirt, *"Die Heimat reicht der Front die Hand." Kulturelle Truppenbetreuung im Zweiten Weltkrieg 1939-1945. Ein deutsch-englischer Vergleich*, 357, 365, 367–368.

152. Jakob Geimer, Museumsstiftung Post und Telekommunikation, Berlin, 3.2002.0894.

153. Stader (ed.), *Ihr daheim und wir hier draussen. Ein Briefwechsel zwischen Ostfront und Heimat, Juni 1941–März 1943*, 43–44.

CHAPTER 7

1. Moltke, *Letters to Freya. 1939–1945*, 187–188.

2. For the German military culture or "way of war," see Citino, *The German Way of War. From the Thirty Years' War to the Third Reich*.

3. Glantz, *Soviet Military Deception in the Second World War*, 47–56.

4. Ziemke, *The Red Army 1918–1941. From Vanguard of World Revolution to US Ally*, 307.

5. Halder, *Kriegstagebuch: Tägliche Aufzeichnungen des Chefs des Generalstabes des Heeres 1939–1942*. Bd. III, 303.

6. Megargee, *War of Annihilation. Combat and Genocide on the Eastern Front, 1941*, 112.

7. Kirchubel, *Operation Barbarossa 1941 (2): Army Group North*, 85.

8. Boog et al., *Germany and the Second World War*, Vol. IV: *The Attack on the Soviet Union*, 649–651.

9. Adamovich and Granin, *Leningrad under Siege. First-Hand Accounts of the Ordeal*, 84–85.

10. Karl Nünnighoff, Museumsstiftung Post und Telekommunikation, Berlin, 3.2008.1388.

11. Rumors of relief, being brought off the line and rested, or even being transferred out of the Soviet Union altogether, were a common occurrence on the Eastern Front and appear to have pervaded most of the divisions. By the autumn of 1941, however, such rumors circulated so often that many disregarded such ideas in order to save themselves the eventual disappointment. Stahel, *Operation Typhoon*, 205; Stahel, *The Battle for Moscow*, 136.

12. Rudolf Oehus, Museumsstiftung Post und Telekommunikation, Berlin. This letter has no archive reference number and must be located by name and date.

13. Prüller, *Diary of a German Soldier*, Landon and Leitner (eds.), 120–121. In the last days of October, Prüller's division was redeployed to the north and came under new army and army group command structures.

14. Machemer and Hardinghaus (eds.), *Wofür es lohnte, das Leben zu wagen. Briefe, Fotos und Dokumente eines Truppenarztes von der Ostfront 1941/42*, 98.

15. Jarausch (ed.), *Reluctant Accomplice. A Wehrmacht Soldier's Letters from the Eastern Front*, 313–314.

16. *Uffz.* X. M. (11 800), Collection BfZ; also cited in Manoschek (ed.), *"Es gibt nur eines für das Judentum: Vernichtung." Das Judenbild in deutschen Soldatenbriefen 1939–1944*, 49.

17. Prüller, *Diary of a German Soldier*, Landon and Leitner (eds.), 121–122.

18. For the most complete study of urban combat on the Eastern Front, see Wettstein, "Urban Warfare Doctrine on the Eastern Front," in Kay, Rutherford and Stahel (eds.), *Nazi Policy on the Eastern Front, 1941. Total War, Genocide and Radicalization*, 45–72; Wettstein, *Die Wehrmacht in Stadtkampf*.

19. Machemer and Hardinghaus (eds.), *Wofür es lohnte, das Leben zu wagen. Briefe, Fotos und Dokumente eines Truppenarztes von der Ostfront 1941/42*, 99–100.

20. In fact, in 1941, there were no British bombers deployed on the Eastern Front. By November 1941, the Soviet Union was receiving Lend-Lease transports with British fighters, but the only air crews from the Royal Air Force came from the 151 Fighter Wing at Vianga airfield (twenty-seven kilometers northeast of Murmansk on the Barents Sea). Ostensibly, its role was to provide training for Soviet pilots and ground crews in the newly arriving Hurricane fighters, yet the proximity of Vianga airfield to Finnish and German airbases meant a combat role soon became inevitable. Bergström, *Barbarossa—The Air Battle: July–December 1941*, 79–80; Mellinger, *Soviet Lend-Lease Fighter Aces of World War 2*, 23–24.

21. Bähr and Bähr (eds.), *Kriegsbriefe Gefallener Studenten, 1939–1945*, 331.

22. Fritz Pabst, Museumsstiftung Post und Telekommunikation, Berlin, 3.2002.0306.

23. There was, of course, censorship in Nazi Germany, but the sheer volume of letters reduced its impact, and soldiers appeared to have expressed themselves with relative frankness, especially when it came to military matters.

24. In this case the unit's mail bag was reviewed by the censor, and clearly people from home had written information that was forbidden, but this suggests that postal communication was largely open and honest in spite of official regulations. Letters that fell afoul of the censor typically had objectionable passages rendered illegible. Criticisms of Hitler or the Nazi party, however, were far less common. Vaizey, *Surviving Hitler's War. Family Life in Germany, 1939–48*, 55.

25. Pabst is referring to the explosions and subsequent fires in Kiev, which took place in September. He also discussed this in his letter from 5 October.

26. In fact, some 33,771 Jews were shot.

27. Kurt Miethke, Museumsstiftung Post und Telekommunikation, Berlin, 3.2002.0912.

28. Miethke is guarding a Soviet POW camp.

29. Bähr and Bähr (eds.), *Kriegsbriefe Gefallener Studenten, 1939–1945*, 112–113.

30. The mythology of death in the Third Reich was as near as the regime came to a pseudo-state religion. The cult of death even had its very own saints, none of whom was more celebrated than Horst Wessel, the leader of an SA troop who was killed by Communists in 1930 after he was implicated in the murder of one of their members. His funeral was a lavish affair in which Goebbels himself gave the eulogy and a song was played that Wessel himself had written. "The Flag on High" (also known as the Horst Wessel song) was then adopted as the official anthem of the Nazi movement. Having been written in 1929 at the height of the Nazi street battles with the KPD (Communist Party of Germany), the lyrics took on special meaning in context of the latter Nazi-Soviet war. The first verse includes the refrain "Comrades shot by the Red Front and reactionaries, march in spirit within our ranks." Such a blood sacrifice elevated the victim to the status of national martyrdom and, in accordance, Hitler had the more somber "Day of National Mourning" (*Volkstrauertag*) reinvented as "Heroes Memorial Day" (*Heldengedenktag*) with pageantry, national pride, and military glorification at the center of proceedings. Yet it was the onset of war that gave full meaning to the cult of death and bore out sacrifice and conflict as central tenets of Nazism. Baird, *To Die for Germany. Heroes in the Nazi Pantheon.*

31. Buchbender and Sterz (eds.), *Das andere Gesicht des Krieges*, 85–86.

32. Klaus Becker, Museumsstiftung Post und Telekommunikation, Berlin, 3.2002.0224.

33. This process is addressed in the introductory chapter describing the war as a transformative event in which men experienced first "shock" and then a process of "renormalisation." Heer, "How Amorality Became Normality: Reflections on the Mentality of German Soldiers on the Eastern Front," in Heer and Naumann (eds.), *War of Extermination. The German Military in World War II 1941–1944*, 329–344.

34. Mühleisen (ed.), *Hellmuth Stieff Briefe*, 132–133.

35. Criticism of Hitler was extremely rare in letters from 1941, but as a general staff officer Hellmuth Stieff had a clear-eyed understanding of the war and Hitler's role in it. In 1943 Stieff joined the anti-Hitler conspiracy and was executed in 1944 after the failure of the July plot.

36. As of 26 November 1941, the *Ostheer* had sustained 743,112 casualties in the war against the Soviet Union. That equaled 23 percent of the total German invasion force on 22 June 1941, and even this figure did not include those released from duty on account of sickness. Overall, by the end of November, more than a quarter of a million men (262,297 German troops) had been killed outright or died of their wounds. With the reserves of the Replacement Army long since exhausted, the *Ostheer* was now some 340,000 men short, which, according to the OKH, meant that the combat strength of the infantry divisions was reduced by 50 percent. Halder, *Kriegstagebuch: Tägliche Aufzeichnungen des Chefs des Generalstabes des Heeres 1939–1942.* Bd. III, 319.

37. Bähr and Bähr (eds.), *Kriegsbriefe Gefallener Studenten, 1939–1945*, 112.

38. Scheuer (ed.), *Briefe aus Russland. Feldpostbriefe des Gefreiten Alois Scheuer 1941–1942*, 48.

39. Bähr and Bähr (eds.), *Kriegsbriefe Gefallener Studenten, 1939–1945*, 112–113.

40. On the belt buckle of every soldier in the German Army were inscribed the words "*Gott mit uns*" (God is with us), and for many Christian men in the *Ostheer*, this was their most redeeming thought. To soldiers seeking to endure the hardships of war, religion offered a guise of protection and deliverance, while prayer became an emotional sanctuary for personal redemption and spiritual salvation. See Faulkner Rossi, *Wehrmacht Priests. Catholicism and the Nazi War of Annihilation.*

41. Helmut Nick, Museumsstiftung Post und Telekommunikation, Berlin, 3.2002.0274.

42. This was a common trope within the German Army at the time and often repeated by members of the *Wehrmacht* in their postwar publications, but the claim is illogical and has been debunked by numerous social studies of the Red Army.

43. Many German accounts give an impression of Soviet soldiers or partisans that tend to reflect the dehumanizing depictions of Nazi propaganda. Yet such accounts may also be a result of the trauma of war and the desire to distance one's self from involvement in an otherwise barbarous action. In that sense, Nazi propaganda not only offered "explanations" for Soviet actions (they did not fear death) but also provided coping strategies for the wholesale killing that was sometimes demanded in the East.

44. Dollinger (ed.), *Kain, wo ist dein Bruder? Was der Mensch im Zweiten Weltkrieg erleiden musste—dokumentiert in Tagebüchern und Briefen*, 106.

45. Dollinger (ed.), *Kain, wo ist dein Bruder? Was der Mensch im Zweiten Weltkrieg erleiden musste—dokumentiert in Tagebüchern und Briefen*, 108–109.

46. Jackson and Böhme (eds.), *"Beim Militär hat man immer sein Totenhemd an . . ." Feldpostbriefe von drei gefallenen Brüdern aus dem Odenwald 1939–1944*, 79–80.

47. Machemer and Hardinghaus (eds.), *Wofür es lohnte, das Leben zu wagen. Briefe, Fotos und Dokumente eines Truppenarztes von der Ostfront 1941/42*, 102–104.

48. Stehmann, *Die Bitternis verschweigen wir. Feldpostbriefe 1940–1945*, 141.

49. Elmar Lieb, Museumsstiftung Post und Telekommunikation, Berlin, 3.2002.7255. Guderian's 2 Panzer Group was redesignated 2 Panzer Army on 6 October 1941.

50. Although German propaganda presented Soviet culture as something perverse and inherently negative, there was in fact a rich artistic, literary, and musical heritage carried over from the Czarist period. See Stites (ed.), *Culture and Entertainment in Wartime Russia*.

51. Kurt Miethke, Museumsstiftung Post und Telekommunikation, Berlin, 3.2002.0912.

52. Machemer and Hardinghaus (eds.), *Wofür es lohnte, das Leben zu wagen. Briefe, Fotos und Dokumente eines Truppenarztes von der Ostfront 1941/42*, 112.

53. A worthwhile recent study into fatherhood in the SS offers some instruction on attitudes generally within the Nazi state. Carney, *Marriage and Fatherhood in the Nazi SS*, Chapter 4.

54. Bähr and Bähr (eds.), *Kriegsbriefe Gefallener Studenten, 1939–1945*, 67.

55. Ltr., Dr. Heinrich Haape, to his fiancée, 10.11.41.

56. The problem of the German railways was in part due to seasonal factors—German locomotives affixed their water pipes external to their boilers, meaning that 70 to 80 percent of them burst when the water froze—yet there were also systemic failures in the organization and management of the railways. German prewar planning assumed the widespread capture of broad-gauge Soviet trains and only insignificant damage to the Soviet rail network. The general disappointment of this optimistic expectation forced heavy reliance on the immediate eastward extension of the standard-gauge rail lines, while the deficit in locomotives and rolling stock had to be borne by the already overstrained *Reichsbahn* (German railways). The railroad troops (*Eisenbahntruppe*) charged with carrying out the conversion were faced with critical shortages of both manpower and materials, making rapid progress impossible. Indeed, a total of only one thousand motor vehicles (mostly inferior French and British models) was allocated to the *Eisenbahntruppe* across the whole of the Eastern Front. As the distances grew, emphasis was placed on the speed of the conversion rate rather than the quality of the work, and consequently train speeds had to remain very low. Meanwhile, the coexistence of Soviet and German railways, although the latter were constantly being pushed forward, was never entirely eliminated, and the transfer points became bottlenecks. Security along the lines was also extremely poor as Army Group Center's security divisions proved totally inadequate to prevent even the nascent Soviet partisan movement from sabotaging tracks and sometimes derailing trains. Schüler, "The Eastern Campaign as a Transportation and Supply Problem," in Wegner (ed.), *From Peace to War. Germany, Soviet Russia and the World, 1939–1941*, 205–222.

57. Machemer and Hardinghaus (eds.), *Wofür es lohnte, das Leben zu wagen. Briefe, Fotos und Dokumente eines Truppenarztes von der Ostfront 1941/42*, 112.

58. *O'Gefr.* Joseph B. (25 341), Collection BfZ.

59. Buchbender and Sterz (eds.), *Das andere Gesicht des Krieges*, 86.

60. Prüller, *Diary of a German Soldier*, Landon and Leitner (eds.), 123.

61. Karl Nünnighoff, Museumsstiftung Post und Telekommunikation, Berlin, 3.2008.1388.

62. *Uffz.* Karl R. (35 672), Collection BfZ.

63. Goebbels fumed in his diary at the disastrous effect Otto Dietrich, the Reich's press chief who publicly announced that the war in the East had been decided, had had in raising false expectations. Dietrich later claimed that his statements had been dictated to him by Hitler. However, Goebbels himself was in no small measure to blame for the overblown expectations of the German population. He had directed the fanfare of victory announcements, sometimes at Hitler's behest, which for weeks had acted to sow the seeds of hope of an impending end to the war.

64. Jarausch (ed.), *Reluctant Accomplice. A Wehrmacht Soldier's Letters from the Eastern Front*, 313–314.

65. As a result of the distances and the time of year, the condition of the prisoners arriving in the German camps in November was generally very poor. Accordingly, mortality rates rose dramatically, especially in camps located in Ukraine and Belarus. Streit, *Keine Kameraden. Die Wehrmacht und die sowjetischen Kriegsgefangenen, 1941–1945*, 130–137.

66. Wm. Josef L. (22 633 C), Collection BfZ.

67. *Gefr.* Hans Joachim C. (06 742 C), Collection BfZ.

68. H.D., Museumsstiftung Post und Telekommunikation, Berlin, 3.2002.0280.

69. König (ed.), *Ganz in Gottes Hand*, 124.

70. Machemer and Hardinghaus (eds.), *Wofür es lohnte, das Leben zu wagen. Briefe, Fotos und Dokumente eines Truppenarztes von der Ostfront 1941/42*, 115.

71. The popular Soviet writer Ilya Ehrenburg gained satirical mileage out of the plight of Germany's soldiers but ended his article "Freezing Them Out" with a warning that was probably more truthful than the usual hyperbole of his propaganda. Ehrenburg wrote, "How the German soldiers freezing in the fields of Russia must envy their compatriots in Africa! . . . They are rushing toward Moscow like frozen men rushing to the fire. . . . They are ready to come under fire for a pair of felt boots or a woman's warm jacket. That's why they are now doubly dangerous. . . . In terror they say to each other: 'This is only November.'" Goebbels also fumed in his diary about British propaganda "representing the situation on the Eastern Front as especially catastrophic." He accused them of reporting hundreds of thousands of Germans dying as a result of the winter weather. It was a particularly sensitive point for Goebbels, as he was well informed about the condition of the troops (he had daily military briefings) and, on 14 November, expressed grave concerns about the impact of the freezing conditions on the already ebbing morale of the German population. He knew that the cold and suffering of the men at the front, not to mention the inability of the army to deliver enough winter uniforms, would soon be reported back to the German public in hundreds of thousands of letters.

72. Jarausch (ed.), *Reluctant Accomplice. A Wehrmacht Soldier's Letters from the Eastern Front*, 324–325.

73. The "experts" is a reference to the SS killing squads.

74. Machemer and Hardinghaus (eds.), *Wofür es lohnte, das Leben zu wagen. Briefe, Fotos und Dokumente eines Truppenarztes von der Ostfront 1941/42*, 119.

75. On the unique role of Russian emigrants who served within the German Army in the East with the special rank of *Sonderführer*, see Beyda, "'Iron Cross of the Wrangel's Army': Russian Emigrants as Interpreters in the Wehrmacht," in *The Journal of Slavic Military History*, vol. 27, no. 3 (July 2014), 430–448.

76. Anton Böhrer, Museumsstiftung Post und Telekommunikation, Berlin, 3.2002.0889.

77. In fact, Hitler's speech was on 8 November, the text of which can be found in Domarus, *Hitler. Speeches and Proclamations 1932–1945: The Chronicle of a Dictatorship. Volume IV. The Years 1941 to 1945*, 2504–2513.

78. Johannes Hamm, Museumsstiftung Post und Telekommunikation, Berlin, 3.2002.7184.

79. After a failed campaign in 1695, Peter the Great successfully extended his rule all the way to the Sea of Azov in 1696, defeating the Crimean Tatars backed by the Ottoman Turks.

80. Buchbender and Sterz (eds.), *Das andere Gesicht des Krieges*, 86–87.

81. Beermann (ed.), *Soldat Werner Beermann Feldpostbriefe 1941–1942*, 168.

82. Prüller, *Diary of a German Soldier*, Landon and Leitner (eds.), 123–124.

83. Hammer and Nieden (eds.), *Sehr selten habe ich geweint. Briefe und Tagebücher aus dem Zweiten Weltkrieg von Menschen aus Berlin*, 260; Dollinger (ed.), *Kain, wo ist dein Bruder? Was der Mensch im Zweiten Weltkrieg erleiden musste—dokumentiert in Tagebüchern und Briefen*, 110.

84. Alexander and Kunze (eds.), *Eastern Inferno. The Journals of a German Panzerjäger on the Eastern Front, 1941–43*, 124–125.

85. A Potemkin village is any construction (real or imagined) built solely to deceive others into thinking that a situation is better than it really is. The term comes from stories of a fake portable village built solely to impress Empress Catherine II by her former lover Grigory Potemkin during her journey to Crimea in 1787. While modern historians claim accounts of this portable village are exaggerated, the term "Potemkin village" has acquired popular usage in numerous languages.

86. Buchbender and Sterz (eds.), *Das andere Gesicht des Krieges*, 87.

87. Mühleisen (ed.), *Hellmuth Stieff Briefe*, 134–137.

88. According to Nicolaus von Below, Hitler's *Luftwaffe* adjutant, "The army Quartermaster-General, General Wagner, stated that work on winter clothing was in hand and that sufficient quantities would be made available to men in the field. Hitler took note of the report and appeared satisfied." In fact, according to Colonel Wilhelm von Rücker, attached to the planning staff of the Quartermaster-General's office, "a few hundred additional trains would have to have been sent" to meet the needs of the troops for the coming winter. Not only was there not the transport capacity for winter equipment but other higher priority materials, such as fuel and ammunition, were also decidedly underresourced by the quartermaster-general.

89. Such casual statements even from a staunch critic of the Nazi regime, and later a member of the resistance movement, warns against underestimating the extent of National Socialist thinking within the German Army in 1941. There is a growing body of research on the contrasting activities and attitudes of resistance figures early in the war; see Hürter, "Auf dem Weg zur Militäropposition. Tresckow, Gersdorff, der Vernichtungskrieg und der Judenmord. Neue Dokumente über das Verhältnis der Heeresgruppe Mitte zur Einsatzgruppe B im Jahr 1941," in *Vierteljahreshefte für Zeitgeschichte*, vol. 52, no. 3 (2004); Gerlach, "Men of 20 July and the War in the Soviet Union," in Heer and Naumann (eds.), *War of Extermination: The German Military in World War II 1941–1944*; Gerlach, "Hitlergegner bei der Heeresgruppe Mitte und die 'verbrecherischen Befehle,'" in Ueberschär (ed.), *NS-Verbrechen und der militärische Widerstand gegen Hitler*.

90. Erich Dohl, Museumsstiftung Post und Telekommunikation, Berlin, 3.2009.1998.

91. *Wm.* Artur W. (21 573 B), Collection BfZ.

92. Jarausch (ed.), *Reluctant Accomplice. A Wehrmacht Soldier's Letters from the Eastern Front*, 327.

93. *O.Gefr.* Fritz N. (20 123), Collection BfZ.

94. Machemer and Hardinghaus (eds.), *Wofür es lohnte, das Leben zu wagen. Briefe, Fotos und Dokumente eines Truppenarztes von der Ostfront 1941/42*, 123–125.

95. Machemer is referring to withdrawals of the panzer group around Rostov.

96. Buchbender and Sterz (eds.), *Das andere Gesicht des Krieges*, 87.

97. Hellmuth H., Museumsstiftung Post und Telekommunikation, Berlin, 3.2002.7139.

98. Edgar Steuerwald, Museumsstiftung Post und Telekommunikation, Berlin, 3.2002.1234.

99. On German food policy in the occupied areas of the Soviet Union, see Pohl, *Die Herrschaft der Wehrmacht: Deutsche Militärbestzung und einheimische Bevölkerung in der Sowjetunion 1941–1944*, Section VII: *Ernährungspolitik*; Collingham, *The Taste of War. World War II and the Battle for Food*, Chapter 9: Germany Exports Hunger to the East.

100. Franz Siebeler, Museumsstiftung Post und Telekommunikation, Berlin, 3.2002.1285.

101. The Germans captured Rostov on 20 November.

102. Heinz Rahe, Museumsstiftung Post und Telekommunikation, Berlin, 3.2002.0985.

103. In the early months of Operation *Barbarossa*, the vast areas conquered by Germany would remain under military occupation, but as soon as the situation allowed it, a more permanent form of administration for these territories would be instituted. By the start of September 1941, the new civilian-administered *Reich Commissariat Ostland* was created, supporting mass repression and the retention of the hated Soviet collective farms. This quickly dispelled the myth of benevolent German rule and fueled sympathies for underground Communist propaganda. *Ostland* consisted of Lithuania, Latvia, and Belorussia (1 September) and Estonia (incorporated on 5 December 1941). *Reich Commissariat Ukraine* was created by Hitler's decree on 20 August 1941, but the first transfer of Soviet Ukrainian territory from military to civil administration took place on 1 September 1941. There were further transfers on 20 October and 1 November.

104. Klaus Becker, Museumsstiftung Post und Telekommunikation, Berlin, 3.2002.0224.

105. This was completely untrue; German bombers, especially over heavily defended targets like Moscow, could not hope to drop their loads with any degree of accuracy.

106. Erich Dohl, Museumsstiftung Post und Telekommunikation, Berlin, 3.2009.1998.

107. Upper Silesia (known in German as Oberschlesien) is the southeastern part of the historical and geographical region of Silesia (located today mostly in Poland, with small parts in the Czech Republic).

108. Mühleisen (ed.), *Hellmuth Stieff Briefe*, 138.

109. Machemer and Hardinghaus (eds.), *Wofür es lohnte, das Leben zu wagen. Briefe, Fotos und Dokumente eines Truppenarztes von der Ostfront 1941/42*, 131–133.

110. While most associate the devastating German "scorched-earth" policies with the retreats of 1943–1944, they in fact began in late 1941. Although such actions were typically (although not always) aimed at denying the Red Army important logistical support, the burning of homes and appropriation of vital possessions condemned countless Soviet civilians to death over the winter.

111. Bähr and Bähr (eds.), *Kriegsbriefe Gefallener Studenten, 1939–1945*, 122–123.

112. *Oblt.* August D. (00 319), Collection BfZ.

113. Rudolf Oehus, Museumsstiftung Post und Telekommunikation, Berlin. This letter has no archive reference number and must be located by name and date.

114. *O'Gefr.* Joseph B. (25 341), Collection BfZ.

115. On 4 November, German intelligence reported one hundred British tanks were being unloaded at Archangel. Soviet sources indicate that ninety-six had been issued to tank battalions of the Red Army by 20 November. These were to be found at Tula in the south, west of Moscow at Mozhaisk, and farther north near Kiln and Istra. 4 Panzer Group noted that after a battle on 25 November, three destroyed British tanks were discovered, while on 27 November the 5 Panzer Division noted intelligence from POWs that two of the three opposing Soviet tank battalions consisted of British tanks. The British tanks sent to the Soviet Union were in fact

little better suited to the Russian late autumn and winter conditions than the German tanks. The British Valentine and Matilda, like the German models in 1941, had much narrower tracks than the Soviet T-34 and KV-1. Accordingly, while Soviet tanks could still perform in up to seventy centimeters of snow, the British tanks were only capable of operating in up to forty centimeters. There was even a suggestion that British tanks should be held back from service until March 1942, as they were "apparently African vehicles." By the end of 1941, some 466 British tanks (259 Valentines, 187 Matildas, and the remainder apparently Tetratchs) had been delivered to the Soviet Union along with 699 British and American planes. See Hill, "British Lend-Lease Aid and the Soviet War Effort, June 1941–June 1942," in *The Journal of Military History*, vol. 71, no. 3 (July 2007), 788, 792.

116. Golovchansky, Osipov, Prokopenko, Daniel and Reulecke (eds.), *"Ich will raus aus diesem Wahnsinn." Deutsche Briefe von der Ostfront 1941–1945. Aus sowjetischen Archiven*, 234–235.

117. Erich Dohl, Museumsstiftung Post und Telekommunikation, Berlin, 3.2009.1998.

118. Stehmann, *Die Bitternis verschweigen wir. Feldpostbriefe 1940–1945*, 146–147.

119. Ltr., Dr. Heinrich Haape, to his fiancée, 27.11.41.

120. As it turned out, Haape's leave would be canceled, and he remained with his unit for the winter battles.

121. Buchbender and Sterz (eds.), *Das andere Gesicht des Krieges*, 88.

122. This was left unanswered by the author of the letter.

123. *O.Gefr.* H. S. (04 497 A), Collection BfZ.

124. *L'Inconnue de la Seine* (The Unknown Woman of the River Seine) was an unidentified young woman whose death mask became a popular fixture on the walls of artists' homes after 1900. Her visage inspired numerous literary works.

125. Machemer and Hardinghaus (eds.), *Wofür es lohnte, das Leben zu wagen. Briefe, Fotos und Dokumente eines Truppenarztes von der Ostfront 1941/42*, 144–145.

126. Scheuer (ed.), *Briefe aus Russland. Feldpostbriefe des Gefreiten Alois Scheuer 1941–1942*, 51.

127. Erich Dohl, Museumsstiftung Post und Telekommunikation, Berlin, 3.2009.1998.

CHAPTER 8

1. Glantz and House, *When Titans Clashed. How the Red Army Stopped Hitler*, 108.

2. Stahel, *The Battle for Moscow*, 292–293.

3. Hürter (ed.), *Ein deutscher General an der Ostfront. Die Briefe und Tagebücher des Gotthard Heinrici 1941/42*, 122.

4. Bücheler, *Hoepner. Ein deutsches Soldatenschicksal des Zwanzigsten Jahrhunderts*, 162.

5. Lopukhovsky and Kavalerchik, *The Price of Victory. The Red Army's Casualties in the Great Patriotic War*, 154.

6. Boog et al., *Germany and the Second World War*, Vol. IV: *The Attack on the Soviet Union*, 652.

7. Meyer (ed.), *Generalfeldmarschall Wilhelm Ritter von Leeb: Tagebuchaufzeichnungen und Lagebeurteilungen aus zwei Weltkriegen*, 418; Megargee, *Inside Hitler's High Command*, 146–147.

8. Shepherd, *Hitler's Soldiers. The German Army in the Third Reich*, 180.

9. Adamovich and Granin, *Leningrad under Siege. First-Hand Accounts of the Ordeal*, 87.

10. Boog et al., *Germany and the Second World War*, Vol. IV: *The Attack on the Soviet Union*, 625–626.

11. Kirchubel, *Operation Barbarossa 1941 (1): Army Group South*, 86.

12. Bähr and Bähr (eds.), *Kriegsbriefe Gefallener Studenten, 1939–1945*, 109.

13. Ibid., 371.

14. Ibid., 88–89. Harald Henry was killed in action on 22 December 1941, northwest of Moscow.

15. Prüller, *Diary of a German Soldier*, Landon and Leitner (eds.), 124–125.

16. Bähr and Bähr (eds.), *Kriegsbriefe Gefallener Studenten, 1939–1945*, 68.

17. Anton Böhrer, Museumsstiftung Post und Telekommunikation, Berlin, 3.2002.0889.

18. Urbanke and Türk, *Als Sanitätsoffizier im Rußlandfeldzug. Mit der 3. Panzer-Division bis vor Moskaus Tore*, 542.

19. *O'Gefr.* Joseph B. (25 341), Collection BfZ.

20. Stehmann, *Die Bitternis verschweigen wir. Feldpostbriefe 1940–1945*, 148.

21. Erich Dohl, Museumsstiftung Post und Telekommunikation, Berlin, 3.2009.1998.

22. In addition to the toll taken on German vehicles during the summer, the low temperatures introduced a whole host of new complications. Many trucks and some of the guns developed "cold breaks" in the already brittle, and scarcely replaceable, springs and suspension. The narrower track width made the nominal ground pressure ratio much higher, which reduced traction and mobility, especially in snow and ice. There was an absence of calks for the tracks, making it almost impossible for the tanks to climb frozen slopes. Optical instruments suffered from frost, causing distortions that affected tanks as well as the artillery and caused shells to be inaccurately fired, sometimes landing "short" on German positions. The oils in the buffering systems of the German artillery were freezing, which highlighted the lack of low-temperature lubricants and graphite. Similarly affected were the sliding parts of machine guns and bolt-action rifles, which routinely jammed even with constant cleaning.

23. *Lt.* Gerhard S. (04 601 C), Collection BfZ.

24. Sudeten Germans, also known as German Bohemians, were ethnic Germans living in the lands of the Bohemian Crown, which later became an integral part of the state of Czechoslovakia. In the Sudeten crisis of 1938, Pan-Germanist demands saw the Sudetenland annexed to Germany, a result that was later confirmed by the major powers in the Munich Agreement.

25. Johannes Hamm, Museumsstiftung Post und Telekommunikation, Berlin, 3.2002.7184.

26. Erich Dohl, Museumsstiftung Post und Telekommunikation, Berlin, 3.2009.1998.

27. Machemer and Hardinghaus (eds.), *Wofür es lohnte, das Leben zu wagen. Briefe, Fotos und Dokumente eines Truppenarztes von der Ostfront 1941/42*, 155, 162.

28. Golovchansky, Osipov, Prokopenko, Daniel and Reulecke (eds.), "Ich will raus aus diesem Wahnsinn," 47–48.

29. *Gefr.* Hans Joachim C. (06 742 C) Collection BfZ.

30. Italics in the original.

31. Urbanke and Türk, *Als Sanitätsoffizier im Rußlandfeldzug. Mit der 3. Panzer-Division bis vor Moskaus Tore*, 555.

32. *True to Type. A Selection from Letters and Diaries of German Soldiers and Civilians Collected on the Soviet-German Front*, 36–37.

33. Dollinger (ed.), *Kain, wo ist dein Bruder? Was der Mensch im Zweiten Weltkrieg erleiden musste—dokumentiert in Tagebüchern und Briefen*, 111.

34. Buchbender and Sterz (eds.), *Das andere Gesicht des Krieges*, 90.

35. *Wm.* Joseph L. (22 633 C), Collection BfZ.

36. Mühleisen (ed.), *Hellmuth Stieff Briefe*, 140.

37. Beermann (ed.), *Soldat Werner Beermann Feldpostbriefe 1941–1942*, 181.

38. The issue of inexperienced and sometimes downright incompetent Soviet officers launching wasteful frontal attacks was addressed by Marshal Zhukov, the commander of the

Western Front, who became so incensed by these massed assaults against defended German positions that he issued a special order on 9 December, which opened, "I order: 1. Categorically forbid you to conduct frontal combat with enemy covering units and to conduct frontal combat against fortified positions." As cited in Glantz, *Barbarossa*, 194. Yet the problem remained over the course of the winter and led to another order by Zhukov in March 1942, which noted, "the criminal negligent attitude of commanders of all levels to the preservation of Red Army men of the infantry." As cited in Hill, *The Great Patriotic War of the Soviet Union, 1941–45. A Documentary Reader*, 88 (Document 65).

39. The Japanese attacked Pearl Harbor on 7 December 1941.

40. *Uffz. Karl R.* (35 672), Collection BfZ.

41. Mühleisen (ed.), *Hellmuth Stieff Briefe*, 141–142.

42. This was the opening stage of what would be the Soviet winter offensive that would force withdrawals in every army of Bock's (later Kluge's) Army Group Center.

43. While the railways were the crucial artery delivering supplies to the front, the other arm of the logistical apparatus was the truck-based transport fleets (*Grosstransportraum*) bridging the railheads with the front. These motorized transport columns were already in grave difficulties even before the Soviet winter offensive, with just 15 percent of truck depots across the Eastern Front remaining operational in November 1941. As an indication of what that meant, each army would on average need to transport between 2,500 and 3,000 tons of supplies a day, but Second Panzer Army could manage just 360 tons a day, and the other armies were no better. The declining fleet of trucks was further reduced by a critical lack of antifreeze oil and "cold breaks" in the leaf springs.

44. *True to Type. A Selection from Letters and Diaries of German Soldiers and Civilians Collected on the Soviet-German Front*, 37–38.

45. Postenrieder, *Feldzug im Osten 2.8.1941–19.4.1942*, 204.

46. Prüller, *Diary of a German Soldier*, Landon and Leitner (eds.), 126.

47. On the next day (14 December), all leave was canceled, and Prüller was forced to remain with his unit for Christmas.

48. Machemer and Hardinghaus (eds.), *Wofür es lohnte, das Leben zu wagen. Briefe, Fotos und Dokumente eines Truppenarztes von der Ostfront 1941/42*, 175–177.

49. As of 1 December, the Red Army fielded some 4.2 million men, and this figure does not include the Stavka reserves. At the same time, the *Ostheer* directed barely three million men, maintained a rough parity in tanks, and fielded far fewer aircraft and artillery pieces. What was worse was that Soviet industry, even under the pressure of switching to wartime production as well as managing an unprecedented evacuation of essential industry from threatened regions, still managed to surpass Germany's year-on-year armament production. The Khar'kov tractor factory was one shining example. Having been evacuated to the Urals in October, the factory shipped its first trainload of T-34s on 8 December 1941. Indeed, Soviet tank production rose from 2,794 in 1940 to 6,590 in 1941 and 24,446 in 1942. By contrast, German output was consistently less, and in 1942 German industry was outproduced by some 15,246 Soviet tanks (a total of only 9,200 panzers were built in the course of the year). A similar pattern emerged for Soviet aircraft and artillery production, which, combined with British and American production totals, made the industrial imbalance decisive long before the supposed turning points at Stalingrad or Kursk. See table of production in Stahel, *Operation Typhoon*, 29.

50. Postenrieder, *Feldzug im Osten 2.8.1941–19.4.1942*, 204.

51. Klaus Becker, Museumsstiftung Post und Telekommunikation, Berlin, 3.2002.0224.

52. Buchbender and Sterz (eds.), *Das andere Gesicht des Krieges*, 90–91.

53. Stehmann, *Die Bitternis verschweigen wir. Feldpostbriefe 1940–1945*, 151.

54. *True to Type. A Selection from Letters and Diaries of German Soldiers and Civilians Collected on the Soviet-German Front*, 37–38.

55. The 87 Infantry Division was, in fact, not cut off.

56. Postenrieder, *Feldzug im Osten 2.8.1941-\-19.4.1942*, 212–213.

57. The Messerschmitt Bf 110 was a twin-engine heavy fighter known as a *Zerstörer* (Destroyer). It was armed with two 20mm cannons and four 7.92mm machine guns. Its aerodynamics resulted in a contested service history, which clearly worsened as the war progressed and allied fighters improved.

58. Dollinger (ed.), *Kain, wo ist dein Bruder? Was der Mensch im Zweiten Weltkrieg erleiden musste—dokumentiert in Tagebüchern und Briefen*, 111.

59. Meyer-Timpe (ed.), *"Träume recht süß von mir." Eine deutsche Freundschaft in Briefen 1940–1943*, 128.

60. Kempowski (ed.), *Das Echolot. Barbarossa '41. Ein kollektives Tagebuch*, 465–466.

APPENDIX 1

1. Megargee, *Inside Hitler's High Command*, 238; *Handbook on German Military Forces*, 5-7; Buchner, *The German Infantry Handbook 1939–1945*, 6.

APPENDIX 2

1. Glantz, *Barbarossa. Hitler's Invasion of Russia 1941*, 246–248; Boog et. al., *Das Deutsche Reich und der Zweite Weltkrieg. Bd. 4: Der Angriff auf die Sowjetunion*, 186–187; *Gliederung und Stellenbesetzung des Feldheeres, Stand: B-Tag, H.Qu. O.K.H., den 19.6.1941*, in Kurt Mehner (ed.), *Die Geheimen Tagesberichte der deutschen Wehrmachtführung im Zweiten Weltkrieg 1939–1945. Bd. III: 1. März 1941–31. Oktober 1941*.

2. The "Rear Army Area" formations were responsible for security behind the fronts of the army groups.

3. Sixth Army had temporarily assigned six of its infantry divisions to 1 Panzer Group to support the latter's breakthrough at the border; hence, its order of battle on 22 June 1941 was relatively modest.

APPENDIX 3

1. The army group was still led by GFM Fedor von Bock. Boog et al., *Germany and the Second World War*, Vol. IV: *The Attack on the Soviet Union*, 668–669; *Schematische Kriegsgliederung vom 2.10.1941 (GenSt.d.H.Op.Abt. III/Prüf.Nr.: 17 125)*, in Thies, *Der Ostfeldzug—Ein Lageatlas*.

2. The 454 Security Division was in the process of being transferred from Army Group South.

Bibliography

Archival Materials

1. NATIONAL ARCHIVES & RECORDS ADMINISTRATION (NARA) (COLLEGE PARK, MD)

a. Still Pictures Department. RG 242-GAP-286B-4: "German troops in Russia 1941"
b. Microfilm Department. RG 242: Captured German Records Microfilmed at Alexandria, VA.
   User Guides to Records of the German Field Commands

2. AIR FORCE HISTORICAL RESEARCH AGENCY (AFHRA) (MAXWELL AFB, AL)

"Berichte aus Russland Sommer 1941." (*Hauptmann Herbert Pabst. Staffelkapitän und Gruppen-kommandeur in einer Sturzkampfgruppe*) (Karlsruhe Document Collection [KDC]: G/VI/3d).
"Der Luftkrieg im Osten gegen Russland 1941." Aus einer Studie der 8. Abteilung. 1943/1944 (KDC: G/VI/3a).
"Die deutschen Flugzeugverluste im ersten Monat (22.6.41-17.7.41) des Krieges gegen Russland." Nach einer Zusammenstellung der 6. Abteilung des Generalstabes der deutschen Luftwaffe (KDC: G/VI/3a).
Plocher, Hermann. *The German Air Force Versus Russia, 1941* (No. 153, 1965).
———. *"Einsatz gegen Moskau im Jahre 1941"* (KDC).
Schwabedissen, Walter. *The Russian Air Force in the Eyes of German Commanders* (No. 175, 1960).
Suchenwirth, Richard. *Command and Leadership in the German Air Force* (No. 174, 1969).

3. US ARMY MILITARY HISTORY INSTITUTE, CARLISLE BARRACKS

(Foreign Military Studies [FMS] prepared by former *Wehrmacht* officers in late 1940s and 1950s for the US Army in Europe):

D-034: "Diseases of Men and Horses Experienced by the Troops in Russia." Dr. Erich Rendulic. 1947.

D-035: "The Effect of Extreme Cold on Weapons, Wheeled Vehicles and Track Vehicles." Dr Erich Rendulic. 1947.

D-187: "The Capture of Smolensk by the 71st Motorized Infantry Regiment on 15 July 1941." Genlt. Wilh. Thomas. 1947.

D-247: "German Preparations for the Attack against Russia (The German Build-up East of Warsaw)." Genlt. Kurt Cuno. 1947.

P-052: "Combat in Russian Forests and Swamps." Gen. Hans von Greiffenberg. 1951.

P-190: "*Verbrauchs- u. Verschleisssätze während der Operationen der deutschen. Heeresgruppe Mitte vom 22.6.41 – 31.12.41.*" Gen. Rudolf Hofmann & Genmaj. Alfred Toppe. 1953.

T-6: "Eastern Campaign, 1941–42. (Strategic Survey)." Genlt. Adolf Heusinger. 1947.

T-28: "Battle of Moscow (1941–1942)." Gen. Hans von Greiffenberg et al. n.d.

T-34: "Terrain Factors in the Russian Campaign." Gen. Karl Allmendinger et al. 1950.

4. BIBLIOTHEK FÜR ZEITGESCHICHTE (BFZ) (STUTTGART, GERMANY)

Flugblattpropaganda im 2. Weltkrieg (1941), Mappe 92-22; 92-26; 92-32; 92-36; 92-38 and 92-40.

Albert M. (05 042) (Eisb.Bau-Btl. 511)

Friedrich G. (L 29 759) (Stab/Z.G. 26)

Fw. Hans M. (28 193 B) (79 ID)

Fw. Herbert E. (07 874), (SS "DR")

Gefr. Adolf M. (05 905 D) (260 ID)

Gefr. Alfons L. (29 549) (Br.Bau-Btl. 159)

Gefr. Eberhard W. (06 323 E) (5 ID)

Gefr. Ewald M. (01 137) (125 ID)

Gefr. Ferdinand B. (19 685) (125 ID)

Gefr. Ferdinand M. (22 200) (167 ID)

Gefr. Franz B. (17 736) (198 ID)

Gefr. Fritz G. (19 768 B) (101 le.Inf.Div.)

Gefr. G. (13 517 A) (11 PD)

Gefr. Gu. (13 517 A) (11 PD)

Gefr. Hans B. (38 051) (269 ID)

Gefr. Hans F. (07 735) (Flak-Lehr-Rgt.)

Gefr. Hans Joachim C. (06 742 C) (23 ID)

Gefr. Heinz B. (05 854) (23 ID)

Gefr. Heinz B. (26 391) (291 ID)

Gefr. Heinz Sch. (20 158) (Pi.Rgts.Stab 514 z.b.V.)

Gefr. Heinz T. del B. (11 320 B) (Res.Laz. Obornik/Warthegau)

Gefr. Herbert R. (N11.15) (45 ID)

Gefr. Jean Z. (25 130) (Nb.Werf.Rgt. 51)

Gefr. Josef B. (25 144 C) (23 ID)

Gefr. Ludwig B. (04 650) (296 ID)

Gefr. Martin W. (09 378 B) (52 ID)

Gefr. Otto St. (46 010) (H.Gr.Nord)

Gefr. Paul B. (L 46 281) (Flak-Sondergeräte-Werkst.Zug 13)

Gefr. Werner R. (37 717) (Zug Art.M.P.L.715)
Gefr. Wilhelm H. (13 063) (Stab/Bau-Btl.46)
Geo. S. (18 719 A) (Art.Rgt. 70)
Hptm. Friedrich M. (20 305) (73 ID)
Lt. Ernst E. (05 714) (13 PD)
Lt. Gerhard S. (04 601 C) (29 ID [mot.])
Lt. Helmut D. (04 255 C) (4 MD)
Lt. Helmut H. (39 057) (258 ID)
Lt. Joachim H. (18 967) (131 ID)
Lt. Otto Sch. (22 353 D) (73 ID)
Lt. Willibald G. (N02.5) (57 ID)
Mj. Hans R. (21 688) (7 PD)
Mj. Hans Sch. (33 691) (H.G.Süd)
Oblt. August D. (00 319) (131 ID)
Oblt. Richard D. (35 232) (7 PD)
O.Gefr. Ferdi B. (05 261) (197 ID)
O.Gefr. Franz F. (01 096) (12 PD)
O.Gefr. Fritz N. (20 123) (35 ID)
O.Gefr. Heinz B. (05 854) (23 ID)
O.Gefr. H.S. (04 497 A) (131 ID)
O.Gefr. Joseph B. (25 341) (2 PD)
O.Gefr. Konrad F. (09 624 A) (1 ID)
O.Gefr. Werner E. (21 389) (73 ID)
Paul R. (NO2.1) (44 ID)
Peter Sch. (18 055) (19 PD)
Sold. Albrecht B. (19 997) (20 PD)
Sold. Alfred V. (42 616) (36 ID [mot.])
Sold. Carlheinz B. (25 328) (SS-Div. "Wiking" [mot.])
Sold. Hans M. (21 999 B) (262 ID)
Sold. Heinz Sch. (41 455) (101 le.ID)
Sold. Manfred V. (02 544) (32 ID)
Sold. Max Sch. (09 390 E) (17 ID)
Sold. Rudolf B. (20 149) (H.Gr.Nord)
Sold. Rudolf L. (L 35 512) (4./Ln.Rgt. 12)
Sold. Sepp P. (L 34 818) (l.Res.Flak-Abt. 717)
Sold. S.K. (16 120 C) (78 ID)
Sold. Waldo P. (11 668) (5 ID)
Sold. Werner F. (34 911) (H.Gr.Mitte)
SS-Sturmm. Eugen F. (09 239) (SS-Rgt. 4, 2. SS-Brigade [mot.])
SS-Sturmm. Hans T. (47 888) (AOK Norwegen)
St.Fw. Christoph B. (L 34 215) (Trsp.Kol.d.Lw.9/VII)
Uffz. Edmund M. (L 09 244) (Luftwaffe Flak-Rgt. 49)
Uffz. Egon N. (06 209 E) (6 ID)
Uffz. Heinz B. (29 524 C) (125 ID)
Uffz. Heinz H. (19 836) (6 ID)
Uffz. Heinz H. (28 743) (Nachsch.Btl. 563)
Uffz. Karl R. (35 672) (5 PD)
Uffz. Max F. (38 088 C) (256 ID)
Uffz. Rudolf F. (10 203) (267 ID)

Uffz. Willy P. (19 279 D) (167 ID)
Uffz. X.M. (11 800) (707 ID)
Werner R. (N97.3) (8 PD)
Willi F. (10 273 E) (198 ID)
Wm. Artur W. (21 573 B) (129 ID)
Wm. Josef L. (22 633 C) (129 ID)
Wolfgang A. (04 089) (1 ID)

5. MUSEUMSSTIFTUNG POST UND TELEKOMMUNIKATION (BERLIN, GERMANY)

Anton Böhrer, 3.2002.0889 (294 ID)
Edgar Steuerwald, 3.2002.1234 (H.Gr.Süd)
Elmar Lieb, 3.2002.7255 (2 PzGr)
Erich Dohl, 3.2009.1998 (16 Armee)
Franz Siebeler, 3.2002.1285 (14 PD)
Fritz Pabst, 3.2002.0306 (6 Armee)
Georg Fulde, 3.2002.0202 (Luftwaffe)
Gerhard Kunde, 3.2002.1941 (68 ID)
Hans Albring, 3.2002.0211 (Ostfront)
Hans Simon, 3.2002.1288 (12 ID)
H.D., 3.2002.0280 (16 PD)
Heinz Rahe, 3.2002.0985 (13 PD)
Hellmuth H., 3.2002.7139 (50 ID)
Helmut Nick, 3.2002.0274 (Ostfront)
Jakob Geimer, 3.2002.0894 (H.Gr.Süd)
Johannes Hamm, 3.2002.7184 (1 PzGr)
Karl Nünnighoff, 3.2008.1388 (16 PD)
Klaus Becker, 3.2002.0224 (H.Gr.Mitte)
Klaus K., 3.2002.0817 (H.Gr.Mitte)
Kurt Marlow, 3.2002.0884 (68 ID)
Kurt Miethke, 3.2002.0912 (H.Gr.Süd)
R.B., 3.2002.7227 (31 ID)
Rudolf Oehus, (no archive reference number) (H.Gr.Süd)
Walter Neuser, 3.2002.0947 (H.Gr.Mitte)

6. BUNDESARCHIV-MILITÄRARCHIV (BA-MA) (FREIBURG, GERMANY)

MSg 1/1147 & 1/1148, *Tagebuch Gen. Lemelsen* (*"Russlandfeldzug" Bd. I: 6. Jun-8. Okt 41 and Bd. II: 10. Okt 41-24. Apr 42*)
N 19/9, *Nachlass von Weichs. Erinnerungen, Ost-Feldzug bis Frühjahr 1942.*
RH 20-9/16: *KTB AOK 9*
RH 21-2/927: *KTB Pz.AOK 2*
RH 21-2/928: *KTB Pz.AOK 2*
RH 26-6/8: *KTB 6. Inf.-Div.*
RH 26-6/16: *Anlagenband 1 zum KTB Nr. 5 der 6. Inf.-Div.*

RH 27-1/58: *KTB 1. Pz.-Div.*
RH 27-2/22: *KTB 2. Pz.-Div.*
RH 27-7/46: *KTB 7. Pz.-Div.*
RH 27-18/20: *KTB 18. Pz.-Div.*
RH 27-19/23: *KTB 19. Pz.-Div*
RW 2/ v. 145,149,153: *Wehrmacht-Untersuchungsstelle: "Kriegsverbrechen der russischen Wehrmacht 1941/42"*

7. STAATS- U. PERSONENSTANDSARCHIV (DETMOLD, GERMANY)

D 107/56 Nr. 4: *"Aus Briefen des Adjutanten Inf.Rgt. 18, Oberleutnant Juerg von Kalckreuth."*
D 107/56 Nr. 10: KTB Inf.-Rgt. 18, *"Der russische Sommerfeldzug mit dem I.R. 18"* (15.6.-30.9.41)

8. INSTITUTE FÜR ZEITGESCHICHTE (IFZ) (MUNICH / BERLIN)

MS 506: *"Feldzug gegen Russland im Rahmen der 2. Panzer-Armee, 20.6.-4.12.1941."* Feldpost-briefe und Tagebuchnotizen Uffz. Robert Rupp.

9. THE HOOVER INSTITUTION ARCHIVES (STANFORD UNIVERSITY, PALO ALTO, CALIFORINA)

H 08-22/9: *Nachlass Generalfeldmarschall Fedor von Bock* (KTB 22.6.-5.1.42) (Copy of Bock diary from the German Federal Military Archives [BA-MA] in Freiburg, Germany.)

Primary and Secondary Sources
(Books, personal memoirs, letters, diaries—published and unpublished materials)

Adamovich, Ales, and Daniil Granin. *Leningrad under Siege. First-Hand Accounts of the Ordeal.* Barnsley, England: 2007.

Alexander, Christine, and Mark Kunze (eds.). *Eastern Inferno: The Journals of a German Pan-zerjäger on the Eastern Front, 1941–43.* Philadelphia and Newbury: 2010.

Aliev, Rostislav. *The Siege of Brest 1941. The Red Army's Stand against the Germans during Operation Barbarossa.* Mechanicsburg, PA: 2015.

Andres, Kurt Werner. "Panzersoldaten im Russlandfeldzug 1941 bis 1945. Tagebuchaufzeich-nungen und Erlebnisberichte." Unpublished manuscript; courtesy of author.

Bähr, Walter, and Dr. Hans W. Bähr (eds.). *Kriegsbriefe Gefallener Studenten, 1939–1945.* Tübingen and Stuttgart: 1952.

———. *Die Stimme des Menschen. Briefe und Aufzeichnungen aus der ganzen Welt. 1939–1945.* Munich: 1961.

Baird, Jay W. *To Die for Germany. Heroes in the Nazi Pantheon.* Bloomington, IN: 1990.

Bartov, Omer. *The Eastern Front, 1941–45, German Troops and the Barbarisation of Warfare.* London: 1985.

———. *Hitler's Army. Soldiers, Nazis, and War in the Third Reich.* Oxford: 1992.

Beak, Gisela (ed.). *Feldpostbriefe eines Landsers 1939–1943*. No place of publication: 2000.

Beermann, Hartmut (ed.). *Soldat Werner Beermann Feldpostbriefe 1941–1942*. Wrocław: 2012.

Bellamy, Chris. *Absolute War. Soviet Russia in the Second World War*. New York: 2007.

Belke, Friedrich-August. *Infanterist*. Unpublished personal memoir; courtesy of author.

Bergström, Christer. *Barbarossa—The Air Battle: July–December 1941*. Hersham, England: 2007.

Bergström, Christer, and Andrey Mikhailov. *Black Cross Red Star. Air War over the Eastern Front*. Vol. I: *Operation Barbarossa* 1941. Pacifica, CA: 2000.

———. *Black Cross Red Star. The Air War over the Eastern Front*. Vol. II: *Resurgence*, January–June 1942. Pacifica, CA: 2001.

Berkhoff, Karel C. *Harvest of Despair. Life and Death in Ukraine under Nazi Rule*. Cambridge, MA: 2004.

Bidermann, Gottlob Herbert. *In Deadly Combat. A German Soldier's Memoir of the Eastern Front*. Lawrence, KS: 2000.

Bock, Fedor von. *Generalfeldmarschall Fedor von Bock. The War Diary 1939–1945*. Klaus Gerbet (ed.). Atglen, PA: 1996.

Boog, Horst, et al. *Germany and the Second World War*, Vol. IV: *The Attack on the Soviet Union*. Oxford: 1998.

Boog, Horst, et al. *Das Deutsche Reich und der Zweite Weltkrieg*. Bd. 4: *Der Angriff auf die Sowjetunion*. Stuttgart: 1983.

Bopp, Gerhard. *Kriegstagebuch. Aufzeichnungen während des II. Weltkrieges, 1940–1943*. Hamburg: 2005.

Braithwaite, Rodric. *Moscow 1941. A City and Its People at War*. New York: 2006.

Bremer, Walter H. *Die Verlorene Jugend. Jahrgang 1923. Geschriebene und gezeichnete Skizzen über den 2. Weltkrieg und dessen Vorbereitungen*. No date or place of publication.

Buchbender, Ortwin. *Das tönende Erz. Deutsche Propaganda gegen die Rote Armee im Zweiten Weltkrieg*. Stuttgart: 1978.

Buchbender, Ortwin, and Reinhold Sterz (eds.). *Das andere Gesicht des Krieges. Deutsche Feldpostbriefe 1939–1945*. Munich: 1982.

Bücheler, Heinrich. *Hoepner. Ein deutsches Soldatenschicksal des Zwanzigsten Jahrhunderts*. Herford, Germany: 1980.

Buchner, Alex. *The German Infantry Handbook 1939–1945. Organization, Uniforms, Weapons, Equipment, Operations*. Atglen, PA: 1991.

Carney, Amy. *Marriage and Fatherhood in the Nazi SS*. Toronto: 2018.

Citino, Robert M. *The German Way of War. From the Thirty Years' War to the Third Reich*. Lawrence, KS: 2005.

Collingham, Lizzie. *The Taste of War. World War II and the Battle for Food*. New York: 2012.

Conversino, Mark J. *Fighting with the Soviets: The Failure of Operation Frantic 1944–1945*. Lawrence, KS: 1997.

Currilla, Wolfgang. *Die deutsche Ordnungspolizei und der Holocaust im Baltikum in Weissrussland*. Paderborn, Germany: 2006.

Dear, I. C. B. (ed.). *The Oxford Guide to World War II*. Oxford: 1995.

deGraffenried, Julie K. *Sacrificing Childhood. Children and the Soviet State in the Great Patriotic War*. Lawrence, KS: 2014.

Die Wehrmachtberichte 1939–1945. Bands 1–3. Munich: 1985.

DiNardo, Richard L. *Mechanized Juggernaut or Military Anachronism? Horses and the German Army of World War II*. New York: 1991.

Dinglreiter, Joseph. *Die Vierziger. Chronik des Regiments*. Published by the *Kameradschaft Regiment 40*. Augsburg, Germany: n.d.

Dollinger, Hans (ed.). *Kain, wo ist dein Bruder? Was der Mensch im Zweiten Weltkrieg erleiden musste—dokumentiert in Tagebüchern und Briefen*. Munich: 1983.

Domarus, Max. *Hitler: Speeches and Proclamations 1932–1945. The Chronicle of a Dictatorship. Volume IV. The Years 1941 to 1945*. Wauconda, IL: 2004.

Duesel, Dr. Hans H. (ed.). *Gefallen! . . . und umsonst—Erlebnisberichte deutscher Soldaten im Russlandkrieg 1941–1945*. Privately published, 1993.

Dunn, Walter S., Jr. *Stalin's Keys to Victory: The Rebirth of the Red Army*. Westport, CT: 2006.

Echternkamp, Jorg, et al. *Germany and the Second World War*, Vol. 9/II: *German Wartime Society 1939–1945: Exploitation, Interpretations, Exclusion*. Oxford: 2014.

Edele, Mark. *Stalin's Defectors. How Red Army Soldiers Became Hitler's Collaborators, 1941–1945*. Oxford: 2017.

Ehrenburg, Ilya. *Russia at War*. London: 1943.

Ellis, Frank. *Barbarossa 1941. Reframing Hitler's Invasion of Stalin's Soviet Empire*. Lawrence, KS: 2015.

Elmshäuser, Konrad, and Jan Lokers (eds.). *"Man muss hier nur hart sein." Kriegsbriefe und Bilder einer Familie (1934–1945)*. Bremen, Germany: 1999.

Filippenkov, Michael. *Konev's Golgotha. Operation Typhoon Strikes the Soviet Western Front, October 1941*. Solihull, England: 2016.

Forczyk, Robert A. *Tank Warfare on the Eastern Front 1941–42*. New York and London: 2013.

———. *Panzerjäger vs KV-1. Eastern Front 1941–43*. Oxford: 2012.

Fritz, Stephen G. *Frontsoldaten. The German Soldier in World War II*. Lexington, KY: 1995.

Fritzsche, Peter. *Life and Death in the Third Reich*. Cambridge, MA: 2008.

Fröhlich. Elke (ed.). *Die Tagebücher von Joseph Goebbels, Teil I: Aufzeichnungen 1923–1941*, Vol. 9. Munich: 1998.

———. *Die Tagebücher von Joseph Goebbels, Teil II: Diktate 1941–1945*, Vol. 2. Munich: 1996.

Fuchs Richardson, Horst (ed.). *Your Loyal and Loving Son. The Letters of Tank Gunner Karl Fuchs, 1937–41*. Dulles, VA: 1987.

———. *Sieg Heil! War Letters of Tank Gunner Karl Fuchs 1937–1941*. Hamden, CT: 1987.

———. *Your Loyal and Loving Son. The Letters of Tank Gunner Karl Fuchs, 1937–41*. Washington, DC: 2003.

Garden, David, and Kenneth Andrew (eds.). *The War Diaries of a Panzer Soldier. Erich Hager with the 17th Panzer Division on the Russian Front 1941–1945*. Atglen, PA: 2010.

Gilbert, Martin. *Second World War*. Toronto: 1989.

———. *The Holocaust. The Jewish Tragedy*. London: 1986.

Glantz, David M. *Soviet Military Deception in the Second World War*. London: 1989.

———. *Forgotten Battles of the German-Soviet War (1941–1945)*. Vol. I: *The Summer-Fall Campaign (22 June–4 December 1941)*. Privately published: 1999.

———. *Barbarossa. Hitler's Invasion of Russia 1941*. Charleston, SC: 2001.

———. *Atlas and Operational Summary. The Border Battles 22 June–1 July 1941*. Privately published: 2003.

———. *Colossus Reborn. The Red Army at War, 1941–1943*. Lawrence, KS: 2005.

———. *Barbarossa Derailed. The Battle for Smolensk 10 July–10 September 1941*, Vol. I: *The German Advance to Smolensk, the Encirclement Battle, and the First and Second Soviet Counteroffensives, 10 July–24 August 1941*. Solihull, England: 2010.

Glantz, David M., and Jonathan House. *When Titans Clashed. How the Red Army Stopped Hitler*. Lawrence, KS: 2015.

Golovchansky, Anatoly, Valentin Osipov, Anatoly Prokopenko, Ute Daniel and Jürgen Reulecke (eds.). *"Ich will raus aus diesem Wahnsinn." Deutsche Briefe von der Ostfront 1941–1945. Aus sowjetischen Archiven.* Hamburg: 1993.

Gorodetsky, Gabriel. *Grand Delusion. Stalin and the German Invasion of Russia.* New Haven, CT: 1999.

Grossmann, Horst. *Die Geschichte der rheinisch-westfälischen 6. Infanterie-Division 1939–1945. Dörfler Zeitgeschichte,* n.d. (First published 1958.)

Gschöpf, Dr. Rudolf. *Mein Weg mit der 45. Inf.-Div.* Nürnberg: 2002. (First published 1955.)

Guderian, Heinz. *Erinnerungen eines Soldaten.* Heidelberg, Germany: 1951.

———. *Panzer Leader.* New York: 1952.

Günther, Helmut. *Hot Motors, Cold Feet. A Memoir of Service with the Motorcycle Battalion of SS-Division "Reich" 1940–1941.* Winnipeg: 2004.

Haape, Dr. Heinrich. *Moscow Tram Stop. A Doctor's Experiences with the German Spearhead in Russia.* C. W. H. Luther (ed.). Guilford, CT: 2020.

———. *Feldpostbriefe.* Courtesy of Johannes Haape.

Hahn, Jochen. *"Feldzug gegen Russland."* Collection of field post letters; courtesy of R. Mobius.

Halder, Franz. *Kriegstagebuch: Tägliche Aufzeichnungen des Chefs des Generalstabes des Heeres 1939–1942,* Bd. II: *Von der geplanten Landung in England bis zum Beginn des Ostfeldzuges (1.7.1940–21.6.1941),* Hans-Adolf Jacobsen and Alfred Philippi (eds.). Stuttgart: 1963.

———. *Kriegstagebuch: Tägliche Aufzeichnungen des Chefs des Generalstabes des Heeres 1939–1942,* Bd. III: *Der Russlandfeldzug bis zum Marsch auf Stalingrad (22.6.1941–24.9.1942),* Hans-Adolf Jacobsen and Alfred Philippi (eds.). Stuttgart: 1964.

———. *The Halder War Diary 1939–1942,* Charles B. Burdick and Hans-Adolf Jacobsen (eds.). Novato: 1988.

Hammer, Ingrid, and Susanne zur Nieden (eds.). *Sehr selten habe ich geweint. Briefe und Tagebücher aus dem Zweiten Weltkrieg von Menschen aus Berlin.* Zurich: 1992.

Handbook on German Military Forces. Baton Rouge, LA: 1990. Originally published by US War Department as TM-E 30-451 (March 1945).

Hart, Dr. S., and Dr. R. Hart and Dr. M. Hughes. *The German Soldier in World War II.* Osceola: 2000.

Hartmann, Christian. *Wehrmacht im Ostkrieg: Front und militärisches Hinterland 1941/42.* Munich: 2009.

Haupt, Werner. *Die Schlachten der Heeresgruppe Süd. Aus der Sicht der Divisionen.* Friedberg, Germany: 1985.

———. *Heeresgruppe Nord 1941–1945.* Bad Nauheim, Germany: 1966.

———. *Army Group South. The Wehrmacht in Russia 1941–1945.* Atglen, PA: 1998.

———. *Army Group North. The Wehrmacht in Russia 1941–1945.* Atglen, PA: 1997.

———. *Army Group Center. The Wehrmacht in Russia 1941–1945.* Atglen, PA: 1997.

———. *Die deutschen Infanterie-Divisionen. Dörfler Zeitgeschichte,* n.d.

Heinemann, Werner. *Pflicht und Schuldigkeit. Betrachtungen eines Frontoffiziers im Zweiten Weltkrieg.* Berlin: 2010.

———. *Feldpostbriefe.* Collection of field post letters; courtesy of his daughter, Birgit Heinemann.

Herbert, Ulrich. *Hitler's Foreign Workers. Enforced Foreign Labor in Germany under the Third Reich.* Cambridge: 1997.

Hill, Alexander. *The Great Patriotic War of the Soviet Union, 1941–45. A Documentary Reader.* Abingdon, England: 2010.

Hinze, Rolf. *Hitze, Frost und Pulverdampf. Der Schicksalsweg der 20. Panzer-Division.* Meerbusch: 1996. (6. Auflage)

————. *19. Infanterie- und Panzer-Division. Divisionsgeschichte aus der Sicht eines Artilleristen.* Düsseldorf: 1997.

————. *Die 19. Panzer-Division. Bewaffnung, Einsätze, Männer. Einsatz 1941–1945 in Russland.* Dörfler Zeitgeschichte, n.d.

Hirt, Alexander. *"Die Heimat reicht der Front die Hand." Kulturelle Truppenbetreuung im Zweiten Weltkrieg 1939–1945. Ein deutsch-englischer Vergleich* (PhD dissertation submitted to the Georg-August University, Göttingen, 2008).

Hoth, Hermann. *Panzer-Operationen. Die Panzergruppe 3 und der operative Gedanke der deutschen Führung Sommer 1941.* Heidelberg: 1956.

Hubatsch, Walther (ed.). *Hitlers Weisungen für die Kriegsführung 1939–1945. Dokumente des Oberkommandos der Wehrmacht.* Frankfurt: 1962.

Humberg, Martin. *Das Gesicht des Krieges. Feldpostbriefe von Wehrmachtssoldaten aus der Sowjetunion 1941–1944.* Wiesbaden: 1998.

Hürter, Johannes (ed.). *Ein deutscher General an der Ostfront. Die Briefe und Tagebücher des Gotthard Heinrici 1941/42.* Erfurt, Germany: 2001.

Jacobsen, Hans-Adolf (ed.). *Kriegstagebuch des OKW (WFSt.), Bd. I: 1. August 1940–31. Dezember 1941.* Frankfurt: 1965.

Jackson, David A., and Klaus Böhme (eds.). *"Beim Militär hat man immer sein Totenhemd an . . . ": Feldpostbriefe von drei gefallenen Brüdern aus dem Odenwald 1939–1944.* Bickenbach, Germany: 2005.

Jarausch, Konrad H. (ed.). *Reluctant Accomplice. A Wehrmacht Soldier's Letters from the Eastern Front.* Princeton, NJ: 2011.

Jentz, Thomas L. (ed.). *Panzer Truppen. The Complete Guide to the Creation and Combat Employment of Germany's Tank Force, 1933–1942.* Atglen, PA: 1996.

Johnson, Eric A., and Karl-Heinz Reuband. *What We Knew. Terror, Mass Murder, and Everyday Life in Nazi Germany.* Cambridge, MA: 2005.

Jones, Michael. *The Retreat. Hitler's First Defeat.* London: 2009.

Kallis, Aristotle A. *Nazi Propaganda and the Second World War.* New York: 2005.

Kaltenegger, Roland. *Die Stammdivision der deutschen Gebirgstruppe. Weg und Kampf der 1. Gebirgs-Division 1935–1945.* Graz-Stuttgart: 1981.

Kassimeris, George (ed.). *The Barbarization of Warfare.* New York: 2006.

Kay, Alex J. *Exploitation, Resettlement, Mass Murder. Political and Economic Planning for German Occupation Policy in the Soviet Union, 1940–1941.* Oxford: 2006.

Keegan, John. *The Second World War.* New York: 1989.

Keilig, Wolf. *Das Deutsche Heer 1939–1945. Gliederung, Einsatz, Stellenbesetzung.* Bad Nauheim, Germany: 1956.

Kempowski, Walter (ed.). *Das Echolot. Barbarossa '41. Ein kollektives Tagebuch.* Munich: 2002.

Kershaw, Ian. *Hitler 1936–1945: Nemesis.* New York: 2000.

Kershaw, Robert J. *War Without Garlands. Operation Barbarossa 1941/42.* New York: 2000.

Kesselring, Albert. *Soldat Bis Zum Letzten Tag.* Bonn: 1953.

Kipp, Michaela. *Großreinemachen im Osten. Feindbilder in deutschen Feldpostbriefen im Zweiten Weltkrieg.* Frankfurt: 2014.

Kirchubel, Robert. *Operation Barbarossa 1941 (1): Army Group South.* Oxford: 2003.

————. *Operation Barbarossa 1941 (2). Army Group North.* Oxford: 2005.

————. *Operation Barbarossa 1941 (3). Army Group Center.* New York: 2007.

————. *Hitler's Panzer Armies on the Eastern Front.* Barnsley, England: 2009.

————. *Atlas of the Eastern Front 1941–45.* Oxford: 2016.

Klee, Ernst, Willi Dressen and Volker Riess (eds.). *"The Good Old Days." The Holocaust as Seen by Its Perpetrators and Bystanders.* Old Saybrook, CT: 1991.

Klein, Peter (ed.). *Die Einsatzgruppen in der besetzten Sowjetunion 1941/42. Die Tätigkeits- und Lageberichte des Chefs der Sicherheitspolizei und des SD.* Berlin: 1997.

Kleindienst, Jürgen (ed.). *Sei tausendmal gegrüßt. Briefwechsel Irene und Ernst Guicking 1937–1945.* Berlin: 2001.

Knappe, Siegfried (with Ted Brusaw). *Soldat. Reflections of a German Soldier, 1936–1949.* New York: 1992.

Koch, Magnus. *Fahnenfluchten. Deserteure der Wehrmacht in Zweiten Weltkrieg—Lebenswege und Entscheidungen.* Paderborn, Germany: 2008.

König, Franz (ed.). *Ganz in Gottes Hand. Briefe Gefallener und Hingerichteter Katholiken 1939–1945.* Vienna: 1957.

Kreuter, Georg. *Persönliches Tagebuch.* Unpublished diary; courtesy of Klaus Schumann.

Krivosheev, G. F. (ed.). *Soviet Casualties and Combat Losses in the Twentieth Century.* London: 1997.

Krylova, Anna. *Soviet Women in Combat. A History of Violence on the Eastern Front.* Cambridge: 2010.

Kühne, Thomas. *The Rise and Fall of Comradeship. Hitler's Soldiers, Male Bonding and Mass Violence in the Twentieth Century.* Cambridge: 2017.

Kurowski, Franz. *Balkenkreuz und Roter Stern. Der Luftkrieg über Russland 1941–1944.* Friedberg, Germany: 1984.

Kummer, Kurt. *Tagebuch.* Unpublished diary; courtesy of Christoph Nehring.

Latzel, Klaus. *Deutsche Soldaten—nationalsozialistischer Krieg? Kriegserlebnis—Kriegserfahrung 1939–1945.* Paderborn, Germany: 1998.

Letzte Lebenszeichen. Briefe aus dem Krieg. Published by the German War Graves Commission (*Volksbund Deutsche Kriegsgräberfürsorge e.V.*). Kassel, Germany: 2010.

Liddell Hart, Basil. *The Other Side of the Hill.* London: 1999.

Lierow, Dr. Hans. *Persönliches Tagebuch.* Unpublished diary; courtesy of his son, Dr. Med. Konrad Lierow-Mueller.

Liulevicius, Vejas G. *The German Myth of the East. 1800 to the Present.* Oxford: 2009.

Longerich, Peter. *The Unwritten Order. Hitler's Role in the Final Solution.* Stroud, England: 2005.

Lopukhovsky, Lev. *The Viaz'ma Catastrophe, 1941. The Red Army's Disastrous Stand against Operation Typhoon.* Solihull, England: 2013.

Lopukhovsky, Lev, and Boris Kavalerchik. *The Price of Victory. The Red Army's Casualties in the Great Patriotic War.* Barnsley, England: 2017.

Lubbeck, William with David B. Hurt. *At Leningrad's Gates. The Story of a Soldier with Army Group North.* Philadelphia: 2006.

Luther, Craig W. H. *The First Day on the Eastern Front: Germany Invades the Soviet Union, June 22, 1941.* Guilford, CT: 2018.

———. *Barbarossa Unleashed. The German Blitzkrieg through Central Russia to the Gates of Moscow. June–December 1941.* Atglen, PA: 2013.

Machemer, Hans, and Christian Hardinghaus (eds.). *Wofür es lohnte, das Leben zu wagen. Briefe, Fotos und Dokumente eines Truppenarztes von der Ostfront 1941/42.* Berlin: 2018.

Magenheimer, Heinz. *Moskau 1941. Entscheidungsschlacht im Osten.* Selent, Germany: 2009.

Mallmann, Klaus M., Andrej Angrick, Jürgen Matthäus and Martin Cüppers (eds.). *Die "Ereignismeldung UdSSR" 1941: Dokumente der Einsatzgruppen in der Sowjetunion.* Darmstadt, Germany: 2011.

Manoschek, Walter (ed.). *"Es gibt nur eines für das Judentum: Vernichtung." Das Judenbild in deutschen Soldatenbriefen 1939–1944.* Hamburg: 1995.

Manstein, Erich von. *Verlorene Siege.* Bonn: 1998.

————. *Lost Victories*. Novato: 1984.

Markwick, Roger D., and Euridice Charon Cardona. *Soviet Women on the Frontline in the Second World War*. London: 2012.

Maurer, Karl-Wilhelm. *Die hessisch-thüringische 251. Infanterie-Division: wird im Zweiten Weltkrieg vom Jäger zum Gejagten*. Norderstedt, Germany: 2008.

Maurer, Rudolf. *Tagebuch, Notizbuch, Feldpostbriefe*. Courtesy of Karl-Wilhelm Maurer.

Mawdsley, Evan. *Thunder in the East. The Nazi-Soviet War 1941–1945*. London: 2005.

Megargee, Geoffrey P. *Inside Hitler's High Command*. Lawrence, KS: 2000.

————. *War of Annihilation. Combat and Genocide on the Eastern Front, 1941*. Oxford: 2006.

Mehner, Kurt (ed.). *Die Geheimen Tagesberichte der deutschen Wehrmachtführung im Zweiten Weltkrieg 1939–1945*. Bd. III: 1. März 1941–31. Oktober 1941. Osnabrück: 1992.

Meier-Welcker, Hans. *Aufzeichnungen eines Generalstabsoffiziers 1939–1942*. Freiburg: 1982.

Mellinger, George. *Soviet Lend-Lease Fighter Aces of World War 2*. Oxford: 2006.

Merridale, Catherine. *Ivan's War. Life and Death in the Red Army, 1939–1945*. New York: 2006.

Messenger, Charles. *The Last Prussian. A Biography of Field Marshal Gerd von Rundstedt*. Barnsley, England: 2011.

Meyer-Detring, Wilhelm. *Die 137. Infanterie-Division im Mittelabschnitt der Ostfront*. Dörfler Zeitgeschichte, n.d. (First published, *Verlag der Kameradschaft* 137. I.D., 1962.)

Meyer-Timpe, Ulrike (ed). *"Träume recht süß von mir": Eine deutsche Freundschaft in Briefen 1940–1943*. Frankfurt: 2004.

Moutier, Marie (ed.). *"Liebste Schwester, wir müssen hier sterben oder siegen." Briefe deutscher Wehrmachtssoldaten 1939–45*. Munich: 2015.

Mühleisen, Horst (ed.). *Hellmuth Stieff Briefe*. Berlin: 1991.

Müller-Hillebrand, Burkhart. *Das Heer 1933–1945*, Bd. III: *Der Zweifrontenkrieg. Das Heer vom Beginn des Feldzuges gegen die Sowjetunion bis zum Kriegsende*. Frankfurt: 1969.

Muller, Richard. *The German Air War in Russia*. Baltimore: 1992.

Müller, Rolf-Dieter, and Gerd R. Ueberschär. *Hitler's War in the East 1941–1945. A Critical Assessment*. Oxford: 2009.

Müller, Sven Oliver. *Deutsche Soldaten und ihre Feinde. Nationalismus an Front und Heimatfront im Zweiten Weltkrieg*. Frankfurt: 2007.

Murray, Williamson, and Allan R. Millett. *A War to Be Won. Fighting the Second World War, 1937–1945*. Uncorrected page proof, 2000.

Mutzenbecher, Geert-Ulrich. *Feldpostbriefe an meine Eltern: 1941–1945*. Oldenburg, Germany: 2009.

Nafziger, George F. *The German Order of Battle. Panzers and Artillery in World War II*. London: 1999.

————. *The German Order of Battle. Infantry in World War II*. London: 2000.

————. *The German Order of Battle. Waffen SS and Other Units in World War II*. London: 2001.

Nehring, Walther K. *Die Geschichte der deutschen Panzerwaffe 1916–1945*. Stuttgart: 2000.

Neitzel, Sönke, and Harald Welzer. *Soldaten. On Fighting, Killing and Dying: The Secret World War II Tapes of German POWs*. London: 2011.

Oberkommando der Wehrmacht (ed.). *Kampf gegen die Sowjets. Berichte und Bilder vom Beginn des Ostfeldzuges bis zum Frühjahr 1942*. Berlin: 1943.

Overmans, Rüdiger. *Deutsche militärische Verluste im Zweiten Weltkrieg*. Munich: 2004.

Overy, Richard. *Russia's War*. London: 1997.

Pabst, Helmut. *The Outermost Frontier: A German Soldier in the Russian Campaign*. London: 1957.

Paul, Wolfgang. *Geschichte der 18. Panzer-Division 1940–1943.* n.p.: 1989.

Piekalkiewicz, Janusz. *Moscow 1941. The Frozen Offensive.* London: 1981.

Pietrow-Ennker, Bianka (ed.). *Präventivkrieg? Der deutsche Angriff auf die Sowjetunion.* Frankfurt: 2011.

Pine, Lisa. *Hitler's "National Community." Society and Culture in Nazi Germany.* London: 2017.

Pleshakov, Constantine. *Stalin's Folly. The Tragic First Ten Days of WWII on the Eastern Front.* Boston: 2005.

Pohl, Dieter. *Die Herrschaft der Wehrmacht: Deutsche Militärbesatzung und einheimische Bevölkerung in der Sowjetunion 1941–1944.* Nördlingen, Germany: 2011.

Pöppel, Martin. *Heaven and Hell. The War Diary of a German Paratrooper.* Staplehurst, England: 1996.

Postenrieder, Heinz. *Feldzug im Osten 2.8.1941–19.4.1942.* n.p.: 2010.

Prüller, Wilhelm. *Diary of a German Soldier.* H. C. Robbins Landon and Sebastian Leitner (eds.). New York: 1963.

Rass, Christoph. *"Menschenmaterial." Deutsche Soldaten an der Ostfront: Innenansichten einer Infanteriedivision 1939–1945.* Paderborn, Germany: 2003.

Reddemann, Karl (ed.). *Zwischen Front und Heimat. Der Briefwechsel des münsterischen Ehepaares Agnes and Albert Neuhaus 1940–1944.* Münster, Regensberg: 1996.

Reese, Roger R. *Why Stalin's Soldiers Fought.* Lawrence, KS: 2011.

Reese, Willy Peter. *A Stranger to Myself.* New York: 2005.

Reinhardt, Klaus. *Moscow—The Turning Point. The Failure of Hitler's Strategy in the Winter of 1941–42.* Oxford: 1992.

———. *Die Wende vor Moskau. Das Scheitern der Strategie Hitlers im Winter 1941/42.* Stuttgart: 1972.

Rhein, Ernst-Martin. *Das Rheinisch-Westfälische Infanterie-/Grenadier-Regiment 18 1921–1945.* Privately published, 1993.

Richardson, William, and Seymour Freidin (eds.). *The Fatal Decisions.* London: 1956.

Risse, S. *"Das IR 101 und der 2. Weltkrieg."* Unpublished report; courtesy of Klaus Schumann.

Römer, Felix. *Der Kommissarbefehl. Wehrmacht und NS-Verbrechen an der Ostfront 1941/42.* Paderborn, Germany: 2008.

Rossi, Lauren Faulkner. *Wehrmacht Priests. Catholicism and the Nazi War of Annihilation.* Cambridge: 2015.

Rubenstein, Joshua, and Ilya Altman (eds.). *The Unknown Black Book. The Holocaust in the German-Occupied Soviet Territories.* Bloomington, IN: 2008.

Rühle, Brunhild (ed.). *Die Feldpostbriefe des Adelbert-Ottheinrich Rühle 1939 bis 1942.* Heusenstamm, Germany: 1979.

Rundbrief Nr. 50, Traditionsverband Inf.Rgt. 37/184/474. Osnabrück, Germany: 1993. Courtesy of G. Wegmann.

Rutherford, Jeff. *Combat and Genocide on the Eastern Front. The German Infantry's War, 1941–1944.* Cambridge: 2014.

Rutherford, Jeff, and Adrian Wettstein. *The German Army on the Eastern Front. An Inner View of the Ostheer's Experiences of War.* Barnsley, England: 2018.

Sahm, Christiane (ed.). *Verzweiflung und Glaube. Briefe aus dem Krieg 1939–1942.* Munich: 2007.

Scheuer, Günter (ed.). *Briefe aus Russland. Feldpostbriefe des Gefreiten Alois Scheuer 1941–1942.* St. Ingbert, Germany: 2001.

Schick, Albert. *Die 10. Panzer-Division 1939–1943.* Cologne: 1993.

Schneider-Janessen, Karlheinz. *Arzt im Krieg. Wie deutsche und russische Ärzte den zweiten Weltkrieg erlebten.* Frankfurt: 2001.

Seaton, Albert. *The Russo-German War 1941–1945*. London: 1971.

———. *The German Army 1933–45*. New York: 1982.

Sebastian, Mihail. *Journal, 1935–1944*. London: 2003.

Shepherd, Ben. *War in the Wild East. The German Army and Soviet Partisans*. Cambridge, MA: 2004.

———. *Hitler's Soldiers. The German Army in the Third Reich*. New Haven, CT: 2016.

Showalter, Dennis. *Hitler's Panzers. The Lightning Attacks that Revolutionized Warfare*. New York: 2009.

Slepyan, Kenneth. *Stalin's Guerrillas. Soviet Partisans in World War II*. Lawrence, KS: 2006.

Snyder, Louis L. *Encyclopedia of the Third Reich*. Hertfordshire, Great Britain: 1998.

Spaeter, Helmuth. *Die Geschichte des Panzerkorps Grossdeutschland*, Bd. I. Privately published, 1958.

Stader, Ingo (ed.). *Ihr daheim und wir hier draussen. Ein Briefwechsel zwischen Ostfront und Heimat, Juni 1941–März 1943*. Cologne: 2006.

Stahel, David. *Operation Barbarossa and Germany's Defeat in the East*. Cambridge: 2009.

———. *Kiev 1941. Hitler's Battle for Supremacy in the East*. Cambridge: 2012.

———. *Operation Typhoon. Hitler's March on Moscow, October 1941*. Cambridge: 2013.

———. *The Battle for Moscow*. Cambridge: 2015.

Stahel, David (ed.). *Joining Hitler's Crusade. European Nations and the Invasion of the Soviet Union*. Cambridge: 2018.

Stargardt, Nicholas. *The German War. A Nation under Arms, 1939–1945*. New York: 2015.

Stehmann, Siegbert (Gerhard Sprenger, ed.). *Die Bitternis verschweigen wir. Feldpostbriefe 1940–1945*. Hannover: 1992.

Steinert, Marlis G. *Hitler's War and the Germans. Public Mood and Attitude during the Second World War*. Ohio: 1977.

Stites, Richard (ed.). *Culture and Entertainment in Wartime Russia*. Bloomington, IN: 1995.

Streit, Christian. *Keine Kameraden. Die Wehrmacht und die sowjetischen Kriegsgefangenen, 1941–1945*. Bonn: 1997.

Stützel, Rudolf. *Feldpost. Briefe und Aufzeichnungen eines 17-Jährigen 1940–1945*. Hamburg: 2005.

Thies, Klaus-Jürgen. *Der Zweite Weltkrieg im Kartenbild*, Bd. 5: Teil 1:1: *Der Ostfeldzug Heeresgruppe Mitte 21.6.1941-6.12.1941. Ein Lageatlas der Operationsabteilung des Generalstabes des Heeres*. Bissendorf, Germany: 2001.

Tilemann, Walter. *Ich, das Soldatenkind*. Munich: 2005.

True to Type. A Selection from Letters and Diaries of German Soldiers and Civilians Collected on the Soviet-German Front. London. This book makes no reference to its editor or date of publication.

Trevor-Roper, H. R. (ed.). *Hitler's War Directives 1939–1945*. London: 1964.

Tsouras, Peter G. (ed.). *Fighting in Hell. The German Ordeal on the Eastern Front*. New York: 1995.

Ueberschär, Gerd R., and Wolfram Wette (eds.). *"Unternehmen Barbarossa." Der deutsche Überfall auf die Sowjetunion 1941*. Paderborn, Germany: 1984.

Ueberschär, Gerd R., and Lev A. Bezymenskij (eds.). *Der deutsche Angriff auf die Sowjetunion 1941. Die Kontroverse um die Präventivkriegsthese*. Darmstadt, Germany: 1998.

Urbanke, Axel, and Hermann Türk. *Als Sanitätsoffizier im Rußlandfeldzug. Mit der 3. Panzer-Division bis vor Moskaus Tore*. Bad Zwischenahn, Germany: 2016.

Vaizey, Hester. *Surviving Hitler's War. Family Life in Germany, 1939–48*. London: 2010.

Vierkorn, Karl-Gottfried. *Feldpostbriefe*. Courtesy of author.

Wagner, Elisabeth (ed.). *Der Generalquartiermeister. Briefe und Tagebuchaufzeichnungen des Generalquartiermeisters des Heeres General der Artillerie Eduard Wagner.* Munich: 1963.

Wegner, Bernd (ed.). *Zwei Wege nach Moskau. Vom Hitler-Stalin-Pakt bis zum "Unternehmen Barbarossa."* Munich: 1991.

Welch, David. *The Third Reich: Politics and Propaganda.* London: 1993.

Wessler, Wilhelm. *Tagebuch.* Unpublished diary; courtesy of author.

Wette, Wolfram. *The Wehrmacht. History, Myth, Reality.* Cambridge, MA: 2006.

Wettstein, Adrian. *Die Wehrmacht in Stadtkampf.* Paderborn, Germany: 2014.

Will, Otto. *Tagebuch eines Ostfront-Kämpfers. Mit der 5. Panzerdivision im Einsatz 1941–1945.* Selent, Germany: 2010.

Winchester, Charles D. *Hitler's War on Russia.* Oxford: 2007.

Woche, Klaus-R. *Zwischen Pflicht und Gewissen. Generaloberst Rudolf Schmidt 1886–1957.* Berlin-Potsdam: 2002.

Wray, Major Timothy A. *Standing Fast: German Defensive Doctrine on the Russian Front during World War II. Prewar to March 1943.* Fort Leavenworth, KS: 1986.

Ziemke, Earl F. *The Red Army 1918–1941. From Vanguard of World Revolution to US Ally.* London: 2004.

Ziemke, Earl F., and Magna E. Bauer. *Moscow to Stalingrad: Decision in the East.* New York: 1988.

Articles and Essays

Assmann, Vice Admiral Kurt. "The Battle for Moscow. The Turning Point of the War," in *Foreign Affairs,* January 1950.

Beyda, Oleg. "'Iron Cross of the Wrangel's Army': Russian Emigrants as Interpreters in the Wehrmacht," in *The Journal of Slavic Military History,* vol. 27, no. 3, July 2014.

Beyda, Oleg, and Igor Petrov. "The Soviet Union," in *Joining Hitler's Crusade. European Nations and the Invasion of the Soviet Union, 1941.* Cambridge: 2018.

Edele, Mark. "Take (No) Prisoners! The Red Army and German POWs 1941–1943," in *The Journal of Modern History,* no. 88, June 2016.

Förster, Jürgen. "Zum Russlandbild der Militärs 1941–1945," in Hans-Erich Volkmann (ed.), *Das Russlandbild im Dritten Reich.* Cologne: 1994.

Fritze, Lothar. "Did the National Socialists Have a Different Morality?," in Wolfgang Bialas and Lothar Fritze (eds.), *Nazi Ideology and Ethics.* Newcastle upon Tyne: 2014.

"Gegen Kritik immun," interview by Gerhard Spörl and Klaus Wiegrefe, in *Der Spiegel,* 23/1999.

Gerlach, Christian. "Hitlergegner bei der Heeresgruppe Mitte und die 'verbrecherischen Befehle,'" in Gerd R. Ueberschär (ed.), *NS-Verbrechen und der militärische Widerstand gegen Hitler.* Darmstadt, Germany: 2000.

———. "Men of 20 July and the War in the Soviet Union," in Hannes Heer and Klaus Naumann (eds.), *War of Extermination: The German Military in World War II 1941–1944.* New York/Oxford: 2006.

Hagelstam, Sonja. "Families, Separation and Emotional Coping in War: Bridging Letters Between Home and Front, 1941–44," in Tiina Kinnunen and Ville Kivimäki (eds.), *Finland in World War II. History, Memory, Interpretations.* Boston: 2012.

Heer, Hannes. "How Amorality Became Normality: Reflections on the Mentality of German Soldiers on the Eastern Front," in Hannes Heer and Klaus Naumann (eds.), *War of Extermination. The German Military in World War II 1941–1944*. New York/Oxford: 2006.

Herzog, Dagmar. "Hubris and Hypocrisy, Incitement and Disavowal: Sexuality and German Fascism," in Dagmar Herzog (ed.), *Sexuality and German Fascism*. New York: 2005.

Hill, Alexander. "British Lend-Lease Aid and the Soviet War Effort, June 1941–June 1942," in *The Journal of Military History*, vol. 71, no. 3, July 2007.

Hillgruber, Andreas. "The German Military Leaders' View of Russia Prior to the Attack on the Soviet Union," in Bernd Wegner (ed.), *From Peace to War. Germany, Soviet Russia and the World, 1939–1941*. Oxford: 1997.

Humberg, Martin. "Die Bedeutung der Feldpost für die Soldaten in Stalingrad," in Wolfram Wette and Gerd R. Ueberschär (eds.), *Stalingrad. Mythos und Wirklichkeit einer Schlacht*. Frankfurt: 2012.

Hürter, Johannes. "Auf dem Weg zur Militäropposition. Tresckow, Gersdorff, der Vernichtungskrieg und der Judenmord. Neue Dokumente über das Verhältnis der Heeresgruppe Mitte zur Einsatzgruppe B im Jahr 1941," in *Vierteljahreshefte für Zeitgeschichte*, vol. 52, no. 3, 2004.

Kay, Alex J., and David Stahel. "Reconceiving Criminality in the German Army on the Eastern Front, 1941–1942," in Alex J. Kay and David Stahel (eds.), *Mass Violence in Nazi Occupied Europe*. Bloomington, IN: 2018.

Kilian, Katrin. "Postal Censorship from 1939 to 1945," at http://www.feldpost-archiv.de /english/e11-zensur.html.

———. "Moods in Wartime: The Emotions Expressed in Forces Mail," in Jorg Echternkamp et al., *Germany and the Second World War*. Volume IX/II: *German Wartime Society 1939–1945: Exploitation, Interpretations, Exclusion*. Oxford: 2014.

Kühne, Thomas. "Gruppenkohäsion und Kameradschaftsmythos in der Wehrmacht," in Rolf-Dieter Müller and Hans-Erich Volkmann (eds.), *Die Wehrmacht. Mythos und Realität*. Munich: 1999.

———. "Male Bonding and Shame Culture: Hitler's Soldiers and the Moral Basis of Genocidal Warfare," in Olaf Jensen and Claus-Christian W. Szejnmann (eds.), *Ordinary People as Mass Murderers. Perpetrators in Comparative Perspectives*. New York: 2008.

Latzel, Klaus. "Wehrmachtsoldaten zwischen 'Normalität' und NS-Ideologie, oder: Was sucht die Forschung in der Feldpost?" in Rolf-Dieter Müller and Hans-Erich Volkmann (eds.), *Die Wehrmacht. Mythos und Realität*. Munich: 1999.

———. "Feldpostbriefe: Überlegungen zur Aussagekraft einer Quelle," in Christian Hartmann, Johannes Hürter and Ulrike Jureit (eds.), *Verbrechen der Wehrmacht. Bilanz einer Debatte*. Munich: 2005.

Luther, Craig. "German Armoured Operations in the Ukraine 1941: The Encirclement Battle of Uman," in *The Army Quarterly and Defence Journal*, vol. 108, no. 4, October 1978.

Overy, Richard, "Statistics," in I. C. B. Dear and M. R. D. Foot (eds.), *The Oxford Companion to the Second World War*. Oxford: 1995.

Pennington, Reina. "Offensive Women: Women in Combat in the Red Army in the Second World War," in *The Journal of Military History*, vol. 74, no. 3, July 2010.

———. "Women," in David R. Stone (ed.), *The Soviet Union at War 1941–1945*. Barnsley, England: 2010.

Raus, Erhard. "Russian Combat Methods in World War II," in Peter G. Tsouras (ed.), *Fighting in Hell. The German Ordeal on the Eastern Front*. New York: 1998.

Römer, Felix. "The Wehrmacht in the War of Ideologies: The Army and Hitler's Criminal Orders on the Eastern Front," in Alex J. Kay, Jeff Rutherford and David Stahel (eds.), *Nazi*

Policy on the Eastern Front, 1941. Total War, Genocide and Radicalization. Rochester, NY: 2012.

Streit, Christian. "Soviet Prisoners of War in the Hands of the Wehrmacht," in Hannes Heer and Klaus Naumann (eds.), *War of Extermination. The German Military in World War II, 1941–1944.* New York: 2000.

Schröder, Hans Joachim. "Erfahrungen deutscher Mannschaftssoldaten während der ersten Phase des Russlandkrieges," in Bernd Wegner (ed.), *Zwei Wege nach Moskau. Vom Hitler-Stalin-Pakt bis zum "Unternehmen Barbarossa."* Munich: 1991.

Schüler, Klaus. "The Eastern Campaign as a Transportation and Supply Problem," in Bernd Wegner (ed.), *From Peace to War. Germany, Soviet Russia and the World, 1939–1941.* Oxford: 1997.

Shils, Edward A., and Morris Janowitz. "Cohesion and Disintegration in the Wehrmacht in World War II," in *Public Opinion Quarterly*, vol. 12, no. 2, 1948.

Stahel, David. "The Wehrmacht and National Socialist Military Thinking," in *War in History*, vol. 24, 2017.

Volkmann, Hans-Erich. "Das Russlandbild in der Schule des Dritten Reiches," in Hans-Erich Volkmann (ed.), *Das Russlandbild im Dritten Reich.* Cologne: 1994.

Weiner, Amir. "Something to Die for, a Lot to Kill For: The Soviet System and the Barbarization of Warfare, 1939–1945," in George Kassimeris (ed.), *The Barbarization of Warfare.* New York: 2006.

Wette, Wolfram. "Juden, Bolschewisten, Slawen. Rassenideologische Rußland-Feindbilder Hitlers und der Wehrmachtgeneräle," in Bianka Pietrow-Ennker (ed.), *Präventivkrieg? Der deutsche Angriff auf die Sowjetunion.* Frankfurt: 2011.

Wettstein, Adrian. "Urban Warfare Doctrine on the Eastern Front," in Alex J. Kay, Jeff Rutherford and David Stahel (eds.), *Nazi Policy on the Eastern Front, 1941. Total War, Genocide and Radicalization.* Rochester, NY: 2012.

Wiegrefe, Klaus. "Abrechnung mit Hitlers Generälen," in *Spiegel Online*, 27 November 2001.

Websites

www.feldgrau.com
www.feldpost-archiv.de
www.lexikon-der-wehrmacht.de

Index